Fodor's 91 Ireland

Fodor's Travel Publications, Inc.
New York and London

ISBN 0-679-01918-9

Fodor's Ireland

Editor: David Low
Contributors: Suzanne Brown, Georgina Campbell, Allanah Hopkin, Philip Joseph, Pat Mackey, Denise Nolty, Hugh Oram, Nan Richardson, Andrew Sanger.
Art Director: Fabrizio La Rocca
Cartographer: David Lindroth
Illustrator: Karl Tanner
Cover Photograph: Burnett/Stock Boston

Design: Vignelli Associates

Special Sales

Fodor's Travel Publications are available at special discounts for bulk purchases (100 copies or more) for sales promotions or premiums. Special editions, including personalized covers, excerpts of existing guides, and corporate imprints, can be created in large quantities for special needs. For more information write to Special Marketing, Fodor's Travel Publications, 201 East 50th St., New York, NY 10022. Inquiries from the United Kingdom should be sent to Fodor's Travel Publications, 20 Vauxhall Bridge Rd., London, England SW1V 2SA.

MANUFACTURED IN THE UNITED STATES OF AMERICA
10 9 8 7 6 5 4 3 2 1

Contents

Foreword

We wish to express our gratitude to Tim Magennis, Paddy Derivan, Simon O'Hanlon, and Orla Carey at the Irish Tourist Board; and Rhona Blake at Pembroke Public Relations in Dublin; for their assistance in preparation of this guide.

While every care has been taken to ensure the accuracy of the information in this guide, the passage of time will always bring change, and consequently, the publisher cannot accept responsibility for errors that may occur.

All prices and opening times quoted here are based on information available to us at press time. Hours and admission fees may change, however, and the prudent traveler will avoid inconvenience by calling ahead.

Fodor's wants to hear about your travel experiences, both pleasant and unpleasant. When a hotel or restaurant fails to live up to its billing, let us know and we will investigate the complaint and revise our entries where the facts warrant it.

Send your letters to the editors of Fodor's Travel Publications, 201 E. 50th Street, New York, NY 10022.

Highlights '91 and Fodor's Choice

1-800-Shamrock

Highlights '91

Dublin The look of Dublin City Center continues to improve, with more pedestrianized streets and a greater variety of shops. In the South City Center, **Grafton Street** looks resplendent with its new red-brick walkways for shoppers. The street now attracts a myriad of street musicians, so you just might hear the U2 band of the future. The North City Center is also changing; **O'Connell Street** now features recently planted trees, a fountain near the General Post Office, and a new James Joyce statue at the O'Connell Street corner of **North Earl Street,** which has also been pedestrianized.

In 1991 Dublin anticipates an increase in tourism as it becomes the European City of Culture of the year, following in the footsteps of such cities as Athens, Berlin, Glasgow, and Paris. This honor is designated by the European Community. Many buildings are getting a facelift; the **National Gallery's** Milltown Rooms, Irish Rooms, and Shaw Room have already been splendidly renovated. The **Civic Museum** and the **Municipal Gallery** have also been refurbished. A recent addition to the city is the **RHA Gallery,** a large well-lit showcase on Ely Place devoted to contemporary Irish art. Two new museums are scheduled to open in 1991. The **Dublin Writers' Museum** on Parnell Square will commemorate the city's rich literary heritage. The **Irish Museum of Modern Art,** featuring the best of 20th-century Irish art, is due to be unveiled at the Royal Hospital, Kilmainham. A **James Joyce Cultural Center** also plans to open in 1991 on North Great George's Street. A library and an archives will be housed in a restored Georgian mansion.

Dublin Environs The **Millmount Museum** in Drogheda was recently refurbished and is now one of the best exhibition halls in the country, with numerous relics of Drogheda's commercial and industrial past. Two new museums scheduled to open in 1991 in County Kildare are the **Peat Industry Museum** in Lullymore and the **Steam Museum** in Straffan, dedicated to the history of the steam engine in Ireland. 1991 also marks the centenary of the death of Charles Stewart Parnell, the Irish Nationalist political leader; a new **Parnell Park** plans to open near Rathdrum in County Wicklow in time for the commemorative celebrations. Large tracts of land in the north of County Wicklow, near Glendalough, have also been declared a state-owned national park, to guard against undesirable development.

The Southeast In Waterford City's former Viking and Norman area near the waterfront, the **Waterford Heritage Centre** is now open to the public; it houses artifacts from the 10th to the 16th centuries. Part of this complex contains a 13th century church and burial ground with many architectural details still visible. These remains will be incorporated in a special underground exhibition area of a new shopping complex currently under construction.

Sealink British Ferries recently launched a new luxury ferry on the Fishguard—Rosslare sea route. The ferry carries 500 cars and 1,800 passengers; it offers a 220-seat movie theater, 200 cabins with bath, a choice of restaurants, a sauna, and a Jacuzzi. Meanwhile, **Rosslare Harbour,** which serves ferries arriving in the Southeast from Fishguard, Pembroke, Le Havre and Cherbourg, now has one of the most up-to-date boating facilities in Europe. The new terminal has a new train station and includes covered walkways to shops and restaurants.

The Southwest

Cork City Center's pedestrianized **Paul Street** area with its paved piazza has revitalized the whole area between Patrick Street and the river. Paul Street, French Church Street, and Carey's Lane are fast becoming the best addresses in town for lively moderately priced restaurants, adventurous fashion boutiques, specialist book shops, and top-quality craft shops.

Adare Manor in County Limerick is the newest luxury hotel in the region. This vast, gothic Victorian mansion on a 1,000-acre estate is furnished with fine antiques and offers fishing, horsebackriding and a fitness center; an 18-hole golf course will be ready by autumn 1991. The hotel is an ideal touch-down point for transatlantic passengers arriving at Shannon, which is only 25 km (16 mi) away. (*See* Dining and Lodging, Chapter 7.)

As far as tourism is concerned, **Kinsale** is definitely the boom-town of the Southwest. If you want to get acquainted with the town while it still bears some resemblance to a sleepy fishing port, make a point of visiting in 1991. By 1992 a new 90-bed hotel and yacht marina will open on the water's edge in Kinsale's town center. Two of the already existing hotels are building new bedroom wings, and work is about to start on a French-owned 600-bed health spa and conference center close to town. Local residents are fighting a losing battle against the construction of a cluster of 60 holiday homes on an unspoiled stretch of the inner harbor. However, the boom means good business for the dozen or so fine restaurants which thrive in this small town (population 2,000).

The West

The development of regional airports is now making the West more accessible than ever. Travelers can save time by flying direct from the United Kingdom to Carnmore Airport, Galway City, or Horan International Airport at Knock in County Mayo. Flights are also scheduled to these airports from Cork and Dublin, eliminating a three- or four-hour drive.

Theater fans should try to catch a show at the tiny **Druid Theater** in Galway City, the launching pad for many of

Ireland's most talented young actors and directors, such as Mick Lally, Frances Tomelty, and Garry Hynes. The Druid's productions have been acclaimed off-Broadway in New York and in London's West End for their energetic and innovative approach to 20th-century classics.

The West is Ireland's sweater center, and the revival of small-cottage industries producing hand-knitted or hand-loomed sweaters remains important to the area's economy. Most first-time visitors will want to invest in a traditional hand-knitted off-white Aran sweater, with its intricate pattern of stitches. If you already own an Aran, look for unusual and attractive designs, usually in tweedy natural colors, with Gaeltarra and Dawn Seal labels.

The Northwest The work to restore **Parke's Castle** on the eastern shore of Lough Gill has finally been completed. The sturdy fortified tower house has been returned to its original 17th-century condition. At the same time, new facilities have been added, including a video show on the history of the building and the area; it's like a little tour of the region, and quite a good substitute if you don't have a lot of extra time for the real thing.

Knockmuldowney House, the distinguished country house hotel and restaurant at Strandhill, west of Sligo Town, has closed, but its owner-managers, Charles and Mary Cooper, have moved to Charles's family home. They are again offering bed and breakfast, as well as dinner, in one of the most impressive mansions in Ireland, **Markree Castle** at Collooney, 11 km (7 mi) south of Sligo Town. Most of the building is early 19th-century, but part of it dates back originally to 1640. The castle, with oak-paneling, a huge stained glass window, and elaborate plasterwork, stands amid 150 acres of grounds, with lovely gardens. (*See* Dining and Lodging, Chapter 9.)

Northern Ireland The steady decline in serious violent incidents during the last few years, together with decisive new Government initiatives—in education, employment, and housing—to bring to an end the social divisions which led to the unrest, has led to a renewed interest in Northern Ireland as a tourist destination. The Government has also launched a scheme of financial aid to providers of high-quality accommodations in the province. As a result of the changing atmosphere, the number of visitors to Northern Ireland have been noticeably increasing. The total number of tourists in 1989 topped one million, the highest on record for the province. But of course, one of the main attractions of Northern Ireland remains its smaller number of visitors compared to the Irish Republic and other parts of Europe.

Belfast has recently seen some revitalization. Old slum quarters continue to be replaced with fresh new housing. The city center, too, has some attractive construction going up, and run-down areas are scheduled for a complete overhaul (London's lively Covent Garden district is cited as the model for these developments). One such renovated area is situated around St. Anne's Cathedral; the **Northern Ireland Tourist Board** will be moving into new premises opposite the cathedral in 1991.

Derry City, for years considered a worse trouble-spot than Belfast, seems to have entered a new era as well. The high-rise apartment buildings of the unsavory Bogside quarter have been replaced by modern housing; now a substantial area, situated between Shipquay Street and the city walls, will become a new commercial quarter called **The Village.** Barbed wire and army stations on the historic city walls are due to be taken down this year, and guided walks on the ramparts will resume. A scaling down of the army's presence in the town may soon be possible.

Fodor's Choice

No two people will agree on what makes a perfect vacation, but it's fun and helpful to know what others think. We hope you'll have a chance to experience some of Fodor's Choices yourself while visiting Ireland. For detailed information about each entry, refer to the appropriate chapters (given in the left-hand margin) within this guidebook.

Sights to Remember

Dublin
Sunset over the River Liffey

Deserted Georgian squares on a Sunday

Phoenix Park

Dublin Environs
Glendalough Valley

Greystones Harbour at dusk

Japanese Gardens, near Kildare Town

The Lakelands
Birr Castle Demesne, Birr

The Southeast
Irish National Heritage Park, Ferrycarrig

Mitchelstown Cave, Burncourt, Cahir

Woodstock Forest Park, Inistioge

The Southwest
The view of the Blasket Islands from Slea Head

Dusk over Killarney's Lower Lake as seen from Aghadoe Heights

The view of Fastnet Rock Lighthouse from Cape Clear Island

The West
The view of the Aran Islands from the Cliffs of Moher

Clifden's twin spires nestling in the mountains above the sea

Salmon Weir Bridge, Galway

The Northwest
Peat cutters in the bog country

Whitewashed single-story cottages with tied-on thatched roofs

Northern Ireland
Devenish Island viewed from Lough Erne's shore

The Giant's Causeway

Red, white, and blue curbstones in Protestant neighborhoods

Buildings and Monuments

Dublin
Bank of Ireland, College Green

	National Library—the Reading Room
	Royal Hospital, Kilmainham
	Trinity College
Dublin Environs	Castletown House, Celbridge
	Church of Ireland cathedral and round tower, Kildare Town
	Newgrange, Co. Meath
	Russborough House, Blessington
The Lakelands	Boyle Abbey, Co. Roscommon
	Clonalis House, Castlerea
	Clonmacnoise Monastery, Co. Offaly
The Southeast	Brown's Dolmen, Carlow Town
	Kilkenny Castle, Kilkenny City
	Reginald's Tower, Waterford City
	Rock of Cashel, Cashel
	Selskar Abbey, Wexford
The Southwest	Bunratty Castle, Bunratty
	Charles Fort, Kinsale
	Gallarus Oratory, Dingle Peninsula
	Monastic remains, Skellig Michael
The West	Ashford Castle, Cong
	Dún Aengus, Inishmore, Aran Islands
	Kylemore Abbey, Connemara
The Northwest	Creevykeel megalithic court-cairn, near Cliffony
	Donegal Castle, Donegal Town
	Glenveagh Castle, Co. Donegal
Northern Ireland	Belfast's Victorian pubs
	Carrickfergus Castle, Carrickfergus
	Castle Coole, near Enniskillen

Museums and Works of Art

Dublin	Civic Museum
	Guinness Hop Store
	Treasury, at the National Museum
Dublin Environs	Millmount Museum, Drogheda
	Ledwidge Cottage and Museum, Slane
The Southeast	County Museum, Enniscorthy Castle

	Reginald's Tower Museum, Waterford City
The Southwest	Crawford Gallery, Cork
	Fota House, Cobh
	Hunt Collection, Plassey
	Craggaunowen Project, Co. Limerick
The West	Dysert O'Dea Castle, Archaeology Center, Corofin
	Thoor Ballylee, Gort
The Northwest	Glebe Gallery, Church Hill
	Sligo County Museum, Sligo Town
Northern Ireland	Ulster Museum, Belfast
	Ulster Folk Museum, near Belfast

Scenic Drives and Views

Dublin	East pier, Dun Laoghaire
	Hill of Howth
Dublin Environs	Around the shores of Poulaphouca Reservoir, Co. Wicklow
	Banks of Grand Canal, Co. Kildare
	Drive over the Wicklow Gap, near Glendalough
	Hill of Tara, Co. Meath
The Southeast	Vee Gap scenic route, Co. Tipperary
The Southwest	Connor Pass, Dingle Peninsula
	Scenic route from Allihies to Eyeries, Beara Peninsula
	Tunnel road: Glengarriff–Kenmare–Killarney
The West	Atlantic drive around Achill Island
	The Burren: Cliffs of Moher to Ballyvaughan via Doolin and Fanore (coast road), returning to Lisdoonvarna via Corkscrew Hill
	Sky Road, Clifden
The Northwest	Around Lough Gill
	Killybegs to Glencolumbkille, Donegal Bay
	Around Sheephaven Bay
	The road along Errigal Mountain's south side
Northern Ireland	The Glens of Antrim
	Around Lower Lough Erne

Hotels

Dublin	Killiney Castle, Co. Dublin (*Expensive*)

	Shelbourne (*Expensive*)
	Towers (*Expensive*)
	Lansdowne (*Moderate*)
	Ariel House (*Inexpensive*)
Dublin Environs	Rathsallagh House, Dunlavin (*Very Expensive*)
	Moyglare Manor, Maynooth (*Expensive*)
	Tinakilly House, Rathnew (*Expensive*)
	Tulfarris House, Blessington (*Expensive*)
	Ballymascanlon House, Dundalk (*Moderate*)
The Lakelands	Bloomfield Hotel, Mullingar (*Moderate*)
	Prince of Wales Hotel, Athlone (*Moderate*)
The Southeast	Cashel Palace Hotel, Cashel (*Very Expensive*)
	Waterford Castle Hotel, Waterford City (*Very Expensive*)
	Kelly's Strand Hotel, Rosslare (*Expensive*)
	Newpark Hotel, Kilkenny City (*Moderate*)
	Diamond Hill Country House, Waterford City (*Inexpensive*)
The Southwest	Adare Manor, Adare (*Very Expensive*)
	Park Hotel, Kenmare (*Very Expensive*)
	Longueville House (*Expensive*)
	Cahernane Hotel, Killarney (*Expensive*)
	Benner's, Dingle (*Moderate*)
The West	Dromoland Castle, Newmarket-on-Fergus (*Very Expensive*)
	Ballynahinch Castle, Recess (*Expensive*)
	Cashel House Hotel, Cashel Bay (*Expensive*)
	Gregan's Castle, Ballyvaughan (*Expensive*)
	Rock Glen Manor House, Clifden (*Moderate*)
The Northwest	Rathmullan House, Rathmullen (*Expensive*)
	St. Ernan's House, Donegal Town (*Moderate*)
Northern Ireland	Culloden House, Belfast (*Very Expensive*)
	Wellington Park Hotel (*Expensive*)
	Londonderry Arms, Carnlough (*Moderate*)

Bed-and-Breakfasts

Dublin	Kilronan House (*Inexpensive*)
	Iona House (*Inexpensive*)

Dublin Environs Lennoxbrook, Kells (*Moderate*)

Old Rectory Country House, Wicklow Town (*Moderate*)

The Southeast Diamond Hill Country House, Waterford City (*Inexpensive*)

The Southwest Bantry House, Bantry (*Moderate*)

Kathleen's Country House, Killarney (*Moderate*)

Scilly House, Kinsale (*Moderate*)

Tahilla Cove Country House, Tahilla (*Inexpensive*)

The West Currarevagh House, Oughterard (*Moderate*)

Ballinalacken Castle, Lisdoonvarna (*Inexpensive*)

Dun Aengus, Clifden (*Inexpensive*)

The Northwest Coopershill, Riverstown (*Expensive*)

Markree Castle, Collooney (*Expensive*)

Bruckless House, Bruckless (*Moderate*)

Temple House, Ballymote (*Moderate*)

Woodhill Guest House, Ardara (*Inexpensive*)

Northern Ireland Ash-Rowan Guest House, Belfast (*Moderate*)

Jamestown House, Ballinamallard (*Moderate*)

Camera House, Belfast (*Inexpensive*)

Restaurants

Dublin Restaurant Patrick Guilbaud (*Very Expensive*)

Les Frères Jacques (*Expensive*)

Shay Beano (*Expensive*)

The King Sitric (*Expensive*)

Pigalle (*Moderate*)

Gallagher's Boxty House (*Inexpensive*)

Dublin Environs Tinakilly House, Rathnew (*Very Expensive*)

Roundwood Inn, Roundwood (*Expensive*)

Tree of Idleness, Bray (*Expensive*)

The Lakelands Dooley's Hotel, Birr (*Moderate*)

The James Joyce Restaurant, Mullingar (*Moderate*)

The Southeast Cashel Palace, Cashel (*Very Expensive*)

Marfield House Hotel, Gorey (*Very Expensive*)

Waterford Castle, Waterford (*Very Expensive*)

Dwyers of Mary Street, Waterford (*Moderate*)

Neptune Restaurant, Ballyhack (*Moderate*)

The Southwest Arbutus Lodge, Cork (*Expensive*)

The Vintage, Kinsale (*Expensive*)

Beginish, Dingle (*Moderate*)

Dunworley Cottage, Clonakilty (*Moderate*)

The West Drimcong House, Moycullen (*Expensive*)

Claire's, Ballyvaughan (*Moderate*)

Noctan's, Galway (*Moderate*)

The Orchid Room, Sheedy's Spa View, Lisdoonvarna (*Moderate*)

The Northwest Cromleach Lodge, Castlebaldwin (*Moderate–Expensive*)

Restaurant St. John's, Fahan (*Moderate–Expensive*)

Reveries, Rosses Point (*Moderate*)

Northern Ireland Roscoff, Belfast (*Very Expensive*)

Restaurant 44, Belfast (*Expensive*)

MacDuffs, Coleraine (*Expensive*)

After Hours

Dublin Irish music session at O'Donoghue's

National Concert Hall

A play at the Abbey, the Gate, or the Project Arts Centre

Abbey Tavern, Howth

Dublin Environs Singing sessions at Black Bull and Gwent Arms pubs, Drogheda

A pint of Guinness at Moran's Pub, Mornington

Summer concerts at Castletown House, Celbridge

The Southeast Portholes Bar, Hotel Rosslare, Rosslare

Seanachie Pub, Ballymacart

T & H Doolans Bar, Waterford City

The Southwest Gleneagles Hotel, Killarney

Mangan's Brasserie, Cork

O'Flaherty's Pub, Dingle

The West Abbeyglen Castle Hotel, Clifden

Murray's Piano Bar, Hotel Salthill, Galway

West County Hotel, Ennis

The Northwest Abbey Hotel, Donegal Town

Hargadon's Pub and Sligo Park Hotel, Sligo Town

Nancy's and Peter Oliver's pubs, Ardara

Northern Ireland

Grand Opera House, Belfast

Irish music sessions at the Rotterdam, Maddens, and Pat's Bar, Belfast

Ireland

ATLANTIC OCEAN
Malin Head
Tory Island
Rathlin Island
North Channel
Portrush
Coleraine
Ballymoney
Buncrana
Lough Swilly
Lough Foyle
Derry City
Aran Island
Letterkenny
Gweebarra Bay
DONEGAL
Strabane
DERRY
Ballymena
Larne
ANTRIM
Island Magee
Belfast Lough
NORTHERN IRELAND (Great Britain)
Lough Neagh
Belfast
Newtownards
Omagh
Cookstown
TYRONE
Dungannon
Lisburn
Lurghan
Donegal Bay
Ballyshannon
Lower Lough Erne
FERMANAGH
Armagh City
DOWN
ARMAGH
Killala Bay
Sligo Bay
Sligo Town
Upper Lough Erne
Monaghan Town
Newry
Newcastle
LEITRIM
Ballina
SLIGO
MONAGHAN
Lough Conn
Dundalk
Cavan
Dundalk Bay
Achill Island
MAYO
CAVAN
LOUTH
Clare Island
Clew Bay
ROSCOMMON
River Shannon
Irish Sea
Inishturk
Drogheda
Inishbofin
Lough Mask
WEST MEATH
MEATH
Mullingar
Lough

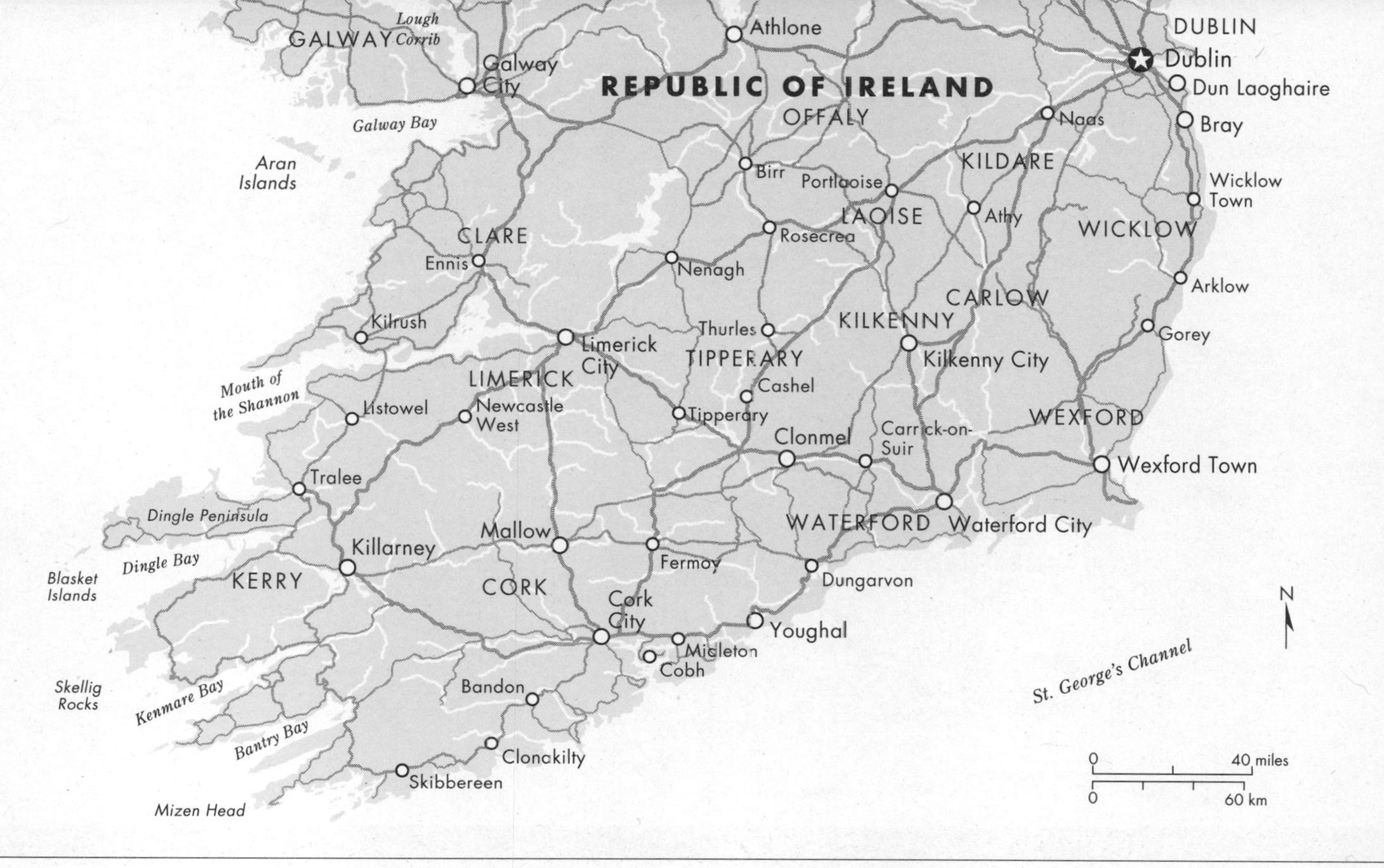
REPUBLIC OF IRELAND
GALWAY
Lough Corrib
Galway City
Athlone
DUBLIN
Dublin
Dun Laoghaire
Bray
Naas
OFFALY
Galway Bay
Aran Islands
Birr
Portlaoise
KILDARE
Wicklow Town
LAOISE
Athy
WICKLOW
CLARE
Rosecrea
Ennis
Nenagh
Arklow
CARLOW
Kilrush
Thurles
KILKENNY
Gorey
Limerick City
TIPPERARY
Kilkenny City
LIMERICK
Cashel
Mouth of the Shannon
Listowel
Newcastle West
Tipperary
WEXFORD
Clonmel
Carrick-on-Suir
Wexford Town
Tralee
Dingle Peninsula
WATERFORD
Waterford City
Mallow
Killarney
Fermoy
Dingle Bay
Dungarvon
Blasket Islands
KERRY
CORK
Cork City
Youghal
Midleton
Cobh
St. George's Channel
Skellig Rocks
Kenmare Bay
Bandon
Bantry Bay
Clonakilty
Skibbereen
Mizen Head
N
0
40 miles
0
60 km

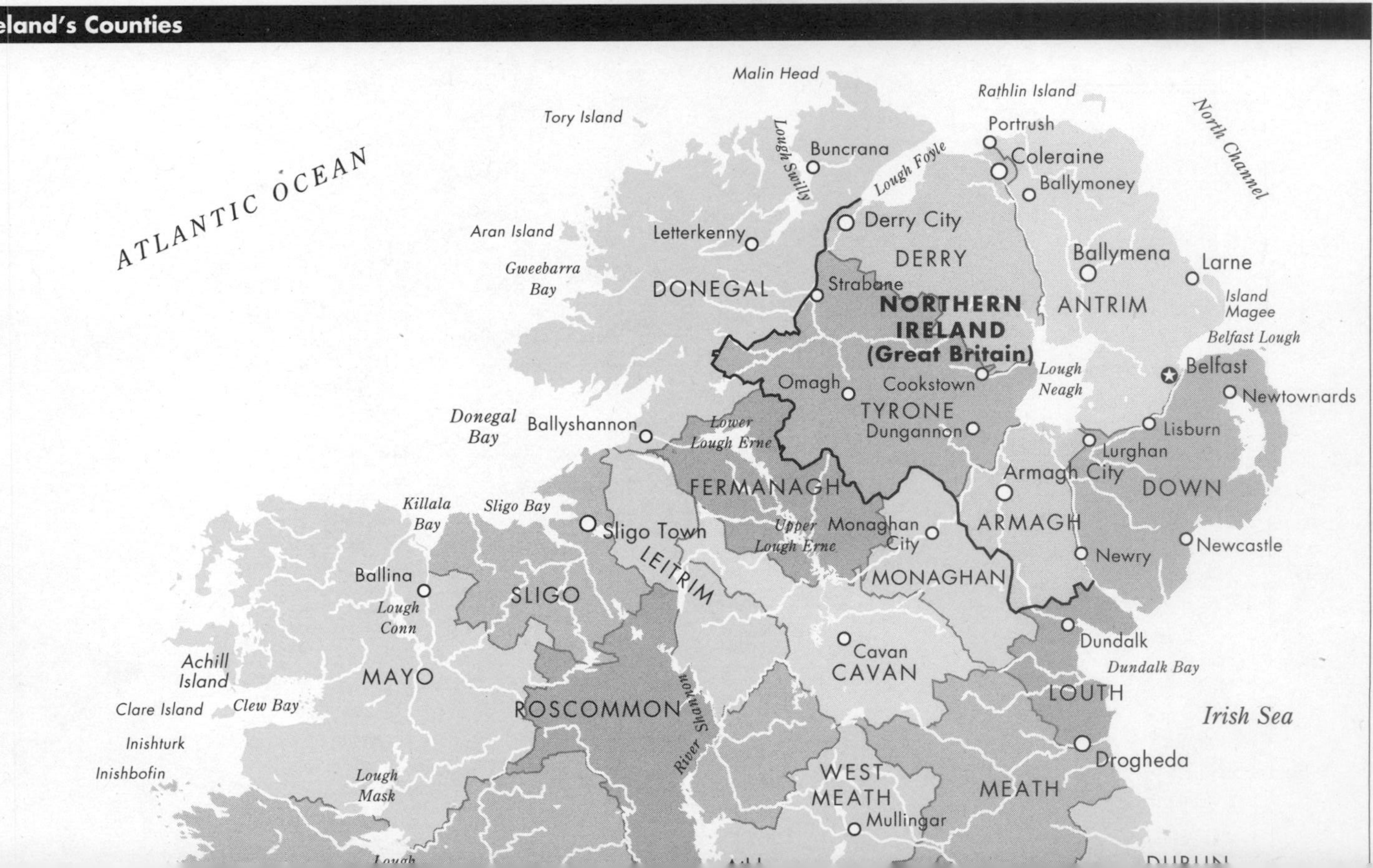
Ireland's Counties
ATLANTIC OCEAN
Malin Head
Tory Island
Rathlin Island
North Channel
Portrush
Coleraine
Ballymoney
Buncrana
Lough Swilly
Lough Foyle
Derry City
DERRY
Aran Island
Letterkenny
Gweebarra Bay
DONEGAL
Strabane
NORTHERN IRELAND (Great Britain)
Ballymena
ANTRIM
Larne
Island Magee
Belfast Lough
Belfast
Newtownards
Omagh
Cookstown
Lough Neagh
TYRONE
Dungannon
Lisburn
Lurghan
Donegal Bay
Ballyshannon
Lower Lough Erne
FERMANAGH
Armagh City
ARMAGH
DOWN
Killala Bay
Sligo Bay
Sligo Town
Upper Lough Erne
Monaghan City
Newry
Newcastle
LEITRIM
MONAGHAN
Ballina
Lough Conn
SLIGO
Dundalk
Dundalk Bay
Achill Island
MAYO
Cavan
CAVAN
LOUTH
Clare Island
Clew Bay
ROSCOMMON
River Shannon
Irish Sea
Inishturk
Inishbofin
Lough Mask
WEST MEATH
MEATH
Drogheda
Mullingar

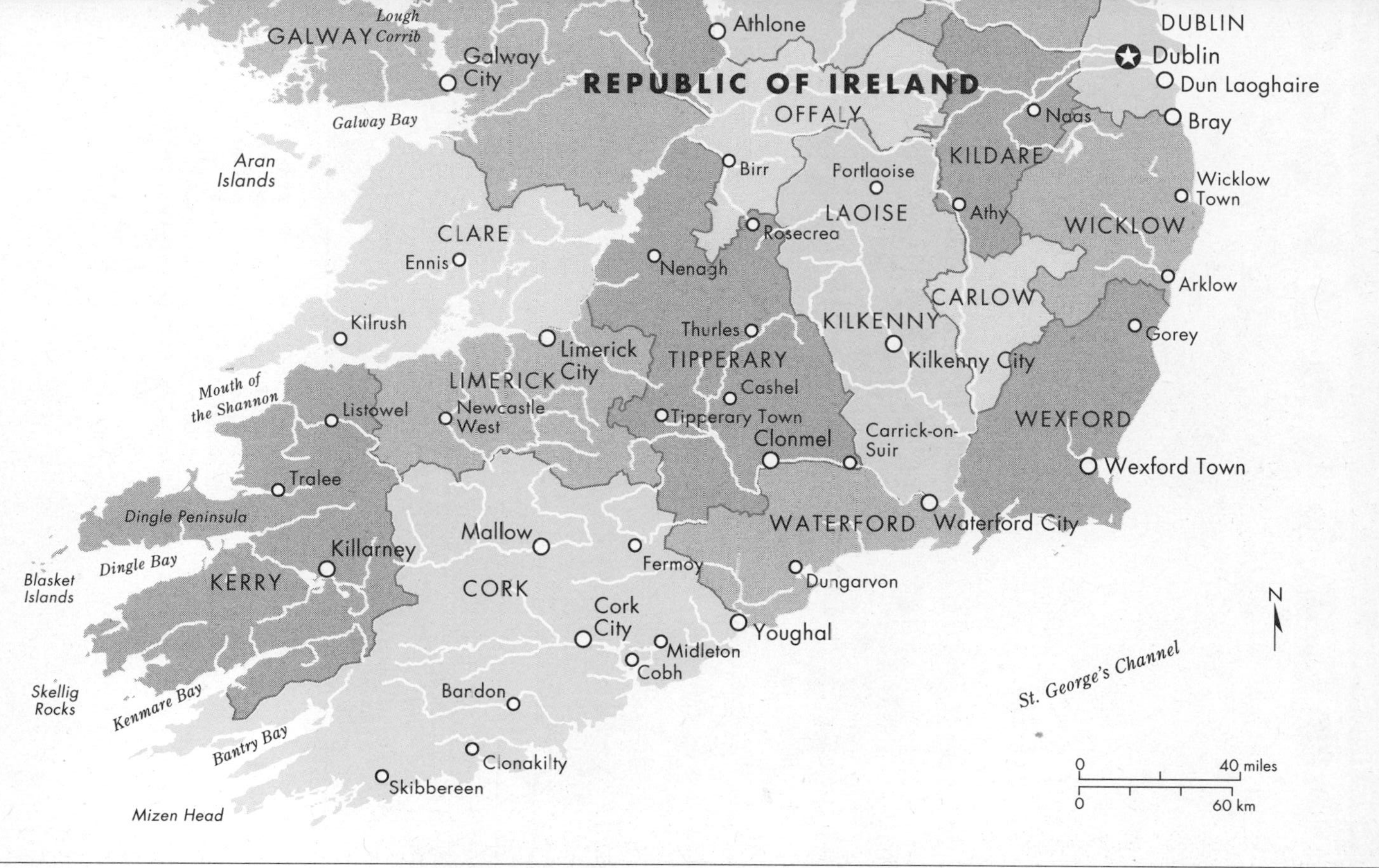

GALWAY
Lough Corrib
Galway City
Athlone
REPUBLIC OF IRELAND
DUBLIN
Dublin
Dun Laoghaire
Naas
Bray
OFFALY
Galway Bay
Aran Islands
Birr
Portlaoise
KILDARE
Wicklow Town
LAOISE
Athy
Rosecrea
WICKLOW
CLARE
Ennis
Nenagh
Arklow
CARLOW
Kilrush
Thurles
KILKENNY
Gorey
Limerick City
TIPPERARY
Kilkenny City
LIMERICK
Cashel
Mouth of the Shannon
Listowel
Newcastle West
Tipperary Town
Carrick-on-Suir
WEXFORD
Clonmel
Wexford Town
Tralee
Dingle Peninsula
WATERFORD
Waterford City
Mallow
Killarney
Fermoy
Dingle Bay
Blasket Islands
KERRY
CORK
Dungarvon
Cork City
Youghal
Midleton
Cobh
N
St. George's Channel
Skellig Rocks
Kenmare Bay
Bardon
Bantry Bay
Clonakilty
Skibbereen
Mizen Head
0 40 miles
0 60 km

World Time Zones

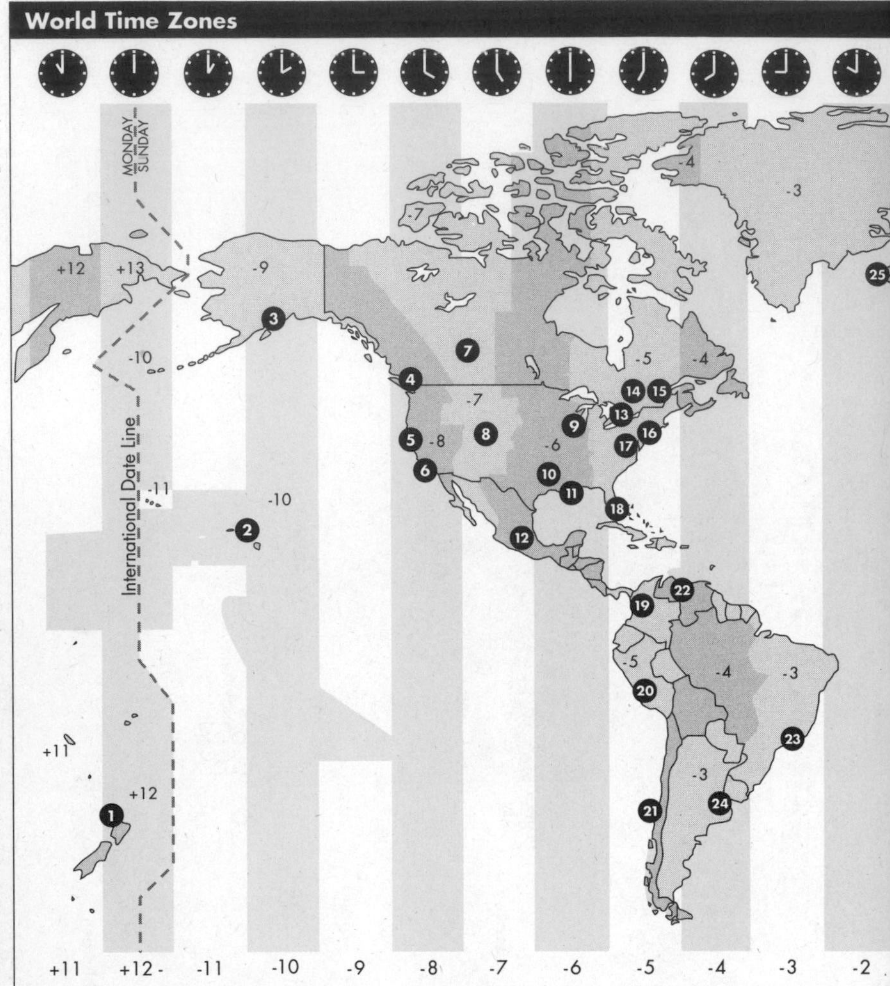

Numbers below vertical bands relate each zone to Greenwich Mean Time (0 hrs.). Local times frequently differ from these general indications, as indicated by light-face numbers on map.

Algiers, **29**
Anchorage, **3**
Athens, **41**
Auckland, **1**
Baghdad, **46**
Bangkok, **50**
Beijing, **54**
Berlin, **34**
Bogotá, **19**
Budapest, **37**
Buenos Aires, **24**
Caracas, **22**
Chicago, **9**
Copenhagen, **33**
Dallas, **10**
Delhi, **48**
Denver, **8**
Djakarta, **53**
Dublin, **26**
Edmonton, **7**
Hong Kong, **56**
Honolulu, **2**
Istanbul, **40**
Jerusalem, **42**
Johannesburg, **44**
Lima, **20**
Lisbon, **28**
London (Greenwich), **27**
Los Angeles, **6**
Madrid, **38**
Manila, **57**

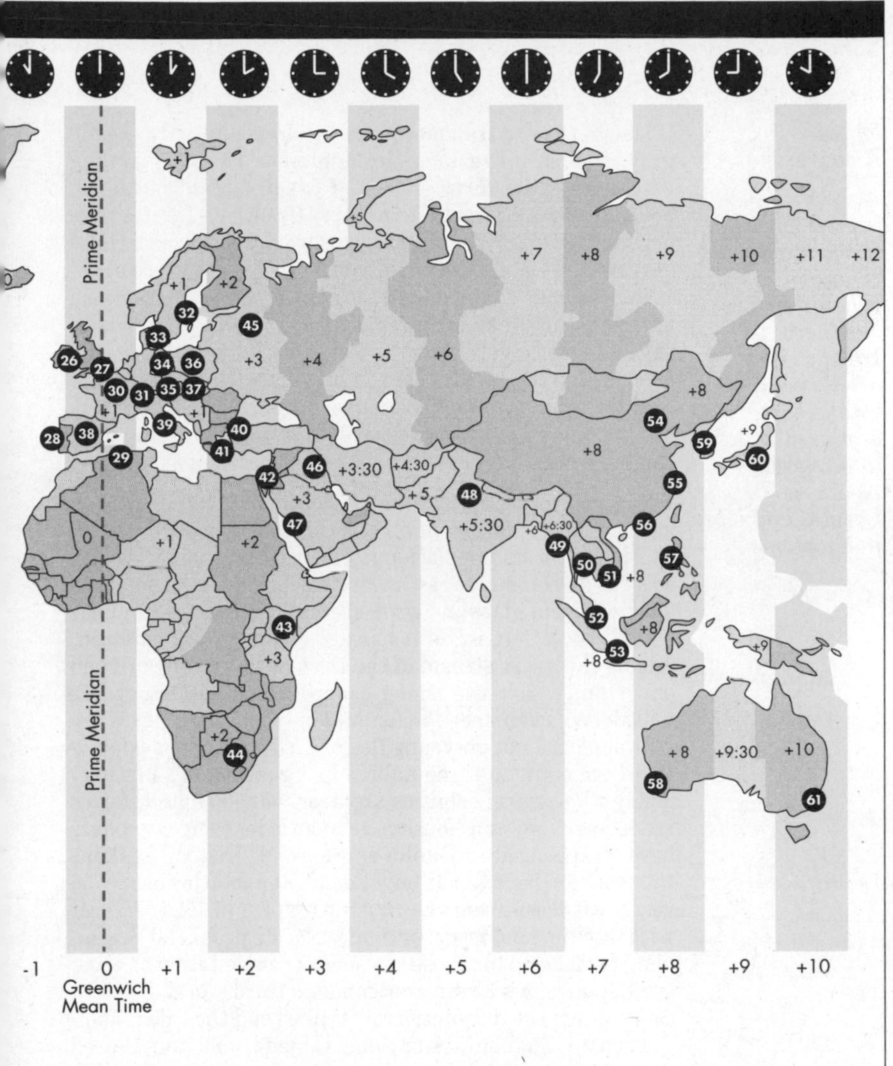

Mecca, **47**
Mexico City, **12**
Miami, **18**
Montreal, **15**
Moscow, **45**
Nairobi, **43**
New Orleans, **11**
New York City, **16**
Ottawa, **14**
Paris, **30**
Perth, **58**
Reykjavík, **25**
Rio de Janeiro, **23**
Rome, **39**
Saigon, **51**
San Francisco, **5**
Santiago, **21**
Seoul, **59**
Shanghai, **55**
Singapore, **52**
Stockholm, **32**
Sydney, **61**
Tokyo, **60**
Toronto, **13**
Vancouver, **4**
Vienna, **35**
Warsaw, **36**
Washington, DC, **17**
Yangon, **49**
Zürich, **31**

Introduction

by Nan Richardson

A frequent visitor to Ireland, Nan Richardson is the co-author of An Eye for an Eye: Northern Ireland. *Her articles and essays have appeared in* Art in America, Aperture, Granta, *and other publications.*

If you journey to Ireland by air, the descent is shrouded in gray, suddenly breaking through mists to that startling patchwork, "the forty shades of green," that leaves you breathless. But if you take the ferry (from say, Le Havre or Cherbourg to Cork or Rosslare; or from Liverpool or Holyhead to Dun Laoghaire or Belfast), you'll see the face of another Ireland, stained with the smell of peat from the braziers, the steaming pots of black tea, the tendrils of smoke from cigarettes passed silently around seated groups. You'll taste the sharp tang of golden whiskey, and hear the sounds of Gaelic-accented English that is the Irish brogue, as well as the noise of children: wheeling, crawling, climbing, laughing, bawling, like some untrammeled force.

While more prosperous countries of the EC vainly encourage barely a replacement birthrate, Ireland overflows with youth: 60% of its population is under the age of 25. But all this has its sober side, as Ireland's chief export is not linen and tweed, cut glass and wool, sheep and fat cattle, or music and literature. It is, as it has always been, her children, joining the great stream of the Irish in search of work and opportunity that the island cannot provide. History has willed it so, ever since the famines of the last century when the young and not-so-young fled or died, reducing a population from eight to three million in a generation's lifetime. Today whole rural counties are nearly depopulated, farms are abandoned, and houses are emptied—their occupants have disappeared to Dublin and beyond. History explains this, too, for Ireland has only been a Republic for barely 50 years, cut loose from the British Empire in 1923 and left with no cities, industry, or market for its products. Scrambling to make up for those centuries of exploitation has cost the Republic, which staggers under a third-world debt and cannot stem the dissolution of families and the tide of emigration to England, Australia, Canada, and the United States. The balladmakers sing emigre's songs, such as "A Long Way from Clare to Here," and it will be an equally long way to solvency for Ireland. For Ireland is two-faced, like the Janus-stones and sheel-na-gigs of its pre-Christian past; it's a complex place where the mystic lyricism of Yeats, the hard Rabelesian passions of Joyce, and the spare, aloof dissection of Beckett grew not only from a rich and ancient culture but also from 20th-century upheavals.

A Friendly People

Simple customs tell a lot. Hospitality in Ireland is counted among the greatest of virtues, a legacy from Celtic times when anyone not offering the traveler food and drink was shamed; the country is justly legendary even now for the friendliness of its people. "You are welcome," people say in greeting the moment you cross the threshold of the poorest house, while total strangers will take you home for tea or supper and strike up conversations with ease and curiosity, entertaining you perhaps with an account of their second cousin's memorable fortnight (a fortnight's worth of stories if you have the time!)

Time, in fact, is one of the greatest luxuries of Ireland. On a fine day, along a lushly green country lane, you may pass a bicycle abandoned against a tree; looking vainly for its owner, you'll find him reclining in the feathery hedgerows or on the long grass, contemplating fast-moving clouds like some philosopher-king. "Oh the dreaming, the dreaming, the heart-scalding bitter, maddening dreaming," cried the playwright George Bernard Shaw, but to knowing travelers in the stressed and industrialized world, this haven of dreamers is a pearl of great price, sought-after and kept secret. Not long ago, in a bar in Crossmaglen, a village in Armagh, a rugged farmer in oilskins and thornproof, chores over and done with (or just put on hold) turned an amused and quizzical eye as I fretted at the lateness of my appointment. "All that rushing about—and what for?" he reprimanded. "Give us a wee one there," he signaled the barman with a lift of his pipe, and pushed his glass to mine to toast the sentiment, "Life's for the living!" And, he concluded with another swallow, "Never put off for tomorrow a drink you can have today."

Much of the real beauty of Ireland is hidden on the back roads. If America is known for its car culture, Ireland is known for its cow culture, ever since the days of the "Tuigne na Cuailnge," or "The Cattle Raid of Cooley," the 8th century epic that is the Iliad of Ireland, describing a marital dispute between the two leaders, King Ailill and Queen Maeve over who had the finest herds in the land. Equal down to the last cow, Maeve had one item that Ailill lusted after: a giant brown bull; to win the wager, the king kidnapped the bull one night, kicking off a 50-year internecine war. Although Irish wealth today is not exactly measured in sirloin pound, the moo-cows seem to own the country lanes, staring haughtily and curiously at interloping motorists, lazily drooping timothy from their soft maws. In the end, with persuasion from harried livery equipped with frisky dogs and long-knobbed sticks, they'll share the road—but all in their time.

Somehow this may help explain why Ireland is what anthropologists call a "lived" culture, one that doesn't put much stock in the outward monuments of achievement; where the most potent history is oral, where storytelling is an art, and where people will travel miles for the "crack," the Irish synonym for a rousing good time. Ireland teaches you patience, reminds you of the rhythms of the natural world, and convinces you, reassuringly, of the essential well-being of man. French traveler LaTochaye wrote in his journals in 1644, after a tour of the island, that "the Irish are very fond of strangers," and Oliver Goldsmith, later in the 18th century, observed, "The natives are peculiarly remarkable for their gaiety and the levity of their dispositions; English transplanted here lose their serious melancholy and become gay and thoughtless, more fond of pleasure and less addicted to reasoning."

The Price of a Pint

Hospitality finds its logical institution in the local pub, the center of social life in Ireland. Even a small town such as Dingle in County Kerry (population 1,000) boasts 52 watering holes, open day and night. Protocol dictates that you enter and greet everyone, taking a seat alone until invited (as you inevitably are) to join a table. Then the ancient custom of rounds begins, with the newcomer offering to buy the first set of drinks, and when the pints are barely half-full (half-empty from an Irish perspective), another imbiber stands the round, and so on, in turn. With a few companions, this makes it nearly obligatory to spend an afternoon in the pub. Similarly, if you're smoking, custom demands that you offer the pack to fellow socializers before you light up yourself. Women are often exempted from these rituals, if, indeed, they are allowed to join in at all, for in rural areas the sight of a woman drinking is still frowned upon, and if they do darken a publican's door they head for the "lounge," a slightly dressed-up version of the same establishment to drink glasses, never pints, even if they have a powerful thirst. Of course, "strangers," female or other, can be nonconformist with impunity.

These social and equitable customs help explain why 10% of Irish personal spending goes to alcohol like some unholy tithe and why these dark village pubs with their scratched wooden counters, dusty tiled floors, and the yeasty smell of Guinness have a feeling of sanctity and remove from wordly cares not unlike a church. It may also explain, incidentally, the historic Irish reputation for wit and bellicosity. The rumor of bellicosity, however, is ill-founded: "The only people in Europe who have never set out to conquer," my friend, a Dublin photographer claimed with pride, but wit flows untapped from unexpected sources. It might come from the use of a borrowed language, perhaps from the need of a subject people for subterfuge, but nuance and irony are the rules of conversation, and anything less would be considered flat-footed. Irish expertise in double-think and forked tongue makes for a universally acknowledged aptitude for legal affairs, a gift for words of imagination and persuasiveness that you can find in the crossroads *shebeen* (pub) much as in Dublin's Leinster House, where the Irish *Dail* (or legislature) sits.

The Grand Tour

You are never very far from anywhere in Ireland, but each of its thirty-two counties have their special character and history, and fierce loyalty from their sons and daughters. Dublin is the millenium-old capital, once a Celtic settlement by the ford of the River Liffey, later a Norse encampment for raiding Viking and Danish pirates, and finally the citadel-seat of the British colonizer's power for centuries. Today it is a graceful mix of fine Georgian buildings, a lively waterfront, wrought iron canals and bridges, an army of booksellers, 800-odd pubs, and a rich cultural life. Ireland chooses to exempt artists from taxes, designating them national resources of sorts, and filmmakers, painters, and writers are part of the local scenery, along with the "rale Dubs," or "jackeens,"—the breezy natives born in the heart of the city between the Grand and Royal canals that divide North and South Dublin into two worlds. Although it can be a sophisticated city, with sushi bars, French restaurants and bold theater, it hasn't lost any of its simple pleasures, like waking to the tinkling of glass bottles with round silver caps, delivered to the stoop by a milkman dressed all in white; afternoon tea at Bewley's with scones slathered with Kerry Gold butter; soda farls heaped with clouds of whipped cream; waitresses in black dresses and starched aprons; or breakfast "the like of which you'll never see again," my landlady promised (though everywhere in Ireland seemed to be competing in this category). The silver pots of dark tea, the wheaten bread and toast in gleaming racks, the eggs, oatmeal, rashers (bacon), and sausages all done up with doilies, sends you out into the permeating mists that the Irish ironically call "soft weather," fortified and content.

Nearby, the scenic Wicklow mountains and rich Boyne valley are home to the wealthier class. The ancestral homes of the dwindling members of the Anglo-Irish ascendancy dot the landscape throughout the country, and lords and baronets down on their luck have turned hoteliers and welcome guests to castle holidays with adaptable grace. Limerick County is famed as horse country. County Tipperary's rolling green flatlands and Galtee mountains are known for champion greyhounds and the stud farms that have turned out winners for generations. The Rock of Cashel, seat of the Kings of Munster for 700 years, (where St. Patrick said his first mass in Ireland) is here, along with Cahir Castle, one of the few places that managed to resist Cromwell's hordes, now restored to its former impressiveness.

The coast of County Wexford was the original beachhead of Ireland named by the Vikings after the consort of their one-eyed god Odin; it still bears the stamp of its fearless, sea-going settlers, in its steep pathways and fine seafood. Wexford is a quick trip to Kilkenny, the finest medieval city in Ireland and known for its artisans. Also nearby is Waterford City, where the crystal of the same name is produced, at the delta of three great rivers—the Nore, Barrow, and Suir. Waterford City has one of the oldest forts in Ireland, Reginald's Tower, built in 1013 and named for the Viking warrior who founded the city. But while the Southeast has its charm, for scenery, generally speaking, go to the counties in the West: from Cork and Kerry to Clare and Galway, from Sligo up to Donegal.

County Donegal, in the far northwest, is among the wildest, most ruggedly beautiful places in the world, with its long rocky coastline, white beaches, turbulent surf, and impressive mountains and plateaus, full of legendary lore of giants and witches, fairies, and pishrogues. Irish is widely spoken here, and the music is famous; traditional groups, such as Clannad and De Dannaan, named after the prehistoric followers of the goddess Dana, are local heroes, and when Enya, daughter of local musicians, hit the top of the charts in Europe and the United States with her Irish-New Age instrumentals, the roof flew off Leo's pub in Gweedore, where spontanteous sessions for the music-loving community are regular happenings.

Galway City is a port and university town, bustling and businesslike, and the departure point for the Aran Islands, celebrated by playwright J.M. Synge in *Riders to the Sea* and Robert Flaherty in his classic documentary film *Man of Aran*. Just to the west of Galway City, lies Connemara, loved by painters, who flock there in summer, by writers (from Yeats to Gogarty to Joyce), and by all seekers of silence and beauty. It, too, is a *Gaeltacht* (Irish-speaking) area, celebrated for its simplicity of lifestyle and genuinely warm natives. Connemara is also known for its ponies, descendants of the Andalusian horses that swam to shore from the Spanish fleet and bred with the local Celtic stock (direct decendants of the original Ice Age horse of 20,000 B.C.)

At the southwestern end of the Republic is County Kerry, full of soft accents and magic places. For centuries, summer travelers here have been thrilled by the surfeit of natural beauty as they've gazed at the black rocks and green waves glistening at Slea Head on the Dingle Peninsula or at the Blasket Islands, where St. Brendan the Navigator was said to have set sail in a wooden *curragh* (boat) to discover the Americas in the 7th century. Sea birds reel and wild donkeys graze among the fuschia hedges awash in crimson velvet flowers, and the fields explode with deep yellow gorse, may-blossom and honeysuckle against a dark blue sky. County Kerry's special events and attractions include Killorgin's annual three-day Puck Fair in mid-summer (when a large billy goat is crowned king and garlanded with flowers, a residue of an old pre-Christian fertility rite) and

Killarney, with its lakes, park lands, and jumping-off places for a drive around the Ring of Kerry.

Nearby Cork, (from the Gaelic "corcaigh," meaning marshes) has always been called "The Rebel County," and a quick tour of all the monuments will tell you why. Michael Collins, the general who won independence for Ireland was assassinated here, and Terence McSweeney, a former mayor of Cork, died on hunger strike here, to name a few. A Venice-like port city of canals and bridges, and a bustling mercantile center, Cork was once home to writers Sean O'Faolain and Frank O'Connor, and is today a city of sport. Its team is always in the championship finals of hurling, that fast and furious ancient game that makes soccer look like kick-the-can, and the city is one of the few places where they still play the traditional, two-thousand-year-old game of bowls that the Irish giant Cuchulain used to excel at. If your taste runs to less athletic entertainment, visit the exquisitely restored village of Kinsale, or the attractive historical and arts centers of West Cork, helped along by an influx of discriminating French and German settlers in this part of Ireland for the last 20 years.

Taking the main road from Dublin to Belfast is a reminder —as you pass bristling watchtowers, sandbagged forts and warpainted soldiers in camouflage who check your papers —that, as another song goes, "one of Ireland's four green fields are still in stranger's hands." While Munster, Leinster, and Connaught are in the south, six of the nine counties of Ulster remained part of Britain in 1921. Today Northern Ireland is definitely worth a trip, and the reward for a little courage is great: here you have the beauty of the Antrim Coast from Carncastle to Bushmills; the Giant's Causeway; the rich farmlands and lakelands of Fermanagh; and the austere beauty of the Mourne Mountains. People are as friendly and helpful here as they are in the Republic, and, probably because of their history, perhaps a little sharper and wittier. Northern Ireland is also fascinating for any follower of history and politics for you get an unforgettable glimpse of the winds of time changing, a scene not unlike the last days of the Raj, as Britain's first colony erodes to be her last.

Digging Up the Past

That sense of otherness which few destinations on this scale, or this accessible, can provide, cannot only be attributed to its evergreen climate and leisurely pace of life but also to the palimpsest of history and legend dug deep under Ireland's rich grassy surface. Its tumultuous past is in evidence everywhere, from the Neolithic tombs and defenses of Newgrange in County Meath and Dun Aengus on Inishmore Island, 5,000 years older than the pyramids of Giza, to the numerous other antiquities and archeological sites, registered and unregistered—standing stones and court graves, mottes and dolmens, raths and cairns, holy wells and mass stones, round towers and Celtic crosses.

The legacy of the first-known Scandinavian settlers in Ireland and the later influx of Bronze Age Celts from Central Europe was an agrarian society based on a democratic kingship, a justice system known as the Brehon laws, and an artisan caste proficient in gold and precious metals. Christianity followed in the 4th century, and while European culture flickered and died in the Dark Ages, priests nurtured knowledge in beehive huts and stone monasteries. About 800 AD Viking longboats scourged the island's coasts, leaving the mark of bright red hair behind on their Irish descendents. Brian Boru, last of the High Kings to sit at Tara, won the Battle of Clontarf against Danish armies in 1014, only to have his successors lose Ireland in 1169 to the Norman Strongbow, opening the door to 800 years of rebellion.

By 1609, the last of the Irish chieftains sailed for exile, making way for the "Plantation" of 200,000 Scottish Lowlanders on native Irish lands. Britain's Oliver Cromwell, "the Avenger," reinforced those Protestant claims, beheading thousands of men, women, and children in his devastating marches. In their wake came the "Penal Code," forbidding the Irish Catholics to practice their religion, exercise law, or own land, vote, and hold office. The crushing blow was the famine that struck after 1845, reducing the once-populous island from eight to three million inhabitants, through death or emigration, creating the first wave of the Irish diaspora and setting the stage for the ultimate uprising, on Easter morning, 1916, when Irish Nationalists proclaimed a republic. England's vengeance on the patriots galvanized the country to the bitter war of independence that ended in the partitioning of Ireland into twenty-six counties in the South and six in the North, a political struggle that continues today. Like many facets of history in Irish life, this conflict is subtle, often below the surface and invisible to the casual observer.

Ireland Today

Present-day Ireland encourages creativity that goes beyond history and tradition. In the music field, internationally known talents have emerged, such as the rock bands U2, the Hothouse Flowers, the Pogues, and In Tua Nua; top-of-the charts singers Sinead O'Connor, Van Morrison, Christy Moore, and Chris de Burgh; and folk musicians Sean Keane, Maggie Barrie, Liam Og O'Flynn, Paddy Reilly, Billy Bragg, and Mary Black. Theater is bursting with talent that often takes the centuries-old route across the water to London, with actors such as Richard Branagh, Brenda Fricker, Stella McCusker, Gabriel Byrne, and Daniel Day-Lewis, not to mention playwrights Brian Friel, Hugh Leonard, John Boyd, Graham Reid, Anne Devlin, John B. Keane, and the late Stewart Parker.

Contemporary filmmakers Pat O'Connor, Jim Sheridan, and Joe Comerford often draw from a rich source of narrative writing provided by novelists Neil Jordan, William Trevor, James Plunkett, Bernard McLaverty, Thomas Kinsella, Edna O'Brien, Benedict Kiely, and John McGahern. Irish poetry is alive and well in the hands of Seamus Heaney, Derek Mahon, Paul Muldoon, Seamus Deane, Tom Paulin, and Medh McGuckian.

While literature is certainly Ireland's single greatest contribution to the arts, with the shadow of giants like Jonathan Swift, Oscar Wilde, Patrick Kavanagh, Brendan Behan, Bernard Shaw and others still casting a shadow, the country shows hidden strengths in other creative fields. In the visual arts, the legacy of Irish Impressionists Jack Yeats and Paul Henry, gave way to painters such as Tom Carr, David Crone, Felim Egan, Jack Pakeham, James Coleman, and Louis de Brocquy, whose subject matter is metaphor, "the secret logic of ambivalence." Meanwhile, a younger generation of artists, including Rita Duffy, Micky Donnelly, Fergus and Diarmuid Delargy, sculptor Ailish O'Connell, and others confront issues of social and political contradiction in their work. In its capacity for regeneration, irrepressible vitality, mordant wit, eerie spirituality, and culturally ingrained generosity, Ireland often seems to move backwards in time to the Tir-na-Og—the mythical land of the ever-young, an alternative world of fairies, pishrogues and hidden supernatural forces that remains alive in the Irish imagination.

1 Essential Information

Before You Go

Government Tourist Offices

Irish Republic Contact the Irish Tourist Board for information on all aspects of travel to and around Ireland.

In the U.S.: 757 Third Ave., New York, NY 10017, tel. 212/418–0800.

In Canada: 10 King St. E, Toronto, Ont. MC5 1C3, tel. 416/364–1301.

In the U.K.: 150 New Bond St., London W1Y 0AQ, tel. 071/493–3201.

Northern Ireland The Northern Ireland Tourist Board (NITB) has its own overseas offices, which are the primary source of information for tourists planning to visit the province. Where there is no NITB office, however, the British Tourist Authority can usually supply information.

Addresses of the NITB are:

In the U.S.: 40 W. 57th St., 3rd Floor, New York, NY 10019, tel. 212/686–6250. **In the U.K.:** Ulster Office, 11 Berkeley St., London W1X 6BU, tel. 071/493–0601; 38 High St., Sutton Coldfield, B72 1UP, tel. 021/354–1431.

British Tourist Authority offices overseas are:

In the U.S.: 2580 Cumberland Pkwy., Suite 470, Atlanta, GA 30339, tel. 404/432–9635; 875 N. Michigan Ave., Chicago, IL 60611, tel. 312/787–0490; 2305 Cedar Springs Rd., Suite 210, Dallas, TX 75201, tel. 214/720–4040; World Trade Center, Suite 450, 350 Figueroa St., Los Angeles, CA 90071, tel. 213/628–3525. **In Canada:** 94 Cumberland St., Suite 600, Toronto, Ont. M5R 3N3, tel. 416/925–6326.

Tour Groups

Care to ride round the Ring of Kerry, kiss the Blarney Stone, or pick up some Irish crystal? Then you might want to consider a package tour of Ireland's most famous highlights. Creative itineraries abound, hitting the traditional tourist spots as well as off-the-beaten-path places you might not be able to get to on your own. They also tend to save you money on airfare and hotels. If group travel is not your thing, look into independent packages. (*See* Package Deals for Independent Travelers, below.)

When considering a tour, be sure to find out (1) exactly which expenses are included, particularly tips, taxes, side trips, meals, and entertainment; (2) the ratings of all hotels on the itinerary and the facilities they offer; (3) the additional cost of single, rather than double, accommodations if you are traveling alone; and (4) the number of travelers in your group. Note whether the tour operator reserves the right to change hotels, routes, or even prices after you've booked, and check out the operator's policy regarding cancellations, complaints, and trip-interruption insurance. Many tour operators request that packages be booked through a travel agent; there is generally no additional charge for doing so.

Listed below is a sampling of operators and packages to give you an idea of what is available. For additional information, contact your travel agent, the Irish Tourist Board, or the Northern Ireland Tourist Board.

General-Interest Tours

Irish Republic

Maupintour (Box 807, Lawrence, KS 66044, tel. 913/843–1211 or 800/255–4266) sweeps through many of the Emerald Isle's highlights on its 15-day "Best of Ireland" tour. For shorter stays, **American Express Vacations** (Box 5014, Atlanta, GA 30302, tel. 800/241–1700 or, in GA, 800/282–0800) offers 10- and 12-day packages. **Trafalgar Tours** (21 E. 26th St., New York, NY 10010, tel. 212/689–8977 or 800/854–0103) has seven- and eight-day packages. **Globus Gateway** (150 S. Los Robles Ave., Pasadena, CA 91101, tel. 818/449–0919 or 800/556–5454) touts a seven-day introduction to Ireland, as well as a 13-day in-depth tour. **Cosmos,** the budget-minded affiliate of Globus Gateway, does an eight-day "Jig Through Ireland." From May to October, **Brian Moore International Tours** (116 Main St., Medway, MA 02053, tel. 508/533–6683 or 800/982–2299) runs 10- and 14-day tours. One-week packages are offered year-round. **CIE Tours International** (122 E. 42nd St., New York, NY 10168, tel. 212/972–5600 or 800/CIE–TOUR) brings you "St. Patrick's Week in Ireland," along with nine other tours ranging from four days to two weeks in length. **TWA Getaway Vacations** (28 S. 6th St., Philadelphia, PA 19106, tel. 800/GETAWAY) hits Ireland's most popular sights in either eight or 12 days. **Delta Air Lines** (Box 1525, Ft. Lauderdale, FL 33302, tel. 305/522–1440 or 800/872–7786) offers a seven-day "Irish Heritage Motorcoach" tour. **Olson-Travelworld** (100 N. Sepulveda Blvd., Suite 1010, El Segundo, CA 90245, tel. 213/615–0711; 800/421–2255; in CA 800/421–5785) offers "three-star" and "five-star" tours that combine Ireland and Britain. **Vacation Ireland** (2 River Rd., Nutley, NJ 07110, tel. 201/284–1171 or 800/634–5085) also has a variety of escorted Emerald Isle tours.

In the United Kingdom, contact **CIE Tours International** (Ireland House, 150–151 New Bond St., London W1Y 9FE, tel. 071/629–0564), which offers a six-night "Irish Adventure Coach" tour.

Northern Ireland

The following companies run escorted tours combining Ireland and Northern Ireland, spending significant time in the North. **Sceptre Charters/Chieftain Tours** (101–13 101st Ave., Ozone Park, NY 11416, tel. 800/221–0924 or, in New York City, 718/738–9400) has a 15-day tour called the "Shamrock Royal" and a seven-day jaunt called the "Claddagh Royal." **Brendan Tours** (15137 Califa St., Van Nuys, CA 91411, tel. 800/421–8446) runs the 13-day "Sights and Sounds of Ireland" tour. **Celtic International Tours** (161 Central Ave., Albany, NY 12206, tel. 800/833–4373) offers the "Sojourn," a six-night trip with stops in the North, and **Brian Moore International** (*see* above) provides the 10-day "Irish Landscape" tour.

Special-Interest Tours

Irish Republic

Cultural: Lynott Tours (Empire State Building, 350 5th Ave., Suite 2619, New York NY 10118, tel. 212/760–0101 or 800/221–2474) customizes tours for groups of 10 people or more. Possible themes include literature, history, and architecture. The leading specialists in cultural tours are **Abercrombie & Kent** (1420 Kensington Rd., Suite 103, Oak Brook, IL 60521, tel. 312/954–2944 or 800/323–7308). Itineraries can include social visits with the owners of Ireland's leading stately homes. U.K. visitors should contact **Elegant Ireland** (15 Harcourt St., Dublin 2, tel.

01/751665). This company offers a customized itinerary with overnight stops at a variety of Irish country homes for dinner, bed, and breakfast. An enthusiastic team at **Hidden Ireland** (Box 2281, Dublin 4, tel. 01/686463) will arrange for you to stay in selected Irish country homes as paying guests. Hunting, shooting, fishing, and golf can be included in the itinerary. Houses range from small shooting lodges to great ancestral homes. Flights, itineraries, and self-driven or chauffeur-driven cars can be provided for groups of two to eight people. Alternatively, select your own destinations from its illustrated brochure.

Day Hiking: British Coastal Trails (150 Carob Way, Coronado, CA 92118, tel. 619/437–1211) features an excellent 11-day hiking tour of Southwest Ireland, held in May, July, and September. The itinerary covers some of the Republic's most scenic areas, including County Clare's lunar-like landscape in the Burren section; a ferry ride across the Shannon Estuary to County Kerry; the Ring of Kerry, including Valentia Island, Hog's Head, and the Dingle Bay coastline; and Killarney's lakes and national park. Walks are frequently away from the tourist track, along footpaths dating back to medieval Ireland, with views of such sites as Galway Bay, the Blasket Islands, and the Cliffs of Moher. The cost of the tour includes accommodations with private bath, an Irish breakfast and dinner daily, and a full-time guide.

Golf: Value Holidays (10224 N. Port Washington Rd., Mequon, WI 53092, tel. 414/241–6373 or 800/558–6850) organizes golf vacations for two or more people at courses such as Ballybunion, Tralee, the Royal Dublin, and Portmarnock. Transportation, accommodations, green fees, caddies, and optional matches are provided. Tours for nongolfers and evening entertainment can also be arranged. **Aer Lingus** (122 E. 42nd St., New York, NY 10168, tel. 212/557–1110 or 800/223–6537) organizes golf tours, as well as special shopping tours.

In the United Kingdom, **Atlantic Golf** (54A Richmond Rd., Twickenham, Middlesex TW1 3BE, tel. 081/891–6451) is a leading specialist in golfing holidays. Ballybunion, Lahinch, and Portmarnock are just three of the famous golf links served by the company. Four days, with unlimited golf, for four people traveling by air starts at £235. Other golf tours are run by **Aer Lingus Holidays** (223 Regent St., London W1R 0AJ, tel. 071/439–7262) and **Abbey Golf Holidays** (27 Victoria St., London SW1 0HD, tel. 071/222–3356).

All Sports: Lismore Tours (106 E. 31st St., New York, NY 10016, tel. 212/685–0100 or 800/547–6673) organizes all aspects of an equestrian holiday, whether you aim to be a spectator at the Budweiser Irish Derby and the Dublin Horse Show, or spend long hours in the saddle, either hunting or trail riding. Lismore also arranges golf, hunting, shooting, and fishing vacations, either in Ireland or in Ireland and Scotland.

Sceptre Charters/Chieftain Tours (*see* General-Interest Tours, above) organizes all aspects of a fishing, shooting, or horseback-riding vacation. Cycling or walking itineraries for groups of more than six can also be arranged.

In the United Kingdom, **B&I Tours** (Ireland House, 150–151 New Bond St., London W1Y 0AQ, tel. 071/491–8682) offers a wide range of packages, all with travel to Ireland on the company's ferries. Short vacations, motoring tours, farmhouse holidays, horseback-riding excursions, golf vacations, fishing holidays, riverboat cruises, bus tours, cottages, and city getaways are all available.

Keen anglers should contact **Cliff Smart Angling Holidays** (141 Queensway, Burton Latimer, Northants NN15 5QQ, tel. 05367/725453), **Angler's World Holidays** (25 Market Place, Bolsover, Chesterfield, Derbyshire, tel. 0246/826350), or **Kings Angling Holidays** (27 Minster Way, Hornchurch, Essex RM11 3TH, tel. 04024/53043). For golfing, fishing, farmhouse, and self-catering holidays, as well as bus tours, contact **PAB Travel** (11 Dale End, Birmingham, B4 7LN, tel. 0212/331252).

Northern Ireland

Golf: Sceptre Charters/Chieftain Tours (*see* General-Interest Tours, above) features an eight-day golf package that includes unlimited golf at four of Northern Ireland's leading courses. **Sunquest Vacations Ltd.** (130 Merton St., Toronto, Ont. M4S 1A4, tel. 416/485–1700 or 800/268–8899) offers a seven-day tour giving access to 10 leading Northern Ireland courses.

Horseback Riding: A residential riding vacation with instruction at all levels (if required) in dressage, show jumping, and cross-country is offered at **Ashbrooke Riding School** (Brookeborough, Co. Fermanagh, tel. 0365/53242). Accommodation is available on Viscount Brookeborough's estate, either as a paying guest of the family or in self-catering units.

Irish/American Heritage: CIE Tours International (*see* General-Interest Tours) offers custom-designed group tours of Northern Ireland in virtually any area of special interest, including family lineage. Heritage holidays for groups or individuals are also arranged by the **Irish Genealogical Association** (162A Kingsway, Dunmurry, Belfast BT17 9 AD, tel. 0232/629595).

Walking: Ulster is encircled by a long-distance footpath called the **Ulster Way,** which is 790 km (491 mi) long. Accompanied walking holidays lasting a weekend or longer can be arranged through David Munnis (Secretary), **Ulster Rambling Federation,** 5 Rowan Rd., Ballymoney, Co. Antrim, tel. 02656/63360.

Package Deals for Independent Travelers

Irish Republic

CIE Tours International (*see* General-Interest Tours) offers a three-night-minimum Dublin hotel package, which includes Irish breakfast daily, airport transfers, sightseeing tours, theater tickets, a four-day bus-and-rail pass, and a discount on rental-car rates. **Pan Am Holidays** (tel. 800/THE TOUR) affords special rates at select hotels in Dublin and Limerick when you fly round-trip on Pan Am; stay for just one night or as many as you choose. **Delta Air Lines** (*see* General-Interest Tours), **CIE Tours** (*see* General-Interest Tours), and **Pan Am Holidays** all offer self-drive packages, which include accommodations at hotels or Irish town-and-country homes, rental car, and full Irish breakfast daily. Some include round-trip airfare. **Brian Moore International Tours** (*see* General-Interest Tours) also has self-drive packages, plus weekend shopping sprees, Dublin weekends, and three-night castle stays. **Vacation Ireland** (*see* General-Interest Tours) serves up fly/drive and city-based packages.

In the United Kingdom, **Aer Lingus Holidays** (*see* Special-Interest Tours) offers a variety of weekends in Ireland, both in

Dublin and elsewhere in the country, including two nights in a castle hotel and cruises on the Shannon. **CIE Tours International** (*see* General-Interest Tours, above) is another leading specialist. **Ryan Tourist Group** (200 Earls Court Rd., London SW5 9QX, tel. 071/244–6355) offers minibreaks in the west of Ireland, including three nights in Killarney, Westport, Galway, Limerick, or Sligo.

Northern Ireland **Celtic International Tours** (*see* General-Interest Tours, above) has self-driven packages of at least three nights, with farmhouse or hotel accommodations, unlimited mileage in a rental car, and Irish breakfast. **Sceptre Charters/Chieftain Tours** (*see* General-Interest Tours) offers the "Royal North Auto Tour," a seven-night self-driven package exclusively in Northern Ireland, with Irish breakfast, first-class hotels, and unlimited mileage in a rental car.

In the United Kingdom, **Scotia Holidays** (57 Bothwell St., Glasgow, Scotland G2 6RF, tel. 0414/440–1094) offers packages for a minimum of two nights if you travel by car ferry, three nights if you travel by plane. A rental car can be provided if you choose to fly. The packages allow you to select from a range of hotels and guest houses. **B&I Tours** (*see* Special-Interest Tours, above) arranges a minimum six-night package in Northern Ireland and/or the Irish Republic, with car ferry and bed-and-breakfast included. Two- to five-night packages can also be organized.

When to Go

The summer remains the most popular time to visit Ireland, and for good reason. The weather is pleasant, the days are long, (daylight lasts until about 10 PM in late June), and the countryside is green and beautiful. But there will be crowds in popular holiday spots, and prices for accommodations are at their peak. As British and Irish school vacations overlap, covering the time from late June to mid-September, families, backpacking students, and other vacationers descend on popular coastal resorts in the South, the West, and the East. Unless you are determined to enjoy the short (July and August) swimming season, you would be well advised to take your vacation in Ireland outside these months.

Fall and spring are good times to travel, though the weather can be unpredictable. When hotels, restaurants, and accommodations are seasonal, they usually close from early or mid-November until mid-March or Easter. During this *off-season*, prices are considerably lower than at the summer peak, but your selection of hotels and restaurants is limited, and many minor attractions also close. St. Patrick's Week in March gives a focal point to a spring visit, but some American visitors may find the saint's-day celebrations a little less enthusiastic than the ones back home. Dublin, however, welcomes its American visitors on March 17 with a parade and then the Lord Mayor's Ball to round off the evening. If you're planning an Easter visit, don't forget that most theaters still close from Thursday to Sunday of Holy Week (the week preceding Easter), and all bars and restaurants, except those serving hotel residents, close on Good Friday.

If you want to feel like the only tourist in town, try a winter visit. Many hotels arrange special Christmas packages with entertainments and outdoor activities. Mid-November to mid-February is either too cold or too wet for all but the keenest golfers; however, horse races and hunting trips abound. There are cheerful open fires in almost all hotels and bars, and with extra time on their hands, people tend to take an added interest in visitors.

Climate What follows are average daily maximum and minimum temperatures for some major cities in Ireland.

Dublin

Jan.	47F	8C	**May**	59F	15C	**Sept.**	63F	17C
	34	1		43	6		49	9
Feb.	47F	8C	**June**	65F	18C	**Oct.**	58F	14C
	36	2		49	9		43	6
Mar.	50F	10C	**July**	68F	20C	**Nov.**	50F	10C
	38	3		52	11		40	4
Apr.	56F	13C	**Aug.**	67F	20C	**Dec.**	47F	8C
	40	4		52	11		38	3

Cork

Jan.	49F	9C	**May**	61F	16C	**Sept.**	65F	18C
	36	2		45	7		50	10
Feb.	49F	9C	**June**	67F	19C	**Oct.**	58F	14C
	38	3		50	10		45	7
Mar.	52F	11C	**July**	68F	20C	**Nov.**	52F	11C
	40	4		54	12		40	4
Apr.	56F	13C	**Aug.**	68F	20C	**Dec.**	49F	9C
	41	5		54	12		38	3

Belfast

Jan.	43F	6C	**May**	59F	15C	**Sept.**	61F	16C
	36	2		43	6		49	9
Feb.	45F	7C	**June**	65F	18C	**Oct.**	56F	13C
	36	2		49	9		45	7
Mar.	49F	9C	**July**	65F	18C	**Nov.**	49F	9C
	38	3		52	11		40	4
Apr.	54F	12C	**Aug.**	65F	18C	**Dec.**	45F	7C
	50	4		52	11		38	3

WeatherTrak provides information on more than 750 cities around the world—450 of them in the United States. Dialing 900/370-8725 will connect you to a computer, with which you can communicate by touch tone at a cost of 75¢ for the first minute and 50¢ a minute thereafter. The number plays a taped message that tells you to dial a three-digit access code for the destination you're interested in. The code is either the area code (in the United States) or the first three letters of the foreign city. For a list of all access codes, send a self-addressed stamped envelope to Cities, Box 7000, Dallas, TX 75209 (tel. 214/869-3035 or 800/247-3282).

Festivals and Seasonal Events

Irish Republic
January At least six major horse races are held at centers such as Thurles (Co. Tipperary), Naas (Co. Kildare), Leopardstown (Co. Dublin), and Gowran Park (Co. Kilkenny). The Point-to-Point season opens; these are small but exciting steeplechases, held in a different spot every Sunday until mid-May. The **Irish Crafts Fair** is held at the Royal Dublin Society.

February At the beginning of the month Dublin Airport hosts an **International Arts Festival,** which will include *artists at work* in the terminal building. This is only one of many arts events to be held during 1991 while Dublin is designated *Cultural Capital of Europe.* The **Cavan International Song Contest** (town and county of Cavan) chooses a winner from international submissions, amateur and professional. In Naas, County Kildare, the **Punchestown Bloodstock Sales** are held; this is one of the most important racehorse auctions in Ireland. There's an **international rugby match** between England and Ireland at Lansdowne Road, Dublin, in the middle of the month.

March **St. Patrick's Day,** March 17, is the focus of the month, with a parade in Dublin featuring guest bands from the United States and a festival of traditional Irish music, the Dublin **Feis Ceoil.** The **World Irish Dancing Championships** take place (venue to be announced). At the end of the month the **International Folk Dance Festival** gets underway at Cobh in County Cork. Motoring enthusiasts take part in the **Circuit of Ireland** rally. The **West of Ireland Golf Championships** takes place at Rosses Point in County Sligo.

April Easter provides one of the biggest events of the racing calendar, the two-day **Irish Grand National** race at Fairyhouse, County Meath, about 19 km (12 mi) from Dublin. The leadership of the Gaelic Football League is decided in the capital at Croke Park. Cork City holds its **International Choral and Folk Dance Festival.**

May This month sees the opening of Ireland's agricultural showcase, the **Royal Dublin Society Spring Show** at Ballsbridge. If you're interested in your ancestors, track down one of the seminars on Irish Origins held in Dublin, Kilkenny, and Tipperary. Festivals include the **Fleadh Nua** (traditional music, song, and dance) at Ennis, County Clare; **Pan Celtic Week,** a celebration of Celtic music, song, and dance in Killarney; a **Maytime Festival** at Dundalk; and a **Mussel Festival** at Bantry.

June Among the many fishing events of the month is the **Lough Swilly International Tope Festival** at Rathmullen, County Donegal. One of the richest and most exciting horse races in the world, the **Budweiser Irish Derby,** is run 48 km (30 mi) from Dublin at the Curragh, headquarters of Irish racing. The **Festival of Music in Great Irish Houses**—a delightful series of classical music concerts is held in different stately homes around the Dublin area. **Bloomsday,** June 16, is celebrated in Dublin with readings and dramatizations of James Joyce's *Ulysses,* preceded by fancy-dress breakfasts and pilgrimages around the city.

July Youghal Sea Anglers holds a deep-sea shark safari in County Cork, and Athlone has a freshwater angling festival on the Shannon. The **Shannon Boat Rally** concludes with the sailing of an armada of small craft up the Shannon from Athlone to Carrick-on-Shannon. Another classic horse race, the **Guinness Oaks,** takes place at the Curragh. On the last Sunday in July many thousands of pilgrims, some in bare feet, climb the rocky slopes of Croagh Patrick (765 m/2,510 ft) in County Mayo to honor St. Patrick.

August The **Dublin Horse Show,** held in the second week of August, attracts the best of Irish bloodstock and a highly fashionable crowd. **The Summer Show of Flowers** is held in conjunction with the Horse Show. For golf enthusiasts, the month begins with the **Amateur Open at Lahinch** in County Clare and ends with the **Carroll's International** at the Royal Dublin. **Puck Fair** is a robust and entertaining occasion held at mid-month at Killorglin, County Kerry. At the end of the month in the same county, the *Rose of Tralee* is selected from among women of Irish descent from around the world; the competition coincides with the **Tralee Races.** The **Connmeara Pony Show** at Clifden, County Galway, attracts a cosmopolitan crowd. **Kilkenny Arts Week** at the end of the month is renowned for interesting classical-music events.

September In Galway, the oyster season opens with appropriate celebrations. The **Hurling and Gaelic Football finals** are played with great excitement at Croke Park in Dublin. The **Matchmaking Festival** in Lisdoonvarna, County Clare, is the traditional place for bachelor farmers to seek a wife; the revival of this informal tradition has become popular with American husband-seekers. The **Cork Film Festival,** the **Sligo Arts Week,** and the **Waterford International Festival of Light Opera** all start at the end of September and run into October, as does the **Dublin Theater Festival.**

October The **Ballinasloe October Fair** in County Galway is one of the biggest and oldest horse and cattle fairs in Europe. The **Wexford Opera Festival** assembles international singers, directors, and conductors, all of whom present unfamiliar operatic gems in a tiny restored Georgian theater, the Theater Royal. Cork swings on the last weekend of October when the town and its environs are taken over by the **Guinness International Jazz Festival.** The **Dublin City Marathon** on the last Monday of the month attracts thousands of runners and engenders a carnival spirit.

November The hunting season starts in November, continuing through April. The Irish Rugby Football season gets under way with hotly contested games between the four provinces: Connacht, Leinster, Munster, and Ulster (in Northern Ireland).

December On **St. Stephen's Day,** December 26, the traditional *Wren Boys* in blackface and fancy dress still demand money and sing in the street, but these days most of the proceeds go to charity. If you miss them on the 26th, you can catch them at the Wren Boy Festival in Bunratty Folk Park on the 30th and 31st.

Northern Ireland

February The **Ulster Harp National** is an exciting steeplechase held at Downpatrick Race Course.

March The **Belfast Musical Festival** sponsors speech, drama, and music competitions for young people (Balmoral, Belfast). **St. Patrick's Day celebrations** include parades and pilgrimages at sites historically associated with the saint (Downpatrick, Newry, and Cultra). The **Horse Plowing and Heavy Horse Show** is an old-time plowing competition held for over 100 years at Fair Head, Ballycastle.

April The **Circuit of Ireland International Motor Rally,** with a 650-mile course, serves as a qualifying round for the **European Rally Championship. Belfast Civic Festival and Lord Mayor's Show** lasts 15 days and includes concerts, competitions, and exhibitions, ending on the first Saturday in May with floats and bands in the streets of Belfast.

May The **Belfast Marathon** is held. Anglers compete in the **P&O European Ferries Classic Fishing Festival** (Fermanagh Lakeland). The **Ballyclare Horse Fair** has horse-dealing in the old style on the village street. The **Royal Ulster Agricultural Society Show** includes international show-jumping and sheep-shearing competitions, parades, bands, and fashion shows (since 1855 at Balmoral, Belfast).

June At the **Belfast Midsummer Jazz and Blues Festival,** international jazz and blues players join local talent (Europa Hotel, Belfast). The **Black Bush Amateur Golf Tournament** is played over four days using four courses (close to the Gaint's Causeway, County Antrim). At the **Fiddle Stone Festival,** fiddlers from all over Ireland converge on the pretty village of Belleek.

July The **City of Belfast International Rose Trials** has over 100,000 roses in a riverside park (Dixon Park, Belfast). The **Northern Ireland Open Amateur Golf Championship** is held on the famous Royal Portrush links (County Antrim). **Battle of Boyne** festivities celebrate this 17th-century battle in which the Protestant William of Orange defeated the Catholic James II (Belfast and other large towns). **Ulster Steam Traction Engine Rally** has vintage cars and field sports at Shane's Castle, Antrim.

August In the **Feast of the Assumption** on the 15th of the month, Hibernians in green sashes march to the music of Gaelic pipers (various Ulster cities). **Oul' Lammas Fair,** on the last weekend of the month, is a big social occasion, with trading in sheep and ponies, and about 100 stalls selling everything from antiques to ropes and ladders (Ballycastle).

September The **Belfast Folk Festival** provides a weekend of Irish folk talent in the center of Belfast. **Opera Northern Ireland** starts its autumn season at the end of the month in the Grand Opera House in Belfast.

October The **Ulster Antiques and Fine Art Fair** takes place at the Culloden Hotel in Belfast on the first weekend of the month.

November The **Belfast Festival** at Queen's University is a major arts festival featuring drama, ballet, cinema, and every kind of music from classical to jazz and folk.

December The **New Year Viennese Ball** is held, with music by Johann Strauss from the Ulster Orchestra (Belfast City Hall).

What to Pack

Clothing In Ireland you can experience all four seasons in one day, so pack accordingly. Even in July and August, the hottest months of the year, a heavy sweater and a good waterproof coat or umbrella are essential. (You may be tempted to buy an Irish handknit sweater or two while you're there, so don't pack more than one!) You should bring at least two pairs of walking shoes: It can and does rain at any time of the year, and rain showers can soak a pair of sneakers in minutes. In the coldest months, December and January, the average maximum temperature is around 7°C (45°F), while in the hottest months, July and August, it's about 19°C (66°F).

The Irish are generally informal about clothes. In the more expensive hotels and restaurants most people dress formally for dinner, but very few places operate a strict dress policy.

Younger travelers should note that old or tattered blue jeans are forbidden in certain bars and discos.

Miscellaneous An extra pair of glasses, contact lenses, or prescription sunglasses is always a good idea; it is important to pack any prescription medicines you use regularly, as well as any allergy medication you may need.

Pack light, because porters and luggage trolleys can be hard to find at New York airports.

Electrical Appliances The standard current in Ireland and Northern Ireland is 220 volts (50 cycles) AC. Most hotels have 220/110v sockets. Some shavers and hair driers have a built-in transformer, which can be set for 220v or 110v. If you will need a plug adapter or travel transformer, buy it before leaving home.

Carry-on Luggage Airlines generally allow each passenger one piece of carry-on luggage on international flights from the United States. The bag cannot exceed 45 inches (length + width + height) and must fit under the seat or in the overhead luggage compartment.

Checked Luggage Passengers are generally allowed to check two pieces of luggage, neither of which can exceed 62 inches (length + width + height) or weigh more than 70 pounds. Baggage allowances vary slightly among airlines, so check with the carrier or your travel agent before departure.

Taking Money Abroad

Traveler's checks and major U.S. credit cards are widely accepted. You'll need cash, however, for some of the smaller restaurants and shops. Although you won't get as good an exchange rate at home as abroad, it's wise to change a small amount of money before you go. This way you won't have to face long lines at airport currency-exchange booths. Most U.S. banks will convert dollars into Irish pounds (Irish Republic) and pounds sterling (Northern Ireland). If your local bank can't provide this service, you can exchange money through **Deak International.** To find the office nearest you, contact them at 630 Fifth Avenue, New York, NY 10011 (tel. 212/635–0515).

For safety and convenience, it's always best to take traveler's checks. The most recognized traveler's checks are American Express, Barclays, Thomas Cook, and those issued through major commercial banks such as Citibank and Bank of America. Some banks will issue the checks free to established customers, but most charge a 1% commission fee. Buy part of the traveler's checks in small denominations to cash toward the end of your trip. This will save you from having to cash a large check and ending up with more foreign money than you need. (Hold on to your receipts after exchanging your traveler's checks; when abroad, it's easier to convert foreign currency back into dollars if you have the receipts. Institutions in the United States always charge a fee, so converting money at home can be expensive.) You can also buy traveler's checks in Irish pounds or pounds sterling, a good idea if the U.S. dollar is falling and you want to lock in the current rate. Remember to take the addresses of offices where you can get refunds for lost or stolen traveler's checks.

Getting Money from Home

There are at least three ways to get money from home: (1) Have it sent through a large commercial bank that has a branch where you are staying. The only drawback is that you must have an account with the bank; if not, you'll have to go through your own bank, and the process will be slower and more costly. (2) Have it sent through American Express. If you are a cardholder, you can cash a personal check or a counter check at an American Express office for up to $1,000; $200 will be in Irish pounds or pounds sterling, and $800 in traveler's checks. There is a 1% commission on the traveler's checks. You can also receive money through an American Express MoneyGram, which enables you to obtain up to $10,000 in cash. It works this way: You call home and ask someone to go to an American Express office—or an **American Express MoneyGram** agent located in a retail outlet—and fill out an American Express MoneyGram. It can be paid for with cash or with any major credit card. The person making the payment is given a reference number and telephones you with that number. The American Express MoneyGram agent calls an 800 number and authorizes the transfer of funds to the American Express office or participating agency where you are staying. In most cases, the money is available immediately on a 24-hour basis. You pick it up by showing identification and giving the reference number. Fees vary with the amount of money sent. For $300 the fee is $30; for $5,000, $195. For the American Express MoneyGram location nearest your home and to find out the locations in Ireland and Northern Ireland, call 800/543-4080. You do not have to be a cardholder to use this service. (3) Have money sent through Western Union, whose U.S. number is 800/325-6000. If you have a MasterCard or Visa, you can have money sent for any amount up to your credit limit. If not, have someone take cash or a certified cashier's check to a Western Union office. The money will be delivered to a bank where you are staying. Fees vary with the amount of money sent and the precise location of the recipient.

Cash Machines Virtually all U.S. banks belong to a network of ATMs (automatic teller machines), which dispense cash 24 hours a day in cities throughout the world. There are some eight major networks in the United States, and some banks belong to more than one. A recent study shows that travelers may actually save money by using ATMs—instead of commercial exchanges—to change money; the rate is better, and no commission is charged.

To receive a card for one of the ATM systems you have to apply for it. Cards issued by Visa and MasterCard may also be used in the ATMs, but the fees are usually higher than the fees on bank cards. There is also a daily interest charge on credit card "loans," even if monthly bills are paid on time. Check with your bank for information on specific ATM locations in Ireland, on fees, and on the amount of cash you can withdraw on any given day.

Irish Currency

The unit of currency in the Irish Republic is the pound or punt, pronounced *poont*. It is divided into 100 pence (abbreviated

100p). **In this guide, the £ sign refers to the Irish pound; the British pound is referred to as the pound sterling and is written UK£.**

Irish notes come in denominations of £100, £50, £20, £10, £5, and £1. Coins are available as 50p, 20p, 10p, 5p, 2p, and 1p. By 1991 it is likely that £1 coins will have begun to replace £1 notes. Dollars and British pounds are accepted only in large hotels and shops geared to tourists. Elsewhere you will be expected to use Irish currency.

At the time of writing (April 1990), the punt stood at around US$1.59, Canadian $1.85, and UK0.96; however, these rates will inevitably change both before and during 1991, making it advisable to keep a sharp eye on the exchange rate during your trip.

The unit of currency in Northern Ireland is the pound sterling, divided into 100 pence. Notes come in denominations of UK£50, UK£20, UK£10, and UK£5, and coins of UK£1, 50p, 20p, 10p, and 1p. At the time of writing (April 1990), the pound sterling stood at around US $1.64, Canadian $1.92, and IR£1.04.

What It Will Cost

The strength of the punt in comparison with the pound sterling is making some headway in reducing Ireland's high cost of living. Dublin, far more expensive than the rest of the country, is reputed to be one of Europe's most expensive cities for the business traveler. The independent traveler who is prepared to make a few not necessarily unpleasant concessions does not have to spend a fortune. A modest hotel in Dublin costs about £80 a night for two; this figure can be reduced to under £60 by staying in a registered guest house, and reduced to under £30 by staying in a suburban bed-and-breakfast (*see* Lodging, below). As far as food goes, lunch, consisting of a good *one dish* plate of bar food at a pub, costs around £4.50; a sandwich at the same pub about £1.20. Dinner in Dublin is more expensive; a fancy restaurant, though not an absolutely top spot, charges about £21 per person, excluding drinks and tip. On the other hand, theater and entertainment in most places is inexpensive —about £8.50 for a good seat, and double that for a big-name pop-music concert. For the price of a few drinks and (in Dublin and Killarney) a small entrance fee of about £1.50, you can spend a fun and memorable evening at a *seisún* (pronounced *say-shoon*) in a music pub. Entrance to most public galleries is free, but stately homes and similar attractions normally charge about £2 per person.

Just about everything is more expensive in Dublin, so add at least 10% to these sample prices, which apply in the rest of the country: cup of coffee, 50p; pint of beer, £1.75; soda, 75p; ham sandwich, £1.20; and 1-mile taxi ride, £2.50.

Northern Ireland is generally inexpensive compared with both the rest of the United Kingdom and the Republic of Ireland. At the time of writing (April 1990) the Irish pound and the pound sterling had almost reached parity, but the lower level of taxation in Northern Ireland still makes dutiable goods such as gasoline, alcoholic drinks, and tobacco much cheaper there. The cost of accommodations and restaurant meals is also less expensive.

Passports and Visas

U.S. Residents All U.S. citizens need a passport to enter both Ireland and Northern Ireland. Applications for your first passport must be made in person; renewals can be obtained in person or by mail. First-time applicants should apply at least five weeks in advance of their departure date to one of the 13 U.S. Passport Agency offices. In addition, local county courthouses, many state and probate courts, and some post offices accept passport applications. Necessary documents include (1) a completed passport application (Form DSP-11); (2) proof of citizenship (birth certificate with raised seal or naturalization papers); (3) proof of identity (driver's license, employee ID card, or any other document with your photograph and signature); (4) two recent, identical, two-inch-square photographs (black-and-white or color), with a white or off-white background; (5) $42 application fee for a 10-year passport (those under 18 pay $27 for a five-year passport). Passports should be mailed to you in about 10 working days—but it can take longer in the early summer.

To renew your passport by mail, you'll need to complete Form DSP-82 and submit two recent, identical passport photographs, a passport less than 12 years old from the issue date, and a check or money order for $35.

A visa is not required for tourists staying in Ireland for up to 90 days, or in the North for up to 180 days. Tourists may be asked to show onward/return tickets. For further information, contact the **Embassy of Ireland** (2234 Massachusetts Ave. NW, Washington, DC 20008, tel. 202/462–3939), the **Embassy of Great Britain** (3100 Massachusetts Ave. NW, Washington, DC 20008, tel. 202/898–4506), or the nearest Consulate General.

Canadians All Canadians need a passport to enter both Ireland and Northern Ireland. Send your completed application (available at any post office or passport office) to the **Bureau of Passports,** External Affairs, Ottawa, Ontario K1A OG3. Include $25, two photographs, a guarantor, and proof of Canadian citizenship. Application can be made in person at the regional passport offices in Edmonton, Halifax, Montreal, Calgary, St. John's (Newfoundland), Victoria, Toronto, Vancouver, or Winnipeg. Passports are valid for five years.

A visa is not required for tourists entering Northern Ireland, but it is required for travelers to the Republic of Ireland. Contact your nearest Consulate General for information.

Britons Neither a passport nor a visa is required for British citizens entering Ireland.

Customs and Duties

On Arrival
Irish Republic Two categories of duty-free allowance exist for travelers entering the Irish Republic: one for goods obtained outside the European Community, on a ship or aircraft, or in a duty-free store within the EC; and the other for goods bought in the EC, with duty and tax paid.

In the first category, you may import duty-free: (1) 200 cigarettes or 100 cigarillos or 50 cigars or 250 grams of smoking tobacco; (2) 2 liters of wine, and either 1 liter of alcoholic drink over 22% volume or 2 liters of alcoholic drink under 22% volume (sparkling or fortified wine included); (3) 50 grams of perfume and ¼ liter of toilet water; and (4) other goods to a value of IR£34 per person (IR£17 per person for travelers under 15 years of age); you may import 12 liters of beer as part of this allowance.

In the second category, you may import duty-free: (1) 300 cigarettes or 150 cigarillos or 75 cigars or 400 grams of smoking tobacco; (2) 5 liters of wine, and either 1.5 liters of alcoholic drink over 22% volume or 3 liters of alcoholic drink under 22% volume (fortified or sparkling wine included); (3) 75 grams of perfumes and ⅜ liter of toilet water; (4) other goods to a value of IR£302 per person (IR£77 per person for travelers under 15 years of age), but no item may exceed IR£65; 12 liters of beer may be imported as part of this allowance.

Goods that cannot be freely imported include firearms, ammunition, explosives, drugs (e.g. narcotics, amphetamines), indecent or obscene books and pictures, oral smokeless tobacco products, meat and meat products, poultry and poultry products, plants and plant products (including shrubs, vegetables, fruit, bulbs, and seeds), domestic cats and dogs from outside the United Kingdom, and live animals from outside Northern Ireland.

Northern Ireland Two levels of duty-free allowance exist for people entering Northern Ireland: one for goods bought outside the European Community (EC) *or* for goods bought in a duty-free shop in an EC country; the other for goods bought in an EC country but not in a duty-free shop.

In the first category you may import duty-free: (1) 200 cigarettes or 100 cigarillos or 50 cigars or 250 grams of tobacco (if you live outside Europe these allowances are doubled); (2) 1 liter of alcoholic drink over 22% volume, or 2 liters of alcoholic drink under 22% volume or of fortified or sparkling wine; (3) two liters of still table wine; (4) 60 milliliters of perfume and ¼ liter of toilet water; and (5) other goods to the value of UK£32.

In the second category you may import duty-free: (1) 300 cigarettes or 150 cigarillos or 75 cigars or 400 grams of tobacco; (2) 1.5 liters of alcoholic drink over 22% volume, or three liters of alcoholic drink under 22% volume or of fortified or sparkling wine; (3) five liters of still table wine; (4) 90 milliliters of perfume and 375 milliliters of toilet water; and (5) other goods to the value of UK£250.

Note that, though it is not classified as an alcoholic drink by EC countries for customs purposes and is thus part of the "other goods" allowance, you may not import more than 50 liters of beer. No animals or pets of any kind can be brought into Northern Ireland without a six-month quarantine. Other items that may not be imported include fresh meats, plants and vegetables, controlled drugs, and firearms and ammunition.

On Departure If you are bringing any foreign-made equipment from home, such as cameras, it's wise to either carry the original receipt with you or register it with U.S. Customs before you leave (Form 4457). Otherwise, you may end up paying duty on your return.

U.S. Residents You may bring home duty-free up to $400 worth of foreign goods, as long as you have been out of the country for at least 48 hours and you haven't made an international trip in 30 days. Each member of the family is entitled to the same exemption, regardless of age, and exemptions may be pooled. For the next $1,000 worth of goods, a flat 10% rate is assessed; above $1,400, duties vary with the merchandise. Travelers 21 or older are entitled to bring in up to one liter of alcohol, 100 cigars (non-Cuban), and 200 cigarettes. Only one bottle of perfume trademarked in the United States may be brought in. However, there is no duty on antiques or works of art more than 100 years old. Anything exceeding these limits will be taxed at the port of entry, and it may be taxed additionally in the traveler's home state. Gifts valued at less than $50 may be mailed to friends or relatives at home duty-free, but you may not send more than one package per day to any one addressee, and packages may not include tobacco, liquor, or perfumes costing more than $5.

Canadians You have a $300 exemption and may also bring in duty-free up to 50 cigars, 200 cigarettes, 2.2 pounds of tobacco, and 40 ounces of liquor, provided these items are declared in writing to customs on arrival and accompany the traveler in carryons or checked-through baggage. These restrictions apply for absences of at least seven days and at most one year. If you are out of Canada for less than seven days and for a minimum of 48 hours, there is a $100 exemption, with the same restrictions on alcohol and tobacco products. Personal gifts should be labeled, "Unsolicited gift—value less than $40." Get a copy of the Canadian Customs brochure "I Declare" for further details. Copies can be obtained at local customs offices.

Britons You can expect tight security coming into Great Britain from both the Irish Republic and Northern Ireland. Customs regulations are the same for Great Britain and Northern Ireland. For details, *see* On Arrival for Northern Ireland, above. Further information can be obtained by contacting **HM Customs and Excise** (Dorset House, Stamford St., London SE1 9PS, tel. 071/928–0533).

Traveling with Film

If your camera is new, shoot and develop a few rolls of film before leaving home. Pack some lens tissue and an extra battery for your built-in light meter. Invest about $10 in a skylight filter: It will protect the lens and reduce haze.

Film doesn't like hot weather, so if you're driving in summer, don't store film in the glove compartment or on the shelf under the rear window. Put it behind the front seat on the floor, on the side opposite the exhaust pipe.

On a plane trip, never pack unprocessed film in check-in luggage; if your bags get X-rayed, say good-bye to your pictures. Always carry undeveloped film with you through security and ask to have it inspected by hand. (It helps to keep your film in a plastic bag, ready for quick inspection.)

The old airport scanning machines, still in use in some countries, use heavy doses of radiation that can make a family portrait look like an early morning fog. The newer models used in all U.S. airports are safe for anything from five to 500 scans, depending on the speed of your film. The effects are cumulative; you can put the same roll of film through several scans without worry. After five scans, though, you're asking for trouble.

If your film gets fogged and you want an explanation, send it to the **National Association of Photographic Manufacturers** (550 Mamaroneck Ave., Harrison, NY 10528). It will try to determine what went wrong. The service is free.

Language

Irish (also known as Gaelic), a Celtic language related to Scottish Gaelic, Breton, and Welsh, is the official national language. Though English is technically the second language of the country, it is in fact the everyday language of the majority of the population. Nowadays all Irish speakers are fluent in English.

Irish-speaking communities are found mainly in sparsely populated rural areas along the western seaboard, on some but not all offshore islands, and in small pockets in West Cork and County Waterford. Irish-speaking areas are known as Gaeltacht. While most road signs in Ireland are given in both English and Irish, within Gaeltacht areas the signs are often in Irish only. A good touring map will give both Irish and English names to places within the Gaeltacht. The most important Irish words a visitor needs to recognize are *Fir* and *Mná*, used frequently outside of public toilets: *Fir* is Men and *Mná* is Women.

Staying Healthy

No special shots are required before visiting Ireland or Northern Ireland. If you have a health problem that might require purchasing prescription drugs while traveling, have your doctor write a prescription using the drug's generic name; brand names can vary widely.

The International Association for Medical Assistance to Travelers (IAMAT) is a worldwide organization offering a list of approved, English-speaking doctors whose training meets British and U.S. standards. Contact IAMAT for a list of physicians and clinics in Ireland that belong to this network. **In the United States:** 417 Center St., Lewiston, NY 14092, tel. 716/754–4883. **In Canada:** 40 Regal Rd., Guelph, Ontario N1K 1B5. **In Europe:** 57 Voirets, 1212 Grand-lancy, Geneva, Switzerland. Membership is free.

Insurance

In the United States

Travelers may seek insurance coverage in three areas: health and accident, lost luggage, and trip cancellation. Your first step is to review your existing health and home-owner policies; some health-insurance plans cover health expenses incurred while traveling, some major medical plans cover emergency transportation, and some home-owner policies cover the theft of luggage.

Health and Accident

Several companies offer coverage designed to supplement existing health insurance for travelers:

Carefree Travel Insurance (Box 310, 120 Mineola Blvd., Mineola, NY 11501, tel. 516/294–0220 or 800/343–3553) provides coverage for emergency medical evacuation. It also offers 24-hour medical phone advice.

International SOS Assistance (Box 11568, Philadelphia, PA 19116, tel. 215/244–1500 or 800/523–8930) does not offer medical insurance but provides medical evacuation services to its clients, who often are international corporations.

Travel Assistance International (1133 15th St. NW, Suite 400, Washington, DC 20005, tel. 202/347–2025 or 800/821–2828) provides emergency evacuation services and 24-hour medical referrals.

Travel Guard International, underwritten by Transamerica Occidental Life Companies (1100 Centerpoint Dr., Stevens Point, WI 54481, tel. 715/345–0505 or 800/782–5151), offers reimbursement for medical expenses—with no deductibles or daily limits—and for emergency evacuation services.

Wallach and Company, Inc. (243 Church St. NW, Suite 100D, Vienna, VA 22180, tel. 703/281–9500 or 800/237–6615) offers comprehensive medical coverage, including emergency evacuation, for trips of 10 to 90 days.

WorldCare Travel Assistance Association (605 Market St., Suite 1300, San Francisco, CA 94105, tel. 415/541–4991 or 800/666–4993) provides unlimited emergency evacuation, 24-hour medical referral, and an emergency message center.

Lost Luggage

On international flights, airlines are responsible for lost or damaged property at rates of up to $9.07 per pound ($20 per kilo) for checked baggage, and up to $400 per passenger for unchecked baggage. If you're carrying valuables, either take them with you on the plane or purchase additional insurance for lost luggage. Some airlines will issue extra luggage insurance when you check in, but many do not. Insurance for lost, damaged, or stolen luggage is available through travel agents or directly through various insurance companies. Luggage-loss coverage is usually part of a comprehensive travel-insurance package that includes personal accident, trip cancellation, and sometimes default and bankruptcy. Two companies that issue luggage insurance are **Tele-Trip** (Box 31685, 3201 Farnam St., Omaha, NE 68131, tel. 800/228–9792), a subsidiary of Mutual of Omaha, and the **Travelers Insurance Co.** (Ticket and Travel Dept., 1 Tower Sq., Hartford, CT 06183, tel. 203/277–0111 or 800/243–3174). Tele-Trip operates sales booths at airports, and it also issues insurance through travel agents. Tele-Trip will insure checked luggage for up to 180 days and for $500–$3,000 valuation. For one–three days, the rate for a $500 valuation is $8.25; for 180 days, $100. The Travelers Insurance Co. will insure checked or hand luggage for $500–$2,000 valuation per person, also for a maximum of 180 days. The rate for one–five days for $500 valuation is $10; for 180 days, $85. Other companies with comprehensive policies include **Access America Inc.,** a subsidiary of Blue Cross–Blue Shield (Box 807, New York, NY 10163, tel. 212/490–5345 or 800/284–8300); **Near Services** (1900 N. MacArthur Blvd., Suite 210, Oklahoma City, OK 73127, tel. 800/654–6700 or 405/949–2500 in Oklahoma City); **Travel Guard International** and **Carefree Travel Insurance** (*see* Health and Accident Insurance, above).

Before you go, itemize the contents of each bag in case you need to file an insurance claim. Be certain to put your home or business address on each piece of luggage, including carry-on bags. If your luggage is lost or stolen and later recovered, the airline will deliver the luggage to your home free of charge.

Trip Cancellation Flight insurance is often included in the price of a ticket when paid for with American Express, Visa, or other major credit cards. It is usually included in combination travel-insurance packages available from most tour operators, travel agents, and insurance agents.

In the United Kingdom We recommend strongly that you take out adequate insurance to guard against health problems, motoring mishaps, theft, flight cancellation, and loss of luggage. Most major tour operators offer holiday insurance, and details are given in brochures. But for free general advice on all aspects of holiday insurance, contact the **Association of British Insurers** (Aldermary House, Queen St., London EC4N 1TT, tel. 071/248–4477). A proven leader in the holiday insurance field is **Europ Assistance** (252 High St., Croydon, Surrey CR0 1NF, tel. 081/680–1234).

Car Rentals

The best deals are on fly/drive packages or pre-booked rentals. Renting a car on impulse for a few days is the most expensive way.

All the major car rental companies have offices in Ireland, as do a number of Irish firms. All you need to rent a car is a valid driver's license; however, some companies will only rent to drivers between 23 and 70 years of age—Hertz and Avis are exceptions. Rental rates include only third-party insurance; a collision damage waiver, which protects against liability in the event of an accident, costs about another IR£50 per week.

Cars range from subcompacts to full-size sedans and chauffeured limousines. Unless automatic transmission is specified in advance, stick-shift cars are supplied. Rates vary according to car type and time of year: Do not expect to pay less than £25 a day, excluding the collision damage waiver. Most companies offer unlimited mileage and deliver the car with a full tank. When you return it the tank is refilled, and you pay the difference. The best place to pick up your car is at a major airport. Principal operators in each region are listed in the regional chapters; the following list gives the head offices of the major companies, all of which deliver nationwide. A full list of approved car rental operators, including their U.S. contact numbers, is available from the Irish Tourist Board.

Avis Rent-a-Car Ltd., 1 Hanover St., East, Dublin 2, tel. 01/776971; **Budget/Flynn Bros. Rent-a-Car,** Ballygar, Co. Galway, tel. 0903/4668; **Dan Dooley/Kenning Rent-a-Car,** Knocklong, Co. Limerick, tel. 062/53103; **Hertz Rent-a-Car,** Hertz House, 19/20 Hogan Place, Lower Grand Canal St., Dublin 2, tel. 01/767476; **Johnson & Perrott Ltd.,** Emmet Place, Cork, tel. 021/273295; **Murrays Europcar Rent-a-Car,** Baggot St. Bridge, Dublin 4, tel. 01/681777.

If you are renting a car in the Irish Republic and intend to visit Northern Ireland, make this clear when you get your car. Similarly, if renting in Northern Ireland and crossing the border, make sure that the rental insurance applies.

In Northern Ireland, as in the Republic, a stick-shift car is supplied unless automatic transmission has been specified. Picking up a car from the airport branches of the main firms can almost double the bill, so compare the airport rate with the city rate before deciding. Keep in mind that a surcharge is applied for dropping the car off in the Republic; it's cheaper to do a round-trip and leave it off where you picked it up (*see* Essential Information, Chapter 1, for car rental firms).

Rail Passes

The **EurailPass,** valid for unlimited first-class train travel through 17 countries, including the Republic of Ireland but not including Northern Ireland, is an excellent value if you plan on traveling throughout Ireland and on the Continent. The ticket is available for periods of 15 days ($340), 21 days ($440), one month ($550), two months ($750), and three months ($930). Prices are reduced for two or more people traveling together, so that a 15-day rail pass, for example, costs $240; between April 1 and September 30, you need a minimum of three in your group to get this discount. For those 25 years old and younger, there is the **Eurail Youthpass,** for one or two months' unlimited second-class train travel at $380 and $500, respectively. For travelers who like to spread out their train journeys, there is the **Eurail Flexipass.** With the 15-day pass ($198), travelers get five days of unlimited first-class train travel, but they can spread that travel out over 15 days. A 21-day pass ($360) gives you nine days of travel; a one-month flexipass ($458) gives you 14 days of train travel.

The EurailPass does not cover Great Britain, and it is available only if you live outside Europe or North Africa. The pass must be bought from an authorized agent in the Western Hemisphere or Japan before you leave for Europe. Apply through your travel agent.

The **BritRail Pass** is not valid for travel in Northern Ireland.

The "Rambler Ticket," for use on Ireland's railroads, bus system, or both, covers all the state-run and federal railways and bus lines throughout the Republic of Ireland. It does not apply to the North or to transportation within the cities. An eight-day bus or rail ticket is $78; a 15-day ticket is $116. The combination eight-day ticket for use on buses *and* trains during a 15-day period is $110; a 15-day ticket good for 30 days costs $156. Children under 16 get a 50% discount. Travelers can take their bikes along on the trains for another $29.

The **Emerald Isle Card,** recently introduced by **CIE Tours International,** gives you unlimited bus and train travel anywhere in Ireland and Northern Ireland, valid within the cities as well. A 15-day pass gives you eight days of travel over a 15-day period; it costs $142, $75 for children. A 30-day pass for 15 days of travel over a 30-day period costs $240, $125 for children.

For more information on Rambler or Emerald Isle tickets, or to book in advance, contact CIE Tours International (122 E. 42nd St., New York, NY 10168, tel. 212/972–5600 or 800/CIE-TOUR).

In Northern Ireland, **Rail Runabout** tickets, entitling you to seven days' unlimited travel on scheduled rail services April–October, are available from main Northern Ireland Railway stations. They cost UK£27.50. Inter rail tickets (UK£155)—as well as Inter rail and boat tickets (UK£180)—are also valid in Northern Ireland; these give you one month of unlimited travel in Europe.

Student and Youth Travel

The **International Student Identity Card** (ISIC) entitles full-time students to rail passes, special fares on local transportation, student charter flights, and discounts at museums, theaters, sports events, and many other attractions. If purchased in the United States, the $10 cost of the ISIC card also includes $2,000 in emergency medical coverage, $100 a day for up to 60 days of hospital coverage, as well as a collect phone number to call in case of emergency. Apply to the **Council on International Educational Exchange** (CIEE, 205 E. 42nd St., New York, NY 10017, tel. 212/661–1414). In Canada, the ISIC is available for CN$10 from the **Association of Student Councils** (187 College St., Toronto, Ont. M5T 1P7).

Travelers under age 26 can apply for a **Youth International Educational Exchange Card** (YIEE) issued by the **Federation of International Youth Travel Organizations** (81 Islands Brugge, DK-2300 Copenhagen S, Denmark). It provides similar services and benefits as the ISIC card. The YIEE card is available in the United States from CIEE (address above) and in Canada from the **Canadian Hostelling Association** (333 River Rd., Vanier, Ottawa, Ont. K1L 8H9, tel. 613/476–3844).

An **International Youth Hostel Federation** (IYHF) membership card is the key to inexpensive dormitory-style accommodations at thousands of youth hostels around the world. Hostels aren't only for young travelers on a budget, though; many have family accommodations. Hostels provide separate sleeping quarters for men and women at rates of $7–$15 a night, per person, and are situated in a variety of facilities, including converted farmhouses, villas, restored castles, and even lighthouses, as well as in specially constructed modern buildings. There are more than 5,000 hostel locations in 75 countries around the world. IYHF memberships, which are valid for one year from the time of purchase, are available in the United States through **American Youth Hostels** (Box 37613, Washington, DC 20013, tel. 202/783–6161). The cost for a first-year membership is $25 for adults 18–54. A renewal is $15. For youths (17 and under) the rate is $10, and for seniors (55 and older) the rate is $15. Family membership for $35 is available for two adults traveling with up to two children. Every national hostel association arranges special reductions for members visiting their country, such as discounted rail fare or free bus travel, so be sure to ask for a list of discounts when you buy your membership.

Council Travel, a CIEE subsidiary, is the foremost U.S. student travel agency, specializing in low-cost charters and serving as the exclusive U.S. agent for many student airfare bargains and student tours. CIEE's 80-page *Student Travel* catalogue and "Council Charter" brochures are available free from any Council Travel office in the United States (enclose $1 postage if ordering by mail). In addition to the CIEE headquarters (205 E. 42nd St.) and branch office (35 W. 8th St.) in New York City, there are Council Travel offices in Berkeley, La Jolla, Long Beach, Los Angeles, San Diego, San Francisco, and Sherman Oaks, CA; New Haven, CT; Washington, DC; Atlanta, GA; Chicago and Evanston, IL; New Orleans, LA; Amherst, Boston, and Cambridge, MA; Minneapolis, MN; Portland, OR; Providence, RI; Austin and Dallas, TX; Seattle, WA; and Milwaukee, WI.

The **Education Travel Center** (438 N. Frances St., Madison, WI 53703, tel. 608/256–5551) is another student-travel specialist worth contacting for information on student tours, bargain fares, and bookings.

Students who would like to work abroad should contact CIEE's **Work Abroad Department** (205 E. 42nd St., New York, NY 10017, tel. 212/661–1414, ext. 1130). The council arranges various types of paid and voluntary work experiences overseas for periods of up to six months. CIEE also sponsors study programs in Europe, Latin America, Asia, and Australia, and it publishes many books of interest to the student traveler. These include ***Work, Study, Travel Abroad: The Whole World Handbook*** ($9.95, plus $1 book-rate postage or $2.50 first-class postage); and ***Volunteer! The Comprehensive Guide to Voluntary Service in the U.S. and Abroad*** ($6.95, plus $1 book-rate postage or $2.50 first-class postage).

The Information Center at the **Institute of International Education** (809 UN Plaza, New York, NY 10017, tel. 212/984–5413) has reference books, foreign-university catalogues, study-abroad brochures, and other materials, which may be consulted by students and nonstudents alike, free of charge. The center is open Monday–Friday 10–4; it's closed on holidays.

Traveling with Children

Publications ***Family Travel Times*** is a newsletter published 10 times a year by **Travel With Your Children** (TWYCH, 80 8th Ave., New York, NY 10011, tel. 212/206–0688). A one-year subscription costs $35 and includes access to back issues and twice-weekly opportunities to call in for specific advice.

Home Exchange Exchanging homes is a surprisingly low-cost way to enjoy a vacation abroad, especially a long one. The largest home-exchange service, **International Home Exchange Service** (Box 3975, San Francisco, CA 94119, tel. 415/435–3497), publishes three directories a year. Membership, which costs $35, entitles you to one listing and all three directories. Photos of your property cost an additional $8.50; listing a second home costs $10. A good choice for domestic home exchange, **Vacation Exchange Club, Inc.** (12006 111th Ave., Unit 12, Youngstown, AZ 85363, tel. 602/972–2186), publishes one directory in February and a supplement in April. Membership is $24.70 per year, for which you receive one listing. Photos cost another $9; listing a second home costs $6. **Loan-a-Home** (2 Park La., Mount Vernon, NY 10552, tel. 914/664–7640) is popular with academics on sabbatical and businesspeople on temporary assignment. There's no annual membership fee or charge for listing your home; however, one directory and a supplement cost $30. Loan-a-Home publishes two directories (in December and June) and two supplements (in March and September) each year. The set of four books costs $40 per year.

Getting There On international flights, children under 2 not occupying a seat pay 10% of adult fare. Various discounts apply to children age 2–12, so check with your airline when booking. Reserve a seat behind the bulkhead of the plane. There's usually more leg room and enough space to fit a bassinet, which the airlines will supply. At the same time, ask about special children's meals or snacks; most airlines offer them. See TWYCH's "Airline Guide," published in the February 1990 issue of ***Family Travel Times*** (and again in February 1992) for more information about the children's services offered by 46 airlines.

Ask the airline in advance if you can bring aboard your child's car seat. At press time, the **Federal Aviation Administration** was considering two alternatives to the present regulations governing child restraint systems aboard an aircraft. The first alternative would require that air carriers provide children under 40 pounds or 3 years of age with a safety seat; the second alternative would require that air carriers allow the use of safety seats brought on board by a parent, guardian, or attendant, provided that a ticket is purchased for the child. For the booklet **"Child/Infant Safety Seats Acceptable for Use in Aircraft,"** write to the Federal Aviation Administration (APA-200, 800 Independence Ave. SW, Washington DC 20591, tel. 202/267-3479).

Hints for Disabled Travelers

The following organizations in the United States provide advice and services:

The **Information Center for Individuals with Disabilities** (Ft. Point Pl., 1st floor, 27–43 Wormwood St., Boston, MA 02210, tel. 617/727–5540) offers useful problem-solving assistance, including lists of travel agents who specialize in tours for the disabled.

Moss Rehabilitation Hospital Travel Information Service (12th St. and Tabor Rd., Philadelphia, PA 19141, tel. 215/329–5715) provides information for a small fee on tourist sights, transportation, and accommodations in destinations around the world.

Travel Industry and Disabled Exchange (5435 Donna Ave., Tarzana, CA 91356, tel. 818/368–5648), for a $15 annual fee, provides a quarterly newsletter and a directory of travel agencies and tours to Europe, Canada, Great Britain, New Zealand, and Australia, all specializing in travel for the disabled.

Mobility International USA (Box 3551, Eugene, OR 97403, tel. 503/343–1284) is an internationally affiliated organization with 500 members. For a $20 annual fee, it coordinates exchange programs for disabled people around the world and offers information on accommodations and organized study programs.

Hints for Older Travelers

The **American Association of Retired Persons** (AARP, 1909 K St. NW, Washington, DC 20049, tel. 202/662–4850) has two programs for independent travelers: (1) the **Purchase Privilege Program,** which comes with membership and offers discounts on hotels, airfare, car rentals, RV rentals, and sightseeing; and (2) the **AARP Motoring Plan,** which furnishes emergency aid (road service) and trip-routing information for an annual fee of $33.95 per person or couple. (Both programs include the member and member's spouse, or the member and another person who shares the household.) The AARP also arranges group tours, including apartment living in Europe and Australia, through **American Express Vacations** (Box 5014, Atlanta, GA

30302, tel. 800/241–1700). AARP members must be 50 or older; annual dues are $5 per person or per couple.

When using an AARP or other discount identification card, ask for reduced hotel rates at the time you make your reservation, not when you check out. At restaurants, show your card to the maître d' before you're seated because discounts may be limited to certain set menus, days, or hours. When renting a car, remember that economy cars priced at promotional rates may cost less than cars available with your discount ID card.

Elderhostel (80 Boylston St., Suite 400, Boston, MA 02116, tel. 617/426–7788) is an innovative 16-year-old educational program for people 60 and older. Participants live in dorms on some 1,200 campuses around the world. Mornings are devoted to lectures and seminars; afternoons, to sightseeing and field trips. Fees for two- to three-week trips, including room, board, tuition, and round-trip transportation, are $1,700–$3,200.

Mature Outlook (6001 N. Clark St., Chicago, IL 60660, tel. 800/336–6330), a subsidiary of Sears Roebuck & Co., is a travel club for people over 50, with hotel and motel discounts and a bimonthly newsletter. Annual membership is $9.95; there are 800,000 members currently. Instant membership is available at participating Holiday Inns.

The **National Council of Senior Citizens** (925 15th St. NW, Washington DC 20005, tel. 202/347–8800) is a nonprofit advocacy group with about 5,000 local clubs across the country. Annual membership is $12 per person or per couple. Members receive a monthly newspaper with travel information and an ID card for reduced-rate hotels and car rentals.

Saga International Holidays (120 Boylston St., Boston, MA 02116, tel. 800/343–0273), an affiliate of Elderhostel, specializes in group travel for people over 60. A selection of variously priced tours allows you to choose the package that meets your needs.

Further Reading

History For two intriguing studies that connect Irish culture and history, consult Constantine FitzGibbon's *The Irish in Ireland* and Sean O'Faolain's *The Irish: A Character Study*, which traces the history of Ireland from Celtic times. J.C. Beckett's *The Making of Modern Ireland*, a concise introduction to Irish history, covers the years between 1603 and 1923. *Modern Ireland*, a provocative new study by R.F. Foster, spans the years between 1600 and 1972. For an acclaimed history of Irish nationalism, refer to Robert Kee's *The Green Flag*.

Special-Interest Readers can choose from several volumes on a specific region. Peter Somerville-Large's *Dublin* is packed with anecdotes relating to the famed Irish city. *Georgian Dublin* by Desmond Guinness, the founder of the Irish Georgian Society, explores the city's architecture, with photographs and plans of Dublin's most admirable buildings. The most up-to-date work on the Aran Islands is Tim Robinson's award-winning *The Stones of Aran: Pilgrimage*. Though a little outdated, *The Aran Islands*, by J.M. Synge, is also worth reading. Tomas Ó Crohán's *The Islandman* provides a good background on Dingle and the Blasket Islands.

Autobiography Several autobiographical accounts by both Irish natives and foreign visitors offer unique perspectives on Ireland. Deborah Tall's *The Island of the White Cow* chronicles five years spent with an Irish professor on an island off the coast of Connemara. In *An Only Child* and *My Father's Son*, Frank O'Connor, a well-known fiction writer, recounts his years as an Irish revolutionary and later as an intellectual in Dublin during the 1920s. Niall Williams and Christine Breen, an American-Irish couple who started anew by moving to the County Clare countryside, recount their experiences in *O Come Ye Back to Ireland* and *When Summer's in the Meadow*. In *Round Ireland in Low Gear*, Eric Newby, a British travel writer, writes of his bicycle journey with his wife around the Emerald Isle. Christy Brown's *My Left Foot*, recently made into an award-winning film, is the autobiographical account of an artist crippled with cerebral palsy.

Fiction Ireland has a long, impressive history of great novelists and story writers. For a literary history exploring the influence of Ireland's changing landscape on its writers, look at *A Writer's Ireland*, by William Trevor. Samuel Beckett, the well-known playwright, fills his story collection *More Pricks than Kicks* with Dublin characters; if you enjoy literary gamesmanship, you may also want to try Beckett's trilogy—*Molloy*, *Malone*, and *The Unnamable*. James Joyce, certainly one of the most acclaimed writers of the 20th century, is world renowned for *Ulysses*, a classic, linguistically innovative work, which follows a group of Dublin characters through the course of a single day; shorter introductions to Joyce's writing include *Portrait of the Artist as a Young Man*, and *Dubliners*, a story collection.

Maeve Blinchy's *Light a Penny Candle* traces the friendship of two women, one of whom escapes to Ireland during World War II. If you're drawn to tales of unrequited love, turn to Elizabeth Bowen's stories and her novel, *The Last September*, set in Ireland during the Irish Civil War. Coming-of-age novels include *Under the Eye of the Clock*, a somewhat autobiographical work by Christopher Nolan, which takes as its subject a handicapped youth discovering the pleasures of language; and *Fools of Fortune*, by William Trevor, which treats the loss of an ideal childhood, brought about by a changing political climate.

Thomas Flanagan's *The Year of the French* is a historical novel about the people of County Mayo, who revolted in 1798 with the help of French revolutionaries. *A Nest of Simple Folk*, by Sean O'Faolain, follows three generations of an Irish family between 1854 and 1916. Leon Uris's *Trinity* covers the years 1840–1916, as seen through the eyes of British, Irish Catholic, and Ulster Protestant families. Jennifer Johnston, admired for her verbal economy, sets her best novels (including *The Captains and the Kings*, *The Gates*, and *How Many Miles to Babylon*) in the declining world of the Anglo-Irish "big house" in the early 20th century. In *No Country for Young Men*, Julia O'Faolain writes of two Irish families struggling to overcome the effects of the Irish Civil War. Bernard MacLaverty's two novels *Cal* and *Lamb* deal with modern-day Irish political and social barriers that can stand in the way of love.

If you prefer reading a more magical rather than a realistic novel, take a look at James Stephens's *A Crock of Gold*, a charming and wise fairy tale written for adults, or Flann O'Brien's *At Swim-Two-Birds*, a surrealistic tale full of Irish folklore.

Edna O'Brien writes often about romantic relationships in a trilogy of short novels titled *The Country Girls* and a collection of stories called *A Fanatic Heart*. Wayward characters, such as loners, prostitutes, and immigrants, abound in Desmond Hogan's volume of stories, *A Link with the River*. Other superbly crafted story collections, full of acute observations of Ireland's social and political landscape, include Benedict Kiely's *The State of Ireland*, Mary Lavin's *Collected Stories*, Frank O'Connor's *Collected Stories*, and William Trevor's *Stories*.

Theater Ireland claims a range of fine playwrights as well. Samuel Beckett, who moved from Ireland to Paris and began writing in French, is the author of the comic modernist masterpiece *Waiting for Godot*, among many other plays. *The Importance of Being Earnest* is perhaps the most acclaimed work of Oscar Wilde, a major proponent of "art for art's sake" and a dramatist, poet, and wit of the late 19th century. Among the many plays of George Bernard Shaw, who grew up in Dublin, are *Arms and the Man*, *Major Barbara*, *Pygmalion*, and *Saint Joan*.

The history of Irish theater includes a good number of controversial plays, such as J.M. Synge's *The Playboy of the Western World*, which was considered morally outrageous at the time of its opening in 1907, and is still appreciated today for its poetic language. Sean O'Casey wrote passionately about social injustice and working-class characters around the time of the Irish Civil War in such plays as *The Plough and the Stars* and *Juno and the Paycock*. *The Quare Fellow*, by Brendan Behan, challenged accepted mores in the 1950s and could only be produced originally in London. Behan is also well known for his play *The Hostage* and *Borstal Boy*, his memoirs. Two playwrights who have been recognized more recently internationally are Hugh Leonard (*Da* and *A Life*) and Brian Friel (*Philadelphia, Here I Come!*, *The Faith Healer*, and *The Aristocrats*), whose work often illuminates Irish small-town life.

Poetry No list of Irish literature would be complete without mention of the country's poets. The most celebrated of these is William Butler Yeats, whose poems often describe the Irish landscape, including the Sligo and Coole countryside. A favorite poet among the Irish people themselves is Patrick Kavanagh, whose distinguished career was devoted to writing exceptionally about ordinary lives. Thomas Kinsella's *Poems 1956–1973* and Seamus Heaney's *Selected Poems* are both highly recommended. Kinsella is also the editor of *The New Oxford Book of Irish Verse* and a translator of Irish (Gaelic) poetry. Heaney is considered one of today's most compelling Irish poets since Yeats; Northern Ireland serves as the setting for many of his recent poems.

Periodical *Ireland of the Welcomes* (U.S. and Canada: Box 2745, Boulder, CO 80322; Europe and elsewhere: Box 84, Limerick, Ireland), a magazine published six times a year by the Irish Tourist Board, features articles on aspects of Irish culture and travel, including driving tours.

Arriving and Departing

Visitors have a choice of three types of flights: nonstop—no changes, no stops; direct—no changes, but one or more stops; and connecting—two or more planes, one or more stops.

From North America by Plane

Irish Republic
Airports and Airlines

The main post of arrival for transatlantic flights is **Shannon Airport** (tel. 061/61444) on the west coast, 25½ km (16 mi) west of Limerick City. Shannon is a small airport, with only one modest terminal building. If you have some time to pass there, visit the duty-free shop, the first of its kind to open. It's stocked with last-minute buys such as sides of smoked salmon, handmade chocolates, whole farmhouse cheeses, and sweaters and tweed caps. Shannon is the place where Irish coffee—black coffee and sugar, bolstered with a shot of Irish whiskey and topped with whipped cream—was invented; sipping a cup at the airport is another good way to pass the time. All transatlantic flights touch down at Shannon, even if their destination is Dublin. The Shannon–Dublin flight takes 30–40 minutes.

Dublin Airport (tel. 01/379900) is 9.5 km (6 mi) north of the city center. Most of the flights it handles come from Europe, the United Kingdom, or inside of Ireland. It has just one terminal building, but the well-stocked duty-free shop boasts an unusual concession: Books can be sold prior to their official launch, so you can pick up the latest work by your favorite author even before it's been reviewed in the papers.

Only two airlines have regularly scheduled flights from the United States: **Aer Lingus** (212/557–1110 or 800/223–6537) and **Delta** (800/722–9230 or 800/241–4141). **Aer Lingus** flies from New York, Chicago, or Boston to Shannon or Dublin. **Delta** flies from Atlanta to Shannon or Dublin. A number of charter flights operate from the United States and Canada between May and September. No direct commercial flights are scheduled from Canada.

Flying Time

The shortest scheduled transatlantic flight to Shannon leaves from Boston (Aer Lingus); it takes five hours and 35 minutes. If you're flying on to Dublin, there is a 45-minute stopover at Shannon and then a 40-minute onward flight. New York to Shannon takes about 6½ hours; Chicago to Shannon, 7½ hours; and Atlanta to Shannon, seven hours.

Northern Ireland
Airports

No scheduled transatlantic flights are available to Belfast, although some charter flights can be found in the summer. For details, check with your travel agent. Otherwise, pick up a connecting flight to Belfast in Shannon, Dublin, London, or Manchester. Two airports serve Belfast: **Belfast International Airport at Aldergove** (tel. 0232/229271), 24 km (15 mi) from the city, handles all international traffic, and **Belfast Harbour Airport** (tel. 0232/57754), 6½ km (4 mi) from the city, handles local and U.K. flights only. In addition, **Eglinton,** Derry's airport, receives flights from Manchester and Glasgow in the United Kingdom (Loganair).

Enjoying the Flight

If you're lucky enough to be able to sleep on a plane, it makes sense to fly at night. Many experienced travelers, however, prefer to take an afternoon flight to Ireland and arrive in the evening, just in time for a good night's sleep. The air on a plane is dry, so it helps to drink a lot of nonalcoholic beverages while flying; drinking alcohol contributes to jet lag, as does eating heavy meals on board. Feet swell at high altitudes, so it's a good idea to remove your shoes at the beginning of your flight. Sleepers usually prefer window seats to curl up against; those who like to move around in the cabin should ask for aisle seats. Bulkhead seats (located in the front row of each cabin) have more legroom, but seat trays are attached rather awkwardly to the arms of the seat rather than to the back of the seat ahead. Generally, bulkhead seats are reserved for the disabled, the elderly, or parents traveling with babies.

Discount Flights

The major airlines offer a range of tickets that can increase or decrease the price of any given seat by more than 300%, depending on the day of purchase. As a rule, the further in advance you buy the ticket, the less expensive it is but the greater the penalty (up to 100%) for canceling. Check with airlines for details.

The best buy is not necessarily an APEX (advance purchase) ticket on one of the major airlines. These tickets carry certain restrictions: They must be bought in advance (usually 21 days); they restrict your travel, usually with a minimum stay of seven days and a maximum of 90; and they also penalize you for changes—voluntary or not—in your travel plans. But if you can work around these drawbacks (and most travelers can), they are among the best-value fares available.

Charter flights offer the lowest fares but often depart only on certain days, and they are seldom on time. You may be able to arrive at one city and return from another; however, you may lose all or most of your money if you cancel your trip. Travel agents can make bookings, though they won't encourage you, since commissions are lower than on scheduled flights. Checks should, as a rule, be made out to the bank and the specific escrow account for your flight. Don't sign up for a charter flight unless you've checked with a travel agency about the reputation of the packager. It's particularly important to know the packager's policy concerning refunds in the event of a canceled flight; some agents recommend that travelers purchase trip-cancellation insurance if they plan to book charter flights. One of the most popular charter operators to Europe is **Council Charter** (205 E. 42nd St., New York, NY 10017, tel. 212/661–0311 or 800/223–7402), a division of the **Council on International Educational Exchange** (CIEE). Other companies advertise in Sunday travel sections of newspapers.

Somewhat more expensive—but up to 50% below the cost of APEX fares—are tickets purchased through consolidators, companies that buy blocks of tickets on scheduled airlines and sell them at wholesale prices. Tickets are subject to availability, so passengers must generally have flexible travel schedules. Here again, you may lose all or most of your money if you change your plans, but at least you will be on a regularly scheduled flight with less risk of cancellation than on a charter. As an added precaution, you may want to purchase trip-cancellation insurance. Once you've made your reservation, call the airline to confirm it. Among the best-known consolidators are **UniTravel** (Box 12485, St. Louis, MO 63132, tel. 314/569–2501 or 800/325–2222) and **Access International** (250 W. 57th St.,

Suite 511, New York, NY 10107, tel. 212/333–7280 or 800/825–3633). Others advertise in the Sunday travel sections of newspapers.

A third option is to join a travel club that offers special discounts to its members. Among such organizations are **Discount Travel International** (114 Forrest Ave., Narberth, PA 19072, tel. 215/668–2182), **Moment's Notice** (40 E. 49th St., New York, NY 10017, tel. 212/486–0503), **Traveler's Advantage** (CUC Travel Service, 40 Oakview Dr., Trumbull, CT 06611, tel. 800/648–4037), and **Worldwide Discount Travel Club** (1674 Meridien Ave., Miami Beach, FL 33139, tel. 305/534–2082). These cut-rate tickets should be compared with APEX tickets on the major airlines.

Smoking As of late February 1990, smoking is banned on all routes within the 48 contiguous states; within the states of Hawaii and Alaska; to and from the U.S. Virgin Islands and Puerto Rico; and on flights of less than six hours to and from Hawaii and Alaska. The rule applies to both domestic and foreign carriers.

On a flight where smoking is permitted, you can request a nonsmoking seat during check-in or when you book your ticket. If the airline tells you there are no seats available in the nonsmoking section, insist on one: Department of Transportation regulations require carriers to find seats for all nonsmokers, provided they meet check-in time restrictions. These regulations apply to all international flights on domestic carriers; however, the Department of Transportation does not have jurisdiction over foreign carriers traveling out of or into the United States.

From North America by Ship

The days are long gone when almost all transatlantic liners made Cobh in County Cork their first or last European port of call. The only regular visitor these days is Cunard's superliner, the *Queen Elizabeth 2*. For the last three years, she has called at Cobh in mid-July and mid-September en route to New York (a four-day trip). Confirmation of her 1991 schedule will be available early 1991 from **Cunard** (555 5th Ave., New York, NY 10017, tel. 212/661–7777 or 800/5–CUNARD). Inclusive tours that coincide with the sailings are offered by **O'Connor Fairways Tours** (800 2nd Ave., New York, NY 10017, tel. 212/661–0550 or 800/288–7609). Rates for the four-day crossing start at around $1,785 per person, including one-way economy-class airfare.

From Britain by Plane

Irish Republic *Airports and Airlines* Flying to Ireland has never been easier, with 11 airlines serving 11 destinations in Ireland from 19 British airports. The major carriers are **Aer Lingus, British Airways,** and **Ryanair.** There are 11 flights every day to Dublin from Heathrow, operated jointly by Aer Lingus and British Airways. Aer Lingus and Dan Air also operate frequent daily flights to Dublin from Gatwick. In addition, flights to Dublin leave from Birmingham, Bristol, East Midlands, Liverpool, Manchester, Leeds/Bradford, Newcastle, Edinburgh, and Glasgow. There are at least two flights daily from Heathrow to Shannon, and three flights daily to Cork. There are also flights to Cork from Birmingham,

Manchester, and Plymouth, and to Dublin, Cork, Knock, Shannon, and Waterford from Luton (near London). Flying time to most Irish airports is around one hour.

The wide range of fares reflects the number of flights available—and the competition: Most fares offer good value. The season you travel, the length of time you stay in Ireland (with all cheaper fares you have to spend at least one Saturday night in the country), and the amount of time between your trip and the purchase of your ticket (generally, the further in advance you make your reservations, the cheaper the flight will be) dictate the cost of the flight. It's always worth shopping around before making your reservation. A range of business-class fares is also available. There are no first-class fares to Ireland.

For reservations and information in Britain: **Aer Lingus** (tel. 071/569–5555); **British Airways** (tel. 071/897–4000); **British Midland** (tel. 071/589–5599); **Brymon Airways** (tel. 0345/717383); **Capital Airline** (tel. 0345/800777); **Loganair** (tel. 041/889–3181); **Manx Airlines** (tel. 0624/824313); **Ryanair** (tel. 071/435–7101); **SAS** (tel. 0345/090900); and **TAP** (tel. 061/499–2161).

Northern Ireland
Airports and Airlines

Frequent flights are scheduled throughout the day to Belfast from Heathrow, Gatwick, and 17 other U.K. airports. Flights take about 1¼ hours from London. British Airways' and British Midland Airways' shuttle services from London are walk-on, no-reservation flights, and the airlines claim that no passenger is turned away; another plane would be employed if necessary. **Belfast International Airport at Aldergrove** is Northern Ireland's principal air arrival point. **Belfast Harbour Airport** receives flights from U.K. provincial airports and from Luton. **Eglinton Airport,** a few miles from Derry City, receives flights from Manchester and Glasgow. Call 0504/261911, 0504/44100, or 0504/43813 for a taxi into town.

British Airways and **British Midland Airways** (*see* above) operate most flights into Belfast, but the cheapest flights are on either **Capital Airlines** (*see* above) or **Brittania** (tel. 0582/405737). Other main airlines flying into Northern Ireland are **Loganair** (*see* above) and **Air UK** (tel. 0345/666777).

From Britain by Ferry, Car, and Bus

By Ferry
Irish Republic

Getting to Ireland by train/ferry is simple, though slow. There are two principal routes: to Dublin from Holyhead on the Isle of Anglesea, and to Rosslare from Fishguard or Pembroke in Wales. Two companies sail the Dublin route: **B&I** (tel. 071/491–8682) and **Sealink** (tel. 0223/647047), whose ferries go to Dun Laoghaire, a few miles south of Dublin. Buses into Dublin from the docks meet all the ferries. Total journey time from London is around 11 hours.

B&I operates the Pembroke–Rosslare route; Sealink operates the Fishguard–Rosslare route. To connect with the Fishguard sailings, take one of the many direct trains from London (Paddington). Sailing time is 4½ hours. A connecting train at Rosslare will get you to Waterford by about 8:30 PM, to Cork by about midnight. For the Pembroke sailings, you have to change at Swansea. Sailing time is again 4½ hours.

The cost of your trip can vary substantially. It's worth spending time with a travel agent and comparing prices carefully;

flying is sometimes cheaper. Fares to Dublin are cheapest, starting at around UK£50 off-season round-trip and rising to UK£80 round-trip in summer. Book well in advance at peak periods. Students and others under 26 should take advantage of the cheap fares offered by **Eurotrain** and **Transalpino.**

For reservations and information, contact: **B&I; Eurotrain** (tel. 071/730–3402); **Sealink;** and **Transalpino** (tel. 071/834–9656).

Northern Ireland Car ferries run to the port of Larne from the Scottish port of Stranraer. Trains leave London (Euston) for Stranraer Harbour several times a day. **Sealink Ferries** (tel. 0776/22620) crosses the water to Larne, where you pick up a train to Belfast. The whole trip is around 13 hours. There is also a nine-hour crossing from Liverpool to Belfast, operated by **Belfast Ferries** (tel. 0519/226234). Trains leave London (Euston) for Liverpool throughout the day.

If you're traveling from Dublin, you can take the Belfast–Dublin Express, which goes nonstop between the two cities in two hours. Six trains run daily in both directions (only three on Sundays).

By Car

Irish Republic All ferries on *both* principal routes to Ireland—Holyhead–Dublin and Fishguard/Pembroke–Rosslare—take cars. Fishguard and Pembroke are relatively easy to reach by road. The car trip to Holyhead, on the other hand, is sometimes difficult: Delays on the A55 North Wales coastal road are not unusual.

For reservations and information, *see* From Britain by Ferry, above.

Northern Ireland Car ferries to Belfast leave from Liverpool; those to Larne, from the Scottish ports of Stranraer and Cairnryan. For more information, *see* From Britain by Ferry, above.

Many roads from the Republic into Northern Ireland have been closed, but a score of legitimate crossing points, as well as another score of "unapproved" routes, exist. There's an army checkpoint, with relatively few formalities, at all approved frontier posts. The fast N1/A1 connects Belfast to Dublin (161 km/100 mi); there are sometimes border delays on this road.

By Bus

Irish Republic Numerous bus services run between Britain and Ireland. Those traveling with young children should beware the long hours and possible delays. All bus services use either the Holyhead–Dublin or Fishguard/Pembroke–Rosslare ferry routes.

Services are operated by **National Express–Supabus** (tel. 071/730–0202), a consortium of British bus companies, and **Slattery's** (tel. 071/724–0741), an Irish bus operator. Supabus has services from all major British cities to more than 90 Irish destinations. Slattery's has services from London, Manchester, Liverpool, and North Wales to Dublin, Tralee, Listowel, Ennis, and Galway.

Northern Ireland Buses to Belfast run from London and from Birmingham, making the Stranraer–Larne crossing. For reservations and information, contact **National Express** (tel. 071/730–0202).

Staying in the Irish Republic

Getting Around

By Plane Ireland is not a large country, so air travel does not play a big role in internal travel; however, an increase primarily in internal business travel has led to the development of provincial airports, some of which now have regular daily flights from the United Kingdom. They can also be very useful to vacationers. See relevant regional chapters for details on airports at Kerry, Sligo Town, Galway, Knock, Waterford, and Derry City (for Donegal). Several flights daily are scheduled between Shannon, Dublin, and Cork, with a flying time of 30–40 minutes between each city. There is also a regular air service to all three of the Aran Islands from Galway Airport. Operated by Aer Arann, the flights take 15–25 minutes, weather permitting (*see* Chapter 8).

By Car A car is the ideal way to explore Ireland, a country of small back roads and predominantly rural attractions. Roads are generally good, although four-lane two-way roads are the exception rather than the rule. Most National Primary Routes (designated by the letter "N") have two lanes with generous shoulders on which to pass. In general, traffic is light, especially off the National routes, but it's wise to slow down on the smaller, often twisty roads. The general speed limit in Ireland is 88 kph (55 mph) on the open road and either 48 kph (30 mph) or 64 kph (40 mph) in urban areas. Beware of high speeds on the back roads; you may find a herd of cattle or a donkey and a cart around the next corner.

Road signs are generally in both English and Irish (Gaelic). The Republic is currently undergoing a slow changeover from miles to kilometers. There simply is not enough money in the road budget to change all the signs at once: you'll understand why when you see how many signs can be attached to a single post in rural Ireland. As a general rule, distances on the new *green* signposts (which cover most of the National Primary Routes) are in kilometers. Most white signposts are older, and they give the distance in miles. (The *new* white signposts, however, give the distance in kilometers!)

Because of the coexistence of both old and new signs, the route number is not always referred to on the signpost, particularly when traveling on a National Secondary Road (also N-numbered routes) or a Regional road (R-numbered routes). In these cases, the name of the next town on your itinerary is more important to know than the route number: Neither small local signposts nor local people refer to roads by these relatively new official numbers.

The Irish, like the British, drive on the left-hand side of the road. Safety belts must be worn by the driver and front passenger, and children under 12 must travel in the back. It is also compulsory for motorcyclists and their passengers to wear helmets.

Traffic signs are the same as in the rest of Europe, and roadway markings are standard. Note especially that a continuous white line down the center of the road prohibits passing. Barred markings on the road and flashing yellow beacons indicate a crossing, where pedestrians have the right of way. At a junction of two roads of equal importance, the driver to the right has the right of way.

Despite the relatively small amount of traffic, parking in towns can be a problem. Signs with the letter *P* indicate that parking is permitted, but a stroke through the P warns you to stay away or you'll be liable for a fine of £15 to £40. In Dublin and Cork, parking lots are your best bet, but check the rate first in Dublin; they can vary wildly.

Drunk-driving laws are strict. Like the United Kingdom, Ireland has a Breathalyzer test, which the police can administer anytime. If you refuse to take it, the odds are you'll be prosecuted anyway. As ever, the best advice is not to drink if you're going to be driving.

By Train Ireland's train services are operated by the state-owned **Irish Rail (Iarnrod Éireann),** the rail division of **CIE (Coras Iompair Éireann).** They are generally reliable, reasonably priced, and comfortable. All the principal towns are easily reached from Dublin, though services between provincial cities are roundabout. If you want to go to Cork City from Wexford, for example, you have to go via Limerick Junction. It is often quicker, though perhaps less comfortable, to take a bus.

Most mainline trains have two classes: standard and super-standard. A round-trip ticket is usually cheapest to buy. For information on long-term passes, *see* Rail Passes, above.

By Bus The long-distance services are operated by Irish Bus (**Bus Éireann**), a subdivision of CIE. Bus Éireann also provides local services in Cork, Galway, Limerick, and Waterford. Expressway bus services, with the most up-to-date buses, cover the major routes throughout the country.

Buses are a cheap and flexible way of exploring the countryside. Bear in mind that outside the peak season, services are limited, and some routes (e.g. Killarney–Dingle) disappear altogether. There is often only one service a day on the Express routes—and one a week to some of the more remote villages! To ensure that your proposed bus journey is feasible, buy a copy of Bus Éireann's timetable—45p from any bus terminal.

Many of the destination indicators on bus routes are in Irish, so make sure you get on the right bus. For example, a bus to Wicklow marked "Baile Átha Cliath" would in fact be going to Dublin, as that is the Irish name for the capital. Asking someone to translate is often the best way to avoid a mishap.

By Ferry Ferries provide two very useful short cuts. If you're traveling from County Kerry to County Clare and the West of Ireland, you can take the ferry from Tarbert (in County Kerry), leaving every hour on the half hour. Going the other way, ferries leave from Killimer (in County Clare) every hour on the hour. The boat takes 30 minutes to cross the Shannon Estuary. It costs £5 per car, £1 for foot passengers.

A 10-minute car ferry crosses the River Suir between Ballyhack in County Wexford and Passage East in County Waterford. It not only saves you a boring drive through New Ross on the N25 but also introduces you to two pretty fishing villages, Ballyhack and Arthurstown. It operates continuously during daylight hours and costs £3 per car, 70p for foot passengers.

Many, but not all, of Ireland's offshore islands can be reached by ferry. There are regular services to the Aran Islands from Galway City, Rossaveale in County Galway, and Doolin in County Clare. Ferries also sail to Inishbofin and Arranmore off the Donegal coast, and to Bere, Sherkin, and Cape Clear islands off the coast of County Cork. The islands are all small enough to explore on foot, so the ferries are for foot passengers and bicycles only. Other islands—the Blaskets and the Skelligs in Kerry, Rathlin, and Tory off the Donegal coast—can be reached by private arrangements with local boatmen (*see* relevant regional chapters). Full details on ferries to the islands are available in *Islands of Ireland* (£1.50), available from the Irish Tourist Board.

Telephones

Public pay phones are located in all towns and villages. They can be found in street booths and in bars and shops, some of which display a sign saying "You can phone from here." There are currently at least three different models of pay phones in operation; read the instructions or ask for assistance. A local call costs 20p for three minutes; long-distance calls within Ireland are around 60p for three minutes. The whole country is covered by a direct dialing (STD) system. If you have trouble getting through, dial 10 for operator assistance; however, if the operator has to connect your call it will cost at least one third more than direct dial. Do not make calls from your hotel room unless it's absolutely necessary. Practically all hotels add 200% to 300% to the cost of a call.

International calls can only be made from the most up-to-date pay phones. Most towns and villages have this facility in the post office; in Cork City and Dublin, the general post offices are located on Oliver Plunkett Street and O'Connell Street, respectively.

Calls can be dialed directly to over 75 countries worldwide, with access to 120 more via the operator. International dialing codes can be found in all telephone directories. The international prefix from Ireland is 16. Calls to the United States cost about £4.50 for three minutes, less after 10 PM and on Saturdays, Sundays, and bank holidays. Calls to Canada cost the same.

For calls to Great Britain, dial 03 before the exchange code (031 for London), followed by the local number. Calls to Britain cost about £2.10 for three minutes, about one third less after 6 PM and on Saturdays, Sundays, and public holidays.

For operator assistance, dial 10. To call the international operator in the Dublin area, dial 114; in all other areas, dial 10. The international operator covers collect calls, person-to-person calls, and calls to ships.

For international telegrams, dial 196; for audio conference calls, dial 114. To find out the time, dial 1191; the weather forecast is 1199. For directory inquiries within Ireland and Northern Ireland, dial 190.

Mail

Postal Rates Airmail rates to the United States and Canada are 50p for letters, 32p for postcards. Mail to all European countries goes by air automatically, so airmail stickers or envelopes are not required. Rates are 30p for letters, 26p for postcards. These rates may change before or during 1991, so be sure to check them.

Receiving Mail Mail can be held for collection at any post office free of charge for up to three months. It should be addressed to the recipient "c/o Poste Restante." In Dublin, use the General Post Office (O'Connell St., Dublin 1, tel. 01/728888).

Tipping

In some hotels and restaurants a service charge of around 12% —rising to 15% in some plush spots—is added to the bill. If in doubt, ask whether service is included. In places where it is included, tipping is not necessary unless you have received particularly good service. But if there is no service charge, add a minimum of 10% to the total.

Tip taxi drivers about 10% of the fare displayed by the meter. Hackney cabs, who make the trip for a prearranged sum, do not expect tips. There are few porters and plenty of baggage trolleys at airports, so tipping is usually not an issue; if you use a porter, 50p is the minimum. Tip hotel porters about 50p per large suitcase. Hairdressers normally expect about £1. You don't tip in pubs, but for waiter service in a bar or hotel lounge, or a Dublin lounge bar, leave about 20p.

Opening and Closing Times

Most shops are open from 9 to 5:30 or 6, Monday–Saturday. Once a week—normally Wednesday, Thursday, or Saturday—they shut at 1 for the afternoon. These times do *not* apply to Dublin, and they can vary from region to region, so it's best to check locally. Larger shopping malls usually stay open late once a week—generally until 9 PM—on Thursday or Friday.

Banks are open from 10 to 12:30 and 1:30 to 3, Monday–Friday. They remain open until 5 one afternoon per week; again, the day of week varies locally.

Pubs are open Monday–Saturday from 10:30 AM to 11:30 PM June–September, closing at 11 the rest of the year. The famous Holy Hour, which required city pubs to close from 2:30 to 3:30, was abolished in 1988, and afternoon opening is now at the discretion of the owner or manager; few bother to close. On Sundays, the pubs are open from 12:30 to 2 and from 4 to 11. All pubs are closed on Christmas Day and Good Friday, but hotel bars are open for residents.

Shopping

Few visitors leave Ireland without purchasing at least a tweed hat or a hand-knitted Aran jersey, and if not one of these, then a linen tablecloth or a piece of Waterford crystal. All four items are reasonably priced investments that, given a little care, will last a lifetime.

Irish crafts have come a long way over the last 20 years. The range of Irish-made goods available in the shops is no longer limited to the ethnic and the traditional: high-fashion garments and household goods combining traditional materials with the very best modern designs have added a new dimension to the market.

The best selection of shops and the most sophisticated goods are found in Dublin—especially if high fashion and antiques are among your tastes. Cork City offers less choice but quite a few surprises, and Galway features craft galleries and off-beat boutiques.

A logical shopping scheme would entail tweeds in County Donegal, Aran sweaters in County Galway, Waterford crystal in Waterford, and so on, but the dedicated shopper soon realizes that most craft shops sell a mix of goods drawn from all over the country. If you're after something a little different, keep an eye open for signs indicating "craft workshops": There are at least 16 of them around the country. In each of these workshops, you'll find independent crafts people with different skills selling directly from their studios. Craft workshops have helped increase the variety and quality of Irish souvenirs.

U.S. and Canadian visitors have a great advantage in shopping; they get a refund of the **value added tax**—called VAT—which currently accounts for a hefty 25% of the purchase price of many goods and 10% of those that fall outside the *luxury* category. Most items of interest to visitors, right down to ordinary toilet soap (but excluding children's clothing), are rated at 25%. Most crafts outlets and department stores operate a system called Cashback, which enables U.S. and Canadian visitors to collect VAT rebates in the currency of their choice at Dublin or Shannon Airport on departure. Otherwise, refunds can be claimed from individual stores after returning home. Forms for the refunds must be picked up at the time of purchase, and the form must be stamped by customs before leaving Ireland. Most major stores deduct VAT at the time of sale if goods are to be shipped overseas; however, there is a shipping charge.

Antiques Top-quality antique shops are concentrated in Dublin's Grafton Street area, but it's still possible to pick up modestly priced pieces of 18th- and 19th-century silver, 19th-century pewter, and antique period furniture elsewhere in the country. Try Cork City, Castlecomer, Kilkenny, Galway City, and Limerick.

Crystal Irish lead crystal is justifiably world famous. The best known of all, Waterford Glass, is on sale all over Ireland in department stores and craft shops. The demand is so great that substantial export orders can take weeks or even months to fill. Check out the lesser known crystals—Cork, Dublin, Tyrone, and Galway crystal—and the less formal uncut glass from Jerpoint and Stoneyford.

Drinkables Irish whiskey has an altogether different taste from Scotch whisky, and a different spelling, too. Well-known brands include Powers, Paddy, Jameson, and Bushmills. There are also two excellent Irish liqueurs: Irish Mist, which contains whiskey and honey, and Bailey's Irish Cream, a concoction of whiskey and cream, sometimes drunk on ice as an aperitif.

Edibles Smoked salmon can vary greatly in taste and quality. Make sure it's wild salmon, not farmed, and if the label tells you what sort of wood it was smoked over, opt for oak chips. Nowadays smoked salmon is sold in plastic packages, sliced or unsliced. A cheaper but also delicious alternative is smoked trout. Whole farmhouse cheeses like St. Killian's—a Camembert-like pasteurized cheese—are becoming popular gifts. More exotic and more expensive are the handmade farmhouse cheeses, each from an individual herd of cows. Milleens, Durrus, and Gubbeen are all excellent, though strong when ripe. A milder alternative is the Gouda-like Coolea cheese, found in most duty-free shops.

Jewelry Dublin and Cork City are the best spots for antique jewelry, but do not despair if the prices there are beyond your resources. Beautiful modern reproductions of such Celtic treasures as the Tara brooch are on sale for a fraction of the antique price. Other good buys include Claddagh friendship rings, in silver or gold, and beautiful pieces made by modern silversmiths using polished Connemara marble.

Knitwear Aran sweaters were developed by the women of the Aran Isles to provide a working garment that was warm, comfortable, and weatherproof. The religious symbols and folk motifs woven into distinctive patterns once enabled local people to identify each other's family and locality. Even today, no two Arans are alike: If you want to buy a hand knit, take your time and wait till you find one that really takes your fancy. After all, it should last the rest of your life. Cheaper and less durable Arans are described as "hand-loomed," which is just another way of saying "machine-made," so be sure you are getting what you want. There is a wealth of other types of sweaters: classic blue fisherman's rib sweaters, homespun hand-dyed hand knits, picture sweaters, and sophisticated mohair garments.

Linen A pure linen blouse, like an Aran sweater, can last forever. Designs are classic so they will not date. Linen handkerchiefs for men make useful gifts. Damask tablecloths and crochet-linen place mats make ideal wedding gifts.

Rugs, Shawls, and Blankets All crafts shops sell fleece floor rugs made of goat- or sheepskin. Handwoven shawls made from unspun, undyed wool are even more luxurious than mohair, though not as easy to find. Lightweight woolen blankets in traditional plaids are always popular gifts.

Tableware The Arklow pottery in County Wicklow is famous for its fine china sold at all major department stores. Belleek, on the border with Northern Ireland, produces delicate bone china, which is widely collected. Tableware by Ireland's many ceramic artists, with striking modern designs, can be a real bargain, especially if four or six place settings are ordered at once.

Tweeds The best selection of traditional tweeds is still found in the specialist tweed shops of Counties Galway and Donegal. Weavers can also be found at work in Kerry, Dublin, County Wicklow, and elsewhere in Connemara. Tweeds vary a good deal in type, from rugged-looking garments to clothes with jewellike colors that are popularized by Avoca Handweavers and worn by some of Ireland's most fashionable citizens.

Sports and Outdoor Activities

Participant Sports

Bicycling The combination of numerous side roads and very light traffic makes Ireland an attractive destination for cyclists. The less energetic can concentrate their itinerary on the relatively flat central area of the country; those who brave the mountains of the West and Southwest will be rewarded by magnificent scenery and a wonderfully varied coastline.

Boardsailing and Dinghy Sailing Boardsailing has caught on in the last 10 years. There are numerous locations suitable for the sport: inland lakes, river estuaries, and sheltered harbors. Dinghies can be hired at most of Ireland's sailing schools, which will also teach you how to sail them in five-day courses. Bring your own wet suit, if possible: You'll need it, even in July and August.

Cruising Fully equipped boats are rented by the week on the Shannon and the Grand Canal. It's a simple and relaxing holiday, allowing you to explore lesser-known, but beautiful, corners of Ireland. Boats can accommodate up to eight people and have showers, toilet, and well-equipped galleys. Prices start at about £180 per week.

Fishing Ireland is well known as a game-angling resort: wild Atlantic salmon, wild brown trout, and sea trout abound in the rivers, lakes, and estuaries, and offshore is the deep-sea challenge. Coarse fishing (for all fish that are not trout or salmon) is also available. The salmon season is normally from January 1 to September 30, but dates vary from one district to another. The best period for sea trout is June to late September.

Permits are necessary on privately owned waters or club waters: The latter will cost £5–£15 a day for salmon, £2–£10 for trout. There is no closed season for coarse angling. Besides the permit for the use of a certain stretch of water, those who wish to fish for salmon and sea trout by rod and line must also have a state national license. This costs £25 annually, or £10 for 21 days. It is available in some tackle shops or from the **Central Fisheries Board** (Balngowan House, Mobhi Boreen, Glasnevin, Dublin 9, tel. 01/379206). No license is required for brown trout, rainbow trout, or coarse fish, including pike. Sea angling is available on rocks and piers around the coast. A day of offshore fishing from an open launch costs about £15 per head.

Golf There are nearly 200 golf courses in Ireland, from world-famous championship courses to scenic nine-hole courses. Choose between the challenging links of the Atlantic coast, the more subtle layouts on the eastern seaboard, and the mature parklands of the inland courses. Killarney's two courses are unmatched for scenery; Arnold Palmer says **Portmarnock** (near Dublin) is among the world's best. He himself has designed the new course at **Tralee,** and there's a second 18-hole course at **Ballybunion** designed by Robert Trent Jones. The historic **Royal Dublin** on the shores of Dublin Bay is another course not to be missed.

Green fees average about £7, but can be as much as £25 at the most prestigious places. Only **Waterville** and **Ashville** have electric carts. Very few places rent out clubs.

Hiking The Irish Tourist Board provides free information sheets on long-distance paths, set up throughout the country over the last few years with the consent of local landowners. Routes are indicated by trail markers and signposts. Most are between 30 and 60 km (18 and 37 mi), with the exception of the **Wicklow Way,** the first to be opened and still one of the best, which is 137 km (85 mi) long. Alternatively, you can plan your own walks with the help of a good touring map: Ireland is an excellent walking country, with its mild climate and virtually traffic-free byroads.

Horseback Riding Several riding stables offer all-inclusive holidays combining long days in the saddle with home-cooked food and bed-and-breakfast accommodations. Most stables charge about £7 for an hour's ride, a little more if tuition is included.

Hunting If you're staying in hunting country, your hotel will arrange an introduction to the local hunt. The season runs from November to March, and the meet makes a fine spectacle, with the pink-coated hunt officials and their large, heavy-footed hounds milling around outside the village pub before the start. Special hunting packages can be pre-booked (*see* Special-Interest Tours, above) for real enthusiasts; they make exceptionally memorable holidays.

Jogging Early risers are amazed to find that no one in rural Ireland drives much before 8 AM, turning the place into a jogger's paradise. Phoenix Park is the place to go in Dublin; most hotels are a 10- or 15-minute jog from the park. The many long sandy beaches around the country are popular with runners, but you may find yourself sharing space with a string of race horses: Beaches are favorite spots for practice gallops.

Sailing There are several companies around the coast offering bare-boat charters to experienced skippers, but cruises must be booked well in advance. The coastline is endlessly varied and remarkably uncrowded compared with, say, the southern coast of England. Formalities are minimal, harbor dues are low, and facilities are extremely simple.

Tennis Tennis has gained in popularity over the last few years, but it's not really suited to the rainy Irish climate. More than 100 hotels and guest houses have hard or grass courts—usually just one or two—and the cities and larger towns have public courts. Fees are low, but finding equipment to rent can be difficult.

Spectator Sports

Gaelic Games Gaelic football and hurling are played in most parts of the Republic. Gaelic football is an extremely fast and rough form of football (closer to rugby than American football), which involves two teams of 15 who kick and run around a field with a round, soccer-like ball. The rules of this game are complicated, but the skill and speed of the players is exciting and impressive to watch, even if you don't quite understand what is going on. Hurling, considered by many to be the fastest field game in the world, also involves two teams of 15 who use three-foot wood sticks with a broad base to agressively catch and hurl a leather-covered ball toward goalposts; the game can often result in several injuries. Gaelic games are organized by the Irish Gaelic Athletic Association (GAA) and can be observed free of charge at local GAA fields and sports centers around the Republic. Inter-provincial games and All-Ireland finals are played throughout July and August at the GAA stadiums in Cork and Dublin. Croke Park in Dublin is the setting for the end of the annual All-Ireland finals. Tickets for these matches can be hard to obtain, but the events are also televised.

Horse Racing There is a horse race somewhere in Ireland almost every day of the year. The flat season runs from March to November; steeplechases are held throughout the year. Several courses—about 28 of them altogether—are within easy reach of Dublin. Irish classics are run at the Curragh in County Kildare, and the **Irish Grand National** is at Fairyhouse in County Meath. Some of the best meetings are held in the summer at smaller courses: Killarney in mid-July, Galway in late July–early August, Tramore in mid-August, Tralee in late August, and Listowel at the end of September.

Beaches

Ireland has over 3,200 km (2,000 mi) of coastline, with an abundance of beaches—or strands, as they are called locally. Some are small rocky coves with shingle where you can enjoy utter privacy; others, like Tramore, County Waterford; Courtown, County Wexford; Salthill near Galway; and Bundoran in County Donegal are long sandy beaches fronting a bustling resort town. The Irish like their beaches kept simple, so you will not find much in the way of facilities outside the resort towns. At most, there might be a public toilet, or an isolated hotel or bar, but don't count on it. If bathing is unsafe there will probably be a notice to that effect, or a red flag. You should not assume that bathing is safe in the absence of any warnings: Ask locally to make sure. Few people swim outside the months of July and August, but beaches remain popular with walkers and runners throughout the year.

Dining

The quality and variety of Ireland's restaurants has improved greatly in the past 15 years. The soggy vegetables and overcooked meat that once characterized Irish hotel and restaurant food are becoming increasingly hard to find. A new generation of imaginative chefs has begun to capitalize on what are some of the best raw materials in the world for gourmet cooking.

Lavish hospitality has always been a characteristic of Irish society, and the generous portions offered in Irish hotels and restaurants prove the point. Breakfast starts with fruit juice, followed by cereal or porridge, and then a *fry* consisting of bacon, sausage, egg, and tomato, with local variations such as potato cakes or black pudding. This is accompanied by toast or soda bread (whole-meal bread made with bicarbonate of soda and buttermilk instead of yeast), orange marmalade, and a pot of tea or coffee.

Many people find that this is enough to keep them going until teatime or early dinner. Others tide themselves over with a one-dish pub lunch—an open smoked-salmon sandwich or a bowl of Irish stew (mutton, potatoes, onions, carrots, and parsley, simmered together).

Most towns have at least one restaurant of some sort. In less commercial areas such as the midland counties, the best bet is usually the local hotel. Irish pubs have taken over the role filled elsewhere by cafés and coffee shops. Most pubs serve tea, coffee, and sandwiches, and many offer simple bar food at lunchtime. Requests for tea, coffee, and food (and the presence of small children) are generally not welcome in the evenings, when the main business becomes the provision of alcoholic drinks.

Many Irish people eat their main meal at midday, so most restaurants are open at lunchtime—from 12:30 to 2:30. Dinner service begins at around 6, but 7:30 to 8:30 is the most popular time to eat. The many small Irish restaurants make reservations advisable on weekends and during the peak season. As you will see from the listings, in all but the fanciest top spots, informal dress is acceptable—casual but neat. This does not include beachwear, shorts, skimpy or tattered T-shirts, and torn or cutoff jeans.

Ireland is renowned for its dairy products, its meat, and its seafood. The dominant school of cooking, best described as Irish with a French accent, combines classic French and traditional Irish cooking, and includes some nouvelle cuisine influence as well. Irish cream and butter are blended with wine and herbs to produce light sauces that complement rather than dominate the excellent meat and fish. Steak, which appears on nearly all menus, is always a reliable option. A juicy, charbroiled sirloin needs no embellishment—but if you want it rare, be sure to ask. Lamb and pork are both of high quality. Lamb is at its best from March to September, which is also the best time for seafood—lobster, crab, prawns, fresh salmon, trout, mussels, scallops, sea urchin, sole, brill, monkfish, turbot, skate, and, except in summer, oysters. The coast is never more than an hour and a half away, so you can expect all seafood to be freshly caught and high in quality.

Winter travelers can look forward to sampling the game. Kerry venison is a famous specialty beginning in October; the pheasant season starts on November 1 and lasts for about three months. Quail, woodcock, wild duck, rabbit, and hare all appear frequently on the menus of the better restaurants—either roasted or in pâtés and pies.

Several exceptionally good Irish cheeses have been developed recently, notably Cashel Blue, St. Killian, Coolea, Milleens, and Durrus. Many of the various fruits and vegetables are still imported, but outside Dublin, the best places limit themselves to the locally grown seasonal crop. The more old-fashioned restaurants offer at least two kinds of potatoes, sometimes more: chipped (french fried), boiled, sautéed, mashed, and *dauphinois* (sliced in a gratin dish), to name a few. But usually the Irish like their potatoes plainly boiled in their jackets, piled high on a serving dish and bursting open. Peel one on your side plate, smother it with butter, and you'll understand why.

Nowadays most restaurants have a license to serve alcoholic drinks. There are two kinds of licenses: a wine license allows a restaurant to serve wine and wine-based drinks such as sherry and vermouth; however, it cannot serve spirits or beer of any sort—canned, bottled, or draft. Restaurants with a full license can serve the full range of liquors and beers.

To help visitors on a budget, more than 360 restaurants participate in a *tourist menu* scheme. Up to three three-course menus are available at set prices—£5.75, £7.90, and £12. The Irish Tourist Board's *Dining in Ireland* (£2) gives full details on participating restaurants. Some places limit this menu to lunchtime and early evening.

Lodging

Accommodations in Ireland range from deluxe renovated castles and stately homes to thatched cottages and farmhouses. Room standards are rising all the time, especially in the middle and lower price ranges. Pressure on hotel space reaches a peak from June to September, but it's always a good idea to reserve in advance. Many Irish hotels can be booked directly from the United States. Ask your travel agent for details. The **Irish Tourist Board's Central Reservations Service** in Dublin (14 Upper O'Connell St., Dublin 1, tel. 01/747733) makes reservations in hotels and other accommodations; local tourist offices do the same.

The Irish Tourist Board (ITB) has an official grading system and publishes a list of "approved accommodations," which includes hotels, guest houses, bed-and-breakfasts, farmhouses, hostels, and camping parks. For each accommodation, the list gives a maximum charge that no hotel may exceed without special authorization. Prices must be displayed in every room, so if the hotel oversteps its limit, do not hesitate to complain to the hotel manager and/or the ITB.

Ideally, visitors should sample a range of accommodations. The very expensive country-house hotels and renovated castles offer a unique combination of luxury and history. Less impressive, but equally charming, are any number of provincial inns and country hotels with simple but adequate facilities. Many visitors, seeking to meet a wide cross section of Irish people, prefer a different B&B every night. Others enjoy the simplicity of self-catering for a week or two in a thatched cottage.

Guest Houses Some guest houses, particularly in Dublin, are hard to distinguish from hotels, and they're cheaper as well; however, less is expected in terms of public rooms, bars, restaurants, and front-desk service, so, in general, guest houses are not for the business traveler. Most are owner-run, and with good standards of cleanliness and hospitality, they're often ideal for vacationers. They must have at least five bedrooms, but in Dublin and major cities they're often much bigger; many offer bathrooms in the suites, and TV and direct-dial phones in the bedrooms. The larger guest houses are sometimes built above an existing bar or restaurant. Others are part of a large family home. The cost at these places may or may not include an optional evening meal.

Bed-and-Breakfasts This is a well-established and well-regulated form of accommodation in Ireland. B&Bs are classified by the Irish Tourist Board as either town homes, country homes, or farmhouses. Many now have at least one bedroom with a bathroom, but don't expect this as a matter of course. B&Bs often charge an extra 50p–£1 for a bath or shower. If this is taken in the family bathroom, you should ask first whether you can use the facility. Many travelers do not bother booking a B&B in advance. They are so plentiful in rural areas that it's often more fun to leave open the decision, allowing yourself a choice of final destinations for the night.

Farm Vacations Many Irish farms offer holidays with part board or full board on a weekly basis. These are listed in the ITB's illustrated publication "Farm Holidays in Ireland" (£1). You will notice at once from the booklet that very few Irish farmhouses are picturesque: they are more likely to be modern bungalows or undistinguished two-story houses than creeper-clad Georgian mansions—though exceptions do exist. Room and part board—breakfast and an evening meal—costs from £120 to £150 per week.

Cottages In more than 30 locations there are clusters of holiday cottages for rent. Although built in the traditional style, they have central heating and all the other conveniences of modern life. A three-bedroom cottage equipped for six adults is around £230 per week in mid-season. It is essential to reserve in advance. The ITB's publication *Self-Catering* (£2) lists individual properties and clusters of traditional cottages available by the week. For information on booking, contact the ITB.

Camping This is the cheapest way of seeing the country, and facilities for campers and caravaners are improving steadily. An abundance of coastal campsites compensates for the shortage of inland ones. All are listed in *Guest Accommodation* (£3.50), available from the ITB. Rates start at about £2 per tent, £3 per caravan overnight.

Youth Hostels **An Oíge** (The Irish Youth Hostels Association, 39 Mountjoy Sq., Dublin 1, tel. 01/363111) has a chain of 40 youth hostels ranging from a castle in Kilkenny to cottages at Killary Harbour on the edge of the Atlantic. You must have an International Youth Hostel card to stay in an Irish youth hostel, and it is advisable to book in advance if you're traveling in summer. Charges for adults are £4.50 per night in city hostels, around £3.80 in rural hostels. All have a curfew and are closed between 10 AM and 5 PM.

Another 65 hostels are linked together in the **Association of Independent Hostels.** These budget accommodations range from small cottages to rambling old mansions, each with an informal, friendly atmosphere. Some hostels have private rooms and all offer self-catering kitchens and hot showers. There is no late-night curfew at independent hostels, and no daytime closing rules either. Many have a small shop and offer evening meals of wholesome (often vegetarian) home-cooked food. For a copy of a leaflet listing Independent Hostels and their facilities and locations, write to **Patrick O'Donnell, Dooey Hostel** (Glencolumcille, County Donegal, tel. 073/30130).

Credit Cards

The following credit card abbreviations have been used: AE, American Express; CB, Carte Blanche; DC, Diners Club; MC, MasterCard (known as Access in the Republic); V, Visa. It's a good idea to call ahead to check current credit card policies.

Staying in Northern Ireland

Getting Around

By Car The road network in Northern Ireland is excellent and, outside Belfast, uncrowded. Road signs and traffic regulations conform to the British system. The speed limit is 48 kph (30 mph) in towns, 96 kph (60 mph) on country roads, and 112 kph (70 mph) on two-lane roads and motorways.

There are plenty of parking lots in the towns (usually free except in Belfast), and visitors are advised to use them. Control zones in town centers, where parking is prohibited, are indicated by yellow signs: CONTROL ZONES. NO UNATTENDED PARKING. An unattended car in a control zone is treated as a security risk.

If you are crossing into the Republic, be sure to use an approved road. Crossing the border on the clearly marked unapproved roads is strictly prohibited. Approved roads connect the following towns on either side of the border (the Northern Ireland town is first; the Republic town, second):

Newry–Greenore, Newry–Dundalk (via Killeen).

Armagh–Dundalk (via Newtown Hamilton).

Crossmaglen–Carrikmacross.

Armagh–Castleblayney, Armagh–Monaghan.

Roslea–Monaghan.

Enniskillen–Clones, Derrylin–Belturbet, Enniskillen–Swanlinbar.

Enniskillen–Manorhamilton, Enniskillen–Ballyshannon (via Belleek).

Kesh–Pettigo.

Castlederg–Castlefin, Strabane–Lifford.

Derry–St. Johnston.

Derry–Bridgend, Derry–Muff, Derry–Newton Hamilton.

Posts are normally manned from 8 AM to 8 PM, and some are manned until midnight. On both sides of the border, formalities are quick and friendly; a lengthier stop is more likely at a checkpoint a mile or so from either side of the border. North of the frontier you may be stopped by either the army or the police. Have your passport or driver's license handy.

By Train The state-owned **Northern Ireland Railways** has three main rail routes, all operating out of Belfast's **Central Station** (tel. 0232/230310). These are north to Londonderry, via Ballymena and Coleraine; east to Bangor along the shores of Belfast Lough; and south to Dublin and the Irish Republic.

Other than on the Dublin line, all trains are one class only, with reasonably priced fares similar to those in the Republic. The Belfast–Dublin nonstop express takes about two hours.

For information on long-term passes, *see* Rail Passes, Before You Go, above.

By Bus All services are operated by the state-owned **Ulsterbus** company. Services are generally good, with particularly useful links to those towns not served by train. In addition, there is a **Freedom of Northern Ireland** ticket costing about UK£17 for seven days' unlimited travel. A one-day ticket costs UK£6. Ulsterbus also operates a wide range of bus tours. (For details, *see* Essential Information, Chapter 1.)

Telephones

Northern Ireland is part of the United Kingdom telephone system. A local call costs 10p.

If you are dialing Northern Ireland from the Republic, codes are different than they would be otherwise. For example, the code for Belfast is 0232 from anywhere within the United Kingdom including Northern Ireland, or indeed from anywhere in the world, but from the Republic of Ireland it's 084. This is explained in detail in phone directories on both sides of the border. In the Republic, you can find the appropriate code for a Northern Ireland number either in the phone directory or by dialing 10. For all operator services in Northern Ireland, dial 100.

Mail

Postal Rates Airmail rates to the United States and Canada are 32p for letters and postcards (not over 10 grams). To the rest of the United Kingdom and the Irish Republic, rates are 19p for first-class letters and 14p for second class. These rates may well increase before or during 1991.

Tipping

Northern Ireland follows Great Britain, rather than the rest of Europe, in keeping tipping to a minimum. In restaurants, check the bill to see if service is included. If it isn't, tip about 10% if you're satisfied with the service you've received. Taxi drivers don't normally expect tips, but again, tip about 10% of the fare if you think it's appropriate.

Opening and Closing Times

Shops in Belfast are open 9 to 5:30, Monday–Friday, with a late closing on Thursday, usually at 9 PM. Elsewhere, shops close for the afternoon once a week, usually Wednesday or Thursday, but it's best to check locally. In addition, most smaller shops close for an hour or so at lunch.

Bank hours are 9:30 to 12:30 and 1:30 to 3, Monday–Friday. All banks are closed on Saturdays.

Post offices are open 9 to 5:30, Monday–Friday, and 9 to 1 on Saturday. Some close for an hour at lunch.

Pubs in Northern Ireland are open from 11:30 AM to 11 PM Monday–Saturday, and 12:30 PM to 2 PM and 7 PM to 10 PM on Sundays. Sunday opening is at the owner or manager's discretion.

Shopping

The range of Irish-made goods is roughly similar to that available in the Republic (*see* Staying in the Irish Republic, above). Most Irish linen is made in Northern Ireland; other items of interest include delicate, Belleek porcelain, Carrickmacross lace, musical instruments (such as harps and bagpipes), Tyrone Crystal, and silver jewelry and ornaments using polished Mourne granite. Keep an eye out also for traditionally woven tweed and wall hangings—as well as items of clothing—designed by handweavers. Bushmills whiskey is made in County Antrim.

Sports and Outdoor Activities

Fishing With a long coastline (750 km, 466 mi), part of it on the Atlantic and the other on the Irish Sea, Northern Ireland offers plenty of choices for shore angling and offshore excursions. Rivers and lakes, including large *loughs* such as Strangford, Neagh, and Erne, add to the variety.

To game fish in Northern Ireland, first you need a rod license. The **Foyle Fisheries Commission** (FFC, 8 Victoria Rd., Londonderry BT47 2AB, tel. 0504/42100) distributes licenses for game fishing in the Foyle area, and the **Fisheries Conservancy Board** (FCB, 1 Mahon Rd., Portadown, Craigavon, Co. Armagh BT62 3EE, tel. 0762/334666) handles all other regions. A license costs between UK£5 and UK£10 for 15 days. You must also obtain a permit from the owner of the waters in which you plan to fish. Most of the waters are owned by the **Department of Agriculture** (Fisheries Division, Stormont, Belfast BT4 3PW, tel. 0232/63939), which charges about UK£10 for a 15-day permit, UK£3.50 for a daily one. If you plan to fish outside the jurisdiction of the Department of Agriculture, you must obtain a permit from one of the local clubs. For more information, and for Department of Agriculture permits and FFC and FCB rod licenses, contact the Northern Ireland Tourist Bureau.

Some of the same regulations apply to coarse fishing (for all fish that are not trout or salmon). A rod license is required by the FCB, though the cost is much less than that of the game-fishing license; the FFC requires no license for coarse fishing. In addition, you need a permit from the owner of the waters in which you plan to fish.

Golf Northern Ireland has 60 golf courses in a territory the size of Connecticut. These include some of the most challenging and scenic golf courses in the world. In Newcastle, the **Royal County Down Golf Club,** which features two 18-hole courses, is considered one of the finest courses in the world. Visitors are welcome. In general, green fees are modest (about UK£9 per day), and reductions are made for groups. There are plenty of caddies, but motorized carts are not available.

Hiking For serious hikers there is the challenge of the 790-km (491-mi) **Ulster Way,** a footpath that travels through spectacular coastal scenery.

Horseback Riding and Pony Trekking These are popular sports throughout the area, particularly in the forest parks and the Glens of Antrim. Several Northern Ireland hunting clubs welcome visitors and will provide a mount if you have an introduction to the master of the hunt. This can be arranged through the Northern Ireland Tourist Board.

Sailing Two of the best places for offshore sailing are Strangford Lough and Ballyholme Bay, Bangor. Lough Erne is a popular inland sailing spot; you can rent a craft at Kesh in County Fermanagh for sailing there.

Dining

Visitors can choose from a number of pleasant restaurants in Northern Ireland, mainly in the middle and lower price range. "Where to Eat" (UK£1.25), published by the Northern Ireland Tourist Board, contains a comprehensive list of places. Prices are notably lower than in the Republic, but the style and presentation of the food is similar.

Lodging

Hotels and other accommodations in Northern Ireland are similar to those in the Republic of Ireland. The Northern Ireland Tourist Board publishes a complete list—called "Where to Stay" (UK£1.95)—of hotels, guest houses, farmhouses, bed-and-breakfasts, self-catering accommodations, youth hostels, and camping and trailer parks; prices and full information are included. There is more of a choice in the middle and lower price ranges than at the top.

Information on the nine hostels in Ulster is provided by **The Youth Hostel Association of Northern Ireland** (56 Bradbury Place, Belfast, tel. 0232/324733). All hostels should be booked in advance for July and August.

Credit Cards

The following credit card abbreviations have been used: AE, American Express; CB, Carte Blanche; DC, Diners Club; MC, MasterCard (known as Access in Northern Ireland); V, Visa. It's a good idea to call ahead to check current credit card policies.

Great Itineraries

Introduction to Scenic Ireland (One Week)

Although Ireland is not a large country, a week allows only enough time for a quick overview. A car is essential for this itinerary.

Day 1: Arrive in Shannon. Have a look at Bunratty Castle and Folk Park before heading south for Killarney. Take a break in Rathkeale for a tour of Castle Matrix.

Day 2: In Killarney, take a full-day organized tour through the Gap of Dunloe and on the Killarney lakes by jaunting car (pony and trap) and boat.

Day 3: Choose between the lush sub-tropical vegetation of the Ring of Kerry or the rugged mountains of the Dingle Peninsula. Both options involve a full-day trip, either by car or organized excursion from Killarney.

Day 4: Head for Galway City by crossing the Shannon estuary on the ferry from Tarbert to Killimer. Follow the coast road through Kilkee, Ennistymon, and Ballyvaughan past the spectacular Cliffs of Moher and into the extraordinary limestone landscape of The Burren.

Day 5: After a walk around Galway City, drive through the famous blue and purple Connemara landscape to Castlebar, continue then on to Sligo and "Yeats Country."

Day 6: Set off early for Dublin. After a lunch in one of Dublin's famous pubs, spend the afternoon on a walking and shopping tour of the City Center.

Day 7: Take the time to see the famous *Book of Kells* in Trinity College's Old Library (closed Sunday) before heading for the airport.

An Extended Tour of Scenic Ireland (Two Weeks)

The scenic contrasts within Ireland are remarkable. The classical splendor of the great buildings in and around Dublin, the rural simplicity of the West Coast, the lush vegetation of the Southwest, the ruggedness of Sligo and Donegal counties, and the neatness of the Antrim Coast are all just a few hours' drive from each other. Listen for the astonishing variety of accents that you'll hear along the way—conclusive proof that there is no such thing as a "typical" Irish accent.

Day 1: Walk around Dublin City Center, taking time to see the *Book of Kells* at Trinty College and the State Apartments at Dublin Castle.

Day 2: Visit Boyne Valley by car or by organized tour, stopping at the Hill of Tara, Slane Castle, and the megalithic tombs at Newgrange, Knowth, and Dowth.

Day 3: Take a trip to County Wicklow, either by car or organized tour, taking in such sights as Powerscourt Estate, Glendalough, Mount Usher Gardens, and Russborough House at Blessington.

Day 4: Drive to Cork City via Kildare Town (stopping there perhaps to look at the National Stud or the Japanese Gardens) and the Rock of Cashel.

Day 5: Walk around Cork City and visit Kinsale, stopping there overnight to sample one of the latter's many fine restaurants.

Day 6: Proceed to Killarney with a short detour to Blarney if you wish to kiss the famous stone. Spend the afternoon riding around the Muckross Estate in a jaunting car.

Day 7: Either take a tour through the Gap of Dunloe by jaunting car and on the lakes by boat, or drive around the Ring of Kerry, one of Europe's premier scenic routes.

Day 8: Head north from Killarney travelling up the West Coast toward Galway City. Cross the Shannon estuary by ferry from Tarbert to Killimer and follow the coast road through Kilkee, Ennistymon, and Ballyvaughan past the Cliffs of Moher to the extraordinary limestone landscape of The Burren.

Day 9: If the weather is fine, head for Rossaveale and take a day trip to the middle Aran Island, Inishman—or fly there from Oranmore Airport. If the weather is unsuitable for visiting the Aran Islands, take a driving tour through the famous Connemara landscape, following the coast road to Clifden and returning to Galway City on the inland Maam Cross road.

Day 10: Head for Westport; for an unforgettable view of Clew Bay and its many islands, climb the mountain of Croagh Patrick. If the weather is unsuitable, take a drive to Achill Island, which is connected to the mainland by a highway.

Day 11: Drive through "Yeats Country" in County Sligo to Donegal Town, turning left at Donegal Town to visit Donegal tweed country–Ardara, Gweedore, and Dunfanashy.

Day 12: Head through Letterkenny toward Derry City. Before crossing the border to Northern Ireland, stop at the Grianan of Aileach, a huge stone fort dating from 1700 B.C. Drive through Derry City to the Causeway Coast, stopping overnight in Portrush or Bushmills.

Day 13: Spend the morning climbing over the Giant's Causeway and then drive through the Glens of Antrim to Belfast.

Day 14: Leave Belfast, and return over the border to the Republic, through Newry and Bundalk to Dublin.

Ireland by Rail (One Week)

All too many travelers who use Shannon as their gateway to Europe miss the opportunity of taking a quick look around Ireland before continuing their journey. This tour starts in Shannon and ends in Dublin, where you can either proceed by plane to mainland Europe or take a ferry to the United Kingdom. While not as flexible as travel by rental car, rail travel in Ireland is a less expensive alternative (especially on a rail pass). Your range of destinations can be extended by taking local buses and organized excursions.

Day 1: The bus from Shannon Airport to Limerick passes Bunratty Castle and Folk Park (both worth a look). Take a walk around old Limerick City and visit St. John's Castle and the city walls.

Day 2: Proceed by train to Killarney. After lunch, take a half-day excursion either to the Gap of Dunloe or (in bad weather) an organized orientation tour.

Day 3: Take an organized tour to either the Ring of Kerry or the Dingle Peninsula.

Day 4: Travel to Cork City by train. Explore the city on foot either before or after an organized excursion to Blarney Castle or a ride on the regular bus to the lovely port of Kinsale.

Day 5: Take the train to Kilkenny City and spend the day exploring this historic place.

Day 6: Get an early train to Dublin and allow a full day to explore the City Center on foot. Spend an evening at one of the traditional music pubs.

Day 7: Head for the airport or the ferry in the Dublin vicinity.

Great Irish Houses and Castles (8–12 days)

Although it is physically possible to accomplish this tour in 8 days, we suggest you allow 3 or 4 more days, if possible, to relieve the somewhat hectic pace. The itinerary is best undertaken between June and September when the maximum number of houses are open to the public. Outside these months, you may often find that it is possible to view a house by phoning a day or so in advance and making an appointment, even if the house is officially closed. This tour will appeal to those with an interest in history, architecture, or interior decoration. You might wish to stay at one of the grand and often historic country house hotels along the way.

Day 1: The Dublin Castle State Apartments and the Royal Hospital, Kilmainham are two must-sees in the Dublin. A walk along the inner city stretch of the River Liffey provides excellent views of two of architect James Gandon's Georgian masterpieces, the Custom House and the Four Courts. South of the river, Georgian domestic town architecture at its best can be seen at Merrion Square and on the continuation of its east side, Fitzwilliam Street.

Day 2: Head north of Dublin to visit Slane Castle, Newbridge House, and Malahide Castle.

Day 3: Castletown House in Celbridge, County Kildare, is one of Ireland's most magnificent Georgian structures; it serves as the headquarters of the Irish Georgian Society, which works hard to preserve Ireland's Georgian heritage. Russborough House near Blessington, County Wicklow, has a good European art collection.

Day 4: Take the main road to Cork City, turning off at New Inn just beyond Monasterevin to visit Emo Court. You will pass the Rock of Cashel en route to Cahir, with a castle in the town center that is worth visiting.

Day 5: Fota House and Arboretum are located on the edge of Cork Harbour; Riverstown House and Dunkathel House are both situated near the village of Glanmire, just outside the city on the Dublin road.

Day 6: A short detour from the main Killarney road will lead you to Blarney Castle and Blarney House. Muckross House in Killarney, a mid-Victorian manor house, is one of the least interesting on the tour, but it should be seen for its attractive location.

Day 7: From Killarney, head north to the Shannon estuary, on whose shore you will find Glin Castle, the ancestral home of the FitzGeralds. Take the Rathkeale road to Limerick in order to visit Castle Matrix; also stop at Cratloe Woods, on the other side of Limerick City, the only remaining 17th-century "longhouse" still inhabited. Stay overnight in or near Limerick City or Ennis.

Day 8: If you have enough time, visit Knappogue Castle and Bunratty Castle in the morning before heading for the airport.

2 Portraits of Ireland

Bogland

for T. P. Flanagan

by Seamus Heaney

Born in County Derry, Seamus Heaney is one of Ireland's most respected living poets. A new edition of his Selected Poems *appeared in 1990.*

We have no prairies
To slice a big sun at evening—
Everywhere the eye concedes to
Encroaching horizon,

Is wooed into the cyclops' eye
Of a tarn. Our unfenced country
Is bog that keeps crusting
Between the sights of the sun.

They've taken the skeleton
Of the Great Irish Elk
Out of the peat, set it up
An astounding crate full of air.

Butter sunk under
More than a hundred years
Was recovered salty and white.
The ground itself is kind, black butter

Melting and opening underfoot,
Missing its last definition
By millions of years.
They'll never dig coal here,

Only the waterlogged trunks
Of great firs, soft as pulp.
Our pioneers keep striking
Inwards and downwards,

Every layer they strip
Seems camped on before.
The bogholes might be Atlantic seepage.
The wet centre is bottomless.

Ireland at a Glance: A Chronology

ca. 6000 BC Mesolithic (middle Stone Age) hunter-gatherers migrate from Scotland to the northeastern Irish coast.

ca. 3500 BC Neolithic (new Stone Age) settlers (origins uncertain) bring agriculture, pottery, and weaving. They also build massive megaliths—stone monuments with counterparts in England (Stonehenge), Brittany (Carnac), and elsewhere in Europe.

ca. 700 BC Celtic tribes begin to arrive via Britain and France; they divide Ireland into "fifths" or provinces, including Ulster, Leinster, Connaught, Meath, and Munster.

ca. AD 100 Ireland becomes the center of Celtic culture and trade without being settled by the Romans.

432 Traditional date for the arrival of St. Patrick and Christianity; in fact, Irish conversion to Christianity began at least a century earlier.

ca. 500–800 Golden Age of Irish monasticism; as many as 3,000 study at Clonard (Meath). Irish missionaries carry the faith to barbarian Europe; art (exemplified by the *Book of Kells*, ca. 700) and Gaelic poetry flourish.

795 First Scandinavian Viking invasion; raids continue for the next 200 years. Viking towns founded include Dublin, Waterford, Wexford, Cork, and Limerick.

1014 Vikings decisively defeated at Clontarf by Irish troops under King Brian Boru of Munster. His murder cuts short hopes of a unified Ireland.

1066 Normans (French descendents of Viking invaders) conquer England and set their sights on Ireland as well.

1169 Dermot MacMurrough, exiled king of Munster, invites the Anglo-Norman adventurer Richard FitzGilbert de Clare ("Strongbow") to help him regain his throne, beginning a pattern of English opportunism and bad decisions by the Irish.

1172 Pope Alexander III confirms Henry II, king of England, as feudal lord of Ireland. Over the next two centuries, Anglo-Norman nobles establish estates, intermarry with the native population, and act in a manner similar to the neighboring Celtic chieftains. Actual control by the English crown is confined to a small area known as "the land of peace" or "the Pale" around Dublin.

1366 Statutes of Kilkenny attempt belatedly to enforce ethnic divisions by prohibiting the expression of Irish language and culture and intermarriage between the Irish and English, but Gaelic culture prevails, and the Pale continues to contract. Constant warfare among the great landowners keeps Ireland poor, divided, and isolated from the rest of Europe.

1477–1513 Garret Mor ("Gerald the Great") FitzGerald, eighth earl of Kildare, dominates Irish affairs as lord deputy (the representative of the English crown).

1494 Henry VII removes Kildare from office (he is soon reinstated), and initiates Statute of Drogheda (Poyning's Law), which is in force until 1782—Irish Parliament can only meet by consent of the king of England.

1534–40 Henry VIII's break with the Catholic Church leads to insurrection in Ireland, led by Garret Mor's grandson Lord Offaly ("Silken Thomas"). He is executed with five of his brothers.

1541 Parliament proclaims Henry VIII king of Ireland (his previous status was merely a feudal lord). Irish magnates reluctantly surrender their lands to him as their overlord. Hereafter, a constant English presence is required to keep the peace; no single Irish family replaces the FitzGeralds.

1558–1603 Reign of Queen Elizabeth I; her fear of Irish intrigue with Catholic enemies of England leads to expansion of English power, including the Munster "plantation" (colony) scheme and the division of Ireland into English-style counties.

1580–88 Edmund Spenser, an administrator for the Crown in Ireland, writes *The Faerie Queene*.

1591 Trinity College, Dublin, is founded.

1595–1603 Rebellion of Hugh O'Neill, earl of Tyrone (Ulster). Defeats England at Yellow Ford (1598), but assistance from Spain is inadequate; Tyrone surrenders at Mellifont six days after Queen Elizabeth's death.

1607 The Flight of the Earls, and the beginning of "the Troubles." The earl of Tyrone and his ally Tyrconnell flee to Rome; their lands in Ulster are confiscated and opened to Protestant settlers, mostly Scots.

1641 Charles I's policies provoke insurrection in Ulster and, soon after, Civil War in England.

1649 August: British leader Oliver Cromwell, having defeated Charles and witnessed his execution, invades Ireland, determined to crush Catholic opposition. Massacres at Drogheda and Wexford.

1652 Act of Settlement—lands of Cromwell's opponents are confiscated, and owners are forced across the Shannon to Connaught. Never fully carried out, this policy nonetheless establishes Protestant ascendancy.

1678 In the wake of the Popish Plot to assassinate King Charles II, Catholics are barred from British parliaments.

1683 Dublin Philosophical Society founded, modeled on the Royal Society of London.

1689 Having attempted, among other things, to repeal the Act of Settlement, King James II (a Catholic) is deposed and flees to Ireland. His daughter Mary and her husband William of Orange assume the throne.

1690 James is defeated by William III at the Battle of the Boyne.

1704 First laws of the Penal Code are enacted, restricting Catholic landowning; later laws prohibited voting, education, and military service among the Catholics.

1775 American War of Independence begins, precipitating Irish unrest. Henry Grattan (1746–1820), a Protestant barrister, enters the Irish Parliament.

1778 Land clauses of Penal Code are repealed.

1782 Grattan's Parliament—Grattan asserts independence of Irish Parliament from Britain. Britain agrees, but independence is easier to declare than to sustain.

1798 Inspired by the French Revolution and dissatisfied with the slow progress of Parliament, Wolfe Tone's United Irishmen rebel but are defeated.

1800 The Irish Parliament votes itself out of existence and agrees to Union with Britain, effective January 1, 1801.

1823 Daniel O'Connell (1775–1847), "the Liberator," founds the Catholic Association to campaign for Catholic Emancipation.

1828 O'Connell's election to Parliament (illegal, because he was a Catholic) leads to passage of Catholic Emancipation Act in 1829; later, he works for repeal of the Union.

1845–48 Failure of potato crop leads to famine; thousands die, others migrate.

1848 "Young Ireland," a radical party, leads an abortive rebellion.

1856 Birth of George Bernard Shaw, playwright (d. 1950).

1858 Fenian Brotherhood founded in New York by Irish immigrants with the aim of overthrowing British rule. A revolt in 1867 fails, but it compels Gladstone, the British prime minister, to disestablish the Anglican Church (1869) and reform landholding (1870) in Ireland. The government also increases its powers of repression.

1865 Birth of William Butler Yeats, the great Irish poet (d. 1939).

1871 Isaac Butts founds parliamentary Home Rule Party, soon dominated by Charles Stewart Parnell (1846–91, descendant of English Protestants), who tries to force the issue by obstructing parliamentary business.

1881 Gladstone's second Land Act opposed by Parnell, who leads a boycott (named for Captain Boycott, its first victim) of landlords.

1882 Phoenix Park murders—British officials murdered by Fenians. Prevention of Crime bill that follows suspends trial by jury and increases police powers. Acts of terrorism increase. Parnell disavows all connection with Fenians. Birth of James Joyce, novelist (d. 1941).

1886 Gladstone introduces his first Home Rule Bill, which is defeated. Ulster Protestants fear Catholic domination and revive Orange Order (named for William of Orange) to oppose Home Rule.

1890 Parnell is named co-respondent in the divorce case of Kitty O'Shea; his career is ruined.

1893 Second Home Rule Bill passes Commons but is defeated by Lords. Subsequent policy is to "kill Home Rule with kindness" with land reform, but cultural nationalism revives with founding of Gaelic League to promote Irish language. Yeats, John

Synge (1871–1909), and other writers find inspiration in Gaelic past.

1898 On the anniversary of Wolfe Tone's rebellion, Arthur Griffith (1872–1922) founds the Dublin newspaper the *United Irishman*, preaching *sinn fein* ("we ourselves")—secession from Britain; Sinn Fein party founded 1905. Socialist James Connolly (executed 1916) founds the *Workers' Republic*.

1904 Abbey Theatre opens in Dublin.

1912 Third Home Rule Bill passes Commons but is rejected by Lords. Under new rules, however, Lords' veto is null after two years. Meanwhile, Ulster Protestants plan defiance; the Ulster Volunteers recruit 100,000. Radical Republicans such as Connolly, Patrick Pearse, and others of the Irish Republican Brotherhood (IRB) preach insurrection and recruit their own volunteers.

1914 Outbreak of war postpones implementation of Home Rule until peace returns. Parliamentarians agree, but radicals plan revolt.

1916 Easter Uprising—IRB stages insurrection in Dublin and declares independence; the uprising fails, but the execution of 15 leaders by the British turns public opinion in favor of the insurgents. Yeats writes "a terrible beauty is born."

1919 January: Irish Parliamentarians meet as the *Dail Éireann* (Irish Assembly) and declare independence. September: Dail suppressed; Sinn Fein made illegal.

1920–21 War breaks out between Britain and Ireland: the "Black and Tans" versus the Irish Republican Army (IRA). Government of Ireland Act declares separate parliaments for north and south and continued ties to Britain. Elections follow, but the Sinn Fein majority in the south again declare themselves the Dail Éireann under Eamonn de Valera (1882–1975), rejecting British authority. December 1921: Anglo-Irish Treaty grants the south Dominion status as the Irish Free State, allowing the north to remain under Britain.

1922 De Valera and his Republican followers reject the treaty; civil war results. The Irish Free State adopts a constitution; William T. Cosgrave becomes president. In Paris, James Joyce's *Ulysses* is published.

1923 De Valera is arrested and the civil war ends, but Republican agitation and terrorism continues.

1932 De Valera, who had founded the *Fianna Fáil* party in 1926, is elected president.

1932–36 Tariff war with Britain.

1938 New constitution creates Republic of Eire with no ties to Britain.

1969 The annual Apprentice Boys' march in Londonderry, Northern Ireland, leads to rioting between Catholics and Protestants. British troops, called in to keep the peace, remain in Northern Ireland to this day.

1972 Republic of Eire admitted to European Economic Community. Troubles continue in the north—January 30, British troops shoot 13 unarmed demonstrators on "Bloody Sunday." Stormont (the Northern Parliament) is suspended and direct rule from London is imposed. Acts of terrorism on both sides leads to draconian law enforcement by the British.

1986 Anglo-Irish Agreement signed, giving the Republic of Eire a stronger voice in northern affairs.

Irish Miles

by Frank O'Connor

Born in County Cork, Frank O'Connor (1903–66), a pseudonym for Michael O'Donovan, was a Republican rebel and one of Ireland's best-loved fiction writers. The essay reprinted here is taken from the first chapter of Irish Miles, *a chronicle of a bicycle trip around Ireland taken by O'Connor, his wife, and a friend.*

Exploring the Boyne Valley in the early days of our married life, before we yet knew what we were looking for and when anything from a high cross to a keep could lure us off our road, Célimène and I came on the prehistoric necropolis of Newgrange. Prehistory or high crosses, all were the same to us. It was a showery day, and after cycling a mile and a half in the rain to find the caretaker so kindly provided by the Board of Works, we found he had already gone back to the tombs with a couple of military officers. We returned. The rain cleared off as quickly as it had begun, and the blue plains of Meath sparkled and steamed all round us, and there in the heart of them was the great tumulus, overgrown with grass and bushes, and surrounded by its circle of monoliths. The two officers were there, but the caretaker had gone off to find some candles—the Board of Works, as we learned later, hasn't yet heard of electric light and will probably drop dead when it does. Dwarfed by the tall stones with their mysterious patterns, the two young men, one plump and cheery, the other slim and good-looking, looked damned unhistoric. Somehow you could never imagine them turning into spirals and trumpets in the National Museum or being lectured on as a style or period. We nodded to one another and tried not to look too self-conscious, but all the same the atmosphere was rather like that of a doctor's waiting-room. The slim officer broke the silence in a rather startling way.

"I wonder would you consider it—what's the word?—if I said this was Egyptian?"

"It's been called a lot of things in its time," I replied, so taken aback that I broke into a Belfast accent which made the other officer hoot with delight. He obviously thought I was a great card.

"Up the Six Counties!" he said.

"No, but I mean it," the first officer went on eagerly—he was a different type entirely; clever and highly strung. "I understand that all these spirals and things are really sun symbols."

"I think you'd be quite safe in calling them anything," said I. "You couldn't very well be contradicted."

"Oh, yes," he said, by no means satisfied with the reply. "I read that in a book somewhere. I wish I could remember the name of it. It's the same thing as you find in the Pyramids."

We were interrupted by the caretaker bringing back the bits of sacred candle which looked as if they might be contemporary, and we solemnly lit them and crawled after him through the depths of the hillside, under the great half-human shoulders of crude stone, giving ourselves a crick in the neck while we tried to study the patterns on them. In the central chamber we were able to stand, and the officer flicked his torch rapidly up the walls to the roof. I knew I ought to feel moved, but while I tried to remember that this was the heart of Irish prehistory, I found myself watching the shadows which the candle-light threw on the young, warm, eager faces. The second officer didn't seem to be altogether sure of himself, and waited for me to make another joke just to reassure him that history didn't apply to him. Personally, at that moment I very much doubted if it did. I felt sure he would get out of it somehow. But his friend was absolutely determined on the point.

"It was the Milesians who built this, wasn't it?" he asked, looking about him.

"It's supposed to have been the Tuatha De Danann," said I. "Whoever the blazes the Tuatha De Danann were."

"That's right," he said quickly. "They were priestly johnnies, weren't they?"

"At any rate, the people who came after them adopted them as gods," said I.

"That's just the same thing that happened in Crete," he said. "Crete was a daughter-civilization of Egypt. It was started by a priestly caste, just like the Tuatha De Danann, and then the Dorians came and booted them out. The Dorians were soldiers. That's how civilization began. It's all in a book I read once, but I can't remember the name of it. Can you?"

"No," I said firmly, "I can't."

"But that's what happened here all right," he said with conviction. "The Milesians were a military caste; they came from the Mediterranean, and booted out the priestly johnnies and took over the show."

I was just on the point of suggesting that I didn't notice any shortage of priestly johnnies, but decided that, having once talked in a Belfast accent, the less I had to say about the clergy the better. The other officer mightn't understand that I was joking.

"That's how civilization began," the first officer continued eagerly, "with priests and soldiers. It all centres on the Mediterranean. The first time it happened was on the banks of the Nile. A lot of priestly johnnies learned to calculate the time of the Nile floods so that they could have three crops of wheat instead of one. It's all in that book I've been telling you about if only I could remember the name."

I was just as glad he couldn't. I shouldn't have been able to believe in its existence. History simply vanished before the pair of them with their eagerness and good looks. I had no doubt it must be subjective. We left them with real regret, and cycled on uphill through a wooded glen, and downhill again into a secluded valley. This was Mellifont, Honey Fountain, St. Malachy's first settlement in his attempt to Europeanize the Irish Church. A French master-builder had supervised its erection, but his monks and the Irish monks didn't agree on the principles of architecture, so after some time they returned to France. But he must, I believe, have been still in Ireland at the time of the consecration, and seen all the famous figures of the tragedy which led up to the Norman invasion. They were all there: O'Connor, the last Irish king; his ruffianly lieutenant, O'Rourke, with his middle-aged wife Darvorgilla, and her lover-to-be, Diarmuid MacMurrough, prince of Leinster, a ruffian even more abominable than her husband. A pretty gang of thieves they were, and Brother Robert of Citeaux must have had a rare time showing them the marvels of this new type of architecture. Up to this, they had seen nothing but the little churches of out-of-the-way monasteries which they were so fond of burning, but this great type of Cistercian architecture with its massive walls and vaulted roofs must have posed them some nice problems in arson. Not that we saw much of it. There was a ruined tower on the right, a tiny, ruined parish church on the side of the hill, an old mill where they sold picture postcards, and the octagon of a lavabo in beautiful European Romanesque. They were cutting the hay, and perhaps if we had come a day later we might have seen a bit more of the lay-out, but now there was nothing to assist us except a big blue notice-board, the contents of which I had to read to Célimène, who fondly believed that there ought to be something to guide us. It ran:

"'Abstract of a Letter of the Lord Abbot of Mount St. Joseph, Roscrea, dated June 10th, 1929, to Very Rev. Francis Canon—, P.P. Mellifont.

"'Mellifont Abbey Items.

"'3,000,000 Masses celebrated, Community assembled in Choir 1,160,000 times to say Divine Praises, 4 Bishops, 2 of them Archbishops of Armagh, 25 Abbots and 3,000 Monks buried in Monastery. These Items—'"

"'Items is good'," interrupted Célimène.

"'These Items'," I continued firmly, "'have been Drawn Up by a Young Monk who was asked to make a *Special* Study of your Questions.'"

"Is he in the Board of Works too?" asked Célimène.

"His father was a labouring man in regular employment," I added.

"Is that there?" she asked in surprise, screwing up her eyes to look at the board.

"No," I said. "I just made it up."

That sprightly pair of lads had cast a spell on the day. We went on to Monasterboice, skipping back a couple of centuries to the days of the Culdees. They were making the hay there, too. We looked for a while at the beautiful old crosses, and then had our lunch and fell fast asleep propped up against a grave. We might of course have dreamed of some old abbot or stone-cutter, in which case this chapter would have been much more exciting, but the fact is that we didn't dream at all. There was no history on us, and in the cool of the evening we cycled under awnings of blue shadow into the little village of Slane. It was dark on the steep road down to the river, with its great avenue of trees and Gothic gateway. By the bridge was a handsome old mill and mill-house, and the great span of the slow, sedgy Boyne. On the far bank a few country boys were playing pitch-and-toss by the light of an electric torch.

We went back and stood in the square. In the whole square there are only four houses; four three-story houses set back a little from the four corners, with flanking walls leading to pavilions in the shape of coach-houses, each facing on to a different road. There were two wrought-iron lanterns in each roadway. That was all; four houses, eight coach-houses, sixteen arches, eight lanterns; and even then the lanterns are now only stumps, the arches hidden with shrubbery. One house belongs to the police, another to the doctor, while the parish priest's house has had its roof raised, and its little Georgian panes replaced by stained glass.

But it is clear that the architect had another story in mind when he found the solution to the problem of his square. I feel sure it was a love story, and that from one of the small-paned Georgian windows he intended some woman to look out night after night on the eight lanterns which shut in her little world, and the carriages that rolled in and out of it with their officers, duellists and squireens from Trim and Drogheda. Was she married, and, if so, for whom did he intend the other two houses? Was it perhaps one of the four-sided comic intrigues that 18th-century dramatists delighted in? The sense of the past swooped down and enveloped us. Below on the riverbank it all began, ages and ages ago, with priestly johnnies and soldier johnnies, and all the trouble they started hasn't yet come to an end.

I feel sure the architect's tale had a happy ending, for though the Gothic gateway under the trees may have been in existence, it had not yet set the fashion for unhappy love, Shelley's poetry and Robert Emmet's speech from the dock. Wolfe Tone, rationalism and married love were still the rage, and I fancy the architect saw a carriage waiting one night on the road down to the river, a coach-house door opening quietly, and a young woman tripping out with lifted skirts. Then a few whispered words, and the carriage rattled over the bridge in the direction of Dublin.

So, at least I fancy, but it is all hard to read, and it is only when darkness falls, and the four old houses cease to whisper correct, serious, official things to one another about the decline in morals and the decay of children's teeth, compulsory Irish and the licensing of dogs, that the old wrought-iron lanterns seem to glow again, the four houses become a string quartet, and the tune they play a Boccherini minuet or a Mozart serenade, melancholy and gay.

The Stone Walls of Ireland

by Richard Conniff

Author Richard Conniff is a former managing director of Geo *magazine.*

The walls look as though they have been there forever: mottled with lichen and bearded with moss; woven together with vines, hedges, and trees; running, in more than one place, straight across a shallow stream bed, as if the wall were there before the water; emerging, in other places, from the low tide mark, as if the walls splashed ashore with the first settlers in Ireland, 8,000 years ago.

"All the people are dead now who was building walls," a man known locally as the Kaiser assured me one afternoon in County Kerry. It was the sort of remark you heard everywhere in Ireland: the walls were built "centuries ago, I suppose." Even "thousands and thousands of years ago." Or "in olden times." And what did he himself do for a living, I asked the Kaiser. Well, he built walls.

Long ago, of course? Not at all, he said. There was the one in Ballyferriter, built a year or two ago to "close up" around a man's house, and another outside the church. There was a fine new wall across from the pub in Ventry. There was the wall he was going to be building soon around Paudy O'Shea's new pub. And of course there was Sean Moran's wall on the Conor Pass Road in Dingle—I must've heard about it—a wall of such magnificence that people stopped their cars dead in the middle of the road to admire it: "You'd *have* to stop to look at it," he said, as if to explain away their poor driving habits. "You'd be blind if you didn't." He would show it to me himself, in fact.

The following Saturday, as arranged, we headed off around the tip of the Dingle Peninsula, stopping at a number of places not listed, including Sean Moran's wall—a structure of double thickness, six feet in height, around a field where sheep grazed. "The best wall around, I'd say, in Kerry," the Kaiser ventured, on his own craftsmanship. "There are no sheep going to be coming out of there soon. Or cattle."

As we drove, he talked about his craft. The common stone in the area was red sandstone, which breaks away in relatively flat tablets well suited to construction. "There's a bed for every one," the Kaiser explained. "You put it there and say, 'Get in it.'" It was sound material for a wall like, well, Sean Moran's. He'd set the stones there so snugly, he said, that "you couldn't pass a blade of grass across it with a pliers. Sean Moran'll be dead and rotting before it falls down.

You'd travel a long time before you saw the likes of that again. You'd travel all Ireland, I suppose."

He lamented the tendency to use barbed wire and electric fencing, which give no shelter for the crops or the animals. Some farmers even bulldozed stone walls to make bigger fields. Sean Moran, of course, would need no wiring. One local man so admired the towering wall at Moran's place that he went out every day with his dog and gazed at it for a half-hour at a time, until one day the dog (gone mad with boredom) got away from him and was killed (doubtless by a driver who was looking at the wall instead of the road). "A lot of people came out to look at it when it was built. Thousands of people. All Dingle came." The wall achieved its rightful status as a conversation piece; it became that estimable thing in Irish country life—a "talking point." For its builder, anyway.

The Kaiser complained about a local farmer who wanted a wall built. "He told me, 'My cattle don't wear glasses looking at the wall. I don't want no fancy work.' The man had red trousers on and a white jacket and he only wanted a plain wall. 'Something thrown up. No fancy work.' And then he put in this big white stone that looks like the arse of a tank in there." Sean Moran's wall, by contrast, was a subtle masterpiece. "You don't see the likes of that in Connemara, do you? You'd travel the world. 'Tis a job forever and ever. And no cement."

Any comparison with Sean Moran's wall is of course invidious, but in that regard it was like a number of others we passed that day on the Dingle Peninsula: dry stone walls, built "forever and ever," of a sort that would make even a modern wall-builder think the craft was one practiced mostly long ago, in days gone by. At the end of the peninsula, for instance, the ancient fort of Dunbeg walls off a small promontory from attack by land. The final line of defense is a massive stone barrier stepped up on the inside with walkways for men fighting with their backs to the Atlantic. No one really knows who built it, or against what foe. Farther on toward Slea Head, the slopes are dotted with beehive huts, monastic dwellings huddled together within small stone circles built high to shut out the world. Around the forts and these anchoritic retreats, the land is of a sort to keep monks and other farmers thin. But it is also well walled, and the field walls, too, look as if they have been there forever. Some of them are sod and stone. The grass grows sideways on them, and they look like yard-high ridges—elongated fins—of lawn. Elsewhere the walls are densely packed piles of flat sandstone. They run up to the mountaintops, enclosing fields pitched at an angle of 30 degrees. The scenery, out to the Blasket Islands, is spectacular, but it's the slope that takes your breath away.

If these walls appear ancient, it may be with good reason. A few Irish walls are as modern as Sean Moran's, and many are of far more recent vintage than a passer-by would surmise. But archeologists have established that the building of walls in Ireland goes back to the Neolithic Age. They have found walls running *underneath* a prehistoric burial cairn in County Down. There, and all along the coast from Kerry to Antrim, farmers cutting turf have stumbled onto field walls—whole systems of walls, in some cases—hidden for millennia by the peat blanket. These subterranean walls run, in one case, from the waterline to a point 600 feet above sea level. At another site, the buried farm has much the shape of a modern one, with half-acre tillage plots, fields of 3 or 4 acres, and a long straight fence more than a mile long, apparently separating one family's holdings from another's. The blanket peat that hid these old fields began to build up around 1000 B.C., as a result of early land clearing and deforestation. The walls beneath this blanket are thus probably 3,000 to 4,000 years old and are compounded of stone and sod, in the same manner as walls built on the present surface within the last century. In some places, the old walls emerge from the turf and continue on the surface as present-day boundaries. Like modern countrymen, prehistoric farmers doubtless cast a cool, appraising eye on one another's fields from across such walls.

But while the Irish landscape abounds in prehistoric and Early Christian antiquities, the walls generally do not date back that far, and the sense of continuity between modern walls and those of prehistoric farmers is an illusion. Most walls in Ireland went up no earlier than the agricultural revolution. The network of walls and hedges that we think of as timelessly defining the Irish countryside was, in fact, cast over the landscape like a web beginning in about 1750. Before that, much, if not most, of Ireland was, in effect, a great unfenced cow pasture. "Their fields lie open and unclosed," declared *Advertisements for Ireland* in 1623. Where proper fields existed, an anonymous writer added a few years later, they were "no better fenced than a midwife's toothless gums." In Donegal, in the middle of the 19th century, a landlord declared: "We suppose it would not be believed that in this district, until very lately, fences were altogether unknown."

Indeed, the Irish seem to have had something close to a split personality on the subject of walls. Scattered across the landscape by their pastoral, cattle-herding way of life, with nothing like the security of a town or village nearby, early Irish farmers commonly walled themselves in. The strongest farmers put up their houses within raths or ringforts, a form associated with Celtic settlers of the first millennium A.D. Thirty thousand of these raths survive around Ireland, visible, in the words of a Kerry farmer, as "old roundish rings of mouldy stone and sods." These grassy corrugations in the earth are all that remain even of Tara, once the seat of power over much of Ireland.

The raths are so well preserved partly because grazing was always more important in Ireland than the plow, but also because farmers regarded the raths as "fairy forts" and would not touch them. In Ulster in 1958, for example, a Land Commission work crew was building a fence in the course of rearranging land holdings in a congested district. "But an ancient rath lay in the path of the fence," a local newspaper reported. "The workmen refused to dig holes in the rath. They said they would die soon if they lifted a sod. A Land Commission supervisor suggested that two of the oldest men in the locality might have no fear of death. Two men, one of 97, the other 95, were asked and indignantly refused. They said that life was 'as sweet as the fairy music they often heard from the rath.'" Such caution has given the Irish landscape the quality of a palimpsest, with the earthworks of earlier civilizations still visible in the modern fields. But that is changing. Unfearing bulldozers now frequently level raths, and at Tara the raths sometimes serve as a sort of makeshift dirt bike course. Carrot-haired boys on fat-wheeled bicycles rise and disappear over the humpy landscape as if pedaling over waves.

The raths were once a place for a farmer to drive his livestock, to protect his wealth from hit-and-run cattle raiders. What field walls existed seem mostly to have been huddled around these refuges and around monastic sites. They formed the tillage plots of the "infield." But beyond them, in the "outfield," Irish farmers seem to have felt something like an abhorrence for walls. The occasional crop planted in a portion of the outfield would necessarily be enclosed, to keep the animals from trampling it. But the enclosure would be wicker, with stakes driven into the ground and rods woven around them. When the crop came in, the fence came down. The rods served as fuel in winter, and the outfield survived as open range. . . .

As English landlords and settlers took over [in Ireland] during the 17th century, widespread fencing of the land began almost immediately. Their methods had obvious and impressive advantages. In County Meath, for example, 5,000 acres of "waste sheep walk" were drained, limed, and fenced off into arable fields of ten acres each, for settlement by French and English Protestants.

These fences were elaborate affairs. An 18th-century visitor described them as typically consisting of an earthen embankment between drainage ditches 6 feet wide and 5 feet deep. The bank was usually planted with hedges and with trees for lumber. (In Ireland, for unknown reasons, the word "ditch" came to apply to the raised bank, rather than to the trenches from which it was formed. The word is now used to denote almost any form of raised boundary, including an unmortared—but not a mortared—stone wall; a mortared stone wall is known as a "wall." By the same logic, the word "moat" or "mote" refers in Ireland not to a water-filled trench around a castle, but to the raised and fortified platform enclosed by the trench; it derives from the Norman French word for "mound." The traveler in Ireland must therefore be prepared to hear about people climbing ditches and walking, like Christ, on moats. These are merely lexical differences, not miracles.)

The single most important benefit of enclosing the countryside was that it made the livestock farming for which Ireland was best suited more systematic and productive. Confining the movement of cattle within an enclosed field meant that the grass would be grazed more thoroughly and the manure concentrated in a field that could subsequently be planted with crops. With cattle no longer wandering freely over the open outfield, more land came under cultivation. Crop rotation was possible, along with the use of hay and roots as winter fodder.

Unfortunately for the Irish, the countryside that was being fenced in had been their common grazing ground. Not only were their ancient ways being supplanted by new and foreign methods; they were themselves being forced out, especially in the fertile lowlands. They responded, in places, by hacking down the landlords' hedges to burn for winter fuel. Later, in the 18th century, secret societies like the Ribbonmen vented their anger at a variety of grievances by mutilating the landlords' livestock. In Munster, the Whiteboys burned the alien settlers' crops and leveled walls across former common grazing ground. By then, however, the walls had already wrought a singular, irreversible change in Irish life: they had made the herder obsolete. . . .

But if enclosure ended one way of life, it also began another, drawing out the latent Irish mania for walls. . . . The walls entered not just every field, but every life and every aspect of life. They became drying racks, clotheslines, coat hooks, scratching posts, hiding places for poteen, and dumps for weapons. They served as shelter for outdoor classrooms—the so-called hedge schools—when formal education of Catholics was for a time outlawed. The walls were a place for lovers to hide, and also for eavesdroppers. They were instruments of spite and weapons for assault, but they were also children's playthings. (Outside Mullingar, for instance, children running small stones across the resonant coping stones have worn a long groove in a "musical wall"; the groove is generations old, but it is also still fresh.) They were a source of entertainment and of "divilment," which was and is a national sport.

As boundaries, the walls became manifestations of the Irish fondness for small fiefdoms and the gleeful cultivation of petty divisions, but they were at times also instruments of self-destructive generosity by enabling the land to be further and further subdivided. For peasant and landlord alike, the walls were a way of showing wealth, power, craftsmanship. As such, like Sean Moran's wall, they were talking points. They were also objects of delight entirely on their own. If the walls closed off the Irish from certain wilder, more naturalistic feelings, still they had a beauty of their own, to which the Irish were hardly blind. (*Tarry Flynn*, Patrick Kavanagh's novel of country life in County Monaghan, is, for example, shot through with walls and hedges. One moment the excitable protagonist is counting the stones in a wall as an exercise in self-control; the next he is suffused with lyrical feelings: "The snails climbing up the stones of the fences and the rushes and thistles in the meadow beyond seemed to be putting a quilt of peace around his heart.")

Finally, of course, the walls had something to do with the business of farming. They were a place to put stones when the fields were being picked clean. They were a way to mark field boundaries. And they were barriers to keep cattle in the pasturage and donkeys out of the cabbages. Indeed, building good walls quickly became synonymous with sound farming in Ireland. It was something that got into the blood. The story is told of County Galway farmers who had complained all their lives about the miserable land, where stones grew like mushrooms and walls divided farms less into fields than into cubicles. In time, the Land Commission relocated them to the rich, wide fields of County Meath. They complained then, of course, that they hadn't enough stones to build a decent fence. There is a saying, still repeated in parts of Ireland: "You can tell a farmer by his ditches."

3 Dublin

Introduction

by Hugh Oram

Based in Dublin, journalist and broadcaster Hugh Oram writes frequently about European travel, particularly about Ireland. He also works on historical documentaries.

Dublin: of all the capital cities in Europe, it is the most intimate in scale and easiest to explore. Although one of its names in Irish (Gaelic), *Dubhlinn*, means "dark pool," most visitors to the city find it a friendly, lighthearted place. Its setting is definitely an added attraction: it is looped around the edge of Dublin Bay, and to the immediate south of the city rise the Wicklow Mountains, (620 m/2,000 ft) high. From many neighborhoods of the city's southern suburbs, these mountains appear to block off the ends of the streets. From north to south, Dublin stretches 16 km (10 mi), and from its central area, immediately adjacent to the port area and the River Liffey, the city spreads westwards for an additional 10 km (6 mi); in total, it covers 28,000 acres.

As recently as 1600, Dublin was little more than a large village, with a population of 15,000. Much of its huge growth in population has occurred during this century; the capital has become the center for government offices and many new service industries. As a result, many people from other parts of Ireland have settled in here. Greater Dublin, with its 1 million residents, now claims nearly one-third of the population of the whole Irish Republic. Yet the city hardly ever seems too crowded, except for a few jam-packed pedestrian-only streets.

The population of Dublin is remarkably heterogeneous, reflecting the many invasions and settlements of the city over the years. From 1880 onwards, Jewish people fled the pogroms of eastern Europe and came to live in Ireland, and until the 1950s, the capital had a substantial Jewish population. (Much of the younger Jewish population has left the city to live in Israel and other countries.) Over the past decade, a large number of Middle Easterners and many American, Dutch, German, and Japanese immigrants have settled here.

Dublin first became a crossroads in Ireland some 1,500 years ago. Four of the main thoroughfares that traversed the country led to the site of present-day Dublin. Today, the area where the city's first inhabitants, members of the Gaelic order, built their dwellings is known as the Liberties; sections of the first town walls, dating back nearly 1,000 years, can still be seen off Thomas Street.

In 837, Norsemen from Scandinavia carried out the first outside attack on Dublin, arriving in a fleet of 60 long ships. Four years later, the Vikings built their first port here and used it for raiding large tracts of the countryside. Despite the resistance of the Irish against Viking rule, the Norsemen made Dublin one of the principal centers of their empire, from Russia in the east to Ireland in the west and Iceland in the north. The power of the Scandinavians was finally broken by the Irish at the Battle of Clontarf in 1014, which took place north of Dublin. Native rule, however, was short-lived; the Anglo-Normans landed in County Wexford, in southeast Ireland, in 1169; a mere two years later, King Henry II of England finally subdued some of the Irish chieftains and granted Dublin its first charter.

Through the Middle Ages, the city developed as a trading center, though fraught with political difficulties; the last remaining relic of medieval trade in Ireland can be seen nearly opposite the Christ Church Cathedral, in Tailor's Hall. In 1651, English soldier Oliver Cromwell occupied and ransacked Dublin. Not until the 18th century did Dublin reach a period of glory, when a golden age of enlightened patronage by wealthy members of the nobility turned the city into one of Europe's most prepossessing. Still, until the early 19th century, social and economic power rested exclusively in Protestant hands.

New streets and squares, such as Merrion and Fitzwilliam squares, were constructed with a classical dignity and elegance. Handel, the German-born English composer, wrote much of his great oratorio, the *Messiah,* in Dublin, where it was first performed in 1742. Many other crafts, such as bookbinding and silvermaking, flourished to cater to the needs of the often titled and usually wealthy members of society. Ireland was granted a certain measure of political autonomy by the British, and in the new government buildings (now the Bank of Ireland) in College Green, opposite Trinity College, the independent parliament met for the first time in 1783.

However, this period of glory was short-lived; in 1800, the Act of Union brought Ireland and Britain together in a common United Kingdom, and the seat of political power and patronage moved from Dublin to London. Dublin quickly lost its cultural and social sparkle, as many members of the nobility moved to London. The 19th century proved to be a time of political turmoil and agitation, although Daniel O'Connell, a lord mayor of Dublin, won early success with the introduction of Catholic emancipation in 1829.

During the late 1840s, Dublin escaped the worst effects of the famine, caused by potato disease, that blighted much of southern and western Ireland. New industries, such as mineral-water manufacturing, were established, and with an emerging Victorian middle class introducing an element of genteel snobbery to the city, Dublin began its rapid outward expansion. Until the mid-19th century, Dublin extended little beyond St. Stephen's Green, but with the sudden demand for additional housing by the newly wealthy, many new suburbs were established, such as Ballsbridge, Rathgar, and Rathmines on the south side, and Clontarf and Drumcondra on the north side.

At the same time, Dublin's cultural activity blossomed, particularly in literature. Two main literary movements grew up side by side. In 1893, Douglas Hyde, later the first president of Ireland, founded the Gaelic League (Conradh na Gaelige) with the aim of restoring the Irish language. At the same time, W. B. Yeats played a pivotal role in the Irish literary renaissance; with the foundation of the Abbey Theatre in 1904 and the coming to prominence of other playwrights like Sean O'Casey and J. M. Synge, Irish literature thrived. The cultural ferment of Dublin in the first decade of this century inevitably had its political apotheosis in the uprising of 1916, which lasted a week, damaging many buildings in the central O'Connell Street area of the city. In 1919, the war aimed at winning independence from Britain began in County Tipperary and lasted for three years. Dublin was comparatively unscathed during this period, but during the Civil War, which followed the setting up of the Irish Free State in December 1921, more harm came to a number of the city's historic buildings, such as the Four Courts and

Dublin Exploring *(Boxes Refer to Detail Maps)*

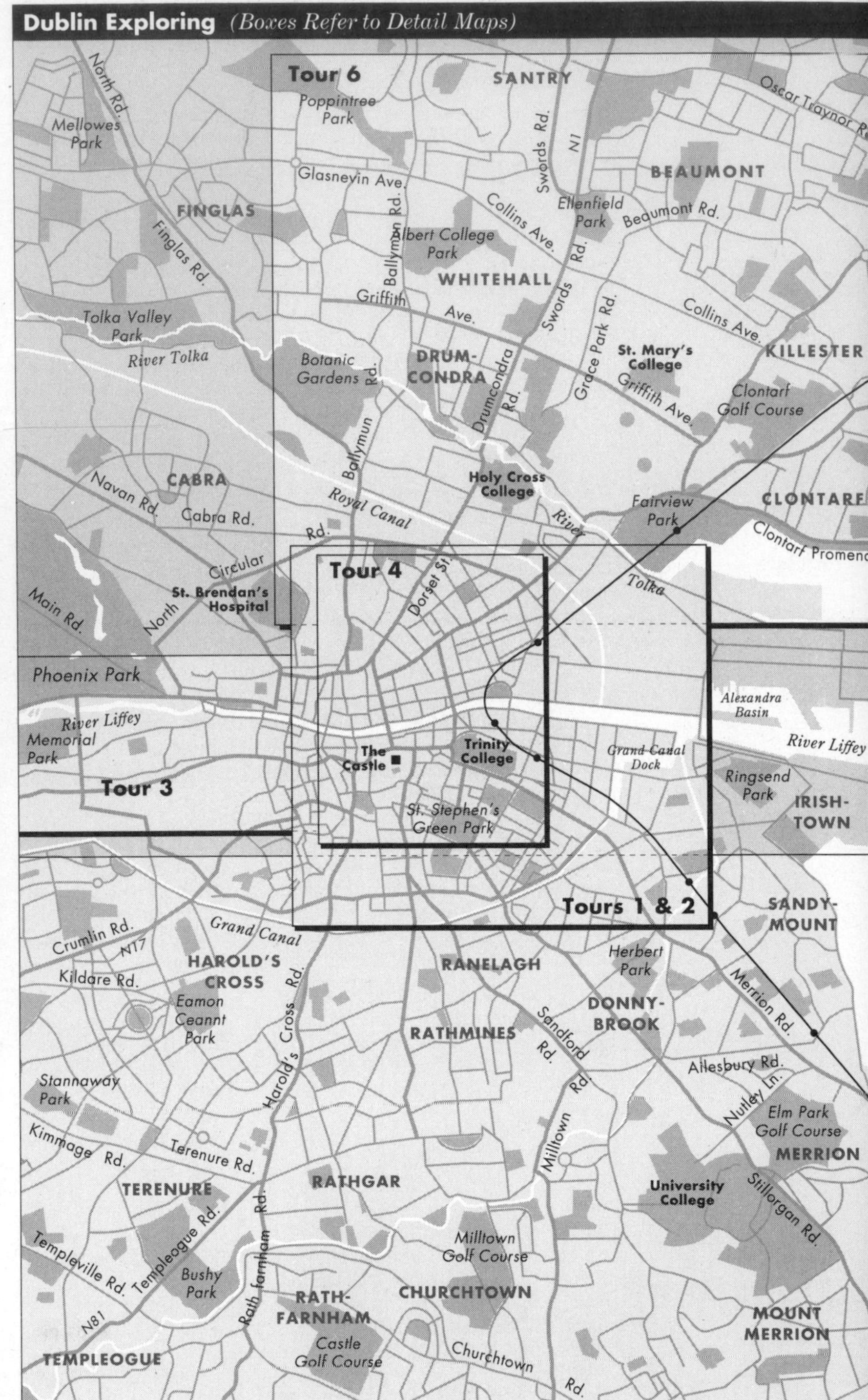

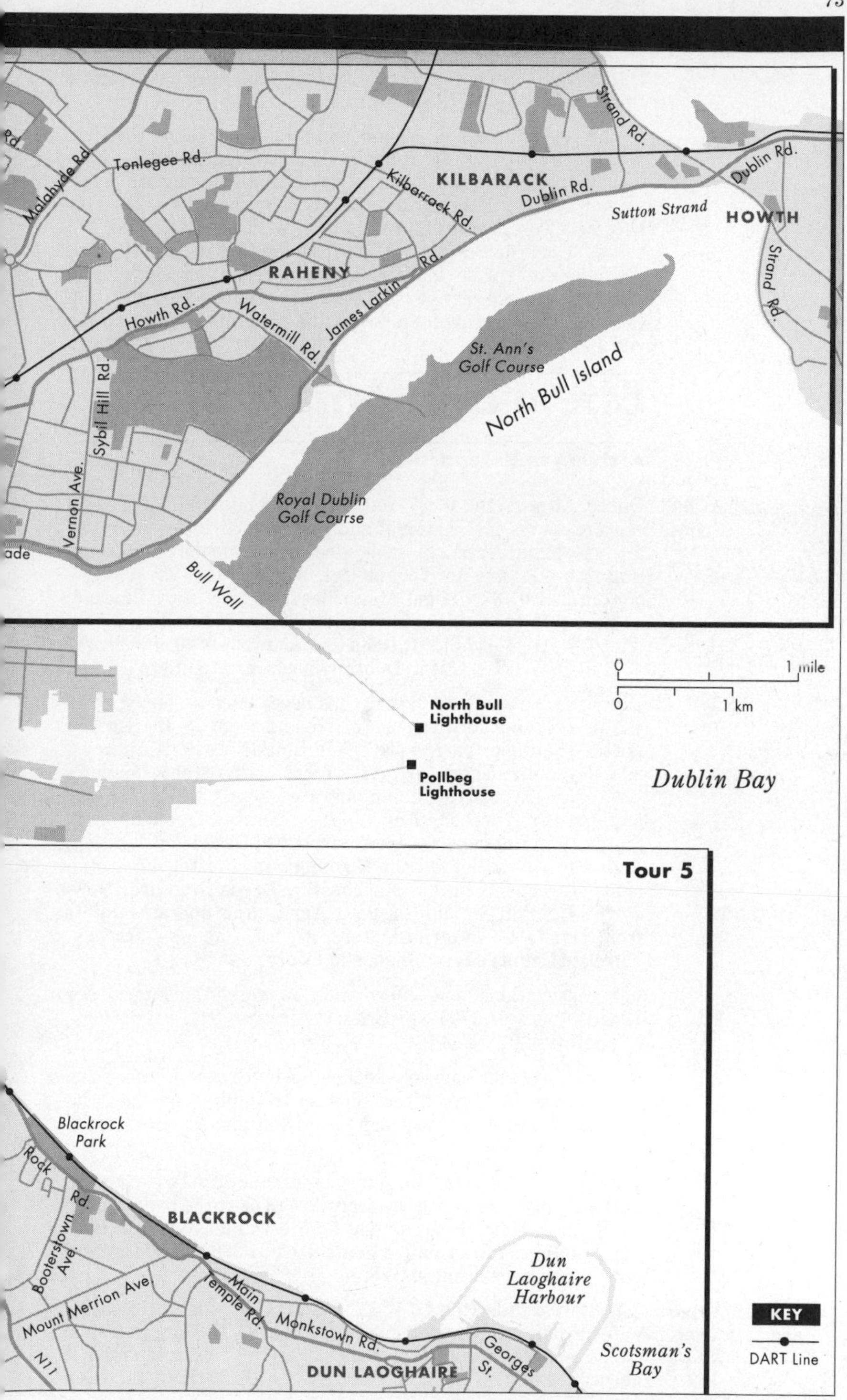

Rd.
Malahyde Rd.
Tonlegee Rd.
Strand Rd.
KILBARACK
Kilbarrack Rd.
Dublin Rd.
Dublin Rd.
Sutton Strand
HOWTH
Strand Rd.
RAHENY
Rd.
James Larkin
Howth Rd.
Watermill Rd.
St. Ann's
Golf Course
North Bull Island
Sybil Hill Rd.
Vernon Ave.
Royal Dublin
Golf Course
ade
Bull Wall
0
1 mile
0
1 km
North Bull
Lighthouse
Pollbeg
Lighthouse
Dublin Bay
Tour 5
Blackrock
Park
Rock
Rd.
BLACKROCK
Booterstown
Ave.
Mount Merrion Ave.
Main
Temple Rd.
Monkstown Rd.
Dun
Laoghaire
Harbour
Georges
St.
Scotsman's
Bay
N11
DUN LAOGHAIRE
KEY
DART Line

the Custom House, which both burned down. The capital had to be rebuilt during the 1920s. After the Civil War was over, Dublin entered a new era of political and cultural conservatism that continued until the late 1950s.

In the 1960s, an era of economic optimism pervaded the city, with many new internationally oriented businesses established. Much of this enthusiasm waned again during the recessionary years of the 1970s, but then in the 1980s, the city became a world center for rock music, with artists such as Bob Geldof, Chris de Burgh, and U2. With the 1990s, a new spirit of economic enterprise is underway with a recently opened international financial services center, next to the two-centuries-old Custom House, drawing many leading business clients to the city.

Essential Information

Arriving and Departing

Airport and Airlines

Dublin Airport (tel. 01/379900), 9½ km (6 mi) north of the city center, serves international and domestic airlines. Only two airlines have regularly scheduled flights from the United States to Dublin: **Aer Lingus** (tel. 212/557–1100 or 800/223–6537 in U.S; 01/370011 in Dublin) flies from New York, Chicago, or Boston to Dublin, and is scheduled to start handling flights from Los Angeles in 1991; **Delta** (tel. 800/722–9320 or 800/241–4341 in U.S.; 01/794744 in Dublin) flies from Atlanta to Dublin.

Flying to Ireland from Britain has never been easier, with 11 airlines serving destinations in Ireland from 19 British airports. The major carriers are Aer Lingus, British Airways, and Ryanair. There are 11 flights daily from London's Heathrow Airport to Dublin, operated jointly by Aer Lingus and British Airways. Aer Lingus operates frequent daily flights from London's Gatwick Airport to Dublin. In addition, flights to Dublin leave from Birmingham, Bristol, East Midlands, Liverpool, Luton, Manchester, Leeds/Bradford, Newcastle, Edinburgh, and Glasgow. Aer Lingus operates flights from Dublin to Waterford, Cork, Kerry, Shannon, Galway, Knock in County Mayo, Sligo, and Derry.

For reservations and information in Dublin, contact: **Aer Lingus** (tel. 01/370011); **British Airways** (tel. 01/610666); **Ryanair** (tel. 01/797444).

Major European carriers such as Air France, Lufthansa, Sabena, and KLM run direct services to Dublin from most European capital cities and major regional airports, especially those in Germany.

When you arrive at Dublin Airport, currency can be exchanged at the Bank of Ireland in the arrivals hall or at the bank branch in the main check-in area. Just before you leave the arrivals hall, the **Tourist Information Center** (tel. 01/376387) will answer any questions relating to Dublin.

Between Airport and City Center

By Bus

The **Dublin Bus** (tel. 01/734222) starts outside the arrivals gateway; pay the driver inside the coach. The single fare is £2.50. Service runs all day, from 7:30 AM to 11 PM, at intervals of about 30 minutes, as far as **Busaras** (tel. 01/302222), the main provincial bus station in the city center. Journey time from the airport to the city center is normally 30 minutes, but it may be longer in heavy traffic.

By Taxi A taxi is a quicker alternative than the bus to get from the airport to Dublin center. A line of taxis waits by the arrivals gateway; the fare for the 30-minute journey to any of the main city-center hotels is about £10. It's advisable to ask about the fare before leaving the airport.

Getting Around

Traveling around Dublin by public transport is comparatively easy, although a car is useful for getting around the outlying suburbs. The city center, with its maze of one-way streets and parking restrictions, is best negotiated on foot.

By Train An electric railway system, the **DART** (Dublin Area Rapid Transport; tel. 01/366222) connects Dublin with Howth to the north and Bray to the south on a fast, efficient line. There are 25 stations on the route, which is the best means of getting to seaside destinations such as Howth, Blackrock, Dun Laoghaire, Dalkey, Killiney, and Bray. The service starts at 6:30 AM and runs until 11:30 PM; at peak periods, 8–9:30 AM and 5–7 PM, trains arrive every five minutes. At other times of the day, the intervals between trains are 15 to 25 minutes.

Tickets can be bought at stations, but it is also possible to buy weekly (£8) or monthly (£39) tickets from the **Irish Rail Travel Centre** (35 Lower Abbey St., tel. 01/366222). Individual fares begin at 65p and range up to £2.40. There are heavy penalties for traveling the DART without a ticket.

Diesel train services run from Connolly Station (Amiens St.) to more distant locations like Malahide, Skerries, and Drogheda to the north of Dublin, and Wicklow and Arklow on the south side.

By Bus Dublin offers an extensive network of buses, but due to heavy traffic, bus service is not always reliable. Fares begin at 45p and have to be paid to the driver on entry to the bus, another cause of delays. Some bus services run on cross-city routes, but most buses start in the city center. Buses to the north of the city begin in the Lower Abbey Street/Parnell Street area, while those to the west begin in Middle Abbey Street and in the Aston Quay area. Routes to the southern suburbs begin at Eden Quay and in the College Street area. A number of services are links to DART stations, and another regular bus route connects the two main provincial railway stations, Connolly and Heuston. For Dublin Bus information, call 01/734222.

By Taxi The taxi service in Dublin is comparatively inexpensive, with a pick-up charge of £2 and a further charge of about £1.50 a mile thereafter. Many taxi stands are located through the city center and suburbs, listed in the Dublin telephone directory, where a cab may be picked up at most times of the day and night. Alternatively, you may phone a taxi company and ask for a cab to meet you at your hotel, but this may cost up to £4 extra. Although the taxi fleet in Dublin is large, the cabs are non-standard and some cars are neither spacious nor in pristine condition. Local taxi companies include **VIP Taxis** (tel. 01/

783333), **Metro** (tel. 01/683333), and **Mercs and Perks** (tel. 01/421341).

By Hired Car Two companies will supply a car with a driver for an individual guided tour of the city, which will cost between £50 and £100 a day, depending on the size of car: **Co-op Taxis** (tel. 01/777777) and **Tailors' Tours** (tel. 042/76393).

By Rental Car Renting a car in Dublin is extremely expensive, with high rates and a 10% local tax. Gasoline is also expensive by U.S. standards, at around 60p a liter. Peak-period car-rental rates begin at around £150 a week for the smallest models, like a Fiat Uno. Dublin has many car rental companies, and it pays to shop around and to avoid "cowboy" outfits. Some reliable car rental firms in the Dublin vicinity are: **Avis** (Jury's Hotel, tel. 01/683394; 51 Grafton St., tel. 01/778877; Hanover St., tel. 01/774010; Dublin Airport, tel. 01/372369), **Hertz** (O'Connell St., tel. 01/788862; Leeson St. Bridge, tel. 01/602255; 19 Hogan Place, tel. 01/765921; Dublin Airport, tel. 01/429333), and **Murray's Rent-a-Car** (Baggot St. Bridge, tel. 01/681777; Dublin Airport, tel. 01/378179).

Important Addresses and Numbers

Tourist Information The main Dublin **Tourist Information Office** (14 Upper O'Connell St., tel. 01/747733) is open weekdays 9–5:30 and Saturday 9–1. Because the office is located in one of the busiest areas of town, you are advised to go there as early as possible. The head office of the **Irish Tourist Board** (Baggot St. Bridge, tel. 01/765871) is open weekdays 9–6. Tourist Information Offices are also located at Dublin Airport (arrivals level, tel. 01/376387), which is open daily 8–8, and at St. Michael's Wharf (Dun Laoghaire, tel. 01/806984), which is open daily 7 AM–8 PM.

Emergencies For **gardai** (police), **ambulance,** or **fire,** dial 999.

Medical Check the main newspapers to see which public hospitals offer emergency services on any given day. For minor ailments, hotels have access to their own doctors and also to private hospitals, such as the Blackrock Clinic, south of Dublin.

Dentists The **Dublin Dental Hospital** (20 Lincoln Pl., tel. 01/679–4311) has emergency facilities and lists of dentists offering emergency care.

Embassies Embassies are open weekdays 9–5, but are closed for lunch 1–2.

U.S. Embassy (42 Elgin Rd., tel. 01/6888777).
Canadian Embassy (65 St. Stephen's Green, tel. 01/781988).
British Embassy (31 Merrion Rd., tel. 01/695211).
Australian Embassy (Fitzwilton House, Wilton Terr., tel. 761517).

Travel Agencies **American Express** (116 Grafton St., tel. 01/772874).
Thomas Cook (118 Grafton St., tel. 01/771721).

Lost and Found **Dublin Bus:** contact its headquarters (59 Upper O'Connell St., tel. 01/734222).
Railways, including the DART: contact **Iarnrod Éireann/Irish Rail** (Travel Centre, 35 Lower Abbey St., tel. 01/366222).

Opening and Closing Times

Dublin is gradually becoming a 24-hour city, even though the bus and DART train services close down for the night at 11:30 PM. Many taxis run all night, so there is no problem getting around. Many of the clubs on the Leeson Street Strip stay open until 4 AM or later. Even Sunday, once a day of sabbatical rest in Dublin, is lively in Continental style. Many smaller city-center shops and boutiques are open on Sundays; department stores are occasionally open on Sundays.

Banks are open weekdays 10–12:30 and 1:30–3. On Thursdays, they remain open until 5. Banks may have lunchtime opening shortly. Most branches now have automatic cash dispensers.

Post offices are open weekdays 9–1 and 2–5:30. On Saturdays, they are open 9–12:30. Main post offices are open Saturday afternoons, too. The General Post Office (GPO) on O'Connell Street, which has foreign exchange and general delivery facilities, is open Monday–Saturday 8–8. On Sunday, it is open 10:30–6:30.

Museums are normally open Tuesday–Saturday and also Sunday afternoon. Monday is the usual closing day.

The city's main **stores** are open Monday–Saturday 9–5:30 or 9–6. Department stores are closed on Sunday. Smaller specialty stores open on Sunday as well, usually 10–6.

Crime

Crime, often drug related, is a problem in Dublin, so visitors should watch over their wallets, handbags, and other personal possessions. Great care should be taken when parking a car not to leave any valuables inside, even under a raincoat on the back seat or in the trunk. Certain areas demand caution: The city center is where pedestrians and motorists should be especially careful. Another danger area for parking cars is in the vicinity of the Guinness Brewery Hop Store and Irish Whiskey Corner (*see* Tour 3: Dublin West, below). Side streets off O'Connell Street can also be dangerous, especially at night.

Guided Tours

Orientation Tours

Bus Éireann (tel. 01/366111) provides a four-hour city sightseeing tour that covers the main sights in the city-center, including St. Patrick's Cathedral, Trinity College, the Royal Hospital, and Phoenix Park. The company also features day tours to country destinations, out of the main bus station, Busaras, in Dublin.

Dublin Bus (tel. 01/734222) offers a three-hour city-center tour, taking in sights similar to the Bus Éireann tour (*see* above). During the summer, this tour runs daily, using open-topped buses in fine weather. The company also conducts a north-city coastal tour, going to Howth, and a south-city tour, traveling as far as Enniskerry.

Gray Line Tours (tel. 01/619666) runs city-center tours that cover the same sights as the Bus Éireann and Dublin Bus itineraries (*see* above).

Special-Interest Tours

DART Train Tours Guided tours of Dublin using the DART system are organized by **Views Unlimited** (8 Prince of Terrace, Bray, tel. 01/860164 or 862861).

Horse-Drawn Carriage Tours Horse-drawn carriage tours are available around Dublin and in Phoenix Park. For tours of the park, contact the **Office of Public Works** (tel. 01/613111). For other tours through the city, contact **Paddy Sarsfield** (tel. 01/755995).

Pubs Evening tours of the literary pubs of Dublin are offered by **Colm Quilligan** (tel. 01/540228).

Walking Tours **Tour Guides Ireland** (Glendenning House, Wicklow St., tel. 01/794291) conduct walking tours of the city, including Georgian Dublin. **Eamonn MacThomais** offers entertaining walking tours of the Liberties and Literary and Georgian Dublin; tours begin at 2 PM on weekends at the statue of Molly Malone's barrow, Grafton Street. Tourist Information Offices also provide leaflets describing walking tours that follow signposted itineraries.

Exploring

Highlights for First-time Visitors

Book of Kells at Trinity College (*see* Tour 1)
Chester Beatty Library (*see* Tour 5)
Guinness Brewery Hop Store (*see* Tour 3)
Howth Peninsula (*see* Tour 6)
Hugh Lane Municipal Art Gallery (*see* Tour 2)
Merrion Square (*see* Tour 1)
National Gallery of Ireland (*see* Tour 1)
Phoenix Park (*see* Tour 3)
Royal Hospital, Kilmainham (*see* Tour 3)
St. Stephen's Green (*see* Tour 1)

Tour 1: South City Center

Numbers in the margin correspond with points of interest on the Tours 1 and 2: Dublin City Center map.

A good place to start your tour of Dublin is the city-center area south of the River Liffey; it contains a majority of the city's historic buildings and monuments. Let's begin south of O'Connell Bridge and Westmoreland Street at College Green, once a Viking meeting place and burial ground. East of College Green
1 stands **Trinity College,** the sole college of Dublin University, Ireland's oldest, dating back to 1592, when it was founded by England's Queen Elizabeth I on the site of the confiscated Priory of All Hallows. For centuries, Trinity was the preserve of the Protestant church, and it is only within the past 30 years that final prohibitions barring Catholics from studying there have been lifted. Among the distinguished alumni of the college are Jonathan Swift, Thomas Moore, Sheridan LeFanu, George Berkeley, Oscar Wilde, J. M. Synge, Bram Stoker, and Samuel Beckett. Trinity served as a stand-in for an English university in the popular 1983 movie *Educating Rita*.

Trinity's grounds cover 40 acres, and most of its buildings were constructed in the 18th and early 19th centuries. The extensive West Front, with a classical portico in the Corinthian style, faces onto College Green; now grimy with age, it was built between 1755 and 1759, possibly the work of Theodore Jacobsen, architect of London's Foundling Hospital. Statues of orator Edmund Burke and dramatist Oliver Goldsmith are positioned close to the front gate. Parliament Square, the cobbled quadrangle that is the visitor's first introduction to the grounds, also dates back to the 18th century. On the right of the square, you'll find the Theatre, or Examination Hall, which features an impressive organ retrieved from an 18th-century Spanish ship and a gilded oak chandelier from the old House of Commons; concerts are sometimes held here. The Chapel, which stands on the left of the quadrangle, has stucco ceilings and fine woodwork. Both the Theatre and the Chapel were designed by Scotsman William Chambers in the late-18th century. The looming Campanile, or bell tower, erected in 1853, dominates the center of the square. *College information, tel. 01/772941. Grounds are open daily 8AM–10PM.*

At the right-hand corner of the second quadrangle, called Library Square, the **Old Library** houses Ireland's most valuable collection of ancient volumes and priceless manuscripts; the most famous of these is the Book of Kells, a splendidly illuminated version of the Gospels, designed by unknown monks, perhaps in Kells, County Meath, in the 9th century. The 680-page book was rebound in four volumes in 1953, and two of these are usually displayed at a time, with pages turned periodically, in the library's two-story Long Room. This room, which is 13 m (41 ft) wide by 65 m (210 ft) long, has a high-pitched barrel-vaulted ceiling and contains approximately 200,000 of the 3 million volumes in Trinity's collection. Since the 1801 Copyright Act, the college has received a copy of every book published in Britain and Ireland, and a great number of these publications must be stored in other parts of the campus and beyond. The carved Royal Arms of Queen Elizabeth I, above the library exit, is the only surviving relic of the original college buildings. *Admission: £1.75 adults, free for students under 18. Open weekdays 9:30–4:45, Sat. 9:30–12:45.*

At the east end of the Old Library stands the **New Berkeley Library,** built in 1967. Behind the Old Library, you'll find the concrete Arts and Social Sciences Buildings, with an entrance on Nassau Street; this complex houses the **Douglas Hyde Gallery of Modern Art,** which concentrates on contemporary art exhibitions and has its own bookshop. *Tel. 01/772941, ext. 1116. Admission: 50p. Open Mon.–Thurs. 11–6, Fri. 11–7, Sat. 11–4:45.*

In the Thomas Davis Theatre in the Arts Building, Trinity recently introduced the **Dublin Experience,** an elaborate audiovisual presentation devoted to the history of the city over the past 1,000 years. *Tel. 01/772941. Admission: £2.50, £4 with the Old Library and the Book of Kells. Open May–Oct., daily 10–5.*

Directly opposite the front entrance of Trinity College in College Green stands one of Dublin's most striking buildings, now
2 serving as a branch of the **Bank of Ireland.** This grand structure, with a facade incorporating Corinthian pillars into its Ionic porticos, was first designed by Sir Edward Lovett Pearce to house the Irish Parliament, which resided here for 17 years; when the Parliament was abolished in 1803 under the Act of Union, the building was bought by the Bank of Ireland. Today

Bank of Ireland, **2**
Bewley's Café, **7**
Carmelite Church, **5**
City Hall, **3**
Dublin Castle, **4**
Dublin Civic Museum, **6**
Garden of Remembrance, **24**
Gate Theatre, **26**
Genealogical Office, **10**
GPO (General Post Office), **28**
Heraldic Museum, **11**
Hugh Lane Municipal Art Gallery, **23**
Huguenot Cemetery, **17**
Leinster House, **13**
Merrion Square, **20**
Mountjoy Square, **21**
National Gallery of Ireland, **19**
National History Museum, **18**
National Library, **12**
National Museum, **14**
O'Connell St., **27**
Pro-Cathedral, **29**
Rotunda Maternity Hospital, **25**
Royal Irish Academy, **9**
Shelbourne Hotel, **16**
St. Ann's Church, **8**
St. Francis Xavier, **22**
St. Stephen's Green, **15**
Trinity College, **1**

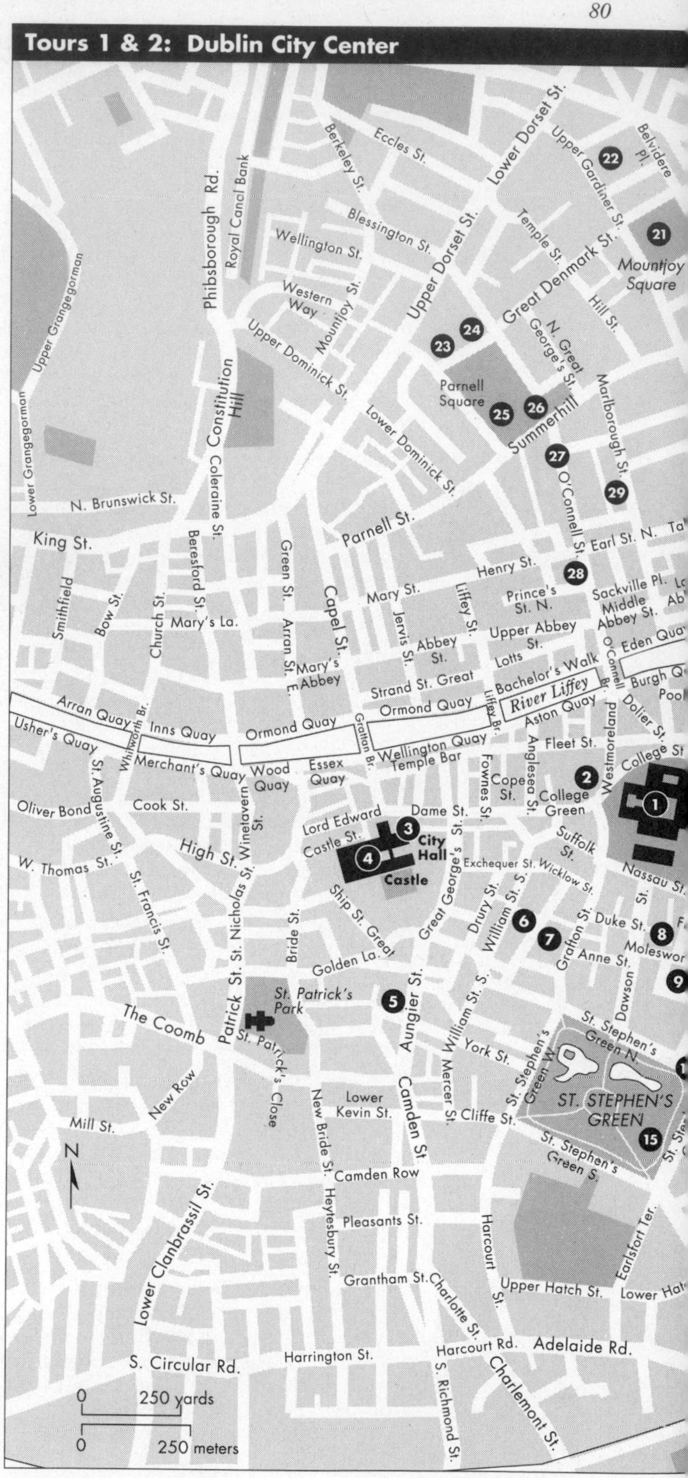

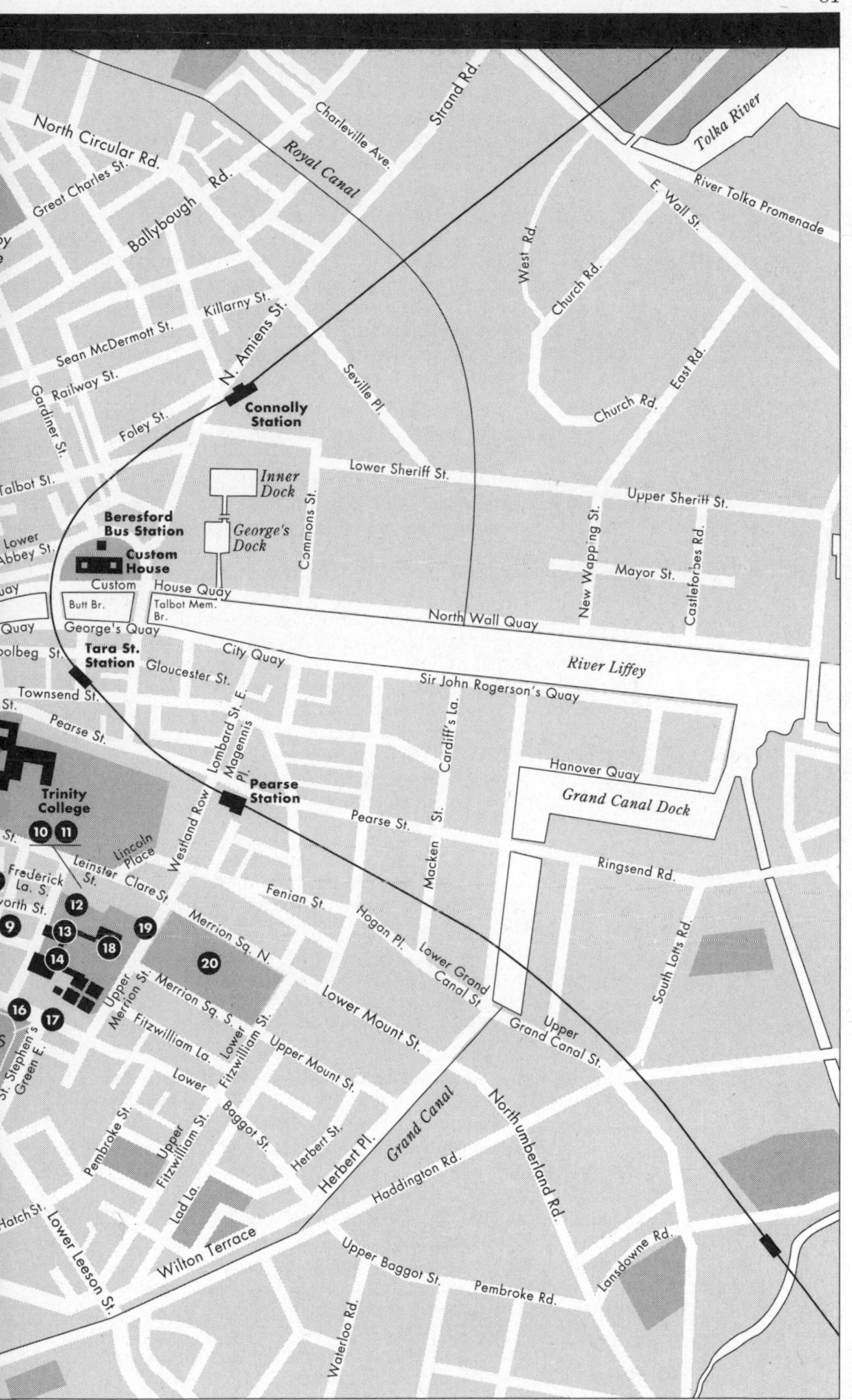

North Circular Rd.
Great Charles St.
Ballybough Rd.
Charleville Ave.
Royal Canal
Strand Rd.
Tolka River
River Tolka Promenade
E. Wall St.
West Rd.
Church Rd.
Killarny St.
Sean McDermott St.
N. Amiens St.
Railway St.
Gardiner St.
Seville Pl.
East Rd.
Church Rd.
Foley St.
Connolly Station
Lower Sheriff St.
Upper Sheriff St.
Talbot St.
Inner Dock
George's Dock
Commons St.
Beresford Bus Station
Custom House
Lower Abbey St.
New Wapping St.
Mayor St.
Castleforbes Rd.
Custom House Quay
Butt Br.
Talbot Mem. Br.
North Wall Quay
Quay
George's Quay
Tara St. Station
City Quay
Gloucester St.
River Liffey
Townsend St.
Sir John Rogerson's Quay
Pearse St.
Lombard St. E.
Magennis Pl.
Cardiff's La.
Hanover Quay
Trinity College
Pearse Station
Westland Row
Grand Canal Dock
Pearse St.
10
11
Lincoln Place
Macken St.
Ringsend Rd.
Frederick La. S.
Leinster St.
Clare St.
Fenian St.
12
Hogan Pl.
9
13
19
Merrion Sq. N.
18
14
20
Lower Grand Canal St.
South Lotts Rd.
Upper Merrion St.
Merrion Sq. S.
Lower Mount St.
16
17
Fitzwilliam La.
Lower Fitzwilliam St.
Upper Grand Canal St.
St. Stephen's Green E.
Upper Mount St.
Lower Baggot St.
Grand Canal
Northumberland Rd.
Pembroke St.
Upper Fitzwilliam St.
Herbert St.
Herbert Pl.
Haddington Rd.
Lad La.
Hatch St.
Lower Leeson St.
Wilton Terrace
Upper Baggot St.
Lansdowne Rd.
Pembroke Rd.
Waterloo Rd.

the main banking hall is set in the old Court of Requests where citizens' petitions were heard. The former House of Lords, which may be viewed by small groups upon request, features a coffered ceiling, an exquisite 18th-century Waterford glass chandelier, and two large tapestries depicting the Battle of Boyne and the Siege of Derry. *College Green, tel. 01/776801. Admission free. Open weekdays 10–12:30 and 1:30–3; Thurs. until 5.*

From the Bank of Ireland, turn left on to College Green, which
becomes Dame Street; continue for less than 1 km (½ mi) to
3 Cork Hill and **City Hall,** the seat of the Dublin Corporation, the
elected body that governs the city. This edifice, with its great domed entrance hall, was built as the Royal Exchange in 1769 and contains many notable historical artifacts, including 102 royal charters and the mace and sword of the city. *Tel. 01/6796111. Admission free. Open weekdays 9–5.*

4 Behind City Hall (west) is **Dublin Castle,** the seat of British administration in Ireland from the 13th century to 1922. It is now heavily restored and is used mostly for government and conference purposes. In the Lower Castle Yard, the Record Tower, built by King John between 1208 and 1220, and the earliest of several towers on the site, is the largest remaining relic of the original Norman buildings. Guided tours are offered around the principal State Apartments (on the southern side of the Upper Castle Yard), which are furnished with rich Donegal carpets and illuminated by Waterford glass chandeliers; today these elaborate rooms are largely used for ceremonial occasions. The largest and most impressive of these chambers, St. Patrick's Hall, with its gilt pillars and painted ceiling, is used for the inauguration of Irish presidents. The Round Drawing Room, in Bermingham Tower, dates from 1411 and was rebuilt in 1777; a number of Irish leaders have been imprisoned in the tower, from the 16th century to the early 20th century. The blue oval Wedgwood Room contains Chippendale chairs and a marble fireplace.

Also on the castle grounds is the **Church of the Holy Trinity** (formerly called Chapel Royal), designed in the early 19th century by Francis Johnston, who also designed the original General Post Office building on O'Connell Street. Carved oak panels and stained glass depicting viceroys' coats of arms grace the interior. *Castle St., tel. 01/777129. Admission to State Apartments: £1. Open weekdays 10–12:15 and 2–5; Sat., Sun., and public holidays 2–5. Call ahead, because apartments are sometimes closed for state occasions.*

From the main entrance of the castle, turn right on to Cork Hill and Dame Street until you reach South Great George's Street on your right. The covered markets here (open Mon.–Sat. 9–6), a Victorian legacy, have changed little despite their restoration; you'll find many lines of food, fashion, and trinkets for sale.

Time Out Take a look at the **Long Hall Pub** (51 S. Great George's St.), one of Dublin's most ornate traditional taverns, full of lamps, woodwork, mirrors, and chandeliers, all at least 100 years old. The pub serves sandwiches, beers, and whiskies.

South Great George's Street eventually turns into Aungier
5 Street. The inside of the **Carmelite Church** on Whitefriar

Street, off Aungier Street, contains an unusual bequest from an early 19th-century pope, Gregory XVI, who gave the prior of the church, in recognition of the latter's work, the remains of St. Valentine, the patron saint of lovers, who was martyred in Rome about AD 269. *Tel. 01/758821. Admission free. Open daily 8–8.*

Return to the market area on South Great George's Street; behind the shops on the right, approached by a pedestrian walk-
6 way, is the **Dublin Civic Museum.** In the 18th century, the building housed the City Assembly Hall, precursor of City Hall. The museum's small, esoteric collection includes Stone Age flints, Viking coins, old maps and prints of the city, and the sculptured head of British admiral Horatio Nelson, which used to top Nelson's Pillar, beside the General Post Office on O'Connell Street (*see* below); the column was toppled by an explosion in 1966 on the 50th anniversary of the Easter Rising. Often, the museum runs exhibitions relating to the city. *South William St., tel. 01/679–4260. Admission free. Open Tues.–Sat. 10–6, Sun. 11–2.*

From the museum, walk east passing Clarendon Street and the Catholic **St. Theresa's Church;** continue along Johnson's Court, beside the church, onto Grafton Street.

Part of Dublin's most famous chain of coffee houses, dating
7 back to 1840, **Bewley's Café** on Grafton Street with its dark wood and marble tables is renowned for its stained-glass windows by Harry Clarke (1889–1931), Ireland's most distinguished early 20th-century artist in this medium. The café, which serves reasonably priced tea, coffee, meals, and desserts, is a fine place in which to observe Dubliners of all ages and occupations. On the first floor, a small museum deals with Bewley's history. (Other branches of Bewley's are located at South Great George's and Westmoreland streets.) *Tel. 01/776761. Open weekdays 10–6.*

Cross Grafton Street and walk east along South Anne Street to
8 **St. Ann's Church** (Church of Ireland) on Dawson Street. Its plain neo-Romanesque granite exterior, designed in 1868, belies its rich, 18th-century Georgian interior, with polished wood balconies and ornate plasterwork. *Dawson St., tel. 01/762186. Admission free. Open weekdays 10–3 and Sun. for services. Closed Sat.*

9 Steps away from the church is the **Royal Irish Academy,** which houses Thomas Moore's library, old scientific texts, and a large collection of ancient Irish manuscripts, including the 11th–12th century Book of the Dun Cow. *19 Dawson St., tel. 01/762570. Admission free. Open weekdays 9:30–5:30.*

From Dawson Street, walk along Molesworth Street, where you'll pass the **Freemasons Hall** (tel. 01/761337), a large 18th-century building with a pillared portico. At the end of the street, turn left on to Kildare Street. At 2 Kildare Street, the
10 full records of the **Genealogical Office** can help people who are searching for Irish ancestors. *Tel. 01/618811. Open weekdays 9:30–5:30.*

11 At the same address, you'll find the **Heraldic Museum,** founded in 1911 and once located in Dublin Castle. It now displays a collection of family coats of arms. *2 Kildare St., tel. 01/614877. Open weekdays 10–12:30 and 2–4:30.*

12 West of the museum stands the **National Library.** Its main Reading Room opened in 1890 to contain the collections of the Royal Dublin Society. Beneath its dramatic domed ceiling, countless authors have researched and written their books over the years. The library accommodates an important collection of first editions and works by Irish writers, including ones by Swift, Goldsmith, Yeats, Shaw, Joyce, and Beckett. Virtually every book ever published in Ireland is kept here, as well as an unequaled selection of old maps and an extensive collection of Irish newspapers and magazines. *Kildare St., tel. 01/765521. Admission free. Open weekdays 10–6.*

13 Next to the library you'll find the impressive **Leinster House** (Kildare St., tel. 01/789911) constructed in 1745 as a lavish town house for the duke of Leinster and now the seat of the Dáil Éireann (House of Representatives) and the Seanad Éireann (Senate), which constitute the National Parliament. The public is admitted to the Dáil visitors' gallery only with an introduction from a member of the House; local Tourist Information Offices can make arrangements.

14 The **National Museum** is located west of Leinster House. Extensively renovated in recent years, the museum features several rooms devoted to artifacts from prehistoric Ireland, including carved stones, weapons, and jewelry. The Treasury collection, including some of the museum's most renowned pieces, is open permanently. Among the priceless relics on display are the 8th-century Ardagh Chalice, a two-handle silver cup with gold filigree ornamentation; the bronze-coated iron St. Patrick's Bell, the oldest surviving example (5th–8th centuries) of Irish metalwork; the 8th-century Tara Brooch, an intricately decorated piece made of white bronze, amber, and glass; and the 12th-century bejeweled oak Cross of Cong, covered with silver and bronze panels. Another room is devoted to the 1916 Easter Rising and the War of Independence (1919–1921); displays include uniforms, weapons, banners, and a piece of the flag that flew over the General Post Office during Easter Week, 1916. Other exhibits showcase Irish glass, lace, and instruments, including pipes, harpsichords, and 17th- and 18th-century harps. At press time, however, several rooms were closed temporarily because of staff shortages.

In contrast to the convoluted late-Victorian architecture of the main museum building with its balustrades and fancy ironwork, the design of the **National Museum Annexe** (located around the corner on Merrion Row, just past the Shelbourne Hotel) is purely functional; it houses temporary shows of Irish antiquities. *National Museum, Kildare St., tel. 01/618811; Annexe, 7–9 Merrion Row, tel. 01/601117. Admission free, except for certain exhibitions. Open Tues.–Sat. 10–5, Sun. 2–5.*

Across from the National Museum, at 30 Kildare Street, a plaque records that Bram Stoker, creator of the 19th-century classic horror story *Dracula*, once lived here, quite peacefully.

Time Out Right opposite the main museum entrance, **Cunningham's** (35A Kildare St., tel. 01/762952), a cozy tearoom and snack bar, serves all kinds of tantalizing sandwiches and salads.

15 At the south end of Kildare Street lies **St. Stephen's Green,** a verdant city-center square, with extensive lakeside walks. It was an open common until 1663, but the houses and buildings

that now stand on its four sides were not constructed until the late-18th century. (Unfortunately, several of these old structures have been modernized without charm.) Lord Ardiluan, a member of the Guinness brewery family, paid for the space to be laid out as a public park in 1880. The green features flower gardens, formal lawns, a Victorian bandstand, and an ornamental lake that is home to many waterfowl. Among the park's many statues are a memorial to Yeats by Henry Moore, and the Three Fates, a dramatic group of bronze female figures watching over Man's destiny by a fountain.

On the north side of the green—referred to in the 18th century as the Beaux Walk—you'll find the imposing Victorian-era
16 redbrick **Shelbourne Hotel** (27 St. Stephen's Green, tel. 01/766471), where in a first-floor suite, the Irish Free State's constitution was drafted in 1921. A center for Dublin's high society, the Shelbourne is a friendly place despite its grandeur, and nonguests can stop here comfortably for a drink or meal (*see* Lodging, below).

17 Next to the Shelbourne Hotel is the **Huguenot Cemetery,** the last such burial ground in Dublin, which was used in the late-17th century by French Protestants who had fled persecution in their native land. The gates to the cemetery are rarely open, but you can observe its grounds from the street.

From the corner of Merrion Row and Lower Baggot Street,
18 turn left onto Upper Merrion Street, where the **Natural History Museum** houses a collection of mounted mammals and birds, with examples of extinct species, including skeletons of prehistoric giant deer. *Merrion Sq. W, tel. 01/618811. Admission free. Open Tues.–Sat. 10–5, Sun. 2–5.*

19 The **National Gallery of Ireland,** on Merrion Square West, owes its existence to William Dargan (1799–1867), who was responsible for building much of Ireland's railway network in the 19th century (he is honored by a statue on the front lawn). The building was designed by Francis Fowke, who was also responsible for London's Victoria and Albert Museum. Rated as one of the best smaller public museums in Europe, the National Gallery contains more than 2,000 paintings, with a large number representing the Irish School, including the work of Jack B. Yeats, the brother of W. B. Yeats and considered by many to be one of Ireland's finest painters. The collection also includes work by French Impressionists, a small selection of Dutch masters (including some fine Rembrandts), and exceptional paintings from the 17th-century French, Italian, and Spanish schools. *Merrion Sq. W, tel. 01/615133. Admission free. Open Mon.–Wed. and Fri.–Sat. 10–6, Thurs. 10–9, Sun. 2–5.*

20 Across from the gallery, you'll come to **Merrion Square,** created in the late-18th century after the construction of the surrounding homes. This oasis of lawns and flower beds takes you away from the roar of city traffic. During the famine years of 1845–1847, soup kitchens were established here to feed starving refugees. The square has formerly been the home to several distinguished Dubliners, including Oscar Wilde's parents, Sir William and "Speranza" Wilde (No. 1), Irish national leader Daniel O'Connell (No. 58), and authors W. B. Yeats (No. 52 and 82) and Sheridan LeFanu (No. 70). Visitors can walk past the houses and read the plaques on the house facades, which identify the former inhabitants. Until 50 years ago, the square was a

fashionable residential area, but today, most of the houses are used for commercial purposes.

Tour 2: North City Center

The northern part of the city center beyond the River Liffey—a mixture of densely thronged shopping streets and run-down sections of once genteel homes—is less attractive today than the south city center. But during the 18th century, most of the upper echelons of Dublin society lived in the Georgian houses around Mountjoy Square and shopped along Capel Street, which was lined with pricey shops that carried such items as fine furniture and silver. However, with the construction of Merrion Square on the south side (completed in 1764) and the nearby Fitzwilliam Square (completed in 1825), the city's fashionable social center switched decisively and permanently from north to south of the River Liffey. Although some of the illustrious inhabitants in the north city center clung to their houses, this area gradually became more run down over time.

21 Off Upper Gardiner Street, **Mountjoy Square,** built in the mid-18th century, once had four sides of elegant terraced houses, but today, only the northern side remains intact. Irishman Brian Boru, who led his soldiers to victory against the Vikings in the Battle of Clontarf in 1014, was said to have pitched camp before the confrontation on the site of Mountjoy Square. Playwright Sean O'Casey once lived here at No. 35 and used the square as a setting for *The Shadow of a Gunman.*

22 A block and a half north of the square stands the Jesuit **St. Francis Xavier,** one of the city's finest churches in the classical style, begun in 1829, the year of Catholic Emancipation, and completed three years later; the building is designed in the shape of a Latin cross, with a distinctive Ionic portico and an unusual coffered ceiling. The striking *faux*-green marble high altarpiece, decorated with lapis lazuli, came from Italy. The church appears in James Joyce's story "Grace." *Upper Gardiner St., tel. 01/363411. Admission free. Open daily 8–6.*

A walk west from Mountjoy Square along Gardiner Place and
Great Denmark Street leads you to Parnell Square and the
23 **Hugh Lane Municipal Art Gallery,** built originally as a town
house for the earl of Charlemont in 1762 and named after an art benefactor who drowned on the *Lusitania,* which was sunk off the County Cork coast in 1915. The small museum features an impressive collection of paintings and sculpture by 19th- and early 20th-century French and Irish artists and strikingly displayed stained-glass work by Harry Clarke and Evie Hone. *Parnell Sq., tel. 01/741903. Admission free. Open Tues.–Sat. 9:30–6, Sun. 11–5.*

24 The **Garden of Remembrance,** which faces the gallery, was
opened in 1966 to commemorate all those who died fighting for
Irish freedom. The garden has a large plaza at its entrance;
steps lead down to the fountain area, which has a sculpture by
contemporary Irish artist Oisin Kelly based on the mythologi-
cal Children of Lir, who were turned into swans. Most of the
25 remainder of Parnell Square is occupied by the **Rotunda Maternity Hospital** (Parnell St., tel. 01/730700), founded in 1745 as
the first of its kind in Ireland or Britain. The hospital, with a
three-story tower and copper cupola, was designed on a grand
scale by architect Richard Cassels (1690–1751). Its exquisite

chapel features elaborate plasterwork, appropriately honoring motherhood, executed by Bartholomew Cramillion in 1757–1758.

26 Parnell Square is also the site of the **Gate** (Cavendish Row, tel. 01/744045), one of Dublin's main theaters. For five decades, from the 1930s to the 1970s, Michéal MacLiammóir and Hilton Edwards staged many startling and memorable productions here by Irish playwrights and introduced Dublin audiences to foreign writers. Orson Welles and James Mason both performed here early in their careers. Today the Gate continues to mount exciting plays, particularly by young Irish dramatists.

27 Parnell Square leads to the top (north) end of **O'Connell Street,** Dublin's most famous thoroughfare. Previously known as Sackville Street, its name was changed in 1924, two years after the setting up of the Irish Free State. After the devastation of the 1916 Easter Rising, the street had to be almost entirely reconstructed until the end of the 1920s. The main attraction of the street, Nelson's Pillar, a Doric column towering over the city center and a marvelous vantage point, was blown up by an unknown group in 1966, the year that the 50th anniversary of the Easter Rising was celebrated.

At the corner of Henry and O'Connell streets, you'll see the
28 massive **General Post Office** (known as the **GPO**), with the original facade and Ionic portico designed by the neoclassical architect Francis Johnston in the early 1800s. The building was destroyed during the Easter Rising and was then rebuilt in its original style; it reopened in 1929. Inside the main concourse of the building, the bronze sculpture depicts the dying Cuchulainn, a leader of the Red Branch Knights in Celtic mythology. *O'Connell St., tel. 01/728888. Open Mon.–Sat. 8–8, Sun. 10:30–6:30.*

From the GPO, cross O'Connell Street and walk down Cathe-
29 dral Street to Marlborough Street and the Catholic **Pro-Cathedral,** built between 1815 and 1825. Although the severely classical church design is on a suitably epic scale, the building was never granted full cathedral status. The church's facade with its six-pillared portico is based on the Temple of Theseus in Athens; the interior is modeled after the Grecian-Doric style of St. Philippe du Roule of Paris. The Pro-Cathedral has been used over the years for important state funerals. A Palestrina choir, in which the great Irish tenor John McCormack began his career, sings in Latin here every Sunday at 11. *Marlborough St., tel. 01/745441. Admission free. Open daily 8–6.*

Time Out **Café Kylemore** (1 Upper O'Connell St., at North Earl St., tel. 722138) offers a plain menu, but its neo-Viennese decor is charming, with many unusual prints on the walls. **Conway's** (Parnell St., near Upper O'Connell St.), the second-oldest pub in Dublin, was founded in 1745; little has changed in it since Victorian times. Among its antique furnishings is a real gem: a 130-year-old, eight-day grandfather clock.

Tour 3: Dublin West

Numbers in the margin correspond with points of interest on the Tour 3: Dublin West map.

If you follow the River Liffey upstream from the north city center, keeping to the north bank, the streets along the quays lead
30 you to the classical edifice of the **Four Courts,** the seat of the
Irish Law Courts. Built between 1786 and 1802, this massive structure was designed by architect James Gandon, who was also responsible for another Dublin landmark, the **Custom House,** downstream on the same side of the River Liffey. In 1922, during the Irish Civil War, the Four Courts was almost totally destroyed by shelling, and the adjoining Public Records Office was gutted, destroying many priceless legal documents, including innumerable family records; restoration to the building's original style took 10 years. Today, the stately Corinthian portico and the circular central hall are worth viewing. The upper rotunda of the Four Courts' distinctive lantern dome provides a good view of the city. *Inns Quay, tel. 01/725555. Admission free. Open weekdays 10–4.*

Around the corner from the Four Courts on Church Street is
31 the Anglican **St. Michan's Church,** dating from 1685 and on the
site of an 11th-century Danish church. The church, which is architecturally undistinguished except for its 37-m (120-ft) bell tower, features an 18th-century organ, supposedly played by Handel, and the Stool of Repentance, the only one still in existence in the city; parishioners who were termed "open and notoriously naughty livers" used it to do public penance. St. Michan's main claim to notoriety, however, is down in the vaults, where the totally dry atmosphere has preserved a number of corpses in a remarkable state of mummification. They lie in open caskets, and strong-hearted visitors can shake hands with a former religious crusader or nun. Most of the preserved bodies are thought to have been Dublin tradespeople. *Church St., tel. 01/724154. Admission free. Open weekdays 10–12:45 and 2–4:45, Sat. 10–1.*

From St. Michan's, turn left from Church Street onto May
32 Lane and continue through to the **Irish Whiskey Corner.**
Jameson's Whiskey Distillery was built here in 1791. After local distilleries merged in 1966 to form Irish Distillers, part of the old Jameson's complex was converted into the new group's head office and one of the bonded warehouses was turned into a whiskey museum. Visitors can watch a short audiovisual history of the industry, which actually had its origins 1,500 years ago in Middle Eastern perfume making. Mementos of whiskey-making on display include antique posters and a large scale model of an old distillery; you can also view a reconstruction of a former warehouse, where the colorful nicknames of former barrel makers are recorded. In the Ball o' Malt bar, you're invited to taste the different blends of Irish whiskey and compare them against bourbon and scotch. *Bow St., tel. 01/725566. Guided tour: £2. Tours weekdays 3:30 PM.*

From the whiskey museum, turn right on Bow Street and make a left on to King Street North; proceed to Blackhall Place and
33 then make a left on to Arbour Hill, the location of **Arbour Hill**
Cemetery, where the leaders of the 1916 Easter Rising are buried. A total of 14 Irishmen were executed by the British; these included Patrick Pearse, who led the rebellion, and James Connolly, a labor leader wounded in the battle. The burial ground is a simple but formal area, with the names of the dead leaders carved in stone, beside an inscription of the proclama-

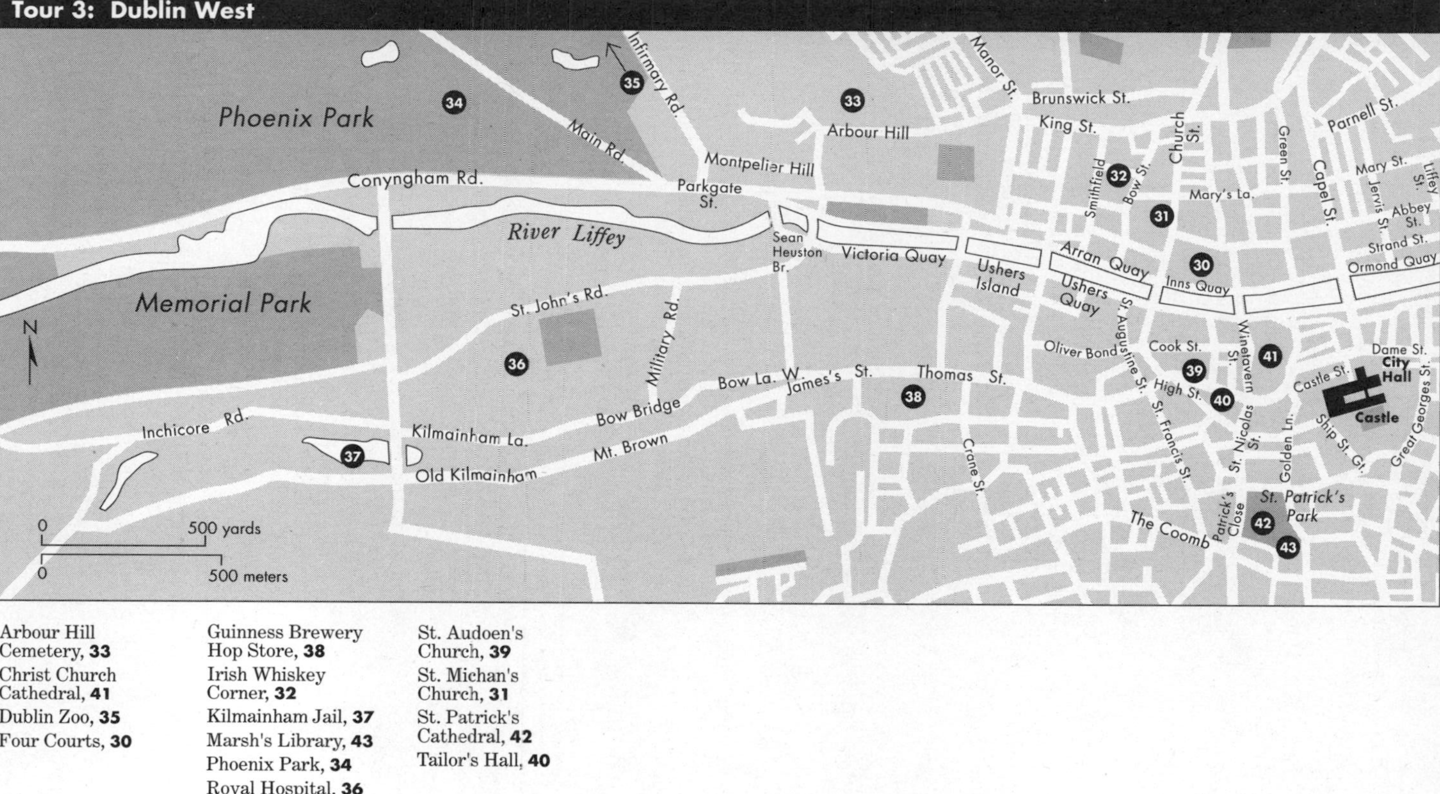

Arbour Hill Cemetery, **33**
Christ Church Cathedral, **41**
Dublin Zoo, **35**
Four Courts, **30**
Guinness Brewery Hop Store, **38**
Irish Whiskey Corner, **32**
Kilmainham Jail, **37**
Marsh's Library, **43**
Phoenix Park, **34**
Royal Hospital, **36**
St. Audoen's Church, **39**
St. Michan's Church, **31**
St. Patrick's Cathedral, **42**
Tailor's Hall, **40**

tion they issued during the uprising. *Arbour Hill. Admission free. Open Mon.–Sat. 9–4:30, Sun. 9:30–12.*

Walk south toward the quays and then west along Parkgate Street, a distance of 1 km (½ mi).

Time Out **Ryans Pub** (Parkgate St., tel. 01/776097) is one of Dublin's last genuine late Victorian-era pubs; it has changed little since its last (1896) remodeling. Its dark-mahogany bar counters and old-fashioned lamps and snugs (small drinking alcoves) create a restful setting.

At the end of Parkgate Street, opposite the bus depot, entrance
34 gates lead to the 1,752 attractive acres of **Phoenix Park,** Europe's largest public park, with lakes, woods, gardens, and expansive playing fields. The main road that bisects the park for 4 km (2½ mi) was laid out by Lord Chesterfield, a lord lieutenant of Ireland, in the 1750s; old-fashioned gas lamps that line both sides of the road were recently renovated. By the entrance to the park is the People's Garden, a charming and colorful flower garden.

Among the park monuments worth noting are the Phoenix Column erected by Lord Chesterfield in 1747 and the 60-m (198-ft) obelisk, built in 1817 to commemorate the duke of Wellington, the Irish general who defeated Napoleon for the British. A much more recent edifice marks the visit to Ireland by Pope John Paul II in 1979, when he addressed more than a million people here. Both the president of Ireland and the U.S. ambassador have official residences in the park, but neither building is open to the public. The Garda Siochana (police) has its headquarters here; a small museum (tel. 01/771156) contains many relics of Irish police history, including old uniforms. *Park: tel. 01/213021. Admission free. Open all day.*

35 **Dublin Zoo** may be found on the northern fringes of the Phoenix Park; founded in 1830, it is the third-oldest public zoo in the world. Many animals from tropical climes are housed in barless enclosures, while Arctic species swim the lakes, complementing the deer that roam free in the adjoining park. The zoo is one of the few places in the world where lions will breed in captivity. The children's corner features goats, guinea pigs, and lambs. *Tel. 01/775283. Admission: £2. Open daily 9:30 AM–sunset.*

Return to the main park entrance and walk east on Parkgate Street to the Sean Heuston Bridge; cross the River Liffey to the Heuston Railway Station, continue past the station's main entrance, cross St. John's Road, and walk on Military Road to
36 the **Royal Hospital** on Kilmainham Lane. Built in the late-17th century to house military pensioners, it is a replica of Les Invalides in Paris. After the founding of the Irish Free State in 1922, the building fell into disrepair, but over the last 15 years, a huge restoration program has returned the whole edifice to its former glory. The structure consists of four galleries around a courtyard with a grand dining hall and a chapel with a stucco ceiling and fine wood carvings. Today the Royal Hospital offers a series of musical events and art exhibitions, and a museum of modern art is scheduled to open in 1991. *Kilmainham La., tel. 01/718666. Admission free, but individual shows may have separate charges. Open Tues.–Sat. 2–5, Sun. noon–5. Guided tours every 30 min on Sun.*

Immediately beyond the front gates of the Royal Hospital
37 grounds lies **Kilmainham Jail,** a grim, forbidding structure where leaders of the 1916 Easter Rising, including Patrick Pearse and James Connolly, were held before being executed in the prison yard. In the 19th century, other inmates here were the revolutionary Robert Emmet and Charles Stewart Parnell, a leading politician. You can visit the cells, a chilling sight, while the guided tour and a 30-minute audiovisual presentation relate a graphic account of Ireland's political history over the past 200 years from a nationalist viewpoint. *Inchicore Rd., tel. 01/535984. Admission: £1.50. Open June–Sept., daily 11–6; Oct.–May, Wed. and Sun. 2–6.*

From the jail, turn right (east) onto Old Kilmainham, which turns into Mount Brown, James's Street, and then Thomas Street (a 1½-km/1-mi walk). Here you'll reach the vast
38 **Guinness Brewery** complex, the largest brewery in Europe, where a 19th-century **Hop Store** has been skillfully converted into a museum and exhibition space for art shows. An elaborate audiovisual presentation details Guinness's history since the brewery was established on this spot in 1759. The show ends with the curtain going up on the kind of old-fashioned pub, with mahogany decor, mirrors, and snugs, that has become hard to find in modern Dublin. *Guinness Hop Store, Crane St., tel. 01/536700. Admission: £1. Open weekdays 10–3; show every 20 min.*

Return to Thomas Street and continue east for 1 km (½ mi) in the direction of the south city center. Thomas Street becomes Cornmarket and then High Street, where you'll find the Catho-
39 lic **St. Audoen's Church,** with an elegant classical interior, completed in 1847, and a striking Corinthian pillared portico, added at the end of the 19th century. The church provides a well-produced audiovisual presentation, which tells the story of ancient Ireland before the arrival of the Vikings 1,200 years ago. St. Patrick and the Celtic gods figure prominently in the show. *High St., tel. 01/679–1855. Admission: £1.50. Open daily 10–4:30.*

An alley below the church takes you to the 13th-century archway of the only remaining stretch of Dublin's medieval city
40 wall. South of the church across the road stands **Tailor's Hall,** built in 1706–07; the only surviving guildhall or crafts workers' center in Dublin, the structure is now the headquarters of An Taisce, the Irish National Trust, committed to restoring ancient buildings. Visitors can request to see the exquisite 18th-century interior, especially the main hall with its lofty ceiling, tall Queen Anne windows, and a carved balcony for musicians. The basement bar has an authentic early 18th-century stone fireplace. *Back La., tel. 01/544794. Admission free. Open weekdays 9–5.*

If you return to High Street and walk east, the street quickly
41 becomes Christ Church Place, where you'll reach **Christ Church Cathedral,** one of two Protestant cathedrals in Dublin, built on the site of a Viking wooden church founded in 1038; this church was replaced by a new stone church in 1173, constructed by the Norman invader Strongbow, who is said to be buried here. The cathedral was largely reconstructed from 1871 to 1878 in early Gothic style. Remains from the 12th-century building include the north wall of the nave, the west bay of the choir, and the transepts, featuring fine stonework with pointed

arches and supporting columns. *Christ Church Pl., tel. 01/778099. Admission free. Open May–Sept., Mon.–Sat. 10–5, Sun. between church services; Oct.–Apr., Tues.–Fri. 10–12:45 and 2:15–4:30, Sun. between services.*

Next walk west from Christ Church Place on Nicholas Street, which turns into the nearby incline of Patrick Street; this leads
42 you to **St. Patrick's,** the national cathedral of the Church of Ireland. Sir Benjamin Guinness, of the brewing family, paid for its renovation in the 1860s. The original building, dedicated in 1192, was an unsuccessful attempt to assert supremacy over Christ Church Cathedral. In the present-day St. Patrick's, a memorial to Jonathan Swift, the writer of *Gulliver's Travels,* is located in the south aisle; Swift was dean of the cathedral between 1713 and 1745. Other interesting tributes include the 17th-century Boyle Monument with its numerous painted figures of family members and the monument to Turlough O'Carolan, the last of the Irish bards and one of the country's finest harp players. To the immediate north side of the cathedral is a small park, with statues of many of Dublin's literary figures. *Patrick St., tel. 01/754817. Admission: 80p adults, 30p students. Open Mar.–Oct., weekdays 9–6; Mar.–Apr., Sat. 9–4; May–Oct., Sat. 9–5; Easter–Oct., Sun. 10–11:15 and 12:45–3. Nov.–Feb., weekdays 9:30–12:30 and 1:30–6, Sat. 9–4, Sun. 12:45–3.*

43 Near the cathedral entrance is **Marsh's Library,** the oldest public library in Ireland, founded and endowed in 1701 by Narcissus Marsh, the Archbishop of Dublin. Housed in a modest two-story brick Georgian building approached through a small garden, the library stores a priceless collection of 200 manuscripts and 25,000 16th- to 18th-century books; many of these rare volumes are locked inside cages, as are any readers who wish to look at them. In recent years, the library has been restored with great attention to its original architectural details, especially in the book stacks. *St. Patrick's Close, off Patrick St., tel. 01/543511. Admission free. Open May–Sept., weekdays 9–6, Sat. 9–4, Sun. 10–11 and 2:15–3; Oct.–Apr., weekdays 9–12:30 and 1:30–6, Sat. 9–12:30 and 1:30–4, Sun. 10–11 and 2:15–3.*

Tour 4: James Joyce's Dublin

Numbers in the margin correspond with points of interest on the Tour 4: James Joyce's Dublin map.

James Joyce (1882–1941), one of Ireland's greatest 20th-century writers, used his incredibly detailed knowledge of Dublin as the basis for his major achievements: *Dubliners, A Portrait of the Artist as a Young Man, Ulysses,* and *Finnegans Wake;* in fact, he never wrote about any other place. He was, however, unsentimental about his native city, and at one time referred to it as the Center of Paralysis. Joyce spent the first 22 years of his life in Dublin and the last 36 in exile, in several locations, including Trieste, Paris, and Zurich. Yet he knew and remembered Dublin so well that he used to claim that if the city were destroyed, it could be rebuilt in its entirety from his written works, particularly *Ulysses.*

Begin your tour of Joyce's Dublin in the very heart of the city,
44 on **Prince's Street,** next to the General Post Office. The office of the old and popular *Freeman's Journal* newspaper (published

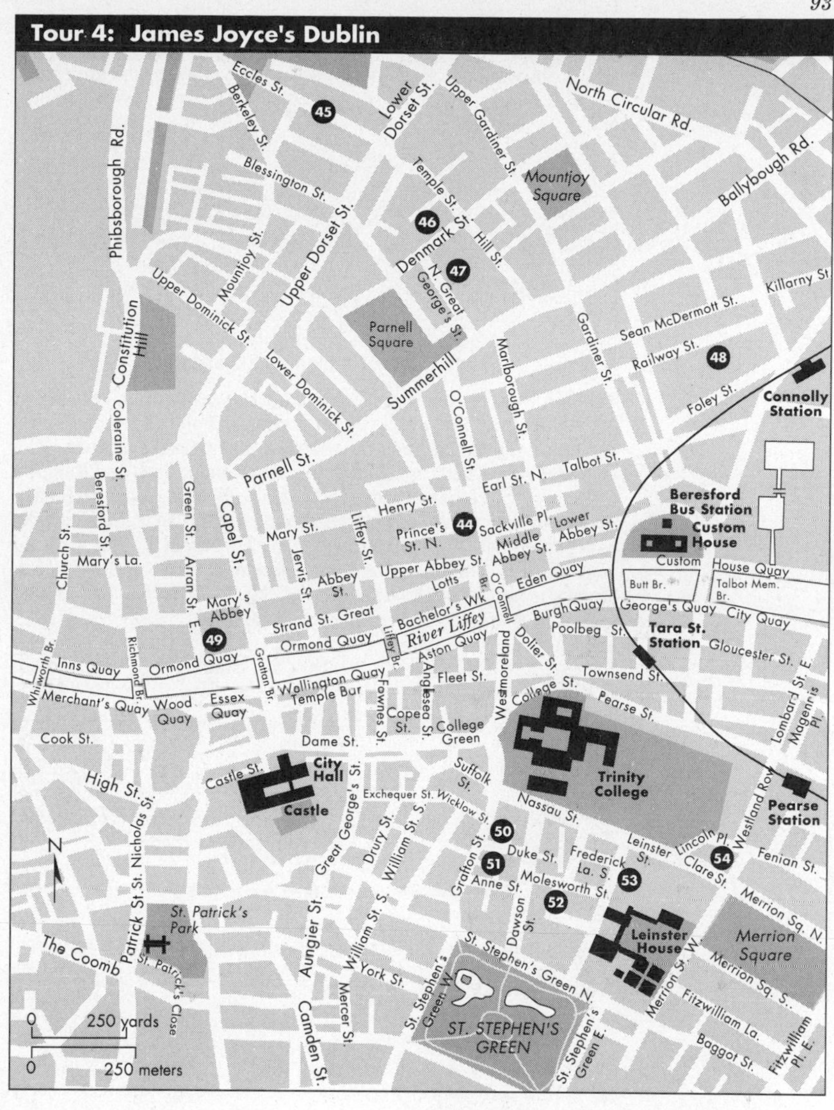

Bailey Restaurant, **50**
Bella Cohen's Brothel, **48**
Belvedere College, **46**
Davy Byrne's Pub, **51**
Eccles Street, **45**
James Joyce Cultural Centre, **47**
Molesworth Street, **52**
National Library, **53**
New Ormand Hotel, **49**
Prince's Street, **44**
Sweny's Pharmacy, **54**

1763–1924) was located here, but the building was destroyed
during the 1916 Easter Rising. The central character of *Ulysses*, Leopold Bloom, a newspaper advertisement canvasser,
worked at the *Freeman's Journal* office. Next, travel northward up O'Connell Street and Parnell Square, into Dorset
45 Street, before turning right, then first left into **Eccles Street.**
No. 7 no longer exists, but the site is revered by Joycean scholars, since this was the fictional home of Bloom. Cross Dorset
Street and walk down Temple Street into Great Denmark
46 Street, where you'll find **Belvedere College** (tel. 01/774795), a
well-preserved 18th-century mansion where Joyce studied between 1893 and 1898. You can visit the interior during term
time (September–June, excluding holidays). The entrance lobby, the classrooms, the rich Venetian plasterwork, and the
staircase with bronze Apollo medallions are worth a look.

47 The **James Joyce Cultural Centre,** off Great Denmark Street at
35 North Great George's Street, is due to open in 1991 as a center for Joycean studies and events related to the author. The
restored 18th-century Georgian town house, once the dancing
academy of Professor Dennis J. Maginni, will house a library
and archives. Turn left at the foot of North Great George's
Street and continue through to Parnell Street before turning
right into the much redeveloped Lower Gardiner Street. Retrace your steps in the direction of the Custom House, with its
green cupola dominating the foot of the street. Take the second
48 turn left, into Railway Street; No. 82 was the site of **Bella
Cohen's Brothel,** a key location in Bloom's travels around
Dublin on June 16, 1904. This immediate area contained many
such houses of ill repute in the early years of this century. From
here, return to the city center and travel westward along the
49 quays, toward the Guinness Brewery. The **New Ormond Hotel**
(Upper Ormond Quay, tel. 01/721811), an afternoon rendezvous
spot for Leopold Bloom, has been restored in recent years, and
plaques in the Siren Suite Ballroom and Malachy's Bar note
their connections with Joyce's writings. On Bloomsday, June
16 of each year, special Joyce-related events are organized at
the hotel.

Return once more to the city center, eastward along the quays
to O'Connell Bridge; walk south on Westmoreland and Grafton
50 streets to the **Bailey Restaurant** (tel. 01/773055) on Duke
Street, which will be on your left off Grafton. Inside the restaurant, the actual door from No. 7 Eccles Street is carefully pre-
51 served (*see* above). Right across the road from Bailey's is **Davy
Byrne's Pub** (tel. 01/711298), another historic Dublin hostelry
frequented by Joyce; here Bloom, on his peregrinations, has a
glass of burgundy and a Gorgonzola cheese sandwich. Then he
leaves the pub and walks to Dawson Street, where he helps a
52 blind man cross the road. He then walks along **Molesworth
Street** (which leads eastward) from Dawson Street; next he en-
53 ters the **National Library** (tel. 01/618811; *see* Tour 1: South City
Center, above), on Kildare Street at the far end of Molesworth
Street, where he has a near meeting with Blazes Boylan, his
wife's lover. In the library, Bloom looks for a copy of an advertisement.

Walk north on Kildare Street toward the grounds of Trinity
College, and head east on Leinster Street. On Lincoln Place, at
54 the back of Trinity College, **Sweny's Pharmacy,** which appears
in *Ulysses*, remains close to its original Joycean splendor. No

other establishment mentioned by James Joyce in his literary works, whether shop or pub, has changed so little since early this century. Sweeney's still has its black and white exterior and atmospheric interior, with its potions and phials. The shop is at the west end of Westland Row, at the other end of which is the Pearse railway station, a stop on the DART electric line.

Four other destinations related to Joyce and his writings are located outside of Dublin's city center.

Brighton Square. From Kildare Street, you can take a 5-km (3-mi) bus journey by the 15A or 15B bus, or by taxi, to the southern suburb of Rathgar, a genteel neighborhood even today. James Joyce was born at 41 Brighton Square, on February 2, 1882. Joyce spent the first two years of his life here; during the next 20 years, he lived at more than 20 addresses in the city.

James Joyce Martello Tower (Sandycove, tel. 01/809265). Sandycove Station on DART (*see* Tour 5: Dublin Southside, below).

One Martello Terrace (Bray, Co. Wicklow, tel. 01/868407). Bray Station on DART (*see* County Wicklow in Chapter 4, Dublin Environs).

Sandymount Strand (Sandymount). Sandymount Station on DART (*see* Tour 5: Dublin Southside, below).

Tour 5: Dublin Southside

Numbers in the margin correspond with points of interest on the Tour 5: Dublin Southside map.

South of City Center Take the 47A bus from Hawkins Street in the city center to the suburb of Rathfarnham, where you may explore the 50-acre
55 **St. Edna's Park,** which features a charming small-scale lake and nature trails. St. Edna's 18th-century house has been turned into a museum commemorating Patrick Pearse, leader of Dublin's 1916 Easter Rising. In the early years of this century, the house was a progressive boys' school, which Pearse and his brother Willie founded. The museum preserves Pearse family memorabilia, documents, and photographs. *Grange Rd., Rathfarnham, tel. 01/934208. Admission free to park. Open daily 10–sunset. Admission free to museum. Open May–June, daily 10–12:30 and 2–6; Sept.–Apr., the museum closes sometime between 3:30 and 5:30, depending on the month. Call ahead.*

Leaving the park, turn on to Grange Road and walk up the hill for about 1 km (½ m), turning left at the T junction and continu-
56 ing for a further ½ km (¼ mi), as far as **Marlay Park,** an extensive parkland with woodlands and nature walks; it is also the start of Wicklow Way, a well-defined walking route that crosses the Wicklow Mountains for 48 km (30 mi), through some of the most rugged landscapes in Ireland. Marlay Park has a cobbled courtyard, which is home to brightly plumaged peacocks. Surrounding this courtyard are crafts workshops, where visitors are welcome to watch the crafts people in the process of bookbinding and making jewelry and furniture. *Grange Rd., Rathfarnham, tel. 01/942834. Admission free. Open weekdays 9:30–5.*

Ballsbridge To reach the prestigious suburb of Ballsbridge, take the DART local train to Sydney Parade; the No. 7 or 8 bus from Eden

Tour 5: Dublin Southside

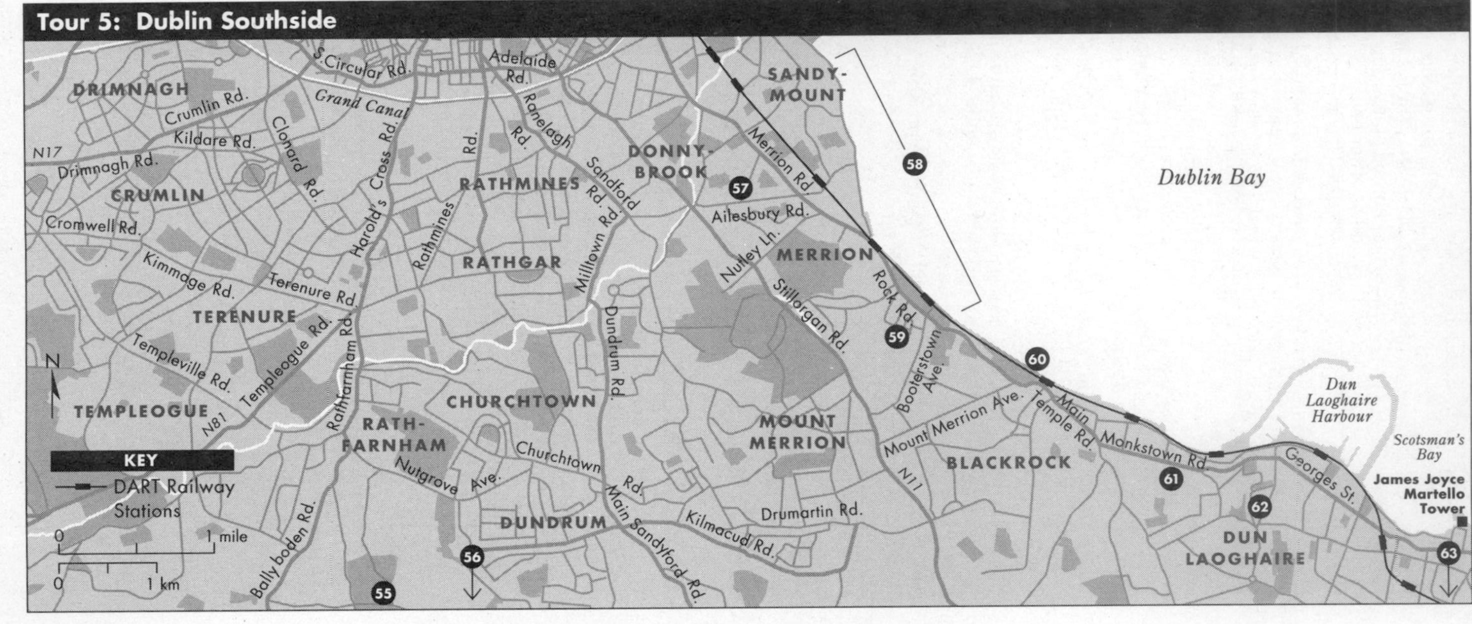

Blackrock, **60**
Booterstown, **59**
Chester Beatty Library, **57**
Dalkey, **63**
Dun Laoghaire, **62**
Marlay Park, **56**
Monkstown, **61**
Sandymount Strand, **58**
St. Edna's Park, **55**

Quay; or the No. 45 bus from Burgh Quay in the city center. From the DART station, walk west on Ailesbury Road to
57 Shrewsbury Road, where you'll reach the **Chester Beatty Library,** with one of the most significant collections of Islamic and Far Eastern art in the Western world. Sir Alfred Chester Beatty (1875–1968), a Canadian mining millionaire, donated the collection to Ireland. Among the library's exhibits are clay tablets from Babylon dating from 2700 BC, Japanese color wood-block prints, Chinese jade books, and Turkish and Persian paintings. *20 Shrewsbury Rd., Ballsbridge, tel. 01/692386. Admission free. Open Tues.–Fri. 10–5, Sat. 2–5. Conducted tours, Wed. and Sat. 2:30.*

Next return east from the museum, walk the length of Ailesbury Road, cross the DART railway line, and continue on
58 Sydney Parade Avenue until you reach **Sandymount Strand.** This beach stretches for 5 km (3 mi) from Ringsend to Booterstown. It was cherished by James Joyce and his beloved from Galway, Nora Barnacle, and figures as one of the settings in *Ulysses.* When the tide goes out, the beach extends for 1½ km (1 mi) from the foreshore, but the tide sweeps in again very quickly. A small park lies between the main Strand Road and the beach. You can take a bracing walk along the 1½-km (1-mi) breakwater at Ringsend, approached by passing the electricity-generating station. Poolbeg Lighthouse stands at the end of this seawall walk. About ½ km (¼ mi) inland from Sandymount Strand is the village of the same name, built round a large green that is lined with small shops. Some of the stores sell antiques, and you can also stop for a drink at one of the plain but cozy pubs. From the green, the No. 2 or 3 bus will take you back to the city center, or you can return by the DART train.

Outer Southern Suburbs

The outer southern suburbs of Dublin offer a choice of attractions with historical and literary associations, enough for several day trips. These destinations can be reached most easily by the DART local train or by car, taking the R118 from the corner of Lower Merrion Street and Merrion Square. Near
59 **Booterstown,** along the R118 on the way south to Blackrock, lies the largest wildlife preserve in the Dublin area. Many fairly rare migratory species of birds, such as curlews, herons, and kingfishers, come to nest here; information boards along the road describe these birds for visitors. Also on this main road you'll pass Glena, the house where Athlone-born John McCormack, the world-famous tenor, died in 1945.

60 Continue on 3 km (2 mi) to **Blackrock,** a bedroom community with a popular shopping center, fine sea views, and swimming. Idrone Terrace, above the DART railway station, provides a view across the bay to Howth Peninsula. The old-fashioned lamps on the terrace were recently renovated.

61 **Monkstown,** 3 km (2 mi) south beyond Blackrock on Temple and Monkstown roads (the R119) to Dun Laoghaire, boasts two architectural curiosities. The first is a strange-looking **Anglican Parish Church** in the main square, built in 1833. Its architect, John Semple, was inspired by two entirely different styles, the Gothic and the Moorish, which blend into an unlikely composite of towers and turrets. The church is only open during Sunday services. About 1 km (½ mi) south of town you'll find the well-preserved ruins of **Monkstown Castle,** a 15th-century edifice

with a keep, a gatehouse, and a long wall section, all surrounded by greenery.

62 Once a Protestant stronghold of the old ruling elite, **Dun Laoghaire,** a further 2½ km (1½ mi) beyond Monkstown along Monkstown Crescent (the R119), was once called Kingstown, after the British monarch, King George IV, disembarked for a fleeting visit in 1821. The town reverted to its original Irish name 99 years later. In some of the neo-Georgian squares and terraces behind George's Street, the main thoroughfare, a little of the community's former elitist elegance can still be felt.

Dun Laoghaire has long been known for its great harbor, enclosed by two piers, each 2½ km (1½ mi) long. The harbor was constructed between 1817 and 1859, using granite quarried from nearby Dalkey Hill; the west pier has a rougher surface and is less favored for walking than the east pier, which features a bandstand where musicians play during summer. The workaday business here includes freight services and passenger-ship sailings to Holyhead in north Wales, 3½ hours away. Dun Laoghaire, however, is also a yachting center with the members-only Royal Irish, National, and Royal St. George yacht clubs, all founded in the 19th century, lining the harbor area.

The first railway in Ireland was built from Westland Row (now Pearse Station) in Dublin to Dun Laoghaire, opening in 1834. Much of the original station's entrance and booking hall has been converted into the fine but expensive **Restaurant na Mara** (Railway Station, Harbour Rd., tel. 01/806767), a fish restaurant owned and run by the Irish Rail company.

The former Mariners' Church, west of the harbor and across from the Royal Marine Hotel and the People's Park, now houses the **National Maritime Museum.** The former nave of the church makes a strangely ideal setting for such exhibits as the French longboat captured at Bantry, County Cork, in 1796, as part of an aborted French invasion. A particularly memorable exhibit is the old optic from the Baily Lighthouse on Howth Head, across Dublin Bay; the herringbone patterns of glass reflected light across the bay until 20 years ago. *Haigh Terr., Dun Laoghaire, tel. 01/800969. Admission: £1. Open May–Sept., Tues.–Sun. 2:30–5:30; Oct.–Apr., weekends 2:30–5:30.*

From the harbor area, **Marine Parade** leads alongside Scotsmans Bay for 1¼ km (¾ mi), as far as the **Forty Foot Bathing Pool,** once a male-only preserve but now sometimes used by brave women.

A few steps away stands the **James Joyce Martello Tower,** originally built in 1804 as one of a series along Ireland's east coast, when Napoleon's invasion seemed imminent. Its first civilian tenant in 1904 was Oliver St. John Gogarty, a medical student who was known for his poetry and ready wit; Joyce spent time with Gogarty at the tower, and described it in the first chapter of *Ulysses,* using his friend as a model for the character of Buck Mulligan. The tower now houses a Joyce Museum, founded in 1962 thanks to Sylvia Beach, the first publisher of *Ulysses,* in Paris. The exhibition hall contains first editions of most of Joyce's works. Joycean memorabilia include his waistcoat, embroidered by his grandmother, and a tie that he gave to Samuel Beckett. The gunpowder magazine stores the Joyce Tower Library, including a death mask made of Joyce on January 13,

1941. *Tel. 01/808571 or 01/809265. Admission: £1.50. Open Apr.–Oct., Mon.–Sat. 10–1 and 2–5, Sun. 2:30–6. Rest of year, by appointment.*

Time Out **Marine Parade** has a choice of fine restaurants, serving international cuisine, such as **Les Relais des Mouettes** (tel. 01/809873) for classical French cuisine and **Pier 3** (tel. 01/842234), a converted house with simply prepared but substantial dishes, such as mignon of pork and grilled minute steak in mustard sauce.

From the James Joyce Tower at Sandycove, walk the short distance to the main Sandycove Road and continue for 1 km (½ mi)
63 to the next seaside village, **Dalkey.** Along Castle Street, its
main thoroughfare, you'll observe substantial stone remains,
resembling small turreted castles, of two 15th- and 16th-
century fortified houses. From the center of the village, walk
up the coastal Coliemore Road as far as Coliemore Harbour,
where small boats during the summer make the 15-minute
crossing to **Dalkey Island,** which is uninhabited except for a
herd of goats. The island, which is covered in long grass, has its
own Martello tower. Return to the mainland and continue up
the hill to Vico Road, where you'll have astounding bay views
(similar to those near Italy's Bay of Naples) as far as Bray in
County Wicklow. Return to Dalkey Village by Sorrento Road.

Tour 6: Dublin Northside

Numbers in the margin correspond with points of interest on the Tour 6: Dublin Northside map.

Glasnevin Dublin's northern suburbs remain predominantly working class and largely residential but they do offer a few places worth an extra trip. To reach the suburb of **Glasnevin,** drive from the north city center by Lower Dorset Street, as far as the bridge over the Royal Canal. Turn left, go up Whitworth Road, by the side of the canal, for 1 km (½ mi); at its end, turn right onto Prospect Road and then left onto the Finglas Road, the N2. You may also take the No. 40 or 40A bus from Parnell Street, next to Parnell Square, in the north city center.

64 **Glasnevin Cemetery,** on the right-hand side of Finglas Road, is the best-known burial ground in Dublin; it contains the graves of many distinguished Irish leaders, including Eamon De Valera, a founding father of modern Ireland and a former Irish *taoiseach* (prime minister) and president. Other notables interred here include 19th-century poet Gerard Manley Hopkins and Sir Roger Casement, an Irish rebel hung for treason by the British in 1916. The cemetery is freely accessible all day.

65 From the eastern side of the cemetery, enter the **National Botanic Gardens,** which date back to 1795 and feature more than 20,000 different varieties of plants, a rose garden, and a vegetable garden. The main attraction is the curvilinear range of greenhouses, more than 124 m (400 ft) long, designed and built by a Dublin ironmaster, Richard Turner, between 1843 and 1869. The Palm House, with its striking double dome, was built in 1884 and houses orchids, palms, and tropical ferns. In recent times, these buildings have become run down, but an extensive restoration program is under way. Visitors here can stroll along the River Tolka. *Glasnevin Rd., tel. 01/374388. Ad-*

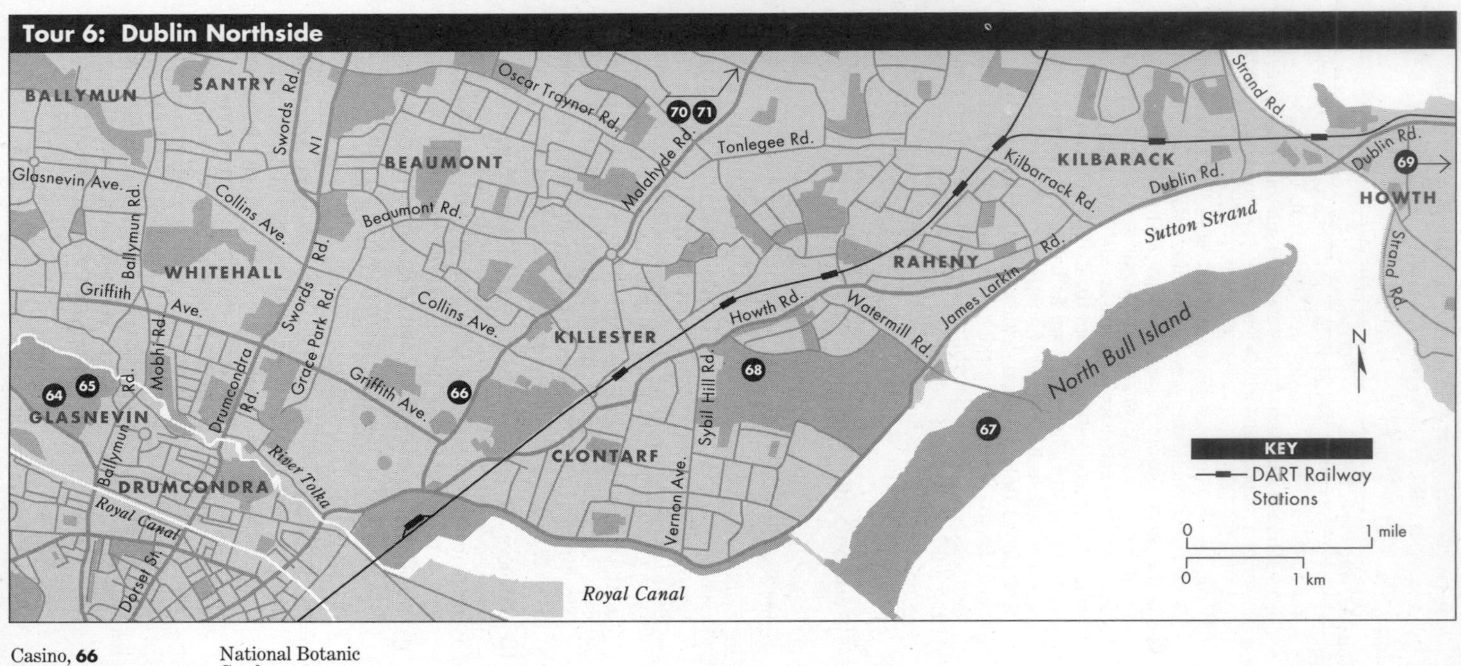

Casino, **66**
Glasnevin Cemetery, **64**
Howth, **69**
Malahide Castle, **70**
National Botanic Gardens, **65**
Newbridge House, **71**
North Bull Island, **67**
St. Anne's Park, **68**

mission free. Open summer, Mon.–Sat. 9–6, Sun. 11–6; winter, Mon.–Sat. 10–4:30, Sun. 11–4:30.

Marino Casino

To reach the Casino in the suburb of Marino by car, take the Malahide Road from Dublin's north city center for 4 km (2½ mi). You can also take a No. 20A or 24 bus to the Casino from Eden Quay in the north city center.

66 The **Casino** is one of Dublin's most exquisite, yet also most underrated, architectural landmarks; a former summerhouse that had nothing to do with gambling, it rests on part of what was once Lord Charlemont's estate. The main grand mansion was demolished in 1921, but the delightful small-scale Palladian-style casino, built between 1762 and 1771 from a plan by William Chambers, was luckily saved. Although it remained in a decayed state for years, it has now been fully restored, complete with ornate fireplaces and authentic period furnishings in the 16 rooms. Outside, four stone lions grace the terrace, while on the roof, gracious urns hide the chimneys. *Malahide Rd., Marino, tel. 01/331618. Admission: £1. Open June–Sept., daily 10–6:30.*

North Bull Island

To reach North Bull Island from Dublin's north city center by car, take the Clontarf Road for 4 km (2½ mi) to the causeway that leads out to Bull Wall, a walkway that stretches for 1½ km (1 mi) seawards, as far as the North Bull Lighthouse. Bull Wall
67 also extends on the southern end of **North Bull Island,** a 5-km- (3-mi-) long island created in the last century by the action of the tides. With its vast beach and dunes, it serves as a nature conservancy area and an interpretive center that details bird life on the island, including mallards, moorhens, and sandpipers. Telescopes and binoculars are available to rent, and guided tours can be arranged daily. *Center, tel. 01/338341. Open daily 9–6.*

The most northerly causeway from the island, halfway along the inland side, leads to the main James Larkin Road, which at
68 this point fronts **St. Anne's Park.** The green area features extensive rose gardens, with many prize species, and woodland walks. The park is freely accessible all day.

Howth

From Dublin, you can easily get to Howth by the DART train, which takes about 30 minutes, or by the No. 31B bus from Lower Abbey Street in the city center. By car, take the Howth Road from the north city center for 16 km (10 mi) to Howth.

69 **Howth,** a fishing village set at the foot of a long peninsula, was an island with inhabitants as long ago as 3250 BC. Its name is derived from the Norse *hoved,* meaning head. The village served as the point for the sea crossing to Holyhead in north Wales between 1813 and 1833, but it was then superseded by the newly built harbor at Kingstown (now Dun Laoghaire), on the other side of Dublin Bay. Today, Howth Harbour is home to an extensive fishing fleet, and it also features a new marina. Both arms of the harbor pier form extensive walks. **Ireland's Eye,** an island with a prominent craglike profile, is separated from the harbor by a channel nearly 1½ km (1 mi) wide. In calm weather, local boatmen make the crossing to the island, where visitors will find an old stone church on the site of a 6th-century monastery and also a Martello tower dating back two centuries.

At the King Sitric Restaurant on the East Pier (*see* Dining, below), a 2½-km (1½-mi) cliff walk begins, leading to the white

Baily Lighthouse, which was built in 1814. At times, the cliff path is narrow, with sheer drops to the sea, but the views out over the Irish Sea are very rewarding. The lighthouse, approached by a footpath on a narrow spit of land, may be visited by obtaining written permission in advance from the Commissioners for Irish Lights (Lower Pembroke St., Dublin 2, tel. 01/682511). From the car park above the lighthouse, you'll have access to perhaps the best views in the Dublin area, over the entire bay as far south as Dun Laoghaire, Bray, and the north Wicklow coast. Much of Dublin can also be seen.

North of the lighthouse at Howth Summit, you can take a local bus to complete the circuit of the peninsula. The 5½-km (3½-mi) journey takes about 10 minutes. Just before the DART station at Howth, disembark for the **Transport Museum.** The star of the collection here is the open-topped Hill of Howth tram. Until 1959, a tram service ran from the railway station in Howth, over the summit and back down to the station. Volunteers have spent several years restoring the tram, which stands alongside other unusual vehicles, such as old horse-drawn bakery vans. *Tel. 01/480831. Admission: £1. Open weekends and public holidays 2–5.*

Next door to the museum lie the **Howth Castle Gardens,** at the rear of the Deerpark Hotel. The rambling castle, which dates back to 1464 and has been much altered in the intervening centuries, is not open to the public. However, visitors can revel in the beautiful gardens. A formal garden with high beech hedges was laid out in the early 18th century, and the rhododendron garden boasts many rare varieties, which can be seen in full flower during April, May, and June. The grounds also feature the ruins of a tall, square 16th-century castle and a Neolithic dolmen (a prehistoric free-standing structure made from boulders). *Tel. 01/322624. Admission free. Open daily 8–sunset.*

Malahide To reach Malahide by car from Dublin, drive from the north city center on the R107 for 14½ km (9 mi). You can also get to Malahide by taking a train from Connolly Station, Dublin, which runs every hour and takes about 20 minutes. A bus to Malahide also leaves from Talbot Street, near Connolly Station; while service is more frequent (every 15 minutes), the ride takes about an hour.

70 Southwest of **Malahide** village stands **Malahide Castle,** which was occupied by the Anglo-Irish and aristocratic Talbot family from 1185 until 1976, when it was sold to the Dublin County Council. The great expanse of parkland around the castle includes a botanical garden with more than 5,000 species and varieties of plants, all clearly labeled. The castle itself is a combination of styles and periods; the earliest section, the three-story tower house, dates from the 12th century. The medieval Great Hall is the only one in Ireland that is preserved in its original form, while the National Portrait Gallery features many fine portraits of the Talbot family and 18th- and 19th-century Irish notables. Other rooms are well-furnished with authentic 18th-century pieces. *Malahide, Co. Dublin, tel. 01/452655. Admission: £2.15. Open weekdays 10–5, weekends 2–5.*

If you're driving, continue from Malahide through Swords on the coastal road (the R106) for 8 km (5 mi), turning off the N1
71 road as signposted to **Newbridge House** in Donabate. (You can

also travel from Malahide to Donabale by train, which takes about 10 minutes. From the Donabale train station, the walk to the Newbridge House grounds takes 15 minutes.) This 18th-century mansion, now publicly owned, features its original furnishings, and its drawing room is considered to be one of the best examples of Georgian domestic design in Ireland. The kitchens of the house are furnished with their original utensils, while in the courtyard, visitors find crafts workshops and some examples of old-style transportation, such as coaches. Beyond the walled garden are innumerable acres of parkland and an animal farm. *Donabate, Co. Dublin, tel. 436534. Admission: £2.10 adults, £1 children. Open Apr.–Oct., weekdays 10–5, Sun. and bank holidays 2–6; Nov.–Mar., Sun. and bank holidays 2–5.*

Dublin for Free

Bank of Ireland (College Green, tel. 01/776801). (*See* Tour 1: South City Center, above.)

Dunsink Observatory, north of Phoenix Park, is one of the oldest in the world, dating back to 1783. A small museum section features astronomical instruments. As the location is isolated, visitors are recommended to either drive there or take a taxi. *Castleknock, Dublin, tel. 01/387911. Open Mar.–Aug., 1st and 3rd Sat. of the month, 8–10 PM.*

Guinness Hop Store (Crane St., off Thomas St., tel. 01/536700). Visitors to the Hop Store can enjoy a complimentary half-pint of Guinness stout, brewed in Dublin since 1759, at the ground-floor bar (*see* Tour 3: Dublin West, above).

Four Courts (Inns Quay) (*see* Tour 3: Dublin West, above).

The **Irish Stock Exchange,** though now computerized, has a delightfully old-fashioned air compared with that of Wall Street. Visitors can take a seat in the tiny spectators' gallery. *28 Anglesea St., opposite Blooms Hotel, tel. 01/778808. Gallery open to the public weekdays 9:30–10:30 and 2–2:45.*

Lunchtime concerts are presented free during the summer by brass bands and other musical ensembles in the bandstand in the heart of St. Stephen's Green (*see* Tour 1: South City Center, above) and in other parks around the city, such as Herbert Park in Ballsbridge.

Marlay Park Craft Courtyard (Grange Rd., Rathfarnham, tel. 01/942834) (*see* Tour 5: Dublin Southside, above).

Rathborne's Candle Factory (East Wall Rd., tel. 01/743515 or 749222), Ireland's oldest candle-making firm, dates back to 1488. You can make an appointment to watch the candle-making process.

Tower Design Centre (Pearse St., tel. 01/775655) (*see* Shopping, below).

What to See and Do with Children

Dublin Zoo (Phoenix Park, tel. 01/775283) (*see* Tour 3: Dublin West, above).

Fry Model Railway is a museum on the grounds of Malahide Castle, 16 km (10 mi) north of the city, offering a unique collection of models of Irish trains from their introduction in 1834 until the present day. They are displayed on an authentic layout built by a master craftsman, Tom Tighe, and feature city landmarks such as the River Liffey and the Hill of Howth. An hourly train runs from Dublin's Connolly Station to Malahide. *Tel. 01/*

452337. Admission: £2.25 adults, £1.15 children. Open weekdays 10–5, Sat. 11–6, Sun. 2–6.

Lambert Puppet Theatre (Clifton La., Monkstown, Co. Dublin, tel. 01/800974) stages regular puppet shows and also has a puppetry museum. Visitors can take the DART train from the city center to the Monkstown and Seapoint stations.

Marlay Park (Grange Rd., Rathfarnham, tel. 01/942834), on the southern fringes of the city, provides a free ride for children every Saturday 3–6 PM, on the model steam railway. The No. 47B bus from Hawkins Street in the city center stops outside the park (*see* Tour 5: Dublin Southside, above).

Museum of Childhood, located in a large 19th-century house, has a fascinating collection of dolls and toys. *20 Palmerstown Park, Rathmines, tel. 01/973223. Admission: £1 adults, 75p children under 12. Open July–Aug., Wed. and Sun. 2–5:30. Rest of year, Sun. 2–5:30. Closed Oct.*

The **National Wax Museum** is Ireland's only such museum, accommodating more than 100 wax replicas. A favorite with many children is the Chamber of Horrors. *Granby Row, tel. 01/726340. Admission: £2.50 adults, £1.50 children. Open Mon.–Sat. 10–5:30, Sun. noon–5:30.*

Newbridge House (Donabate, Co. Dublin, tel. 01/436534) features Tara's Palace, a doll's house that was made to raise funds for children's charities. The palace has 25 rooms, all fully furnished in miniature. The exterior of the doll's house is based on the facades of three great Irish houses—Carton, Castletown, and Leinster (*see* Tour 6: Dublin Northside, above).

Shopping

Dublin's central shopping area, from O'Connell to Grafton streets, is the best place in Ireland for concentrated general and specialty shopping, at prices competitive with most other European countries. The big department stores stock the internationally renowned fashion lines and accessories, while alongside of them stand small, owner-managed boutiques that make shopping in the city a personalized and pleasurable event. Prices can be higher in the smaller shops, but the department stores are less likely to stock specifically Irish crafts lines.

Shopping in central Dublin can mean pushing through crowds, especially in the afternoons and on weekends. Most large shops and department stores are open Monday–Saturday 9–6. While department stores are closed on Sundays, most smaller specialty shops stay open Sunday 10–6. Shops with later closing hours are noted below.

Shopping Districts

O'Connell Street The main thoroughfare of the city offers perhaps too many fast-food outlets, but it also has some worthwhile stores. One of Dublin's largest department stores, Clery's, faces the General Post Office (GPO), and on the same side of the street as the post office is Eason's, another big department store.

Henry Street Running westwards from O'Connell Street, this street features Arnotts department store and a host of smaller, specialty stores selling records, footwear, and fashion. Henry Street's continuation, Mary Street, has a branch of Marks & Spencer.

Dublin Shopping

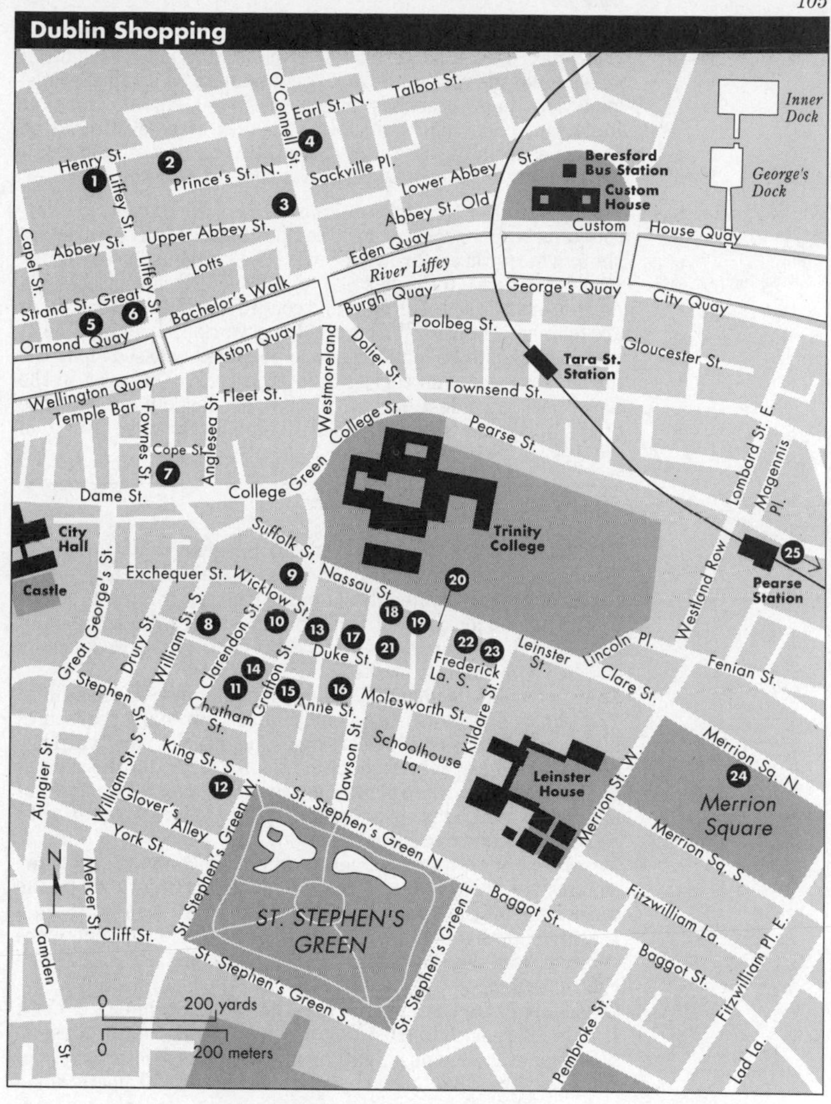

Arnotts, Grafton St., **9**
Arnotts, Henry St., **2**
Best of Irish, **11**
Blarney Woollen Mills, **20**
Brown Thomas, **13**
Claddagh Records, **7**
Clery's, **4**
Dublin Woollen Company, **6**
Eason's, **3**
Fred Hanna's, **19**
Gael Linn, **24**
Greene's, **23**
HMV, **14**
Hodges Figgis, **17**
Kevin & Howlin, **18**
Kilkenny Shop, **22**
Marks and Spencer, Grafton St., **15**
Marks and Spencer, **1**
Powerscourt Townhouse Centre, **8**
Royal Hibernian Way, **16**
St. Stephen's Green Centre, **12**
Switzers, **10**
Tierneys, **12**
Tower Design Centre, **25**
Waterstone's, **21**
Winding Stair, **5**

Grafton Street Dublin's main shopping street is now closed to vehicles for most of the day. Two substantial department stores face each other here, while the rest of the street is taken up by smaller shops, many of them branches of international chains, such as Benetton, Next, and Principles. Smaller streets off Grafton Street, especially Duke Street, South Anne Street, and Chatham Street, have interesting crafts and fashion shops.

Francis Street The new hub of Dublin's antiques trade, this street and surrounding areas such as the Coombe offer a concentration of shops where you can browse at will. The largest shop in the district is Cooke's (79 Francis St., tel. 01/542057), a veritable emporium of antiques of all ages and conditions. The smaller shops are more specialized. With a whole network of dealers, if what you want cannot be found, you will be quickly passed along the line to someone who carries what you seek. This area in the Liberties, the oldest part of the city, has largely replaced the quays upstream from O'Connell Bridge as the chief source of antiques.

Specialty Shopping Centers

Blackrock (Blackrock, Co. Dublin) is technically outside of Dublin's city center, but it deserves special mention as one of the most customer friendly shopping centers around. It's built on two levels, looking onto an inner courtyard, with the giant Superquinn Center, cafés, and restaurants. Blackrock can be reached conveniently on the DART train line.

Powerscourt (S. William St.), a fashionable town house built in 1771, housed a wholesale textile company for many years until it was updated nearly 15 years ago. The interior courtyard has been thoroughly refurbished and roofed over; on the dais at ground-floor level, live piano music is often heard. Two floors of galleries have a maze of small crafts shops, interspersed with coffee shops and restaurants.

Royal Hibernian Way (between S. Anne and Duke sts., off Dawson St., tel. 01/679–5915), a small development, stands on the former site of the two-centuries-old Royal Hibernian Hotel, a coaching inn that was demolished in 1983. The stylish shops are small in scale and include a branch of Leonidas, the Belgian chocolate firm.

St. Stephen's Green Centre (NW corner of St. Stephen's Green), Dublin's largest and most ambitious shopping center, resembles a giant greenhouse, with ironwork in the Victorian style. On three floors overlooked by a vast clock, the 100 mostly small shops sell a variety of crafts, fashions, and household goods.

Tower Design Centre (Pearse St., tel. 01/775655) is the most imaginative of Dublin's crafts centers, fashioned from an 1862 sugar-refinery tower. Taken over in 1978 by Ireland's Industrial Development Authority, the tower now houses more than 35 separate crafts firms. On the ground floor, visitors can stop at workshops devoted to heraldry, stained glass, and Irish pewter; the sixth floor features hand-painted silks, handknits, and silver jewelry.

Department Stores

Arnotts has two stores; its main one on Henry Street (tel. 01/721111) has three levels. On the top floor, the exhibition hall often has unusual art shows with a Dublin theme. The other store on Grafton Street (tel. 01/721111) concentrates exclusively on fashions.

Brown Thomas (Grafton St., tel. 01/679–5666) is Dublin's most elegantly decorated department store, with many international fashion labels on sale.

Clery's (O'Connell St., tel. 01/786000) has four floors of merchandise; the ground floor has a *bureau de change*.

Eason's (O'Connell St., tel. 01/733811) is a multipurpose store with four floors. The basement, with its rows of souvenirs, and the ground floor, with an especially large book section, are particularly worth browsing in.

Marks and Spencer main store on Mary Street (tel. 01/728833) has a larger range of fashions and foods than its three-story shop on Grafton Street (tel. 01/679–7855).

Switzers (Grafton St., tel. 01/776821) remains a middle-of-the-road department store; the ground floor carries a good selection of Royal Doulton porcelain, Wedgwood china, and Waterford crystal.

Specialty Shops

An increasing number of Irish-made crafts and souvenir lines reflect an increasing demand by visitors for specifically Irish goods. Some newer specialty shops sell nothing else.

Books Books are ideal presents from Ireland. With nearly 1,000 titles now published a year in Ireland, the breadth and choice of material is quite impressive. The range of texts is particularly wide in relation to Irish history and travel and the production quality of such titles compares very favorably with such books published outside Ireland.

Fred Hanna's (27 Nassau St., tel. 01/771255) sells old and new books, with a good choice of travel and Irish books.

Greene's (Clare St., tel. 01/762544) carries an extensive range of secondhand volumes.

Hodges Figgis (54 Dawson St., tel. 01/774754) stocks 1½ million books on three floors.

Waterstone's (7 Dawson St., tel. 01/679–1260), a large branch of a British chain, has two floors featuring a fine selection of Irish books.

The Winding Stair (40 Lower Ormond Quay, tel. 01/733292) features second-hand books and a café that overlooks the River Liffey.

CDs, Records, Tapes An increasing amount of Irish-recorded material, covering traditional folk music, country and western, rock, and even a smattering of classical music, is now available on records, compact discs, and tapes. **HMV** (65 Grafton St., tel. 01/679–5334; and 18 Henry St., tel. 01/732899) is one of the larger record shops in town. **Claddagh Records** (2 Cecilia St., tel. 01/679–3664) and **Gael Linn** (26 Merrion Sq., tel. 01/767283) specialize in traditional Irish music and Irish-language recordings.

China, Crystal, Ceramics Ireland is synonymous with Waterford crystal, which is available in a wide range of products, including relatively inexpensive items such as ashtrays or sets of glasses. But other lines are now gaining recognition, such as Cavan, Galway, and Tipperary crystal. At **Dublin Crystal** (Carysfort Ave., Blackrock, Co. Dublin, tel. 01/887932), visitors can watch the crystal being cut. The best city-center retail outlets are **Blarney Woollen Mills** (tel. 01/710068) and **The Kilkenny Shop** (tel. 01/777066), both on Nassau Street, and **Best of Irish** (Westbury Hotel, Harry St., tel. 01/679–1233). The above outlets are also good for Irish-made ceramics, such as Belleek, Galway, and Donegal Parian. **Tierneys** (St. Stephen's Green Centre, tel. 01/782873) carries a good selection of crystal and china.

Irish Tweeds Suits and other garments, such as skirts for women and jackets for men, come ready-made in this durable and popular cloth. It can also be bought by the length for making your own clothes. The tweed on sale in Dublin comes from two main sources, Donegal and Connemara; labels inside the garments guarantee their authenticity. The following are the largest retailers of Irish tweeds in the city: **Dublin Woollen Company** (Metal Bridge Corner, tel. 01/775014); **Kevin & Howlin** (31 Nassau St., tel. 01/770257); **Blarney Woollen Mills** (College Park House, Nassau St., tel. 01/710068); and **The Kilkenny Shop** (Nassau St., tel. 01/777066).

Outdoor Markets

Dublin has a number of open-air markets, selling mostly men's and women's fashions. **Moore Street** is open from Mondays to Saturdays, 9–6; stalls lining both sides of the street sell fruits and vegetables. The traditional Dublin repartee here is renowned in the city. Other open markets are only open at the weekends. A variety of bric-a-brac is sold at the **Liberty Market** on Meath Street, open on Fridays and Saturdays, 10–6, and Sundays, 12–5:30. The indoor **Christchurch Market,** opposite St. Audeon's Church, is open Saturdays and Sundays, 10–5; come here for antiques and bric-a-brac.

Hotel Shops

Several of the leading hotels have shops. The **Berkeley Court** (Lansdowne Rd., Ballsbridge, tel. 01/601711) features a crafts shop and boutique that is open all year, adjoined by a branch of Weir's, the Grafton Street jewelers. The Irish gift shop and boutique in the adjacent **Jury's** (Northumberland Rd., tel. 01/605000) stocks a wide selection of Irish tweeds and crystalware. The **Burlington** (Upper Leeson St., tel. 01/605222) has a small crafts shop with pottery and jewelry.

Sports, Fitness, and Beaches

Participant Sports

Bicycling Dublin streets have no special lanes for bicycles, but the flat countryside to the north and the west of Dublin and the mountains to the south are ideal territories for cycling. Bicycles cost around £25 a week to hire, with an equivalent amount charged for deposit. Nearly 20 firms in the Dublin region rent out bicycles; Tourist Information Offices have a full list. Some of the best firms include **Joe Daly** (Lower Main St., Dundrum, tel. 01/981485), **McDonald's** (38 Wexford St., tel. 01/752586), and **Ryan's** (115 Upper Dorset St., tel. 01/305090).

Bowling Bowling continues to be a popular sport in Dublin; two kinds are played locally. The sedate, outdoor variety is played at a dozen outdoor areas; among the most attractive of these are **Herbert Park** (Ballsbridge, tel. 01/695637) and **Moran Park** (Dun Laoghaire, tel. 01/801179). The city has three indoor bowling centers: **Crumlin Super Bowl** (Crumlin Rd., tel. 01/559659), **Dundrum Bowl** (Dundrum, tel. 01/980209), and **Stillorgan Bowl** (Stillorgan, tel. 01/881656).

Fitness Centers Two major fitness centers in the Dublin vicinity are **Fitzwilliam** (Appian Way, tel. 01/603988), a privately owned club offering a swimming pool, 10 tennis courts, six squash courts, a gym, and a sauna; and **RiverView Sports Club** (Beech Hill, Clonskeagh, tel. 01/830322), with a full gymnasium and sauna facilities. Both clubs offer temporary memberships.

Golf The Dublin region is an idyllic place for golfers, with a total of 24 18-hole courses and around 15 nine-hole courses, with several more in the development stage. Major 18-hole courses include **Deer Park** (Howth, tel. 01/322624), with appealing views of the water; **Elm Park** (Donnybrook, tel. 01/693438), in a south city suburb location, but with a rural ambience; **Foxrock** (Torquay Rd., tel. 01/893992), in an exclusive residential area; **Newlands** (Clondalkin, tel. 012/592903), an inland course west of Dublin; **Portmarnock** (Portmarnock, tel. 01/324674), one of Ireland's premier courses, situated above a beach northeast of Dublin city center and host to several international tournaments; **Sutton** (Sutton, tel. 01/323013), a seaside course north of Dublin; and **Woodbrook** (Bray, tel. 01/824799), south of Dublin city center, with stunning mountain views and sea breezes.

Horseback Riding About 20 riding stables in the greater Dublin area hire out horses by the hour or the day, for novices and experienced riders. A few of these stables also operate as equestrian centers with full tuition facilities. Some major stables in the vicinity include **Ashton Equestrian Center** (Castleknock, tel. 01/383236), **Castleknock Riding Center** (Castleknock, tel. 01/201104), and **Riding and Driving Club** (Willow Rd., Dundrum, tel. 01/986112).

Jogging Joggers can enjoy running in Dublin's 40 parks and open squares and along the footpaths of the city's main roads after 6 PM, when traffic has become less heavy. The south city center around Merrion Square is ideal for the sport, but only after business hours and during weekends.

Squash Dublin has about 10 privately owned squash centers; **Squash Ireland** (tel. 01/801515) runs four main centers in various city locations.

Swimming Dublin has 12 public pools, but only two can be recommended to visitors, at **Townsend Street** (off Tara St., tel. 01/770503) and **Williams Park** (Rathmines, tel. 01/961275). **Fitzwilliam** (Appian Way, tel. 01/603988), a private fitness club, features a fine pool and offers temporary memberships. Privately owned pools open to the public for a small fee are located at **Dundrum Family Recreation Center** (Meadowbrook, Dundrum, tel. 01/980183), **Fitzpatrick's Killiney Castle Hotel** (Killiney, tel. 01/851533), **Jury's Hotel** (Ballsbridge, tel. 01/605000), **St. Vincent's** (Navan Rd., tel. 01/384906), and **Terenure College** (Templeogue Rd., tel. 01/908822). For hardier spirits, there is year-round sea swimming at the **Forty Foot Bathing Pool** in Sandycove, County Dublin. Traditionally open only to men, it now admits women.

Tennis Tennis is one of Dublin's most popular participant sports, and some public parks have excellent tennis facilities that are open to visitors. Among these are **Bushy Park** (Terenure, tel. 01/900320), **Herbert Park** (Ballsbridge, tel. 01/684364), and **St. Anne's Park** (Dollymount, tel. 01/313697); these parks each have six courts. Several private tennis clubs are open to visitors, such as **Donnybrook** (Brookvale Rd., tel. 01/692838), with six courts; **Fitzwilliam** (Appian Way, tel. 01/603988), with eight outdoor and two indoor courts; and **Kilternam Tennis Centre** (Kilternam Golf and Country Club Hotel, Kilternan, tel. 01/953729), with four outdoor and four indoor courts. For more information, contact the **Irish Lawn Tennis Association** (22 Upper Fitzwilliam St., tel. 01/610117).

Spectator Sports

Football Although football, played in Ireland with a soccerlike ball, is the country's latest big-time sport, following some impressive international wins, facilities for watching it are not so ideal. **Dalymount Park,** north of the city center, is the main center for international matches.

Gaelic Games The traditional Gaelic games of Ireland, including football and hurling, still attract a large following with intensely exciting big national matches, full of roaring crowds as they cheer on their county teams; games are held at **Croke Park,** the main stadium, located just north of the city center. For details of matches, contact the **Gaelic Athletic Association** (Croke Park, tel. 01/363222).

Horse Racing Horse racing is one of the great sporting loves of the Irish; nothing attracts the crowds like a race meeting. The sport is closely followed, with keen interest in betting, but the social side of attending racing is also important to Dubliners. The main course in Dublin is **Leopardstown** (tel. 01/893607), an ultramodern course on the south side. In the greater Dublin region, other courses include **Fairyhouse** (Co. Meath, tel. 01/256167) and **Curragh** (tel. 045/41205), west of Dublin, a setting for classic races on the vast Curragh plain.

Rugby International rugby matches are staged at the vast **Lansdowne Road Stadium,** normally during the winter and spring. Local matches are played every weekend, also during the winter and spring. For details, contact the **Irish Rugby Football Union** (62 Lansdowne Rd., tel. 01/684601).

Beaches

The immediate Dublin area has two main beaches. On the north side of the city lies **Bull Island,** created over the years by the action of the tides and offering an almost 3-km- (2-mi-) long stretch of fine sand. The No. 30 bus from Lower Abbey Street stops by the walkway to the beach. The main beach for swimming on the southside of the city is situated at **Killiney,** 13 km (8 mi) south side of the city center; this shingly beach stretches for 3 km (2 mi). The DART train station is right by the beach. Much nearer the city center, **Sandymount Strand** is a long expanse of fine sand where the tide goes out nearly 3 km (2 mi), but it is not suitable for swimming or bathing because the tide races in so fast. The strand also can be reached easily by the DART train.

Dining

by Georgina Campbell

A resident of Howth in County Dublin, Georgina Campbell is the food writer for Dublin's The Sunday Press *and Irish correspondent for* Taste, *a London-based gourmet magazine.*

Until recently, most Irish people thought of going out for a meal as a treat reserved for special occasions, such as birthdays and anniversaries, and the most likely dining choice was usually the local hotel restaurant. During the last two decades, however, Ireland has experienced a gastronomic revolution. A new interest in dining out has paved the way for smaller, more individualized restaurants to do well, often in the well-tried French tradition of family ownership, with a chef-patron overseeing every detail. Many of these chefs have studied abroad and been influenced by recent trends; a disproportionately high number of recommended restaurants can be described as French. Nevertheless, although nouvelle cuisine will undoubtedly have a long-term effect on presentation, regional food is making a comeback, which is a positive trend. Traditional Irish dishes used to be thought too ordinary for restaurant menus, but talented young chefs are now keen to revive them, and, indeed, to demonstrate the goodness of Irish ingredients in any way possible. The Green movement is also on Ireland's side, with the potential of unpolluted Irish produce at last being properly valued.

Not many restaurants in Dublin have yet had the courage to specialize entirely in traditional Irish food, but two establishments reviewed below that concentrate on Irish cuisine—Oísins and Gallagher's Boxty House—are excellent in their own fashion. Meanwhile, even what is probably the smartest Dublin restaurant, Restaurant Patrick Guilbaud, at least makes a gesture (albeit more Gallic than Gaelic) toward regional specialties.

The hotels, conscious of having lost their dining business to smaller restaurants, are fighting back, creating fine gourmet restaurants, such as the Aisling at the Shelbourne, the Kish at Jury's, the Berkeley Room at the Berkeley Court, the Russell Room at the Westbury, and now the Alexandra at the new Conrad/Hilton. Yet despite the improved standards at these places, they still tend to lack atmosphere and generally aren't worth the price, compared to the independent restaurants. Getting good value for your money is, in fact, a big problem when dining in Ireland. In a comparable British city, lively ethnic restaurants provide above-average meals at reasonable prices, but the ones that exist in Dublin tend to be at the top end of the market. Still, good and less expensive restaurants are starting to fill in the gaps in the market.

Situated as it is, beside the sea and with easy access to fresh fish from all around the coast, Dublin offers several places to eat where seafood is the specialty. These restaurants feature not only the traditional cockles and mussels (although these dishes are reappearing on menus) but also wild salmon and oysters from the clear Atlantic waters of the west coast; deep-sea fish trawled off the Donegal coast and the Irish Sea; and lobsters, crabs, and more unusual creatures, such as sea urchins, from rocky coastal waters. Pork, bacon, lamb, and beef still

The Bad Ass Café, **7**
Bewley's, **3**
Burdock's, **8**
Caesar's, **9**
Café Klara, **20**
Celtic Mews, **22**
Cornucopia Wholefoods, **11**
Eastern Tandoori, **17**
Fat Freddy's Pizza Warehouse, **6**
Gallagher's Boxty House, **2**
The Grey Door, **24**
Independent Pizza Company, **18**
The Kilkenny Kitchen, **14**
La Vie en Rose, **15**
Le Caprice, **10**
Les Frères Jacques, **5**
Mitchells Cellars, **21**
Oisins Irish Restaurant, **23**
Paddy Kavanagh's, **25**
Pasta Fresca, **19**
Peers Café, **12**
The Periwinkle Seafood Bar, **13**
Pigalle, **1**
Restaurant Patrick Guilbaud, **26**
Shay Beano, **16**
Stately's, **4**

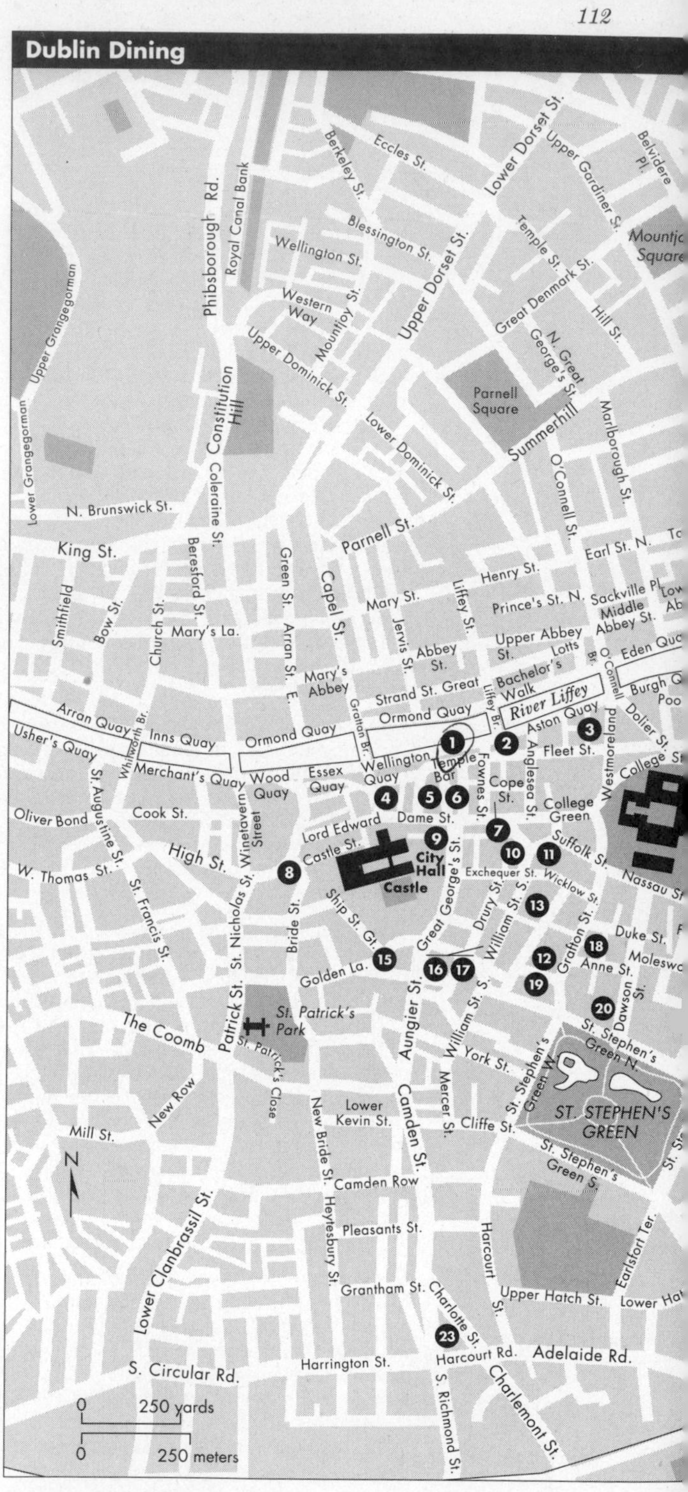

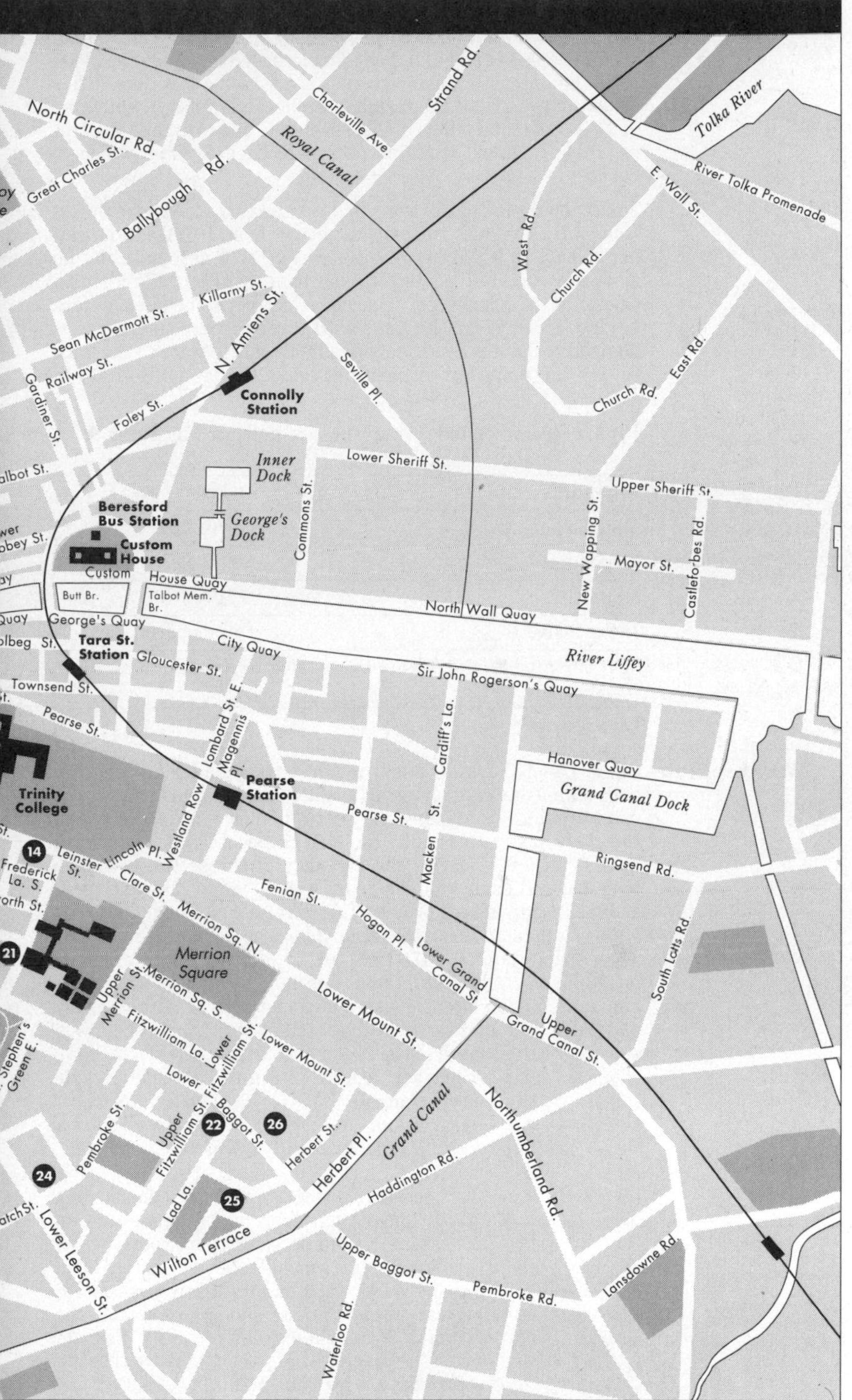
North Circular Rd.
Great Charles St.
Ballybough Rd.
Charleville Ave.
Strand Rd.
Royal Canal
Tolka River
River Tolka Promenade
E. Wall St.
West Rd.
Church Rd.
Killarny St.
Sean McDermott St.
N. Amiens St.
Railway St.
Gardiner St.
Seville Pl.
East Rd.
Church Rd.
Foley St.
Connolly Station
Lower Sheriff St.
Inner Dock
Upper Sheriff St.
Beresford Bus Station
George's Dock
Commons St.
New Wapping St.
Castleforbes Rd.
Custom House
Mayor St.
Custom House Quay
Butt Br.
Talbot Mem. Br.
North Wall Quay
George's Quay
Tara St. Station
City Quay
Gloucester St.
River Liffey
Townsend St.
Sir John Rogerson's Quay
Pearse St.
Lombard St. E.
Magennis Pl.
Cardiff's La.
Hanover Quay
Grand Canal Dock
Trinity College
Pearse Station
Westland Row
Pearse St.
Macken St.
Ringsend Rd.
Leinster St.
Lincoln Pl.
Frederick La. S.
Clare St.
Fenian St.
Merrion Sq. N.
Hogan Pl.
Lower Grand Canal St.
South Lotts Rd.
Merrion Square
Upper Merrion St.
Merrion Sq. S.
Lower Mount St.
Upper Grand Canal St.
Fitzwilliam La.
Lower Fitzwilliam St.
Lower Mount St.
Stephen's Green E.
Lower Baggot St.
Upper Fitzwilliam St.
Pembroke St.
Herbert St.
Herbert Pl.
Grand Canal
Northumberland Rd.
Haddington Rd.
Lad La.
Wilton Terrace
Lower Leeson St.
Upper Baggot St.
Pembroke Rd.
Lansdowne Rd.
Waterloo Rd.
14
21
22
24
25
26

provide the backbone for traditional dishes such as Dublin coddle, Irish stew, and corned beef with cabbage, but game, such as venison and quail, has also increased in popularity. Perhaps the biggest culinary success story of the last decade has to be the growth of the farmhouse cheese industry: whenever you see Irish farmhouse cheese on the menu, make a point of trying it; you'll now find dozens of cheeses from which to choose.

Dining hours in Dublin are much the same as elsewhere in Europe, with the main rush at lunchtime from 1 to 2 and at dinner from 8 to 9. VAT (value added tax) will automatically be added to your bill—a 10% tax on food, a 25% tax on drinks. Check to see, however, if service has been included before paying: if so, it can be paid with a credit card and there is no need to leave a tip. If not, it is more considerate to the staff to pay the main bill by card but leave the tip (10%–15%) in cash.

Highly recommended restaurants are indicated by a star ★.

Category	Cost*
Very Expensive	over £20
Expensive	£15–£20
Moderate	£10–£15
Inexpensive	under £10

**per person, without tax (10%), service, or drinks*

City Center

Very Expensive

Celtic Mews. Turn off busy Baggot Street under an archway and, immediately on your right, you'll find this long-established oasis of calm in a Georgian mews. Over the years, the chefs have successfully blended classical French and Irish cooking styles. Despite the elegance of the setting—a deep wine-colored background sets off a collection of fine antiques, as black-tied waiters provide full silver service at polished or white-clothed tables—the atmosphere is cozy and informal. The cuisine tends toward richness; if you enjoy a bit of showmanship, try the Celtic filet mignon, cooked at the table and served with a mushroom-and-tomato sauce with whiskey and cream. Simpler tastes will be satisfied with an upscale version of traditional Irish stew, made with center loin lamb chops. If you seek privacy, ask for one of the banquette-style tables. *109A Lower Baggot St., tel. 01/760796. Reservations advised. Dress: casual but neat. Dinner only. Closed Sun., bank holidays, Easter weekend, Christmas. AE, DC, MC, V.*

La Vie En Rose. This recently opened restaurant consists of a long, narrow room with unexciting decor, but the credentials of the French proprietor-chef are impeccable: his experience at several highly praised restaurants includes seven years as head chef at London's Le Gavroche. The restaurant is well-situated, just a five-minute walk from St. Stephen's Green and the Grafton Street shopping area. The cuisine is classic French, with a nouvelle flair in the presentation. You might try the *flan de poivrons doux aux trois sauces* (flan made of green, red, and yellow sweet peppers served with three sauces), and follow this with the *tresse de poissons, sauce verte* (plait of salmon and brill served with a slightly creamed spinach sauce). The desserts are especially good; don't miss the ices laced with liqueurs and crunchy nuts, served in delicate brandy-snap baskets. Stick to the house wines, which offer a good value—the wine list is short and painfully pricey. Avoid the tables near the door. *6A Upper Stephen's St., tel. 01/781771. Reservations advised; weekend reservations required. Jacket required; jacket and tie suggested. Closed Mon. dinner, Sat. lunch, Sun., bank holidays. AE, MC, V.*

★ **Restaurant Patrick Guilbaud.** Discreet to the point of austerity, the modern and quiet ambience features pink and gray decor and large hanging plants. The formality of the service attracts the local business community, as does the air of professional calm, combined with absolute reliability; corner tables are often in demand for meetings. Officially, the cuisine is "classic and nouvelle French," yet, in keeping with the current revival of interest in regional food, a selection of homemade black pudding, sweetbreads, and *crúbeens* (pigs' trotters) served with a pepper and red wine sauce, appears on the menu, alongside more predictable dishes, such as casserole of Dublin Bay prawns and lobster served with aromatic butter. *46 James Pl., Lower Baggot St., tel. 01/764192 or 01/601799. Reservations advised. Jacket and tie suggested. Closed Sat. lunch, Sun., bank holidays. AE, DC, MC, V.*

Expensive

★ **Les Frères Jacques.** Housed in a late Victorian corner house next door to the Olympia Theatre, this restaurant offers something special, exemplified by the Gallic charm of *le patron* and the nostalgic prints of Paris and Deauville on the green-papered walls. The French waiters, dressed in white Irish linen and black bow ties, are all very proper, yet the atmosphere is far from stiff; romantic souls will enjoy the piano player who performs in the evening. Expect traditional French cooking, with the emphasis on the changing seasons. You'll find a good choice of game in season. Fish lovers can dive into delights such as fresh turbot stuffed with mushroom duxelles, served with basil sauce; also recommended is the *magret de canard*—roast breast of duck, served with a ginger and grapefruit sauce. Chocolate marquise, well laced with rum and served with two sauces, provides a suitably dramatic ending. *74 Dame St., tel. 01/679–4555. Reservations advised. Dress: casual but neat. Lunch weekdays; dinner Mon.–Sat. Closed Sun., holidays. AE, DC, MC, V.*

The Grey Door. Located just off Fitzwilliam Square and only a five-minute walk from St. Stephen's Green, this establishment, right in the heart of Georgian Dublin, takes its style from the elegance of the restored terraced building it occupies. The menu offers a unique combination of classical Scandinavian and Russian cuisine—the owners call it "the food of the Tsars." The restaurant, which is richly furnished with antiques and gleaming cut glass, is suitably sumptuous. Although the building is large (there's a less expensive, informal restaurant, Blushes Bistro, in the basement and a beautiful private dining room upstairs), the ground-floor restaurant is small and intimate, with tables in the front half of the room grouped around a magnificent Georgian fireplace, complete with open fire. Specialties include gravlax (dill-cured salmon) served with a light mustard sauce and dill potatoes, and beef Novgorod, a center cut fillet, panfried and served on sauerkraut, fried barley, vegetables, garlic butter, and sour cream. The extensive wine list begins with a flourish—an 1892 Château Margaux, Premier Grand Cru, at £550—but the house wines are more accessible at £9.50; a good selection is available in the £10–£15 range. *23 Upper Pembroke St., tel. 01/763286 or 01/766011. Reservations advised. Dress: casual but neat. Closed Sun., holidays. AE, CB, DC, MC, V.*

★ **Oísins Irish Restaurant.** A restaurant that demonstrates the goodness of traditional Irish cuisine at its best is a rare treat, not to be missed. Although true to their origins, all the old favorites at Oísins have actually been improved by a lightness of touch that is utterly modern. Up-to-date sauces add interest to otherwise familiar dishes; garnishes, especially, provide color and a variety of texture pleasing to the modern palate. Situated on the first floor of a Victorian terrace, with a little bar below, this small, intimate, and relaxing place features modern Irish art on the walls, pottery on the polished tables, and a piano player performing the old airs in the corner. Dinner consists of a six-course menu, starting with a house specialty—tasty little sausage slices flambéed in *poítin* (a spirit made from potatoes). The next course includes appetizer-size portions of dishes, such as Dublin coddle (the traditional Saturday-night dish, for after the pub—bacon, sausages, onion, carrot, and potatoes, all boiled together) and, perhaps, a chowder made with cockles and mussels. Among the main course choices are Irish stew and other specialties such as baked ham and spiced beef. If you want a really Irish dessert, go for the carrageen moss pudding, a cold sweet based on a seaweed and served with Bailey's Irish Cream. *31 Upper Camden St., tel. 01/753433 or 01/783635. Reservations advised. Dress: casual but neat. Dinner only. Closed Sun.–Mon., Christmas week, Easter week. No credit cards.*

The Pavilion Restaurant. This restaurant is uniquely situated, on the first floor of a Victorian building (Haughton House) in the middle of Dublin Zoo in Phoenix Park, about a 10-minute drive from the city center. The place recently changed hands and is now under French management. The smart decor includes a parquet floor, a cool, understated color scheme, heavy linen napery, white china, and sparkling glasses. The French menu leans toward *cuisine moderne*—warm salads, chicken breast with wild mushroom sauce, beef and pepper sauce with fettuccine. If you go for dinner, when the zoo is closed, ask for directions beforehand. *Dublin Zoo, Phoenix Park, tel. 01/775283. Reservations advised. Jacket suggested. Dinner Fri.–Sat. only. Closed Sat. lunch, Dec. 25–26, Jan. 1. AE, DC, MC, V.*

★ **Shay Beano.** This tiny French restaurant positively exudes designer chic. After you squeeze through the minuscule lobby straight from the street, a mouthwatering display of desserts on a side table will grab your attention within seconds, making the cool gray and chrome decor take second place. The white-clothed tables are simply set but boast a serious array of fine glasses. The owner-chef excels in "cuisine moderne," and the dishes that currently please him include *roti de veau et son jus, lié au pinot noir d'Alsace* (roast veal with its juices, Alsace rose wine, and wild mushrooms) and an unusual appetizer, fresh black pasta, colored with olive puree and served with fresh ginger and chilies. The menu comes in French, without translations, and the chef has a reputation for doing things his way (rather than the customer's), but it's usually worth putting up with such minor eccentricities. Sunday lunch is a special occasion, a relaxed sort of marathon that is more expensive than weekday lunches. *37 St. Stephen's St. Lower, tel. 01/776384. Reservations advised. Dress: casual. Closed Sun. dinner. DC.*

Moderate

Caesar's. The friendly, efficient staff and good food make for a warm atmosphere at this unpretentious Italian restaurant, with its rows of white-clothed tables. This is a good place for a late meal after visiting the Olympia Theatre across the road. Fresh pasta is made on the premises daily; fresh fish (especially prawns) and veal are other specialties. Favorite dishes include veal parmigiana or prawns with garlic and wine, served, perhaps, with spaghetti *alla carbonara* as a side dish. Across the road, you'll find a sister restaurant, Nico's (53 Dame St., tel. 01/773062), which is run on the same lines but also serves lunch. *18 Dame St., tel. 01/679-7049. Reservations advised. Dress: casual but neat. Dinner only. Closed Sun., holidays. AE, DC, MC, V.*

Café Klara. Don't miss this brasserie just opposite the Mansion House and a stone's throw from St. Stephen's Green. The food is variable and the service erratic, but behind its restrained 18th-century facade lies one of the finest Georgian rooms in Dublin today. The building was previously known as Engineers Hall, and the main room used as a ballroom. Today, the room, which has been restored with great verve, makes a wonderfully elegant backdrop for a bustling, fashionable restaurant. Mirrors are used to great effect—which is appropriate as this is a place where Dublin's smart society comes to be seen by each other. The owners describe the cooking style as "traditional French with *cuisine moderne* influences," which may explain the occasional confusion of the menu. Typical dishes may include a warm pigeon salad (thinly sliced pink pigeon breast on top of a mixture of salad greens, served hot with a nut oil and raspberry vinegar dressing) on the one hand, or chicken casserole grand mère (jointed chicken with shallots, turned vegetables, and a rich red wine sauce), on the other. *35 Dawson St., tel. 01/778611. Weekend reservations advised. Dress: casual but neat. Closed Dec. 25–26. MC, V.*

Le Caprice. Situated right in the city center, this Italian restaurant features white linen–covered tables and lots of bric-a-brac and busy decorations. The place also has a reputation for a real party atmosphere later in the evening if the pianist is in the right mood or if musicians from the nearby National Concert Hall happen to be among the guests and an impromptu session gets going. The menu includes several old favorites, traditional Continental dishes such as prawn cocktail, deep-fried scampi, roast duckling à l'orange, and so on. Go, instead, for the pasta dishes such as tortellini *alla panna* (cooked in broth, drained, and heated in cream) or *melanzane* parmigiana (a sort of pie made of aubergines, interspersed with layers of mozzarella cheese and tomato sauce) and finish up with *cassata*, the classic Sicilian ice cream with candied fruit. *12 St. Andrew's St., tel. 01/679-4050 or 01/770033. Reservations accepted. Dress: casual but neat. Dinner only. Closed New Year's Day, Good Friday, Easter Sunday, Dec. 24–26. AE, DC, MC, V.*

★ **Eastern Tandoori.** This popular Indian restaurant makes no concessions to European tastes; although it's on the ground floor of a modern office block in the very center of town, the decor is traditional Indian, with beautiful brasses, wall plaques, and lanterns (all specially imported from India). The staff wears traditional waistcoats and shirts, and Indian music plays in the background. The menu includes an extensive vegetarian choice, but no European alternatives for the faint-hearted. The cuisine tends to be aromatic rather than burning hot; chicken is a specialty—try, for instance, tandoori makhan chicken (spring chicken marinated in yogurt, herbs, and spices, first cooked over charcoal, then in butter with tomatoes and cream, and served topped with nuts). Or sample the hotter pasanda (lean pieces of chicken, lamb, or beef, cooked in an almond sauce with fresh cream, highly spiced, and also served with nuts). *34 South William St., tel. 01/710428 or 01/710506. Reservations advised. Dress: casual but neat. AE, DC, MC, V.*

★ **Pigalle.** Housed in a very old building at the archway leading to Ha'penny Bridge, this charming restaurant built up a strong local following within six months of opening in 1988; it's located in an interesting area of antique shops, galleries, characterful little shops, and restaurants (now dubbed Dublin's Left Bank). The place features pleasantly old-fashioned decor, a relaxed atmosphere, and good food. Moroccan by birth, the owner-chef trained in the south of France. The menu is unashamedly French. It changes daily, but typical dishes include *le gateau aux asperges fraîches* (fresh asparagus tart), *filet de truite saumonée à l'oseille et au muscadet* (fillet of sea trout with sorrel and muscadet), or *magret de canard au calvados et aux pommes* (duck breast with calvados and apples). Try to get the window table overlooking bustling Crown Alley. *14 Temple Bar, tel. 01/719262 or 01/679–6602. Reservations advised; weekend reservations required. Dress: informal. Lunch weekdays; dinner Mon.–Sat. Closed Sun., 1 wk at Christmastime. MC, V.*

Stately's. This restaurant, which opened in 1989, occupies the first floor of the corner house opposite City Hall and Dublin Castle; with four theaters within a short walking distance and convenient hours, it is a good choice for a meal before or after the performance. The cool monochromatic art deco decor is warmed by a hint of peach; a good selection of Irish art covers the walls. The best tables stand beside the dining room's pièce de résistance, a fine 19th-century Venetian "piano-mobile" window overlooking the main thoroughfare. The traditional Continental menu, with some Irish influence, offers few surprises, but everything is fresh and homemade. Typical dishes and desserts include Irish oak smoked salmon, seafood au gratin, beef and Guinness casserole, chicken in a black cherry sauce with port, chocolate mousse, and cheesecake. Vegetarian meals are a specialty here; a vegetarian table d'hôte menu is available at a couple of pounds less than the regular one. *82 Dame St., tel. 01/679–8606. Reservations accepted. Dress: casual but neat. Dinner only (but inquire about booking private lunch parties). Closed Sun., holidays. AE, DC, V.*

Inexpensive

The Bad Ass Café. This lively restaurant in the Left Bank area between the Central Bank and Ha'penny Bridge, set in a converted warehouse, retains a distinctly barnlike atmosphere, with primary colors used inside and out. Bulbs and floor alike are bare, but there's plenty to watch—notably the old-fashioned cash shuttles whizzing around the ceiling. Although the food (pizzas, burgers, etc.) is unexceptional and the wine is frankly awful, the place can be great fun and is popular with all age groups. Children will enjoy the special Kidz Bizz menu and the ongoing coloring competition. *9–11 Crown Alley, tel. 01/712596. Reservations only for groups of 8 or more. Dress: casual. Open daily 9 AM–"late." Closed Jan. 1, Good Friday, Dec. 25–26. AE, MC, V.*

Bewley's. This famous chain of coffeehouses is dear to the nation's hearts; recent threat of closure provoked an unprecedented emotional response, even from respected national figures. Although no longer under family ownership, Bewley's now seems safe and a massive restoration program is well under way. Completed branches have now returned to their original style, with dark mahogany trim, stained-glass windows, bentwood chairs, and the much-loved waitresses in black dresses with white aprons and headbands. Specialties include the traditional Irish breakfast (eggs, bacon, sausage, black-and-white pudding, tomatoes, and mushrooms) and a wide range of home-baked breads, cakes, and pastries, which can be washed down with Bewley's own teas or coffees—the shops have 11 blends of tea and 15 of coffee from which to choose. *Westmoreland St., Grafton St., South Great George's St., and suburban branches, tel. 01/776761 (head office). No reservations. Dress: casual. Open daily 8–7. Closed Dec. 25–26. AE, DC, MC, V.*

Burdock's. In the heart of Viking Dublin, next door to the Lord Edward Pub, Dublin's most famous take-out fish-and-chipper is determinedly old-fashioned: Vegetable oil is scorned in favor of real beef drippings; it's also the only chipper in town that still fries over a coal fire. Joining the inevitable queue is part of the fun. As your meal should be consumed as quickly as possible, the traditional place to sit and eat is on the steps of St. Patrick's Cathedral. *Werburgh St., tel. 01/540306. Dinner only. Closed Tues. and Sun. No credit cards.*

Cornucopia Wholefoods. Vegetarian restaurants often provide the best value for the money, and this spot is no exception. Access is through the Cornucopia unrefined food shop (which offers plenty of distractions on the way), and the restaurant features lots of well-cared-for plants, as well as recycled paper and handmade pottery for sale. The seating consists of bar stools at high, glass-topped, narrow tables; locals often slip advertisements under the glass, which makes for some interesting reading. The menu includes red lentil soup, avocado quiche, vegetarian spring roll, and vegetarian curry, all of them regular favorites. *19 Wicklow St., tel. 01/777583. No reservations. Dress: casual. Open weekdays 8 AM–9 PM, Sat. 8–6. Closed Sun. No credit cards.*

Fat Freddy's Pizza Warehouse. Fat Freddy and his cat occupy the ground floor of this white-walled, timber-floored 18th-century warehouse in the lively Temple Bar area; various bands and artists add to the atmosphere (and noise level) in the practice rooms upstairs. Although this is mainly a student hangout, no upper age limit exists here—anyone who appreciates a good pizza (not to mention Grandma's homemade apple pie) is welcome. Customers have a reasonable choice apart from pizzas, including baked potatoes with various fillings, quiches, lasagna, and chili con carne, as well as half a dozen wines. *20 Temple La., Dame St., tel. 01/679–6769. Weekend reservations advised. Dress: casual but neat. MC, V.*

★ **Gallagher's Boxty House.** Located in a late Victorian building behind the Central Bank, right in the heart of the thriving Temple Bar area, this highly original restaurant features a lovely country ambience, with lots of dark-green decor complementing the antique pine furniture and trim, the stone floors, and the handmade pottery; everything is Irish made. The main dish, Boxty, is a traditional Irish potato bread or cake that has been cleverly adapted by the Gallaghers to make a potato pancake that is thin enough to wrap around all kinds of fillings, such as bacon and cabbage, chicken with leeks, and smoked fish. Other recommended dishes include bacon and cabbage with parsley sauce and champ (potato mashed with spring onions, milk, and butter), followed by brown bread and Bailey's ice cream or the superb bread and butter pudding. Expect to share a table. *20 Temple Bar, tel. 01/772762. No reservations. Dress: casual. Closed Christmas and Good Friday. V.*

Independent Pizza Company. This small operation just off Grafton Street claims their crusts are lighter and crisper than those of their rivals, but in fact it's probably the "fresh ingredients only" policy practiced here that makes regulars swear the pizzas are the best in town. The modern and spacious city-center place opened only recently (the original store is north of the river, in Drumcondra); it features black and gray decor, lots of plants everywhere, and a lemon tree in the back. *8 South Anne St., tel. 01/679–5266. No reservations. Dress: casual. Closed 4 days around Christmas and Good Friday. No credit cards.*

The Kilkenny Kitchen. Uniquely situated in a modern shop specializing in the best of Irish craftsmanship and overlooking Trinity College, this tweed-carpeted self-service restaurant decorated with natural wood showcases wholesome home cooking in the traditional style. The menu includes a house quiche (combining Irish bacon, herbs, and fresh vegetables), a good traditional Irish stew, casseroles, and an imaginative selection of salads. The choice of Irish farmhouse cheeses and the home-baked scones, bread, and cakes are all tempting. Lunchtime is busy; expect to share a table. *6 Nassau St., tel. 01/777066. No reservations. Dress: casual. Open Mon.–Sat., 9–5. Closed Sun., public holidays. AE, MC, V.*

Mitchells Cellars. Situated comfortingly in the vaulted basement of a wine shop, this place hasn't really changed since the early '70s: It still has the same bustling lunchtime crowd, the quarry-tiled floor, white-washed walls, red and white lampshades hanging over pine tables, waitresses neatly dressed in navy and white—and much the same menu. Country French–influenced home cooking dominates on the menu, which includes soups and pâtés, quiche lorraine and salads, beef braised in Guinness, and chocolate and brandy meringue. The restaurant's perennial popularity may be attributed to its attachment to the revered wine merchants upstairs (there's usually something interesting on the wine list at the right price) and to its location just off St. Stephen's Green. Get here early, or expect a line. *21 Kildare St., tel. 01/680367. No reservations. Dress: casual but neat. Lunch only. Closed Sun.; Sat. in June, July, and Aug.; bank holidays; Dec. 24–28. AE, CB, DC, MC, V.*

Paddy Kavanagh's. Tucked away in a lane behind the Bord Failté (Tourist Board) head office, Paddy Kavanagh's isn't a place you're likely to come across by chance, but it's very popular with local office workers. This informal, friendly place in an old building has been transformed into an atmosphere well-suited to the restaurant's reputation for good home cooking—the decor features country tones of dark green and terra-cotta and plenty of natural wood. The main dishes tend to be fairly traditional and homey; fish pie is a typical specialty. Tasty vegetarian alternatives and an unusually wide range of salads are also on the menu. This weekday place opens early, with breakfast from 8 AM; it closes following afternoon tea. *6 Pembroke Row, tel. 01/765056. Limited reservations accepted for lunch. Dress: casual but neat. Open Mon.–Thurs. 8–5, Fri. 8–4. Closed weekends, 1 wk at Christmas. No credit cards.*

Pasta Fresca. Situated on one of Dublin's most interesting thoroughfares, just off Grafton Street, this stylish little Italian restaurant and delicatessen squeezes a surprising number of people into a small area; it's comfortable, however, once you're settled, and the high ceiling does create a sense of space. Antipasto *misto* (assorted sliced Italian meats) makes a good appetizer—or go for a single meat like prosciutto (Italian cured ham), or *carpaccio della casa* (wafer-thin slices of beef fillet, with fresh Parmesan, olive oil, lemon juice, and black pepper). The main courses consist mainly of Pasta Fresca's own very good versions of well-known dishes such as spaghetti *alla bolognese*, cannelloni, and lasagna *al forno*. The pasta is freshly made each day. You'll find lines at lunchtime. *3–4 Chatham Street, tel. 01/679–2402 or 01/679–8965. Reservations accepted; weekend reservations advised. Dress: casual but neat. Open daily 8 AM–11 PM. Closed public holidays. No credit cards.*

Peers Café. This stylish modern daytime restaurant is situated over the Acquiesce shop on the fashionable Grafton Street. There's a hint of the '30s and art nouveau in the pretty yellow and blue design, and the best tables—beechwood with a blue-gray marbled inset—stand near the window, overlooking the bustling street and flower sellers down below. The cooking, mainly Continental, is outstanding for its wholesomeness and its low cost. The menu includes homemade soups, such as watercress or leek and potato; a roast, such as roast stuffed pork with mustard sauce; and Parson's Hat, a pastry stuffed with fish. Desserts include rich pastries and sweets like black currant and lime yogurt mousse. *41 Grafton St., tel. 01/719795. Reservations accepted. Dress: casual but neat. Breakfast weekdays, lunch Mon.–Sat. Closed Sun., bank holidays. No credit cards.*

The Periwinkle Seafood Bar. This informal daytime restaurant is located in what was once the stable area of Lord Powerscourt's town house (now imaginatively converted into Dublin's most attractive shopping center); it features the original low arched ceiling and even the cauldron that was once used to prepare the horses' bran mash. The modern quarry-tile floor, pine tables, and chunky pottery complement the old building's architecture; the kitchen is open, with a gray marble counter the only barrier. Expect home cooking with a leaning toward Cordon Bleu: the emphasis is on freshness, quality, and simplicity. Sample the seafood chowder, served with homemade brown bread, or the toasted crab claws in garlic butter, cheese, and breadcrumbs. *Unit 18, Powerscourt Townhouse Centre, South William St., tel. 01/679–4203. No reservations. Dress: casual. Open 10:30–5. Closed Sun., Christmas, Easter, bank holidays. No credit cards.*

Suburbs and County Dublin

Very Expensive ★

Colin O'Daly's Park Restaurant. This restaurant (15 minutes from the city center on the DART train or by taxi) shows what an Irish chef-proprietor devoted to the *cuisine moderne* style can do with local ingredients. The setting is an old stone parish hall, with a conservatory reception area; the style is formal and sophisticated, yet also friendly. The innovative dishes receive an attractive presentation. You might start off with a tartlette of scrambled eggs with crabmeat, followed by pan-fried escalope of veal with a veal liver mousse and mustard-seed sauce. The crab will almost certainly be from nearby Dalkey's harbor, the mustard will be Irish whole-grain mustard (made in Limerick). Game, when in season, is a specialty here. *40 The Mews, Blackrock, Co. Dublin, tel. 01/886177. Reservations required. Jacket advised; jacket and tie advised in the evening. Closed Sun., bank holidays. AE, DC, MC, V.*

★ **Le Coq Hardi.** This successful restaurant, close to the city center and most of the major hotels, is consistently popular with the business community. Rosewood furniture, gilt-framed pictures and mirrors, Irish linen, Newbridge silver, and Rosenthal china create a reassuring, clublike atmosphere. The house style is classical French, with some concessions to *cuisine moderne* in the choice and presentation of vegetables. Specialties include "smokies," an appetizer made with Scottish smoked haddock, marbled with tomato, double cream, and Irish cheese and baked "en cocotte" (in an ovenware dish), and *coq* Hardi, which is chicken filled with potatoes, mushrooms, and special herbs, wrapped in bacon, oven-baked, and finished with Irish whiskey. Their outstanding wine list concentrates on the great wines of Bordeaux, Burgundy, Loire, and Champagne; bear in mind, however, that there is very little under £15. *35 Pembroke Rd., Ballsbridge, tel. 01/689070 or 01/684130. Reservations required. Jacket required; tie advised. Lunch weekdays; dinner Mon.–Sat. Closed Sun. AE, DC, MC, V.*

Expensive

Abbey Tavern. Situated in the fishing port of Howth, 14 km (9 mi) north of the city center, this Old World tavern is only a five-minute walk from the DART station. The ancient building's original stone walls, flagged floors, and old gas lights are more effective than anything a decorator might conceive; blazing turf fires add to the historic atmosphere. The upstairs restaurant specializes in fish dishes, with the traditional Irish and Continental cuisine. Sole Abbey—fillet of sole stuffed with prawns, mushrooms, and herbs—is a house specialty, and fresh Dublin Bay prawns can be cooked to order. Traditional Irish music is offered in a different part of the building. *Abbey St., Howth, Co. Dublin, tel. 01/390282. Reservations advised; weekend reservations required. Jacket suggested. Dinner only: Apr.–Sept., daily; Oct.–Mar., closed Sun. eves. AE, DC, MC, V.*

Ayumi-Ya Japanese Restaurant. This is Dublin's first Japanese restaurant, located in a small shopping complex 8 km (5 mi) from the city center. Customers have a choice of seating at regular tables; on the floor, Japanese-style; or at *teppan-yaki* (iron-grill) tables (offered by reservation). Japanese decorations and porcelain are used throughout and the waiting staff wear kimonos or Japanese-style shirts. The Japanese proprietor-chef is a qualified dietician and has won numerous awards for her cuisine. Choices include *sushi* and *sashimi* (a selection of ultrafresh, thinly cut raw fish), *tempura* (a deep-fried selection of prawns, vegetables, and fish), beef teriyaki, and *teppan-yaki*, which the chef cooks right at the tables; this is the only restaurant in Ireland offering this iron-grill style of cooking. *Newpark Centre, Newtownpark Ave., Blackrock, Co.*

Dublin, tel. 01/831767. Reservations advised; weekend reservations required. Dress: casual but neat. Closed Sat.–Sun. lunch, Sun. dinner, Mon., Dec. 25–26, Jan. 1–2. AE, DC, MC, V.

Beaufield Mews. A 10-minute taxi ride from the city center, this 18th-century coach house and stables still has its original cobbled courtyard and is even said to be haunted by a friendly monk. Inside it's all black beams, old furniture, and bric-a-brac, including stable artifacts. The most desirable tables overlook the courtyard or the garden, or are, less predictably, "under the nun" (the nun in question is a 17th-century portrait). The traditional food makes use of the best of seasonal ingredients; you'll find old favorites like roast glazed duckling à l'orange, but also fresh wild salmon steaks simply grilled or poached and served with hollandaise sauce. The menu also includes game in season—venison and pheasant are specialties—and homemade ice cream. *Woodlands Ave., Stillorgan, Co. Dublin, tel. 01/886945. Reservations required. Dress: casual but neat. Dinner only (other meals by arrangement). Closed Sun., Mon., bank holidays. AE, DC, V.*

Bon Appetit. Owner-chef Patsey McGuirk brought a loyal folthe staff of black-jacketed waiters. Patsey's wife, Catherine, manages the front of the house. The traditional Continental menu includes entrées such as escargots and mushrooms in garlic and cream sauce, and a generous choice of desserts. Especially recommended are sole McGuirk, boned sole stuffed with prawns and turbot and baked with white wine and cream, and duckling Montmorency, served with black cherries and a cherry brandy and orange sauce. *9 James's Terr., Malahide, Co. Dublin, tel. 01/450314. Reservations advised. Jacket and tie advised. Lunch weekdays; dinner Mon.–Sat. Closed Sundays, bank holidays, Christmas week. AE, DC, MC, V.*

Broph's. Near the American Embassy and over a (very exclusive) nightclub, Broph's restaurant is upstairs in a Georgian terraced building. It's interestingly furnished in warm colors—Afghan rugs on the terra-cotta walls, lamps, and wall lights all create a relaxing atmosphere. The chef-owner takes pride in making imaginative use of the best Irish ingredients in his own style. For instance, he may take some wild sea trout, make it into *quennelles* (dumplings), and serve them in a delicate sauce with saffron and chives; another evening, he may fan out a panfried duck breast, give it a game glaze, and add baby corn for color. Desserts tend to be classical, but often with a twist—crème brûlée, for example, comes with a pretty net of caramelized sugar spun over it. *16 Merrion Rd., Ballsbridge, tel. 01/602236 or 01/605288. Reservations advised; weekend reservations required. Dress: casual but neat. Lunch weekdays, dinner Mon.–Sat. Closed Sun., bank holidays. AE, DC, V.*

Digby's Restaurant and Wine Bar. Situated in a terraced Georgian house on the seafront in Dun Laoghaire, this is a well-established favorite with locals. The smart upstairs restaurant is often used for special occasions; the rustic stone-flagged wine bar on the ground floor, for inexpensive, casual meals. In the restaurant, recently redone in pinks and grays with art deco mirrors, owner-chef Paul Cathcart practices what he calls "cuisine marchais" to emphasize the seasonal nature of his approach to fresh products—using a lot of game in winter and seafood in summer, for instance. For starters, you might try aubergine cake (sliced panfried eggplant layered with tomato and basil and baked with grated sheep's cheese) and follow with steamed medallions of monkfish with wild mushrooms. If you still have room, you can order chocolate pecan truffle pie. *5 Windsor Terr., Dun Laoghaire, Co. Dublin, tel. 01/804600 or 01/809147. Reservations advised. Dress: casual but neat. Dinner Wed.–Mon.; lunch Sun. only. Closed Tues., Dec. 25–26, Good Friday, bank holidays. AE, DC, MC, V.*

★ **The King Sitric.** This well-known seafood restaurant is a main attraction in the fishing port of Howth, north of the city center; it's situated in a Georgian house on the harbor front, with the yacht marina and port on one side, and with sea views from the upstairs bar/reception area. The restaurant consists of a series of rooms on the ground floor, furnished traditionally with antiques and white linen; try to get a table in the middle, near the kitchen. The menu makes little concession to non–fish eaters, although there's usually some alternative, such as chicken Kiev or some game, when in season. But who could resist fish that is so utterly fresh? Lobster, caught just yards away in Balscadden Bay, is the big treat; it's best at its simplest, in butter sauce. Crab is equally fresh and scrumptious here, dressed with mayonnaise or mornay sauce. *Calmar frites* (deep-fried squid) is a special starter served with fresh tomato or tartar sauce. For dessert, don't miss the house specialty meringue Sitric (hollow meringues, filled with homemade vanilla ice cream, covered with dark chocolate sauce, and scattered with flaked almonds). *East Pier, Howth, Co. Dublin, tel. 01/325235 or 01/326729. Reservations advised; weekend reservations required. Jacket advised; jacket and tie suggested. Dinner only. Closed Sun., bank holidays, and at Christmas and Easter, 10 days each. AE, DC, MC, V.*

★ **Roche's Bistro.** About a 15-minute drive out of Dublin and handy to the airport, Roche's is part of an old terraced house in the main street of a pretty coastal town. Orla Roche is a Francophile, and it shows—the particular brand of relaxed Gallic charm and good country French cooking found here is rare in Ireland. The small and cozy place, with white walls covered with French prints and antique copper utensils, has cheerful blue-and-white-check tablecloths and an open coal fire in winter. The cooking is done in full view of clients, in a minuscule kitchen behind the bar. Seafood figures strongly on the wide-ranging menu. You might start with a mousseline of scallops (scallops pureed with egg white, Noilly Prat, cream, and grated orange zest, cooked in a mold and served with orange *beurre blanc*) and follow with breast of duck with cassis. *12 New St., Malahide, Co. Dublin, tel. 01/452777. Reservations accepted; weekend reservations advised. Dress: casual but neat. Lunch Mon.–Sat., dinner Thurs.–Sat. AE, DC, MC, V.*

Trudi's. Situated in a late-19th-century building on Dun Laoghaire's main street, this informal bistro has become something of an institution, with a devoted local clientele. The restaurant has two floors, with a small wine bar on the ground floor and an intimate upper balcony area. The menu reflects seasonal changes, with food prepared to allow the natural flavor of ingredients to predominate. Typical entrées include braised lambs' tongues with mustard sauce and poached salmon with watercress sauce, in the summer. Game in season is served. *107 Lower George's St., Dun Laoghaire, Co. Dublin, tel. 01/805318. Reservations advised, especially on weekends. Dress: casual but neat. Dinner only. Closed Sun.–Mon., Dec. 25–26, Good Friday. AE, DC, MC, V.*

The Wine Epergne. This delightful restaurant, a 10-minute drive from the city center, has a strong local following. Once a Victorian shop (and still connected to Findlater's Wine Merchants next door), it now features polished floors, Turkish carpets, Victorian furniture, and old cutlery that is charmingly mismatched. The feeling of being in a private home is emphasized by the family portraits on the walls. The country house–style food includes reassuring childhood favorites, such as fishcakes and hearty homemade soups complemented by game in season, such as pheasant with madeira sauce or venison with whiskey and orange sauce. For dessert, try the rich chocolate mousse, homemade ice cream, or bread-and-butter pudding. *147 Upper Rathmines Rd., tel. 01/967811. Reservations advised. Jacket suggested. Dinner Tues.–Sat. Closed Sat. lunch, Sun.–Mon., Christmas Eve–mid-Jan. MC, V.*

Moderate

China-Sichuan Restaurant. This restaurant has the distinction of being state-owned by the Szechuan Province of the People's Republic of China; the ingredients (and the chefs) are supplied directly from China. The establishment is situated in an ordinary terraced building about a 15-minute drive from the city center. The focal point here is a giant ceramic water-lily fountain. Traditional scarlet lanterns and velvet-covered booths set in private areas help create an intimate ambience. Recommended specialties include duck skin stuffed with seafood, and whole steamed sole. Desserts are unexceptional. *4 Lower Kilmacud Rd., Stillorgan, Co. Dublin, tel. 01/884817 or 01/889560. Reservations required. Jacket and tie required. Closed Good Friday and 3 days at Christmas. AE, MC, V.*

The Old Schoolhouse. Although it's a half-hour drive from the city center, this attractively converted Victorian schoolhouse is only a five-minute drive from the airport. The stone-walled garden makes a delightful setting for al fresco dining in summer; guests can relax in the reception/lounge area of the recently added conservatory. Inside, you'll find an informal atmosphere, with old pine furniture and local pottery complementing the original wood floors and paneled walls. Traditional Irish home cooking is served, with the emphasis on fresh fish and steaks. Recommended dishes include the lemon sole stuffed with crab, or Irish potato cakes with crispy bacon. A vegetarian option is always available, such as mushrooms in garlic butter, followed by spinach roulade and salad. *Coolbanagher, Swords, Co. Dublin, tel. 01/402846. Reservations advised. Dress: casual but neat. Closed Sat.–Sun. lunch, Sun. dinner. AE, DC, MC, V.*

The Orchid Szechuan Restaurant. Just outside the city center, in the basement of an early Victorian terraced house, this pretty Chinese restaurant with its unusual cool, monochromatic black color scheme, is one of the friendliest dining spots in town. The chef, from Hong Kong's Riverside Restaurant, has a talent for turning an ordinary meal into a banquet with specialties like hot-and-sour soup, king prawns with hot garlic sauce, and crispy deep-fried shredded fillet of beef with spicy sauce. *120 Pembroke Rd., Ballsbridge, tel. 01/600629. Reservations accepted; weekend reservations advised. Jacket and tie suggested. Closed Dec. 24–26. AE, DC, MC, V.*

Lodging

Dublin's city center and the immediate south side of the city offer a number of first-class hotels. Rates for these hotels are reasonable by international standards, although suites, usually a bedroom and a sitting room, are increasingly popular but very expensive, at around £500 a night. Some city-center hotels are located in drab parts of town, such as Upper O'Connell Street. For travelers with their own cars, it is worth considering a location out of the city center, such as Dalkey and Killiney, where the surroundings are more pleasant.

The city also has a good choice of less expensive accommodations, with many moderately priced and inexpensive hotels offering basic but agreeable rooms. Bed-and-breakfast establishments, long the mainstay of the economy end of the market, have upgraded their facilities and now provide rooms with their own bathrooms or showers, as well as multichannel color televisions and direct-dial telephones, for around £20 a night per person.

A new development in Dublin is the renting of apartments and houses to visitors; the travelers usually cook their own meals. Most of these apartments and houses provide maid service that is responsible for daily cleaning. These apartments and houses are well decorated and furnished, offering travelers total freedom to come and go as they please.

Bord Failté (Irish Tourist Board) publishes a complete self-catering guide, for £3; these recommended properties can be booked through any Tourist Information Office (*see* Important Addresses and Numbers in Essential Information, above).

Category	Cost*
Expensive	over £80
Moderate	£40–£80
Inexpensive	under £40

**all prices are for a double-size room, except where stated, and include a 10% local sales tax (VAT) and a 12½% service charge.*

Highly recommended hotels are indicated by a star ★.

City Center

Expensive **Berkeley Court.** Opened more than a decade ago, this quietly elegant hotel with efficient service in the verdant residential district of Ballsbridge attracts both local and foreign celebrities. Although the glass-and-concrete exterior is designed in a modern blocklike style, the vast, recently renovated lobby is more attractive, with plush carpeting, roomy sofas, white tiles, and antique planters. The large bedrooms are decorated in light pastel shades, with antiques or reproductions of period furniture; bathrooms feature marble tiling. The Berkeley Room restaurant offers improved table d'hôte and à la carte menus; the more informal Conservatory restaurant, with hanging plants and large windows, serves grilled food and snacks. The hotel is a 10-minute cab ride from the city center. *Lansdowne Rd., Dublin 4, tel. 01/601711. 187 rooms, including*

20 suites. Facilities: 2 restaurants, 2 shops, hairdresser, barbershop, Jacuzzis in suites. AE, DC, MC, V.

Conrad. Rising seven stories, Dublin's latest new expensive hotel opened in 1989 and is well placed opposite the National Concert Hall and within a two-minute walk of St. Stephen's Green. Gleaming light-colored marble graces the large, formal lobby. Bedrooms are furnished with sand-colored decor and natural wood furniture, offer uninspiring views of the adjacent tower blocks, and are rather cramped. The air-conditioning/heating systems can also be quite noisy. The suites, however, are spacious enough with stylish, dark-colored furniture in the sitting area. On the first floor, guests have a choice of two restaurants: The airy Plurabelle serves informal lunches and evening meals, and the more enclosed Alexandra room, with heavy wood paneling and drapes, has formal menus emphasizing elaborately prepared fish, fowl, and meat dishes. In the basement, the Alfie Byrne Bar, named in honor of Dublin's lord mayor for most of the 1930s, has a black bar counter in the center of the room that some may find a bit gloomy. Overall, the hotel has a sophisticated ambience; while the service is efficient, it lacks the spontaneous Irish warmth that can be found in smaller establishments. *Earlsfort Terr., Dublin 2, tel. 01/765555. 179 rooms, 9 suites. Facilities: 2 restaurants. AE, DC, MC.*

Jury's and the Towers. These two hotels offer striking contrasts in decor and design. Jury's is a seven-story, concrete-and-glass blocklike building; it adjoins the Towers, which is the same height with a light finish to its facade. Jury's, the older hotel, dating back 30 years, offers large, plainly decorated bedrooms with light walls and brown drapes; furnishings are functional but uninspired, especially for an expensive hotel. The Towers' bedrooms are a third larger than those of Jury's, with subtle, sand-colored decor, complemented by natural built-in wood furniture. Both the large beds and the armchairs are blissfully comfortable. Rooms also have plenty of storage space. Suites are even grander, with their own sitting rooms and kitchenettes. Entry to the Towers is restricted to guests, who can enjoy their own lounge and well-stocked reading room. All shop and restaurant facilities are located in Jury's. The Kish serves only fish and features an elaborate bar; the Embassy Room has a green garden-theme decor; and the Coffee Dock, with light fare, is open 23 hours a day. The Dubliner's Bar, in a setting reminiscent of a farmhouse kitchen, has a collection of memorabilia, old photographs, and newspaper clippings, as well as a 100-year-old printing press. Although both hotels are popular with businesspeople and vacationers, you'll probably be happier at the Towers, if you can afford the extra cost. *Ballsbridge, Dublin 4, tel. 01/605000. Jury's, 300 rooms, 8 suites; the Towers, 100 rooms, 4 suites with kitchenettes. Facilities: 2 restaurants, coffee shop, bar, pool, shop/boutique, Irish cabaret in summer. AE, DC, MC, V.*

★ **Mont Clare Hotel.** Rarely has a Dublin hotel undergone such a complete personality change; this establishment used to be a rather drab place offering modest accommodations and undistinguished dining facilities. A brand new wing, however, opened in 1990, and all the bedrooms in the original part of the hotel were refurbished to match the standards of the new section. Bedrooms feature deep-pile carpeting and vibrant colors, such as deep-red walls and white ceilings. All rooms provide a computerized minibar, individual heat/air-conditioning con-

Ariel House, **16**
Berkeley Court, **15**
Blooms, **5**
Burlington, **12**
Conrad, **9**
Dublin International Youth Hostel, **2**
Gresham, **3**
Iona House, **1**
Isaac Tourist Hostel, **4**
Jury's/The Towers, **14**
Kilronan House, **10**
Lansdowne, **13**
Leeson Court, **11**
Mont Clare Hotel, **6**
Montrose House, **18**
Mount Herbert, **17**
Shelbourne, **8**
Westbury, **7**

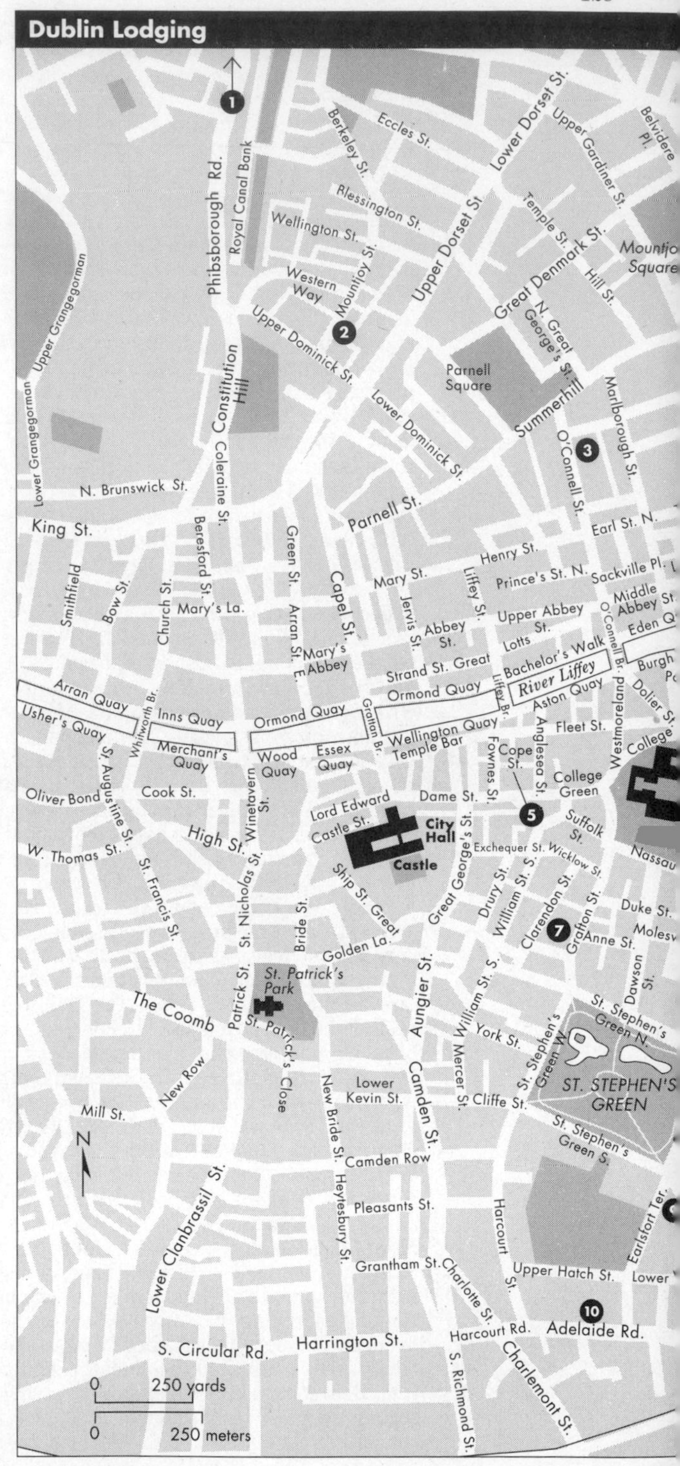

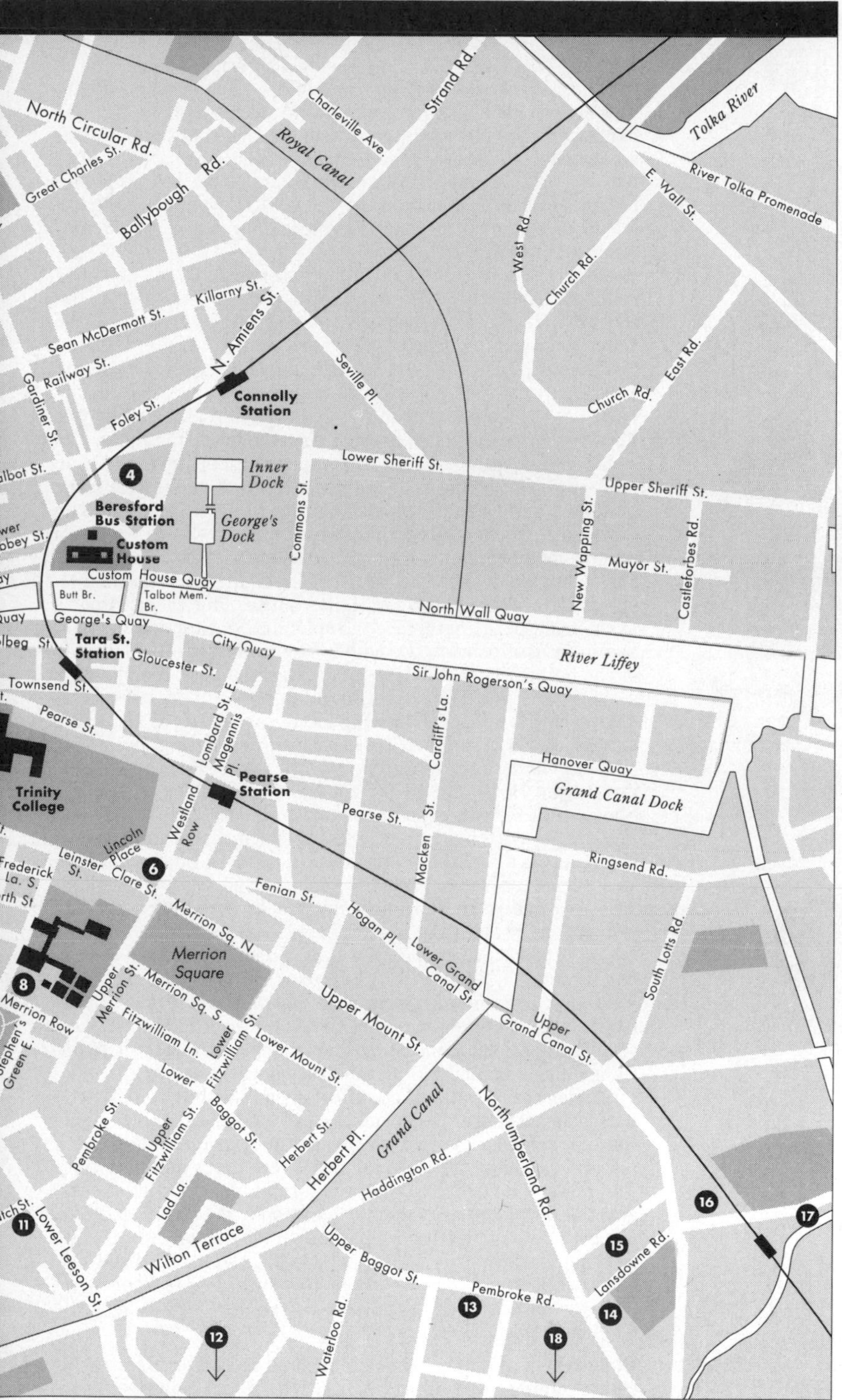

North Circular Rd.
Great Charles St.
Ballybough Rd.
Charleville Ave.
Royal Canal
Strand Rd.
Tolka River
River Tolka Promenade
E. Wall St.
West Rd.
Church Rd.
Killarny St.
Sean McDermott St.
N. Amiens St.
Railway St.
Gardiner St.
Seville Pl.
East Rd.
Church Rd.
Connolly Station
Foley St.
Lower Sheriff St.
Inner Dock
Talbot St.
4
Upper Sheriff St.
Beresford Bus Station
Commons St.
George's Dock
New Wapping St.
Castleforbes Rd.
Abbey St.
Custom House
Mayor St.
Custom House Quay
Butt Br.
Talbot Mem. Br.
North Wall Quay
George's Quay
Tara St. Station
City Quay
River Liffey
Gloucester St.
Sir John Rogerson's Quay
Townsend St.
Lombard St. E.
Magennis Pl.
Cardiff's La.
Pearse St.
Hanover Quay
Trinity College
Pearse Station
Grand Canal Dock
Westland Row
Pearse St.
Lincoln Place
Macken St.
Ringsend Rd.
Frederick La. S.
Leinster St.
6
Clare St.
Fenian St.
Merrion Sq. N.
Hogan Pl.
Lower Grand Canal St.
South Lotts Rd.
Merrion Square
Upper Merrion St.
Merrion Sq. S.
8
Merrion Row
Upper Mount St.
Upper Grand Canal St.
Stephen's Green E.
Fitzwilliam Ln.
Lower Fitzwilliam St.
Lower Mount St.
Lower Baggot St.
Northumberland Rd.
Pembroke St.
Upper Fitzwilliam St.
Herbert St.
Grand Canal
Herbert Pl.
Haddington Rd.
Lad La.
16
17
11
Lower Leeson St.
Wilton Terrace
Upper Baggot St.
15
Lansdowne Rd.
Pembroke Rd.
13
14
Waterloo Rd.
12
18

trols, trouser presses, tea- and coffee-making facilities, and an in-house film channel. The immaculate bathrooms have marble floors and wall tiles. Corridors seem a bit cramped, and guests may not find the low ceilings in the older rooms to their liking. The new Goldsmith's Restaurant specializes in Irish fish and beef, while the Merrion Lounge serves Irish bar food, such as sandwiches and stews. The location of the hotel could not be better, just behind Trinity College and near St. Stephen's Green, Grafton Street, and museums. *Merrion Sq., Dublin 2, tel. 01/616799 or 01/619555. 74 rooms. Facilities: restaurant, bar, parking. AE, DC, MC, V.*

★ **Shelbourne.** This grand old Dublin hotel may have an imposing redbrick front with white trim, but you'll find it far from unfriendly. Its guest book contains names ranging from the Dalai Lama to Laurel and Hardy to Richard Burton to Peter O'Toole. (In the 19th century, writer William Makepeace Thackeray stayed here for six shillings and eight pence a day.) The blazing open fire in cold weather in its bustling lobby, flanked by two huge rose brocade sofas, is proof that the hotel has not lost its sense of past grandeur. The Shelbourne first opened in 1824, in modest houses facing St. Stephen's Green; over the years, the buildings were expanded considerably, but also became run down until, between 1986 and 1988, £7 million was lavished on a tip-top refurbishment. No two bedrooms are the same size or shape, but all have fine, carefully selected furniture and luxurious drapes, with splendid antiques in the older rooms. Rooms at the front of the hotel face the splendid St. Stephen's Green, and in the distance are the Dublin mountains; it's the only side of the hotel with good views. Although the back rooms face a service yard, you'll find them far quieter. The impressive suites have separate bedrooms, sitting rooms, and dressing areas; the largest, with a mininetwork of interconnecting rooms, is named in honor of the late Princess Grace of Monaco, who visited in the 1960s and 1970s. On the ground floor, the Horse Shoe Bar is a small, popular rendezvous spot; tea in the adjoining lounge, with its deep, comfortable armchairs and views of the green, is a real Dublin tradition. The distinguished Aisling Restaurant serves a varied, expensive menu with excellent seafood appetizers and such entrées as crab, duck, grilled salmon, and veal. *St. Stephen's Green, Dublin 2, tel. 01/766471, fax 01/616006. 165 rooms, 22 suites. Facilities: 2 restaurants, bar, lounge, gift shop/newsagent, parking. AE, DC, MC, V.*

Westbury. This hotel has an excellent location, right off the fashionable shopping mecca of Grafton Street in the city center. The spacious main lobby is furnished with attractive antiques and comfortable armchairs where guests sit to take afternoon tea. Despite these efforts, the Westbury offers little period atmosphere. Bedrooms are rather utilitarian, with pastel color schemes; suites, which combine European decor with tasteful Japanese screens and prints, are much more inviting. The flowery Russell Room serves formal lunches and dinners, and the downstairs Sandbank, a seafood restaurant and bar, features decor imitating a Joycean-period establishment. The food and service can be disappointing. *Grafton St., Dublin 2, tel. 01/746881 or 01/679–1122. 160 twin/double rooms, 43 suites. Facilities: 2 restaurants; shops in Westbury Mall beside hotel entrance. AE, DC, MC, V.*

Moderate

Blooms. This establishment's location, the Temple Bar area, is fast becoming a new cultural center with its art galleries; Trinity College is also only a five-minute walk away. The hotel is a modern, unexceptional five-story concrete building. Bedrooms, decorated in white and cream, are plain and boxlike yet comfortable. The hotel remains popular with tourists and business visitors. *Anglesea St., Dublin 2, tel. 01/715622. 86 rooms. Facilities: restaurant, bar. AE, DC, MC, V.*

Burlington. Opened in 1969, the first and largest of Dublin's modern hotels has an impersonal glass-and-concrete facade, but the staff here is quite friendly and attentive. The hotel attracts a number of tour groups. Public rooms are well decorated, especially the large bar, with mahogany counters and hanging plants to enhance the conservatory-style setting. The generous-size bedrooms have large picture windows. For such a big hotel, the Burlington is surprisingly lacking in sports and health facilities, and the pool was removed to make way for the bar extension. *Upper Leeson St., Dublin 4, tel. 01/605222. 450 rooms. Facilities: 2 restaurants, nightclub, gift shop/newsagent, Irish cabaret in summer. AE, DC, MC, V.*

Gresham. This old hotel, dating back to 1859, has been substantially refurbished within the past five years, but it is located in a drab part of town. In the past, the hotel attracted many celebrities, such as Richard Burton and Elizabeth Taylor, but more recent VIPs have gravitated to newer and more expensive accommodations. Bedrooms are reached via long windowless corridors. The somewhat antiquated bathrooms lend character to the bland modern-repro style of the newly decorated rooms, which are nevertheless clean and comfortable. The Gresham's restaurant is still a pleasant place to stop for lunch and dinner, with an emphasis on meat and fish dishes. Although you're right near the historic GPO, you'll also have to watch out in the area for pickpockets. *Upper O'Connell St., Dublin 1, tel. 01/746881. 198 rooms. Facilities: restaurant, bar, nightclub/disco. AE, DC, MC, V.*

★ **Lansdowne.** In the leafy suburb of Ballsbridge, convenient to the city center, this small establishment offers a very friendly ambience. The cozy, modest rooms are painted in pastel shades, and they have all the basics. The basement bar is a popular hangout for local business people and fans of the international rugby matches held at nearby Lansdowne Road; photos of sports personalities hang on the walls. Next to the bar is the Bonne Bouchée Restaurant, which serves lunch and dinner, specializing in seafood and grilled steaks. *27 Pembroke Rd., Dublin 4, tel. 01/684079 or 01/682522. 28 rooms. Facilities: bar, restaurant, TV. AE, DC, MC, V.*

Leeson Court. Two 18th-century terraced houses have been combined to form this recently opened hotel, which stands close to St. Stephen's Green and is just around the corner from the new Conrad (*see* above). The first sight to greet arrivals are two enormous bookcases in the lobby, filled with an enticing selection of old volumes. The tiny breakfast room is a real pleasure, with blue table linen, walls, and curtains, and a view of the garden. The small bedrooms are all cheerfully decorated in matching colors, with thick carpeting and stained-wood furnishings. The tiled bathrooms are surprisingly spacious. Although the windows in the front are double-glazed against traffic noise, some sounds do filter in, especially around 9 AM and 6 PM. The wood-paneled Darby O'Gill bar looks like a very old-fashioned country pub; during the late evening, there is real Irish music to set a lively mood. The conservatory at the back of the hotel faces a pleasant patio and beer garden. A nightclub is located in the basement but it is fully sound-insulated from the rest of the building. *26–27 Lower Leeson St., Dublin 2, tel. 01/763380. 20 rooms. Facilities: bar, nightclub, restaurant. AE, DC, MC, V.*

Inexpensive

★ **Ariel House.** This redbrick Victorian guest house, dating from 1850, stands conveniently near bus routes and the DART line, a five-minute ride to the center of Dublin; it is also just down the road from the Berkeley Court and Jury's (*see* above). Michael O'Brien, the amiable owner, returned to Ireland from San Francisco and London, and he turned his home into this immaculate lodging with a new extension in the back. The lobby, lounge, and restaurant are graced with Victoriana and lace curtains in the Irish-style; the lounge features comfortable leather chairs, a white marble fireplace, lovely oil portraits, a Waterford crystal chandelier, and an exquisite Japanese doll. Bedrooms are plain with light walls and contemporary furniture, though some rooms in the main house have high ceilings. Number 27, which faces a neat garden, is especially charming with Victorian-style furniture and a Jacuzzi. A well-prepared breakfast is served in the cozy dining room with a special glass-roofed area and fine wood furnishings. This is a good economical alternative to the more expensive hotels. The owner plans to expand the hotel in 1991. *52 Lansdowne Rd., Dublin 4, tel. 01/685512. 20 rooms. Facilities: restaurant, TV and phones in rooms. AE, DC, MC, V.*

Dublin International Youth Hostel. Housed in a converted convent, it offers dormitory accommodations (up to 25 people per room) and also family-size rooms that can take up to four people. This is a spartan, low-cost alternative to hotels; nonmembers of the international youth hosteling organization can stay for a small extra charge. The hostel is located north of Parnell Square, near the Mater Hospital. *51 Mountjoy St., Dublin 1, tel. 01/301766. 500 beds. Facilities: restaurant. No credit cards.*

Iona House. This north-side family-run guest house was converted from a large Victorian redbrick home. The genial Shoulderdice family make sure travelers have a comfortable visit at a reasonable price. All the modestly furnished rooms offer showers and TVs. *5 Iona Pk., Dublin 9, tel. 01/306217. 14 rooms. No credit cards.*

Isaac Tourist Hostel. This cheap alternative for young people has bunk beds in a dormitory situation. Bathrooms are also shared. You can't get any cheaper (around £5 a night), but if you're prepared to pay around £12 a night, you can get a private room. The hostel is close to the Busaras bus station and the city center. *2 Frenchman's La., Dublin 1, tel. 01/363877. 3 single rooms, 10 double rooms; otherwise, dormitory accommodations. No credit cards.*

★ **Kilronan House.** This guest house, only a five-minute walk from St. Stephen's Green, remains a longtime favorite with vacationers, perhaps because of the friendly welcome they receive from the Murray family, who have run the place for the past 30 years. The large, late-19th-century terraced house, with a white facade, was well-converted, and the owners can be commended for updating decor and furnishings each year. Bedrooms are pleasantly furnished, with plush carpeting and pastel-colored walls. Another welcome plus for visitors, and rather rare in Dublin hotels, let alone guest houses, are the orthopedic beds, which guarantee a restful night's sleep. *70 Ade-*

laide Rd., Dublin 2, tel. 01/755266. 12 rooms. Facilities: TV, radio, direct-dial phone in room, tea-making equipment. No credit cards.

Montrose House. Located on a secluded road near Herbert Park in Ballsbridge, this small 19th-century redbrick guest house features lovely gardens that rival the floral splendor of the nearby park. Your welcome here will be warm, but the clean, no-frills rooms have no individual bath or shower facilities. Breakfast is the only meal served. *16 Pembroke Pk., Ballsbridge, Dublin 4, tel. 01/684286. 5 rooms. No credit cards.*

Mount Herbert. This rather sprawling hotel, derived from combining a number of large Victorian-era houses, overlooks fine rear gardens in the residential Ballsbridge district, right near the main rugby stadium and a 10-minute bus ride from Dublin center. The simple rooms are painted in light shades with little furniture besides the beds, but all of them have bathrooms and TVs. Guests can relax in the lounge, and a large restaurant, overlooking the back garden, serves three meals a day, with unpretentious dinners of steaks and stews. The place is a great favorite with budget-minded visitors from all over the world who seek comfortable accommodations. *7 Herbert Rd., Dublin 4, tel. 01/684321. 120 rooms. Facilities: restaurant, shop. AE, DC, MC, V.*

Suburbs and County Dublin

Expensive

Dublin International. The only hotel at Dublin Airport, this low-rise redbrick structure with a plain exterior features roomy but characterless sleeping accommodations. The lively bar features music during the weekends, while the usually crowded dual-level Garden Room restaurant serves mostly fish and meat entrées, as well as a good selection of vegetarian dishes. Some of the public rooms display interesting photographs from the early days of Irish aviation. *Dublin Airport, Dublin 1, tel. 01/379211. 187 rooms. Facilities: bar, restaurant, gift shop/newsagent. AE, DC, MC, V.*

★ **Killiney Castle.** A 13-km (8-mi) drive from the Dublin city center, this hotel is more agreeably situated than any lodging in the capital, for its lofty location allows guests sweeping views over south Dublin and parts of Dublin Bay. The original part of the hotel is a 19th-century stone castle, with a substantial modern addition where you'll find the bedrooms. Although some of these rooms are narrow, many are furnished with antiques and four-poster beds; they also feature large bathrooms and plenty of storage space. Ask for a room at the front of the building; the nighttime view over the lights of Dublin is spectacular. Restaurants include Jesters, in the basement disco, which has a mediocre grill menu, and Truffles, on the ground floor, which serves more-formal breakfasts, lunches, and dinners. The health center offers treadmills, bicycles, a sauna, squash and tennis courts, and a 25-m (82-ft) indoor heated pool, and the hotel is convenient to golfing, horseback riding, and fishing. At the side of the hotel stands Killiney Hill, a viewpoint in a public park; the seaside village of Dalkey and Killiney Beach are both within comfortable walking distance. *Killiney, Co. Dublin, tel. 01/851533. 94 rooms. Facilities: 2 restaurants, health center, parking. AE, DC, MC, V.*

Moderate

Dalkey Island. To get to this converted 19th-century two-story mansion on the edge of the sea, you take a pleasant drive out to

Dalkey, a seaside village 13 km (8 mi) south of the city center; the village is also easily accessible by DART train. In the lobby, you'll find a photograph that shows the house 70 years ago. Although the pale pastel rooms are a bit cramped, they all look out to the Dalkey Island, and their balconies are useful in the summer. You'll find the service here friendly and informal. The relaxing bar and restaurant are popular with local residents. *Coliemore Harbour, Dalkey, Co. Dublin, tel. 01/850377. 20 rooms. Facilities: restaurant. AE, DC, MC, V.*

Kilternan Golf Hotel. This grand, rambling hotel, with extensions added to a 19th-century mansion, features a splendid setting that looks out on the rugged, wooded mountains around Enniskerry. The 16-km (10-mi) journey from Dublin center can be tedious when the traffic is slow moving, especially from 5 to 6 PM on weekdays, but the hotel's location is more than ample reward. Each of the spacious bedrooms has a double and a single bed, as well as a balcony and private bath. Ask for a room that overlooks the golf course and Scalp Mountain. The extensive sports facilities feature an artificial ski slope, a golf course, and a tennis court; the full gym includes exercise bicycles and a sauna. *Kilternan, Dublin 18, tel. 01/955559. 53 rooms. Facilities: restaurant, sports gym, TV. AE, DC, MC, V.*

Montrose. This well-designed hotel, located near the Irish TV and radio studios (RTE) and across the road from University College's Belfield campus, features large, relaxing bedrooms that were recently repainted. It is only a 15-minute cab ride from the city center. *Stillorgan Rd., Dublin 4, tel. 01/693311. 190 rooms. Facilities: bar, restaurant, gift shop/newsagent, hairdresser. AE, DC, MC, V.*

Royal Marine. A 19th-century seaside edifice, this hotel has been totally overhauled in recent years, and its public areas, bar, and restaurant have been completely modernized. The comfortable, capacious bedrooms have also been refurnished with contemporary decor; the eight suites with four-poster beds and separate sitting rooms preserve the lofty ceilings of the original building. Ask for a room at the front of the hotel, facing a gorgeous view of Dun Laoghaire harbor. *Dun Laoghaire, Co. Dublin, tel. 01/801911. 90 rooms. Facilities: restaurant. AE, DC, MC, V.*

Skylon. This modern five-story hotel, designed as a square box, with a concrete-and-glass facade, is located on the main road into the Dublin city center from the airport. The generous-size rooms have been plainly decorated in cool pastel shades; they have little furniture other than the double beds and a couple of easy chairs. The ground-floor area has been substantially renovated, with a large bar and a restaurant. The cooking is adequate but uninspired, with dishes such as grilled steak, poached cod, and omelets. *Upper Drumcondra Rd., Dublin 9, tel. 01/379121. 92 rooms. Facilities: bar, restaurant, gift shop/newsagent. AE, DC, MC, V.*

Tara Tower. A seven-story minitower in the Doyle chain, this unpretentious, informal hotel is not far from the Booterstown bird sanctuary. Its best rooms face Dublin Bay, stretching to the Howth peninsula. On the ground floor, you'll find a large bar and a restaurant attractively refurbished with rustic woodwork. The menu includes grilled fish, steaks, and omelets, but the food quality varies. The hotel service, though, is very personable. *Merrion Rd., Dublin 4, tel. 01/694666. 88 rooms. Facilities: bar, restaurant, gift shop/newsagent. AE, DC, MC, V.*

The Arts and Nightlife

Compared with most large cities, nightlife in Dublin may seem comparatively staid, beginning around 10 PM and continuing until 4 AM. The plethora of pubs, some 900 in the city, are one source of entertainment, and many in the city center offer musical performances, often folk or jazz. For a good listing of cultural and evening events, consult *The Irish Times*, which has a daily guide to what's happening in Dublin and in the rest of the country, as well as complete film and theater schedules; *The Evening Herald* and *Evening Press*, with useful listings of theaters, cinemas, and pubs offering live entertainment; and *In Dublin*, a fortnightly guide to all film, theater, and musical events around the city.

The Arts

Classical Music The main theater for classical music performance is the **National Concert Hall** (Earlsfort Terr., tel. 01/711888), which stages orchestral concerts and smaller recitals throughout the year. The **Royal Hospital Kilmainham** (Military Rd., tel. 01/718666) also presents frequent classical concerts.

Films Dublin has two dozen cinema screens in the city center, but only a few in the suburbs, that show a selection of current releases made in Ireland and abroad. Two theaters popular with movie buffs are the **Lighthouse** (Middle Abbey St., tel. 01/679–2644) and the **Screen** (College St., tel. 01/714988). **The Irish Film Institute** (6 Eustace St., tel. 01/679–5744) has ambitious plans for a new Irish film center, including two theaters.

Theater For theatrical productions, the main venues are the **Abbey** (Lower Abbey St., tel. 01/744505), which stages mainstream traditional plays, mostly Irish, and its sister theater at the same address, the **Peacock,** which offers more experimental drama. The Abbey originally opened in 1904 and became an important center for the Irish cultural renaissance. Poet W. B. Yeats and Lady Gregory, an aristocratic writer and patron of the arts, were prominent in the early Abbey, encouraging young playwrights such as J. M. Synge. The original theater burned down in 1951, but it reopened with a modern design in 1966.

The **Gate** (Cavendish Row, Parnell Sq., tel. 01/744045; *see* Tour 2, above) stages a range of contemporary plays, while the **Gaiety** (South King St., tel. 01/771717) and the **Olympia** (Dame St., tel. 01/778962) both provide family-style entertainment. The **Project Art Centre** (39 E. Essex St., tel. 01/712321), the **Andrew's Lane Theatre** (9–11 Andrew's La., tel. 01/679–5720), and the **Tivoli** (Francis St., tel. 01/535998) present experimental productions.

Nightlife

Irish Cabarets/ Dance Clubs **Leeson Street,** off St. Stephen's Green, is a main nightclub area from 10 PM to 4 AM. Clubs on this street include **Fanny Hills, Suesey Street,** and **Von B's.** Dress at these places is informal, but jeans and sneakers are not welcome. Drink prices can be exorbitant, up to £20 for a mediocre bottle of wine.

Abbey Tavern (Howth, Co. Dublin, tel. 01/390307) offers a rip-roaring cabaret with rousing Irish traditional songs.

Bracmor Rooms (Churchtown, tel. 01/988664) presents Irish and international stars in cabaret, with backing groups.

Burlington Hotel (Upper Leeson St., tel. 01/605222) features a well-performed Irish cabaret, with dancing, music, and song.

Jury's Hotel (Ballsbridge, tel. 01/605000) stages a similar cabaret show to that at the Burlington Hotel.

Pink Elephant (S. Frederick St., tel. 01/775876), a noted night spot with a young crowd, has a full bar and books the latest rock stars.

Irish Music and Dancing

Comhaltas Ceoltóiri Éireann (35 Belgrave Sq., Monkstown, tel. 01/800295) offers boisterous summer evenings of genuine Irish music and dancing.

Pubs

Bad Bob's Backstage Bar (34 E. Essex St., tel. 01/775482), is a very popular pub with the young; the late-night crowd enjoys its live rock music.

Bartley Dunnes (32 Lower Stephen St., tel. 01/533137), with its near dark interior, attracts black-leather-and-chain-clad young people; its atmosphere is unusual because of its clientele, but it can be fun.

Brazen Head (Bridge St., tel. 01/779549), Dublin's oldest pub, dates back to 1688; with its stone walls and open fires, it has changed little over the years. The place is renowned for traditional music performances, as well as for lively sing-along sessions on Sunday evenings.

Dockers (5 Sir John Rogerson's Quay, tel. 01/771692) is a trendy, riverside establishment, just round the corner from Windmill Lane Studios, where U2 and other noted bandsr noted bands record. Bono of U2 is a frequent visitor here. You'll find sing-alongs here by the piano.

Doheny & Nesbitt (5 Lower Baggot St., tel. 01/762945), a traditional spot with dark wooden decor and smoke-darkened ceilings, has hardly changed over the years. Its snugs are favoredsonalities.

Horse Shoe Bar (Shelbourne Hotel, St. Stephen's Green, tel. 01/766471) has comparatively little space for drinkers around the semicircular bar; it's a popular meeting pllar meeting place for Dublin's smart social set, including politicians.

McDaid's (3 Harry St., tel. 01/679–4395) attracted boisterous Brendan Behan and other leading writers in the 1950s; its wild literary reputation still lingers, although the bar has been discreetly modernized and Dublin's prry generation is altogether quieter.

Mother Redcap's Tavern (Back La., tel. 01/538306) opened two years ago. It's an authentic re-creation of a 17th-century Dublin tavern, with stone walls from an old flour mill, beams, and plenty of old prints of the city, as well as trendy Victorian posters.

Neary's (1 Chatham St., tel. 01/777371), with an exotic Victorian-style interior, was once the haunt of music-hall artists, as well as of a certain literary set. Today, actors and actresses actresses from the adjacent Gaiety Theater enliven the scene.

O'Donoghue's (15 Merrion Row, tel. 01/762807), a cheerful smoky hangout offers impromptu musical performances that often spill out onto the street.

Ryan's Pub (28 Parkgate St., tel. 01/776097) is one of Dublin's last genuine late Victorian-era pubs, which has changed little since its last 1896 remodeling. Its dark mahogany counters, old-fashioned lamps, and snugs create a marvelously restful setting.

Slattery's (129 Capel St., tel. 01/727971) has an undistinguished decor, but it remains one of the city's best traditional music showcases, with performances held almost every night.

Stag's Head (1 Dame Court, tel. 01/6793701) dates back to 1770 and was rebuilt in 1895; it has a smoky atmosphere and an unusual counter, fashioned from Connemara red marble.

Toner's (139 Lower Baggot St., tel. 01/763090), though billed as a Victorian bar, actually goes back 200 years, with an original flagstone floor to prove its antiquity, as well as wooden drawers running up to the ceiling, a relic of the days when bars doubled as grocery shops.

4 Dublin Environs

by Hugh Oram

Only an hour or two from Dublin, you can find yourself deep in the countryside, with landscape ranging from County Wicklow's magnificent rugged mountain scenery, to County Kildare and County Meath's flat pastoral lands rich in historical remains. Newgrange in County Meath is perhaps Ireland's most important prehistoric site. Astride the River Boyne in County Louth is Drogheda, a fascinating town settled by the Vikings in the early 10th century. The Dublin environs also have an impressive eastern coastline stretching from Counties Wicklow to Louth, punctuated by delightful harbor towns and fishing villages. The coast is virtually unspoiled for its entire length.

Essential Information

Important Addresses and Numbers

Tourist Information To answer questions on travel in the Dublin environs and for help in making lodging reservations, contact one of the following Tourist Information Offices: **Dublin City Center** (Upper O'Connell St., tel. 01/747733), **Dublin Airport** (tel. 01/376387), **Dun Laoghaire** (tel. 01/806984), **Dundalk** (tel. 042/35484), or **Mullingar** (tel. 044/48650).

Mullingar is the head office of tourism covering the counties of Wicklow, Louth, Meath, and Kildare. During the summer, temporary Tourist Information Offices are open throughout the environs, in towns such as Arklow, Bray, and Wicklow Town, in County Wicklow; Drogheda, in County Louth; Trim, in County Meath; and Athy, Kildare, Naas, and Newbridge, in County Kildare.

Emergencies For **police, fire,** or **ambulance,** dial 999.

Getting Around

By Car The easiest and best way to tour Dublin's environs is by car, because public transportation is infrequent to the more outlying areas. Dublin Airport offers a choice of a dozen car rental companies, and all the main national and international firms have branches in Dublin's city center. Some reliable car rental firms in the Dublin vicinity include: **Avis** (Jury's Hotel, tel. 01/683394; 51 Grafton St., tel. 01/778877; Hanover St., tel. 01/774010; Dublin Airport, tel. 01/372369), **Hertz** (O'Connell St., tel. 01/788862; Leeson St. Bridge, tel. 01/602255; Dublin Airport, tel. 01/429333), and **Murray's Rent-a-Car** (Baggot St. Bridge, tel. 01/681777; Dublin Airport, tel. 01/378179).

By Bus Bus services link Dublin with main and smaller towns in the environs. All bus services for the region depart from Busaras, the central bus station, at Store Street. For bus inquiries, contact: **Bus Éireann** (tel. 01/366111).

By Train Train services run the length of the east coast, from Dundalk to Arklow, with many intervening stops, including Dublin, where the main stations are Connolly Station (Amiens St.) and Pearse Station (Westland Row). From Heuston Station, trains run westwards to Newbridge, The Curragh, and Kildare Town. For train inquiries, contact: **Iarnród Éireann (Irish Rail,** tel. 01/366222).

Guided Tours

Bus Éireann (tel. 01/366111; information available Mon.–Sat., 9–7, Sun., 10–7) runs guided bus tours to many of the historic and scenic locations throughout the Dublin environs on a daily basis during the summer. Most tours depart from Busaras Station, Dublin, but some leave from regional destinations, such as Dun Laoghaire.

Gray Line (tel. 01/619666), a privately owned touring company, also runs many guided bus tours throughout the Dublin environs between May and September.

Exploring the Dublin Environs

Numbers in the margin correspond with points of interest on the Dublin Environs map.

County Wicklow

East Wicklow Begin your tour of the eastern part of County Wicklow, often called the Garden of Ireland, in its main town and administrative center,
1 **Wicklow Town,** 51 km (32 mi) south of Dublin on the N11, about one hour's driving time. Frequent train services to Wicklow Town run about every two hours from Connolly and Pearse Stations in Dublin. Buses leave from Dublin about every two hours. Train and bus times are both about 1¼ hours.

The English name of Wicklow derives from the Danish words *Wyking alo* (Viking meadow). The town's Main Street is attractive, divided into two levels and framed by trees. On this street at the entrance of the town are the extensive ruins of a 13th-century Franciscan friary, which was closed down under the 16th-century dissolution of the monasteries in the area. Inquire at the nearby priest's house (Main St., tel. 0404/67196) to view the ruins. Also on Main Street is a statue in honor of the town's most famous resident, Captain Robert Halpin (1836–1894). Wicklow has long had a strong seafaring tradition, but Halpin's career culminated in his commanding the *Great Eastern,* the pioneer mid-19th-century ironclad steamship that laid the first transatlantic cable. A grateful British government awarded Halpin a substantial pension, and he used the money to build Tinakilly House, 3 km (2 mi) on the Dublin side of the town, which is now a hotel and restaurant (*see* Dining and Lodging, below).

The most appealing area of Wicklow Town lies around the harbor. Harbour Road leads down to the pier; several alleyways connect this road to Main Street. A bridge across the River Vartry leads to a second, smaller pier, which is situated at the northern end of the harbor. From this end, follow the shingle beach, which stretches for 5 km (3 mi); behind the beach is the broad Lough, a lagoon noted for its wildfowl. Immediately to the south of the harbor, perched on a promontory that is a good viewing point for much of the Wicklow coastline, is the ruin of the **Black Castle.** This structure was built in 1176 by Maurice Fitzgerald, an Anglo-Norman lord who arrived with the English invasion of Ireland in 1169. The freely accessible ruins ex-

Dublin Environs

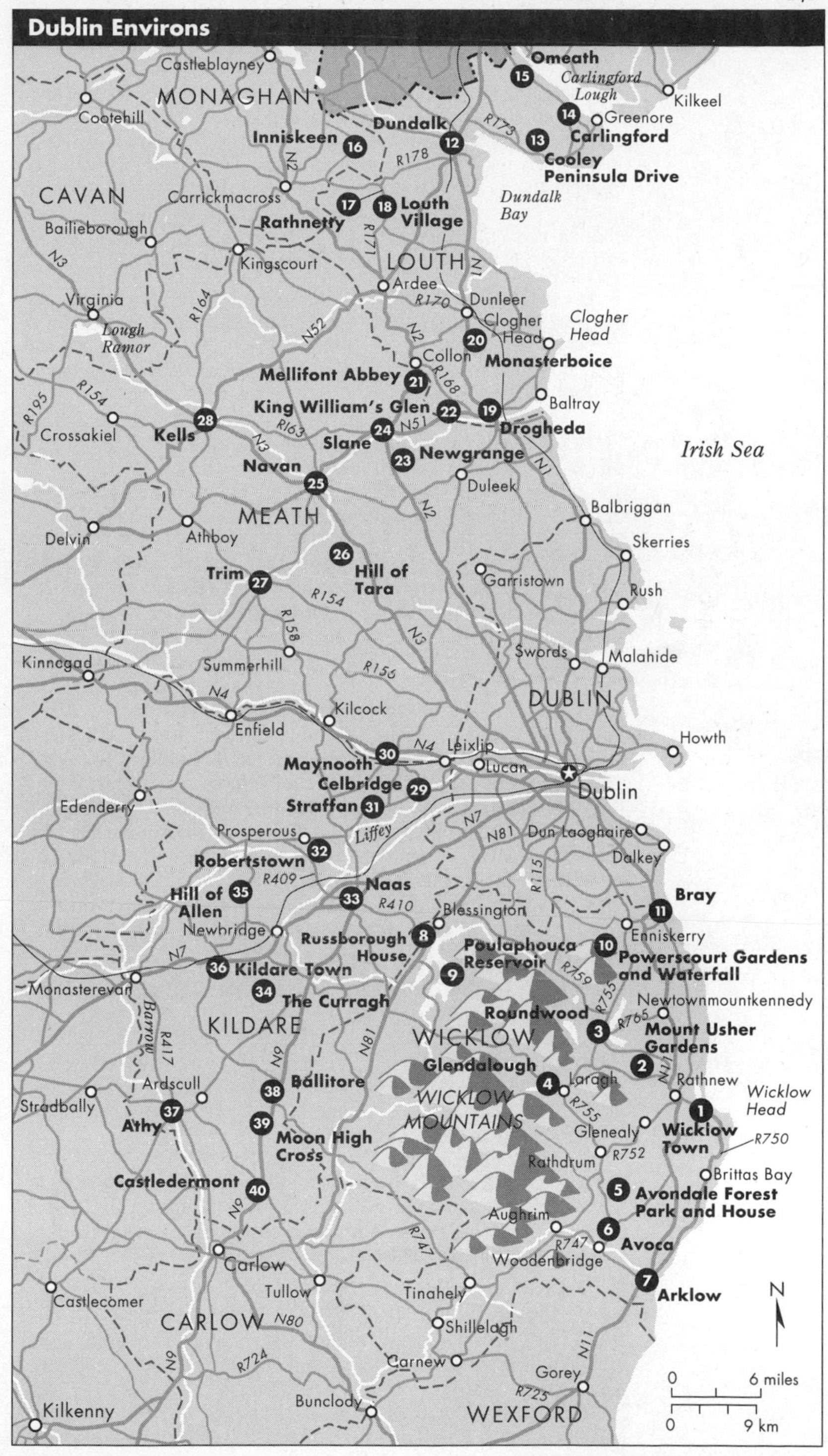

tend over a large area; with some difficulty, you can climb down to the water's edge.

Between one bank of the River Vartry, which flows into the harbor, and the road to Dublin stands the 18th-century **St. Lavinius Church** (Church of Ireland). The building is worth a visit to investigate the Romanesque door from a medieval church, the pews, the 12th-century stonework, and the atmospheric graveyard. The church is topped off by a green onion-shaped cupola, made from copper, which was added as an afterthought in 1771. *Admission free. Open daily 10–6.*

At press time, work was partially completed to transform the old town jail, just above Market Square, into a heritage center that will trace the stormy history of the county and also act as a genealogical center. The center is scheduled to open sometime in 1991.

Time Out **Pizza del Forno** (Main St., tel. 0404/67075) serves inexpensive pizzas and steaks, as well as vegetarian dishes. With its red-and-white-check tablecloths, low lighting, and pizza oven blazing away, it provides an agreeable stop for the whole family.

From Wicklow Town, travel 6½ km (4 mi) north along the R750 and N11 roads to **Ashford.** Just before the village of Ashford,
2 turn directly off the main road into **Mount Usher Gardens.** At the entrance to the gardens, you'll find a cluster of crafts shops, including a pottery workshop, as well as a bookshop. You pass through the self-service restaurant to reach the gardens, which cover more than 20 acres on either side of the narrow River Vartry. Edward Walpole, who owned a Dublin textile firm, took over the ancient mill in 1868 and converted the site to gardens. Succeeding generations of the Walpole family maintained the grounds so that today the gardens, under new ownership, have more than 5,000 species, including eucalypti, azaleas, camellias, and rhododendrons. Visitors can wander along the garden paths, through woodland glades, and across bridges that span the river. *Tel. 0404/40116. Admission: £2 adults, £1.30 children. Open Mar. 17–Oct. 31, Mon.–Sat. 10:30–6, Sun. 11–6.*

From Ashford, drive north on the N11; after 11 km (7 mi), you'll reach the small town of **Newtownmountkennedy.**

Time Out **Harvey's Bistro** (tel. 01/819203), on the Dublin end of Newtownmountkennedy, is a two-story cottage that has been converted into a restaurant; it specializes in tasty Irish home cooking, with dishes such as corned beef and cabbage.

Turn off by the Catholic St. Joseph's Church on Newtownmountkennedy's main street and take the R765 west for 9½ km (6 mi)—past the reservoirs that supply Dublin's drinking water—as far as Roundwood.

3 **Roundwood,** standing 279 m (900 ft) above sea level, is the highest village in Ireland. It consists of little more than a broad main street, although the Sunday-afternoon market held in the village hall, where cakes, jams, and other homemade goods are sold, can be a lively affair. From the main street, by the Roundwood Inn (*see* Dining and Lodging, below), a minor road leads west for 8 km (5 mi) to two lakes, **Lough Dan** and **Lough**

Tay, lying deep between forested mountains like Norwegian fjords.

Leave Roundwood by driving south on the R755, the main road
4 to **Glendalough** for 9½ km (6 mi). (Glendalough can also be easily reached from Dublin by taking the St. Kevin's bus service, which departs daily at 11:30 AM from the front of the Royal College of Surgeons on St. Steven's Green; cost: £7 round-trip.) This valley with two lakes, situated between forested mountains, is the setting of some of Ireland's most significant monastic ruins. The 6th-century missionary St. Kevin, a descendant of the royal house of Leinster, came to the valley to live as a hermit. According to one tale, St. Kevin was pursued here by a stunning redhead named Kathleen, whom he proceeded to throw from a cliff into one of the nearby lakes. Whether or not the story is true, St. Kevin did indeed found a monastery here. Despite the attacks of the Vikings in the 9th and 10th centuries, the religious settlement continued to develop, only waning when English forces overran it in 1398. Substantial ruins were left behind, which can be viewed today. Most of the buildings among the ruins are open all day and are freely accessible. The best introduction to the glories of the valley and lakeside is the new **Visitor Center,** which has models of Glendalough and an audiovisual presentation that tells its whole history. *Tel. 0404/45325. Open Mar.–May and Sept.–Oct., daily 10–5; June–Aug., daily 10–7.*

The **Teampaill na Skellig** (Church of the Oratory), on the south shores of the Upper Lake in Glendalough, is probably the oldest building on the site, dating from St. Kevin's time. A little to the east of this oratory is **St. Kevin's Bed,** a tiny cave in the rockface, about 9¼ m (30 ft) above the level of the lake, where St. Kevin lived his hermit's existence in the 6th century. It is not easily accessible; you approach the cave by boat, but climbing the cliff to the cave can be dangerous and is not recommended. At the southeast corner of the Upper Lake is **Reefert Church,** also dating from the 6th century, whose ruins consist of a nave and a chancel. The saint also lived in the adjoining ruined beehive hut with five crosses, which marked the original boundary of the monastery. At this point, you'll have a superb view up the valley.

The ruins by the edge of the Lower Lake are the most important part of the whole Glendalough site. The gateway, beside the Royal Hotel, is the only surviving entrance to an ancient monastic site anywhere in Ireland. Inside, you'll observe an extensive graveyard, with many elaborately decorated crosses. The perfectly preserved, six-story **Round Tower,** which was built around the 11th or 12th century, stands 31 m (100 ft) high. The entrance to the first story stands 8 m (25 ft) above ground level. The largest building here, and on the entire Glendalough site, is the 7th- to 9th-century **Cathedral,** which is substantially intact, with the nave, chancel, and ornamental oolite limestone window, which may have been imported from England. The nave is small for a large church, only 9 m (30 ft) wide by 15½ m (50 ft) long.

South of the cathedral is the 3½-m- (11-ft-) high Celtic **St. Kevin's Cross.** Made of granite, it is the best-preserved such cross on the site. **St. Kevin's Church,** an early barrel-vaulted oratory with a high-pitched stone roof, is also worth a visit. Besides exploring all the ruins, you can also take extensive walks around the lakes; the scenery around the Upper Lake is particularly awesome.

From Glendalough, drive for 1½ km (1 mi) to the crossroads of Laragh; from here take the R755 to Rathdrum, a distance of 21½ km (13½ mi), and drive on the R752 for a further 16 km (10 mi) to Wicklow Town.

South of Wicklow Town

From Wicklow Town, drive to Rathnew on the R750 for 3 km (2 mi), then turn left in Rathnew onto the R752 in the direction of Rathdrum. After 5 km (3 mi), you'll pass the small village of Glenealy; continue on for 8 km (5 mi) to Rathdrum; 1½ km (1 mi) south of the town, signposted off the R752 to Woodenbridge, is
5 the entrance to **Avondale Forest Park,** the location of **Avondale House.**

Avondale House resonates in Irish history, for this was the home once owned by Charles Stewart Parnell, the 19th-century nationalist leader, who fell in love with a married woman named Kitty O'Shea; when her husband instituted divorce proceedings in 1890, the revelation of Parnell's affair during court hearings quickly ruined his political career. The house, built in 1779, was acquired by John Parnell, great-grandfather of Charles Stewart, in 1795; Charles was born here in 1846. The two-story dwelling was used by the political leader as a residence and for social occasions, until his premature death in 1891.

The whole house has been flawlessly restored, with the reception and dining rooms on the ground floor filled with Parnell memorabilia, including many political cartoons of his time, which portray his efforts to secure home rule for Ireland. The surrounding estate and forest park are equally impressive. The park, which extends to 523 acres, mainly on the west bank of the Avondale River, was the first forest in Ireland to be taken over by the state, in 1904; in subsequent years, a forestry school has been active here. Visitors can take a 5½-km (3½-mi) walk along the river or stroll along a pine trail and an exotic tree trail. They may also observe the ruins of a teahouse and the stump of a 350-year-old beech tree, with all the rings marked in relation to historic events in Ireland and the world. *Tel. 0404/46111. Admission: 50p. Car park fee: £2. Open May–Sept., daily 10–1 and 2–6; Oct.–Apr., weekends noon–6.*

Return to the main road, the R752, and continue south for a fur-
6 ther 6½ km (4 mi) to **Avoca,** a small hamlet set amid heavily forested hills at the confluence of the Rivers Avonbeg and Avonmore. At this deeply peaceful setting, beneath a riverside tree, the great poet Thomas Moore (1779–1852) composed his poem "The Meeting of the Waters," in 1807. You can take some pleasant forest walks here, and visit **Avoca Handweavers** (tel. 0402/5105), the oldest handweaving mill in Ireland, with colorful tweed fabrics for sale.

Three km (2 mi) south of Avoca is another attractive village, **Woodenbridge,** situated at a meeting of the Rivers Aughrim and
7 Avoca. Continue for 8 km (5 mi) on the R747 to **Arklow,** the only industrialized town in County Wicklow; it has a fertilizer factory. The town is also an important fishing and maritime town in the county; though much of its appearance is somewhat grim, you can take restful walks along the river bank and around the harbor area. At the **Arklow Pottery Factory** on the quays, you

can take guided tours and look at its crafts shop. *Tel. 0402/32401. Open weekdays 9:30–1 and 2–4:45, weekends 10–4:45.*

Arklow has a small **Maritime Museum,** set in the public library building by the railway station; it traces the distinguished seafaring traditions of the town. *Tel. 0402/32868. Admission: £1 adults, 50p children. Open June–Sept., weekdays 10–1 and 2–5.*

To the immediate north of Arklow, off the R150 coastal road, are sandy beaches and quiet coves. The largest beach on **Brittas Bay** is popular in the summer with those on holiday from Dublin.

From Arklow, drive on the R747 road, passing Aughrim, a lovely little town, after 14½ km (9 mi). From Aughrim, take the R747, passing another small village, Tinahely; continue 8 km (5 mi) south of Tinahely on the R749 road, as far as **Shillelagh,** an attractive one-street village, lined with stone cottages. About 3 km (2 mi) to the east of Shillelagh is **Coolattin Wood,** one of the last original native woods left in Ireland, with impressively tall oak trees. The timber for the roof of Dublin's St. Patrick's Cathedral came from here.

From Shillelagh, return to Wicklow Town via Carnew, Gorey, and Arklow on the R725/N11, a total of 77 km (48 mi).

West Wicklow

8

Russborough House is one of the highlights of the western part of County Wicklow; it is situated just off the N81, 3 km (2 mi) south of Blessington, which can also be reached from Dublin by bus. To reach Russborough House from Wicklow Town by car, drive in the direction of Ashford on the main N11 road (in the direction of Dublin); then take the minor road that leads to Glendolough. From here, take the R758 across the Wicklow Gap as far as the main N81 road. When you reach the N81, turn right in the direction of Dublin; this road will lead directly to Russborough.

Faced in gray Wicklow granite, this outstanding Palladian structure, built between 1740 and 1750, was designed by the architect Richard Castle, the first earl of Milltown. From the main block of the house, two semicircular loggias reach out to embrace the wings.

The main rooms of the building are elaborately decorated in baroque-style plasterwood, executed by the Francini brothers, Italian craftsmen who were active in Dublin in the mid-18th century. The house belongs to Sir Alfred Beit, the nephew of a German entrepreneur, and the Beit art collection that is on display includes works by Gainsborough, Goya, Rubens, and Velázquez, as well as bronzes and porcelain. Russborough looks out over an impressive artificial lake to the mountains of Wicklow; the extensive woodland on the estate is open to visitors. *Tel. 045/652329. Admission: £2.50, upstairs £1. Open Easter, Oct. 31, Sun., and public holidays, 2:30–5:30; June–Aug., daily 2:30–5:30.*

Leave the grounds of Russborough House, turn right onto the main N81 road, and travel north for 3 km (2 mi) to **Blessington,** with its very wide main street lined on both sides by tall trees. This small market town, founded in the second half of the 17th century, used to be a stop on the Dublin–Waterford mail-coach service in the mid-19th century, and until 1932 a quaint steam train ran from here to Dublin, along the side of the main road.

9 Near Blessington is the great **Poulaphouca Reservoir,** which provides water for Dublin. At the southern end of the reservoir lie two glens of outstanding natural beauty, Poulaphouca and Hollywood. Near the latter glen are fine views from the summit of Church Mountain. You can drive around the entire perimeter of the reservoir, on minor roads.

From Blessington, drive north on the N81 for 8 km (5 mi), then turn right onto the R759 and continue through wild upland country for 25½ km (16 mi) to the Sally Gap, a bleak crossroads. At this junction, turn left onto the R115 for a further 13 km (8 mi) to Glencree; from here drive another 25½ km (16 mi) east along minor roads to Enniskerry.

The village of **Enniskerry** is a pretty spot, built around a central square and surrounded by the wooded Wicklow Mountains.
(Enniskerry can also be reached directly from Dublin by taking
the No. 44 bus from the Dublin quays area.) The main reason to
10 visit here, however, is the estate of the **Powerscourt Gardens
and Waterfall.** The grounds were originally granted to Sir
Richard Wingfield, the first viscount of Powerscourt, by King
James I of England in 1609. Richard Castle, the architect of
Russborough House (*see* above) designed the grand Powerscourt House in the Palladian style; it was constructed between
1731 and 1740. In 1974 the house burned down, although there
are now plans to restore the house to its original splendor, complete with antique furnishings and paintings. However, the
Powerscourt Gardens, which were laid out from 1745 to 1767
and redesigned from 1843 to 1875, survive beautifully and are
considered among the finest in Europe. The gardens were originally planned by Daniel Robertson, who drew his inspiration
from two sources: the Villa Butera in Sicily, and copious
amounts of sherry.

The gardens feature sweeping terraces, antique sculptures, and a circular pond and fountain flanked by winged horses; you have a magnificent view of the Italianate patterned ramps, lawns, and pond across the Dargle Valley to Sugar Loaf Mountain, one of Ireland's most dramatic vistas. The grounds include many specimen trees, an avenue of monkey puzzles, a parterre of brightly colored summer flowers, and a Japanese garden. The kitchen gardens, with their modest rows of flowers, are a striking antidote to the classical formality of the main sections. The gardens also offer a restaurant, a crafts center, and a children's play area. *Tel. 01/867676. Admission: £2 adults, £1 children. Open Mar.–Oct., daily 9–5:30.*

The equally renowned Powerscourt Waterfall, with a spectacular height of nearly 124 m (400 ft), is situated 5 km (3 mi) south of the gardens; it is the highest falls in the British Isles. *Admission: £1 adults, 50p children. Open daily 10:30–7, or until dusk in winter.*

From Enniskerry, travel 8 km (5 mi) along the road that skirts
11 the River Dargle toward **Bray,** an unspectacular seaside community that offers a good sea walk along a 1½-km- (1-mi-) long
promenade. (Bray may also be reached easily by the DART
train from Dublin.) At the top of Main Street, the Heritage
Center in the town hall houses many artifacts from Bray's history, such as old photographs and household items. *Tel. 01/
868205. Admission free. Open Wed., Sat., Sun. 2–6.*

Bray is perhaps more well known for **One Martello Terrace,** immediately by the harbor, where James Joyce (1882–1941) lived between 1887 and 1891. The writer used this house as setting for the Christmas dinner in *A Portrait of the Artist as a Young Man*. Today the house is privately owned but if you catch the owners on a good day, you may persuade them to show you the dining room. Although the residence has been renovated, the dining room portrayed in Joyce's novel still maintains the spirit of his time.

Immediately off the Bray–Greystones Road just south of Bray, the **Kilruddery Gardens,** dating from the 17th century, have fine beech hedges, Victorian statuary, and a parterre of lavender and roses. *Tel. 01/863405. Admission: £2. Open summer, daily 1–5.*

County Louth

Dundalk and the Cooley Peninsula 12

The first stop on our tour of County Louth, **Dundalk,** lies 83 km (52 mi) from Dublin on the N1, about a 1½-hour drive. Frequent train services run to Dundalk from Dublin's Connolly Station, departing at roughly 1½-hour intervals. The fastest express train is one hour. Buses to Dundalk leave Dublin about every 1½ hours; the trip takes about two hours.

The history of Dundalk, the main town of County Louth, dates back to the early Christian period, around the 7th century. The area near the town is closely connected with Cuchulainn, a renowned figure in Irish mythology. Today, it is a frontier town, only 9½ km (6 mi) from the Northern Ireland border, and few traces of its past remain. The remnants of two early religious foundations do survive, however; on Mill Street, the **bell tower** of a Franciscan monastery with Gothic windows dates from the 13th century, while the Church of Ireland's **St. Nicholas,** on Market Square, incorporates a 15th-century tower. The church was rebuilt in 1707 and has a large, early 19th-century transept. In the graveyard lies the tomb of Agnes Galt, sister of Robert Burns, the 18th-century Scottish poet. The church is open only during services.

In the town center stands the Catholic **St. Patrick's Cathedral,** built between 1835 and 1847 when the Gothic revival was at its height. It is largely modeled on the 15th-century King's College chapel, at Cambridge in England, with its buttresses and mosaics lining the chancel and the side chapel walls. *Open daily 8–6.*

Other 19th-century buildings in Dundalk include the **Market House,** the **Town Hall,** and the **Courthouse,** which is the most impressive of these, built in the 1820s in a severe Greek-revival style, with Doric columns supporting the portico. The Courthouse stands north of St. Patrick's Cathedral.

On the seaward side of Dundalk, extensive salt marshes and mud flats lie on the edge of Dundalk Bay. This area is one of the largest bird sanctuaries in Ireland: Species such as brant geese, curlews, and oystercatchers are regular visitors. Leave Dundalk by the N1 road, driving northwards for 6½ km (4 mi) to Ballymascanlon. Behind the Ballymascanlon Hotel (*see* Dining and Lodging, below), you'll find the neolithic **Proleek Dolmen,** a huge mushroomlike stone structure that dates back to the third millennium BC. Its capstone weighs nearly 50 tons.

13 From Ballymascanlon, you can begin the **Cooley Peninsula Drive.** Continue for 9½ km (6 mi) along the R173 road to **Gyles Quay,** a small coastal village with a clean, safe beach. From the village, you'll have excellent views southward along the County Louth coast to Clogher Head. The R173 continues round the east of the peninsula to **Greenore,** a distance of 11 km (7 mi). The town was built in Victorian times as a ferry-boat terminal, and today it has become a port for container traffic.

Continue 5 km (3 mi) eastwards from Greenore along the R176
14 to **Carlingford,** a small fishing town dating from medieval times. **King John's Castle,** a massive 13th-century fortress, still dominates the entrance to Carlingford Lough. An unusual feature of this structure is the west gateway, which is only wide enough to admit one horseman. At present, out of the historic buildings in the town, only the castle is freely accessible to the public. Other remnants from the medieval days include a tower from the town wall and one of its gates, which later became the town hall. The 15th-century **Mint Tower House** with mullioned windows also survives. The final survivor from the Middle Ages is **Taaffe's Castle,** a 16th-century fortified town house.

Carlingford also has some striking thatched cottages, but what makes it particularly attractive is its natural setting; the mountains of the Cooley Peninsula rise up from behind the town, the Carlingford Lough lies at its front, and the Mountains of the Mourne rise only 5 km (3 mi) away across the lough.

From Carlingford, drive for 6½ km (4 mi) northwest along the
15 R173 to reach **Omeath,** the final town on the peninsula.

Omeath was until recently the last main *Gaeltacht* (Irish-speaking) village in this vicinity. On the eastern side of the village, you'll find the open-air Calvary and Stations of the Cross at the monastery of the Rosminian Fathers. Jaunting cars (traps pulled by ponies) take visitors to the site from the quayside, which has stalls selling all kinds of shellfish from the nearby lough, including oysters and mussels. A ferry service runs from the quay to Warrenpoint, across the lough in Northern Ireland.

A narrow road climbs the mountains behind Omeath; as you climb higher, the views become ever more spectacular, stretching over the Mountains of the Mourne in the north and as far south as Skerries, 32 km (20 mi) north of Dublin. This narrow road leads back to Dundalk.

16 At **Inniskeen,** 14½ km (9 mi) west from Dundalk and just over the county boundary in Monaghan, the area's most famous poet is commemorated at the **Inniskeen Folk Museum,** in a converted church next to a well-preserved round tower. Patrick Kavanagh (1906–1969), born and raised here, became one of Ireland's leading poets and was brought back to the village for burial. *Tel. 042/78102. Donations appreciated. Open May–Aug., Sun. 2–5; other times, call for an appointment.*

17 In **Rathnetty,** 4.8 km (3 mi.) southwest of Dundalk on the R171, the landmark known as **Cuchulainn's Stone** is said to be the place where the ancient hero threw away his swords. He is reputed to have bound himself to this stone, so that even in death, he would face his enemies standing. Not until a bird perched on his shoulder could his adversaries be sure that Cuchulainn was really dead.

Continue for 1.6 km (1 mi) southwest on the R171 off of the
18 R178, to the small village of **Louth,** set on a hill affording commanding views of the surrounding countryside. St. Patrick, Ireland's patron saint, was reputed to have built his first church in this village in the 5th century. He made St. Mochta the first bishop of Louth; still standing in the village is the excellently preserved **St. Mochta's House,** an oratory dating from the 10th century, with a high-pitched stone roof. The house is freely accessible, but visitors should watch out for cattle in the surrounding field.

From Louth, continue on the R171 passing **Ardee,** a market town with a broad main street. Ardee features two 13th-century castles that are presently closed to the public. **St. Mary's Church of Ireland** on Main Street incorporates part of a 13th-century Carmelite church. Proceed south from Ardee to Drogheda, taking the N52, the R168, and the N51 for a total of 20 km (12½ mi).

Drogheda

Drogheda is one of the most enjoyable historic towns to visit on
19 the east coast of Ireland. It was colonized in 911 by the Danish Vikings; two centuries later, the town was taken over by Hugh de Lacy, the Anglo-Norman lord of Trim, in the neighboring county of Meath. At first, two separate towns existed on the northern and southern banks of the River Boyne. By the 14th century, Drogheda was not only heavily walled and fortified but also unified, making it one of the four most important towns in Ireland. Today it is an industrial town, with cement-making one of its key industries, but its setting on the River Boyne dispels any grim industrial feeling. Even the new ring road, which runs along the southern bank of the river, has not done too much visual damage to the urban landscape.

Originally, Drogheda had 10 gates in its town walls, but only one survives today: **St. Laurence's Gate,** with two four-story drum towers, is one of the most perfect examples in Ireland of a medieval town gate. Nearby, on Chord Road, is the **Siena Convent,** with a delightfully peaceful little chapel, well worth a visit. *Admission free. Open daily 8–8.*

From the St. Laurence's Gate, walk down the steep incline to the dock area, 400 yards away. The northern bank of the river is lined with the imposing warehouses built in the 18th century; this modern port is one of the busiest on the east coast. Towering over the river is the great length of the railway viaduct. Built around 1850 as part of the railway line from Dublin to Belfast, it is still used and is a splendid example of Victorian engineering; because of its height above the river, the viaduct remains the most prominent landmark in the town.

The center of the town, around West Street, is the historic heart of Drogheda. The bank building on the corner of West and Shop streets, called the **Tholsel,** is an 18th-century square granite edifice with a cupola; it used to house the town hall. Further along West Street is **St. Peter's,** a Roman Catholic parish church, built in striking Gothic style. It features a rather macabre point of interest for visitors: The preserved head of St. Oliver Plunkett is on display; he was a primate of Ireland who was martyred at Tyburn in London, in 1681. At the far end of West Street, where it becomes Narrow West Street, turn left toward the river, where you'll reach a well-preserved 13th-century tower. Rising 31 m (100 ft), it is the only remaining portion of an Augustinian foundation.

On the heights above West Street, approached by streets and laneways that climb upwards, you'll reach Fair Street. The 19th-century gray stone **Courthouse** displays 17th-century municipal charters, and a sword and mace presented to the town council by William III after the Battle of the Boyne in 1690. *Admission free. Open weekdays 9–5:30.*

At the eastern end of Fair Street, turn left into the grounds of **St. Peter's Church of Ireland,** built in a severe 18th-century style, with a tower and a steeple. The building is rarely open, except for Sunday services, but it has an impressive interior, with wooden pews, memorial tablets, an organ loft, and statuary. However, if the church is closed, you'll still have access to the fine views over the town from the churchyard. From this vantage point, Drogheda, despite all its recent development, still looks very much like a medieval town, with its uneven lines of slate roofs and chimneys.

The most striking feature on the horizon, seen from here, is the great mound of Millmount, on the other side of the river. You can reach this landmark off the Dublin Road, immediately south of the town center. The tower on top of this mound was built comparatively recently—two centuries ago—but the mound is said to be the site of an 11th-century BC burial place. The gateway to the top of the mound is usually open during the day; if you go to the top, you'll have more extensive views across Drogheda.

The old British Army barracks forming a square at the foot of the tower have been renovated and contain crafts workshops, including a weaver's shop, and the recently refurbished **Millmount Museum.** The museum houses many relics of eight centuries of Drogheda's commercial and industrial past, including painted banners of the old trade guilds; a circular, leather-covered coracle (the traditional fishing boat on the River Boyne); and many instruments and utensils from domestic and factory use. Rather surprisingly, the museum does not have many mementos of the most infamous episode in Drogheda's history, when the English leader Oliver Cromwell sacked the town in 1649, killing 3,000 people. *Tel. 041/36391. Admission free. Open summer, daily 3–6; Nov.–Apr., Wed.–Sun. 3–6. Crafts shops open all year, Mon.–Sat. 9:30–6.*

North of Drogheda

From Drogheda's center, take the minor road north that follows the northern bank of the River Boyne estuary for 11 km (7 mi) to **Baltray,** which still bears a close resemblance to an 18th-century Irish fishing village; from Baltray, continue north another 8 km (5 mi) to the fishing village of **Clogherhead.** Take a walk above the local harbor to the heights of Clogher Head for outstanding views north to the Mountains of the Mourne and south to Skerries.

From Clogherhead, take the R170 for 23 km (15 mi) to Dunleer, then turn south onto the N1 Dublin–Belfast road, returning in the Drogheda direction for 13 km (8 mi) to the small village of
20 **Monasterboice,** with its fine collection of high crosses. The 10th-century **Muireradach Cross,** which stands nearly 6 m (20 ft) high, is considered to be the best-preserved example of a high cross anywhere in Ireland; it features elaborate panels depicting biblical scenes, including a centerpiece of the Last

Judgment. From the adjacent Round Tower, 34 m (110 ft) high, the extent of the former monastic settlement at Monasterboice can be ascertained. The key to the tower door is held at the nearby gate lodge.

From Monasterboice, drive 9½ km (6 mi) west, passing through the small village of **Collon,** laid out in the 18th century with just a single main street. Continue 8 km (5 mi) south of Collon on the R168 and then take the signposted right turn down the minor
21 road to **Mellifont Abbey,** founded in 1142 as the first Cistercian monastery in Ireland; only fragments of the original ground plan survive. Some arches of the Romanesque cloister still exist, and substantial portions of the abbey buildings can still be seen, including the two-story chapter house, in the 12th-century English-Norman style. This structure was once a daily meeting place for the monks and now stores a collection of medieval glazed tiles. The lavabo is a curious structure, originally octagonal; it is now roofless, and only four walls are left.

West of Drogheda

King William's Glen lies 6½ km (4 mi) west of Drogheda, off the
22 N51, following the northern bank of the River Boyne. A portion of King William's Protestant army hid here before the Battle of the Boyne (1690), in which they were victorious, and the nearby site of the battle is marked; many of the Protestant-Catholic conflicts in present-day Northern Ireland can be traced to the immediate aftermath of this battle. Part of the battle site is also incorporated in the nearby **Townley Hall Estate,** which offers forest walks and a nature trail. Continue on a further 13 km (8 mi) west, branching off the N51, onto the signposted minor road leading to the prehistoric sites at Dowth, Knowth, and Newgrange.

The megalithic tombs of Dowth and Knowth are still in the excavation process and are not yet open to the public, but you can
23 visit **Newgrange,** one of the most spectacular prehistoric tombs in Europe. It was built in the fourth millennium BC, with some 250,000 tons of stones that were brought to the site by people with only a primitive knowledge of architectural technology. How they transported the thousands of stones to the site remains a mystery, but the grave may have been the world's earliest observatory. The mound above the tomb is more than 11 m (36 ft) at the front; white quartz stones were used for the retaining wall. The tomb is so carefully constructed that on the day of the winter solstice, the rays of the rising sun hit a roof box above the entrance to the grave. Then the rays shine for about 20 minutes down the passageway that leads to the interior and illuminate the burial chamber. Visitors to the interior of this Bronze Age tomb may see the effect re-created artificially. The geometric designs on some stones at the center of the burial chamber continue to baffle experts. The entire history of the site is narrated in the adjoining interpretive center. *Tel. 041/24488. Admission: £1.50. Open mid-June–mid-Sept., daily 10–7; Apr.–mid-June and mid-Sept.–mid-Oct., Mon.–Sat. 10–5, Sun. 2–5. Rest of year, Tues.–Sat. 10–1 and 2–5, Sun. 2–5.*

Return to the N51 and continue westwards for 5 km (3 mi) to the
24 agreeable crossroads village of **Slane.** Here you can visit the **Slane Castle demesne** (estate) and take a fine walk to a 16th-century building known as the **Hermitage,** constructed on the site where St. Erc, a local man who was converted to Christianity by St. Patrick and led a hermit's existence. Another pleas-

ant tree-lined walk takes you along the River Boyne. The castle itself is not generally open to the public, but it does have a nightclub and a restaurant.

The **Old Mill Transport Museum,** situated near the River Boyne, features about 20 antique cars, as well as old commercial vehicles, motorcycles, horse-drawn carts, and bicycles. You can also stop here for tea. *Tel. 041/51827. Admission: £1. Open May–Aug., daily noon–6; Sept.–Apr., Sun. 2–6.*

About 1½ km (1 mi) to the north of Slane is the 155-m- (500-ft-) high **Slane Hill,** where St. Patrick proclaimed the arrival of Christianity in 433 by lighting the Paschal Fire. From the top of the hill, you'll have sweeping views of the Boyne valley; on a clear day, the panorama stretches from Trim to Drogheda, a vista extending for 40 km (25 mi).

Ledwidge Cottage and Museum is located about 1 km (½ mi) east of Slane, on the road to Drogheda. This humble stone, slate-roofed cottage formerly belonged to Francis Ledwidge (1887–1917), a farm laborer who wrote lyric poetry. Just as he was beginning to win acknowledgment for his work, he joined the British Army and was killed in action in World War I. His cottage has now been furnished as it was in his time, a tribute to his short life. *Tel. 041/24285. Admission: £1. Open Mon.–Wed. 10–1 and 2–6; Sat. 10–1 and 2–7; Sun. 2–6.*

Time Out The **Conyngham Arms Hotel** (tel. 041/24155), at the crossroads in Slane, is an agreeable, family-run establishment with a self-service buffet during the day and set meals at dinner, including such entrées as chicken cooked in Irish-whiskey cream sauce, and shrimp scampi.

County Meath

Navan and the Hill of Tara

25

Begin your tour of County Meath at **Navan,** which is 48 km (30 mi) from Dublin on the N3. Allow one hour's driving time. Navan is 27 km (17 mi) on the N51 from Drogheda, about a half-hour drive. No trains run from Dublin to Navan, but buses leave Dublin every 1½ hours; the journey takes about 1¼ hours.

Navan, the main town of County Meath, is a busy market and mining town of considerable antiquity, with evidence of prehistoric settlements, but its real development did not begin until the 12th century, when Hugh de Lacy, lord of Trim, had the place walled and fortified, making it a defensive stronghold of the English Pale in eastern Ireland. On the main thoroughfare, Trimgate Street, the Catholic **St. Mary's Church,** built in 1839, features an interesting late-18th-century wood carving of the Crucifixion, the work of a local artist, Edward Smyth, who at the time was the greatest sculptor Ireland had produced since the Middle Ages. On Fridays, the Fair Green, beside the church, is the site of a bustling outdoor market. *Church open daily 8–8.*

You'll have the best view of the town from the motte of Navan, an artificial hill that may have once been the tomb of a prehistoric queen, but was more likely an Ice Age gravel deposit; it was adapted for use by D'Angulo, a 12th-century baron. D'Angulo was responsible for the first fairs in Navan. He also built a defensive castle on the hill, and today from its summit, visitors have panoramic views of the area and the River Blackwater. Navan also offers a tree-lined walk along the Ramparts, the towpath of the now disused Navan–Drogheda canal. With some dif iculty, because of the undergrowth, you can walk along the canal for 13 km (8 mi), as far as Slane.

26 The **Hill of Tara** is situated 13 km (8 mi) south of Navan; follow the main N3 road in the direction of Dublin. The hill is signposted to the right; take the minor road for 1½ km (1 mi). The site was originally the location for an Iron Age Celtic hill fort, surrounded by multiple ring forts; some of these were ruined in the 19th century by religious zealots from England who thought that they would find the ark of the covenant here. The hill gained prominence when used as the residence of one of the high kings of Ireland until the 11th century; the site became an inspiration for many Irish legends. The last king to live here was Malachy II, who died in 1022. While the Hill of Tara was used as a royal residence, a great national assembly (*feis*) was held here every three years, when laws were passed and tribal disputes were settled. Tara's influence waned with the arrival of Christianity.

Today on the hill, all that can be seen are a modern statue of St. Patrick and a pillar stone that may have been the coronation stone of the early kings. In the graveyard of the adjacent Anglican church, you'll find a pillar with the worn image of a pagan god and a Bronze Age standing stone. However, the main attraction of the Hill of Tara is its height: It stands more than 155 m (500 ft) above sea level, and from its top on a clear day, you can see across the flat central plain of Ireland, with the mountains of east Galway rising nearly 160 km (100 mi) away.

Trim

27 Return from the Hill of Tara to Navan; 16 km (10 mi) south of Navan is **Trim,** which has some of the finest medieval ruins in Ireland. In 1359, the town was walled on the instructions of the English king and its fortifications were strengthened; several parliaments were held here in the 15th century. Oliver Cromwell captured the town in 1649 and killed most of its inhabitants.

On the southern side of the town, **Trim Castle,** the largest Anglo-Norman fortress in Ireland, is by far the most imposing ruin in present-day Trim. In 1173, it was built by Hugh de Lacy on a site that slopes down to the placid waters of the River Boyne; it was soon destroyed and then rebuilt from 1190 to 1200. The ruins cover two acres and include an enormous keep with 21-m- (70-ft-) high turrets, flanked by rectangular towers; the outer castle wall is almost 500 yards long, and five D-shaped towers survive. The castle remains are freely accessible at all times. Facing the river is another ruin, that of the Royal Mint, an indication of Trim's political importance in the Middle Ages.

The **Yellow Steeple** overlooks the town from a ridge opposite the castle. Dating from 1368, it is a remnant of the 13th-century Augustinian abbey of St. Mary's. Much of the tower was destroyed in 1649 to prevent its falling into Cromwell's hands, and today, only the striking, 38-m- (125-ft-) high east wall remains. On Loman Street, the Church of Ireland cathedral, **St. Patrick's,** is of recent origin, dating back to the early 19th century, but the square tower belongs to an earlier structure, built in 1449. The town hall on Castle Street has records of Trim dating back to 1659; these papers may be seen during business hours on weekdays. The nearby Education Centre (tel. 046/31158), also on Castle Street, has regular exhibitions of historical material.

Several places of interest lie on the outskirts of Trim. At **Newtown,** 1¼ km (¾ mi) east of Trim on the banks of the River Boyne, is the ruin of what was the largest cathedral in Ireland, built by Simon de Rochfort, the first Anglo-Norman bishop of Meath, in 1210. At **Laracor,** 3 km (2 mi) south of Trim on the R158, there is a wall left of the rectory where Jonathan Swift, the great 18th-century satirical writer, was rector from 1699 to 1714. Nearby are the walls of the cottage where Esther Johnson, the "Stella" who inspired much of Swift's writings, once lived. From Laracor, continue for 8 km (5 mi) southeast along the R158 to **Summerhill,** one of the most pleasant villages of south County Meath; it has a large square and a village green with a 15th-century cross. Adjacent to Summerhill is **Cnoc an Linsigh,** an attractive area of forest walks with picnic sites, ideal for a half day's meandering. Many of the lanes that crisscross this vicinity of County Meath provide delightful driving between high hedgerows and afford occasional views of the lush pastoral countryside.

Kells
28

From Navan take the N3 northwest for 16 km (10 mi) to **Kells,** where St. Columba founded a monastery in the 6th century. In the 9th century, a group of monks from Iona in Scotland took refuge at Kells after being expelled by the Danes. Early in that century, these monks wrote and illustrated the Book of Kells, the Latin version of the four Gospels, and one of Ireland's greatest medieval treasures. During the mid-17th-century Cromwellian wars, it was removed to Trinity College, Dublin, for safekeeping and remains there to this day, where it is on view in the Old Library (*see* Chapter 3). A facsimile copy is on display in the Church of Ireland **St. Columba's,** in Kells. In the church graveyard stand four elaborately carved high crosses, while the stump of a fifth is in the marketplace; during the 1798 uprising, it was used as a gallows. Near the church is **St. Columba's House,** a small two-story 7th-century building measuring about 24 feet square; it is nearly 40 feet high with a steeply pitched stone roof, similar in appearance to St. Kevin's Church at Glendalough in County Wicklow (*see* County Wicklow, above) and Cormac's Chapel at Cashel in County Tipperary (*see* Chapter 6). Also adjacent to the church is the nearly 31-m (100-ft) high Round Tower, in almost perfect condition, dating from before 1076. Unusually, its top story has five windows, each pointing to an ancient entrance to the medieval town.

County Kildare

North Kildare
29

Celbridge, the first stop on our tour of County Kildare, is 24 km (15 mi) from Dublin; take the N4 road out of Dublin. Between Lucan and Leixlip, turn onto the R403 and continue on the last 6½ km (4 mi) to Celbridge. The drive from Dublin will take 30 minutes. No train service runs between Dublin and Celbridge. The Dublin City No. 67 bus leaves Middle Abbey Street, Dublin, at intervals of about one hour; the journey to Celbridge takes about one hour.

Celbridge is a rather nondescript market town, with a straggling main thoroughfare, but at the eastern end of this street, the gateway leads into one of Ireland's architectural glories, **Castletown House.** This immaculate Palladian-style house, with colonnaded wings at each side of the main building, was built in 1722 for William Conolly, the speaker of the Irish House of Commons. The house was designed by Alessandro Galilei, an Italian architect who created interiors as pleasing as the neoclassical facade. The intricate plasterwork in the halls was executed by the Italian Francini brothers; at the back of the house, the long gallery, painted in the blue Pompeian style and decorated with Venetian chandeliers, is the most notable of all the public rooms, which also include an 18th-century print room and a red drawing room. Downstairs, you'll find the nursery and the Victorian kitchen. The gardens are designed in the formal 18th-century style, with clipped hedges and neat lawns. The entire property is in an excellent state of preservation; the Irish Georgian Society was responsible for the renovation of both the house and the gardens. *Tel. 01/628–8502. Admission: £2.50. Open Apr.–Oct., weekdays 10–5, Sat. 11–6, Sun. 2–6; Nov.–Mar., weekends and public holidays 2–5.*

From Celbridge, take the R403 west and turn north on the
30 R406 to **Maynooth.** This tiny university town houses St. Patrick's College, a center for the training of Catholic priests that also serves as a lay university, much expanded in recent years. The ruins of **Maynooth Castle** are at the entrance to the college; the oldest part of the castle is the keep, which probably dates from the 13th century; although the keep and the great hall are still in reasonable condition, much of the castle was destroyed in 1647. The key to the castle can be obtained from Castleview House, opposite. *Tel. 01/628–5222. Admission free. Open June–Sept., daily 3–6. At other times, by appointment.*

At the eastern end of Maynooth is **Carton House**, once the residence of the dukes of Leinster. The house was designed about 1740 in the classical style by Richard Castle, who also designed Russborough House, near Blessington (*see* County Wicklow, above). The grounds feature The Shell House, whose interior is decorated entirely with sea shells. *Tel. 01/628–6250. Admission: £1.50 adults, 50p children. The house can be seen by appointment.*

From Maynooth, take the minor road due south for 13 km (8
31 mi), to the village of **Straffan,** attractively situated on the banks of the River Liffey. The butterfly farm in Straffan is the only one of its kind in Ireland, featuring a tropical house with exotic plants, butterflies, and moths. Mounted and framed butterflies are available for sale. *Tel. 01/627–1109. Admission: £1. Open May–Aug., daily 10–6.*

Straffan's **Steam Museum** at Lodge Park, scheduled to open in spring of 1991, plans to cover the Irish history of steam-working engines. The museum will feature steam engines, on view in the courtyard attached to an 18th-century house, and a collection of locomotive models. *By appointment, tel. 01/628–8412.*

From Straffan, follow the R403 for 16 km (10 mi) westwards; in
32 Prosperous, take the signposted turn to **Robertstown,** 2½ km (1½ mi) southwest. Here you can take scenic walks along the canal and boat trips on the water during the summer. The renovated late-18th-century canal hotel at Robertstown is now used for candlelighted dinners and musical entertainment. Dinners

are preceded by an hour-long trip up and down the canal on the boat *Eustace. Tel. 01/452655 or 045/60020. Canal trip and dinner cost about £21 per person. Canal trips and dinners are offered in May and Sept. on Sun. and public holidays; June, July, and Aug., they are offered daily.*

From Robertstown, drive eastwards for 5 km (3 mi) along the minor road, then turn right onto the R409. Just past this junction is **Mondello Park,** where frequent motor races are held;
33 drive for a further 11 km (7 mi) into **Naas,** a busy market town that St. Patrick is said to have visited more than once. Today, however, Naas is best known for the **Punchestown Racecourse,** which is located 3 km (2 mi) from the town. The racecourse has a wonderful setting amid rolling plains, and 16 km (10 mi) away, the west Wicklow Mountains form a spectacular backdrop. Although horse races are held regularly here, the most popular event is the April steeplechase festival.

Time Out **Lawlor's Restaurant** (tel. 045/97085) at Poplar Square in Naas has been catering for visitors to the racecourse since the last century with its tradition of hearty meals of fish and steaks. Light meals are served in the bar, and as a gesture to modern tastes, vegetarian dishes are also available.

The Curragh and Kildare Town

About 8 km (5 mi) south of Naas, past the uneventful town of **Newbridge,** the **Curragh** starts; this broad plain, bisected by
34 the main N7 road, is Ireland's major racing center, where each year several classic international horse races awarding substantial prize money are held; these meetings attract the upper echelons of Irish society, who enjoy intermingling four loves: horse racing, betting, champagne, and the social whirl. The Curragh is also the location for a large camp used by the Irish Army, whose main barracks are situated here; one of its prize relics is the armored car once used by Michael Collins, a leading Irish political leader who was assassinated in 1922. It can be seen with permission from the commanding officer (tel. 045/41301).

If time permits, a detour worth taking lies 8 km (5 mi) north-
35 west of Newbridge: the **Hill of Allen,** which is an outstanding landmark in the vicinity, rising 209 m (676 ft) high. Because it is one of the few high points on the surrounding plain, it offers wonderful views. The hill also has a special place in Irish mythology, since it was the site of one of three royal palaces in Leinster, some 1,500 years ago; Fionn Mac Cumhaill, the hero of many Irish folk tales, also lived here.

From the Curragh, continue along the N7 for a further 5 km (3
36 mi) to **Kildare Town,** one of the most enjoyable towns to visit in this part of the country. **St. Brigid's Cathedral** (Church of Ireland), with its stocky tower, is immediately off the market square in the center of town. St. Brigid founded a religious settlement here in the 5th century; the present cathedral is a restoration of a building that dates from the 13th century. By the mid-17th century, the cathedral was in decline; it was partially rebuilt about 1686, but restoration work wasn't completed until much later, between 1875 and 1896. The stained-glass west window of the cathedral depicts three of Ireland's greatest saints: Brigid, Patrick, and Columba. *Admission free. Open daily 10–6.*

Outside, in the graveyard of the cathedral, but immediately adjacent to the main door, is the 33-m- (108-ft-) high Round Tower, the second highest in Ireland, possibly dating from the 12th century. Energetic visitors can climb the stairs to the top, for extraordinary views across much of the Midlands. *Tel. 045/41654. Admission: 60p adults, 30p children. Open May–Sept., daily 10–6; Oct.–Apr., Sun. 2–5.*

South of the town about 2½ km (1½ mi), clearly signposted to the left of the market square, are the **Japanese Gardens,** considered by many experts to be the finest in Europe. They were founded in the early years of this century by Lord Wavertree, a brewing millionaire, who also owned the National Stud (*see* below), immediately adjacent. A Japanese gardener, Tassa Eida, laid out the gardens between 1906 and 1910, and they have been kept in perfect condition ever since. The gardens symbolize the passage of man through life. With miniature lakes, little rivers spanned by bridges, and a profusion of Asian trees and flowers, the gardens form an absolute oasis. The section depicting eternity has been created in the Japanese Karesansui style, with emblematic features in sand and stone. Visitors can visit a small tearoom and also a garden center, with a good selection of bonsai trees. *Tel. 045/21617. Admission: £1.50. Open Easter–Oct., weekdays 10:30–5, Sat. 10:30–5:30, Sun. 2–5:30.*

The **National Stud,** where breeding stallions are stabled, is a main center of Ireland's racing industry. On application, visitors can tour the Stud and its fine selection of Thoroughbred horses. You can also enjoy the **Irish Horse Museum,** a small, modern building where displays are devoted to the history of the horse in Ireland. Its most outstanding exhibit is the skeleton of Arkle, the Irish racehorse that won outstanding victories in races in Ireland and England during the late 1960s. The museum also contains medieval evidence of horses, such as bones from 13th-century Dublin, and also some early examples of equestrian equipment. *Admission and hours for the museum are the same as for the Japanese Gardens; the entrance fee to the Gardens covers the museum.*

Time Out

The **Silken Thomas** (tel. 045/22232), a pub in the market square of Kildare Town, re-creates an Old World atmosphere with open fires, dark wood decor, and leaded lights.

South Kildare

From Kildare Town, take the N7 for 11 km (7 mi) to Monasterevin on the banks of the Grand Canal; then take the R417 for 19 km (12 mi) south as far as Athy. For most of its distance, the road runs in close proximity to the River Barrow, one of Ireland's major waterways; from the road, you'll have fine views across the river to the low range of wooded hills on the
37 County Laois side of the river. **Athy** is an industrial and market town on the River Barrow, which widens considerably here. Overlooking the river, by the bridge, is a 16th-century castle, now a private house, that was built by the earl of Kildare to defend this strategic crossing. On the other side of the bridge from the castle is a pleasant park and the Catholic church, built in a pentagonal shape between 1963 and 1965; its striking interior features Stations of the Cross by George Campbell, a noted Irish artist; statues; and a crucifix on the high altar, by local artist Brid ni Rinn. *Admission free. Open daily 8–6.*

Northeast of Athy, 6½ km (4 mi) off the N78, is the **Motte of
Ardscull,** a large hillock by the roadside; from the crossroads
here, turn right onto the minor road that leads for 8 km (5 mi)
38 eastward toward **Ballitore,** a former Quaker settlement in the
18th and 19th centuries. An old schoolhouse here has been converted into a small Quaker museum. Among the pupils at the school was Edmund Burke (1729–1797), the great orator and political philosopher. *Tel. 045/31109. Admission: £1. Open sporadically, usually Sun. afternoons.*

Ballitore also has the **Crookstown Heritage Centre,** an old mill that has been converted into a museum of the flour milling and baking industries. *Tel. 0507/23248. Admission: £1 adults, 50p children. Open Apr.–Sept., daily 9–7, or on request.*

From Ballitore go to the main N9 road and drive south for 3 km (2 mi), as far as Timolin, where you'll reach the **Irish Pewter Mill,** a splendid tribute to an old Irish craft. Jugs, plates, and other items made from pewter are for sale. *Tel. 0507/24164. Open weekdays 9:30–5; adjoining crafts center is also open weekends.*

Continue for a further 1½ km (1 mi) south on the N7, and at the
Moone Post Office, take the signposted right turn, con-
39 tinuing for 3 km (2 mi) to the **Moone High Cross,** an ancient
Celtic cross that stands 5½ m (17½ ft) high, with 51 sculptured
panels showing scriptural scenes. From the main road at
Moone, continue southwards on the N7 for 3 km (2 mi), as far as
40 **Castledermot.** On the left-hand side of the village, you'll find an
almost perfectly preserved 10th-century round tower together with two high crosses, equally well conserved, on the grounds of the local church. From the church gate, you can walk back to the main road along the footpath that is totally enclosed by trees. On the right-hand side of the road in the village, the substantial ruins of a Franciscan friary, mostly dating from the 14th century, are freely accessible.

From Castledermot, you can return to Naas on the N7 (43 km/27 mi).

Dining and Lodging

by Georgina Campbell and Hugh Oram

Highly recommended restaurants and hotels are indicated by a star ★. For further information about dining and lodging, *see* Chapter 1, Essential Information, and Chapter 3, Dublin.

Dining

Category	Cost*
Very Expensive	over £20
Expensive	£15–£20
Moderate	£10–£15
Inexpensive	Under £10

**per person, without tax (10%), service, or drinks*

Lodging

Category	Cost*
Expensive	over £80
Moderate	£40–£80
Inexpensive	under £40

** all prices are for a double-size room, except where stated, and include a 10% local sales tax (VAT) and a 12% service charge.*

County Wicklow

Blessington
Dining and Lodging

Tulfarris House. A restored 18th-century Georgian house in the grand style, this hotel features a comfortable sitting room with a large window facing the gardens and a marble fireplace. The 21 charming bedrooms, including some suites, all have private baths; the more expensive rooms are not only larger; they also have striking views out across Poulaphouca Lake. The French restaurant in the main house specializes in more expensive cuisine, while the courtyard bistro serves plainer fare. Isolated on its own grounds, the property offers sports facilities, including its own nine-hole golf course by the lakeside, trout and coarse fishing, croquet, and peaceful walks through its own woods. *Blessington, Co. Wicklow, tel. 045/64574. 21 rooms with baths. Facilities: 2 restaurants, bar, golf course, fishing, croquet, leisure center with swimming pool, gymnasium (including exercise bicycles, sauna, steam room). AE, DC, MC, V. Expensive.*

Bray
Dining
★

The Tree of Idleness. This Greek-Cypriot restaurant, located on the extreme southern stop on the DART line from Dublin, happens to be one of the best restaurants in the country. Located near the seafront on the ground floor of a Victorian house, this pleasant dining spot specializes in classic dishes and good hearty portions. Roast lamb stuffed with feta cheese and olives is highly recommended. The extensive wine list includes Greek and Cypriot house wines. *Bray, Co. Wicklow, tel. 01/863498. Reservations advised. Dress: casual but neat. DC, MC, V. Dinner only. Closed Mon., Christmas, last week of Aug. and first fortnight of Sept. Expensive.*

Dunlavin
Dining and Lodging
★

Rathsallagh House. Joe and Kay O'Flynn's delightful home is well signposted, 56 km (35 mi) southwest of Dublin on the edge of the Wicklow Hills. Set in 500 acres of parkland in some of the most beautiful countryside in the east of Ireland, this large, comfortable farmhouse was converted from Queen Anne stables in 1798 when the original house burned down; it's now run as a Grade A country-house hotel. Double rooms are each decorated in different colors and have large bathtubs. The homey atmosphere is accentuated by the ample cupboard space and the good selection of books in each room. Kay's talents in the kitchen are legendary, and the equally famous relaxed atmosphere belies a high standard of professionalism. Although the dining room is small, tables are tastefully set with linen cloths and napkins, silver cutlery, enormous wine glasses, candles, and fresh flowers. French doors open onto the croquet lawn and, on cool evenings, guests have a welcoming fire blazing in the grate. In the kitchen, homegrown vegetables and fruit complement hearty roasts of local lamb or beef. Specialties include twice-baked cheese soufflé and warm salad of pigeon breast. Sports facilities include a small golf course, a tennis court, an indoor heated swimming pool, and a sauna. *Near Dunlavin, Co. Wicklow, tel. 045/53112. 10 rooms with bath. Facilities: bar, restaurant (Very Expensive). DC, MC, V. Moderate.*

Glendalough
Dining and Lodging

Royal Hotel. This old-fashioned 19th-century hotel, which sits in the glen at Glendalough, was recently refurbished. Upstairs, the cozy bedrooms, all with private baths, are decorated in quiet pastel colors; four rooms are triples. Downstairs, the bar has been modernized and the main restaurant, a long room with grand windows, looks out onto the Glendalough monastery and wooded mountain scenery, with the sound of running water from the stream outside. The rather plain menu features fish and meat dishes, but helpings are hearty. The hotel is a favorite stopping point in the area for visitors from around the world. *Glendalough, Co. Wicklow, tel. 0404/5135. 17 rooms with bath. Facilities: bar, restaurant. AE, DC, MC, V. Moderate.*

Rathnew
Dining and Lodging
★

Tinakilly House. This impressive Victorian mansion, situated on seven acres, was built in the 1870s by Captain Robert Halpin, a Wicklow man who made his fortune at sea. The great lobby at the entrance to the house stores mementos of Captain Halpin and his nautical exploits, including paintings and ship models. The house has been lovingly restored by William and Bee Power; the whole home is filled with impeccable Victorian antiques, and woods used originally in its construction, such as mahogany and pitch pine, have been meticulously replaced. All bedrooms have private baths, and some offer four-poster beds, Jacuzzis, and fine views of the Wicklow landscape. Second-floor rooms are larger than the third-floor attic rooms, which are snug yet comfortable. The seven acres of Victorian gardens feature giant California redwoods at each end of the tennis court. Guests for meals are welcomed into the spacious bar before they proceed to the enchanting two-room restaurant, overlooking attractive gardens and tended by an efficient staff dressed in red and white. The basically Irish country-house cuisine shows definite French nouvelle influences in presentation. Bee Power's famous brown bread is baked in the kitchen, whose specialties include roast breast of Barbary duck with fruit sauce, Wicklow lamb, and quail. *Rathnew, Co. Wicklow, tel. 0404/69274. 14 rooms with bath. Facilities: restaurant (Very Expensive), bar, tennis court, golf and horseback riding nearby. MC, V. Expensive.*

Hunter's Hotel. This old coaching inn, first opened in 1830, has a lovely rural setting on the banks of the River Vartry, only 2½ km (1½ mi) east of Rathnew Village. A delightful Old World atmosphere has been maintained in the period prints, beams, and antique furnishings; the inn is a favorite place with local hunters and many foreigners. The magnificent garden stretches down to the river. All bedrooms are cozily furnished with Victorian-style flower-print wallpaper. Only 10 rooms have private tiled bathrooms; communal bathrooms for the remaining rooms can be rather Spartan. Ask about Room 17 on the ground floor, with a private garden entrance. Original Georgian furnishings have been extended to the dining room, where window tables are much in demand. In the summer, afternoon tea with homemade scones and jams served in the garden is particularly delightful. The restaurant serves traditional country-house cuisine using homegrown produce in such entrées as roast Wicklow lamb with herbs and mint sauce, and baked sea trout with herbs and parsley butter, served with garden vegetables. *Rathnew, Co. Wicklow, tel. 0404/40106. 18 rooms, 10 with bath. Facilities: restaurant (Moderate–Expensive), bar. AE, DC, MC, V. Moderate.*

Roundwood
Dining
★

Roundwood Inn. South of Dublin on the Glendalough road, amid spectacular scenery, you come to the highest village in the Wicklow Hills and this 17th-century inn. Furnished in a traditional style, with wooden floors and diamond-shaped windows, this place is remarkable for having changed so little over the years. Although the inn is best-known for good, reasonably priced bar food—homemade broth, Irish stew, Galway oysters, or smoked Wicklow trout—eaten at sturdy tables beside an open fire, the more expensive restaurant offers a combination of Continental and Irish cuisines, reflecting the traditions of the German proprietor, Jurgen Schwalm, and his Irish wife, Aine. In the long dining room, the most coveted of the dark wooden tables are the ones in front of the big log fires. Local produce features prominently on the menu, especially roasts like rack of Wicklow lamb, prime Irish beef, and local game in winter. Wiener schnitzel is a house special, and the feather-light fresh cream *gâteau* dessert is not to be missed. *Roundwood, Co. Wicklow, tel. 01/818107 or 01/818125. Reservations required. Dress: casual but neat. MC, V. Closed Sun. dinner and Mon. except on public holidays, Christmas Day, Good Friday. Expensive.*

Wicklow Town
Dining and Lodging

Grand Hotel. On the main Dublin road just as you come into Wicklow Town, this solid redbrick Victorian edifice has been thoroughly refurbished in recent years. Downstairs the bar serves plain yet tasty meals all day until 9 PM, while the large restaurant offers more elaborate lunch and dinner menus, featuring fish and lamb specialties of the region. Upstairs, on two floors, the clean and simple rooms all have private baths. The hotel makes no pretense to luxury, but it offers a very friendly and comfortable ambience. *Wicklow Town, Co. Wicklow, tel. 0404/67337. 14 rooms with bath. Facilities: bar, restaurant, TV and direct-dial phones in rooms. AE, DC, MC, V. Moderate.*

★ **Old Rectory Country House.** Once a 19th-century rectory, this splendid country house in the Greek-revival style stands on a hillside just off the main road from Dublin on the approach to Wicklow Town. Owners Paul and Linda Saunders have successfully transformed the interior with dark marble fireplaces, bright colors, original oil paintings, and antique and contemporary furniture, all blending together beautifully. The light, spacious rooms with private baths are decorated in white and pastel shades with Victorian antique furniture. The small and intimate dining room and bow-tied waiters create just the right level of formality. Linda's innovative country-house cooking is based on pure ingredients, especially seafood and organic vegetables, and she specializes in salads and desserts, often including, or garnished with, edible flowers and herbs. Specialties include fillet of black sole stuffed with salmon and spinach terrine, and roast sea trout with a fresh herb sauce. Don't miss the house dessert, "Swan Lake" meringues, piped in the shape of swans and cygnets. *Wicklow Town, Co. Wick-*

low, tel. 0404/67048. 5 rooms, all with bath. Facilities: restaurant. AE, MC, V. Closed Oct.–Easter. Moderate.

County Louth

Ardee
Dining

The Gables House and Restaurant. Situated just off the Dublin–Derry road (the N2), not far from the Dundalk junction, this restaurant was originally a 1940s house built on a school playground. The place features traditional decor, with antique mahogany furniture, deep-burgundy velvet curtains, and oil paintings by local artists. Mats on the polished tables, silver cutlery, linen napkins, lace coasters, and gleaming lead crystal glasses all contribute to the intimate atmosphere. Expect generous portions and a French-influenced cooking style; dishes include, seafood from the Celtic Sea—poached wild salmon, turbot, hake, and prawns, finished in a sauce of carrots, celery, and chives (the colors of the Irish flag)—and a chocolate mousse with Frangelico liqueur and chopped hazelnuts layered with meringue. *Dundalk Rd., Ardee, Co. Louth, tel. 041/53789. Reservations advised. Dress: casual but neat. AE, DC, MC, V. Dinner only. Closed Sun.–Mon.; first fortnight of June and middle fortnight of Nov. Moderate–Expensive.*

Collon
Dining

Forge Gallery Restaurant. This well-established restaurant is located in a converted forge north of Dublin on the N2, just north of Slane. The reception area displays paintings by local artists for sale. Warm tones of rose and plum work well with the antique furniture; the old fireplace contributes real warmth to the atmosphere. A minstrels' gallery overlooks the dining room. The cuisine is a mixture of French provincial with a strong hint of traditional Irish in winter, when old favorites like silversides or boiled mutton with caper sauce appear on the menu. Two popular specialties are salmon and crab in phyllo pastry, and the Rendezvous appetizer with prawns and scallops in a cream and garlic sauce. Be sure to try one of the seasonal homemade soups. *Collon, Co. Louth, tel. 041/26272. Reservations advised; weekend reservations required. Dress: casual but neat. MC, V. Dinner only. Closed Sun.–Mon.; 4 days at Christmas and all of Jan. Moderate–Expensive.*

Drogheda
Dining and Lodging

Boyne Valley Hotel. A converted 19th-century mansion that once belonged to a brewing family in Drogheda, this hotel is situated on extensive parkland; although housing developments are located on adjoining land, they are not intrusive. The hotel is approached by a 1-km- (½-mi-) long drive. Bedrooms are adequately comfortable, with uninspired decor. The new wing of the hotel, completed in 1990, has double rooms, all with private bath and contemporary furnishings. Other additions to the hotel include an attractive, plant-filled conservatory bar looking out over the parkland and the basement, which has been converted into the Sennhof Restaurant. With its wooden beamed ceiling and many posters from Switzerland, it offers an authentic Swiss menu, which includes such delicacies as *berner platte*, a mixture of many kinds of meat, such as pork and lamb. The wine list carries Swiss wines, a real rarity for Ireland. *Dublin Rd., Drogheda, Co. Louth, tel. 041/37737. 36 rooms with bath. Facilities: bar, restaurants, pitch-and-putt golf course. AE, DC, MC. Moderate.*

Dundalk
Dining and Lodging

Ballymascanlon Hotel. This converted Victorian mansion standing on its own grounds, just north of Dundalk, has long had a fine reputation in the area for comfort and good cuisine. All bedrooms have private baths, and the hotel offers a sports complex with an indoor heated swimming pool, a small gymnasium, and a sauna. Other sports facilities include two squash courts, two tennis courts, and a nine-hole golf course. The main restaurant, serving Irish and French cuisine, specializes in fresh seafood entrées, such as lobster in season; the menu also includes vegetarian platters. The hotel grounds also feature an unusual historical artifact, a prehistoric monument known as the Proleek Dolmen. *Dundalk, Co. Louth, tel. 042/71124. 36 rooms with bath. Facilities: 2 bars, restaurant, pool, table tennis, billiards, squash, tennis, golf, gym. AE, MC, V. Moderate.*

County Meath

Kells
Dining and Lodging

Lennoxbrook. This fine country home, run by Paul and Pauline Mullan, dates back over 200 years; it is situated 5 km (3 mi) north of Kells on the N3 road from Dublin to Cavan. The Mullans are the fifth generation of the family to occupy the house, which is filled with antiques and family heirlooms. Upstairs, the five rooms, all doubles, are furnished in the old style, with finely patterned wallpaper and period furniture; they share two bathrooms. Dinner may include freshly caught fish or locally raised lamb. The house is convenient to the Newgrange monument. *Kells, Co. Meath, Tel. 046/45902. 5 rooms. Facilities: restaurant. No credit cards. Moderate.*

Kilmessan
Dining and Lodging

Station House Hotel and Restaurant. For anyone who likes the atmosphere of old railways, or simply good food served in unusual surroundings, the Flynn family's establishment is recommended. You reach the place by traveling up the N3 from Dublin to Navan and turning off the main road at the sign for the Hill of Tara, 9½ km (6 mi) before Navan. Continue down the side road for 6½ km (4 mi), past the Hill of Tara to Kilmessan. The railway station was once the junction for a hub of lines linking Dublin with County Meath, but it was closed down in 1952. The Flynns did a restoration job but kept the main features of the station. Diners can have their aperitifs on what was the old platform, while the old ticket office forms the dining room. The emphasis here is on local produce, including meat, vegetables, and fish, despite the inland location. The Early Express Menu offers a four-course meal for around £10 between 6 and 8 PM nightly. Bedrooms are pleasantly decorated in a floral style; only half the rooms have private baths. Outside, the grounds have been well landscaped, but remnants of the old train station may still be seen, such as the signal box, the turntable for engines, and the engine shed (part of it used for bedrooms). *Kilmessan, Co. Meath, tel. 046/25239. 10 rooms, 5 with bath. Facilities: bar, restaurant. AE, MC, V. Moderate.*

County Kildare

Castledermot
Dining
★

Doyle's Schoolhouse Country Inn. Situated on the main Waterford–Dublin road (the N9) in south County Kildare, bordering on Counties Wicklow and Carlow, this renovated 1930s schoolhouse is slightly off the main tourist trail, but it has a strong local following. Small, intimate, and furnished with a homey mixture of antiques and newer furniture, the cozy atmosphere is appropriate to owner-chef John Doyle's wholesome country-house cooking, with a strong seasonal bias; entrées might include pike baked with sorrel stuffing served with cream and mustard sauce in the summer, or roast venison and pheasant in the autumn and winter. Especially recommended are the country pâtés and rough terrines, usually based on pork with legs of pheasant or duck liver. *Castledermot, Co. Kildare, tel. 0503/44282. Reservations advised; reservations required Sun.–Mon. Dress: casual but neat. AE, DC, MC, V. Lunch Sun. only; Apr.–Oct., informal lunch daily; dinner Nov.–Mar., Tues.–Sat.; Apr.–Oct., nightly. Moderate–Expensive.*

Dining and Lodging

Kilkea Castle. Built in the 12th century as a defensive Anglo-Norman castle, this was the home of the FitzGerald family for centuries. The castle is said to be haunted by apparitions and the sounds of battle, even in its new role as a luxury hotel. Eleven rooms are situated in the castle itself, while the rest are found around the adjacent courtyard. Although most rooms are rather plainly furnished, all have private baths; bedrooms in the castle tend to be more luxuriously furnished. The restaurant is now located in what was the great hall of the castle; in these grand surroundings, typical Irish dishes are served, such as sirloin steak and grilled salmon steak. The hotel features its own sports complex and river fishing. *Castledermot, near Athy, Co. Kildare, tel. 0503/45156. 46 rooms with bath. Facilities: 2 bars, restaurant, heated indoor swimming pool, gymnasium, sauna, 2 tennis courts, river fishing for trout, clay-pigeon shooting, bowls, archery; horseback riding nearby. AE, DC, MC, V. Very Expensive.*

Maynooth
Dining and Lodging

Moyglare Manor. Situated only a half-hour drive southwest of Dublin, this imposing Georgian mansion, set on 16 pastoral acres dotted with cows and sheep, is renowned for its magnificent antique furnishings. The gracious drawing room has velvet chairs, oil paintings, and thickly draped windows. The grand bedrooms feature four-poster canopy beds, roomy wardrobes, marble fireplaces, and comfortable chintz armchairs. Some of the bathrooms alone are as large as a room in a modern home. A cocktail bar is decorated with portraits of residents of the house over the past 150 years. Despite the grandeur of the surroundings, the romantic dining room can be pleasantly intimate, with a large mahogany sideboard, silver dishes, and fine crystal. The traditional French menu includes *crêpes au bruyère* and baked plaice stuffed with shrimps. Desserts tend to be rich and sophisticated; white-chocolate mousse is a typical choice. *Maynooth, Co. Kildare, tel. 01/628–6351 or 01/628–6469. 17 rooms with bath. Facilities: restaurant, 2 bars, tennis court; horseback riding nearby. AE, DC, MC, V. Expensive.*

Newbridge
Dining and Lodging

Hotel Keadeen. This modern, single-story hotel is set beside the main N7 Dublin–Limerick road. The unpretentious, well-maintained rooms feature contemporary furnishings with matching floral wallpaper and bedcovers. You can have lunch in the lounge bar, or lunch and dinner in the main restaurant, which overlooks neatly manicured lawns and flower beds. *Newbridge, Co. Kildare, tel. 045/31666. 37 rooms with bath, including 1 suite, 3 studios. Facilities: 2 bars, restaurant, parking, TV. AE, DC, MC, V. Moderate.*

Prosperous
Dining and Lodging

Curryhills House Hotel. This Georgian farmhouse with modern additions and elegantly landscaped surroundings stands on the flat plain of Kildare, 11 km (7 mi) northwest of Naas on the

R403. The spacious bedrooms are unremarkably furnished but relaxing, and they all have either a bath or a shower. The basement restaurant serves local country-style specialties, such as turkey raised by the owners and served with mushrooms. The bar is a popular local meeting spot, and during weekends, traditional Irish music livens up the atmosphere. The hotel offers no sports facilities, but guests can participate in coarse angling, horseback riding, and golf nearby. *Prosperous, near Naas, Co. Kildare, tel. 045/68150. 10 rooms. Facilities: bar, restaurant. AE, DC, MC, V. Moderate.*

5 The Lakelands

Introduction

by Pat Mackey

A resident of Waterford, Pat Mackey is the author of the travel guides Sunny South East by Hook and by Crooke *and* Lakeland.

Located in the heart of Ireland amid lakes, rivers, and canals, the Lakelands comprise seven counties—Cavan, Laois, Westmeath, Longford, Offaly, Roscommon, and Monaghan. Even if you choose only to drive through the area, you'll have plenty to see along the way. Winding roads lead repeatedly to breathtaking vistas, prehistoric and medieval ruins, placid waters, and acres and acres of rich pastures and low-lying bogs.

From the Neolithic period until the 17th century, much of the area was inhabited by lake dwellers who lived on artificial islands called crannogs. Designed for protection against the raids of neighboring tribes, these crannogs were sometimes connected to the mainland by causeways. More often than not, however, a cunning system of underwater stepping-stones led to and away from the islands. If you knew precisely where the stepping-stones lay, you could avoid the deep water and reach dry land without difficulty.

In more recent times, the region has been associated with several acclaimed poets and writers. County Monaghan was the birthplace of Patrick Kavanagh, a 20th-century writer known for his long poem *The Great Hunger* and for his novel *Tarry Flynn.* Oliver Goldsmith, the 18th-century poet, playwright, and novelist, spent much of his life in Lissoy, outside of Athlone. Turlough O'Carolan, a 17th-century blind bard known as the Prince of Harpists, was buried in County Roscommon after a life of traveling around Ireland performing the songs he composed. Other notable writers from the Lakelands include the 19th-century novelist Maria Edgeworth, and the 20th-century poet and playwright Padraic Colum.

Essential Information

Arriving and Departing by Plane

Airports The principal international airport serving the Lakeland region is **Dublin Airport** (tel. 01/370555). **Connaught International Airport** (tel. 094/67222) in Knock, County Mayo, is much smaller, and **Sligo Regional Airport** (tel. 071/68280) has daily flights from Dublin on Aer Lingus. Car rental facilities are available at Dublin and Knock Airports. For more information on these airports, *see* Chapters 3 (Dublin) and 8 (The Northwest).

Arriving and Departing by Car, Train, and Bus

By Car Mullingar, the regional capital, and Boyle are on the main N4 route between Dublin and Sligo. It takes one hour to go from Dublin to Mullingar (55 km/34 mi), and two hours from Mullingar to Sligo. To get from Mullingar to the southeast of the country, you can take the N52 to the N7 and follow that into Limerick—a trip (150 km/94 mi) of about three hours. The R390 from Mullingar leads you east to Athlone, where it connects with the N6 to Galway. The drive (120 km/75 mi) takes about 2½ hours.

By Train A direct rail service links Mullingar to Dublin, with three trains every day making the 1½-hour journey. It costs £10 one-way and £18 round-trip. Contact **Irish Rail** (tel. 01/366222) for information.

By Bus **Bus Éireann** (tel. 01/366111) runs an express bus from Dublin to Mullingar in 1½ hours, with a round-trip fare of £6. Buses depart three times every day. A regular-speed bus, leaving twice daily, makes the trip in two hours.

Getting Around

By Car Most of the winding roads in the Lakelands are uncongested, although you may encounter an occasional animal or agricultural machine crossing the road. If you're driving in the north of Counties Cavan and Monaghan, be sure to avoid "unapproved" roads crossing the border into Northern Ireland. The approved routes into Northern Ireland connect the towns of Monaghan and Aughnacloy, Castlefinn and Castlederg, Swalinbar and Enniskillen, Clones and Newtownbutler, and Monaghan and Rosslea. Those driving a rented car should make sure it has been cleared for cross-border journeys. You can rent a car at **Hamill Car and Van Rentals** (Dublin Rd., Mullingar, Co. Westmeath, tel. 044/48682).

By Train Trains from Mullingar, departing twice daily every weekday and Sunday, stop at Longford (35 min), Carrick-on-Shannon (1 hr), Boyle (1¼ hr), and Sligo (2 hr).

By Bus The express buses leaving Dublin (*see* Arriving and Departing by Bus) make stops at Mullingar (1½ hr), Longford (2¼ hr), Carrick-on-Shannon (3 hr), Boyle (3¼ hr), and Sligo (4¼ hr). There is also a daily bus from Mullingar to Athlone, and an express service connecting Galway, Athlone, Longford, Cavan, Clones, Monaghan, and Sligo. Details of all bus services are available from Bus Éireann depots at the following locations: **Athlone Railway Station** (tel. 0902/72651), **Cavan Bus Office** (tel. 049/31353), **Longford Railway Station** (tel. 043/45208), **Monaghan Bus Office** (tel. 047/82377), **Sligo Railway Station** (tel. 071/60066), and **Bus Éireann** (Dublin, tel. 01/366111).

Important Addresses and Numbers

Tourist Information Offices Information is available from Tourist Information Offices in **Mullingar** (Dublin Rd., tel. 044/48650), **Athlone** (Church St., tel. 0902/94630), **Birr** (Emmet Sq., tel. 0509/20110), **Roscommon** (The Square, tel. 0903/26342), **Boyle** (Bridge St., tel. 0709/62145), **Cavan** (Farnham St., tel. 049/31942), and **Monaghan** (Market House, tel. 047/81122).

Hospitals and Pharmacies For medical and ambulance service, contact Mullingar's **General Hospital** (tel. 044/40221). You can buy pharmaceutical supplies from **Fairgreen Pharmacy** (Quinnsworth Shopping Centre, Mullingar, tel. 044/48471).

Exploring

Numbers in the margin correspond with points of interest on The Lakelands map.

Tour 1: Counties Westmeath and Offaly

1 This tour begins at **Mullingar,** the capital of County Westmeath. Set between two lakes—Lough Owel to the north and Lough Ennel to the south—Mullingar is the center of a fine cattle-raising area, as you'll be able to tell from the large cattle markets around the town.

In medieval times, Mullingar was the site of two priories, one built in 1227 for the Canons Regular of St. Augustine and the other in 1237 for the Dominican order. Unfortunately, neither one survived the many burnings and plunderings of the Middle Ages. The most visible and best-known sight nowadays is the **Catholic Cathedral of Christ the King,** an imposing neoclassical structure whose two towers rise 42 m (140 ft) above the town. Finely carved stone work decorates the front of the cathedral, and the spacious interior has mosaics of St. Patrick and St. Anne by Russian artist Boris Anrep. *Admission free. Open daily 9–5:30.*

The Military and Historical Museum in Mullingar is also worth a visit, but you must call ahead of time to arrange one. On display here are weapons from the two world wars, boats made out of oak from the 1st century AD, and uniforms and other articles of the old IRA. *Columb Barracks, tel. 044/48391. Admission free. Open to the public by appointment only.*

If you have more time in Mullingar, consider a short excursion to the area just north of the city. A drive on the R394 takes you
2 to **Castlepollard,** a neatly planned 19th-century town with a central village green. **Tullynally Castle** (originally Packenham Hall), the ancestral seat of the earls of Longford and the principal sight in the area, lies just outside the town. Built in the 17th century, the house was transformed at the beginning of the 19th century into a neo-Gothic castle, with an elaborate facade of turrets and towers, an immense kitchen and servants' hall, and surrounding woods and walled gardens. *Tel. 044/61159. Admission to castle and gardens: £2 adults, £1 children; admission to gardens only: £1 adults, 50p children. Gardens open June–Sept., daily 10–5; castle rooms open July 15–Aug. 15, daily 2:30–6.*

3 Three km (2 mi) east of Castlepollard are the remains of **Fore Abbey,** founded by St. Fechin in AD 630. The abbey's oldest existing structure, St. Fechin's Church, dates from the 10th century and probably marks the site of the original monastery. In the 13th century, the de Lacy family added a Benedictine priory; with its square towers and loophole windows, this imposing structure resembles a castle more than an abbey. Nearby is the beautiful Lough Derravaragh, dubbed the Lake of the Oaks for the vast oak forest that once stood there. Lough Derravaragh, Lough Owel, and Lough Ennel—all close to Mullingar—offer a variety of water sports and fishing.

From Mullingar, the R392 leads to Moyvore and then on to
4 Ballymahon. You can take the N55 south to **Lissoy,** site of the

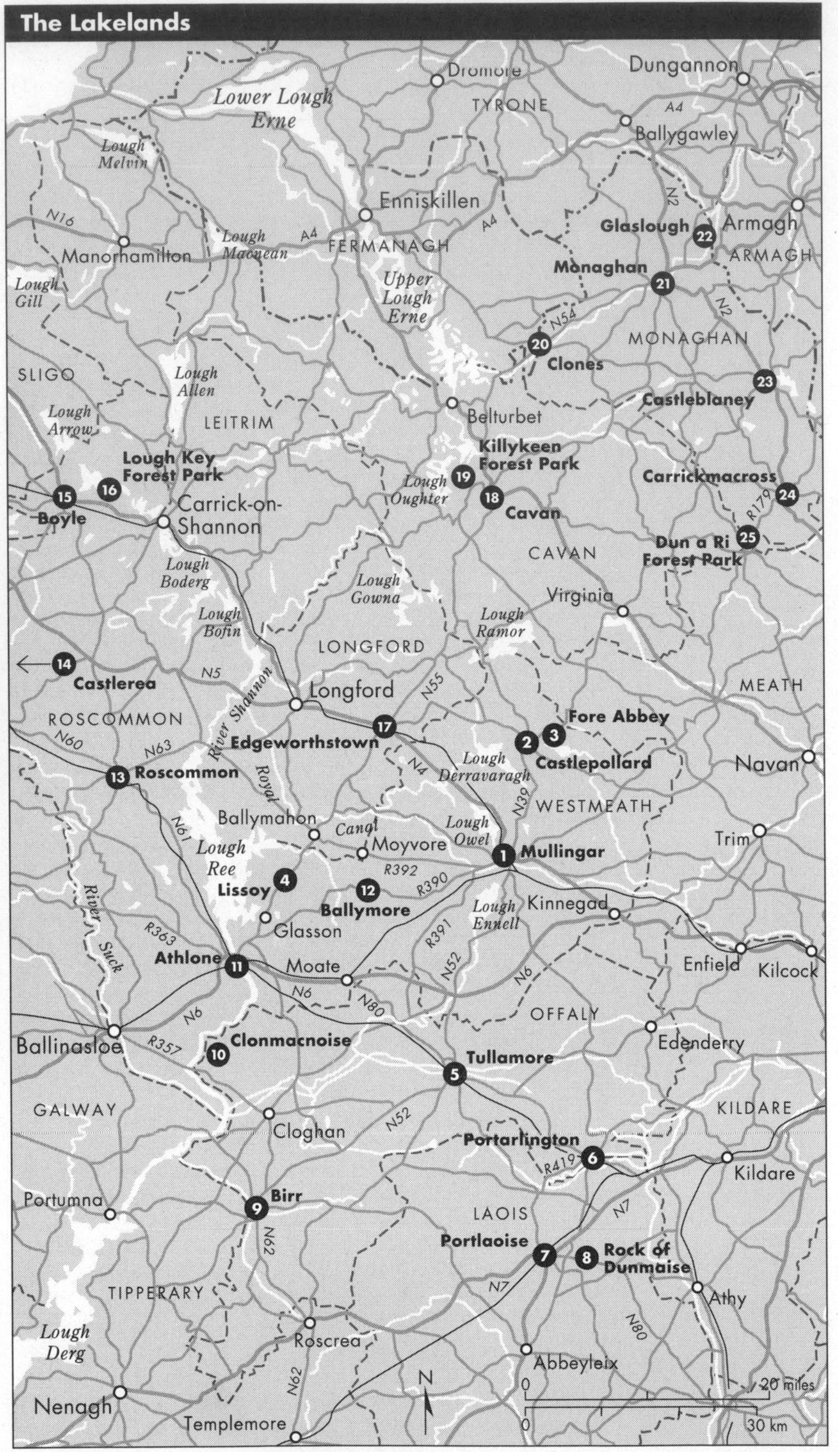
The Lakelands
Dromore
Dungannon
Lower Lough Erne
TYRONE
A4
Ballygawley
Lough Melvin
Enniskillen
N2
N16
Glaslough
22
Armagh
Lough Macnean
A4
A4
Manorhamilton
FERMANAGH
ARMAGH
Monaghan
21
Lough Gill
Upper Lough Erne
N2
N54
MONAGHAN
20
Clones
SLIGO
Lough Allen
23
Castleblaney
Belturbet
Lough Arrow
LEITRIM
Killykeen Forest Park
19
Lough Key Forest Park
Carrickmacross
15
16
Lough Oughter
18
24
Carrick-on-Shannon
Cavan
R179
Boyle
25
Dun a Ri Forest Park
Lough Boderg
CAVAN
Lough Gowna
Virginia
Lough Bofin
Lough Ramor
14
LONGFORD
Castlerea
N5
River Shannon
N55
MEATH
Longford
ROSCOMMON
17
Fore Abbey
3
2
N60
Edgeworthstown
N63
River
Lough Derravaragh
Castlepollard
Navan
N4
13
Roscommon
Royal
N39
WESTMEATH
Ballymahon
Canal
Lough Owel
Trim
N61
Moyvore
Lough Ree
1
Mullingar
R392
4
R390
Lissoy
12
Ballymore
Lough Ennell
Kinnegad
River Suck
Glasson
R391
R363
Athlone
11
Moate
N52
Enfield
Kilcock
N6
N6
N80
N6
OFFALY
Ballinasloe
Clonmacnoise
R357
10
Edenderry
Tullamore
5
GALWAY
KILDARE
Cloghan
N52
Portarlington
R419
6
Kildare
Portumna
Birr
9
N7
LAOIS
N62
Portlaoise
Rock of Dunmaise
7
8
TIPPERARY
N7
Athy
N80
Lough Derg
Roscrea
Abbeyleix
N
0
20 miles
N62
Nenagh
0
30 km
Templemore

boyhood home of 18th-century writer Oliver Goldsmith (a plaque marks the spot), and then continue to Glasson, called the "village of the roses" by Goldsmith. You'll understand why if you're there in the summer, when roses bloom profusely around local cottages.

The N55 south connects at Athlone with the N6, which takes
you east to the village of Moate. From here, the N80 leads you
south past **Durrow Abbey**—where the Book of Durrow, a trea-
sured copy of the Gospels, was written in the 10th century—
5 and finally to **Tullamore,** a busy market town and the center of a
fertile agricultural area. As one legend has it, the Charleville family, who had financed much of Tullamore's development, launched a balloon in 1785 to celebrate the coming-of-age of the young Lord Charleville. Unfortunately, the balloon set fire to the town, causing considerable damage to many of the properties the family had helped to build. The Charleville family later repaired and improved the town. Their Gothic mansion, built by Francis Johnston, is privately owned and usually closed to the public; check with the local Tourist Information Office to see if it has reopened.

Continuing south on the N80 to Portlaoise, you can take a small
detour near Mountmellick onto the R423, which takes you to
6 the charming Old World town of **Portarlington,** founded in 1666
and settled later by the French Huguenots. Back on the N80
7 south again, follow signs to **Portlaoise,** called Maryborough
during the Middle Ages. There isn't much to see in the town,
8 but just 6½ km (4 mi) east on the N80 lies the **Rock of
Dunmaise,** a mound about 45 m (150 ft) high with the remains of a castle at its peak. Originally a Celtic fortress plundered by Vikings, it was passed from one Irish family to another until Oliver Cromwell's men finally besieged and destroyed it in the 17th century. The views of the countryside from the top of the mound are superb.

From Portlaoise, the N7 going southwest leads you to the N62,
9 which takes you into **Birr.** Only the foundations remain of the
old **Birr Castle** of the O'Carrolls, but the great central tower has been incorporated into the present mansion. On the grounds of the castle is a small museum, which houses the well-known telescope built by the third earl of Rosse in 1842. The largest telescope in the world at the time, it was subsequently used to discover the composition of the nebulae and the structure of the Milky Way. The earls of Rosse still live in the mansion, which can only be visited by special arrangement, but the 100 acres of gardens are open to the public. *Tel. 0509/20056. Admission mid-Sept.–Apr.: £2 adults, £1 children; May–mid-Sept.: £2.50 adults, £1 children. Open daily 9–1 and 2–6.*

The N62 north takes you from Birr to Athlone, but we suggest
10 you take a small detour at Cloghan to **Clonmacnoise,** one of the
most significant religious sites in Ireland. Among the well-preserved remains of the 6th-century monastic settlement here are two round towers, six churches, and two high crosses. *Tel. 0905/74195. Admission: £1 adults, 40p children. Open mid-June–Sept., daily 9–7; Oct.–May, daily 10–6.*

11 Follow signs from here back to the N62 north and on to **Athlone,**
a manufacturing town set just below Lough Ree straddling the River Shannon. Most of the town now lies on the east bank of the river, around the 19th-century **St. Mary's Church.** Accord-

ing to tradition, the tower standing beside the church holds a bell from the religious settlement at Clonmacnois. Near the river on the east bank are the remains of a 13th-century Franciscan abbey.

The most recognized historical site in Athlone is **Adamson Castle,** a 13th-century castle on the west bank of the river. As Athlone, the gateway to the province of Connaught, gained in strategic importance, the castle became a military stronghold. In 1690, a small force of James II's men, under the command of Colonel Richard Grace, defended the city successfully against 10,000 soldiers fighting for William of Orange. In the following year, however, James's men succumbed to William's army, and the earldom of Athlone was awarded to the victorious commander, General Ginkel. Declared a national monument in 1969, the castle now houses a museum with a collection of artifacts relating to the Athlone district. *Main St., tel. 0902/92166. Admission: £1 adults, 40p children. Open Mon.–Sat. 11–1 and 3–6.*

From Athlone, the N55 meets up with the R390, which takes
12 you east to **Ballymore,** a small village with the ruins of a 14th-
century castle. Continue on the R390 and follow the signs back
to Mullingar.

Tour 2: Roscommon to Monaghan

13 **Roscommon,** the principal town in County Roscommon, provides a good starting point for our second tour. It isn't a particularly beautiful or significant place, but a leisurely walk by the classical 18th-century **courthouse** (now the Bank of Ireland), with a striking tower and dome, and the **old county jail** (now a cluster of stores) can be especially enjoyable. Several other sights around the town also deserve mention. The 13th-century Norman **Roscommon Castle,** situated just to the north of the town, has a turbulent history, beginning four years after its construction when Irish invaders captured and destroyed it. Rebuilt several years later, the castle suffered continuous sieges until it was finally conquered by Oliver Cromwell's forces. Not far from the castle are the remains of the 13th-century **Dominican Priory.**

14 From Roscommon, the N60 leads you northwest to **Castlerea,** a busy and prosperous town—sometimes called the "crossroads of Connaught"—situated at the juncture of the Rivers Suck and Francis. **Clonalis House,** the major attraction here, is a Victorian mansion built on the site of the ancestral home of the prominent O'Connor family. The house features a range of historical artifacts—including costumes, uniforms, and lace, all belonging to the O'Connors. You can also see the harp used by the 17th-century blind bard Turlough O'Carolan. *Tel. 0907/20014. Admission: £1.50 adults, 75p children. Open June–Sept., Mon.–Sat. 11–5:30, Sun. 2–6.*

15 The R361 takes you north from Castlerea to **Boyle,** at the foot of the Curlew Mountains on the banks of the River Boyle. Lough Gara and Lough Key, on either side of the town, make it an attractive spot for fishing. On the north side of the town lie the well-preserved ruins of a 12th-century **Cistercian Abbey.** *Tel. 079/62604. Admission: 80p adults, 30p children. Open mid-June–mid-Sept., daily 10–6.*

16 Just east of the town is the **Lough Key Forest Park** (tel. 079/62363), surrounding one of the most beautiful lakes in Ireland. Within the park, you'll find picnic sites, a caravan and camping park, a deer compound, forest walks, a bog garden, nature trails, and facilities for boating, fishing, and cruising.

Leaving Boyle on the N4 going southeast, you'll pass Carrick-
17 on-Shannon and Longford before arriving at **Edgeworthstown** (also called Mostrim), noted for its fairs and markets. **Edgeworthstown House,** at the eastern end of the town, was once the residence of the celebrated Edgeworth family, one of whom—Maria Edgeworth (1767–1849)—became a well-known novelist and essayist. Now a nursing home, it is no longer open to the public.

From here, turn north onto the N55 and follow signs to the
18 town of **Cavan.** Its history centers around the O'Reilly clan, who erected a castle (no longer in existence) in the 13th century and established a mint, the coins of which were legal tender on the European mainland until 1447. Nowadays the town is known for its crystal, and the **Crystal Factory** runs daily tours of its premises, showing visitors the technique for blowing and cutting glass. *Dublin Rd., tel. 049/31852. Admission free. Open weekdays 9–5, except the first 2 wks in Aug.*

Traveling north from Cavan on the N3, you can follow signs to
19 **Killykeen Forest Park.** Organized within the beautiful mazelike network of lakes called **Lough Oughter,** this 600-acre park offers a series of planned and signposted walks and nature trails. *Tel. 049/32541. Admission free. Parking: £1.50. Open Feb.–Dec., daily 9–5; closed Jan.*

Continue past **Butler's Bridge** on the N3 and on to **Belturbet,** a resort village with plenty of fishing and boating. From Belturbet, the R197 leads you east several kilometers to the
20 N54 north, which takes you into **Clones.** In early Christian times, this agricultural town was the site of a monastery founded by St. Tighearnach, who died in Clones in AD 548; an Augustinian abbey replaced the monastery in the 12th century, and its remains can still be seen near the 23-m- (75-ft-) high **Round Tower.** In the central diamond of the town stands a 10th-century Celtic **high cross,** with carved panels representing scriptural scenes.

Follow the N54 northeast from Clones until you reach
21 **Monaghan,** the capital of County Monaghan and another thriving agricultural center. There is a good view of the town from **St. Macartan's Catholic Church** (tel. 047/82300), a neo-Gothic 19th-century structure with a lofty slender spire and a spacious interior. Those with a taste for the history of the region may enjoy a visit to the **Monaghan County Museum,** whose varied collection includes archaeological finds and handcrafted lace, much of it from Carrickmacross (*see* below), a neighboring town famous for its traditional lace. Perhaps the most precious item in the museum is the bronze 13th-century **Cross of Clogher.** *The Courthouse, Clones Rd., tel. 047/82211. Admission: £1 adults, 50p children. Open Tues.–Sat. 10–1 and 2–5; June–Aug., also Sun. 2–6.*

If you have more time in the area, we suggest one of two short excursions inside the county. The first one goes north on the
22 N12 and then on the B45 to **Glaslough,** or "green lake," as the name translates. On the shores of this deep and beautiful lake is

Castle Leslie, originally a medieval castle, rebuilt in 1870 by Sir John Leslie, and now housing an impressive collection of artwork. The house itself may or may not be open, depending on whether the owner is at home, but for much of the year, visitors can tour the garden. Call ahead to make sure the house is accessible. *Tel. 047/88109. Admission: £1 adults, 50p children. Open May–Oct., daily 10–5.*

The second excursion takes you south along the N2 into
23 **Castleblaney,** where Hope Castle, built by Sir Edward Blaney
and later transformed into a convent, lies at the southern
boundary of the town. Continue on the N2 until you reach
24 **Carrickmacross,** known for its lace-making industry. You can
purchase lace and watch it being made at the **St. Louis Convent.**
Tel. 042/61247. Admission free. Open weekdays 10–4.

Just outside the town, about 3 km (2 mi) southwest on the R179,
25 lies **Dun a Ri Forest Park.** The 600 acres of woods here contain
many excellent walking trails. *Tel. 042/67320. Admission free.
Car park: £1. Open daily 10–5.*

Sports and Fitness

Biking

One of the best ways to immerse yourself in the natural beauty of the Lakelands is to tour the region on a bicycle. Twisting roads, generally in good condition, lead from one magnificent view to another, and there are picnic places in the state-owned forests, just off the main road. The Irish Tourist Board recommends two long tours: one of the Athlone-Mullingar-Roscommon area, and another of the Cavan-Monaghan-Mullingar region. But part of the pleasure of traveling on bicycle is breaking away from the prescribed routes and making discoveries on your own. Shops that rent cycles in the Lakelands region include the following: **M.R. Hardiman** (Irishtown, Athlone, Co. Westmeath, tel. 0902/78669), **Brendan Sheerin** (Main St., Boyle, Co. Roscommon, tel. 079/62010), **E. Clerkin** (Main St., Monaghan, Co. Monaghan, tel. 047/81434), and **Leo Hunt** (Main St., Roscommon, Co. Roscommon, tel. 0903/26299).

Boating

There are 300 miles of navigable rivers and island-studded lakes in the region, and several companies rent out charter boats of varying sizes for vacations on the water. Most of these vessels hold from six to eight people, and all are operated by the parties who rent them: **Athlone Cruisers Ltd.** (The Jolly Mariner Marina, Athlone, Co. Westmeath, tel. 0902/72892), **Carrick Craft** (The Marina, Banagher, Co. Offaly, tel. 0902/51187), **Celtic Canal Cruisers Ltd.** (24th Lock, Tullamore, Co. Offaly, tel. 0506/21861), and **Silverline Cruisers** (Banagher, Co. Offaly, tel. 0902/51112).

Fishing

For pike, you'll find the most fruitful areas around Cavan, Clones, Cootehill, Castleblaney, Kingscourt, Carrick-on-Shannon, Boyle, Belturbet, and Butlersbridge. Keep in mind, however, that certain laws have been passed to protect and conserve the dwindling population of Irish pike: You are forbidden to use live fish bait, to fish with more than two rods, to transfer live roach from one water to another, or to kill more than three pike in a day. For rudd fishing, the best places are the waters around Mullingar (Lough Patrick, Lough Analla, and the Royal Canal) and Monaghan (Lough na Glach, Lough Moynalty, Lough Corcrin); and tench fishermen seem to favor Carrick-on-Shannon, Boyle, Strokestown, Lanesborough, Athlone, Carrickmacross, and Shercock.

The Lakelands region hosts several angling festivals, with prize money and fringe events such as sing-alongs, dart games, and card competitions. Castleblayney has a tournament in March; Carrickmacross and Ballinsasloe, in May; Athlone, in July and October; and Cootehill, in September. Contact the Irish Tourist Board for more details on these tournaments.

For information on necessary licenses and permits, *see* Chapter 1, Essential Information.

Golf

The golfing clubs in the region offer fine courses, moderate green fees, and clubs and golf carts for rent. All of the following places welcome visitors: **Athlone Golf Club** (Hoosens Bay, Athlone, Co. Westmeath, tel. 0902/20731), **Mullingar Golf Club** (Belvedere, Mullingar, Co. Westmeath, tel. 044/48629), **Longford Golf Club** (Glack, Longford, Co. Longford, tel. 043/46310), **Portlaoise Golf Club** (The Heath, Portlaoise, Co. Laois, tel. 0502/26533), and **Virginia Golf Club** (Virginia, Co. Cavan, tel. 049/47110).

Walking

Forest park trails (Killykeen, Lough Key, and Dun a Ri forest parks) and narrow country roads invite visitors to tour parts of the Lakelands on foot. One impressive walking trail, to the east of Birr, runs through the Slieve Bloom Mountains, where sights include deep glens, rock formations, waterfalls, and views from mountain peaks.

Dining and Lodging

Dining

Category	Cost*
Very Expensive	over £20
Expensive	£15–£20
Moderate	£10–£15
Inexpensive	Under £10

* *per person, excluding drinks, service, and sales tax (10%)*

Lodging

Category	Cost*
Very Expensive	over £100
Expensive	£70–£100
Moderate	£40–£70
Inexpensive	Under £40

* *double occupancy, not including sales tax (10%)*

Highly recommended restaurants and hotels are indicated by a star ★.

Athlone

Dining and Lodging

The Prince of Wales. Conveniently located in the center of town, the Prince of Wales Hotel, which dates back to 1848, houses a restaurant serving reasonably priced food and drink. The decor is bright and cheerful, with floral drapes and lots of brassware. For an entrée, try the filet Mignon with wine or the veal cutlet with peppers. The hotel offers good service and comfortable, if unspectacular, rooms furnished with Victorian-style beds, chairs, and dressers. *Church St., Athlone, Co. Westmeath, tel. 0902/72626. 42 rooms, all with private bath and shower. AE, DC, V. Closed Dec. 25–27. Moderate.*

Birr

Dining and Lodging

Dooley's Hotel. An old coaching lodge in the center of Birr, Dooley's Hotel features ceilings with oak beams, private alcove lounges, an open-hearth fire, hunting prints, and brass-mounted lamps. The hotel was renovated and modernized to a more elegant standard in 1987, but a rustic atmosphere still pervades the place, and the restaurant has a similar feel. The menu of Irish and Continental dishes includes braised beef with red wine and beef bourguignonne. If noise tends to bother you, ask for one of the quieter rooms in the back. *Emmet Sq., Birr, Co. Offaly, tel. 0509/20032. 18 rooms, all with private bath and shower. AE, DC, V. Moderate.*

Clones

Dining and Lodging

The Creighton Hotel. Upon entering this budget accommodation, visitors from abroad may guess that it's a popular spot for anglers: Fishing prints, trout flies, and glass cases with mounted fish hang from the walls. The Creighton's comfortable rooms are furnished with simple, Victorian-style furniture, although the rooms in the front of the hotel may be noisy. *Fermanagh St., Clones, Co. Monaghan, tel. 047/51284. 18 rooms, all with bath and shower. No credit cards. Inexpensive.*

Monaghan

Dining and Lodging

The Four Seasons Hotel. This comfortable inn occupies a quiet spot just 1½ km (1 mi) outside of Monaghan in the town of Coolshannagh. The lobby's warm earthtones and the sporting prints on the wall give the place a rustic feel, and the bedrooms—with traditional period furniture, floral drapery, and views of the lawns—add to the effect. *Coolshannagh, Co. Monaghan, tel. 047/81888. 25 rooms, all with bath. AE, DC, V. Inexpensive.*

Mullingar

Dining and Lodging

Bloomfield House Hotel. This handsome hotel stands on 8 acres of wooded countryside on the shores of Lough Ennel. Previously a convent, the hotel was converted 10 years ago into its present form. Its past function accounts for the variety of rooms you'll find here, some with ceiling-to-floor windows, and others with small, Georgian-style ones. Of the four suites, two have dining areas and all overlook the lake. *Mullingar, Co. Westmeath, tel. 044/40894. 37 rooms, all with bath and shower. Facilities: restaurant, pitch and putt golf, tennis. AE, DC, V. Moderate.*

★ **Greville Arms Hotel.** Noted for its fine wines and its Irish and Continental cuisine, the James Joyce Restaurant in the Greville Arms Hotel is one of the finest in the Lakelands. It has a warm, cozy atmosphere, a personable staff, and an Old World charm. The windows look onto the Royal Canal, a background to enjoy while you dine on baked trout with almonds or pike fillets in a white wine sauce. The hotel is a 10-minute cab ride from the train station. It has brick walls and antique furniture in the lobby, and rooms are spacious and pleasant. *Pearse St., Mullingar, Co. Westmeath, tel. 044/48563. 33 rooms with bath. Facilities: restaurant. D, MC, V. Moderate.*

Portlaoise

Dining

The Maple Leaf Restaurant. Situated just outside of Portlaoise in Ballybrittas, this is an intimate country restaurant in the Montague Hotel. The brightly colored dining room has polished wood furnishings and floral decorations, and the food combines Irish and Continental cuisine. Some of the best dishes include stuffed quail with croutons, duck with apple sauce, and baked river trout. *Montague Hotel, Ballybrittas, Co. Laois, tel. 0502/26154. Reservations advised. Dress: casual. AE, DC, V. Moderate.*

Roscommon

Dining and Lodging

Abbey Hotel. If a quiet meal in a rural setting sounds attractive, try the Abbey Hotel, a 19th-century manor house on private grounds in the suburbs of Roscommon. The restaurant's outstanding reputation can be attributed to the beautiful surroundings, the French-style cooking, and the excellent service. Overnight guests enjoy large bedrooms and traditional touches. You can walk around the hotel gardens and visit the ruins of a medieval monastery. *Galway Rd., Roscommon, Co. Roscommon, tel. 0903/26240. 20 rooms, all with private bath and shower. AE, DC, V. Moderate.*

Virginia

Lodging

The Park Hotel, Deer Park Lodge. Visitors who tire easily of sightseeing should consider a few days at the Park Hotel, situated on Lough Ramor. It's only a short trip southeast from Cavan on the N3 or southwest from Carrickmacross on the R178, and the facilities at the hotel make the trek worthwhile.

Besides fishing and boating at Lough Ramor, guests can enjoy golf, tennis, and walks in the public park areas. Built as a nobleman's hunting lodge, this recently renovated 18th-century hotel has rooms overlooking the lake and a lobby reminiscent of its past function, with a fireplace, sporting prints, and a mounted deer's head. *Virginia, Co. Cavan, tel. 049/47235. 22 rooms, 19 with bath. Facilities: tennis, golf. AE, DC, V. Closed late Oct.–Feb.*

6 The Southeast

Introduction

by Pat Mackey

There's a salty edge to life down here that you won't find in the rest of Ireland. It radiates inland from the coastal counties' sandy beaches and shipyards, slowly giving way to Carlow's fertile countryside, Tipperary's rocky peaks, and Kilkenny's well-cultivated farmland. The Vikings felt it, and while they overran all of Ireland at one time or another, it was in the Southeast that they made their home. The harbor-dimpled coast and the sunny, warm climate, so unlike the rest of the country, were as difficult to pass up then as they are now. The shoreline, the sunshine, the seafood—the very things that the Vikings found so attractive in the 9th century—are just what draw vacationers to the shores of Wexford and Waterford counties today.

The people of the Southeast pride themselves on their fine beaches and good fishing, but they define themselves by their history. Having been occupied at various times by Celtic, Norse, Anglo-Norman, Welsh, and English settlers, the Southeast heritage is like a patchwork quilt, and each group that passed through contributed a piece of itself to the area. But perhaps it is the more recent history that is remembered most clearly by the people who live here. The rolling green countryside also served as the battlefield for some of Ireland's most important conflicts during her struggle for independence. Wexford was the center of the tragic Rebellion of 1798, in which more than 50,000 poorly armed Irish rebels were cut down by English troops—an event that lives on in the collective memory of the county's residents as if it had just occurred last month, rather than almost 200 years ago.

It seems you can't drive more than a mile or two without tripping over the ruin of some long-abandoned Norman fortress or one of many prehistoric standing-stone dolmens. The Brown's Hill Dolmen, the largest of these ancient markers, can be found in County Carlow. The twin coastal towns of Waterford and Wexford were settled by the Vikings (Waterford's name is derived from the Norse word *Vadrefjord*, Wexford's from *Waesfjord)*, but when they were ousted by the Normans these cities became walled strongholds. Explore either one today and you'll find the ruins of the original stone walls and gates, surrounded and overgrown as the cities expanded into the surrounding countryside.

Kilkenny Town, long an ecclesiastic and political center, is also Ireland's best-preserved medieval town. It is here that you'll find Kilkenny Castle, the 12th-century edifice of stone towers and battlements that served as home to the prominent Anglo-Norman Butler family for centuries. County Tipperary is home to the breathtaking and well-visited Rock of Cashel, ancient seat of the kings of Munster. These fierce rulers, among them the legendary Brian Boru, are some of the most impressive figures in Irish history, and it is only fitting that the cathedral-topped rock that served as their home should be among the most impressive sights in Ireland.

Essential Information

Arriving and Departing by Plane

Airports and Airlines **Waterford Regional Airport** (tel. 051/75580) is located on the Waterford–Ballymacaw road in Killowen. **RyanAir** (tel. 051/78272) schedules flights out of this small regional airport three times daily to Luton, England, and weekly to Liverpool, England.

Between the Airport and Center City Waterford City is 9½ km (6 mi) from the airport. **Suirway Bus Service** (tel. 051/82209) provides transportation between the airport and town, with a station located opposite the Tourist Information Office on Merchant's Quay. A hackney cab from the airport into Waterford will cost approximately £10, and there are car rental facilities at the airport.

Arriving and Departing by Car and Ferry

By Car Waterford, the regional capital, is easily accessible from all parts of Ireland. From Dublin, take the N7 southwest, change to the N9 in Naas, and continue along this highway through Carlow and Thomastown until it terminates in Waterford. The N25 travels east–west through Waterford, connecting it with Cork in the west and Wexford in the east. And from Limerick and Tipperary, the N24 stretches southeast until it, too, ends in Waterford.

By Ferry The region's primary ferry terminal is found just south of Wexford at Rosslare. **Sealink Ferries** (tel. 053/33115) sails directly between Rosslare Ferryport and Fishguard, Wales. Pembroke, Wales, can be reached on the **B+I Lines** (tel. 053/33311), and there are three sailings weekly to France's Le Havre and Cherbourg on **Irish Ferries** (tel. 053/33158).

Rental Cars The major car rental companies have offices at Rosslare Ferryport, and in most large towns rental information can be found through the local tourism office. Typical car rental prices start at about £40 per day with unlimited mileage, and they usually include insurance and all taxes. **Budget** has offices in both Rosslare Harbour (The Ferryport, tel. 053/33318) and Waterford (41 The Quay, tel. 051/21670), as does **Hertz** (tel. 053/33238 in Rosslare Harbour; Cork Rd., tel. 051/72886 in Waterford).

Getting Around

By Train Waterford is linked by **Irish Rail** (tel. 01/366222 in Dublin) service to Dublin. Trains run from Plunkett Station in Waterford to Dublin four times daily, making stops at Kilkenny, Thomastown, and Carlow. The daily train between Waterford and Limerick makes stops at Tipperary and Clonmel. The train between Rosslare and Waterford runs twice daily.

By Bus **Bus Éireann** (tel. 01/366111 in Dublin, 051/73401 in Waterford) makes the Waterford–Dublin journey four times daily for about £8. There are three buses daily between Waterford and Limerick, and three between Waterford and Rosslare. The Cork–Waterford journey is made twice daily. In Waterford the terminal is Plunkett Station.

By Car For the most part, the main roads in the Southeast are of good quality and are free of congestion. Side roads are generally narrow and twisting, and drivers should keep an eye out for farm machinery or animals on country roads.

Important Addresses and Numbers

Tourist Information **South East Regional Tourism Organisation Ltd.** (41 Merchant's Quay, Waterford, tel. 051/75823).

Carlow Tourist Information Office (Hadden Shopping Center, Tullow St., Carlow, tel. 503/31554).

New Ross Tourist Information Office (Harbour Centre, The Quay, Co. New Ross, Wexford, tel. 051/21857).

Tipperary Tourist Information Office (3 James St., Tipperary, tel. 062/51457).

Kilkenny Tourist Information Office (Rose Inn St., Kilkenny, tel. 056/21755).

Rosslare Tourist Information Office (Rosslare Ferry Terminal, Kilrane, Rosslare Harbour, Co. Wexford, tel. 053/33232).

Tramore Tourist Information Office (Railway Sq., Tramore, Co. Waterford, tel. 051/81522).

Lismore Tourist Information Office (Main St., Lismore, Co. Waterford, tel. 058/54646).

Emergency Numbers **Waterford Regional Hospital** (Ardkeen, Co. Waterford, tel. 051/73321).

Garda (Police) Emergency (tel. 999).

Ambulance and Fire (tel. 999).

Guided Tours

Walking tours of historic Wexford, arranged by the **Old Wexford Society**, meet at the Talbot Hotel on Trinity Street (tel. 053/22566) and at White's Hotel on George's Street (tel. 053/22311) every evening during the summer.

Walking tours of Kilkenny are arranged by **Tynan Tours** and operate daily from the Kilkenny Tourist Information Office (Rose Inn St., tel. 056/21755).

Exploring the Southeast

Highlights for First-time Visitors

Brown's Hill Dolmen (*see* Tour 1)
Irish National Heritage Park (*see* Tour 1)
Kilkenny Castle (*see* Tour 2)
Mitchelstown Caves (*see* Tour 2)
Rock of Cashel (*see* Tour 2)
Vee Gap Scenic Route (*see* Tour 2)
Waterford Glass Factory (*see* Tour 2)

Tour 1: Counties Carlow and Wexford

Numbers in the margin correspond with points of interest on The Southeast Ireland map.

County Carlow

Tiny, historic Carlow, the second-smallest of Ireland's counties, is a rural patchwork of rich farmland intersected by the
1 Barrow and Slaney rivers. **Carlow Town,** the county capital, is,
found in the northwest corner of the county along the banks of
the River Barrow. It is in this modern market town that we will
begin our tour.

Carlow Town's rich history dates back long before the 12th-century arrival of the Normans, but one of the town's most prominent sights is the more recently built Roman Catholic **Cathedral of the Assumption** (tel. 503/31227, open daily 10–8) on Tullow Street. Completed in 1883, the Gothic cathedral is notable for its superb stained-glass windows and a famous monument by celebrated Irish sculptor John Hogan.

Another major sight in Carlow Town is the ruins of the 13th-century **Carlow Castle,** found near the Barrow Bridge on the grounds of the Corcoran's Mineral Water factory. This castle withstood a siege by Cromwell's troops in 1650, only to be destroyed accidentally in the early 19th century. It seems that in 1814, Dr. Philip Middleton attempted to renovate the castle for use as a mental asylum, and while setting off explosives to gut the interior, Middleton accidentally demolished all but one wall of the old fortress, leaving it in ruins.

One last stop worth making in Carlow Town is the **County Museum** in the town hall. Among the exhibits at the museum are a reconstructed blacksmith's forge and a historic kitchen. *Centaur St., tel. 503/43299. Admission: 50p adults, 30p children. Open daily May–Sept. 11–5:30, Oct.–Apr. Sun. only 2:30–5:30.*

A brief 3¼-km (2-mi) detour on the road to Tullow (R725) east of Carlow Town will bring you to the famous **Brown's Hill Dolmen.** This stone monument dates from 2000 BC and, with a capstone weighing in at 100 tons, is considered to be the largest such prehistoric marker in Ireland. The dolmen is accessible through a field gate along the road; there is no admission fee.

Double back to Carlow Town and pick up highway N9 south for
2 some 10 km (6¼ mi) into **Leighlinbridge,** the site where the first
bridge over the River Barrow was constructed. As is the case
with so many small Irish towns, many of Leighlinbridge's sons
had to leave their homeland to seek their fortunes in the world:
Some of the more famous offspring from this spot include prominent scientist John Tyndall; Cardinal Patrick Francis Moran,
the first Catholic archbishop of Sydney; and Captain Myles
Kehoe, who battled alongside General Custer at Little Big-
horn.

In Leighlinbridge you'll find the ruins of **Black Castle;** built in the 12th century, this fortress was one of the earliest Norman defenses in Ireland, and has been the scene of countless battles and sieges over the centuries. Just one 400-year-old tower remains standing today.

Just 4¾ km (3 mi) west of Leighlinbridge is the small village of
3 **Old Leighlin,** location of one of Ireland's earliest Christian set-

The Southeast

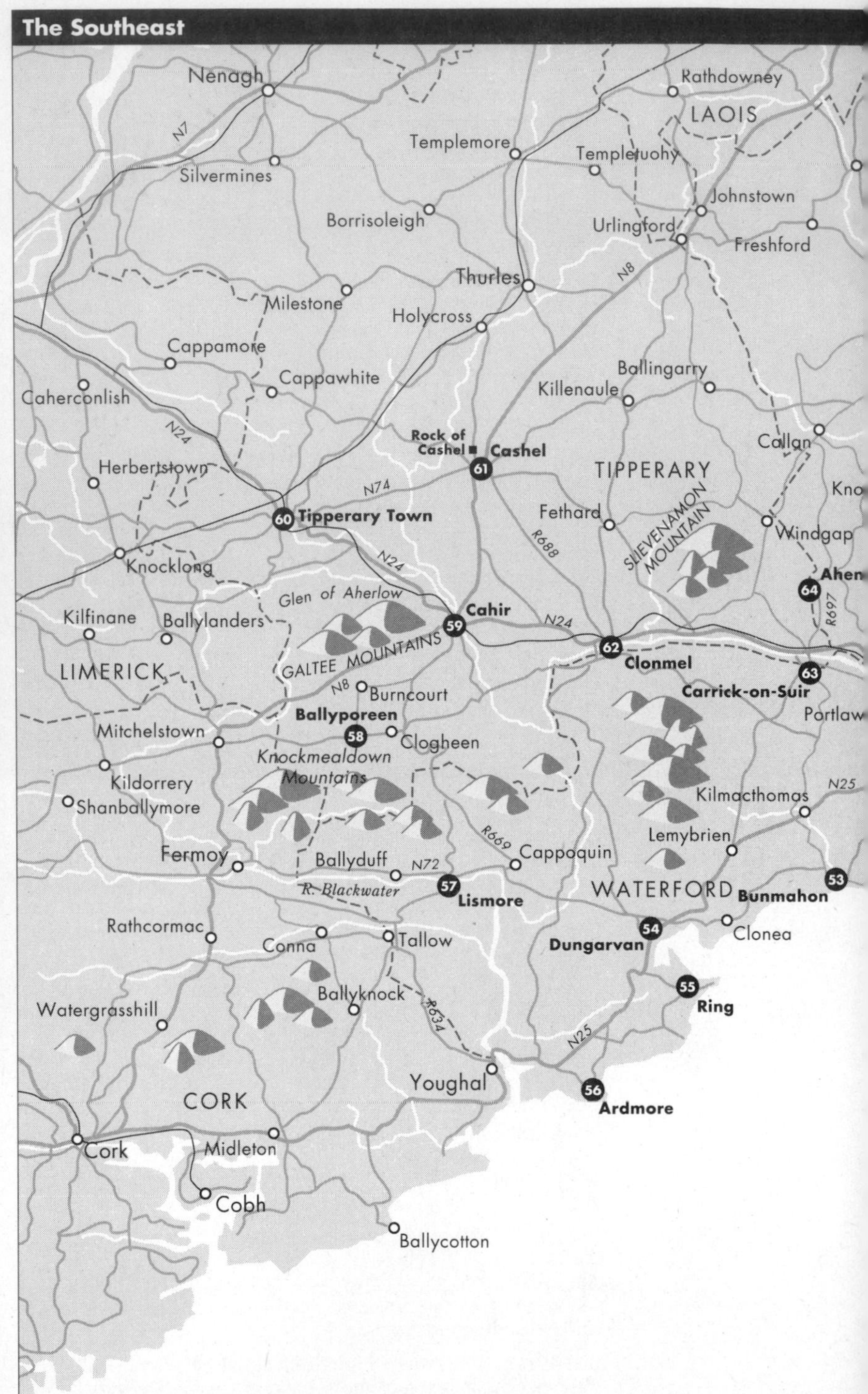

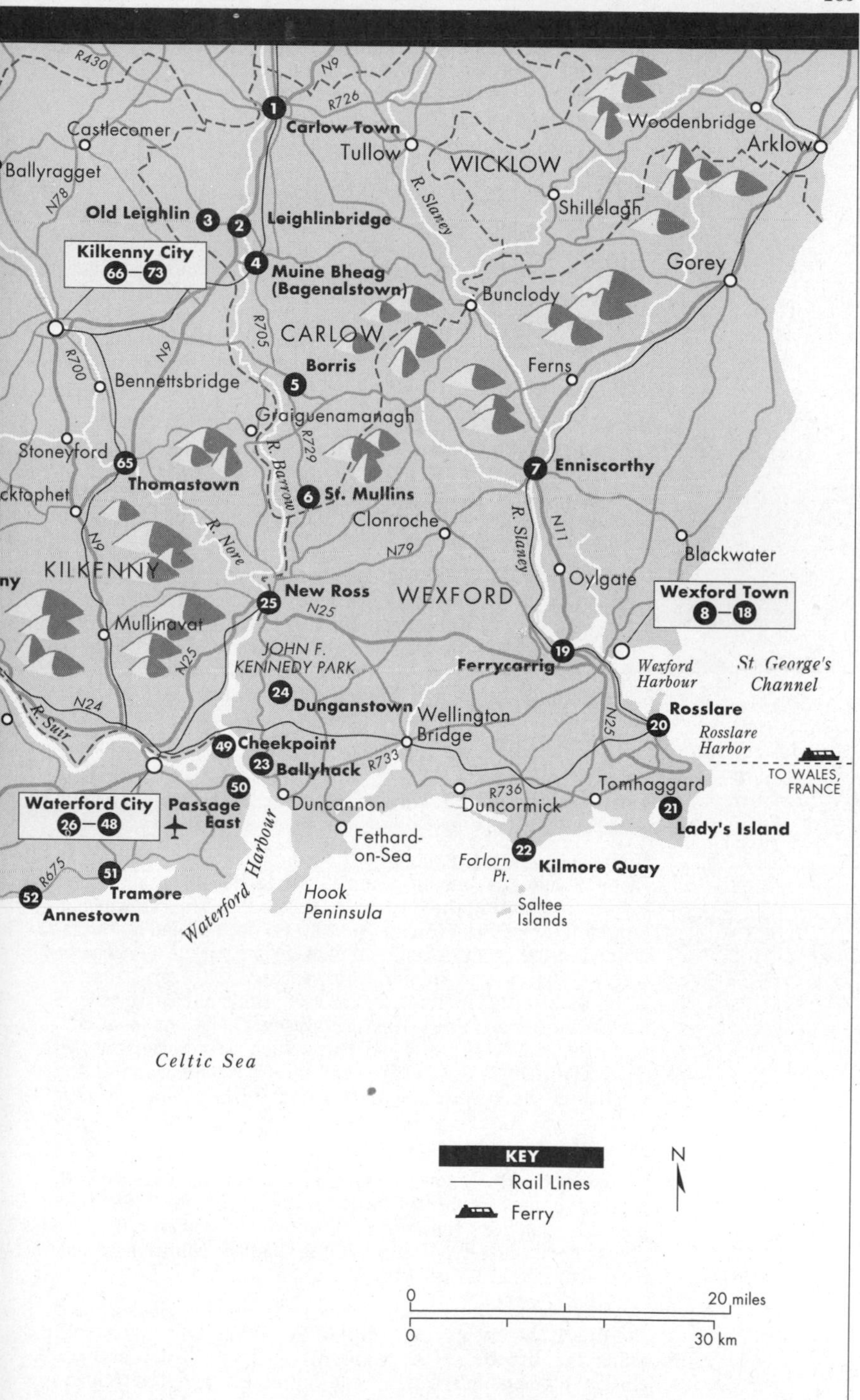

Carlow Town
Castlecomer
Tullow
WICKLOW
Woodenbridge
Arklow
Ballyragget
Old Leighlin
Leighlinbridge
Shillelagh
Kilkenny City
66—73
Muine Bheag
(Bagenalstown)
Gorey
Bunclody
CARLOW
Borris
Ferns
Bennettsbridge
Graiguenamanagh
Stoneyford
Thomastown
Enniscorthy
St. Mullins
Clonroche
Blackwater
KILKENNY
Oylgate
New Ross
WEXFORD
Wexford Town
8—18
Mullinavat
JOHN F. KENNEDY PARK
Ferrycarrig
Wexford Harbour
St. George's Channel
Dunganstown
Wellington Bridge
Rosslare
Rosslare Harbor
Cheekpoint
Ballyhack
TO WALES, FRANCE
Tomhaggard
Waterford City
26—48
Passage East
Duncannon
Duncormick
Lady's Island
Fethard-on-Sea
Forlorn Pt.
Kilmore Quay
Tramore
Annestown
Waterford Harbour
Hook Peninsula
Saltee Islands
R. Slaney
R. Barrow
R. Nore
R. Suir
Celtic Sea
KEY
Rail Lines
Ferry
N
0
20 miles
0
30 km

tlements. A Celtic monastery founded here in the 7th century under St. Laserian was rebuilt in the 12th century as **St. Laserian's Cathedral.** Worth noticing here are the Gothic doorway; the rare, early Christian carvings on the grave monuments; and the nearby holy well.

4 Return to Leighlinbridge and pick up the R705 south to **Muine Bheag** (Bagenalstown). This unusually attractive town was named for its 18th-century founder, Walter Bagenal. The ambitious Bagenal built the town to meet his own high aspirations; he was responsible for the construction of fine public buildings, including a railroad station and a courthouse, all laid out alongside spacious streets and squares. The town's most impressive sight, however, isn't in the town at all. Take the L33 east of town for 3¼ km (2 mi) to reach **Ballymoon Castle.** The massive gatehouse from this 14th-century fortress remains standing, as do three of the towers.

Head back into Bagenalstown and get on the R705 again, heading south. Along this route you'll pass through the pretty vil-
5 lage of **Borris,** where you might like to pause to take a look at the ruins of **Borris Castle.** This is the ancestral home of the Kavanagh family, who are descendants of the ancient kings of the Leinster province.

6 Farther along the R705 you'll pass by the village of **St. Mullins,** founded by St. Moling in the 7th century. Once a great ecclesiastical center, St. Mullins is today home to the ruins of numerous churches and abbeys. The Book of Moling, a Latin copy of the Gospels, contains an inscription that refers to Art MacMurrough Kavanagh. Passed down through the Kavanagh family for centuries, it now resides in a brass-and-silver shrine at Trinity College in Dublin.

County Wexford

Continue south on the R729 from St. Mullins until you reach its junction with the N79. Turn left (east) on the N79 and continue
7 on through the Slaney Valley toward **Enniscorthy.**

Historic Enniscorthy, built on the steeply sloping banks of the River Slaney, is one of County Wexford's most attractive towns. Dominating the town is the castle, built by the Norman knight Maurice Prendergast in 1199 and once owned by the famous English poet Edmund Spenser, author of *The Faerie Queene*. Both the site of fierce battles against Oliver Cromwell and the center of the Rebellion of 1798, the Enniscorthy castle now houses the **County Wexford Museum.** The museum contains thousands of historical items such as a reconstructed dairy and displays of pottery and military memorabilia, and you'll find the curator eager to narrate the exhibits. *Castle Hill, tel. 054/35926. Admission: £1 adults, 30p children. Open weekdays 10–6, weekends 2–6.*

On the east side of town you'll find the famous **Vinegar Hill,** where the most important battle in the Rebellion of 1798 took place. It was here that some 20,000 rebels, armed only with pikes, made a last desperate stand against the continuous bombardment of the British Army's cannon fire.

Before leaving Enniscorthy, you'll want to take a look at both the fine 19th-century **Cathedral of St. Aidan,** which was built under the direction of Augustus Welby Pugin (celebrated architect of London's Parliament building), and the Market

Square statue of Vinegar Hill rebel leader **Father John Murphy,** by Oliver Sheppard.

From Enniscorthy take the N11 south for about 20 km (12.4 mi)
8 into the town of **Wexford,** an ancient place identified on maps by
the Greek geographer Ptolemy as long ago as the 2nd century
AD. The River Slaney empties into the sea here, and wharves line the length of the harbor where Viking traders docked their long ships centuries before. The harbor has silted up since those days, and Wexford is no longer hailed as the famous trading port it once was. Today, her name is most closely associated with excellent seafood, particularly with the famous mussels cultivated in these harbor waters.

Numbers in the margin correspond with points of interest on the Wexford Town map.

9 While you are exploring the waterfront's **Crescent Quay,** be
10 sure to see the bronze **statue of Commodore John Barry,** the Father of the American Navy. Born in 1745 in nearby Bally-
sampson, he settled in Philadelphia by the age of 15 and became
a brilliant naval fighter during the American Revolution. You'll
11 also notice the **Tourist Information Office** along this same
stretch of waterfront.

Walk up Harpers Lane from the Quay and make a left onto Main
Street. On this narrow thoroughfare parallel with the waterfront, boutiques and pubs stand cheek by jowl with bakeries
and vegetable shops, and shopping can prove to be a delightful
experience for visitors seeking provincial Irish charm. Head
toward the center of town, and at the corner of King and Bar-
12 rack streets you'll spot **St. Doologue's church.** This is the center
of the smallest parish—just 3 acres—in the world. If you continue on to the head of King Street, you'll see the birthplace of William Cody, father of the famous American Wild West showman "Buffalo" Bill Cody, in the building that now houses Kelly's.

Return along South Main Street, and make a left onto Bride
Street. From here you can spot rising above the rooftops the
13 graceful spires of the **Immaculate Conception** church on Rowe
14 Street and the **Church of the Assumption** on Bride Street.
These elegant examples of Gothic architecture are known as the **"twin churches,"** because the foundation stones for both were laid on the same day in 1851.

From Bride Street, travel through St. Peter's Square to School
15 Street and the **Franciscan Church.** The ceiling in this church is
worth noticing for its fine, locally crafted stucco work and for
the popular shrine of St. Adjutor, a boy martyr from ancient
Rome. Continue along School Street, turn right onto Rowe
Street, and head downhill, passing the Church of the Immaculate Conception, mentioned above. At North Main Street turn
16 left to reach the **Wexford Bull Ring,** once the scene of bull bait-
ing, a cruel medieval sport that was popular among Norman nobility. This arena was also the sight of another, far more tragic event in 1649, when Cromwell's soldiers massacred 300 panic-stricken townspeople who had gathered here to pray as the army stormed their town.

A few last addresses worth noting as you wander these narrow, winding streets include Oliver Cromwell's temporary residence at 29 S. Main Street; the birthplace of Oscar Wilde's

Church of the Assumption, **14**
Church of the Immaculate Conception, **13**
Commodore John Barry Monument, **10**
Crescent Quay, **9**
Franciscan Church, **15**
St. Doologue's Church, **12**
Selskar Abbey, **18**
Tourist Information Office, **11**
Westgate Tower, **17**
Wexford Bull Ring, **16**

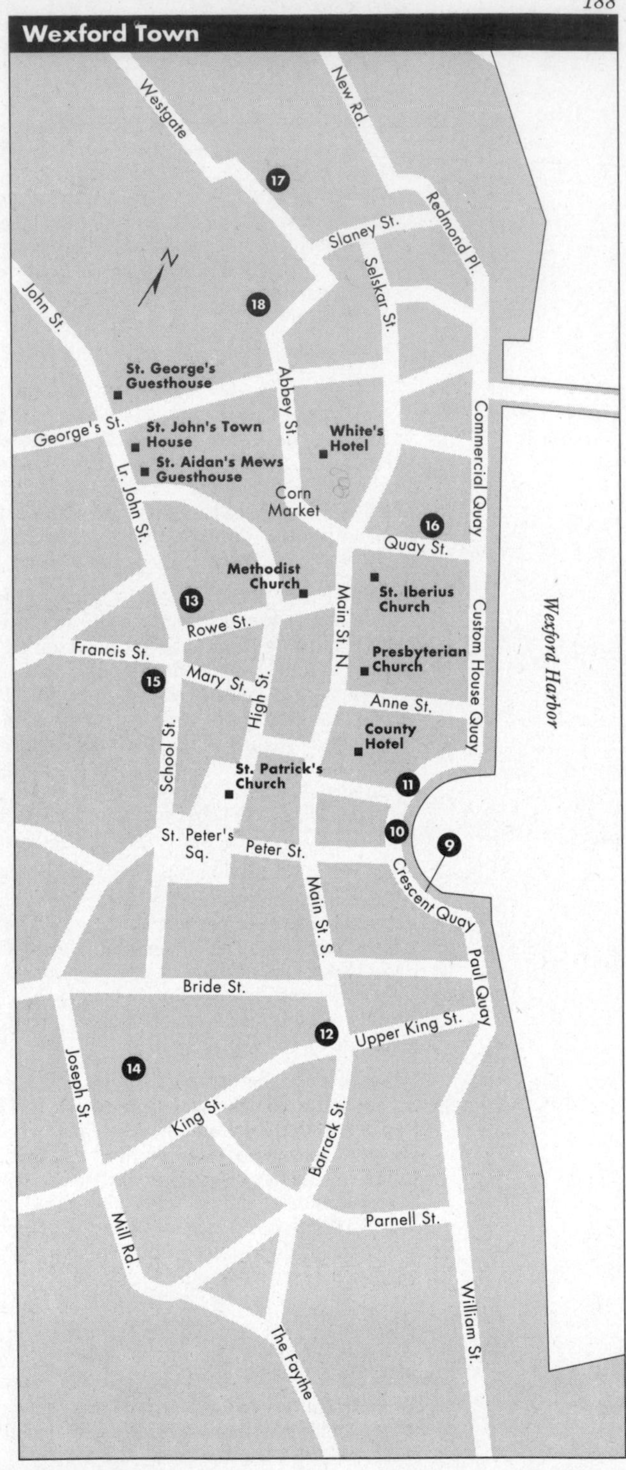

mother, also known as the writer Speranza, in the old rectory on Main Street at the Bull Ring; and the 19th-century poet Thomas Moore's home at the Cornmarket.

Continue along North Main Street and turn left at Slaney Street to reach the remains of the old town walls. There were originally five fortified gateways in the walls, but only the larg-
17 est one, the red sandstone **Westgate Tower,** remains standing today. Near this you'll come across the ruins of the 12th-
18 century **Selskar Abbey,** where the first treaty between the Irish and the Normans was signed in 1169. This is also the spot where, three years later, King Henry II did penance for ordering the murder of the archbishop of Canterbury, Thomas Becket.

Time Out The Wexford **Lodge Restaurant** (Wexford Bridge, tel. 053/23611) is a family-run restaurant specializing in seafood and steaks. There's a fine view of the River Slaney from the dining room.

Numbers in the margin correspond with points of interest on the Southeast Ireland map.

19 **Ferrycarrig,** on the northwestern outskirts of town, is a worthwhile side trip that can be made from Wexford on the N25. This is the home of the **Irish National Heritage Park,** a 35-acre site by the River Slaney where 9,000 years worth of Irish history can be traced through re-creations of Irish monuments and dwellings used through the centuries. Guided tours cover an early Christian monastery, a Viking boatyard, prehistoric homesteads, a dolmen, and Norman fortifications. *Ferrycarrig, Co. Wexford, tel. 053/41733. Admission: £2. Open daily 10–7.*

Double back on the N25 heading south and follow signs for Rosslare Strand. Along the way, just 5 km (3 mi) outside Wexford, you might like to stop in at Johnstown Castle, home of the **Irish Agricultural Museum.** The exhibits at this popular attraction are related to historical Irish agricultural equipment and methods. There is also a display of Irish country furniture. *Johnstown Castle, tel. 053/42888. Admission: £1.25 adults, 50p children. Open Mon.–Sat. 9–12:30 and 1:30–5, Sun. 2–5.*

With its warm, dry climate and seaside setting, it is no wonder
20 that George Bernard Shaw called **Rosslare** "a place of . . . infinite peace." The town is well-known for its fine, sandy beach and 18-hole golf course (tel. 053/32113), though what really put it on the map was the silting of Wexford Harbour, which forced the ferry business to move south and relocate here. To reach the **ferryport** (tel. 053/33115), follow the right fork of the junction of the N25 to Rosslare Harbour. Daily car ferries leave from here to Fishguard and Pembroke in Wales and to Le Havre and Cherbourg in France (*see* Arriving and Departing, above).

21 Return to the N25 and follow signs that lead you past **Lady's Island,** long a popular pilgrimage center for the Irish. Today, pilgrims walk in procession around the shores of the lake, but in centuries past, they had to keep one foot in the water and one on dry land while walking, and they had to abstain from food and drink for three days. Curiously, this stringent penance could be performed by proxy, and many's the early 19th-century noblewoman who paid some local lass to perform the pilgrimage in her place!

From here, follow signs leading southwest through Tomhaggard on to Forlorn Point and the picturesque fishing village of
22 **Kilmore Quay.** Boats can be rented in Kilmore Quay for day trips to the offshore **Saltee Islands,** once a playground for dangerous pirates but today a peaceful sanctuary for some 2,000 birds. Many of these boats are not insured for passengers, however, so ask about their insurance before you hire one.

On leaving Kilmore Quay, make your way north on the R736, then head west through Duncormick and on to Wellington Bridge. Past the bridge, head toward Fethard-on-Sea on the R733. Here, follow signs for Ring of Hook Drive, which will lead around the Hook Peninsula and into **Duncannon.** This Waterford Harbour fishing town boasts a fine beach and a delightful nautical atmosphere which makes it popular with visitors. Its history is marked by the visits of two kings; James II beat a hasty retreat out of Ireland through the Duncannon port after his defeat at the Battle of the Boyne in 1690, and his successor, William III, visited the same spot just two months later—perhaps just to check that James had truly left.

From Duncannon, continue north to the R733 and follow the
23 signs past Arthurstown to **Ballyhack,** terminal for the **Passage East Car Ferry** (Barrack St., Passage East, Co. Waterford, tel. 051/82480). This five-minute ferry journey delivers you across Waterford Harbour to County Waterford. The pretty little fishing village of Ballyhack is highlighted by a castle once owned by the Knights Templars of St. John of Jerusalem. These knights once held the ferry rights by royal charter, and traditionally they were required to always keep a boat at Ballyhack to transport injured knights to the King's Leper Hospital at Waterford.

Time Out Seafood is the reason you come to the **Neptune Restaurant** (tel. 051/89284) in Ballyhack. This delightful restaurant, located in an old schoolhouse, sports a fun, lighthearted ambience.

If you would like to shorten your journey, you can take the ferry from here and pick up the tour again in County Waterford at Passage East. Otherwise, continue your tour north along the Wexford coast of Waterford Harbour, which was created by the convergence of three major Irish rivers, the Barrow, the Nore, and the Suir. An interesting, though inaccurate, story developed around these waters to illustrate Oliver Cromwell's attack on Waterford City. The easternmost point of the harbor's mouth is known as Hook Head, while Crooke was the name of a village on the western shore. It seems that Cromwell devised a plan by which he would take Waterford City "by Hook or by Crooke," meaning that he would knock out the defenses at one of these two towns in order to advance; and thus the phrase came to mean "one way or the other." While the story seems plausible enough, history tells us a different one: In reality Cromwell's troops marched to Waterford overland from the west, a good 20 miles from either of these towns.

Take the R733 north out of Ballyhack for about 15 km (9 mi) to New Ross. Along the way, you may want to make a side trip off R733 to visit the **John F. Kennedy Park,** almost 600 acres of woodland that includes an arboretum, gardens, and a memorial
24 to the late U.S. president. The park is near **Dunganstown,** the ancestral home of the Kennedy family. *Tel. 051/88171. Ad-*

mission: £1. Open daily 10–8 May–Aug., 10–6 Sept. and Apr., 10–5 Oct.–Mar.

25 Situated on the banks of the River Barrow, **New Ross** is one of the oldest towns in County Wexford, and visitors will notice a strong sense of history in the broad quayside and the narrow, winding streets. The town was founded by Isabella de Clare, the earl of Pembroke's daughter, in the early 13th century, and it maintained a good reputation as one of the most prosperous Norman towns in Ireland. Today, situated in the midst of one of the country's richest agricultural areas, New Ross remains an important inland port. For travelers it serves as the gateway to the beautiful Barrow Valley and the settlements of St. Mullins, Inistioge, and Graignamanagh, though it is perhaps best known for its proximity to the John F. Kennedy Park. Popular activities here include golf, fishing, water sports, and sailing.

In the town itself, you may want to explore the tombs and monuments in the ruins of **St. Mary's Abbey** on Church Lane, once one of the largest abbeys in Ireland. Admission is free, but to enter the grounds you'll have to borrow the key from the caretaker, who lives opposite the abbey. Another worthwhile sight is the **Tholsel** (town hall) on Quay Street. Aside from serving as the town's municipal offices, this 18th-century building houses the royal maces of Edward III and Charles II as well as the original town charter from James II. There is also a memorial statue commemorating the Rebellion of 1798. The Norman wall that surrounded the town was originally more than a mile in length, but now only a few pieces remain; among them you might like to investigate the **Three Bullet Gate,** a section of wall with three of Cromwell's cannonballs lodged in it.

Time Out The only floating restaurant in the country, **Galley Cruising Restaurant** (tel. 051/21723) runs marvelous tea and dinner cruises on the River Barrow. Fresh local produce and seafood are emphasized here.

Tour 2: Counties Waterford, Tipperary, and Kilkenny

County Waterford

26 From New Ross, cross the bridge and take the N25 southwest for 22 km (14 mi) to the city of **Waterford,** famous for its exquisite crystal. Like Wexford, Waterford was also founded by the Vikings and boasted a succession of Viking kings. The massive Reginald's Tower, as well as substantial sections of the old Viking wall, remain as evidence of Viking occupation from the mid-9th century through the Norman arrival in the late-12th century. After the Normans evicted the Vikings, they went on to almost double the size of the city and build a wealthy trading port here.

The city prospered under English rule until the 17th century, when it was overrun by Cromwell's forces. Following this, the staunchly Catholic city suffered under economic sanctions imposed by the British government, and it was not until the late-18th century that a renaissance occurred, bringing new growth to the city.

Numbers in the margin correspond with points of interest on the Waterford City map.

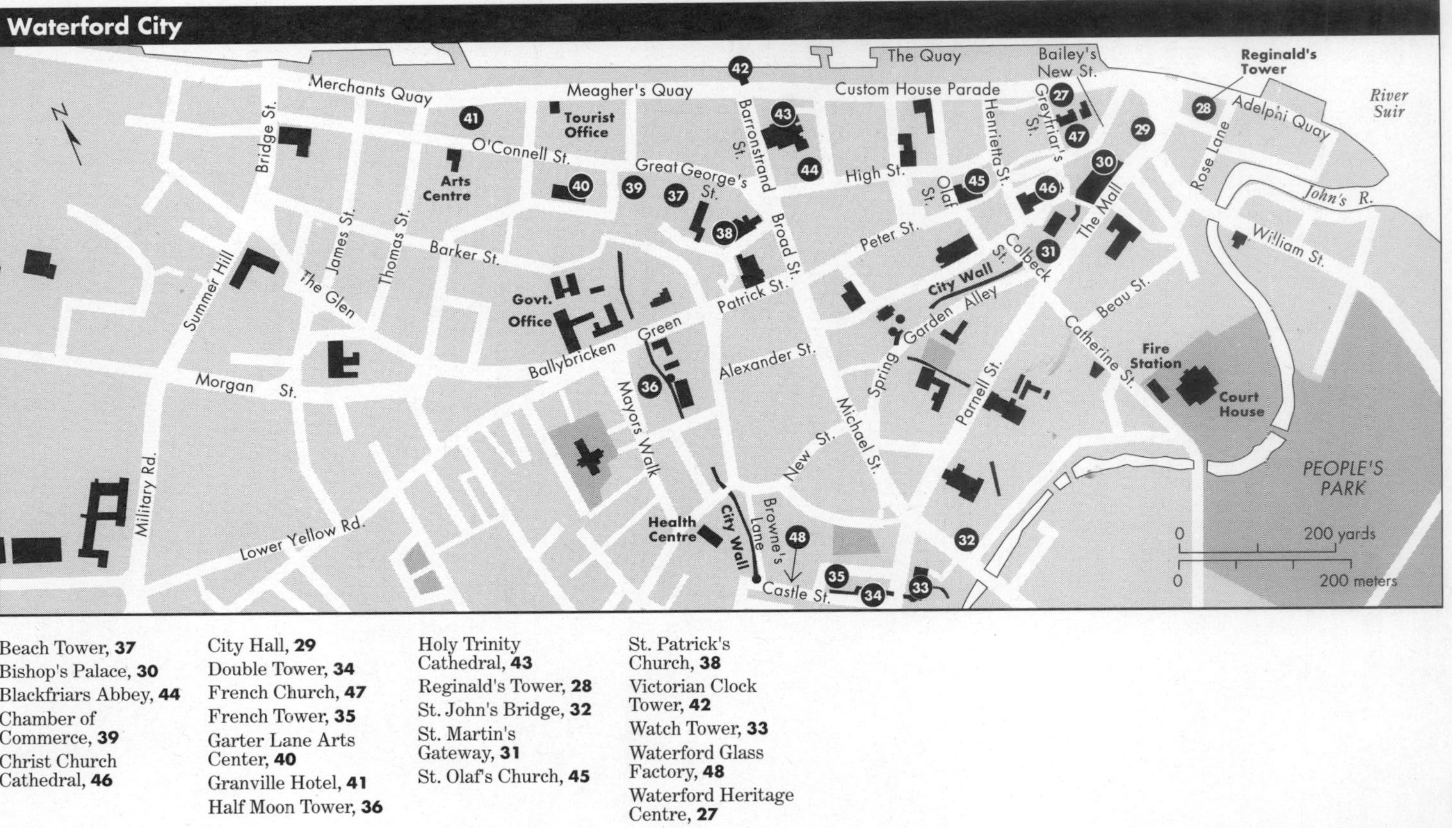

Beach Tower, **37**
Bishop's Palace, **30**
Blackfriars Abbey, **44**
Chamber of Commerce, **39**
Christ Church Cathedral, **46**
City Hall, **29**
Double Tower, **34**
French Church, **47**
French Tower, **35**
Garter Lane Arts Center, **40**
Granville Hotel, **41**
Half Moon Tower, **36**
Holy Trinity Cathedral, **43**
Reginald's Tower, **28**
St. John's Bridge, **32**
St. Martin's Gateway, **31**
St. Olaf's Church, **45**
St. Patrick's Church, **38**
Victorian Clock Tower, **42**
Watch Tower, **33**
Waterford Glass Factory, **48**
Waterford Heritage Centre, **27**

Begin your tour of Waterford at the corner of Greyfriar's Street
and Custom House Parade down at the quays. Here you'll find
27 the **Waterford Heritage Centre,** home to some of the 75,000 historical artifacts excavated from beneath the city in the mid-1980s. Parts of Viking houses were discovered, and they are displayed alongside samples of leatherwork, bone carvings, pottery, and pieces of ornate jewelry—quite an architectural goldmine. *Greyfriars St., tel. 051/73501. Admission: 50p. Open Mon.–Sat. 10–5.*

Make a right on the Parade and head down along the water to
28 the massive **Reginald's Tower,** built by the Vikings almost 1,000 years ago. The walls of this 25-meter- (80-ft-) high circular fortification are 3 meters (10 ft) thick and are lined on the inside with a stairway leading to the top. Since 1955 it has been used as a civic museum, but historically it has served in turn as the residence for a succession of Anglo-Norman kings, including Henry II, John, and Richard II; a mint for silver coins; a prison; and an ammunition storage building. It is also said that Strongbow's marriage was held here. *The Mall, tel. 051/73501. Admission: 50p. Open Mon.–Sat. 10–5.*

29 Proceed south along the Mall to **City Hall,** which was built in 1783 by a local architect, John Roberts. As you enter the imposing yet simply designed building, be sure to notice the Arms of Waterford over the entrance. Also worth investigating is the small display of military memorabilia and the enormous 1802 Waterford glass chandelier hanging in the Council Chamber: a copy of it hangs in Independence Hall in Philadelphia. The Theatre Royal (tel. 051/74402), a lovely old Victorian theater housed inside this building, hosts a yearly opera festival. *The Mall, tel. 051/73501. Admission free. Open weekdays 9–1 and 2–5.*

Time Out The **Reginald** restaurant and pub (The Mall, tel. 051/55087) is worth noting for its unusual decor: A section of the city's 9th-century Viking wall is incorporated into the restaurant's interior. This place is popular for lunch and snacks.

---

30 Alongside City Hall on the Mall is the **Bishop's Palace,** built in
1741 and restored in 1976. Considered to be one of the most imposing town houses in Ireland, it is an example of fine Georgian
architecture. Today, the building is used to house the city engineering offices, but the foyer is open to the public. As you continue along the Mall past the palace, you'll pass the spot where
31 **St. Martin's Gateway,** the southern corner of the Viking defense once stood, on the corner of Colbeck Street. No sign of it remains today.

Farther along the Mall, by this point called Parnell Street,
32 you'll see **St. John's Bridge** on the left, which served as the medieval entrance to the city. Proceed along Parnell and continue
33 onto Manor Street to find the **Watch Tower** on the left side of the
road at the corner of Castle Street. This restored fortification
is a remaining 10.5-m- (35-ft) high section of the old city wall.
Cross the street from here and head up Castle Street, where
34 you'll pass by two similar towers on the right, the **Double Tower**
35 and the **French Tower.** Turn right after the French Tower and
36 head up Brownes Lane to the **Half Moon Tower** and on to the
37 38 **Beach Tower** behind **St. Patrick's Church** (Great George's St.,

open during services only), one of the only surviving mid-18th-century churches in Ireland.

Pick up Great George's Street outside the church and turn left
39 to see the handsome **Chamber of Commerce** building (tel. 051/
72639, open weekdays 9–1 and 2–5). This 18th-century town
house was originally built as a private residence, but since it
was purchased by the city in 1815 it has been open to visitors as
a visual delight, both inside and out. Farther down Great
George's Street, after it becomes O'Connell Street, you can
40 visit the **Garter Lane Arts Centre,** Ireland's largest center for
the arts. Exhibitions, poetry readings, and performances by
the Red Kettle theater group are held here regularly. *O'Connell St., tel. 051/55038. Admission free. Open Tues.–Sat. 10–6.*

Make the first right past the arts center and another right onto
Merchant's Quay. As you walk along the Quay, you can spot the
41 **Granville Hotel,** birthplace of Irish-American hero Thomas
Francis Meagher, on the right side. Meagher (pronounced *Ma-
her*) grew up to become one of the leaders of the Irish Confeder-
ation, was arrested after the rising of 1848, and was sentenced
to life in an Australian penal colony. He escaped and made his
way to the United States in 1852, where he formed an Irish Bri-
gade to fight for the Union during the Civil War. Meagher's illustrious military career eventually led to his appointment as
governor of Montana in 1865.

42 Proceed farther along Merchant's Quay to see the **Victorian
Clock Tower** on the left side, built in 1864 with public donations.
43 Turn right on Barronstrand Street to view **Holy Trinity Cathedral** (tel. 051/74757). Don't let the rather simple-looking exteri-
or fool you—the inside is a rich and expansive space with high,
vaulted ceilings and striking Corinthian pillars. Take a moment to admire the magnificent set of Waterford crystal chandeliers, donated to the church by Waterford Glass.

Pass the cathedral and turn left on Blackfriars Street to reach
44 the ruined tower of **Blackfriars Abbey.** This old Dominican abbey was founded in 1226 on a land grant from Henry III on the
site of what was once Arundel Castle. The Blackfriars returned
the building to the crown in 1541, and it was used as a courthouse for years until it was destroyed by Cromwell's men. You
can visit the grounds free of charge by picking up the key at
City Hall (tel. 051/73501).

Continue along High Street to Olaf Street, and stop to look at
45 the remains of **St. Olaf's Church** (call City Hall for information
at 051/73501) on the right. This Viking church was built in the
9th century by King Sitric, Waterford's founder. Over the centuries it has fallen into ruin, and today it remains much as it
was in 1746, the last time restoration work was attempted.
Continue on High Street to Henrietta Street, and turn right for
46 one block to reach **Christ Church Cathedral.** A church was originally built on this site by the Vikings in 1050, only to be torn
down and replaced during the 18th century with the structure
that stands here today. While visiting, take note of the tomb of
James Rice. On his monument, a high-relief effigy of the man
shows him wrapped in his shroud, in a state of decay, with all
manner of frogs and bugs appearing to climb out of his corpse.

When you leave the church, go right through **Cathedral Square**
to Greyfriars to see, on the right, the roofless ruins of the
47 **French Church,** a 13th-century Franciscan abbey that was

given to a group of Huguenot refugees as a chapel in 1693. Walk toward the Quays from here, and you'll find yourself back at the beginning of this tour.

Last, but certainly not least, is the almost-mandatory trip to
48 the **Waterford Glass factory,** located about 2 km (1¼ mi) from
the quay in Kilbarry. You can reach the world-famous factory
by taking the N25, the main Waterford-to-Cork road, south
from the quay (buses run between the quay and the factory regularly; inquire at the tourist office).

Time Out The **Olde Stand Victorian Pub and Restaurant** (Michael St., tel. 051/79488) serves lunch and bar snacks at reasonable prices. Old paintings, maps of Waterford, and a handcrafted wooden bar add touches of nostalgia.

Guided tours of the glass works illustrate the intricate arts of blowing, cutting, and polishing glass, and though children under 14 are not allowed on the tour, they can watch videos of the process from the showroom. There's an extensive selection of crystal in the showroom and crystal gallery, and it is easy to arrange for delivery overseas. Tours, which take about 40 minutes, should be arranged in advance with the factory directly or through the tourist board. *Cork Rd., Kilbarry, tel. 051/73311. Admission free. Open weekdays 10:15–2:30.*

Numbers in the margin correspond with points of interest on the Southeast Ireland map.

As you leave Waterford City traveling east on the L157 toward
Cheekpoint, be sure to notice **Little Island,** located in the middle of the River Suir. This island is home to the Waterford Castle Hotel, which was at one time the home of noted 19th-
century traveler and translator Edward FitzGerald (*Rubáiyát*
49 *of Omar Khayyám*). In **Cheekpoint,** you'll find plenty of tranquillity and wonderful views of the river. Follow signs from
here south to Passage East, the Waterford terminal of the harbor ferry that connects with Ballyhack in County Wexford.

50 **Passage East**'s rocky slopes are populated by a herd of wild
goats, who some claim are descended from a pair who swam
ashore here following a Greek shipwreck. Whatever their origin, the folks around here consider them to be good luck. Continue through Passage East by following the signs leading you
past Woodstown and Dunmore East and on to the lovely resort
51 of **Tramore.**

The 5-km- (3-mi-) long beach at Tramore is a popular escape for people from Waterford and throughout the entire Southeast, as the many vacation homes and camper parks will attest. You'll find two very different environments along this stretch of sand: The immediate seaside is well populated with bustling amusement arcades and the like, while the upper half of town is markedly more quiet and reserved. At the western end of the beach the sand gives way to rocky cliffs where the Metal Man, a giant cast-iron figure dressed in an 18th-century seaman's costume and facing seaward with outstretched arms, presides. He is posed on top of a great pillar, and it is said that if a young woman hops around the base of the pillar three times on one foot, she will be married within a year. This tale can be traced back to a standing stone which stood on this same spot centuries ago and had been used in ancient Celtic fertility rites.

Time Out The owner/chef of the **Esquire** (The Square, Market St., tel. 051/86237) maintains the restaurant's reputation for fine food with a variety of menus, all emphasizing fresh fish as the specialty.

Eleven km (7 mi) west from Tramore along the R675, you'll
52 come to another resort town, **Annestown,** which also has a good
beach; 8 km (5 mi) beyond this is the former copper-mining cen-
53 ter of **Bunmahon.** During this coastal drive, observe the multitude of unique rock formations scattered along the shore. The coast flattens out again at the beach town of **Clonea** a few miles later, and shortly after this you will find yourself entering
54 **Dungarvan,** the administrative center for the county.

Dungarvan is situated on one of the loveliest stretches of coastline in Ireland, in a pretty valley where the River Colligan empties into Dungarvan Bay. Visitors will find plenty to do here, ranging from sailing, fishing, and mountain climbing to relaxing on the beach or hiking in the woods. The first organized settlement here was founded by St. Garvan in the 7th century, but the valley had been inhabited since the late Stone Age and is rich in archaeological finds worth exploring. You can arrange sailing excursions through the local sailing club (tel. 058/41395 for information), and fishermen will want to contact Cormack Walsh at the Sea Angling Service (29 Abbots Close, Sea Park, tel. 058/43514) in Dungarvan for more information.

Time Out **Merry's** (Lower Main St., tel. 058/41974), once a 17th-century wine merchant's establishment, is today a restaurant with plenty of Old World atmosphere and nostalgic decorations salvaged from former trading days. Food is reasonably priced here, and you'll find filling bar food served throughout the day. At the **Moorings** (Davitt's Quay, tel. 058/41461), you can feast on fresh seafood in a nautical atmosphere.

---

55 West of Dungarvan you'll pass through the village of **Ring,** one of Ireland's distinctive Gaeltachts, or Gaelic-speaking areas. You might like to stop in at the Irish-language college here, **Colaiste na Rinne,** where *ceili* (Irish dancing) is held nightly during the summer (tel. 058/46104).

56 Follow the signs which lead off the N25 to **Ardmore,** a pleasant beach resort with an almost perfect example of an Irish round tower. Standing 31m (97 ft) high, the **Ardmore Tower** was built as a belfry for the nearby monastery and was used by the townsfolk as a place of refuge during battles and raids. Typical of these towers, the doorway was built into the wall some 15 feet above ground level for protection against the Vikings. When everyone was inside, they simply pulled the ladder up into the tower with them. Aside from this tower, you'll find Ardmore sprinkled with historical sights connected to St. Declan, the town's founder. The ruined **Cathedral of St. Declan** is noteworthy for its carvings and altar tombs. **St. Declan's Oratory,** a small cliff-top church where the saint is reputed to be buried, is also of some interest. On the beach below the village you'll find **St. Declan's Stone,** which, according to local legend, floated across the sea bearing the bell and vestments that the saint had inadvertently left behind in Wales.

Return to the N25 and turn left to cross over Youghal Bridge. After the bridge, turn right onto the R634 and follow this through Tallow, the birthplace of famous 19th-century sculptor John Hogan, and on through Ballyduff. Continue east to pick up the N72 into the lovely village of Lismore, on the banks of the River Blackwater.

57 In the 7th century, St. Carthage built a monastery in **Lismore,** and through it the town soon developed a reputation as one of the great educational centers of Europe. However, after centuries of unrest and depredation at the hands of Norman invaders, Lismore was finally destroyed by Raymond le Gros in 1173. The **castle** you can see now in Lismore stands on the very site where the monastery once stood. The castle was built in 1185 by Prince John, who fell in love with Lismore's beautiful scenery and the Blackwater's abundant stock of salmon. Having contracted what he thought was leprosy, the prince also built the Royal Leper Hospital in Waterford—it turned out that his highness suffered from nothing worse than an allergic reactions to "his slavish addiction to wine, gluttony, and lust," according to one observant baron.

The beautiful castle, overlooking the river from a majestic height, eventually became the seat of the bishop of Lismore. During its colorful history it changed hands several times, until it was acquired in the 18th century by the Devonshire family, with whom it has remained ever since. Adele Astaire, sister of Fred Astaire, lived here for many years as the duchess of Devonshire. The Lismore castle is still privately owned, but the grounds are open to visitors. *Tel. 058/54424. Admission to gardens: £1.50 adults, 75p children. Open May–Sept., Sun.–Fri. 1:45–4:45.*

Also worth exploring in Lismore is the ruin of the **Cathedral of St. Carthage,** a Romanesque building with 9th-century grave markers and the pulpit and communion screen from the original Viking Cathedral of Christ Church in Waterford City.

Leave Lismore heading east on the L34 for 6½ km (4 mi) to Cappoquin, and pick up the R669 north into the **Knockmealdown Mountains.** As you travel this road, called the Vee scenic route, you might want to stop and visit the **Mount Melleray Abbey.** The monastery was founded in 1832 by the Cistercian Order of the Strict Observance in what was then a barren, mountainside wilderness. Over the years they have succeeded in transforming this site into more than 600 acres of fertile farmland. The monks maintain strict vows of silence, but visitors are permitted in most areas of the abbey. *Tel. 058/54404. Admission free. Open daily 9–6.*

County Tipperary

The scenic route through the Knockmealdown Mountains is called the Vee Gap because of the hairpin bends in the road, but driving a little slower through here suits most people just fine, because this route offers superb views of the Tipperary Plain stretching ahead for miles. If the visibility is good, you might even be able to see the Rock of Cashel, ancient seat of the kings of Munster located some 32 km (20 mi) away. Just before you enter the Vee Gap, look for a six-foot-high mound of stones on the left side of the road—this marks the grave of Colonel Grubb, a local landowner who requested that he be buried standing up so that he might look over his beloved valley forever.

Continue north through Clogheen and pick up the R655 west to
58 **Ballyporeen,** a town best known as the ancestral home of for-

mer President Ronald Reagan. The special **visitor center** (tel. 052/67106 for information) here documents Reagan's 1984 visit. Five km (3 mi) farther along the R655, turn right on the R665 to reach **Burncourt,** where visitors can stop to inspect the **Mitchelstown Caves.** The motion of water against the rock for millions of years has formed the most extensive cavern system in Ireland, with some caves extending for miles. Through the centuries these caves have provided refuge for rebels and other hunted men, and though they became public knowledge in 1833, they are still surprisingly free of development. *Tel. 052/67246. Admission: £2 adults, 50p children. Open daily 10–6.*

59 From here, take the R665 to the N8 and turn right to reach **Cahir.** This busy market center is located on the River Suir at the crossroads of the heavily traveled N24 and N8. **Cahir Castle,** one of the town's focal points, was built on the river in 1142 and is the largest of its kind in Ireland. A national monument, the castle can be seen on regularly scheduled guided tours given along with an audiovisual show. *Cahir, tel. 052/41011. Admission: £1. Open daily 10–7:30.*

Tipperary Town can be reached by following the N24 northwest from Cahir through the Glen of Aherlow, a lovely stretch of land separating the Galtee Mountains and the Slievenamuck Hills.

Time Out This beautiful woodland setting is the site of the **Glen Hotel** (Glen of Aherlow, tel. 062/56146), a country-style inn with a pleasant, spacious interior. You'll find light snacks, salads, and an à la carte menu available in the dining room here throughout the day.

---

60 The busy market town of **Tipperary** lies in the center of the Golden Vale, one of the richest dairy lands in Ireland. The town was the setting for frequent battles throughout the 14th and 15th centuries, and it played a major role in the Land League agitation of the 19th century. Points of interest about town include a bronze statue of the 19th-century poet and patriot Charles Kickham at the corner of Main Street and Kickham Place; the ruins of a castle built by King John in the late 12th century, on Donohill Road; and the gateway from an Augustinian priory built shortly thereafter, also on Donohill Road.

61 Take the N74 east from Tipperary Town to **Cashel.** With the possible exception of Tara, there is certainly no place in Ireland that commands a greater sense of national importance than Cashel. Legend tells us that the **Rock of Cashel,** a great limestone mound rising up 65 m (200 ft) above the flat countryside, was created by the devil himself. It seems that while flying over Ireland, the devil became quite agitated at the sight of so many good Christian souls, and so he swooped down and spitefully took a bite out of a mountain range found to the north (those mountains are now known as Devil's Bit). Later, while flying over Cashel, the devil was so surprised at seeing St. Patrick below that his mouth gaped open and he spilled his rocky load to the earth—the mound of stone known as the Rock of Cashel.

Cashel has a lengthy history as a center of royal and religious power in Ireland. It was the seat of the Munster kings (including the man who went on to become the high king of Ireland, Brian Boru) from AD 370 until the rock was turned over to the church by King Murtagh O'Brien in 1101. St. Patrick visited Cashel in 450 to baptize King Aengus of Munster, and local legend tells us that during the baptism the saint's crozier accidentally pierced Aengus's foot. The king bore the pain bravely, thinking it to be a part of the ceremony. Legend also tells us that it was here, at Cashel, where St. Patrick illustrated the mystery of the Holy Trinity by using a three-leaf clover, a symbol that has been associated with Ireland ever since.

Primary among the ruins on the rock are a 12th-century round tower, the 13th-century St. Patrick's Cathedral, and the 12th-century Cormac's Chapel. The tower, which stands 30 m (92 ft) high, is in perfect shape and the chapel contains some rather dramatic carvings. There is now a museum that outlines the rock's history, located below the Hall of the Vicars Chorel in the cathedral.

The Coronation Stone of the Munster kings, where Patrick baptized Aengus, dates from as early as the 4th century. Although weathered, the design carved into the stone can still be seen, and St. Patrick's Cross, which dates from the 12th century, stands on top. *Rock of Cashel, tel. 062/61437. Admission: £1. Open May–Sept., daily 9–7:30; Oct.–Apr., daily 9:30–4:30.*

When you leave the rock, you might want to stop down at the town of Cashel itself to look around. The **GPA Bolton Library,** on the grounds of the St. John the Baptist Church of Ireland Cathedral, has a fascinating collection of rare books and manuscripts on display. *John St., tel. 062/61944. Admission: £1 adults, 50p children. Open Mon.–Sat. 9:30–5:30, Sun. 2:30–5:30.*

Also open is the **Cashel Folk Village,** which features a series of reconstructed 18th-century houses and shops as well as a range of tools and other antiques from that period. *Main St., tel. 062/61333. Admission: 50p. Open daily 9:30–8.*

Time Out The **Bishop's Buttery** (tel. 062/61411) in the Cashel Palace Hotel is an informal restaurant found in the cellar of this former bishop's palace. Snacks, light meals, and grills are served, and you may choose between fixed-price or à la carte lunch menus.

Twenty-four km (15 mi) southeast of Cashel on the R688 is the
62 town of **Clonmel,** set in a lovely spot on the banks of the River Suir. Although a settlement had flourished here since before the Viking era of the 9th century, it was not until the early 14th century that the town was walled and fortified. It became a stronghold of the Butler family, Anglo-Normans who became earls of Ormond in the 13th century. Clonmel is noted for being the town that offered Oliver Cromwell the stiffest resistance during his campaign in Ireland in 1650; by the end of a two-month siege here Cromwell had lost more than 2,000 men. It is also remembered for one of its most favorite sons: Laurence Sterne, who wrote the highly original novel *Tristram Shandy,* was born in Clonmel in 1713.

Clonmel's public buildings reflect its prosperous trading history. Among the more notable edifices are the town hall, the West Gate, St. Mary's Cathedral Catholic Church, St. Mary's Church of Ireland, the Franciscan Friary, the courthouse, and a number of fine Georgian houses.

To the north of Clonmel is **Slievenamon,** which means Mountain of the Red-Haired Woman. This evocative name is said to have been given by Fionn MacCumhall (pronounced *Finn Mack cool*), who vowed he would marry the first woman to climb the mountain to the summit where he waited. The first girl to reach him was a beautiful redhead, and the mountain was promptly named in her honor.

Time Out The recently renovated **Gladstone Brasserie** (36 Gladstone St., tel. 052/25077) is set in an early 20th-century post office. The Victorian decor is highlighted with polished wooden floors, and fine-quality snacks and meals are the standard.

About 20 km (12 mi) east of Clonmel on the N24 is another pic-
63 turesque town, **Carrick-on-Suir.** This town is something of an oddity, since it lies partly in County Tipperary and partly in County Waterford: The River Suir, the boundary between the counties, runs through town. The beautifully restored **Ormond Castle** is the central attraction here. The 10th earl of Ormond had this Elizabethan mansion built especially for a proposed visit by Queen Elizabeth I, with whom the earl was reputed to have been personally involved. The proposed visit was never made, though the castle was completed and still stands today. *Tel. 051/40787. Admission: 80p adults, 30p children. Open mid-June–Sept., daily 9:30–5.*

Ten km (6 mi) north of Carrick-on-Suir on the R697 is the little
64 village of **Ahenny,** noted for the two superb 8th-century High Crosses carved with intricate and unique designs found in a village cemetery (open during daylight hours). Double back to the N24 and, before reaching Waterford City, turn left at Granagh onto the N9 toward Kilkenny. You might like to stop off along the N9 at the **Jerpoint Abbey,** a ruined Cistercian monastery dating back to about 1180. Full guide service is available during the summer only, but interesting sculptures and carvings and restored cloisters are accessible year-round. *Tel. 056/21755. Admission: 60p. Open daily 10–6.*

County Kilkenny Continue on the N9 through **Thomastown,** a prosperous market
65 town named for its 13th-century founder, Thomas Fitz-
66 Anthony. From Thomastown take the R700 into **Kilkenny City.**

Numbers in the margin correspond with points of interest on the Kilkenny City map

Kilkenny City is situated on the banks of the River Nore, and for more than a thousand years it has flourished as a civic and ecclesiastical center. The town developed around the 6th-century monastery of St. Canice, and after the Norman invasion it was given to Strongbow, whose heirs erected a castle here in 1192. Kilkenny traditionally served as a central meeting place, and in 1642 it became the seat of the Confederate Irish Parliament representing the Gaelic and Anglo-Norman Catholics. The Confederate Parliament functioned for six years, until Oliver Cromwell attacked and took the city in 1650.

Walking tours of Kilkenny are available through the tourist office (*see* Guided Tours, above), but if you would like to explore the city on your own, start at the corner of Dean Street and Par-
67 liament Street, where you'll find **St. Canice's Cathedral,** which is built on the same spot as St. Canice's original 6th-century monastery. Begun in 1251, this church admirably survived

Black Abbey, **68**
Courthouse, **69**
Kilkenny Castle, **73**
Rothe House, **70**
St. Canice's Cathedral, **67**
Tholsel (Town Hall), **71**
Tourist Information Office (Shee Alms House), **72**

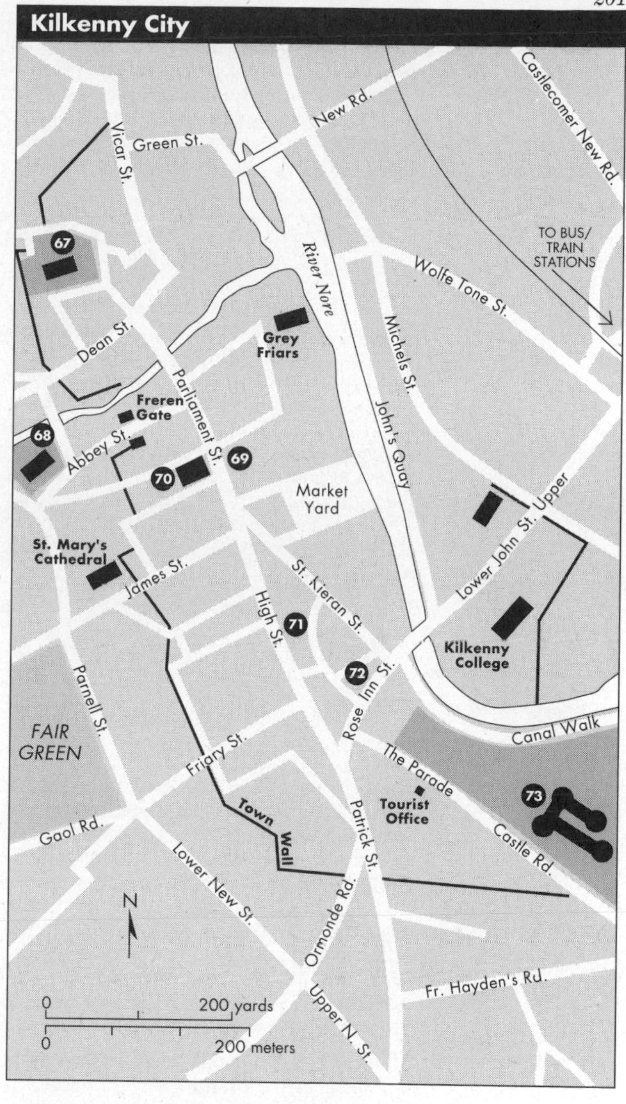

Cromwell's attack on the city and remains one of the finest unruined churches in Ireland. The interior is full of interesting monuments and furniture, and the other buildings on the grounds, including a round tower, a library, and the Bishop's Palace, are also worth investigating. *Dean St. Open daily 9–1 and 2–6.*

68 Across the street from the cathedral, you'll be able to see the back of the **Black Abbey** on the next block south, Abbey Street. Built in 1225, the abbey's nave and transept were restored as a Dominican church. There is a museum displaying a number of historical artifacts located next door in the presbytery. Leave the abbey and make a left down Abbey Street, passing the only town gate, the Black Freren Gate, that is still standing in what

was once a walled city, as well as the Dominican church, both on the left. When you reach Parliament Street, turn right to stroll
69 70 past the **courthouse** on the left and **Rothe House** on the right. Rothe House was built in 1594 as a private residence for a well-to-do merchant, and today it houses a historical museum for the Kilkenny Archaeological Society. *Parliament St., tel. 056/22893. Admission: £1 adults, 50p children. Open Mon.–Sat. 10:30–5, Sun. 3–5.*

Time Out For dining in an unusual setting, take the left fork off Parliament Street onto St. Keiran Street to try **Kytlers Inn** (St. Kieran St., Kilkenny, tel. 056/21064). This restaurant is situated in the cellar of a 16th-century building where Dame Alice Kyteler, a notorious witch, poisoned her four husbands. While the restaurant retains its flagstone and historic decor, you'll find the dishes to be a bit more appealing these days: light snacks, grills, and a fixed-price lunch menu are available.

Farther along on Parliament Street, which is called High
71 Street at this point, you'll notice the town hall, or **Tholsel,** on the right. Built in 1761, this was originally the town toll house, where taxes were collected. Today, the ancient sword and mace of the city are kept here, as well as the municipal records dating back to 1230.

Make a left off High Street onto Rose Inn Street to find the Shee Alms House, on the left side of the street. It was founded as a hospital for the poor in 1582 by Sir Richard Shee and served
72 in that role until 1895. Today, the **Tourist Information Office** is housed here, and CityScope, a sound-and-light show on 17th-century Kilkenny, is presented. *Rose Inn St., tel. 056/21755. Open Mon.–Sat. 9–5:15. CityScope admission: £1.*

High Street will split into Patrick Street and the Parade at Rose Inn Street, and you should veer to the left onto the Parade
73 to reach **Kilkenny Castle.** The castle was built in the 13th century and was once owned by the Butler family. It was almost entirely rebuilt in the 1820s and, now in the hands of the state, is currently undergoing another restoration. Enhanced with gray stone towers and battlements, its features include an impressive portrait gallery, a modern art gallery, full guide service in summertime, a formal rose garden, and acres of rolling parkland. *The Parade, Kilkenny, tel. 056/21450. Admission: £1, grounds free. Open Tues.–Sat. 10–7, Sun. 2–5.*

About 11 km (7 mi) from Kilkenny on the N78 toward Castlecomer is **Dunmore Cave,** a natural limestone cavern that is mentioned in the ancient Book of Leinster as the dwelling place of a giant cat called Lord of the Mice, which was killed by an ancient woman warrior named Aithbel. It is also listed in the Annals of the Four Masters as one of the three darkest places in Ireland, and, as with all other Irish caves, Dunmore was considered to be one of the entrances to hell until well into the 17th century. Such ominous myths have long since been cast aside, however, and since 1940 the cave has been outfitted with stairs, lighting, and walkways to make the eerie beauty of the cave accessible to the public. *Dunmore, tel. 056/67726. Admission: £1. Open daily 10–12:30 and 2–5.*

Continue on the N78 through Castlecomer and turn right at the junction for R430. This will lead you back to Carlow Town and the beginning of our tour of the Southeast.

Shopping

Enniscorthy In Enniscorthy, stop by **Kiltrea Bridge Pottery** (Kiltrea Bridge, Caim, tel. 054/35107) and **Carley's Bridge Pottery** (Carley's Bridge, tel. 054/35312) for handcrafted pottery work.

Tipperary The **Tipperary Crystal** (Ballynoran, Carrick-on-Suir, tel. 051/41188) factory is a similar facility to that at Waterford, and purchases made at this showroom can also be shipped overseas with ease.

Waterford Outside of Waterford City, a visit to the world-famous **Waterford Glass factory** (Cork Rd., Kilbarry, tel. 051/73311) is almost mandatory. The showroom at the factory displays an extensive selection of both Waterford crystal and Wedgwood pottery, and overseas orders are handled promptly. Numerous shopping arcades in Waterford provide ample opportunity for browsing. You'll notice an emphasis on tweeds, knitwear, and crystal in the arcades at Broad Street Centre and George's Court, as well as along The Quay and on Barronstrand and Broad streets. Try **Quay Antiques** (128 The Quay, tel. 051/77784), **Kelly's** department store (75 The Quay, tel. 051/73557), and **Joseph Knox** (3 Barronstrand St., tel. 051/75307) for crystal and china.

Wexford County Wexford is a major center for pottery, leatherwork, weaving, silversmithing, and other crafts. In Wexford City you'll want to visit the **Wool Shop** (39 S. Main St., tel. 053/22247) or **Casket Fabrics** (50 Patrick St., tel. 051/75304) for Aran sweaters, **John Hore's** (31 S. Main St., tel. 053/22200) for handmade Irish linen, and **Lowney Antiques, Ltd.** (61 S. Main St., tel. 053/23140) for your own small slice of Ireland's past.

Sports and Fitness

Participant Sports

Bicycling Maps outlining suggested bicycling routes are available from most tourist board information offices throughout the Southeast. Bikes can be rented through **The Bike Store** in Rosslare, County Wexford (tel. 01/725–339 in Dublin), or through **Raleigh Ireland Rent-A-Bike** (tel. 01/261–333 in Dublin), with locations throughout the region.

Fishing Although most of Ireland's angling is concentrated in the center of the country around the counties of Leitrim, Cavan, and Monaghan, there is good fishing in the Southeast around Carlow Town and in parts of County Waterford. Carlow Town and Graiguenamanagh, both on the River Barrow, are also the sites of a popular angling festival held every May. Contact the **Southern Regional Fisheries Board** (Anglesea St., Clonmel, Co. Tipperary, tel. 052/23971) for further information.

Golf Some of Ireland's best parkland golf courses can be found in the Southeast. Among them are **Carlow Golf Club** (Deerpark, Co. Carlow, tel. 503/31695), **Tramore Golf Club** (Tramore, Co. Waterford, tel. 51/86170), **Kilkenny Golf Club** (Glendine, Co. Kilkenny, tel. 056/22125), **Rosslare Golf Club** (Rosslare Strand, Co. Wexford, tel. 053/32203), **Clonmel Golf Club** (Lyreanearle, Clonmel, Co. Tipperary, tel. 052/21138), and **Courtown Golf Club** (Kiltennel, Gorey, Co. Wexford, tel. 055/21533).

Hiking A number of hiking trails crisscrossing the Irish countryside have been designed and maintained by the National Sports Council, and several of these fine trails are located in the Southeast region. The **South Leinster Way** begins in the County Carlow town of Kildavin and makes its way southwest over Mt. Leinster and the River Barrow, terminating in Carrick-on-Suir. A second trail, the **Munster Way,** picks up where the first ends and leads through the Vee Gap in the Knockmealdown Mountains and on to Clogheen. Contact the tourist board for further information.

Spectator Sports

The people of the Southeast are a sporting lot, and on any given day in this region you're likely to find the stands at the races or the hurling matches full to brimming.

Dog Racing **Greyhound racing** is extremely popular here, and Irish dogs are considered to be among the best in the world. Races are held at night, and the main dog tracks in the Southeast are **Clonmel Greyhound Racetrack** (Davis Rd., Clonmel, Co. Tipperary, tel. 052/21118), **Enniscorthy Greyhound Racetrack** (Showgrounds, Enniscorthy, Co. Wexford, tel. 054/33172), **Waterford Greyhound Racetrack** (Kilcohan Park, Co. Waterford, tel. 051/74531), and **Kilkenny Greyhound Racetrack** (St. James Park, Co. Kilkenny, tel. 056/21214).

Gaelic Football and Hurling Tickets to Gaelic football and hurling matches are available through the **Gaelic Athletic Association** (GAA, Croke Park, Dublin, tel. 01/363222) or at the entrance to the local stadium. In the Southeast, games are played on Sundays at the following county grounds: **Clonmel GAA Grounds** (Western Rd., Clonmel, Co. Tipperary, tel. 52/21806), **Carlow GAA Grounds** (Dr. Cullen Park, Co. Carlow, tel. 503/32414), **Kilkenny GAA Grounds** (Nowlan Park, Co. Kilkenny, tel. 056/22841), **Waterford GAA Grounds** (Walsh Park, Co. Waterford, tel. 056/77798), and **Wexford GAA Grounds** (Wexford Park, Clonard Road, Co. Wexford, tel. 053/24620).

Horse Racing **Horse races** are held regularly at the following tracks in the Southeast: **Gowran Park** (Co. Kilkenny, tel. 056/26126), **Wexford Racecourse** (Bettyville, Co. Wexford, tel. 053/42307), **Tramore Racecourse** (Tramore, Co. Waterford, tel. 051/81574), and **Clonmel Racecourse** (Powerstown Park, Clonmel, Co. Tipperary, tel. 052/22852).

Dining and Lodging

Dining

by Georgina Campbell and Pat Mackey

Category	Cost*
Very Expensive	over £20
Expensive	£15–£20
Moderate	£10–£15
Inexpensive	under £10

**per person, excluding drinks, service, and sales tax (10%)*

Lodging

Category	Cost*
Very Expensive	over £100
Expensive	£70–£100
Moderate	£40–£70
Inexpensive	under £40

**double occupancy, not including sales tax (10%)*

Highly recommended restaurants and hotels are indicated by a star ★.

Ballyhack

Dining **Neptune Restaurant.** Owner-chef Pierce McAuliffe and his wife Valerie have created a wonderfully bright atmosphere in this converted schoolhouse next to the Passage East car ferry at Ballyhack Harbour. A conservatory added to the original dining room contributes light and space, and the yellow-and-blue color scheme reinforces an impression of constant sunshine. The decor is simple, sturdy, and stylish, from the chunky modern cutlery to the unusual nautical accessories. Pierce serves country house–style meals with an emphasis on the fresh seafood for which the Wexford area is famous. Hot crab *bréhat* (mushrooms sautéed in port and cream, baked with white crabmeat and a mustard sauce, and topped with cheese) is a specialty, as is the symphony of seafood, made of shelled crab claws, mussels, scallops, and cockles in garlic butter. Simple steak and chicken dishes are also available, though the more adventurous will want to try the casserole of white pudding, sausages, and duck. Desserts tend to be simple, like his famous apple pie or the homemade ice creams served with liqueurs and seasonal fruits. *Ballyhack Harbour, tel. 051/89284. Reservations advised. Dress: casual but neat. AE, DC, MC, V. Closed Mon. and Dec. 25–Mar. Moderate.*

Borris

Dining **Step House.** Situated on the banks of the River Barrow, this late-Georgian house is the perfect setting for Irish country-house cuisine. Drinks are served beside an open fire in the chintz-draped sitting room before dinner in the equally cozy, candlelit dining room. The food is seasonal: Local pheasant and wild duck is on the menu in winter, and local salmon, mussels, and prawns are served in summer. A Continental influence is found in appetizers like mussels stuffed with garlic butter, and main courses tend to be simple: Poached wild salmon hollandaise is a typical example. When it comes to dessert, don't miss their incredible house special, a chocolate *gâteau* composed of meringue, chocolate mousse, sponge, and chocolate *ganache*—it's so complicated, it takes two days to make! There's a casual, less expensive cellar bistro and bar as well, where you can dine in the courtyard in fine weather. *Tel. 503/73401. Reservations advised. Dress: casual but neat. MC, V. No lunch Tues. and Wed., closed Mon. and Feb. Restaurant Expensive; bistro Moderate.*

Cahir

Lodging

Kilcoran Lodge. This handsome, 19th-century house sits just outside Cahir on the slopes of the Galtee Mountains. The rooms were renovated in 1985, and those facing the front sport the best views of the beautiful heather-covered slopes. Guest rooms are pleasant and have Victorian-style furnishings and comfortable beds. The furnishing in the public areas is discreet and stately, in a 19th-century style, and the entire hotel wears the ambience of a country manor house. *Co. Tipperary, tel. 052/41288. 24 rooms with bath. Facilities: restaurant, pool, health club, nearby fishing and horseback riding. AE, DC, V. Expensive.*

Carlow

Lodging

Royal Hotel. Recently renovated, the Royal is located in the center of town; while this may be convenient, you may also find the busy traffic around the building to be a bit distracting. The lobby and public spaces are decorated with wood trim and heavy, Victorian-style furniture covered with floral prints for color. Guest rooms are comfortable and are also decorated in a floral scheme with Victorian-style furniture. *8-13 Dublin St., Co. Carlow, tel. 503/31621. 30 rooms, 26 with bath. Facilities: restaurant, cable TV. AE, DC, MC, V. Moderate.*

★ **Seven Oaks.** This handsome hotel is in a quiet suburb on the outskirts of town, just a 10-minute ride from the Carlow train station. The building, which was built at the turn of the century, has recently been renovated, and you'll find that the guest rooms in the new section are more spacious than the older ones. The bright, airy public space is filled with modern furniture and plenty of cut glass, which accents the charming rural decor. Guest rooms are also filled with modern furnishings, but again the rural motif is carried throughout with hunting prints and a floral decor. *Athy Rd., Co. Carlow, tel. 503/31308. 16 rooms, 12 with bath. Facilities: restaurant, cable TV. AE, DC, MC, V. Moderate.*

Cashel

Dining

Chez Hans. This small, converted Victorian church at the foot of the Rock of Cashel oozes Old World charm: Dark wood and tapestries provide an elegant background for tables dressed in beige linen. Traditional French cuisine with a hint of nouvelle has been adapted to take advantage of fresh Irish ingredients. Specialties include roast rack of spring lamb with a fresh herb crust and tarragon sauce, and free-range hot chicken, lightly smoked and served with a yogurt, apple, and cider sauce, using locally made cider from Clonmel. Steaks are always excellent here, as is the fish. Owner-chef Hans Matthia has compiled an unusual list of 11 house wines, including two exclusive whites from his sister's vineyard in Germany. *Rockside, tel. 062/61177. Reservations required. Dress: casual but neat. No credit cards. Dinner only, closed Sun., Mon., Dec. 25–26, and the first 3 weeks of Jan. Very Expensive.*

Dining and Lodging ★

Cashel Palace. Located dramatically at the foot of the Rock of Cashel, this 18th-century bishop's palace is an exquisite accommodation. The redbrick-and-stone manor house is set back from the street in its own garden, so despite its central location it is quite tranquil. The public rooms, paneled in pine and filled with Queen Anne antique furniture, are dominated by twin marble fireplaces and carved wood pillars. Perhaps the most striking feature is the sweeping, intricately carved red-pine staircase leading up to the second floor. The richly decorated guest rooms are equally luxurious, filled with four-poster canopied beds and antiques. Request a room facing the back so that you can enjoy the breathtaking view of the Rock of Cashel rising up behind the hotel. The Four Seasons restaurant in the hotel is an elegant dining room done in rich floral drapery, Waterford glass, and formal table settings. The menu here relies heavily on game in season, local lamb and beef, and fresh fish, while the less formal basement restaurant serves simple, light meals all day. *Main St., Co. Tipperary, tel. 062/61411. 17 rooms, 3 suites, all with bath. Facilities: 2 restaurants, bar, gardens, conference facilities. AE, DC, MC, V. Very Expensive.*

Clonmel

Lodging

Clonmel Arms Hotel. Situated in the center of town, this Georgian building is a favorite night spot, with nightly entertainment ranging from jazz music to disco dancing. The hotel was built in the late-18th century, but a new, more comfortable section was added in 1970, and a complete renovation was completed just a few years ago. If you're a light sleeper, you'll want to avoid rooms facing the street and those over the ballroom—they can get a bit noisy. The public spaces are done in a country style, not surprising when you consider the number of outdoorsmen that frequent the hotel. The rooms here are comfortable and well-furnished. *Sarsfield St., Co. Tipperary, tel. 052/21233. 35 rooms, 25 with bath. Facilities: restaurant, lounge, horseback riding and fishing facilities. AE, DC, MC. Expensive.*

Knocklofty House. This splendid 18th-century Georgian mansion is set on 150 acres of parkland. Guest rooms, particularly those in the front, have fine views of the surrounding countryside. The public spaces are decorated with antique furniture from the Georgian period, giving the impression of a manor-house setting. Guest rooms also are done in antiques, with lovely Oriental carpets. *Co. Tipperary, tel. 052/38322. 15 rooms with bath. Facilities: restaurant, 24-hr room service, tennis courts, pool, gym, sauna, Jacuzzi, riding facilities. MC, V. Expensive.*

Minella Hotel. This stately hotel is found in a quiet neighborhood on the banks of the River Suir. The rooms afford fine views of the river, particularly from those in the front and on the east wing. Old World charm is communicated through the comfortable Victorian furnishings and walls decorated with hunting prints. The dining room is oak paneled. *Coleville Rd., Co. Tipperary, tel. 052/22388. 30 rooms with shower. Facilities: restaurant, cable TV, 24-hr room service. AE, DC, MC, V. Expensive.*

Dungarvan

Lodging

Clonea Strand Hotel. This hotel is located on a scenic stretch of Waterford coastline overlooking Clonea Beach, about 3 km (2 mi) outside Dungarvan. The hotel has direct access to a safe swimming beach. The rooms are comfortable and bright, with plenty of modern, natural-wood furnishings. Amenities include coffee/tea–making facilities and hair driers. *Clonea, Co. Waterford, tel. 058/41277. 35 rooms with bath. Facilities: restaurant, cable TV, pool, sauna, gym, bowling alley. AE, DC, V. Moderate.*

Lawlors. This hotel is conveniently located on the busy main road into Dungarvan from Waterford. Built in 1912, the hotel has been renovated and enlarged since then, and you'll find that the newer rooms are more spacious. Try to avoid a room facing front, as you'll be subject to street noise from below—you also miss out on the views available from the rear. Filled with functional, Irish-country furniture, the hotel sports a rural ambience. Guest rooms are done in modern furniture and are brightened with a floral decor. *T.F. Meagher St., Co. Waterford, tel. 058/41122. 52 rooms with bath. Facilities: restaurant, cable TV, pony treks available, nearby fishing. MC, V. Inexpensive.*

Dunmore East

Dining

The Ship Restaurant. This bar/restaurant is found in a 19th-century house overlooking the bay. The dining room is casual and easygoing, with simple, sturdy furnishings; dark wood walls; and a nautical theme. The food is an imaginative mixture of French and Irish influences, and the emphasis is on fresh local seafood. Start off, perhaps, with deep-fried pastry parcels stuffed with fresh crabmeat, or pan-fried prawns with a lemon, verbena, and thyme mousseline. Entrées include grilled or pan-fried black sole, or kabobs of fresh prawns and scallops pan-fried in a chive and hyssop butter. Desserts, such as a chocolate boat filled with white-chocolate mousse on a raspberry *coulis*, are tempting, and there's a good selection of Irish farmhouse cheeses. *Tel. 051/83141 or 051/83144. Reservations accepted. Dress: casual. No lunch; closed Sept.–May, Sun. and Mon. MC, V. Moderate–Expensive.*

Enniscorthy

Lodging

Murphy Flood's Hotel. This recently renovated hotel has a reputation for friendliness. Located on the busy main street in Enniscorthy, you may find the rooms facing the front to be a bit noisy—try instead for rooms in the new section of the hotel, which are a bit bigger. The public areas are filled with polished wood furnishings and trim, and the bright decor is emphasized with lots of glasswork and sunlight. Guest rooms sport a floral decor and functional, modern furniture. *Main St., Co. Wexford, tel. 054/33413. 22 rooms, 16 with bath. Facilities: restaurant, cable TV. AE, MC, V. Moderate.*

Glen of Aherlow

Lodging

Aherlow House Hotel. Set in the middle of a tranquil forest 6½ km (4 mi) outside of Tipperary Town, this popular hotel was once a hunting lodge. Antique furniture fills the inside, and there is lots of pine trim to complete the country atmosphere. Guest rooms are filled with modern furniture, and they have comfortable beds and attractive decor. *Co. Tipperary, tel. 062/*

56147. 10 rooms with bath. Facilities: fishing, pony trekking. AE, DC, V. Inexpensive.

Gorey

Dining **Marlfield House Hotel.** The stylish restaurant in this Regency-period house uses a conservatory and an abundance of greenery to create a light and airy garden atmosphere. Tables are impeccably dressed with white linen, gleaming glasses, silver, and fresh flowers. The sophisticated cuisine is classical with modern leanings, and great emphasis is laid on the use of fresh local ingredients. Dishes include salade *tiède* made with a selection of salad greens and lambs' sweetbreads, duck livers, prawns or mussels, and wild local salmon served with a sorrel or watercress sauce. Chocolate is a specialty, and elegant desserts often combine dark and white chocolate in dishes such as white-chocolate mousse served with dark-chocolate sauce. *Courtown Rd., tel. 055/21124. Reservations required. Jacket and tie suggested. AE, CB, DC, MC, V. Closed Dec. Very Expensive.*

Kilkenny City

Dining **Lacken House Guesthouse and Restaurant.** This well-known restaurant is in the cellar of a Georgian house on the edge of Kilkenny. Owner-chef Eugene McSweeney and his wife Breda have maintained the period character of the house, using traditional furnishings throughout. Formally dressed waiters serve international dishes made with fresh local ingredients. Baked crab *gâteau* would be a typical appetizer—crabmeat blended with a sole mousse, then baked in a *dariole* mold, turned out, and served with an herb and cream sauce. Salmon from the nearby River Nore is the star of the menu in dishes such as cutlet of Nore salmon with a galette of potato and celeriac served with sage butter sauce. For dessert try the homemade ice creams. *Dublin Rd., tel. 056/61085 or 056/65611. Reservations advised. Dress: casual but neat. AE, CB, DC, MC, V. No lunch, closed Sun., Mon., and one week at Christmas. Moderate–Expensive.*

Lodging ★ **The Newpark Hotel.** Set back from the road in the rural suburbs of Kilkenny City, this hotel is a quiet, peaceful escape. The building is relatively new and, having been renovated just a few years ago, is in good shape. All the guest rooms are modern, bright, and airy, though you'll find that those in the rear have the best views. They are decorated in soft, pastel colors and are brightened by floral-patterned drapes. The public spaces in the hotel are done in a country style and are accented with comfortable pine furnishings. *Castlecomer Rd., Co. Kilkenny, tel. 056/22122. 60 rooms with bath. Facilities: restaurant, pool, Jacuzzi, steam room, gym, 2 tennis courts, 18-hole golf course, cable TV, 24-hr room service. AE, DC, MC, V. Moderate.*

Leighlinbridge

Dining **The Lord Bagenal Inn.** This famous old public house beside the River Barrow is today a bar/restaurant with open fires, dim lighting, and an Old World atmosphere. The bar menu is a basic selection of steaks, fresh fish, and some international dishes like chicken Kiev and spare ribs with sweet and sour sauce. The French-style restaurant's menu changes weekly and is considerably more sophisticated. A typical menu might include a homemade soup, avocado pear with prawn dressing, tournedos steak with *chasseur*, or poached or grilled salmon steak served with hollandaise or lime butter sauce. *Carlow Rd., tel. 503/21668. Reservations advised weekends. Dress: casual. DC, V. No dinner Sun. or Mon. Closed Dec. 25 and Good Friday. Moderate.*

Newtown

Dining **Swiss Cottage.** In lovely gardens opposite the People's Park in Newtown, this restaurant is small, rich-toned, and intimate. The dining room itself, where all tables have a view to the gardens, is decorated in delicate shades of blue, gray, and antique rose, and the linen cloths, silver cutlery, and Royal Doulton crockery all help make for an atmosphere of restrained elegance. Look for sophisticated dishes like baked prawns with a curried sabayon, traditional carpaccio with a cream cheese and herb dressing, roulade of free-range chicken with asparagus, and buttered lobster and scallops with lemon and herbs. Desserts tend to be quite traditional, but with a light modern touch —light lemon tart with sauce *anglaise* is typical. *Park Rd., tel. 051/79580. Reservations advised. Dress: casual but neat. DC, MC, V. Closed Dec. 25. Very Expensive.*

Rosslare

Lodging ★ **Kelly's Strand.** Considered to be one of Ireland's best hotels, the family-owned Kelly's is a traditional weekend retreat among the Irish. The recreational facilities here are extensive, including tennis and squash courts, pools, saunas, a golf course, and a health club—not to mention the nearby beach. Guest rooms are done in comfortable, country-style decor, and those facing the front have lovely sea views. The lobby and public spaces employ cane furniture and pastel shades to set a relaxed atmosphere. *Co. Wexford, tel. 053/32114. 89 rooms with bath. Facilities: restaurant, solarium, tennis, squash, 18-hole golf course, health club, saunas, 2 pools, cable TV, 24-hr room service. AE, DC, V. Closed early Dec.–mid-Feb. Expensive.*

The Cedars Hotel. With its new recreation center and recent refurbishment, The Cedars is a good bet for a seaside escape. Located in a quiet area near the beach, the atmosphere here is cool, fresh, and relaxing. Public spaces are decorated with cane furniture, while guest-room pieces are more modern. The rooms pick up the beach atmosphere with their bright drapery and yellow, white, and blue color scheme. *Co. Wexford, tel. 053/32124. 34 rooms with bath. Facilities: restaurant, leisure center. AE, DC, V. Moderate.*

Rosslare Harbour

Lodging **Great Southern Hotel.** Part of a popular Irish hotel chain, the Rosslare Great Southern is located on a rise overlooking the harbor, just a few minutes' walk from the ferry port. It's a modern hotel, and was recently renovated in the cheery seaside colors of blue, green, and white. Lots of glass is used throughout to brighten the interior. The comfortable, modern guest rooms are done in a floral decor, and those facing the rear have views of the sea. *Co. Wexford, tel. 053/33233. 96 rooms with bath. Facilities: restaurant, bar, tennis, nearby golf, health club, saunas, pool, snooker room, children's playground, conference rooms, live entertainment during summer, cable TV, 24-hr room service. AE, DC, MC, V. Closed Jan.–Apr. Moderate.*

Hotel Rosslare. This historic old hotel is located at the top of a cliff, overlooking Rosslare Bay and the ferry port below. Cheery and bright, the spacious public rooms are done in restful pastel shades. The guest rooms have modern, functional furniture and floral decor. Bedrooms have balconies, and those at the rear have the best sea views. Traditional Irish music can be heard live here on summer evenings. *Co. Wexford, tel. 053/33154. 25 rooms, 22 with bath. Facilities: restaurant, bar, beer garden, squash court, billiard room, saunas, nearby beach and golf. AE, MC, V. Moderate.*

Tuskar House Hotel. Found in a quiet area near the ferry port, this small, family-run hotel promises simple pleasures: comfortable rooms and good views of the sea (especially from the rear). The ambience of the public rooms is defined by lots of polished pine, glass, and greenery. In the guest rooms, you'll find functional, modern furniture and a bright, cheery decor. *St. Martin's Rd., Co. Wexford, tel. 053/33363. 20 rooms with bath. Facilities: restaurant. AE, V. Moderate.*

Waterford City

Dining

Dwyers of Mary Street. This unusual restaurant is situated in an old Royal Irish Constabulary barracks (the original bars are still on the downstairs windows). The pink, green, and cream color scheme is pretty and fresh, original paintings grace the walls, and the furnishings are a pleasing mixture of styles—antiques are offset by modern touches, such as Bauhaus chairs. The cuisine is French-influenced country house, and the menu is changed every two weeks. A typical meal might begin with puff pastry pies stuffed with black pudding and apple and served with an apple and cider sauce, followed by brochette of lamb (noisettes of lamb cooked en brochette and served with a red-currant and mint sauce) and seasonal vegetables. Finish with brown bread ice cream—homemade ices are one of chef and co-owner Martin Dwyer's specialties. *Mary St., tel. 051/77478. Reservations advised. Dress: casual. MC, V. Lunch by arrangement only. Closed Sun. in winter, 3 days at Christmas. Moderate.*

Dining and Lodging
★

Waterford Castle. If you've always dreamed of staying in a castle during your visit to Ireland, here's your opportunity. This luxury hotel occupies a genuine stone castle built by the Fitzgerald family in the 17th century. It's located on a 300-acre island in the River Suir, 3 km (2 mi) outside Waterford City, and can only be reached by car ferry. The main hall and drawing room are impressive, filled with ornate antique furniture and tapestries—be sure to notice the fine oak paneling and the great stone fireplace. The guest rooms are quite luxurious, featuring four-poster beds and a lavish decor. The traditional atmosphere in the Leinster Room restaurant is set by the ornate plastered ceiling, the oak furniture, and the deep burgundy Donegal carpet. The cuisine here is traditional also—country-style dishes include poached salmon, asparagus served in puff pastry, and bread and butter pudding. *The Island, Ballinakill, Co. Waterford, tel. 051/78203. 20 rooms, 16 with bath. Facilities: restaurant, tennis, squash, health club, saunas, pool, horseback riding, fishing, cable TV, 24-hr room service. AE, DC, MC, V. Very Expensive.*

Lodging **The Granville Hotel.** Found in the center of the city just five minutes by taxi from the train station, this was the birthplace of the Irish-American Civil War hero and Montana governor Thomas Francis Meagher. Though it was built in the early 19th century, you'll find that the building was recently renovated. The country-manor decor of the public area is emphasized by the use of hunting prints, wood paneling, tapestries, and archways. Guest rooms are warm, filled with reproductions of Victorian furniture and plenty of wood trim. Rooms in the front, and those found over the dining room, may be a bit noisy. *Meagher Quay, Co. Waterford, tel. 051/55111. 74 rooms with bath. Facilities: restaurant, health club, saunas, fishing, pony trekking, cable TV, 24-hr room service. AE, DC, MC, V. Expensive.*

Jury's Hotel. Found on an impressive 35 acres of parkland high above the River Suir, Jury's is a quiet, secluded retreat. All the rooms face south, toward Waterford City, and have panoramic views of the harbor and the surrounding countryside. The large foyer is impressive, with marble and brass trim, and the lobby seating is quite comfortable. Guest rooms are done in bright, pleasant colors, and the furniture is modern and functional. The leisure complex is extensive. *Co. Waterford, tel. 051/32111. 100 rooms, 4 suites, all with bath. Facilities: restaurant, tennis courts, golf course, health club, saunas, Jacuzzis, pool, cable TV, 24-hr room service. AE, DC, MC, V. Expensive.*

★ **The Tower Hotel.** This hostelry is found on The Mall, a quiet section of the city just 10 minutes from the train station by cab. At press time a renovation was in the works, but as it is the public rooms are quite comfortable; they are filled with plenty of fresh flowers and greenery and accented with warm, polished wood trim. The bright, airy guest rooms are comfortable, with modern, functional furniture and a floral decor. Rooms in the rear have good views of the river. *The Mall, Co. Waterford, tel. 051/75801. 81 rooms with bath. Facilities: restaurant, cable TV, 24-hr room service. AE, DC, MC, V. Moderate.*

★ **Diamond Hill Country House.** This guest house is found just 5 km (3 mi) from Waterford City in a quiet cul-de-sac off the Waterford–Rosslare road. Its owners have won several awards for both the fine Irish breakfasts served here and the lovely gardens that surround the house. The country house–style decor in the public space is comfortably accented with tweed fabrics, tapestries, and plenty of greenery. Bedrooms are bright and airy and are filled with modern furniture. *Slieverue, Co. Waterford, tel. 051/32855. 8 rooms, 5 with shower. Facilities: dining room, wine bar, crafts shop, gardens. MC, V. Inexpensive.*

Wexford Town

Lodging **The Talbot Hotel.** One of southeast Ireland's best and most popular hotels, the Talbot is a reliable, comfortable hotel with some pleasant amenities. The hotel features regular live entertainment, especially during the summer, and a well-equipped recreation center. You'll find that the guest rooms are modern, and are decorated with Irish country-style furniture and a floral color scheme. Since the hotel is located on a rather busy street, rooms that face front and rooms found over the ballroom can be noisy. *Trinity St., Co. Wexford, tel. 053/22566. 103 rooms with bath. Facilities: restaurant, pool, squash courts, health club, saunas, cable TV, 24-hr room service. AE, DC, MC, V. Moderate.*

White's Hotel. Housed in a historic 19th-century building conveniently located in the center of town, you'll find White's to be a friendly, convivial place. Its numerous old-fashioned passageways, brass trim, and red velvet decor combine with candlelight and roaring log fires to create a warm ambience. The country-style guest rooms are furnished with Victorian reproductions. Those found in the new addition to the hotel are more spacious. *George's St., Co. Wexford, tel. 053/22311. 76 rooms with bath. Facilities: restaurant, cable TV, 24-hr room service, nearby fishing and pony trekking. AE, DC, MC, V. Moderate.*

The Arts and Nightlife

The Arts

Entertainment in the Southeast is largely confined to the tourist hotels during the summer. These programs of largely Irish entertainment are sponsored by the **Comhaltas Ceoltoiri Eireann (Irish Cultural Association,** 32 Belgrave Sq., Dublin, tel. 01/800295) for visitors. One special performance you won't want to miss is that of the local mummers in County Wexford. Mumming, which combines a style of intricate wooden-sword dancing with spoken verse and incantations, was introduced into County Wexford in the 17th century by shipwrecked sailors from Cornwall, who could trace the dance back to their Moorish origins in North Africa. Contact the Wexford Tourist Information Office (*see* Tourist Information, above) for further information.

Culture buffs won't want to miss the **Garter Lane Arts Centre** (O'Connell St., Waterford, tel. 051/55038), the largest such cultural center in Ireland. Call ahead for a schedule of upcoming concerts, exhibits, and theater productions at the center.

A number of extremely popular cultural festivals are held in the Southeast on an annual basis. The **Waterford International Festival of Light Opera** (tel. 051/74402), the only competitive event of its kind, is a great draw for amateur musical societies from throughout Ireland and Great Britain. The festival runs for 17 nights every September at the Theatre Royal (The Mall, Waterford).

Also worth investigating is the **Wexford Festival Opera** (tel. 053/22141). For more than 30 years this season of professional operatic productions by famous artists from around the world has been held every October at the Theatre Royal in Wexford. Lastly, the **Kilkenny Arts Week** held in late August is a series of classical music performances, concerts, and readings at halls throughout Kilkenny. For more information, contact the Kilkenny Tourist Information Office (*see* Tourist Information, above).

Nightlife

The neighborhood pub is an integral part of Irish life, and travelers who take time to visit some of them will be granted an unvarnished look at Ireland's people—not to mention one of Ireland's favorite pastimes. Wander in, ask the bartender to draw you a pint of Guinness, and strike up a conversation. The stories and local color you'll glean from a chat with your neighbor at the bar are sure to enrich your impressions of Ireland.

While you're traveling through the Southeast, there are a few establishments in particular that you might seek out for their fine entertainment. In County Wexford's Rosslare, visit the **Portholes Bar** at the Hotel Rosslare (Rosslare Harbour, tel. 053/33110) for lively traditional Irish music most evenings during the summer. **T&H Doolan's Bar** (George's St., tel. 051/72764) in Waterford City is another pub that hosts good traditional Irish music most summer nights and on weekends year-round. Also, the **Seanchie Pub** (Ballymacart, Ring, Co. Waterford, tel. 058/46285) is an award-winning place that features traditional music and dancing in the courtyard on Sundays during the summer.

Winners of the National Bar Catering and Pub of the Year Award on a number of occasions, **Langtons Bar** (69 John St., Kilkenny, tel. 056/65133) boasts old-style decor with an emphasis on sports memorabilia. Bar food, snacks, and full lunch or dinner are available.

7 The Southwest

Introduction

by Alannah Hopkin

A resident of Kinsale, Alannah Hopkin is the author of several books, including The Living Legend of St. Patrick.

Cork, Kerry, Limerick, and Clare—the sound of these Southwest Ireland county names has an undeniably evocative Irish lilt. A varied coastline, spectacular scenery, (especially around the famous lakes of Killarney), and a mild climate have long attracted visitors to this region. Although the Southwest contains Ireland's second and third largest cities—Cork and Limerick—its most notable attractions are rural: miles and miles of pretty country lanes meandering through rich but sparsely populated farmlands. Even in the two main cities the pace of life is perceptibly slower than in Dublin. To be in a hurry in the region is to verge on demonstrating bad manners. It was probably a Kerryman who first remarked that when God made time, he made plenty of it.

As you look over thick fuchsia hedges at thriving dairy farms or stop off at a wayside restaurant to sample the region's seafood and locally raised meat, it is hard to imagine that some 135 years ago this area was decimated by famine. Thousands perished in the fields and the workhouses, and thousands more took "coffin ships" from Cobh in Cork Harbour to the New World. Between 1846 and 1849 the population of Ireland fell by an estimated 2½ million. Many small villages in the Southwest were wiped out entirely. The region was battered again in the civil war that was fought with intensity in and around "Rebel Cork" between 1919 and 1921. Economic recovery only began in the late '60s, which led to a boom in hotel construction and renovation—not always, alas, in the most appropriate style to the area.

Outside of Killarney and Shannon, tourist development remains fairly low-key. The area is trying to absorb more visitors without losing too much of what attracts them in the first place: uncrowded roads, unpolluted beaches and rivers, easy access to golf and fishing, and unspoiled scenery where wildflowers, untamed animals, and rare birds (which have all but disappeared in more industrialized European countries) still thrive.

South of the city of Cork, the main business and shopping town of the region, the resort town of Kinsdale is the gateway to a relatively unspoiled coastline containing Roaring Water Bay, with its many islands, and the magnificent natural harbor, Bantry Bay. The southwest coast of the region is formed by three peninsulas: the Beara, the Iveragh, and the Dingle; the road known as the Ring of Kerry makes a complete circuit of the Iveragh Peninsula. Killarney's sparkling blue lakes and magnificent sandstone mountains, inland of the peninsulas, have a unique and romantic splendor, though the area in July and August is packed with visitors. Around the Shannon estuary a traveler moves into "castle country," littered with ruined castles and abbeys as a result of Elizabeth I's attempt to subdue the old Irish province of Munster in the 16th century. Limerick City, too, bears the scars of history from a different confrontation with the English, the Siege of Limerick, which took place in 1691.

Although the Southwest offers several sumptuous country-house hotels, it is basically an easygoing, unpretentious region, where informality and simplicity are the keynotes of hospitality. As in the rest of Ireland, social life centers around the pub, and a visit to your "local" is the best way to find out what's going on. Local residents have not lost their natural curiosity about "strangers," as visitors are called. You will frequently be asked, "Are you enjoying your holiday?" "Yes" is not a good enough answer: What the locals are really after is your life story.

Essential Information

Important Addresses and Numbers

Tourist Information The Irish Tourist Board provide a free information service; their Tourist Information Offices (TIOs) also sell a selection of tourist literature. For a small fee they will book accommodations anywhere in Ireland. TIOs are located in the following places:

Cork City (Grand Parade, tel. 021/273251). **Killarney** (Town Hall, tel. 064/31633). **Limerick** (The Granary, Michael St., tel. 061/317522). **Shannon Airport** (tel. 061/61664). **Skibbereen** (Town Hall, tel. 028/21766). **Tralee** (Godfrey Pl., tel. 066/21288). Open weekdays 9–6; Sat. 9–1.

Bantry (tel. 027/50229). **Clonakilty** (tel. 023/33226). **Cork Airport** (tel. 021/964347). **Dingle** (tel. 066/51188). **Kenmare** (tel. 064/41233). **Kinsale** (tel. 021/772234). **Youghal** (tel. 024/92390). Open weekdays 9–6; Sat. 9–1, July–August only.

Emergencies **Police, Fire,** and **Ambulance:** all areas, tel. 999, toll free.

Doctor/Dentist **Southern Health Board** (tel. 021/545011).

Pharmacies **Cork: Hamilton Long** (66 Patrick St., tel. 021/270548). **Killarney: P. O'Donoghue** (Main St., tel. 064/31813). **Limerick: Roberts James** (105 O'Connell St., tel. 061/44414).

Arriving and Departing by Plane

Airports and Airlines The Southwest has two international airports: Shannon in the West, and Cork on the Southwest coast. **Shannon Airport** (tel. 061/61444), situated 26 km (16 mi) west of Limerick City, is the point of arrival for all transatlantic flights; it also serves some flights from the United Kingdom and Europe. **Cork Airport** (tel. 021/313131), which is located 5 km (3 mi) south of Cork City on the Kinsale road, is used primarily for flights to and from the United Kingdom. Most U.K. flights to the Continent are routed via Dublin, apart from holiday charters. Regular 30-minute internal flights are scheduled between Shannon and Dublin, Shannon and Cork, and Cork and Dublin. **Kerry County Airport** (tel. 066/64350) at Farranfore, 16 km (10 mi) from Killarney, mainly services small planes, but it is gradually increasing its commercial traffic with a daily flight from Dublin and London.

Flights from North America **Aer Lingus** offers direct flights to Shannon Airport from New York. Aer Lingus also provides direct flights to Shannon from Chicago and Boston. **Delta** has direct flights to Shannon from Atlanta. A number of charter flights also operate from the United States and Canada May–September; contact your travel agent and local newspapers for further details.

Flights from the United Kingdom **Aer Lingus, British Airways,** and **Ryanair** offer direct flights to Shannon and Cork City from most major U.K. airports. Ryanair also provides a daily flight from Luton to Kerry.

Between Airports and Major Cities **By Bus.** From **Shannon Airport,** Bus Éireann (tel. 061/61311) runs a regular bus service to **Limerick City** between 8 AM and midnight. The ride takes about 40 minutes and costs £3.

A bus service runs between **Cork Airport** and the **Cork City Bus Terminal** (Parnell Pl., tel. 021/50422) every 30 minutes, on the hour and the half hour. The ride takes about 10 minutes and costs £1.50.

By Taxi. Taxis can be found outside the main terminal building at the Shannon and Cork airports. The ride from Shannon Airport to Limerick City costs about £16; from Cork Airport to Cork City costs about £4.

Arriving and Departing by Other Transportation

By Ferry/Car From the United Kingdom, the Southwest has two ports of entry: Rosslare (in County Wexford) and Cork City. (*See* Chapter 6 for Rosslare ferry details.) From Rosslare Harbour by car, take the N25 to Cork (208 km/129 mi) and allow 3½ hours for the journey. You can pick up the N24 in Waterford for Limerick City (211 km/131 mi) which also takes about 3½ hours.

By Ferry/Bus Train connections between Rosslare Harbour and Cork City, Limerick City, or Tralee all involve changing at Limerick Junction, so the journey time is usually longer than by car or bus. It is quicker and cheaper, if less comfortable, to use the long-distance buses that service the ferries. **International Express Supabus** leaves London's Victoria Coach Station daily and travels overnight via Bristol to Fishguard, then on to Cork, Killarney, and Tralee. Timetables can be obtained from any National Express Coach Station or by calling Supabus (tel. 01/439–9368). An Irish company, **Slattery's** (tel. 01/724 0741), also runs a bus service from London to Cork and Tralee. The journey to Cork via Rosslare by bus and ferry is an arduous one of about 18 hours.

Swansea–Cork Ferries (tel. 0792/456116) operates a 10-hour crossing between the two ports on a comfortable, well-equipped boat. Supabus (*see* above) will get you to the Swansea ferry from anywhere in the United Kingdom.

By Car The main driving access route from Dublin is the N7, which goes direct to Limerick City (192 km/120 mi); from Dublin, pick up the N8 in Portlaoise for Cork City (257 km/160 mi). The journey time between Dublin and Limerick runs just under three hours; between Dublin and Cork takes about 3½ hours.

By Train From Dublin Heuston Station (tel. 01/366222), the region is served by three direct rail links to Limerick City, Tralee, and Cork City. Journey time from Dublin to Limerick is 2½ hours; to Cork, 2¾; to Tralee, 3¾. For passenger inquiries: in Limerick, tel. 061/31555; in Cork, tel. 021/504422; in Tralee, tel. 066/21211.

By Bus Bus Éireann operates Expressway services from Dublin to Limerick City, Cork City, and Tralee. Add approximately one hour to the journey time by train. Most towns in the region are served by the provincial Bus Éireann network (tel. 01/302222 in Dublin, 061/313333 in Limerick, 021/504422 in Cork, and 066/21211 in Tralee).

Getting Around

By Car A car is the ideal way to explore this region, packed as it is with scenic routes, attractive but remote towns, and a host of out-of-the-way restaurants and hotels that deserve a detour. The roads are generally small, two-lane affairs (one in each direction). You will find a few miles of two-lane highway on the outskirts of Cork City, Limerick City, and Killarney, but much of your time will be spent on roads so narrow and twisty that it is not advisable to exceed 40 mph.

Getting around the Southwest is every bit as enjoyable as arriving, provided you set out in the right frame of mind—a relaxed one. There is no point in imposing a rigid timetable on your journey when you are visiting one of the last places in Western Europe where you are as likely to be held up by a donkey cart, a herd of cows, or a flock of sheep as by road construction or heavy trucks.

Car Rentals All the major car rental companies have desks at Shannon and Cork airports:

Shannon Airport: Avis (tel. 061/61643), **Dan Dooley** (tel. 061/61098), **Hertz** (tel. 061/61369), **Irish Car Rentals** (tel. 061/62649), and **Murray's Europcar** (tel. 061/61618).

Cork Airport: Avis (tel. 021/965321), **Hertz** (tel. 021/965849), **Johnson & Perrott** (tel. 021/963313), **Kenning Car Hire** (tel. 021/276611), and **Murray's Europcar** (tel. 021/966736).

In Killarney, try **Killarney Autos Ltd.** (tel. 064/31355).

By Train The rail network, which covers only the inner ring of the region, is mainly useful for moving from one touring base to another. Except during the peak season of July and August, only four trains a day run between Cork (or Limerick) and Tralee. More frequent service is offered between Cork City and Limerick City, but the ride involves changing at Limerick Junction—as does the journey from Limerick to Tralee—to wait for a connecting train. Be sure to ascertain the delay involved in the connection. (For passenger inquiries, *see* Arriving and Departing by Train, above.) The journey from Cork to Tralee takes 2¼ hours; from Cork to Limerick, about 2–2½ hours; from Limerick to Tralee, 3–3½ hours.

By Bus The provincial bus service, which is cheaper and more flexible than the train, serves all the main centers in the region. Additional services are available during the peak summer season. Express services are available between Cork City and Limerick City (twice a day) and between Cork and Tralee (high season only), and among Killarney, Tralee, Limerick, and Shannon (once a day; twice in peak season).

If you plan to travel extensively by bus, a copy of the Bus Éireann timetable (45p from bus terminals) is essential. As a general rule, the smaller the town, and the more remote, the less frequent its bus service. For example, Kinsale, a well-developed resort 29 km (18 mi) from Cork, is served by at least five buses a day, both arriving and departing; Castlegregory, a small village on the remote Dingle Peninsula, only has bus service on Fridays.

The main bus terminals are at Cork (Parnell Pl., tel. 021/504422); Limerick (tel. 061/42433); and Tralee (Casement Station, tel. 066/21211).

Guided Tours

Orientation Tours

CIE, part of the state-run public-transport network, offers a range of day and half-day guided tours from June to September. They can be booked at the bus stations in Cork or Limerick or at any Tourist Information Office (*see* above). A full-day tour costs £10; half-day, £6.50, exclusive of meals and refreshments.

Because distances are not great within the region, Blarney Castle, Killarney, Dingle, and Kinsale can all be visited on a full-day or half-day tour from either Cork City or Limerick City. From Cork, CIE offers orientation tours of the city and excursions to Youghal, Mitchelstown Caves, Gougane Barra National Park, and West Cork, as well as the previously mentioned destinations. No city tours of Limerick are available, but this is the area to take a castle tour and visit some of the Shannon's magnificent castles. CIE also offers overnight stays in a range of 25 destinations, including Killarney, Cork, and Kinsale. The tours are an excellent value at £25 for transport and bed-and-breakfast in a grade A hotel (based on double occupancy).

Full-day and half-day coach tours of Killarney and the Shannon region (during mid-June–Sept. only) are organized by **Gray Line Shannonway Tours** (Limerick Ryan Hotel, Ennis Rd., Limerick, tel. 061/32621). **Shannon Castle Tours** (Limerick, tel. 061/61788) will escort you to an "Irish Night" in Bunratty Folk Park or take you to a medieval banquet at Bunratty or Knappogue Castle; although the banquet isn't exactly authentic, it is a boisterous occasion that is full of goodwill.

Foremost among the Killarney tour operators is **Destination Killarney** (Scott's Gardens, Killarney, Co. Kerry, tel. 064/36238; in the U.S., 319 W. 48th St., Suite 1419, New York, NY 10036, tel. 212/315–5034). Besides offering day and half-day tours of Killarney and Kerry by coach or taxi, the group will prearrange your visit, lining up accommodations, entertainment, special-interest tours, and sporting activities in one package.

A full-day (10:30–5) tour costs about £10 per person, excluding lunch and refreshments. The Killarney Local Circuit tour is an excellent half-day orientation. The unique and memorable Gap of Dunloe tour at £19 includes a coach, boat trip, and horseback ride through the Gap. More conventional day trips can also be made to the Ring of Kerry, the Loo Valley, and Glengarriff; the city of Cork and Blarney Castle; Dingle and Slea Head; and Caragh Lake and Rossbeigh.

The following companies will also organize day and half-day trips by coach or taxi: **Deros Tours** (Main St., tel. 064/31251), **Cronin's Tours** (College St., tel. 064/31521), and **Castlelough Tours** (High St., tel. 064/32496).

Jaunting cars (pony and trap) that carry up to four people can be hired at a stand outside Tourist Information Offices. They can also be found at the entrance to Muckross Estate and at the Gap of Dunloe. A ride costs between £10 and £24, negotiable with the driver, depending on time (1–2 hours) and route. To pre-book a jaunting car, try **Counihan's** (tel. 064/31874).

Special-Interest Tours

Special-interest tours of the region for small or large groups can be prearranged with Valerie Fleury of **Discover Cork** (Belmont, Douglas Rd., Cork, tel. 021/293873). Half-day and full-day tours are individually planned to satisfy each visitor's needs.

Walking Tours

Tourist Trails, which allow the visitor to follow a signposted route while reading an accompanying booklet (60p), have been set up in Cork City, Limerick City, Youghal, Kinsale, and Killarney Town. Booklets can be purchased at local Tourist Information Offices. History buffs should inquire at TIOs for details of guided walking tours, which are organized during the summer by local volunteers.

Exploring the Southwest

If you have only three or four days in the Southwest, you might consider skipping the cities and concentrating on the coast and the mountains. For a short visit, it makes sense to base yourself in Killarney. Reserve one day for an old-style trip through the Gap of Dunloe and the lakes by jaunting car and rowboat. If you have a car, several other attractions can be explored in a day trip.

If, on the other hand, your schedule allows a week or 10 days in the region, you might want to spend a night or two in the Cork City vicinity (taking in Blarney Castle and Fota House), a night in Kinsale, a night in a country-house hotel (such as the Park, Kenmare, or Longueville House at Mallow), and two or three nights in Killarney. Then head west to the Ring of Kerry and the Dingle Peninsula if the weather is good, or north toward Limerick and the Shannon castles if it is not. But don't let passing showers deter you too much. In Killarney, especially, light showers are part of the experience and seldom last long; they can be followed within minutes by brilliant sunshine.

Highlights for First-time Visitors

Blarney Castle (*see* Tour 1)
Bunratty Castle and Folk Park (*see* Tour 4)
Connor Pass (*see* Tour 3)
Craggaunowen Project (*see* Tour 4)
Gap of Dunloe (*see* Tour 3)
Garnish Island (*see* Tour 2)
Great Blasket Island (*see* Tour 3)
Kinsale (*see* Tour 2)
Skellig Islands (*see* Tour 3)
Slea Head (*see* Tour 3)

Tour 1: Cork City and Environs

Numbers in the margin correspond with points of interest on The Southwest and Cork City maps.

1 **Cork,** the major metropolis of the south, is Ireland's second-largest city. Its official population of 138,500 is misleadingly

The Southwest

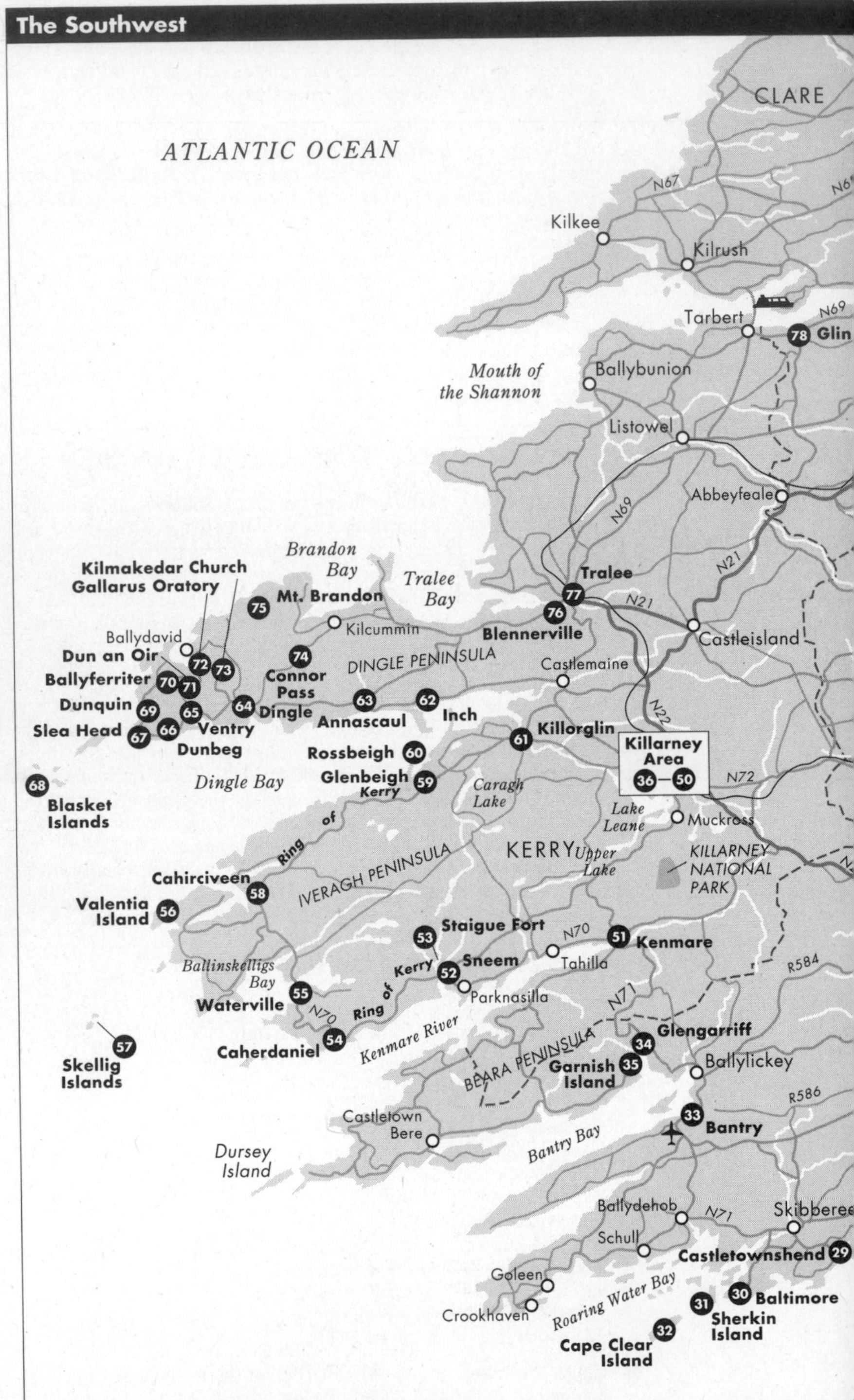

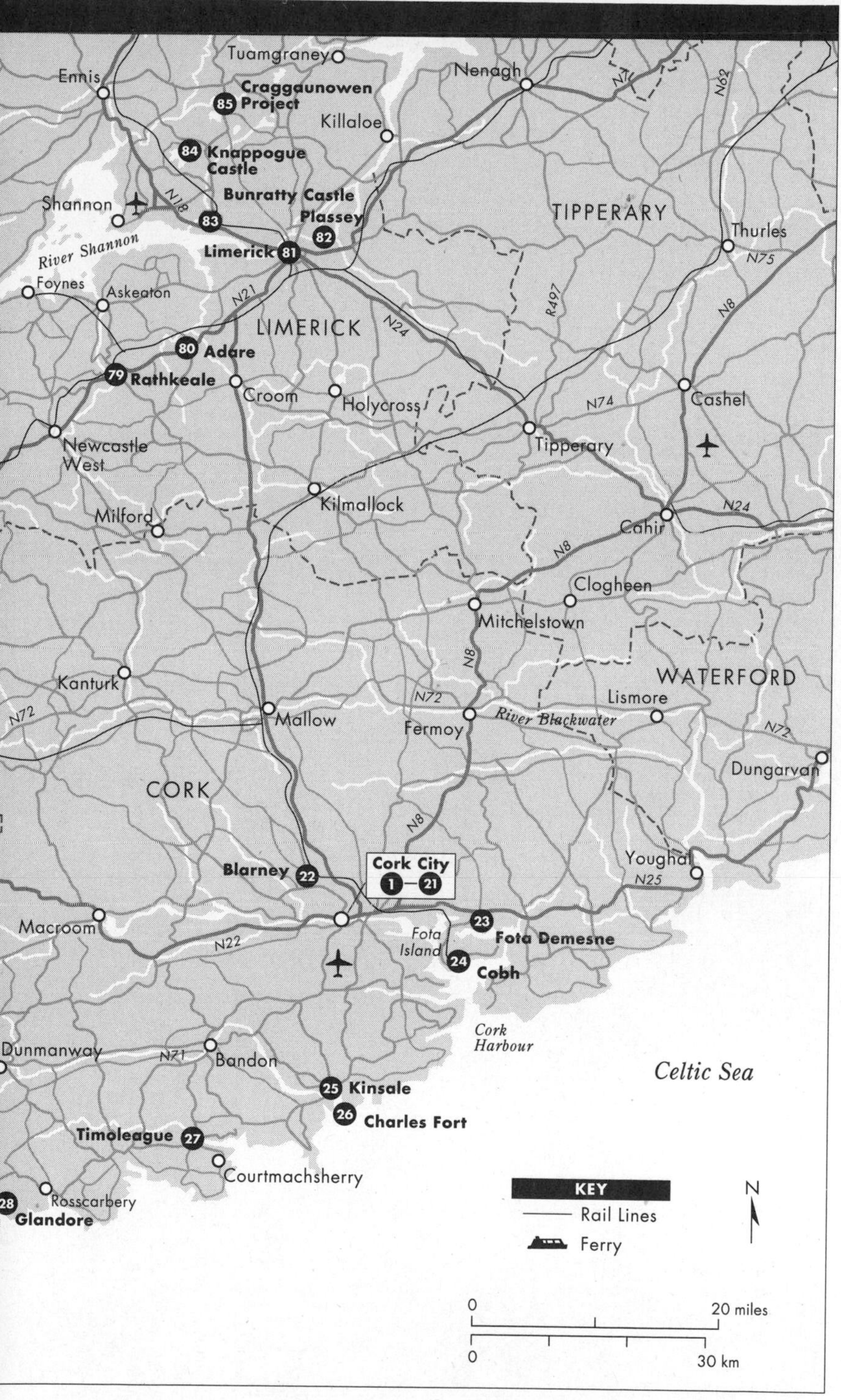
Tuamgraney
Ennis
Nenagh
Craggaunowen Project 85
Killaloe
84 Knappogue Castle
Bunratty Castle
Shannon
N18
83
Plassey
82
TIPPERARY
Thurles
River Shannon
Limerick 81
N75
Foynes
Askeaton
N21
R497
N62
N7
N8
LIMERICK
N24
80 Adare
79 Rathkeale
Croom
Holycross
Cashel
N74
Newcastle West
Tipperary
Kilmallock
Milford
N24
Cahir
N8
Clogheen
Mitchelstown
N8
Kanturk
WATERFORD
N72
Lismore
N72
Mallow
Fermoy
River Blackwater
N72
Dungarvan
CORK
N8
Youghal
Cork City 1—21
Blarney 22
N25
23
Macroom
Fota Island
Fota Demesne
N22
24 Cobh
Cork Harbour
Dunmanway
N71
Bandon
Celtic Sea
25 Kinsale
26 Charles Fort
Timoleague 27
Courtmachsherry
28 Glandore
Rosscarbery
KEY
Rail Lines
Ferry
N
0
20 miles
0
30 km

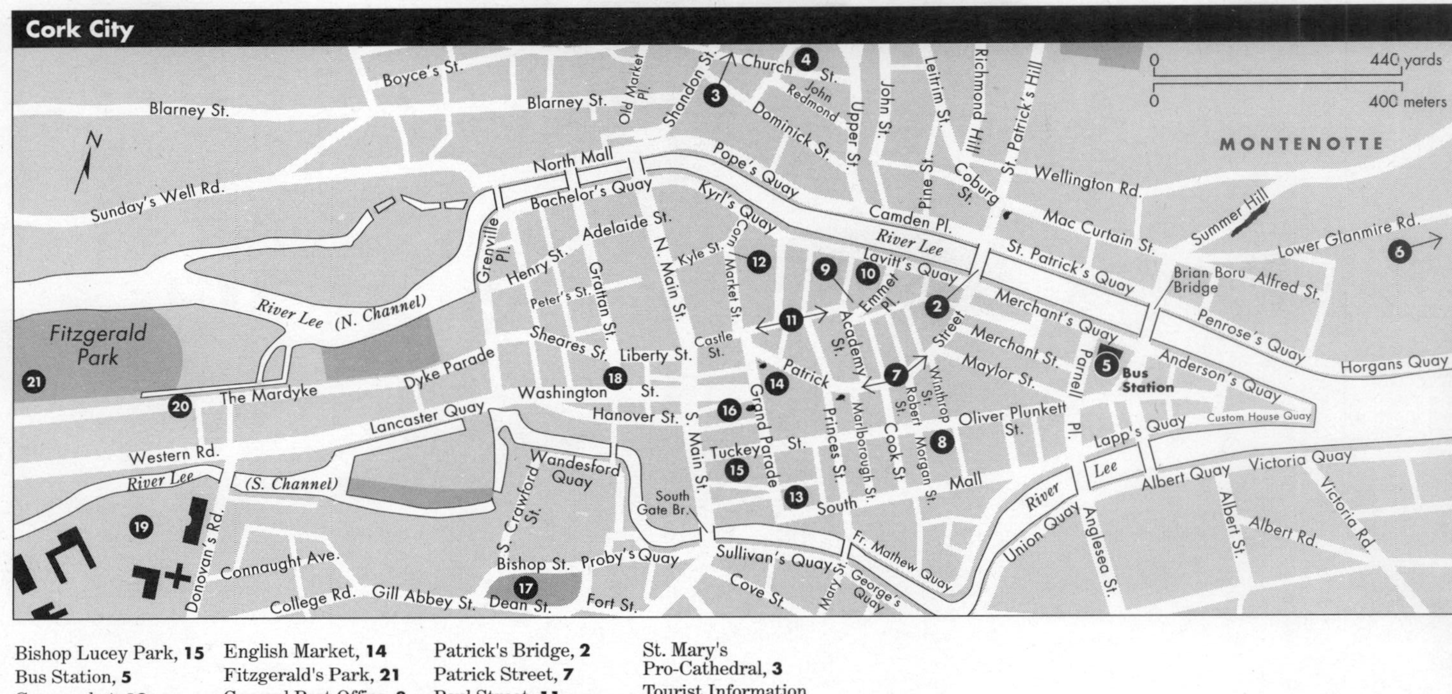

Bishop Lucey Park, **15**
Bus Station, **5**
Cornmarket, **12**
Court House, **18**
Crawford Art Gallery, **9**
English Market, **14**
Fitzgerald's Park, **21**
General Post Office, **8**
Kent (Rail) Station, **6**
The Mardyke, **20**
Opera House, **10**
Patrick's Bridge, **2**
Patrick Street, **7**
Paul Street, **11**
St. Anne's Church (Shandon Steeple), **4**
St. Finn Barre's Cathedral, **17**
St. Mary's Pro-Cathedral, **3**
Tourist Information Office, **13**
Triskel Arts Center, **16**
Univeristy College, **19**

low because it doesn't include the many Corkonians who prefer to live outside the city limits, in pleasant rural areas 10 or 15 minutes' drive from town. In 1185, the city received its first charter from Prince John of Norman England. Major development occurred during the 17th and 18th centuries with the expansion of the butter trade, and many attractive Georgian-style buildings with wide bow-fronted windows were constructed during this time. Cork gets its name from the Irish (Gaelic) word *corcaigh*, which means "marshy place." When the marsh was drained, the River Lee was divided into two streams that now flow through the city, leaving the main business and commercial center on an island. As a result, the city features many bridges and quays, which, although initially confusing, add greatly to the port's unique character.

"Rebel Cork" emerged as a center of the nationalist Fenian movement in the 19th century. The city suffered considerable damage during the civil war in the early '20s, when much of its center was burnt down. Dogged by economic slumps throughout this century, Cork is only now regaining some of its former glory through sensitive commercial development and an ongoing program of inner-city renewal. It is still something of a ghost town after 6 PM, when the business community has gone home.

Cork's main attractions are best visited on foot. Patrick Street
is the main thoroughfare; the best place to get your bearings is
2 at **Patrick's Bridge.** Look across the river to Patrick's Hill,
whose tall Georgian houses are now mainly consulting rooms
for doctors. The hill is so steep that steps are cut into the pave-
ment. The slopes of the hilly north city are dominated by the
3 tower of **St. Mary's Pro-Cathedral** and the Shandon Steeple
with its four-sided clock. If you're interested in tracing Cork
ancestors, the presbytery at St. Mary's has records of births
and marriages dating from 1784. *Cathedral Walk. Admission
free. Open daily 9–6.*

The Bells of Shandon were immortalized in an atrocious ballad
of that name popular in the 19th century. The pepper-pot
4 Shandon Steeple belongs to **St. Anne's Church** on Church
Street, a three-minute walk downhill (toward the city center)
from the Pro-Cathedral. Visitors who are prepared to climb the
120-foot tower can have the bells rung out over Cork at their
request. *Admission free. Open daily 9–6.*

5 From Patrick's Bridge, you can't quite see the **bus station;** still
facing the river, it is one block downstream on the right. The
bridge in front of the bus station, Brian Boru Bridge, leads to
6 **Kent (Rail) Station,** which is north of the river two blocks to the
right.

7 Turn your back on the river and head up **Patrick Street.** On the
left is **Merchant's Quay,** where tall ships that serve the butter
trade used to load up before heading downstream to the open
sea. The design of the large, £30-million shopping center on the
site (built in 1989) evokes the warehouses of old. **Roches Stores,**
on the left, is the largest department store in town, while
Cash's, next door, is the most upscale.

Turn left into Winthrop Street, a pedestrian mall, which leads
8 to the **General Post Office,** a neoclassical building with an elegant colonnaded facade, built on the site of the Theater Royal.
It reopened in 1989 after major refurbishment. The post office

is located on Oliver Plunkett Street, a busy narrow road known for its fashion boutiques and jewelry stores.

Time Out Resist the temptation to nip in to McDonald's on Winthrop Street; try the **Long Valley** instead. This friendly old bar, popular with artists, writers, students, and other eccentrics, serves enormous sandwiches, filled with salad and home-cooked meat, as well as tea, coffee, and pints.

Continue around the graceful curve of Patrick Street—and don't forget to look up. Above some of the standardized plate-glass and plastic shop facades are examples of the bow-fronted Georgian windows that are so typical of old Cork. Cross the street in front of **Penney's** and take Academy Street, which
9 leads to the **Crawford Art Gallery.** Here you'll find an excellent collection of landscape paintings showing views of Cork in the 18th and 19th centuries. Look out for the work of Nathaniel Grogan (1740–1807). The gallery also mounts adventurous exhibitions by contemporary artists from Ireland and abroad. The gallery's cafeteria is one of the best places in town for a light lunch or a tasty home-baked cake. *Emmet Place, tel. 021/273377. Admission free. Open weekdays 9–5, Sat. 9–1.*

10 The **Opera House,** an unfortunate concrete building dating from the '60s, is on the left of the Crawford, but turn right out
11 of the front door instead, crossing into the pedestrianized **Paul Street** area whose development has transformed the city center. The piazza is a popular place for street theater and entertainment. The shops here offer the best in modern Irish design —from Donegal tweeds to hand-blown glass.

If you follow Paul Street in a westerly direction from the
12 Crawford Art Gallery, you'll reach the **Cornmarket,** once the site of a thriving outdoor market. This area has dwindled to a few secondhand clothes dealers, but the shops alongside are worth checking for antiques. Turn left at the crossroads at Paul
13 Street for the Grand Parade, where you will find a **Tourist Information Office** (TIO) at the far end on your left-hand side. *Tourist House, Grand Parade, tel. 021/273251. Open weekdays 9–6, Sat. 9–1.*

If you're curious about food and not squeamish at the sight of it "in the raw," turn right out of the TIO, cross Oliver Plunkett
14 Street, and explore the **English Market.** Note the elaborate Victorian cast-iron construction and the old-fashioned displays of fresh country produce, the styles virtually unchanged since the turn of the century. The stall by the door sells a Cork specialty, tripe (cow's intestines) and drisheen (blood sausage). *Open weekdays 9–5:30, Sat. 9–1.*

Cross the Grand Parade by its central fountain and take a stroll
15 through the green space opposite, **Bishop Lucey Park.** Here you'll see works by contemporary Cork sculptors on permanent exhibition. Turn right at the top into South Main Street. The
16 **Triskel Arts Center** is signposted down an alley on the right. It has a small auditorium, a coffee shop, and interesting exhibitions of contemporary arts and crafts. *Tobin St., tel. 021/272022. Admission free. Open weekdays 11–6, Sat. 11–5, and during advertised performances.*

If churches take your fancy, you will want to make a detour to
17 **St. Finn Barre's Cathedral.** Turn left out of Bishop Lucey Park

and cross the river at South Gate Bridge, turning right on to Proby's Quay. Pause awhile on the quay to savor the atmospheric views of the old quays from what was once the entrance to medieval Cork. The three spires of the 19th-century Gothic cathedral are visible up ahead on Bishop Street. St. Finn Barre, the founder of Cork, established a monastery on this site around 650 AD. The present cathedral belongs to the Church of Ireland. *Admission free. Open daily 9–6.*

Retrace your steps down South Main Street to the busy crossroads at Washington Street. The imposing classical portico
18 across the road belongs to the **Court House,** which dates from the 1830s and is still in use today.

From here, some may prefer to take a No. 5 bus to the Mardyke instead of walking. It is about a mile to the left up Washington Street and the Western Road. Alight near the Doric-porticoed gates of the University College campus.

19 **U.C.C.,** as **University College, Cork** is known, has about 5,000 students. The main quadrangle is a pleasant example of 19th-century university architecture in the Tudor Gothic style, reminiscent of many an Oxford or Cambridge college. Several ancient Ogham stones (pre-Christian standing stones featuring an early form of writing) are on display, as well as occasional exhibitions of archival material from the old library. The Honan Collegiate Chapel, to the east of the quadrangle, was built in 1916 and modeled on the 12th-century Hiberno-Romanesque style (which is best exemplified by the remains of Cormac's Chapel at Cashel). The college chapel contains stonework, textiles, and stained glass executed earlier this century by craftsmen of the Irish revivalist school. *Tel. 021/276871. Admission free. Open weekdays 9–5, but phone ahead during school vacations.*

One block across Western Road beyond the campus entrance is
20 **The Mardyke,** a popular riverside walk where cricket is played
21 on summer weekends. It leads to **Fitzgerald's Park,** where a Georgian mansion, the **Cork Public Museum,** houses a well-planned exhibit of Cork's history from ancient times to the present day. *Tel. 021/270679. Admission free. Open weekdays 11–1 and 2:15–5, Sun. 3–5. Closed Sat.*

Blarney

Numbers in the margin correspond with points of interest on the Southwest map.

22 **Blarney,** which is located 8 km (5 mi) northwest from Cork City on the R617, is a small community built around a village green dominated by the **Blarney Castle** to the north. In the peak season of July and August, or if en route to Killarney, follow the signposts off the main N22 Killarney road at Carrigrohane to avoid inner-city traffic tie-ups. Most first-time visitors wish to make the trip to Blarney Castle so they may acquire the "gift of the gab" by kissing its famous stone. Frankly, this is all a lot of blarney, but the kiss itself does make a good photograph.

To reach Blarney Castle, you'll need to climb 127 steep steps to the battlements. Expect a line from mid-June to September 1; while you wait, you can admire the views of the thickly wooded River Lee valley below. The ruined central keep is all that's left of this mid-15th-century MacCarthy stronghold. The efforts of Cormac MacCarthy to smooth-talk Elizabeth I of England gave the English language the term "blarney" to describe flattering and cajoling conversation. To kiss the stone, you must lie down on the battlements, hold on to a guard rail, and lean your head way back. It's good fun and not at all dangerous.

Visitors can also take pleasant walks around the castle grounds; Rock Close contains weirdly shaped limestone rocks landscaped in the 18th century, and a grove of ancient yew trees is said to have been the center of Druid worship. *Blarney Castle, tel. 021/385252. Admission: £2.50 adults, £1.50 senior citizens, £1 children. Open May, Mon.–Sat. 9–7; June–July, 9–8:30; Aug., 9–7:30; Sept., 9–6:30; May–Sept., Sun. 9:30–5:30; off-season, Sun. 9:30–sundown.*

Blarney Castle House, which is located next door to the Castle, was recently reopened to the public. Built in 1784 in the style of a Scottish baronial mansion, the three-story gray stone building has picture-book turrets and fancy stepped gables. The interior features a fine stairwell and numerous family portraits. *Tel. 021/385252. Admission: £2 adults, £1.50 senior citizens, £1 children. Open June–mid-Sept., Mon.–Sat. noon–6.*

Blarney also probably has more crafts shops than anyplace else in Ireland. Most of these stores are concentrated on the south and west of the village green, a two-minute walk from the castle. A shopping visit here can be profitably used for price comparison and bargain hunting; in spite of appearances, these shops, in general, will not rip you off.

Time Out Instead of braving Blarney's overcrowded bars and restaurants, take a break at the **Angler's Rest** (Leemount, Carrigrohane, tel. 021/871167), a delightful riverside inn with garden tables in the summer and a good choice of bar food. It is midway between Blarney and Cork, off the main N22 Killarney Road on the R579.

Cork Harbour–Fota Island and Cobh

To explore the magnificent Cork Harbour, follow the signposts for Waterford on the N25 along the banks of the River Lee. Alternatively, a suburban rail service from Kent Station (tel. 021/504422 for timetable) has stops at Fota Island and Cobh (pronounced "Cove"), and it offers better harbor views than the road.

The turreted building on the opposite side of the Lee just outside of town is called **Blackrock Castle.** This 16th-century fortification was rebuilt in the 19th century and is now a restaurant and bar (tel. 021/357414). Shortly after you get a glimpse of Blackrock, the road leaves the river. The turning for Fota Island and Cobh (R624) is clearly signposted off the N25 on the right-hand side about 8 km (5 mi) outside town. Turn right
23 again at the gate lodge of the huge **Fota Demesne,** on Fota Island.

The estate's 70-acre **Fota Wildlife Park** serves as an important breeding center for cheetahs and wallabies. It also contains free-ranging monkeys, zebras, giraffes, ostrich, flamingos, emus, and kangaroos. *Tel. 021/812678. Admission: £2.50 adults, £1.25 children and senior citizens. Car park £1.25 per car for all amenities. Open Apr. 7–Oct. 31, weekdays 10–6, Sun. 11–6.*

The other major attraction on Fota Island is **Fota House,** a small Regency hunting lodge dating from the 18th century; it has been carefully restored to give the impression that it is still a family home. The authentic decor provides a perfect background for an important private collection of Irish landscape painting. The collection concentrates on 18th- and 19th-century works and reveals the influence of European trends on Irish art. Behind the house is a magnificent arboretum containing rare trees and shrubs from all over the world, some of them planted as long ago as 1820. *Tel. 021/812555. Admission: arboretum free, house £2 adults, £1 children and senior citizens. Open Mar. 17–Oct. 31, Mon.–Sat. 10–6, Sun. 11–6; Nov. 1–Mar. 16, Sun. 2–6.*

Turn right out of Fota House and continue south on the R624 to Cobh. Note the lush vegetation of this well-sheltered area, whose mud flats are visited by large numbers of migratory birds. Cobh itself faces the open sea, which is some 8 km (5 mi)
24 down the harbor at Roches Point. Both **Cobh** (previously known as Queenstown) and **Roches Point** are familiar landmarks for the many generations who left the port of Cork on immigrant ships for the New World. For a sense of their experience, and the best view of Cobh and St. Colman's Cathedral, an imposing 19th-century Gothic construction made of granite, take a one-hour harbor tour from Kennedy Pier. *Marine Transport, tel. 021/811485. Cost: £2 adults, £1 children. May–Sept., 10, 11, noon, 1:30, and 2:30.*

Cobh was also once the first or last port of call for luxury transatlantic liners, among them the ill-fated *Titanic* and the *Lusitania*. The *Lusitania* was sunk by a German submarine off this coast on May 7, 1915, with the loss of 1,198 lives. Many of the victims are buried in Cobh, with a memorial to them on the local quay.

Tour 2: Kinsale to Glengarriff

This tour takes you on a meandering scenic drive of about 136 km (85 mi) around the unspoiled coast of West County Cork. It starts at the historic old port of Kinsale and travels through a variety of seascapes to the lush vegetation of Glengarriff. The drive from Kinsale to Glengarriff can take about two hours nonstop, but the whole point of taking this tour is to linger anywhere that takes your fancy. The tour is most enjoyable between May and October, when the weather is still warm enough to explore the area on foot.

25 **Kinsale** is 29 km (18 mi) from Cork City past the airport on the R600. This exceptionally beautiful town is built on the slopes of Compass Hill at the top of a wide fjordlike harbor. Its steep narrow streets and tall slated houses feature a Spanish accent that can be traced back to the Battle of Kinsale in 1601, when the Irish and Spanish joined forces here to fight the English—and lost. Subsequently an important fishing port, with the significant presence of a British army and navy, the town today attracts yachtsmen and deep-sea anglers. It is also well-known for its many fine restaurants, which definitely makes a visit here worthwhile.

A signposted walking tour of the town, with an accompanying booklet (60p from the Kinsale Tourist Information Office or Boland's on Pearse St.) will familiarize you with its interesting and varied history. Visit the **museum** in the town's 17th-century Dutch-style courthouse for more insight into the past, and take a look at its fascinating collection of cuttings and memorabilia from the wreck of the *Lusitania* (*see* Cobh, above). The museum staff will also give you details of free guided walks that take place regularly in the summer, or by appointment for groups. *The Old Courthouse, Market Place, tel. 021/772044. Admission: 30p. Open Mon.–Sat. 11–5, Sun. 3–5.*

Leave the town center and return to the point where the main road from Cork City enters Kinsale. Follow the signpost at the
26 water's edge to Summer Cove and **Charles Fort.** This structure was built in the wake of the defeat of the Spanish and Irish forces, on the harbor shore 3 km (2 mi) east of town. If the sun is shining, take the footpath that is signposted Scilly Walk; it winds along the edge of the harbor under tall overhanging trees and then goes through the village of Summer Cove. Charles Fort is one of the best preserved "star forts" in Europe, enclosing some 12 acres on a cliff top. It is sometimes compared to Fort Ticonderoga in New York. In its heyday, it had a population of 2,000; it was in use until 1920, when it was burned out by the Irish Republican Army. *Tel. 021/772684. Admission: £1 adults, 40p children and senior citizens. Open mid-June–mid-Sept., daily 10–6:30; mid-Apr.–mid-June, Tues.–Sat. 10–5, Sun. 2–5. Guided tours on request. Mid-Sept.–mid-Apr., weekdays 8–4:30, except public holidays. No guides off-season.*

Time Out The **Spaniard Inn** (tel. 021/772436) looks out over the town and harbor from a hairpin bend on the road to Charles Fort. Inside, floors covered with sawdust and a big open fire make this fishermen's bar a cozy spot in the winter. In the summer, you can take a pint to the sunny veranda and watch the world go by on land and sea.

Next, leave the town through its center by following the quays and drive west along the Bandon River toward the bridge. The route is signposted to **Ballinspittle** (R600). This grotto with a large statue of the Virgin Mary had a moment of fame in the summer of 1985 when tens of thousands saw the statue move every evening. Fundamentalists smashed the effigy, and its replacement remains immobile, although the pious still stop here to pray.

(If the sun is shining, you may wish to take a brief detour from Ballinspittle village. Follow signposts for the **Old Head of Kinsale** and walk out the headland to enjoy the sea views from the lighthouse.)

The main route takes you through **Garretstown Woods** (signposts for Clonakilty on the R600), which are carpeted with wild bluebells in April; then pass the edge of Courtmacsherry Bay, running alongside a wide saltwater inlet that teems with curlew, plover, and other waders.

Time Out The **Pink Elephant** (Harbour View, Kilbrittain, tel. 023/49608) is an irresistible stopping place in good weather, a pink-painted, moderately priced bar and restaurant with sweeping sea views on its own grounds high above Courtmacsherry Bay. The bar serves soup and sandwiches on homemade brown bread; the restaurant features plain home cooking, including roast or grilled meat and a daily vegetarian special.

The pretty village of multicolored cottages glimpsed across the water is **Courtmacsherry,** whose sandy beaches make it a popular holiday resort. It can be reached by following the signposts from Timoleague.

The R600 continues west to the head of the saltwater inlet (*see*
27 above) and the village of **Timoleague,** which is dominated by a striking ruined abbey that stands at the water's edge. Built in the mid-13th century, it is one of the best-preserved early Franciscan friaries in Ireland. You walk around the back to find the entrance gate. The abbey was sacked by the English in 1642, but like many ruins of its kind, it was used as a burial place until recent times. Ignoring the graves, you can trace the ground plan of the old friary—the chapel, refectory, cloisters, and wine cellar. At one time the friars were famous wine importers.

Timoleague Castle Gardens are signposted in the village. Although the castle has long gone, it has been replaced by a modest early 20th-century house in gray stone; the original gardens have survived. Palm trees and other frost-tender plants flourish in the mature shrubbery; there are two large, old-fashioned walled gardens, one for flowers and one for fruits and vegetables. *Tel. 023/46116. Admission: £1.20 adults, 60p children. Open Easter weekend and mid-May–mid-Sept., daily noon–6.*

The R600 now runs inland to **Clonakilty,** a small market town where many of the shops and businesses have abandoned chrome and plastic materials for traditional hand-painted signs and wooden facades—to very charming effect. Many fine sandy beaches are located nearby; the best of them are found at Inchydoney, which is 3 km (2 mi) outside of town.

This area is the heart of West County Cork, whose small, twisted roads are overhung by tall hedges of *Fuchsia magellanica.* Originally imported as a garden shrub in the mid-19th century, it adapted so well to the balmy sea air that it is widely used here for hedging and is regarded as a weed—albeit a beautiful one with its delicate, drooping mauve-and-red trumpeted flowers. In June, the hedges are offset by tall purple foxgloves, and in August and September by bright purple heather.

The R600 joins the sea again at Rosscarbery, where you leave the main road by turning left at the signpost for Glandore at the end of the causeway. Glandore and Union Hall are twin fishing villages on either side of the landlocked Glandore harbor.
28 **Glandore,** with its steep hill and pretty church, is the more charming of the two; it is a much-favored holiday spot for visitors from the United Kingdom and Germany. The affluence that has come to Glandore has barely touched **Union Hall.** In Glandore you will see expensive yachts on their moorings; in Union Hall simple fishing trawlers tie up at the quay.

Now you are truly in the back of beyond, where the tiny roads
29 do not even have route numbers. However, **Castletownshend** is clearly signposted from Union Hall via Rineen. Castletownshend's main street runs steeply down a hill to the sea. It has an unusual number of graciously designed large stone houses, mostly dating from the mid-18th century when it was an important trading center. Nowadays, this deliciously sleepy place

only comes alive in July and August, when the activity centers on the waters of its sheltered harbor. It was the home of Edith Somerville and Violet "Martin" Ross, authors of the humorous "Resident Magistrate" (R.M.) stories, which in a good-natured way showed the differences between the British and the Irish ways of thinking; the stories were very popular during the early 20th century. The writers' graves can be visited by climbing the 52 steep steps to the cliff-top St. Barrahane's Church, well worth the effort for the view.

Time Out The place to go for a pint and a sandwich in Castletownshend is **Mary Ann's** (tel. 028/36146), one of the oldest bars in the country, whose low-beamed interior is frequented by a very friendly mix of visitors and locals. Writer Edna O'Brien claims that it is her favorite pub in the whole world.

You have only one way out of Castletownshend: the way you came in, up the hill, after which you take the Skibbereen road (the R596). If you have time for a side trip to Sherkin Island or Cape Clear Island, take the Baltimore road (the R595) by turn-
30 ing left at the entrance to Skibbereen. **Baltimore,** once a small
31 fishing village, is now a popular sailing center. **Sherkin Island** is
only a 10-minute ferry trip from Baltimore (7 ferries are scheduled daily; call 028/20125 for times). The island, with a population of 90, offers several safe sandy beaches and abundant wildlife.

32 **Cape Clear Island** is part of the West Cork Gaeltacht (Irish-speaking area). The ferry to the island takes about an hour (cost: £6 round-trip; call 028/39119 for sailing times) and is an exciting trip, as the skipper threads his way through the many rocks and tiny islands of Roaring Water Bay. You have excellent views of the Fastnet Rock Lighthouse, focus of the famous yachting race. Cape Clear can be explored on foot in about an hour, but bird-watchers will want to stay longer. It is the southernmost point of Ireland, and its observatory is famous for records of rare songbird migrants. Large flocks of oceangoing birds can be seen offshore in the summer.

Baltimore, like Castletownshend, is the end of the road, and the visitor must double back to **Skibbereen,** a busy but uninteresting market town. From here take the N71 to Bantry. If you still have an appetite for lovely coastal villages, take a detour at Ballydehob on the R592 to Schull, then the R591 to Goleen and Crookhaven, returning to Bantry through Durrus.

33 On the right-hand side of the road as you enter **Bantry,** you will see the porticoed entrance to **Bantry House.** This magnificent mansion set in Italianate gardens and overlooking the sea was built in the mid-18th century; it was blessed with an extensive art collection (including exquisite 18th-century tapestries and furniture) acquired by the second earl of Bantry during his European grand tour, which gives the house a baroque, Continental air. Some of the rooms are now a little shabby, but the beauty of the location compensates for the lack of polish. Climb to the top of the rear garden for the best views. *Tel. 027/50047. Admission: £2 adults, £1.50 senior citizens, 50p children. Open daily 9–6; till 8 on long summer evenings.*

It is not the town of Bantry that the balladeers celebrate, as a quick glance will confirm, but the glorious sweep of **Bantry Bay,** which is on your left as you climb out of town on the N71.

This is a starker, more magnificent prospect than any encountered so far, and the sparse, windswept vegetation gives an idea of what the wet and windy winters are like on the more exposed part of this coast.

34 The descent into wooded, sheltered **Glengarriff** reveals yet another kind of landscape: It is mild enough down here for subtropical plants to thrive. You are also back on the beaten track with crafts shops, tour buses, and boatmen soliciting your business by the roadside. Do not ignore the boatmen: They can row
35 you over to **Garnish Island,** about 10 minutes offshore, which features beautiful formal Italian gardens, shrubberies with rare subtropical plants, and excellent views from the strange Grecian temple. (The boat trip is subject to negotiation—expect to pay about £4 round-trip.) *Tel. 027/63040. Admission £1.50 adults, 50p senior citizens and children. Open July–Aug., Mon.–Sat. 9:30–6:30, Sun. 11–6; Apr.–June and Sept., Mon.–Sat. 10–6:30, Sun. 1–6; Mar. and Oct., Mon.–Sat. 10–4:30, Sun. 1–5. Last landings 1 hour before closing.*

Tour 3: Killarney, the Ring of Kerry, and the Dingle Peninsula

Killarney, one of the region's most attractive locales, is a year-round, all-weather destination. Because of the area's topography, rain seldom lasts for long among the mountains, and the passing showers, which can be watched as they approach over the lakes, can actually add to your enjoyment of the ever-changing scenery. However, rain can spoil the drive around the Ring of Kerry; much of the enjoyment comes from views across the water to the Beara Peninsula in the east and the Dingle Peninsula in the west. Dingle is also notorious for its heavy rainfall and an impenetrable sea mist that can come down at any time of year. If it does, we recommend you sit it out in Dingle Town or the village of Dunquin, and enjoy the friendly bars, cafés, and crafts shops.

Killarney The lakes and mountains of Killarney are the most celebrated
36 —and the most commercialized—attractions in Ireland. Killarney's heather-clad mountains, lush subtropical vegetation, and deep-blue lakes dotted with wooded isles have made a lasting impression on innumerable visitors, beginning in the 18th century with the English traveler Arthur Young and Bishop Berkeley. Travelers in search of the natural beauty so beloved by the Romantic movement began to flock to the Southwest of Ireland, among them writers Sir Walter Scott and William Thackeray. By the mid-19th century, Killarney's stunning scenery was considered as exhilarating and awe-inspiring as anything in Switzerland or England's Lake District.

The lives of the impoverished natives of this part of Kerry were transformed by the influx of affluent visitors that followed the arrival of the railway in 1854, and the locals became adept at inventing apocryphal legends and farfetched stories to impress the vacationers.

It is the combination of wild mountain scenery and lush subtropical vegetation that attracts today's visitors. The vegetation is splendid at any time of year. The red fruits of the Mediterranean strawberry tree *(Arbutus unedo)* are at their heights in October and November. Also at that time, the bracken turns rust-colored, contrasting with the many evergreens. In late April and early May, the purple flowers of the rhododendron *ponticum* put on a spectacular display. (This Turkish import has adapted so well to the climate that its vigorous growth threatens native oak woods, and many of these purple plants are being dug up by volunteers in a belated effort to control its spread.)

Numbers in the margin correspond with numbered points of interest on the Killarney Area map.

37 The town of **Killarney,** on a flat plain more than a mile from the lakes, is best regarded as a necessary evil in which as little time as possible should be spent. It becomes grossly overcrowded in July and August with Irish and European visitors. The peak season for Americans is September and October. At other times of year, particularly from November to mid-March, when most of the hotels are closed, the town is quiet to the point of eeriness. Given the choice, go to Killarney in April, May, or early October.

If your time in Killarney is limited, try at least to fit the Gap of
Dunloe and the Lower Lake into your itinerary. To reach the
38 **Gap of Dunloe,** drive west 7 km (4½ mi) on the Beaufort road,
Route R562, and follow the signs another 2½ km (1½ mi) to the
39 Gap. You are advised to wait until you reach **Kate Kearney's
Cottage** before hiring a jaunting car (pony and trap) or pony. Kate was a famous beauty who sold moonshine to visitors from her home, contributing greatly, one suspects, to their enthusiasm for the scenery.

Time Out **Kate Kearney's Cottage** (tel. 064/44116) is now, appropriately enough, a pub. It's a good place to pause for a glass of Irish coffee.

The trip through the Gap of Dunloe takes about 90 minutes. The road stretches for 6½ km (4 mi) between MacGillicuddy's Reeks (on your right) and the Purple Mountains. If you are on an organized tour, you can walk or ride (on a pony or in a jaunting car) all the way through to Lord Brandon's Cottage at the head of the Upper Lake and continue by boat. Although cars are banned from the Gap, the first 3 km (2 mi) are busy with horse and foot traffic in the summer, much of which turns back at the halfway point. Five small lakes are strung out beside the track, and massive glacial rocks form the side of the valley creating strange echoes. (Test it out by giving a shout if you feel so inclined.)

At the head of the Gap, the **Upper Lake** comes into view, with
the Black Valley stretching into the hills at the right. From
40 **Lord Brandon's Cottage,** a tea shop serving soup and sand-
wiches (open Easter–Sept., 10–dusk), a path leads to the edge of the lake, and the journey is continued by row boat. It is an old tradition for the boatman to carry a bugle and illustrate the echoes. Look out for caves on the left-hand side when passing through the narrow Middle Lake. The boat passes under Brickeen Bridge and into the **Middle Lake,** whose 30 islands have many legends attached to them, some of which, no doubt, will be recounted by your boatman.

41 The journey ends at **Ross Castle** (closed indefinitely for restoration), a 14th-century stronghold. You can take yourself to

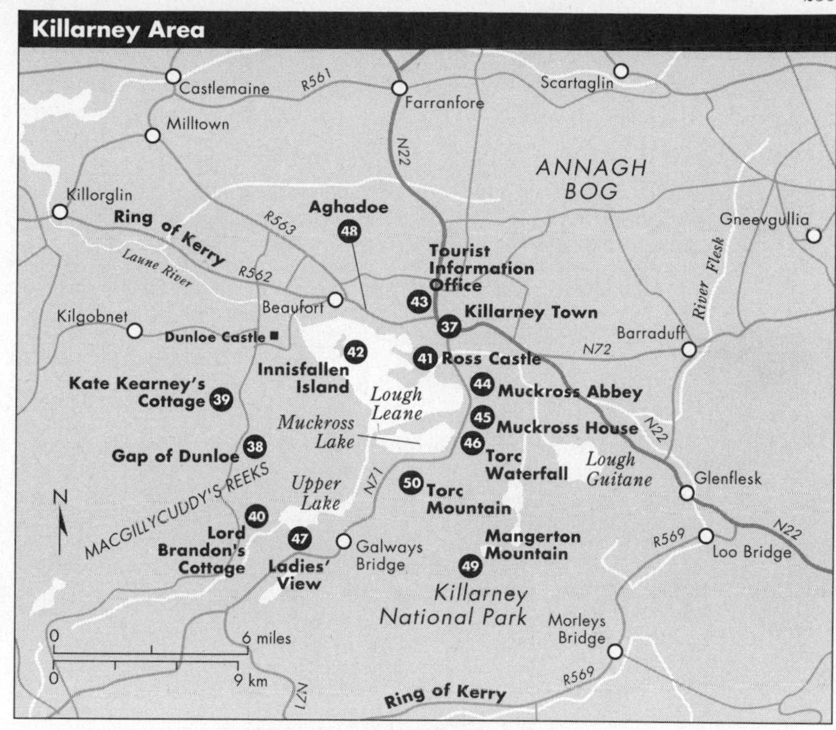

42 **Innisfallen Island** by hiring a rowboat at Ross Castle (cost: £1.50 per hour), or you can join a cruise in a covered, heated launch (cost: £4, also from Ross Castle). The romantic ruins on the island date from the 6th or 7th century. Between 950 and 1350 the *Annals of Innisfallen* were compiled here by the monks. (The book survives in the Bodleian Library in Oxford.)

Time Out Book a table at the **West End House** (Lower New St., tel. 064/32271) and head back into town for a feast of steak or Kerry lamb cooked on an open charcoal grill at this friendly, informal wine bar–restaurant.

Another popular excursion is a half-day trip to Muckross Abbey, Muckross House and Estate, and the Torc Waterfall. Cars are not allowed to tour the grounds of the estate, but a car park is available at the house. Some people choose to make the whole
43 trip by jaunting car, hiring one at the stand near the **Tourist Information Office** (TIO) in Killarney. (The cost of a jaunting car is £10–£24, negotiable with the driver for up to four people. Get an estimate from the TIO.) To save time and money, drive the 4 km (2½ mi) to Muckross Abbey on the N71 Kenmare road, and pick up a jaunting car there. Alternately, hire a bicycle in town, pack a lunch, and make a day of it.

44 **Muckross Abbey** is a 15th-century Franciscan building; even though it was completely wrecked by Oliver Cromwell's British troops in 1652, it is still amazingly complete, although roofless. An ancient yew tree rises up through the cloisters and breaks out over the abbey walls. Three flights of stone steps allow ac-

cess to the upper floors and the living quarters of the monks, where you can visit what was once their dormitory, kitchen, and refectory. *Admission free. Open daily daylight hours.*

45 **Muckross House,** about 1.6 km (1 mile) farther west on the N71, is a 19th-century manor in the Elizabethan style; it now houses the Kerry Folklife Center, where blacksmiths, weavers, basket makers, and potters demonstrate their crafts. One exhibit illustrates Kerry's musical and poetic past, and another deals with old-time farm tools and machinery—some of which are still in use on the smaller farms of Kerry. The informal gardens here are noted for their rhododendrons and azaleas, the water garden, and the outstanding limestone rock garden. *Tel. 064/31440. Admission: £2 adults, £1 children, gardens free. Open Mar. 17–June 30 and Sept.–Oct., daily 9–6; July–Aug., daily 9–7; rest of year, daily 11–5.*

Another 1.6 km (1 mi) west on the N71 (7 km/4½ mi from Killar-
46 ney) is the **Torc Waterfall,** which is about a 10-minute walk from
the car park; after your first view of the roaring cascade, it's
worth the climb up a long flight of stone steps to the second,
less-frequented clearing. If the weather is fine, return to your
47 car and drive on west to **Ladies' View,** a panoramic viewing
point. The N71 continues to Kenmare, from where you can complete the circuit by taking the shorter but very narrow Windy
Gap route, or make a wide sweep via Kilgarvan on the R569 and
48 N22, driving back through the town to **Aghadoe,** 5 km (3 mi)
outside Killarney on the R562 Beaufort–Killorglin road. Here
there is another remarkable view of the Lower Lake with
Innisfallen Island in the distance and the Gap of Dunloe away to
the west. Stand beside Aghadoe's 12th-century ruined church
and round tower and watch the shadows creep across the lake in
the dusk.

The Mangerton track is a walking trail reached by turning left
off the N71 midway between Muckross Abbey and Muckross
House (following signposts). It takes you to the summit of
49 **Mangerton Mountain** (748 m/2,756 ft) in about two hours on
50 foot—rather less should you choose to hire a pony. **Torc Mountain** (537 m/1,764 ft) can be reached off Route N71; it is a satisfying 1½-hour climb. Do not attempt either climb in misty
weather. The Kerry Way, a long-distance walking route,
passes through the **Killarney National Park** on its way to
Glenbeigh (detailed leaflet from TIO). For the less adventurous, four safe and well-signposted nature trails of varying
lengths are available in the National Park. Arthur Young's
Walk (4km/2½ mi) is recommended; it passes through old yew
and oak woods frequented by Sika deer.

From May to September, Killarney offers visitors a lively nightlife, including discos, Irish cabarets, and singing pubs—the latter are a local specialty with a strong Irish-American flavor. But the real pleasure of Killarney is outdoors. Its mild, totally unpolluted air smells of damp woods and heather moors. Few people feel that they have exhausted the area's natural resources in one visit. Most leave with the intention of coming back one day; when they do, they find the fascinating shifts of light, the varied scenery, and the peace of the place as seductive as ever.

The Ring of Kerry

Numbers in the margin correspond with points of interest on the Southwest map.

Because most tour buses travel the Ring of Kerry counterclockwise, we recommend that independent travelers take it clockwise, starting at Kenmare. This is equally convenient for those approaching from Glengarriff (on the N71) and Killarney (also on the N71). The trip covers 176 km (110 mi) on the N70 if Killarney serves as the start and finish; the journey will be 40 km (25 mi) less if you only go between Kenmare and Killorglin; from this latter point, people often choose to travel on to the Dingle Peninsula without returning to Killarney. Allow at least one full day for the Ring—and pray for sunshine, which makes all the difference.

51 In **Kenmare,** a small market town at the head of the sheltered Kenmare River estuary, you'll notice many fine, hand-painted shop signs in town. They may look old, but the revival of this form of folk art dates only from the late 1980s.

Time Out If the weather is clear, you can assemble a picnic at **Mickey and Ned's** (6 Henry St., tel. 064/41591), an excellent deli and café. Don't forget to sample some local handmade farmhouse cheeses —Milleens and Coomkeen are especially fine.

As you drive down the Iveragh Peninsula on the Ring, the Beara Peninsula and its blue-gray mountain ranges, the Caha and the Slieve Miskish, will be across the water on your left-
52 hand side. The village of **Sneem** (from the Irish *an tSnaidhm*—the knot), on the estuary of the Ardsheelaun River, is one of the prettiest in Ireland, although its English-style village green is untypical. Two miles south is the beautiful hotel and wooded estate of **Parknasilla.** The road then runs inland for a few miles before emerging at the coast again at **Castlecove.**

53 **Staigue Fort,** signposted 4 km (2½ mi) inland at Castlecove, is one of the finest examples of an Iron Age stone fort in Ireland. Approximately 2,500 years old, this structure made from local stone is almost circular and about 23 m (75 ft) in diameter, with only one entrance, on the south side. Between the Iron Age (from 500 BC to the 5th century AD) and early Christian times (6th century AD), such "forts" were, in fact, fortified homesteads within which several families of one clan and their cattle lived. The walls at Staigue Fort are almost 4 m (13 ft) wide at the base, 2 m (7 ft) at the top. The walls still stand at 5½ m (18 ft) on the north and west sides. Within the walls are stairs leading to narrow platforms on which the lookouts stood. (Private land must be crossed to reach the fort, and a nominal "compensation for trespass" is often requested by the landowner.)

54 Beyond the next village, **Caherdaniel,** is **Derrynane House.** This home once belonged to the famous politician Daniel O'Connell (1775–1847), "The Liberator," who campaigned for Catholic Emancipation (the granting of full rights of citizenship for Catholics), which became a reality in 1828. The house with its lovely garden and its 320-acre estate now forms **Derrynane National Park.** The south and east wings of the house are open to visitors and still contain much of the original furniture and other items associated with O'Connell. *Derrynane House: Tel. 0667/5113. Admission: £1 adults, 30p children and senior citizens. Open mid-June–Sept., daily 10–1 and 2–7; Oct.–mid-June, Tues.–Sat. 10–1 and 2–5; Sun. 2–5. Park: admission free, open all year.*

55 The village of **Waterville,** which is 5 km (3 mi) north, is famous for game fishing and its 18-hole championship golf course. Salmon and trout fishing are excellent at nearby Lough Currane.

Time Out **The Smuggler's Inn,** situated on a mile-long sandy beach, is a small, family-run guest house and restaurant with a good reputation for seafood. This is an ideal spot for a leisurely lunch or a quick pint and a sandwich. *Cliff Rd., Waterville, tel. 0667/4330. Closed Nov. 3–Feb. 15.*

Just outside Waterville, a scenic detour is signposted from the main Ring to Ballinskelligs, an Irish-speaking area with a fine
56 sandy beach, and **Valentia Island.** Some of the romance of visiting an island has been lost since Valentia was connected to the mainland by a road bridge in 1971. The island still gives its name to weather reports, but the station that monitors the Atlantic weather systems has now moved on to the nearby mainland.

57 From Valentia, the conical-shaped **Skelligs** are visible rising up 217 m (700 ft) out of the Atlantic. The larger rock, Skellig Michael or the Great Skellig, has the remains of a settlement of early Christian monks, which is reached by climbing 600 increasingly precipitous steps. In spite of one thousand years' battering by Atlantic storms, the beehive-shaped living cells, church, and oratory are surprisingly well-preserved.

Because of the ever-increasing stream of tourist traffic to this impressive archaeological site, the rock has been subjected to serious erosion, and local boatmen have been asked to limit the number of landings. Because the other rocks are nature reserves (on which landing is forbidden without a special permit), a round-trip by boat can still be an interesting and rewarding experience, even without landing. Little Skellig has some 20,000 pairs of nesting gannets, and Puffin Island to the north is also a nature reserve with a large population of shearwaters, storm petrels, and about 7,000 pairs of puffins. Boats leave from Knightstown Harbour on Valentia, Ballinskelligs Pier, and Caherciveen (*see* below). Landing is, in any case, only possible in the very calmest of weather. If you are absolutely determined to land on Skellig Michael, and are prepared to wait for the right weather conditions, contact Des Lavelle (tel. 0667/6124). Expect to pay about £12 per head for a half-day look-see cruise—and bad sailors take warning, these waters are exceedingly choppy at the best of times.

The main road, the N70, is joined again just outside
58 **Caherciveen** (accent on the last syllable: Cah-her-sigh-*veen*), the main market town and shopping center for South Kerry, situated at the foot of Bentee Mountain. The impressive church that dominates the main street was built in 1888 to honor the local hero, Daniel O'Connell (*see* Derrynane House, above). Following the tradition in this part of the world, the town has modest terraced houses that are painted in different colors—the brighter the better. The same sign-writers who recently transformed Kenmare with their old-fashioned hand-painted signs have been at work here, too.

The road from Caherciveen to Glenbeigh is one of the highlights of the Ring. On your left is Dingle Bay and the jagged peaks of the Dingle Peninsula, which will, in all probability, be shrouded in mist. If they are not, the gods have indeed blessed your journey. The road runs close to the water here, and beyond Kells it climbs high above the bay, hugging the steep side of Drung Hill before descending to Glenbeigh. Note how different the stark character of this stretch of the Ring is from the gentle, woody Kenmare Bay side.

59 **Glenbeigh** is a popular holiday base, offering excellent hiking in the Glenbeigh Horseshoe, as the surrounding mountains are known, and exceptionally good trout fishing on Lough
60 Coomasaharn. **Rossbeigh,** which is 3 km (2 mi) away, has about 3 km (2 mi) of soft yellow sand backed by high dunes. It faces Inch strand, a similar formation across the water on the Dingle Peninsula.

A signpost to the right just outside Glenbeigh points to **Caragh Lake,** another tempting side excursion to a beautiful expanse of water set among gorse-and heather-covered hills with majestic mountains in the background. A complete circuit of the lake can be made by road; about half of this drive will be right along the lakeshore.

61 **Killorglin,** which is 9½ km (6 mi) beyond Glenbeigh, is a small town on a hill. It's the scene of the famous Puck Fair, a three-day stint of merrymaking that takes place during the second weekend in August. A large billy goat with beribboned horns is installed on a high pedestal to preside over the fair. The origins of the tradition of King Puck are lost in time. While some horse-, sheep-, and cattle-dealing still occurs at the fair, the main attractions these days are free outdoor concerts and extended drinking hours. The crowd is predominantly young and invariably noisy, so avoid Killorglin at fair time if you've come to Kerry for peace and quiet. On the other hand, if you intend joining in the festivities, be sure to book accommodations well in advance.

The Dingle Peninsula

The landscape of the Dingle Peninsula is formed by rugged mountains and cliffs, interspersed with softly molded glacial valleys and lakes. The peninsula's three sides have long sandy beaches and rocky cliffs pounded by the Atlantic Ocean. On the coastal plains, dry stone walls enclose small, irregular fields. The whole area is exceptionally rich in antiquities, especially prehistoric and early Christian remains. The tip of the peninsula—**Corca Dhuibhne (Corcaguiny)**—is officially a Gaeltacht, or area of Irish (Gaelic) speakers, although like all Gaeltacht communities, it is bilingual nowadays, with English as the second language.

The peninsula can be covered in a long day trip of about 160 km (99 mi). From Tralee, Killarney, or Killorglin, head for Castlemaine, and take the coast road (the R561 and R559) to the town of Dingle via Inch. If mist or continuous rain is forecast, postpone the trip until visibility improves.

The head of Dingle Bay is cut off by two sand spits that enclose Castlemaine Harbour. The sand spit on the Dingle side forms
62 the sheltered seaside resort **Inch,** which has a 6½-km-(4-mi-) long sandy beach backed by dunes.

63 **Annascaul,** which is 8 km (5 mi) down the coast road from Inch, near the junction of the Castlemaine and Tralee roads, was an important center for livestock fairs until the 1930s. This explains why such a small village has such a wide street (cattle

trading was carried out in the streets), and also why it boasts such a large number of pubs for such a small population.

Time Out Photographers will be tempted to snap **Dan Foley's** (tel. 066/57257) flamboyantly painted pub. Wander in for a pint, and have a chat with Dan, who is also a magician, a farmer, and an expert on local history.

64 **Dingle,** the chief town of the peninsula, marks the start of the Irish-speaking area. It is backed by mountains and faces a sheltered harbor. In the summer months, its population of 1,400 is doubled by visitors. Dingle offers a good selection of crafts shops and restaurants, but since 1985 its main attraction has been a very friendly and entertaining bottle-nosed dolphin who has taken up residence in the harbor. The Dingle dolphin, or Fungie, as some people call him, will play for hours with swimmers (a wet suit is essential) and scuba divers, and he follows local boats in and out of the harbor. Being wild, it is impossible to predict whether he will stay, but in 1990, his fifth year in residence, boatmen were so confident of a sighting that they were offering trippers their money back if Fungie did not appear. Boat trips (cost: £5 adults, £2 children) leave the pier hourly in July and August between 11 and 6, weather permitting. At other times, call David Donegan at 066/51720.

Time Out Dingle has a wide choice of pubs, but **O'Flaherty's** (Bridge Street at the entrance to the town, tel. 066/51461) is something special. This simple stone-floored bar is a mecca for traditional musicians. Spontaneous music sessions occur most nights in July and August; at other times, they happen less frequently. Even without music, this pub provides a good spot to compare notes with fellow travelers.

65 **Ventry,** the next town along the coast, has a long sandy beach with safe bathing and ponies for hire. Between Ventry and Dunquin, you'll find several interesting archaeological sites on the spectacular cliff-top road along Slea Head. After you pass between two tall hedges of fuchsia bushes about 6 km (3½ mi)
66 outside Ventry, the Iron Age promontory fort, **Dunbeg,** can be seen on the left below the road. A fortified stone wall cuts off the promontory, and the landward side is protected by an elaborate system of earthworks and trenches. Within the enclosure is a ruined circular building, with walls up to 6.35 m (22 ft) wide. Unlike Staigue Fort on the Ring of Kerry, this was not a homestead but was probably used as a refuge in times of danger. *Freely accessible; follow signposts across fields.*

If you continue west along the coast road, you'll see signs indicating "Prehistoric Beehive Huts"—*clocháns* in Irish. These cells are built of unmortared stone on the southern slopes of Mt. Eagle. In the early Christian period, they were used by hermit monks. Some 414 of these huts exist between Slea Head and Dunquin.

The view of the Blasket Islands and the Atlantic Ocean from
67 the top of the towering cliffs of **Slea Head** stops most visitors in their tracks. The long sandy strand below, Coumenole, looks beautiful and sheltered, but swimming here is dangerous. This treacherous stretch of coast has claimed many lives in shipwrecks—most recently in 1982 when a large cargo boat, the *Ranga,* foundered on the rocks and sank. In 1588, four ships

of the Spanish Armada were driven through the Blasket Sound; two made it to shelter, and two sank. One of these, the *Santa Maria de la Rosa,* was only recently found; it is currently being excavated by divers in the summer months.

68 The largest of the **Blasket Islands** visible from Slea Head, the **Great Blasket,** was inhabited until 1953. The Blasket islanders were great storytellers, and were encouraged by scholars of the Irish language to write their memoirs. *The Islandman* by Tomás O Crohán gives a vivid picture of a hard way of life. "Their likes will not be seen again" as O Crohán's catchphrase puts it. The smaller Blasket, Inishvickillane, is owned by the Irish politician Charles J. Haughey (the Irish prime minister, at press time)—known locally as "Charlie"—who traditionally inaugurates the Dunquin Regatta on every August Bank Holiday.

69 **Dunquin** was once the mainland harbor for the islanders. No scheduled ferry service is available; inquire in Dunquin in June, July, and August for boats heading to Great Blasket during the day, depending on the weather (no phone available for the boats). At the pier (signposted from the main road), you will see curraghs (open fishing boats traditionally made of animal hide stretched over wooden laths and tarred) stored upside down. These light canoes (covered in canvas nowadays) are walked to the sea on the heads of three or four men, their legs beneath making each boat look like an enormous black insect. Similar boats are used in the Aran Isles, and when properly handled they prove extraordinarily seaworthy. The pier is surrounded by cliffs of colored silurian rock, which is more than 400 million years old and rich in fossils.

Dunquin is at the center of the Gaeltacht, and it attracts many students of Irish language and folklore. It will be familiar to film buffs, as it was around here that *Ryan's Daughter* was filmed by David Lean in 1969. The movie production gave tourism its first major boost in the area, and its shooting is recalled with affection. The ruins of the film's schoolhouse can be found about 800 m (½ mi) outside Dunquin. You will notice that some of its cut-stone features are actually made of fiberglass. Ask for directions to the building at Kruger's Pub.

Time Out **Kruger's Pub,** well signposted in the town, is the main social center of Dunquin. It has always been frequented by artists and writers—including Brendan Behan—and still is.

Between Dunquin and Ballyferriter the road skirts **Clogher Strand;** this is not a safe spot to swim, but it's a good place to watch the ocean pounding dramatically on the rocks when a storm is approaching or a gale is blowing. Overlooking the beach is Louis Mulcahy's pottery studio. Mulcahy is one of Ireland's leading ceramic artists, producing large pots and urns that are both decorative and functional; he has trained several local people to work in the studio. Visitors are welcome to watch the work in progress and to buy items at workshop prices. *Clogher Strand, tel. 066/56229. Open daily 9:30–6.*

70 **Ballyferriter,** another Irish-speaking town, is mainly a holiday village and a popular center for self-catering vacationers, many of them German or Dutch. Like much of the peninsula, this area is great for walking. A footpath off the road north out of Ballyferriter, signposted Béal Bán, will lead you past a long

71 sandy beach to **Dún an Óir** (the walk is about 2½ km/1½ mi). To reach this former fort by car, take the Dunquin road and turn right after about 800 m (½ mi), following signposts. The site was originally an Iron Age promontory fort, within which an invasion force of about 600 Spaniards and Italians built another fort in 1580. They came to support the Catholic Irish against the Protestant English. The English successfully bombarded the fort from land and sea, and they then slaughtered all survivors, including many innocent local inhabitants. Dún an Óir—which means "fort of gold" in Irish—is now largely obliterated, but folk memory of the massacre is so strong that a memorial was erected on the site in 1980. *Freely accessible.*

Return to the main road and go back through Ballyferriter, following signs for Ballydavid, to visit two of the many important
72 early Christian sites in the area. **Gallarus Oratory,** on the
right-hand side of the main road, is one of the best preserved early Christian churches in the country, dating from the 7th or 8th century. Note the ingenious use of corbeling—successive levels of stone projecting inward from both side walls until they meet at the top, which forms its unmortared roof. The structure is still watertight after more than a thousand years. *Freely accessible.*

73 **Kilmakedar Church,** which is 3 km (2 mi) north of Gallarus, is one of the finest examples of Romanesque (Early Irish) architecture surviving. Although the Christian settlement dates from the 7th century, the present structure was built in the 12th century. Note how the native builders integrated foreign influences with their own local traditions, keeping the blank arcades and round headed windows, but using stone roofs, sloping doorway jambs, and weirdly sculpted heads. Ogham stones and other interestingly carved, possibly pre-Christian stones can be examined in the churchyard. *Freely accessible.*

From Kilmakedar, return to Dingle on the well-signposted
74 main road, then head north across the **Connor Pass,** a mountain
route that passes over the center of the peninsula and offers magnificent views of Brandon Bay, Tralee Bay, and the beaches of North Kerry, with Dingle Bay in the south. It was from Brandon Bay that Brendan the Navigator (487–577) is believed to have set off on his famous voyages in a specially constructed curragh. On his third trip it is possible that he reached Newfoundland or Labrador, then Florida. He was the inspiration for many voyagers, including Christopher Columbus.

75 The summit of **Mt. Brandon** (953 m/3,127 ft) is away on the left as you cross the Connor Pass, and is accessible only to walkers. Do not attempt the climb in misty weather. The easiest way to make the climb is to follow the old pilgrims' path, the Saint's Road; it starts at Kilmakedar Church and rises to the summit from Ballybrack, which is the end of the road for cars. At the summit, visitors will reach the ruins of an early Christian settlement. The top can also be approached from a path that starts just beyond Cloghane (signposted left on descending the Connor Pass); this latter climb is longer and more strenuous.

The main road to Tralee is signposted right at Kilcummin, and runs just inland of Brandon Bay and Tralee Bay, giving glimpses of the latter's long sandy beach at Camp. One approaches Tralee across an uninteresting plain, distinguished only by the black and white sails of the newly restored windmill

76 at **Blennerville.** *Tel. 066/21064. Admission: £1.50 adults; 50p children. Open Apr.–Oct., daily 10–5.*

Tour 4: North Kerry and Shannonside

Because of its proximity to Shannon Airport, the gateway to Ireland for transatlantic visitors, North Kerry and Shannonside have many more formally organized attractions than the rest of the Southwest. For the visitor, the area's well-restored castles help compensate for the lack of dramatic scenery, compared with other parts of the region. This tour takes in the north of County Kerry, the city of Limerick, and those parts of counties Limerick and Clare that border the estuary of the River Shannon.

77 **Tralee** is County Kerry's largest town, with a population of about 16,500. This busy yet unprepossessing place has long been associated with the popular Irish song the "Rose of Tralee," the inspiration for the annual Rose of Tralee International Festival. Irish communities from around the world send young women to join native Irish competitors; one of them is chosen as the "Rose of Tralee." Festival week, the last in August, attracts musicians and entertainers from all over the country, and it coincides with a horse race, so the town is always packed with people. Tralee is also the home of **Siamsa Tíre**—the folk theater of Ireland; it is worth stopping here to catch one of the theater's lively and colorful productions (*see* The Arts, below).

From Tralee, you can take the N69 road, which travels along a plain at the base of the Stack's Mountain for 27 km (16 mi) to **Listowel,** a small, sleepy market town that only really comes alive for its horse race during the third week of September.

Time Out Writer John B. Keane owns and runs the bar that bears his name in the town center. As one would expect, Keane is a great raconteur.

A detour to the left at Listowel on the R553 will take you to the seaside resort of **Ballybunion,** famous for its long sandy beach and championship golf course. The main route along the N69 leads to **Tarbert** (18 km/11 mi) on the Shannon estuary. This is the terminus for the ferry to Killimer in West Clare, a convenient 20-minute shortcut if you're heading for the west of Ireland. The **Shannon,** with a length of 273 km (170 mi), is the longest river in Ireland or Britain. The magnificent estuary, in front of you at this point, stretches westward for a further 96 km (60 mi) before reaching the sea.

78 The N69 continues up the Shannon estuary to **Glin** (5 km/3 mi) and the first of several castles on the itinerary. A Fitz-Gerald castle at Glin, right on the banks of the Shannon, has been standing here for more than 700 years. The present knight of Glin, Desmond Fitz-Gerald, is a keen campaigner for the Irish heritage, and a well-known figure in the country's artistic circles. The current castle dates only from 1785; crenellations and Gothic details were added to the house in the 1820s to make it look more like an ancestral home. The neoclassical hall features elaborate plasterwork with a ceiling painted in the original red and green; the hall opens on to an imposing double staircase. The house also has a unique collection of 18th-century Irish furniture. *Tel. 068/34173. Admission: £2 adults, £1.50 children.*

Open May 1–June 4, daily 10–noon and 2–4; other times by appointment.

Foynes, which is 9 km (5½ mi) up the N69, was the landing place for transatlantic air traffic in the 1930s and '40s. The famous flying boats landed here to refuel before heading on to their European destinations, carrying a diverse range of people, from celebrities to refugees. The town's new museum, which is a must for aviation buffs, recalls the recent history of flying with a range of exhibits and an audiovisual show. *Tel. 069/65416. Admission: £1.70 adults, £1 children. Open July 8–Oct. 29, Mon.–Sat. 10–6; Sun. 2–7.*

The N69 continues to Limerick through **Askeaton,** where the ruins of a 15th-century Desmond stronghold almost cover a rocky islet on the River Deel. On the banks of the river are the well-preserved ruins of a 15th-century Franciscan friary. *Freely accessible.*

Just beyond Askeaton, turn right on the R518 for Rathkeale
79 and Adare. **Castle Matrix,** in **Rathkeale,** dates from 1440, when it was in possession of the earls of Desmond. Confiscated by Elizabeth I, the castle served as a meeting place for the poet Edmund Spenser and Walter Raleigh, when they were young and not yet famous. Raleigh subsequently brought the first potato tubers from North Carolina to Castle Matrix, from where they were distributed throughout south Munster (the old provincial name for the region). In 1962, Colonel Sean O'Driscoll, an American architect, bought Castle Matrix and restored it. The library, which serves as the headquarters of the Irish Heraldry Society, has an interesting collection of documents relating to the "Wild Geese," Irish mercenaries who served in European armies in the 17th and 18th centuries. *Tel. 069/64284. Admission: £2 adults, £1 children. Open May 15–Sept. 15, Sat.–Tues. 1–5.*

80 **Adare** is a lovely village with several thatched cottages amid wooded surroundings on the banks of the River Maigue. The village is also rich in ruins; if you explore the place on foot, you can locate the remains of two 13th-century abbeys, a 15th-century friary, and the keep of a 13th-century Desmond castle.

Beyond Adare, the N21 merges with the N20, which goes
81 straight to the center of **Limerick** (16 km/10 mi), the third-largest city of the Republic, with a population of about 65,000. Oddly enough, no connection at all exists between the city and the facetious five-line verse form known as a limerick.

Like most Irish coastal towns, Limerick was originally a 9th-century Danish settlement. In 1691, the Irish retreated to the walled city of Limerick after the Battle of the Boyne. They were besieged by William of Orange, who made three unsuccessful attempts to storm the city but then raised the siege and marched away. A year later, another of William's armies besieged the city for two months, and the Irish opened negotiations. The resulting Treaty of Limerick was never ratified—it guaranteed religious tolerance—and 11,000 men of the Limerick garrison joined the French army rather than fight in a Protestant "Irish" army. These events and other colorful episodes from Limerick's history are the subjects of a 45-minute *son et lumière* show at **St. Mary's Cathedral** on Bridge Street. The cathedral itself, once a 12th-century palace, features pilasters and a rounded Romanesque entrance that were part of the original structure. Take a close look at the grotesque black oak carvings on the 15th-century misericords in the choir stalls. *Admission to show: £2.50. June 10–Sept. 15, nightly at 7 and 9:15. No advance booking needed.*

Nicholas Street, behind the cathedral, leads to Castle Street and the entrance to **King John's Castle,** built by the Normans in the 13th century. Its north side still bears traces of the 1691 bombardment. If you climb the drum towers, you'll have a good view of the town and the Shannon. *Tel. 061/312344. Admission: 80p adults, 30p children. Open mid-June–mid-Sept., daily 10–6.*

The old part of Limerick is located in this area around the cathedral and the castle, dominated by mid-18th-century buildings with fine Georgian proportions. One of these structures, The Granary, built in 1774 for grain storage, is now the **Tourist Information Office** (Michael St., tel. 061/317522). The main shopping area, which consists mainly of modest chain stores, lies a short 3–4 minute walk to the south on O'Connell Street.

Time Out Just off O'Connell Street, on Honan's Quay, is the **Riverrun Gallery** (tel. 061/40277), which specializes in exhibits of contemporary Irish art; it also has a very pleasant restaurant that serves tasty, health-conscious home-cooked food. *Open Mon.–Sat. 10–5:30.*

---

82 Limerick's university grounds are situated at **Plassey** on the outskirts of the city. The drive there is worth taking (5–10 minutes on the Ring Road signposted Dublin N7) to visit the **Hunt Museum,** located on this small but nicely landscaped campus. The museum contains the finest collection of Celtic and medieval treasures outside the National Museum in Dublin. European art objects are featured as well as ancient Irish metalwork. *Tel. 061/333644. Admission: £1.30 adults, 60p children. Open May–Sept., daily 9:30–5.*

The N18 between Limerick and Shannon Airport is one of the best stretches of road in Ireland—but visitors will soon discover that this four-lane highway is highly untypical. Shannon Airport is located 16 km (10 mi) from Limerick. On the road to the airport is **Bunratty Castle and Folk Park** (16 km/10 mi west of Limerick), one of those rare attractions that appeals to all age groups and manages to be both educational and fun.

83 **Bunratty Castle,** built in 1460, has been fully restored and decorated with 15th- to 17th-century furniture and furnishings. It gives a wonderful insight into the life of those times. As you pass under the walls of Bunratty, look out for the three "murder holes," which allowed defenders to pour boiling oil on attackers below. *Tel. 061/361511. Admission: £3.10 adults, £1.60 children. Open daily 9:30–5:30 (last admission 4:30). Medieval banquets are held here twice nightly*—see *Nightlife, below.*

Bunratty Folk Park in the castle grounds, which re-creates a 19th-century village street, has examples of the traditional rural housing of the region. The park is every bit as quaint as some first-time visitors expect all of modern Ireland to be. The exhibits include a working blacksmith's forge; demonstrations of flour-milling, bread-making, candle-making, thatching, and other traditional skills; and a variety of farm animals in reconstructed small holdings, complete with farmyard smells. An adjacent museum of agricultural machinery cannot compete with the furry and feathered live exhibits. *Tel. 061/361511. Admission: £2.40 adults, £1.20 children. Open daily 9:30–7.*

Time Out No visit to Bunratty is complete without a drink in **Durty Nelly's** (tel. 061/364072) next door, a famous Old World pub that has inspired imitations around the world.

Shannon Airport is signposted to your left shortly after Bunratty, but if you have time before leaving, we suggest turning right at this crossroads. Take the R471 to Sixmilebridge and then turn left on to the R462 and left again at Kilmurry to the R469 for Quin and two more attractions.

84 **Knappogue Castle** at Quin is a 15th-century MacNamara stronghold that has been extensively restored and furnished in the 15th-century style. The castle, which is also a venue for medieval-style banquets, looks spectacular when floodlit. *Tel. 061/71103. Admission: £1.90 adults, £1.15 children. Open May–Sept., daily 9:30–5:30.*

Signposted off the road back to Sixmilebridge about 10 km (6
85 mi) from Quin is the **Craggaunowen Project.** Craggaunowen Castle, a 16th-century tower house, has been restored with furnishings from the period. Especially notable are the two authentic replicas of early Celtic-style dwelling places that have been constructed on the castle grounds. On an island in the lake, reached by a narrow footbridge, is a clay-and-wattle *crannóg*, a fortified lake dwelling; it resembles what might have been built in the 6th or 7th century when Celtic influence was still predominant in Ireland. The reconstruction of a small ring fort shows how an ordinary farmer would have lived in the 5th or 6th century, at the time when Christianity was being established. Tools, cooking utensils, and a cooking pit are featured in this peaceful, open-air exhibit. The two forts are "inhabited" by lively, articulate students, who will answer all your questions about life in the Bronze Age (2000 BC–500 BC) and the Iron Age (500 BC–450 AD). It is a strange experience to walk across the little wooden bridge above reeds rippling in the lake into Ireland's Celtic past as a jumbo jet passes overhead on its way into Shannon Airport—1,500 years of history compressed into an instant. *Tel. 061/72178. Admission: £2.25 adults, £1.30 children. Open May–Sept., daily 10–6.*

Off the Beaten Track

Anne's Grove Gardens, near Castletownroche in north County Cork (midway between Mallow and Fermoy on the N72), were inspired by the ideas of William Robinson, a 19th-century gardener who favored naturalistic planting. Exotic foliage plants border paths winding down to the river; magnificent magnolias and vast numbers of naturalized primulas are among the plants on view. *Tel. 022/26145. Admission: £1.80 adults, £1 children and senior citizens. Open Easter–Sept., weekdays 10–5, weekends 1–6.*

The Beara Peninsula is the one part of the Southwest that most visitors leave out. For a wonderful scenic drive that will take a whole day, turn left at Glengarriff and head south on R572 along the peninsula's edge. You'll have views across Kenmare Bay to the Sheep's Head Peninsula. Pass through Castletownbere, stopping just beyond it at the ruins of **Dunboy Castle and House** (open Easter–Oct., daily 10–7). Then follow signposts for **Dursey Island,** a bird-watcher's paradise, which is still inhabited, but only accessible by cable car. (Cost: 50p. Mon.–Sat. 9, 11, 2:30, and 5; July–Aug., also 7 and 8 PM. For Sunday times, tel. 027/73016.) Return via **Allihies,** where a detour takes you along a precipitous but breathtaking coastal road to **Eyeries,** and then up the edge of the Kenmare River to Kenmare.

Riverstown House, which is located 6 km (4 mi) from Cork on the Dublin road (N20), has been restored with the help of the Georgian Society. It is mainly noted for allegorical plasterwork carried out by the Italian Francini brothers in 1734 and the rococo flowers and foliage adorning the dining room walls. The house is attractively furnished with period furniture. *Tel. 021/821205. Admission: £1.50. Open May–Aug., Thurs.–Sat. 2–6; other times by appointment.*

Shopping

Shopaholics risk severe withdrawal symptoms in the Southwest. Outside Cork City, visitors are mostly faced with crafts and sweaters, and most tourist-oriented crafts shops carry the same lines. The suggestions below should help you to find something a little different. (All shops are in Cork City unless otherwise stated.)

Specialty Stores

Antiques For country-style furniture, try **The Pine Pitch** (Emmet Pl., tel. 021/273131) or **Pinnacle** (44 MacCurtain St., tel. 021/503919). For Georgian and Victorian furniture and objects, go to **James Helen** (3 Cornmarket St., tel. 021/272562) or **Monica's** (24 Oliver Plunkett St., tel. 021/271118). Interesting jewelry, Victoriana, and period clothes can be found at **Victoria's** (2 Oliver Plunkett St., tel. 021/272752). For general bygones and curiosities, try the **Paul Street Antique Market** (no tel.) beside the City Center Car Park. In Killarney, have a look at **J. O'Leary** (32 Main St., no tel.).

Clothing Oliver Plunkett Street and the Paul Street area remain the best bets for clothing in Cork. Try **Richard Alan** (63 Oliver Plunkett St., tel. 021/273759), **Monica John** (13 French Church St., tel. 021/271399), or **Otokio** (82 Patrick St., tel. 021/272619) for sophisticated and expensive styling. Younger and cheaper fashions can be found at **Red Square** (8 Paul St., tel. 021/271716) and **Moderne** (89 Patrick St., tel. 021/270266).

Rainwear **The House of Donegal** (6 Paul St., tel. 021/272447) carries classic rainwear for men and women that should last a lifetime. For more casual weatherproof clothing, try **The Tack Room** (Academy St., tel. 021/272704); for inexpensive rainwear, go to **Penney's** (27 Patrick St., tel. 021/271935) or the main street "drapery store" in any small town.

Sportswear **Matthews** (Academy St., tel. 021/277633) and **Great Outdoors** (23 Paul St., tel. 021/276382) cater to most needs.

Tweeds The best tweed comes from Donegal, and the **House of Donegal** (6 Paul St., tel. 021/272447) features a good stock of it. The shop sells both men's and women's ready-to-wear and made-to-measure, which they will ship home to you.

Crystal **Cash's** (18 Patrick St., tel. 021/276771) has a good selection of Waterford glass, as does **Blarney Woolen Mills** (Blarney, tel. 021/385280). For striking modern uncut crystal, try the **House of James** (10 Paul St., tel. 021/272324).

Irish Crafts For the very best in modern design, check out the **House of James** (10 Paul St., tel. 021/272324). This shop carries Stephen Pearce's tableware and bowls; you can also take a trip to his studio and buy at workshop prices (Kilmahon, Shanagarry, near Cloyne, Co. Cork, tel. 021/646807). **Blarney Woolen Mills** (Blarney, tel. 021/385280) has the largest stock and the most turnover of crafts in the country. The mills sell everything from Irish-made high fashion to Aran handknits to leprechaun key rings. **Boland's** (Pearse St., Kinsale, tel. 021/772161) features some unusual items, including exclusive sweaters, designer rainwear, and linen shirts. **The World of Wool** (Main St., Kinsale; and The Pier, Dingle, no tel.) offers good bargains in hand- and machine-knit sweaters, including mohair. Lisbeth Mulcahy at **The Weaver's Shop** (Green St., Dingle, tel. 066/51688) sells outstanding handwoven, vegetable-dyed woolen wraps, mufflers, and skirt lengths. **Louis Mulcahy**'s pottery (at Clogher, near Dingle, tel. 066/56229; *see* Tour 3, above) sells tableware and decorative bowls and urns. **Peter Wolstenholme** (Pottery Workshop, Courtmacsherry, Co. Cork, tel. 023/46239) produces decorated tableware and witty ceramic objects. The most reliable crafts shops in Killarney are located on Main Street and High Street; they all carry a standard range of crystal, handknits, T-shirts, sweatshirts, and tweed hats.

Sports and Fitness

Outdoor activities are very much a way of life in the Southwest, and, like everything else around the region, such activities are undertaken casually and informally, with a minimum of organization.

Participant Sports

Bicycling Bicycles can be hired by the day or the week. Distances may look small on the map, but hills can be steep. Except on the hottest summer days, you're advised to carry a light waterproof jacket. Traffic is usually light, especially if you seek out alternatives to the National routes (N-numbered roads). Tours 2, 3, and 4 in this chapter are all suitable for cyclists. The Irish Tourist Board publication "Cycling Ireland" (cost: £2) suggests six other bicycling circuits that can be made in the region.

For bicycle rentals, expect to pay about £6 per day with a £30 refundable deposit, or £25 for seven days. Bicycles may be rented at the following establishments. **Blarney: Tony McGrath** (Stoneview, tel. 021/385658); **Cork: Cycle Center** (Kyle St., tel. 021/276255); **Dingle: John Moriarty** (Main St., tel. 066/51316); **Killarney: O'Callaghan Bros.** (College St., tel. 064/31465); **Limerick: Limerick Sports Store** (10 William St., tel. 061/45647); **Skibbereen: N.W. Roycroft** (Ilen St., tel. 028/21235); **Tralee: J. Caball Himself Ltd.** (Staughton's Row, tel. 066/21654).

Fishing The deep-sea fishing season runs from April to October. Boat rental costs about £15 per person per day. Shore fishing is available all along the coast, from Cobh in the east to Foynes in the west. The whole region offers excellent opportunities for lake and river fishing, although most anglers head for Waterville or Killarney. Boats can be hired at Ballycotton, Cork Harbour in Cobh, Midleton, Passage West, Crosshaven, Kinsale, Courtmacsherry, Clonakilty, Castletownshend, Valentia Island, Fenit, and Dingle. Your hotel or the local tourist information office can suggest places that rent boats. The latter will also recommend locations for coarse and game fishing. Fishing tackle, bait, and licenses can be obtained at: **The Cycle Center** (Thomond Shopping Center, Roxboro, Limerick, tel. 061/44900), **O'Neill's** (Plunkett St., Killarney, tel. 064/31970), and **T.W. Murray** (87 Patrick St., Cork, tel. 021/271089).

Golf The Southwest offers a great variety of 18-hole courses from which to choose, many of them world-famous championship clubs set amid wonderful scenery. Greens fees cost around £12 for a full day. Professionals charge about £10 for 30 minutes of instruction. Bring your own clubs: They are not generally available for rental, and not all courses provide golf carts.

Cork Golf Club at Little Island is considered to be the most challenging in the county. The clubs in Waterville and Ballybunion in County Kerry are tricky but highly praised seaside links. Killarney Golf and Fishing Club is unsurpassed for its lake and mountain scenery. Because some clubs cannot welcome greens fees on weekends or on competition days, it is best to phone ahead. The following is a selection of the available 18-hole courses.

Cork City: Douglas Golf Club (Douglas, tel. 021/895297); **Cork Golf Club** (Little Island, tel. 021/35345); **Monkstown Golf Club** (Parkgarriffe, Monkstown, tel. 021/841376); **Muskerry Golf Club** (Carrigrohane, near Blarney, tel. 021/385297). **County Cork: Mallow Golf Club** (Ballyellis, Mallow, tel. 022/21145); **Youghal Golf Club** (Knocknaveny, Youghal, tel. 024/92787). **County Kerry: Waterville Golf Club** (Ring of Kerry, tel. 0667/4133); **Killarney Golf and Fishing Club** (Killorglin Rd., Killarney, tel. 064/31242); **Tralee Golf Club** (Barrow, Ardfert, Tralee, tel. 066/36379); **Ballybunion Golf Club** (Ballybunion, tel. 068/27146). **Shannon: Shannon Golf Club** (near Shannon Airport, Co. Clare, tel. 061/61020).

Health and Fitness Clubs Leisure centers are a new but fast-growing phenomenon in the region, and facilities are constantly being upgraded. Most hotels like to reserve their facilities for guests and local club members. Exceptions are listed below. Expect to pay up to £4 for the use of the pool, about £6 if access to a sauna and a gymnasium are included in the price. Aerobic classes cost about £2 an hour; tennis and squash courts start from £2.50.

Gleneagle Country Club (Muckross Rd., Killarney, tel. 064/31870) provides an indoor pool, a sauna, two tennis courts, and four squash courts.

Jury's Hotel Leisure Center (Western Rd., Cork, tel. 021/507533) has an indoor/outdoor pool, a sauna, a Jacuzzi, two tennis courts, and one squash court.

Jury's Hotel Leisure Center (Ennis Rd., Limerick, tel. 061/327777) features an indoor pool, a sauna, a Jacuzzi, a steamroom, a gymnasium, and one tennis court.

Silver Springs Activity Center (Silver Springs Hotel, Tivoli, Cork, tel. 021/507533) offers an indoor pool, a sauna, a steambath, a Jacuzzi, two squash courts, and three tennis courts (two indoor, one outdoor and floodlit).

Skellig Hotel (Dingle, Co. Kerry, tel. 066/51144) has an indoor pool, a sauna, and one tennis court.

Westlodge Hotel (Bantry, Co. Cork, tel. 027/50360) has an indoor pool, a sauna, two squash courts, one tennis court, and pitch and putt.

Hiking Two signposted long-distance trails for walkers are available in the region, the **Kerry Way** from Killarney to Glenbeigh (57 km/35 mi) and the **Dingle Way** from Tralee to Dingle (50 km/35 mi). Details on the trails are available on free information sheets from the Irish Tourist Board, Sheet 58 for the Kerry Way and Sheet 70 for the Dingle Way. Other good off-the-highway walks can be found in **Killarney National Park; Gougane Barra, Farran,** and **Doneraile Forest Parks** in County Cork; and **Currachase Forest Park,** County Limerick.

Horseback Riding Expect to pay about £6 per hour for a ride, about £9 if lessons are included. Horses and ponies can be hired by the hour at the following places:

County Cork: Hitchmough Riding School (Highland Lodge, Monkstown, near Cork City, tel. 021/371267); **Monatrea Country Club** (Ferry Point, near Youghal, tel. 024/94301); **Pinegrove Riding School** (White's Cross, near Cork City, tel. 021/303857); **County Kerry: El Rancho Horse Holidays,** with four- and seven-day treks on Dingle Peninsula (Ballyard, Tralee, tel. 066/21840); **Glenbeigh Riding Stables** (Glenbeigh, Ring of Kerry, tel. 066/68143); **Killarney Riding Stables Ltd.,** with four and seven day treks in Killarney National Park with accommodation (Ballydowney, Killarney, tel. 064/31686). **County Limerick: Clarina Riding Center** (Clarina, tel. 061/301189); **Rathcannon Equestrian Center** (Kilmallock, tel. 063/90557).

Jogging Most people use secondary roads because they have very little traffic, especially before 8 AM. The many long sandy beaches in the region are also popular with runners.

Water Sports

Bareboat Charters The average cost of a four-berth yacht between 8½ meters and 10½ meters (28 and 35 feet) ranges from £100 per person per week (low season) to £130 (high season). Contact **International Yacht Charters** (c/o Trident Hotel, Kinsale, Co. Cork, tel. 021/772301) and **Rossbrin Yacht Charters** (Rossbrin Schull, Co. Cork, tel. 028/37165).

Boardsailing and Dinghy Sailing The **Oysterhaven Boardsailing Center** (Oysterhaven, near Kinsale, Co. Cork, tel. 021/770738) offers tuition and hire of all equipment, including wet suits, from about £8 per hour. Sailing dinghies as well as sailboards can be hired by the hour (from about £6) or by the day (from about £20) from the following companies, which also offer tuition and residential courses: **Glénans Irish Sailing Club** (head office: 28 Merrion Sq., Dublin, tel. 01/611481) at Castletownbere, Co. Cork; **International Sailing Center** (5 E. Beach, Cobh, Co. Cork, tel. 021/811237);

Baltimore Sailing School (The Pier, Baltimore, Co. Cork, tel. 028/20141).

Traditional Sailing Cruises along the coast of Kerry and Cork with a skipper and a crew on a traditional 13-meter (42-foot) Galway Hooker for up to six people can be booked at **Teach Dearg Restaurant** (Ballydehob, near Skibbereen, Co. Cork, tel. 028/37282). *Cost: £150 per person per week self-catering; £185 per week including meals.*

Spectator Sports

Gaelic Games Gaelic football and hurling are fast-moving games that generate great excitement. The county finals are held in Cork City at Pairc Ui Chaiomh, but tickets are not easy to come by. Ask about more easily accessible local Gaelic Athletics Association (GAA) events at Tourist Information Offices.

Horse Racing The Southwest is good racing country and the breeding ground for many a National Hunt steeplechase winner. Plenty of small lively meetings provide a good day out. **Killarney** sponsors races that are held during early May and mid-July, **Tralee** has races in late August, and **Listowel** in late September. During the summer, two or three evening meetings a year take place at **Limerick** and **Mallow.**

Road Bowling Quite unrelated to 10-pin bowling, this outdoor sport, unique to counties Cork and Armagh, is played on quiet stretches of back roads. Two players compete by throwing a heavy iron ball, either underhand or overhand, along the road for a distance of about a mile. The lowest number of throws wins. Betting is complicated and the stakes can be high, which leads to much leaping and cheering, as well as a celebration afterwards in a nearby pub. Ask about bowling in any country pub, or look for listings in the classified ads of Saturday's *Cork Examiner*.

Sailboat Racing Small regattas, consisting of inshore and offshore sailing races, rowing races, swimming races, and local variations, such as curragh racing (Dingle) or salmon-boat racing (Kinsale), take place all along the coast during the summer. These lighthearted events are fun to watch and provide plenty of ad hoc entertainment. Kinsale and Dingle start the season on the August Bank Holiday (the first Monday in August), and Schull, Baltimore, Bantry, Cobh, Glandore, Lough Ine, and Castletownshend share the remaining August weekends. Details are available from local Tourist Information Offices.

Dining and Lodging

Dining

In Southwest Ireland, diners at one time could only choose between old-fashioned hotel restaurants serving plain roast meat or plain boiled fish or unlicensed tea rooms offering a high tea of cold meat, bread and butter, and cakes. Today the dining scene is diverse enough to suit all tastes. This region pioneered a phenomenon known as "the front parlour restaurant," which is typically operated by the owner-chef and his or her spouse. This kind of establishment usually begins in one room in the family home, often a room that was previously a shop or bar. The space is converted into a four- or five-table restaurant, with a small menu featuring fresh local produce cooked in the Continental style, accompanied by a small selection of wines. If the customer response is good, within a few years more rooms are converted for dining or larger premises are taken.

Most of the leading chefs in the region are French or Swiss trained, often having learned their trade in a fine restaurant abroad before setting up business at home. The result has become known as Hiberno-French or Franco-Irish cuisine; traditional Irish dishes are prepared using fresh local produce, influenced by both classical French cooking and nouvelle cuisine techniques.

The outstanding quality of local meat, game, and seafood is enhanced by sauces making subtle use of the rich cream and butter of the region in combination with leeks, mushrooms, sorrel and other herbs, and wines. Salads and vegetables still tend to be a weak point in the meal because most salad ingredients and vegetables must be imported. Similarly, desserts, apart from those making use of fresh cream, are usually disappointing.

Very few restaurants in Southwest Ireland require jacket and tie or fancy dresses at dinner. Unless it is specified below, rest assured that you will feel entirely at ease with your own interpretation of "casual but neat." In July and August and on weekends from May to October, these places operate under considerable pressure, and it is essential to book a table in advance. Be patient with delays and junior front-of-house staff, who are often catering students obtaining their first work experience.

Category	Cost*
Expensive	over £28
Moderate	£16–£28
Inexpensive	under £16

** per person for appetizer, main course, and dessert, excluding drinks and 10% tip*

Lodging

Accommodations in the Southwest include some of the best country-house hotels in the country, and many more modest establishments with spectacular seaside locations, where you'll receive excellent value for the cost. The region also offers reliable modern hotels with unremarkable decor and some delightfully renovated old-fashioned hotels.

Country-house hotels may appear very grand at first sight, but their main aim is to provide a relaxed stay in beautiful surroundings. A good pair of walking boots and a sensible raincoat are more useful here than a formal wardrobe. If you want to dress for dinner, as some people do, then an outfit suitable for a smart lunch in a large city is more than good enough. Elsewhere, informality is the order of the day.

Facilities have improved greatly over the last 10 years, but perhaps not enough to impress some first-time visitors. Only expensive hotels have fitness centers. However, most hotels can organize golf, deep-sea fishing, freshwater angling, and horseback riding. B&Bs are gradually introducing private bathrooms and, in the larger towns, televisions and direct-dial phones in rooms. The absence of a television or phone is indicated under *Facilities* below, as is the absence of an elevator in hotels with more than two stories.

Few hotels have coffee shops, but in general you can order tea or coffee and a sandwich or light snack at the bar. Bear in mind, if you choose a B&B or guest house without a bar or restaurant, that such provisions rest entirely on the goodwill of your host.

Accommodations in West Cork, Killarney, and Dingle are seasonal: Between November and March, choice is very limited. Outside these months, especially from July to mid-October, hotels are busy, so be sure to book well in advance. Hosts in this region are friendly, and there is a lack of cutthroat competition among them: If your first choice is booked up, ask the hotel to recommend some similar lodging nearby.

Category	Cost*
Very Expensive	over £120
Expensive	£80–£120
Moderate	£60–£80
Inexpensive	under £60

**All prices are for a standard double room, excluding taxes and service.*

Highly recommended restaurants and hotels in city or town are indicated by a star ★.

Adare

Dining ★

Mustard Seed. Fresh flowers adorn the tables of this chic little restaurant in a modest late-Victorian house among the thatched cottages of the village's main street. Chef-owner Dan Mullane's Irish kitchen produces imaginative, health-conscious cooking with daily vegetarian specials such as nut roast with fresh tomato coulis. Unusual dishes such as shark steak add variety to a menu that also includes free-range roast duckling and roast rack of lamb. *Main St., Adare, Co. Limerick, tel. 061/86451. Reservations advised. DC, MC, V. Wine license only. Dinner only. Closed Sun.–Mon. and Feb. Moderate.*

Lodging ★

Adare Manor. One of Ireland's biggest and newest country-house hotels, this vast Victorian edifice, surrounded by a 1,000-acre riverside estate, is a short walk from the village. Until 1988, it was the home of the earls of Dunraven. Its Gothic interior has vast stone arches, tall mullioned windows, heavy Flemish wood carvings, and elaborately decorated ceilings with hanging crystal chandeliers. This place offers grandeur and opulence on a large scale; it is well worth visiting just for a drink in the Tack Room (with music nightly in the summer) and a peek, if you can't pay the hotel rates. The bedrooms are every bit as splendid as the public rooms: More than 50 of them have individually carved fireplaces, and some of the "staterooms" are bigger than the entire ground floor of an ordinary hotel. All rooms have super-king-size beds, fabulous drapes and carpets, and enormous, mostly Victorian antiques that are elaborately carved and ornamented. Try room 203 with its elaborate vaulted, molded ceiling, or room 301, which has 15-foot-tall stone-mullioned windows. *Adare, Co. Limerick, tel. 061/86566. 64 rooms with bath. Facilities: indoor pool, sauna, gymnasium, horse riding, fox hunting by arrangement, clay-pigeon shooting, 18-hole golf (for completion autumn 1991), fishing, 2 bars, 1 restaurant (jacket and tie preferred). AE, DC, MC, V. Very Expensive.*

Dunraven Arms. This two-story Victorian inn in the village center positively oozes Old World charm. Adare is good hunting country, and an equestrian theme pervades the cozy bar and lounges where the dark walls are hung with paintings and prints of horseback riders. The bedrooms, though not large, are comfortably and tastefully decorated with antiques in the traditional style. Try room 6, where Colonel Lindbergh stayed while working on the design of Shannon Airport. *Main St., Adare, Co. Limerick, tel. 061/86209. 45 rooms with bath. Facilities: horseback riding, fox hunting by arrangement, fishing, bicycling, bar, restaurant. AE, DC, MC, V. Moderate.*

Ballylickey

Lodging ★

Ballylickey Manor House. Situated on a hillside overlooking Bantry Bay, this modest 300-year-old whitewashed manor house, surrounded by gardens, has a sophistication unusual for the area. The ambience here is more country-French than Irish—which can be a plus or a minus, depending on your taste. Four rustic chalets stand around the pool, but the best bet is one of the elegant rooms with bay windows in the main house, which was recently rebuilt and redecorated after being gutted by a fire. The French cuisine in the candlelit restaurant is way above average for the region. *Ballylickey, near Bantry, Co. Cork, tel. 027/50071. 11 rooms with bath. Facilities: heated outdoor pool, fishing on grounds, bar, restaurant. V. Closed Nov.–Mar. Moderate.*

Baltimore

Dining

Chez Youen. Mr. Youen, an exuberant Breton, owns and runs this small, rustic restaurant with copperware hanging from low beams above a simple tiled floor. It overlooks Baltimore Harbour and Sherkin Island and specializes in the best local seafood, bought directly from the town's fishing fleet. Lobster is available year-round; other treats on the menu include *coquilles St. Jacques* (poached scallops) and *moules marinières* (mussels in white wine). *Baltimore, Co. Cork, tel. 028/20136. Reservations advised on weekends. AE, DC, MC, V. Wine license only. Closed Nov. 1–Dec. 15. Lunch, Easter–Sept. and Sun.; otherwise dinner only. Moderate.*

Bantry

Lodging

Bantry House. This magnificent mansion overlooking the bay is certainly the best place to stay in town. The Aubusson tapestries and other treasures are kept in the central section of the house, which is open to the public; some plainly decorated rooms in both wings are available for bed-and-breakfast. Be sure to check out the view of Bantry Bay when you wake up—it is breathtaking on a clear day. *Bantry, Co. Cork, tel. 027/50047. 9 rooms, 6 with bath. No TV or direct-dial phone in rooms. No credit cards. Moderate.*

Caragh Lake

Lodging ★ **Ard na Sidhe.** ("Sidhe" is pronounced *Sheen;* it means "hill of the fairies.") This secluded Edwardian mansion, built in the style of an Elizabethan manor, is low and gabled with casement windows set in stone mullions and gray stone walls covered by creeper. The extremely attractive large rooms have coordinated carpets and spreads, and lovely floral drapes on the bay windows. Rooms are better in the main building than in the annex. Antiques and open fires adorn the traditionally furnished lobby and lounges. The hotel also offers delightful, award-winning lakeside gardens. Guests are entitled to use the sporting facilities at the Hotel Europe (*see* Killarney, below) and Dunloe Castle in Killarney. *Caragh Lake, near Killorglin, Co. Kerry, tel. 066/69105. 20 rooms with bath. Facilities: boating and fishing, restaurant, bar. No TV in rooms. AE, DC, MC, V. Closed Oct. 1–Apr. 30. Moderate.*

Castletownroche

Lodging **Blackwater Castle.** If you're approaching the Southwest from Dublin or the east coast, you'll find Castletownroche (on the N72) signposted off the main N8 at Fermoy. The town is located about 45 minutes north of Cork and just over an hour's drive from Killarney. This property, one of the smaller country-house hotels, opened in 1989. Situated on 50 acres of land on a tributary of the Blackwater, it was built around a 13th-century tower. The large, individually designed bedrooms feature French and German antiques. St. Patrick's, a top-floor suite under the eaves, is recommended. The Continental nouvelle cuisine restaurant serves only fresh produce. Most guests here are German at the moment, but the hotel expects to welcome more Americans by 1991. *Castletownroche, Co. Cork, tel. 022/26333. 10 rooms with bath. Facilities: fishing on the grounds, tennis court, restaurant (jacket and tie required), bar. Expensive.*

Clonakilty

Dining ★ **Dunworley Cottage.** Perched on a clifftop about 6 km (4 mi) outside town (well signposted), this tiny renovated cottage in the middle of nowhere has built up a fanatically loyal clientele. The German chef-proprietor, Otto Kunze, who uses only organically produced meat and vegetables and locally caught fish, prepares all dishes to order; service can be a little slow, but the wait will be worthwhile. About a third of the menu is vegetarian. Celeriac deep-fried in butter with blue cheese sauce is typical of Otto's imaginative approach to cooking; his pan-fried duck in a honey, raisin, and brandy sauce is also recommended. Choose a table in the small interior dining room with an open fire or sit in the more spacious glass conservatory, which is drafty in cold weather but has pleasant views of Otto's free-range geese. *Dunworley, Butlerstown, near Clonakilty, Co. Cork, tel. 023/40310. Reservations advised. AE, DC, MC, V. Dinner only Wed.–Sat.; lunch and dinner Sun. Closed Oct. 1–Mar. 16. Moderate.*

Cloyne/Midleton

Lodging **Ballymaloe House.** This place is a favorite hideaway for movie stars and other celebrities; although owner Myrtle Allen is too discreet to name any of them, it is well-known locally that Jeremy Irons is a regular guest. Originally the Allen family's home on a 400-acre farm, the rambling house, covered with creeping plants, has been developed into an informal, easy-going hotel over the past 20 years. The rooms here come in all shapes and sizes. They are homey rather than elegant, but there are good options both in the main house and in the courtyard. Myrtle Allen has done much to revitalize Irish cookery, bringing in French undertones and insisting on using only fresh produce; the food at Ballymaloe remains as close as you can get to home cooking in a restaurant. The hotel is situated only 32 km (20 mi) from Cork City, near the pretty fishing village of Ballycotton. Drive out and sample the buffet lunch if you're based in Cork. Turn off the N25 Waterford road at Midleton for Cloyne, then follow signposts down tiny back lanes for Shanagarry. The last 2 miles are the trickiest, especially in the dark. *Shanagarry, Midleton, Co. Cork, tel. 021/652531. 30 rooms with bath. Facilities: outdoor heated pool, tennis court, deep-sea fishing by arrangement, 8-hole (sic) golf, bar, restaurant (jacket and tie required). No TV in rooms. AE, DC, MC, V. Moderate.*

Cork City

Dining ★ **Arbutus Lodge.** The dining room in this solid Victorian villa is relatively small, ensuring that the highest standards are maintained. The tall ceiling, large bay window, polished mahogany sideboards, plush velvet chairs, original Irish paintings, and intricate fresh-flower arrangements on each table evoke the atmosphere of a luxurious private home, providing the ideal setting for a leisurely sampling of French-Irish haute cuisine. An eight-course "tasting menu" (served only to everyone at the table) provides a perfect introduction to the restaurant's special cuisine. Imported raw ingredients are avoided as much as possible; local meat, fish, and game, which are lightly and appropriately sauced and garnished, are the stars of the show. In winter, try the salmis of roast pheasant with lentils; in summer, the baked sea bass with sea urchin sauce is recommended. Two independent authorities, *The Wine Spectator* and the *Egon Ronay Guide*, recently declared the wine list here to be among the best in the world. If your budget is tight, sample the inexpensive buffet lunch (including tripe and onions, and beefsteak and kidney pie), which is served in the spacious Gallery Bar with panoramic views of the city. *Middle Glanmire Rd., Montenotte, Cork, tel. 021/501237. Reservations required. AE, DC, MC, V. Closed Sun. and Dec. 24–29. Expensive.*

Clifford's. Michael Clifford, once the head chef at the Arbutus Lodge (*see* above), now runs this small yet very fashionable restaurant on the western edge of the city center near the Jury's hotel. Although the interior of the Georgian town house has been modernized, it retains the old cornices and elaborate high ceilings. The high standard of cooking maintained here offers a limited number of choices on a fixed-price set menu. House specialties include spinach soup with miniature chicken quenelles (dumplings), medallions of veal garnished with apples and walnuts, and grilled chicken with Dubonnet and orange sauce. *18 Dyke Parade, Cork, tel. 021/275333. Reservations advised. Jacket and tie. AE, DC, MC, V. Wine license only. Closed Sun. and Mon., as well as Sat. lunch. Moderate.*

Glassialleys. Originally a tiny wine bar, the ambience proved so popular that the owners recently moved to larger, more elegant premises opposite the Cork Opera House and declared the place to be primarily a restaurant—but it is still a small one. Theater goers and artists as well as stylish young executive types contribute to the lively clientele. The irregular-shaped corner room, complete with a circular lookout tower, is simply furnished with marble-topped tables and bentwood chairs standing on a teak-block floor. At night, the wooden shutters on the Georgian windows are closed to enhance the intimate, candlelit atmosphere. The Continental cuisine is reliable and satisfying rather than adventurous, with such dishes as seafood pancakes in white-wine sauce and *kassler* (smoked pork) with mustard sauce. *5 Emmett Pl., Cork, tel. 021/272305. Reservations advised. MC, V. Wine license only. Closed Sun. Moderate.*

Huguenot. Situated in the fashionable Paul Street area, this restaurant has established a reputation, since opening in 1988, for good French (classic-cum-nouvelle) food in relaxed, informal surroundings. The dark, high-ceilinged dining room is dominated by an elaborate, carved mahogany fireplace on one side and a bar on the other. Saddle of rabbit with mushroom and apple and *mille feiulle* of salmon with dill are among the alternating seasonal specialties, served at slightly shabby wooden-topped antique tables by an enthusiastic young staff. *French Church St., Cork, tel. 021/273357. Reservations advised. AE, DC, MC, V. Closed Sun. Moderate.*

★ **The Oyster Tavern.** Fully refurbished in 1989, this grand old Cork eatery, a venerable institution that has served the local population for more than 200 years, is still a favorite for business lunches and family celebrations. You now enter directly into the dark-paneled front bar, with the addition of a cocktail piano that some of the regulars resent. The main attraction of the Oyster is its traditional Old World atmosphere, redolent of a Victorian gentlemen's club with its dark woodwork, original 1790s mirrors, red plush upholstery, and waitresses dressed in black-and-white uniforms. The establishment is famed for its char-grilled steaks, home-smoked salmon, fresh Dover sole on the bone, and crispy roast duckling. Expect no surprises from the menu, but savor the exceptional quality of its basic ingredients. *Market Lane (off Patrick St.), Cork, tel. 021/272716. Reservations advised. AE, DC, MC, V. Closed Sun. and bank holidays. Moderate.*

Chew Chews. The pun in the title refers to the railroad-theme decor of this superior fast-food joint. The nonsmoking section is designed as a 19th-century railway carriage, and a model railway track is suspended from the ceiling, with a locomotive and carriages making a circuit of the spacious rooms every few minutes. Kids usually love this place, and adults appreciate the speed of the table service and the quality of the burgers (the best in town at press time). The menu also includes a daily roast joint, chicken Maryland, salad, and American-style desserts. *Phoenix St. (near the General Post Office), Cork, tel. 021/272708. Reservations advised for large groups. MC, V. Closed Sun. lunch. Inexpensive.*

★ **Halpin's.** By day, this labyrinthine warren of pine booths and tables is a busy self-service restaurant offering an excellent selection of salads, home-baked pizzas, curries, and daily specials. At night, it turns into an intimate waiter-service wine bar, offering the same menu in a more relaxed atmosphere. This establishment is one of the few reputable restaurants in Cork to open on a Sunday evening. *14 Cook St., Cork., tel. 021/271534. Reservations advised lunch and Sat.–Sun. dinner. MC, V. Wine license only. Inexpensive.*

Lodging

★ **Arbutus Lodge.** This two-story Victorian villa is the first choice in Cork for those who like the feeling of staying in a fancy private home; it is only a five-minute drive from the city center (well signposted from St. Luke's Cross) on a hill overlooking the River Lee and the city. The light, airy rooms have been individually decorated with fine antiques and original paintings. The rooms designated as "superior" have vast super-king-size beds (which can unzip into twins on request) and comfortable sofas. Ask for number 14 with its magnificent bay window. The smaller "ordinary" rooms (which fall into the Moderate price category) offer their surprises as well: number 9, for instance, has a magnificent carved oak and walnut four-poster bed. The majority of guests are American, often on their third or fourth visit, but the bar and outstanding restaurant (*see* Dining, above) attracts a lively local clientele. *Middle Glanmire Rd., Montenotte, Cork, tel. 021/501237. 20 rooms with bath. Facilities: restaurant, bar. AE, DC, MC, V. Closed Dec. 24–29. Expensive.*

Imperial. From 1816 until the 1960s, this was Cork's premier hotel. Situated in the heart of the legal and banking district, just around the corner from the smartest shops, the building has an elegant classical facade with pilasters above a generous wrought-iron canopy that distinguishes it from the surrounding offices. The bar and the coffee shop, which are popular meeting places for business executives and affluent shoppers, have been spoiled by overenthusiastic modernization. To savor the Imperial's heritage, ask for an antique-style room with old mahogany furniture and velvet upholstery. The rest of the rooms, in various styles of hotel-modern, are spacious but undistinguished. *South Mall, Cork, tel. 021/274040. 101 rooms with bath. Facilities: 2 bars, 2 restaurants, coffee shop. AE, DC, MC, V. Closed Dec. 24–31. Expensive.*

Jury's. A striking modern smoked-glass-and-steel structure beside the River Lee, Jury's, a five-minute walk from the city center, is a lively spot which attracts a young, Yuppie clientele. Its large, open lobby/restaurant area features a waterfall and much hanging greenery—some of it plastic. Cork's Bar is popular with the locals at lunch and early evening. The plain yet spacious rooms offer quilted spreads, small sofas, and floor-to-ceiling picture windows. Be sure to ask for a room that overlooks the interior patio garden and pool. The hotel's fine classical French restaurant, Fastnet, is the only place in town serving caviar. *Western Rd., Cork, tel. 021/276622. 185 rooms with bath. Facilities: 2 bars, 2 restaurants, sauna, Jacuzzi, gymnasium, indoor/outdoor pool, 2 tennis courts, squash court. AE, DC, MC, V. Closed Dec. 25–26. Expensive.*

Silver Springs. Ten minutes outside town on the Dublin–Rosslare approach road, this 1960s glass-and-concrete hotel is set back from the busy main road among extensive lawns. The large and impersonal lodging is favored by tour buses in summer and business travelers in winter. The main recommendation is its recently added fitness center, which is the best in town. The fanciest and largest rooms, decked out in French-boudoir style in pink-and-gray plush, are located in the newest (1988) wing. *Tivoli, Cork, tel. 021/507533. 107 rooms with bath. Facilities: 2 bars, 2 restaurants, sauna, Jacuzzi, gymnasium, steam room, indoor pool, 2 squash courts, 3 tennis courts (1 outdoor, 2 indoor), bowling, 9-hole golf. AE, DC, MC, V. Closed Dec. 25. Expensive.*

Moore's. An unpretentious establishment on a quiet inner-city stretch of the River Lee, Moore's has many ardent fans who praise the homey atmosphere and the friendly staff. Others complain of the pervasive smell of cooking in the public areas and the twisted narrow corridors that resulted from combining three undistinguished town houses into one. The cozy rooms have plain carpets and blue patterned drapes and spreads, but they vary greatly in size, shape, and outlook. The best bet is a room with a river view. *Morrison's Island, Cork, tel. 021/271291. 35 rooms with bath. Facilities: bar, restaurant. No elevator. AE, DC, MC, V. Moderate.*

Gabriel House. A four-minute uphill hike from the railroad station, and a seven-minute walk from the bus station, this well-run, large Victorian guest house boasts many satisfied customers. The rooms are small, but they all have pleasant views, nice old sash windows, and floral comforters with matching drapes. Refreshments are served 24 hours a day. Guests are encouraged to make themselves at home in the comfortable television lounge. *Summerhill, St. Luke's, Cork, tel. 021/500333. 23 rooms, 21 with bath. Facilities: restaurant, TV lounge. No TV or direct-dial phone in rooms. AE, DC, MC, V. Inexpensive.*

★ **Victoria Lodge.** Built originally in the early 20th century as a Capuchin monastery, this exceptionally well-appointed B&B is located a five-minute drive from the town center; it is also accessible by several bus routes. Breakfast is served in the spacious old refectory with its polished benches and paneled walls still intact, and the common room is now a television lounge and reading room. The simple, comfortable rooms feature brown chenille spreads, cotton curtains, and mahogany bureaus. *Victoria Cross, Cork, tel. 021/542233. 32 rooms with bath. Facilities: TV lounge, no bar, no evening meal. MC, V. Inexpensive.*

Dingle

Dining

★ **Beginish.** Dingle is an oasis in a culinary desert, although this spot would be outstanding whatever the location or the competition. The small rooms feature pale green carpeting, fresh flowers on the pink linen tablecloths, and muted classical music. The food is an imaginative and generous interpretation of French nouvelle cuisine; specialties include brill fillets on leek fondue with white-wine sauce, and fillet of lamb in phyllo pastry with *duxelles*. The wine list, with about 100 choices, includes a good selection of half-bottles. *Green St., Dingle, Co. Kerry, tel. 066/51588. Reservations advised. AE, DC, MC, V. Closed Mon. and Nov.–Mar. Moderate.*

Doyle's Seafood Bar. This establishment is more of a restaurant than a bar, but sandstone slates on the floor, rush-seated chairs, and pine tables create a very casual atmosphere. Because the seafood is so fresh, John Doyle prefers to keep it simple: fillets of plaice (flounder) stuffed with crab with prawn sauce is about the fanciest dish. Crab claws *beurre blanc* and scallops with a chive butter sauce are more typical options. The menu offers a good selection of seafood appetizers and irresistible homemade desserts. Eight very comfortable, moderately-priced bedrooms are available in the adjoining town house—as long as you don't mind the pervasive smell of fish! *John St., Dingle, Co. Kerry, tel. 066/51174. Reservations advised. AE, DC, MC, V. Closed Sun. and mid-Nov.–early Mar. Moderate.*

★ **The Islandman.** The front of this dining spot consists of a bar and a bookshop that blend well with the dark wooden tables, bentwood chairs, and Tiffany lamps of the small restaurant. During the day, it is a popular café-bar. The dinner menu, which caters to more serious eaters, includes venison in a mushroom sauce with red cabbage and potato dumplings; fresh trout or salmon plainly broiled; or vegetarian pasta and a side salad. *Main St., Dingle, Co. Kerry, tel. 066/51803. Reservations advised for dinner. AE, DC, MC, V. Inexpensive.*

Lodging

★ **Benner's.** An American owner has restored this small town-center hotel to its former glory. It should be made a model for many similar establishments around Ireland still suffering from insensitive 1960s modernization programs. All the rooms are individually furnished with country-style stripped-pine antiques, plain pale cream wool carpets, and light green *eau de nil* paintwork. Rooms 2 and 3 have pine four-poster beds, but the largest rooms are 16 and 17 on the third floor. The effect throughout is cheerful and uncluttered, with plump chintz sofas in the lobby and much well-polished wood paneling on the ground floor. The front bar has a busy local trade, especially at lunchtime. *Main St., Dingle, Co. Kerry, tel. 066/51638. 25 rooms with bath. Facilities: 2 bars, restaurant. No elevator. AE, DC, MC, V. Closed Jan.–Feb., but check for 1991. Moderate.*

Skellig (Ostan na Sceilge). This was the product of Ireland's 1960s hotel boom when novelty was much prized. It has left us with a two-story concrete-and-glass bedroom section joined on to a spaceship-like lobby/bar/restaurant/pool complex that is meant to recall, of all things, *clocháns*, the local beehive-shape anchorite cells. Be sure to ask for a second-floor bedroom with a sea view—216, 218, 220, and 222 are the best. The hotel is a five-minute walk from town on the water's edge; it is very popular with Irish families—which means swarms of children—in July and August. The spacious bar and lounge, which feature exposed stone work and wooden beams, are at their best when they're busy and very eerie when they're not. *Dingle, Co. Kerry, tel. 066/51144. 72 rooms with bath. Facilities: bar, restaurant, tennis court, indoor pool, sauna. AE, DC, MC, V. Closed Nov.–Easter. Moderate.*

★ **Alpine.** This three-story concrete hotel is not great on atmosphere, but it compares very favorably with the B&Bs in town, which tend to be small, stuffy, over-furnished, and under-bathroomed. It is just outside town opposite the Skellig (*see* above). The front rooms, with wonderful ocean views, are all plain but clean and have well-appointed bathrooms. *Dingle, Co. Kerry, tel. 066/51250. 14 rooms with bath. No TV or direct-dial phone in rooms. No credit cards. Closed Nov.–Feb. Inexpensive.*

Durrus

Dining ★

Blair's Cove House. This restaurant, in the converted stables of a Georgian mansion overlooking Dunmanus Bay, has a unique atmosphere. The elegance of the gleaming silverware, the pink napery, and the large crystal chandelier contrasts sharply with the building's exposed beams and rough stone walls. In summer, you dine on the covered, heated terrace overlooking the rose-filled courtyard and fountain. The cuisine is French-Irish (the owners are French) with an emphasis on fresh local produce. Try rack of lamb cooked on the open oak-wood grill, or a seafood special such as monkfish in Pernod sauce. *Blair's Cove, Durrus, Co. Cork, tel. 027/61127. Reservations advised on weekends. AE, DC, MC, V. Wine license only. Dinner only Tues.–Sat.; lunch only Sun. Closed Nov. 1–mid-Mar. Moderate.*

Shiro Japanese Dinner House. One of the biggest surprises of West Cork's culinary world in recent years has been the success of this tiny, 15-seat restaurant, which serves authentic Japanese cuisine in an imposing Edwardian house surrounded by palm trees. The room is decorated with accomplished watercolors by the talented hostess, Tokyo-born Kei Pilz. A fixed-price four-course menu is available with a choice of main dishes such as yakitori (chicken roasted on the spit with a sweet sauce) and tempura (fried fish, squid, vegetables, and prawns). *Ahakista, Durrus, Co. Cork, tel. 027/67030. Reservations required. AE, DC, MC, V. Dinner only. Moderate.*

Kanturk

Lodging

Assolas Country House. This lovely 17th-century manor offers an atmosphere more like a dignified family home than a hotel. It is immaculately furnished with period antiques in the individually designed bedrooms. The tableware in the dining room is old Bourke family silver. A large log fire is featured in the drawing room, where you join the other guests for a predinner sherry. Both the well-manicured gardens and the cooking here have won several awards. Kanturk is known for its good fishing and hunting, and it is located within an hour's drive of Cork, Limerick, and Killarney. *Kanturk, Co. Cork, tel. 021/50015. 10 rooms with bath. Facilities: restaurant (dinner only; jacket and tie required), fishing, tennis court, boating. No TV or direct-dial phone in rooms. Closed Nov. 1–Mar. 16. Very Expensive.*

Kenmare

Dining

Lime Tree. This charming old stone house is a popular choice with discerning visitors who prefer not to pay the higher prices at the swanky Park Hotel next door. Entrées from their award-winning menu include mussels in garlic butter and smoked chicken with curried rice salad. *Kenmare, Co. Kerry, tel. 064/41225. Reservations advised. V. Dinner only. Closed Sun. and Nov.–Mar. Moderate.*

Lodging ★

Park Hotel. Formerly a bishop's palace, this establishment is now one of Ireland's premier country-house hotels. Set in extensive grounds with views of the Caha Mountains, the hotel property features terraced lawns that sweep down to the bay. The hotel is a favorite with affluent young executives from Germany and France, as well as from Dublin. The thickly carpeted lobby features a black marble fireplace, a tall grandfather clock, and Victorian chaise longues. Sensuous watercolors of Kerry wildlife by Pauline Bewick, a well-known Irish painter who lives nearby, adorn the dining-room walls. The bedrooms are individually designed with late Victorian furniture faithful to the house's original period; walnut or mahogany bedroom suites have matching wardrobes, chests of drawers, and headboards. Some rooms feature four-poster beds, while others are just as nice with matching twin beds and elaborately carved headboards and footboards. A major renovation during the winter of 1990 upgraded rooms in the 1950s extension by doubling them in size, and the extension was covered with stonework to integrate it into the old 1897 house facade. "Superior deluxe" rooms are the smallest, but big by the standards of other places, with armchairs or sofas in the bedroom area. Park Suite rooms have an entrance hall and a separate sitting area; nine larger suites are also available. All bedrooms have finely equipped bathrooms with glossy Italian marble tiling. Be sure to sample the seafood on the nouvelle-cuisine menu of the renowned restaurant (jacket and tie required). *Kenmare, Co. Kerry, tel. 064/41200. 48 rooms with bath. Facilities: bar, restaurant, fishing, tennis court, horseback riding, golf. TV in rooms on request. DC, MC, V. Closed Jan.–Mar. and Nov.–Dec. 22. Very Expensive.*

Kilfinnane

Lodging

St. Andrew's Villa. This pleasant B&B is located halfway between Cork and Limerick (R515) on the edge of a small rural town that does not see many tourists and consequently makes a big fuss over them. The villa is a modest late-Georgian house, a home-away-from-home surrounded by gardens in which the owners, the Nunans, grow their own food. The bedrooms feature Canadian pine trim and pleasant views over the landscaped gardens and lawns. *Mrs. Patricia Nunan, Kilfinnane, near Kilmallock, Co. Limerick, tel. 063/91008. 4 rooms. Facilities: 2 tennis courts, lunch or dinner on request (BYOB), TV lounge. No TV or direct-dial phone in rooms. No credit cards. Inexpensive.*

Killarney

Dining

Panorama. This vast restaurant in the Hotel Europe, which is a five-minutes drive from town, can seat up to 600 people. All tables enjoy a view of the ever-changing Lower Lake. Wood-framed carver chairs and large tables draped in pink-and-green napery furnish the forbiddingly large room; such a large-scale operation evokes a somewhat anonymous ambience, but the live entertainment most nights helps to lighten the mood. The cuisine is based on French classical cooking, with Irish variations; specialties include loin of Kerry lamb with herb stuffing and a mint-flavored tomato sauce, and turbot poached with julienne vegetables, mousseline sauce, and boiled potatoes. *Killorglin Rd., Fossa, Killarney, Co. Kerry, tel. 064/31900. Reservations advised mid-June–Sept. AE, DC, MC, V. Closed Nov.–Mar. Very Expensive.*

★ **Foley's.** What appears to be a simple front-parlor restaurant behind a small bar with an open fire is in fact a warren of small rooms decorated with half-paneled walls, stained glass, and

Tiffany lamps. The food is far superior to the decor; chef Carol Buckley, daughter of the original owners, trained in a superior French restaurant, and it shows. Typical dishes include roulade of trout stuffed with prawn mousse and grilled T-bone steak with garlic butter, accompanied by superb al dente vegetables. The chef's sauces make generous use of superior Irish cream and butter. The wine list offers over 200 choices, and a pianist entertains during the summer months. *23 High St., Killarney, Co. Kerry, tel. 064/31217. Reservations advised mid-June–Sept. AE, DC, MC, V. Moderate.*

Gaby's Seafood. The tiled floors, pine booths, and red gingham cloths with matching lampshades at this town-center restaurant help create a cheerful, informal bistro atmosphere. The small dining room is usually crowded because of the good seafood. Try the seafood mosaic (seven or eight kinds of freshly caught fish in a cream-and-wine sauce) or lobster Gaby (deshelled, boiled in a cream-and-cognac sauce, and served back in the shell). *17 High St., Killarney, Co. Kerry, tel. 064/32519. Reservations advised. AE, DC, MC, V. Closed Mon. lunch, Sun., and mid-Dec.–mid-Mar. Moderate.*

Sheila's. Sheila's has fed the people of Killarney and its visitors for more than 30 years, and it was recently handed down from mother to daughter. Situated in the town center, it is brightly lighted and simply furnished with stripped pine tables and red paper mats. The unpretentious menu features Irish specials, such as corned beef with cabbage and Irish stew (Kerry lamb stewed with barley, carrots, onion, and potatoes). In a town bedeviled by tourist traps, this friendly spot offers excellent value for the money. *75 High St., Killarney, Co. Kerry, tel. 064/31270. Reservations advisable in high season. Wine license only. MC, V. Closed Christmas–mid-Mar. Inexpensive.*

Lodging

★ **Cahernane.** This 1887 lakeside mansion, set in secluded grounds only a five-minute drive from town, was once the country retreat of the earls of Pembroke. The lobby, with its heavily carved wooden staircase and ornate fireplace, and the lounge, with its shabby Leatherette bucket chairs, retain the slightly gloomy atmosphere of a Victorian hunting lodge. The 12 rooms in the main house offer paneled ceilings, solid teak doors, creaking floorboards, and polished mahogany wardrobes as big as many a modern hotel bedroom. Try room 23 on the third floor, which has an extraordinary window overlooking the lake. The well-concealed modern section, whose bedrooms feature strident purple-and-black contemporary decor, have less charm than the older rooms. *Muckross Rd., Killarney, Co. Kerry, tel. 064/31895. 52 rooms with bath. Facilities: tennis court, mini-golf, croquet, 2 restaurants, bar. No TV or direct-dial phones in rooms; no elevator. AE, DC, MC, V. Closed Nov. 1–Dec. 23, and Jan. 4–Apr. 13. Expensive.*

Europe. The combination of a secluded lakeside location (a five-minutes drive from town) and luxurious but unfussy decor gives this modern five-story hotel the edge over its competitors. Almost all the bedrooms feature solid pine trim, a lake view, and a private balcony. The spacious lounges and lobbies are rather large and impersonal, but they do offer picture windows overlooking the lake and mountains and an imaginative display of old carved timber and valuable antiques. The sports facilities, including an Olympic-size pool, are among the best and most up-to-date in the district. *Killorglin Rd., Fossa, Killarney, Co. Kerry, tel. 064/31900. 176 rooms with bath. Facili-*

ties: indoor pool, sauna, gymnasium, tennis court, fishing, horseback riding, 2 restaurants, 2 bars. AE, DC, MC, V. Closed Nov.–Feb. Expensive.

Great Southern. Built in 1854 just across from the railway station, this three-story building covered with creeping plants is a relic of a past age. In the main section, the high-ceilinged bedrooms feature tall Georgian-style windows and some antiques; rooms in the new wing lack character by comparison, but they all have garden views. The lobby is ennobled by Grecian pillars and large gilt mirrors; blue velvet armchairs surround an open fire. The Victorian-style cocktail bar, a total anachronism, has Persian rugs on its stripped-pine floor, spoon-back bar stools, and an open fire, but it is typical of the slightly faded elegance and informal atmosphere of this much-loved institution. *Killarney, Co. Kerry, tel. 064/31262. 180 rooms with bath. Facilities: indoor pool, sauna, tennis court, 2 restaurants, bar. AE, DC, MC, V. Closed Jan. and Feb. Expensive.*

Gleneagle. This lodging will appeal to sociable people who enjoy plenty of action but are unperturbed by bizarre decor; the main house and its three modern bedroom extensions combine clashing decorating styles and an apparently random selection of carpets and drapes. The hotel is located on the main road to Kenmare, about a five-minute drive from town. It is popular with both Irish and American visitors, and serves mainly a younger crowd. Evening entertainment includes live music at the Eagles Whistle Singing Pub and during mid-June through September, disco music at the Wings Nightclub and top Irish cabaret acts. Ask for a bedroom in the newest (1979) wing, which has a lake view; the rooms are the largest in the hotel, and all have private balconies. *Muckross Rd., Killarney, Co. Kerry, tel. 064/31870. 96 rooms with bath. Facilities: 2 tennis courts, 4 squash courts, practice golf, sauna, indoor pool, bar, restaurant, nightclub. TV in rooms on request. AE, DC, MC, V. Moderate.*

★ **Kathleen's Country House.** Situated on the Tralee road a mile outside town, this imaginatively designed two-story guest house, incorporating traditional slate walls and roofing and large, modern windows, was built in 1979 to owner/manager Kathleen O'Regan-Sheppard's exacting specifications. The rooms are relatively spacious, light, and airy with wooden trim, bright floral comforters, and matching floral curtains. Everything is spotlessly clean. The small second-floor lounge offers pleasant views of the wooded valley and Killarney Town below. The restaurant serves only fresh produce and organic vegetables. *Tralee Rd., Killarney, Co. Kerry, tel. 064/32810. 10 rooms with bath (10 more under construction for 1991). Facilities: restaurant (no smoking) for dinner only. Wine license only or BYOB. No credit cards. Moderate.*

Lake. Set well back from the main road opposite the Gleneagle, this vast 1820s house is a mildly eccentric place with a glorious location and excellent lake views. It appeals mainly to visitors from the United Kingdom and Germany. The authentic Victorian decor of the lobby, stairs, and corridors, including heavy wooden banisters and high ceilings, is diminished by the ill-chosen modern furniture, such as plastic stacking chairs in the restaurant and cheap cane tables and chairs in the sun lounge. Try room 169, which offers polished mahogany furniture and a lake view. Rooms in the new wings have stripped oak trim and pretty print drapes, but you still reach them via long creepy corridors. *Muckross Rd., Killarney, Co. Kerry, tel. 064/*

31035. 65 rooms with bath. Facilities: tennis court, fishing, bar, restaurant. TV in rooms on request. No elevator. AE, DC, MC, V. Closed mid-Oct.–mid-Mar. Moderate.

★ **Arbutus.** Run by the friendly Buckley family since it was built more than 60 years ago, this is a good budget hotel in the town center; it is a short step from the bus and train station and a three-minute walk from the main shopping and dining area. The lobby has an open fire, and the bar is popular with locals. The rooms in the new second-story section are recommended for the extra space and more recent furnishings. *College St., Killarney, Co. Kerry, tel. 064/31037. 36 rooms with bath. Facilities: bar, restaurant. No elevator. AE, DC, MC, V. Closed Dec. 24–Jan. 7. Inexpensive.*

East Avenue. This centrally located mock-timber building dating from 1978 offers a better degree of comfort and cleanliness than many other older hotels nearby. It also has conference and banquet facilities for up to 300 people and holds popular disco evenings every weekend. The cheerful rooms offer gray, blue, and pink decor and white woodwork; the quietest ones are situated in the new (1989) section, which has been well soundproofed. *East Ave., Killarney, Co. Kerry, tel. 064/32522. 56 rooms with bath. Facilities: 3 bars, restaurant (lunch, summer only), disco. AE, MC, V. Inexpensive.*

Linden House. On a busy road just off the main street, this family-run guest house is a plain, functional 1960s suburban home with uninspired olive-green drapes and carpeting and plywood decor; however, it offers an excellent value among the more inexpensive hotels. Its clientele consists mainly of independent travelers from Ireland, Europe, and the United States. The quietest rooms are located in the back. The optional evening meal is a substantial, home-cooked affair. *New Rd., Killarney, Co. Kerry, tel. 064/31379. 20 rooms with bath. Facilities: restaurant (wine license only) for dinner only, TV lounge. No TV or direct-dial phone in rooms. V. Closed Dec. and Jan. Inexpensive.*

Killorglin

Dining

Nick's Seafood and Steak. Owner/chef Nick Foley trained as a veterinary surgeon but finds life in the kitchen more congenial. The old stone town house has a bar-cum-dining room at street level and a quieter dining room on the floor above. Seasonal specials include seafood and game; Foley is known for his cockle-and-mussel soup. In winter, sample the haunch of Kerry venison in red-wine and juniper sauce. All vegetables are grown locally. *Main St., Killorglin, Co. Kerry, tel. 066/61219. Reservations advised. DC, MC, V. Bar food only at lunch. Closed Dec. 24–26. Moderate.*

Kinsale

Dining

Blue Haven. This tastefully decorated old town house has received international acclaim for its seafood. Inexpensive bar lunches are served in the lounge bar, the patio, and the conservatory, which are all decorated with pretty swagged curtains, hanging plants, and nautical brass. The quiet, pastel-colored restaurant overlooks a floodlit garden whose fountain is adorned by cherubs. For dinner, choose between something traditional, such as lobster thermidor or beef *en croute*, or something more unusual, such as chef Jean Michel's special seafood chow mein, featuring the best of the day's catch. *3 Pearse St., Kinsale, Co. Cork, tel. 021/772209. Reservations advised. AE, DC, MC, V. Expensive.*

★ **The Vintage.** This charming, front-parlor restaurant, hidden away in a narrow back street one minute from the center of town, is the outstanding one of its kind. It is patronized equally by discerning locals and celebrities. The original front room has been extended without losing the impression that you are dining in a chic, antique-filled private home. The Swiss-trained owner, Michael Riess, is personally responsible for what comes out of the kitchen, while his Irish wife Marie tends the front of the house. Hot oysters in a sauce of dry white wine, cream, and sorrel, and guinea fowl with red cabbage and apples are among the unusual specialties on the sophisticated international menu. *Main St., Kinsale, Co. Cork, tel. 021/772502. Reservations advised. AE, DC, MC, V. Dinner only. Closed Sun. in winter, 2 weeks in Nov., 3 weeks in Jan.–Feb. Expensive.*

Jim Edwards. One of the most succesful pub/restaurants in Ireland, this place is renowned for the quality of its steaks and seafood. The restaurant is unpretentiously decorated with dark wood tables, dark-green place mats, and red carpets and drapes. The staff, under the personal supervision of the owner and his wife, is friendly and efficient. Portions tend to be exceptionally generous, and children are most welcome. Recommended dishes include the fricassee of seafood and the succulent char-grilled local steak fillet. (The separate bar serves inexpensive fare.) *Market Quay, Kinsale, Co. Cork, tel. 021/772541. Reservations advised weekends and summer. AE, DC, MC, V. Closed Tues. dinner, mid-Nov.–mid-Mar. Moderate.*

1601. Named for the date of the famous Battle of Kinsale, this wine bar has become the in place for the younger crowd who appreciate the jazz piano sessions and the emphasis on organic and wild food, such as nettles, woodland mushrooms, samphire, and dandelion leaves. If you want a quiet meal, dine early. Fresh homemade pasta is recommended here; try the seafood *tagliatele*. The adventurous menu often includes nettle soup and a great salad of warm pigeon breasts in hazelnut oil and apricot vinegar. The dining area is located at the back of the bar, and is decorated with paintings by contemporary Irish artists, all of which are for sale. *Pearse St., Kinsale, Co. Cork, tel. 021/772529. Reservations advised weekends and summer. No credit cards. Inexpensive.*

Lodging

Acton's. Kinsale's biggest hotel is constantly being renovated but never seems to get it right. It has an ideal seafront location on the town pier, but be sure to specify a room with a sea view: The other side overlooks a noisy back street. Although the rooms offer the typical comforts of a modern hotel, they tend to be a bit cramped. The bar and lobby are subject to invasions from the conference groups, bus tours, and weddings, as well as jazz buffs attending the very popular Sunday-brunch jazz sessions. *Pier Rd., Kinsale, Co. Cork, tel. 021/772135. 55 rooms with bath. Facilities: indoor pool, sauna, gymnasium, bar, restaurant. AE, DC, MC, V. Expensive.*

★ **Scilly House.** Californian Karin Young has turned this lovely Georgian house set in an acre of mature gardens into a country inn, right on the edge of town, opposite the Spaniard Inn. All the rooms offer wonderful views of the town, the harbor, and Charles Fort. They feature colonial furniture and old American quilts on the walls, alongside of Karin's watercolors. All the rooms are clean and fresh with a restrained pink-and-white floral motif. In the evenings, host Bill Skelly often leads a singalong around the grand piano in the library. *Scilly, Kinsale, Co. Cork, tel. 021/772413. 6 rooms with bath. Facilities: wine bar, evening meal by arrangement. Wine license only. At press time, credit card policy unconfirmed. Moderate.*

Trident. This is a modern low rise on the water's edge that is popular with visitors who come to Kinsale for deep-sea fishing—mainly all-male Dutch or English groups. The cinderblock modern rooms feature tweed curtains and drapes and large windows overlooking the inner harbor. The Fisherman's Bar offers a congenial spot for conversation between the locals and visiting anglers. *Pier Head, Kinsale, Co. Cork, tel. 021/772301. 40 rooms with bath. Facilities: restaurant, bar. AE, DC, MC, V. Moderate.*

White House. Six comfortable bedrooms are available above this popular bar/restaurant in the town center. They all feature brass bedsteads, matching pink-and-white comforters and curtains, and pine bathroom trim. The friendly atmosphere and good value for the money make it a popular place with those in the know, so you'll need to book well in advance for weekends and the summer. *Pearse St., Kinsale, Co. Cork, tel. 021/772125. 6 rooms with bath. Facilities: bar, restaurant. AE, DC, MC, V. Inexpensive.*

Limerick

Dining

De la Fontaine. Only a discreet black awning indicates the existence of this restaurant, which is on the top floor of a former warehouse in the city center, a short walk to the east of O'Connell Street (turn right on to Roches Street). It offers both a cozy ambience and authentic French "cuisine moderne." The narrow dining room, graced with pretty floral napery and heated by a glowing gas fire, has a high-pitched oak-beamed ceiling. The cooking is chef/owner Alain Bras's interpretation of nouvelle cuisine; recommended dishes include marinated salmon with dill and chicken breast stuffed with a julienne of vegetables in orange and Dubonnet sauce. The restaurant also offers a good wine list. *12 Gerald Griffin St., Limerick, tel. 061/44461. Reservations advised. Wine license only. V. Closed Sun. Moderate.*

Jasmine Palace. Since opening in 1988, this Cantonese restaurant has become one of the most fashionable in town with both old and young sophisticates, possibly because it's the only decent place where you can eat late (last orders at midnight). The large upper-floor room on the busy main street is furnished with a plush carpet, generous-size tables, and divisions of potted plants to create some privacy amid the busy surroundings. Besides the usual fixed-price dinners, the restaurant offers an excellent sizzling chicken and a very good Cantonese roast duck. *O'Connell Mall, O'Connell St., Limerick, tel. 061/42484. Reservations advised. AE, DC, MC, V. Wine license only. Moderate.*

Lodging

★ **Jury's.** Built around a landscaped garden overlooking the Shannon, this modern steel-and-glass hotel offers a quiet location only a four-minute walk from the traffic-filled city center. The bright, airy lobby and lounges are decorated with hanging greenery. Limericks Bar is a popular meeting place for local Yuppies. Although the rooms have painted concrete walls, they are all spacious and feature floor-to-ceiling picture windows overlooking either the interior garden or the river. *Ennis Rd., Limerick, tel. 061/327777. 100 rooms with bath. Facilities: indoor pool, sauna, Jacuzzi, steam room, gymnasium, tennis court, fishing, bar, coffee shop, restaurant. AE, DC, MC, V. Expensive.*

George. Founded in 1820 as the Royal George, this unpretentious hotel is a landmark in Limerick's city center, although its facade has been brutally modernized. It is probably best known these days for the Glory Hole Pub, which presents Irish music nightly. Rooms have also been modernized, but in a more tasteful way than the facade; they are plain but comfortable with white melamine trim. *O'Connell St., Limerick, tel. 061/44566. 58 rooms with bath. Facilities: 2 restaurants, 2 bars, nightclub. AE, DC, MC, V. Inexpensive.*

★ **Glentworth.** A large glass sun lounge dominates the facade of this modern city-center hotel just one block away from O'Connell Street. It is a friendly, practical place to stay, only a few minutes' walk from the bus and rail stations. The Music Bar and Niteclub attract a lively young crowd. Guests can use sporting facilities (swimming, tennis, a gym) at the nearby Thomand College on request. The rooms, decorated in unadventurous tones of beige, are a little small but they are more than adequate for the price range. *Glentworth St., Limerick, tel. 061/43822. 61 rooms with bath. Facilities: 2 restaurants, 3 bars, nightclub. AE, DC, MC, V. Inexpensive.*

Mallow

Lodging **Longueville House.** A large early 18th-century house with Victorian wings and a magnificent conservatory, Longueville is an imposing edifice from the outside, with symmetrical two-story wings flanking the classic three-story central section featuring a porch supported by four pillars. Inside, the hotel is very much a family home. The vast drawing rooms overlook the tranquil lawns of the estate (which is on the Blackwater River); they are furnished with a comfortable mixture of old and new furniture. All the bedrooms are decorated with antiques to a high standard of comfort; the best rooms are the high-ceilinged ones on the first-story front. The President's Room restaurant serves highly acclaimed French-Irish cuisine. In summer it is possible, weather permitting, to dine in the magnificent conservatory. Don't forget to sample a glass of fruity white wine from the Longueville vineyard, which is believed to be the only vineyard in Ireland. Mallow is at the crossroads of the Cork–Limerick and Waterford–Killarney roads, within an hour's drive of all four towns. *Mallow, Co. Cork, tel. 022/147156. 16 rooms with bath. Facilities: fishing, bicycling, restaurant (jacket and tie required), bar. No TV in rooms. AE, DC, MC, V. Closed Dec. 21–Mar. 1. Expensive.*

Parknasilla

Lodging **Parknasilla Great Southern.** A porter in a frock coat and striped gray pants typifies the elegant and slightly stuffy turn-of-the-century atmosphere of this grand old hotel. Among the most famous previous guests have been General de Gaulle, Princess Grace, and George Bernard Shaw, who wrote much of *Saint Joan* while staying here. Although the rooms can be a bit plain, they have been very tastefully decorated in soft pinks and blues. The sheltered coastal location and excellent sporting facilities make it an ideal retreat for an open-air holiday, with superb comfort at the end of the day. *Parknasilla, near Kenmare, Co. Kerry, tel. 064/45122. 60 rooms with bath. Facilities: bar, restaurant (jacket and tie required), tennis court, indoor saltwater pool, sauna, horseback riding, sailing, windsurfing, waterskiing, fishing, golf. AE, DC, MC, V. Closed Nov.–mid-Mar. Very Expensive.*

Quin

Lodging **Ballykilty Manor.** A modest Georgian house on 50 acres of grounds along the River Rine, this is a handy stopover if you're heading for or returning from the west. It is located 16 km (10 mi) from Shannon and 10 km (6 mi) from Ennis. The renovated rooms feature some antique pieces; ask for one at the front of the house overlooking the lawn and the ruins of 15th-century Quin Abbey. *Quin, Co. Clare, tel. 065/25627. 11 rooms with bath. Facilities: restaurant, bar, fishing, pitch and putt, horseback riding and hunting by arrangement. AE, MC, V. Moderate.*

Shannon

Lodging For lodging convenient to Shannon Airport, *see* also listings for Adare, Limerick, and Quin, above.

Shannon International. This pleasant modern low rise is conveniently located just across from the main terminal building at Shannon Airport, making it an ideal first or last stopping place for transatlantic travelers. Try an Irish coffee in the circular bar overlooking the river; the drink was invented at Shannon Airport to fortify passengers on the fueling stop-over that was inevitable in the early days of aviation. The bland yet comfortable rooms have unexceptional contemporary hotel decor, but all will be refurbished by 1991. *Shannon Airport, Co. Clare, tel. 061/61122. 118 rooms with bath. Facilities: restaurant, bar. Closed Nov.–mid-Mar. Moderate.*

Skibbereen

Dining **West Cork Hotel.** Sometimes, plain cooking (just like Ma's) is just what you're in the mood for; this busy, family-run hotel is the place to find it. Ignore the vagaries of the decor, which runs from fake Louis XV to nondescript modern, and concentrate on the vast portions of roast meat, potatoes, and vegetables that are served by attentive waitresses. At dinner, hearty eaters will enjoy the mixed grill. *Bridge St., Skibbereen, Co. Cork, tel. 021/21277. Reservations advised for parties of more than 4. AE, DC, MC, V. Inexpensive.*

Tahilla

Lodging ★ **Tahilla Cove Country House.** An excellent place to escape from the hectic atmosphere that can develop in Killarney in the high season, this is a simple, secluded, out-of-the-way guest house. It has an idyllic seashore location with a private beach, a pier, and an anchorage for boats. The rooms are fairly spacious with floral drapes; all but two have a sea view and sliding doors leading to a balcony. The hosts are exceptionally friendly. *Tahilla,*

Co. Kerry, tel. 064/45104. 9 rooms, 8 with bath. Facilities: restaurant, bar, fishing. No TV or direct-dial phone in rooms. AE, DC, MC, V. Closed Sept. 30–Mar. 31. Inexpensive.

Tralee

Dining **Chez Jean Marc.** Aiming for Parisian sophistication in the depths of Kerry is not easy, but the chef's generous interpretation of nouvelle cuisine at this establishment comes fairly close. The small, cozy room features a pastel pink-and-green decor and an open fire. Some recommended specialties include duck off the bone in caramel and sherry sauce, and Dover sole fillets with crab and salmon mousse in a creamy Riesling sauce. *29 Castle St., Tralee, Co. Kerry, tel. 066/21377. Reservations advised. Dinner only; closed Sun. DC, MC, V. Moderate.*

★ **Skillet.** This is a friendly, relaxed bistro with contemporary paintings hung under low beams and red-and-white-check place mats on the tables. Backpackers and a generally young crowd are attracted by the generous portions and the low prices. Vegetarian lasagna and pan-fried trout with almonds are regular favorites on the menu. *Barrack La., Tralee, Co. Kerry, tel. 066/24561. No reservations necessary. Closed Sun. MC, V. Inexpensive.*

Lodging **Ballyseede Castle.** Located 3 km (2 mi) east of Tralee on the main Killarney road, this former Fitzgerald Castle is approached through an impressive granite gateway. Its location makes it popular with golfers because it is within easy reach of four of the best courses in the region. The castle is an imposing three-story building with Victorian additions. The structure has two magnificent drawing rooms with ornamental plasterwork and marble fireplaces. The individually decorated rooms have been generously furnished with antiques. Try the Yeats room, which is one of the fanciest. *Tralee, Co. Kerry, tel. 066/25799. 13 rooms, 10 with bath. Facilities: restaurant, bar. No TV in rooms. AE, MC, V. Expensive (Inexpensive, if you take a room without bath).*

Brandon. This five-story modern hotel in the center of town is not especially exciting, but it is the only place in Tralee with a pool and a fitness center, and, unlike some of Tralee's other hotels, it's clean and well-run. The decent-size rooms offer plain, modern decor, with uninspiring urban views. The restaurant is well-reputed. Rates shoot up to the Expensive category during the Rose of Tralee Festival (late Aug.) and the Listowel races (third week in Sept.). *Princes St., Tralee, Co. Kerry, tel. 066/23333. 154 rooms with bath. Facilities: indoor pool, sauna, steam room, gymnasium, restaurant, 2 bars. AE, DC, MC, V. Moderate.*

Waterville

Dining **The Huntsman.** Locals agree that this is the best place in town to eat, in spite of the overwhelming bordellolike decor: bright-red carpets, red chairs, and lampshades that tint the light red as well. The specialty here is fresh, plainly cooked fish: lobsters from the tank broiled and served with roe, salmon hollandaise, and scampi Newburg. *Waterville, Co. Kerry, tel. 0667/4124. Reservations advised. AE, DC, MC, V. Open daily until the end of Oct.; weekends only off-season.*

Lodging **Butler Arms.** The white castellated towers at the corners of this imposing but architecturally undistinguished hotel provide a familiar landmark on the Ring. The building has been in the same family for three generations; it has a regular clientele, predominantly male, who come back year after year for the excellent fishing and/or golf facilities nearby. It was a favorite base for family holidays of the late Charlie Chaplin. Although the accommodations are neither smart nor chic, the solid comfort of the rambling old lounges with open turf fires is highly conducive to both conversation and relaxation. *Waterville, Co. Kerry, tel. 0667/4144. 27 rooms with bath. Facilities: restaurant, 2 bars, tennis court, deep-sea and freshwater angling, horseback riding. No TV in rooms. AE, DC, MC, V. Closed Oct. 12–Apr. 15. Expensive.*

The Arts and Nightlife

The Arts

Arts Centers/ Galleries Some of Ireland's finest contemporary painters live and work in the Southwest—such as Pauline Bewick, Tim Goulding, Cormac Boydell, Barrie Cooke, and Maria Simonds-Gooding—but they often choose to exhibit mainly in Dublin and abroad. You may find some of the above artists' prints at the places mentioned below, but the bulk of the work on display is by lesser-known (and less expensive) local artists, some of whom, no doubt, have a big future.

Cork Arts Society (16 Lavitt's Quay, Cork, tel. 021/277749) has a representative selection of fairly conservative oils and watercolors by local artists, all of which are for sale. For more adventurous work in all media, take a look at the **West Cork Arts Center** (North St., Skibbereen, tel. 028/22090), where works are also for sale. In Limerick, don't miss the **Riverrun Gallery** (Honan's Quay, tel. 061/40277), probably Ireland's leading provincial commercial gallery. Offbeat exhibits can also be found at the **Triskel Arts Center** (Tobin St., off S. Main St., Cork, tel. 021/272022) and the **Belltable Arts Center** (69 O'Connell St., Limerick, tel. 061/319866). **J & R Forrester** (83 N. Main St., Bandon, tel. 023/41360) has a small gallery above its craft shop showing well-selected, reasonably priced works.

A thriving community of ceramic artists resides in the Southwest (*see* Shopping, Irish Crafts, above). For a list and location map of potters who welcome visitors, drop in at or phone **J & R Forrester** (*see* above).

Film Outside of the Cork Film Festival in Cork City, held annually in mid-September (details from the **Triskel Arts Center,** *see* Arts Centers/Galleries, above), the Southwest is not a good place for movie buffs. Such screens as there are are dominated by movies for the teenage market. If you want to catch up on the latest horror films, check the listings in the *Cork Examiner* or the *Limerick Leader*.

Theater Ten years ago Cork City had two repertory companies and a ballet. At the time of writing, all that is left is the **Cork Opera House** (Lavitt's Quay, Cork, tel. 021/270022), which hosts touring productions and variety shows. Two new companies are trying to get started: ask at the tourist information office for news of the **Everyman** and the **Granary.**

The **Triskel Arts Center** in Cork and the **Belltable Arts Center** in Limerick (*see* Arts Centers/Galleries, above) have small auditoriums suitable for one-person shows and experimental works.

In Tralee, try to catch the **National Folk Theater of Ireland (Siamsa Tíre).** Language is no barrier to this colorful entertainment, which re-creates traditional rural life through music, mime, and dance. *Godfrey Pl., Tralee, tel. 066/23055. Admission: £4 adults, £3 children. Shows July–Aug., Mon.–Sat.; May, June, and Sept. every Tues. and Thurs. at 8:30.*

Nightlife

Medieval Banquets

Most first-time visitors will not want to miss the medieval banquets held at the Bunratty and Knappogue castles. Both events cater largely to overseas visitors, many of them on organized tours; they will have little appeal for independent travelers in search of "the real Ireland." Medieval banqueting may not be authentic, but it can be a lot of fun. At Bunratty, you'll be welcomed by Irish colleens in 15th-century dress who bear the traditional bread of friendship; you are led off to a honey-and-mead reception. Before sitting down at the long tables in the candlelit great hall, you don a bib: You'll need it, because you'll be eating the four-course meal medieval style—with your fingers! The serving wenches take time out to sing a few ballads or pluck the strings of a harp. This warm-hearted evening of Irish hospitality can be taken in the lighthearted spirit in which it is offered. These banquets are so popular that they must be booked as far in advance as possible. *Bookings for both Bunratty and Knappogue can be made by calling 061/61788. Tickets, including four-course meal, wine, mead, and entertainment: £25.90. Nightly (subject to demand) at 5:45 and 8:45.*

If you can't get a place for a banquet, the next best thing is a *Ceilí* at Bunratty Folk Park; this program features traditional Irish dance and song and a meal of Irish stew, soda bread, and apple pie. *Tel. 061/61788. Cost: £20.75, including wine. May–Sept., 5:45 and 9 PM.*

Pubs, Cabarets, and Discos

Pub entertainment is the key to the Southwest's nightlife and offers far more in terms of value for money, variety, and authenticity than the package market–oriented Irish cabaret options. If the music is in the main bar, you'll seldom have to pay a cover charge. To dance to a fully amplified band in a room adjacent to the bar costs anywhere from £1.50 to £8, depending on the performers. During mid-June through September, you'll find musical entertainment most nights; during other seasons, Thursday through Sunday are the busiest times. Dingle is the best place in the region for traditional Irish music; elsewhere, pubs and clubs offer a mix of traditional, Irish, and folk ballads; country and rock classics; and a touch of New Orleans jazz in Cork and Kinsale. Spontaneous music sessions can take off at any time, especially on the Dingle Peninsula; elsewhere, performances usually begin around 9. Discos and nightclubs are usually attached to hotels or bars; they are open from 10:30 PM until 1 or 2AM. Expect to pay £2.50–£5 entrance fee.

Cork City **Mojo's** (George's Quay, tel. 021/311786) specializes in live rhythm and blues; **De Lacy House** (74 Oliver Plunkett St., tel. 021/270074) attracts a young crowd for rock and folk gigs. Live music (rock and nostalgia) is featured at **Rearden's Mill** (25 Washington St., tel. 021/27169). The **Stradbally Village** (Grand Parade Hotel, tel. 021/274391) offers traditional music and dancing nightly in an indoor reconstructed village. In the same hotel, you'll find live rock music at **Chandra's Nightclub. Mangan's Brasserie** (Carey's La., tel. 021/276531) is the leading night spot for the over-25s to wine, dine, and dance.

County Cork Kinsale and Clonakilty are the liveliest towns for nightlife. Check out the **Spaniard Inn** (Scilly, tel. 021/772436) for live rock and folk groups. **The Shanakee** (Market St., Kinsale, no tel.) is renowned in the area for nightly sing-alongs and ballad sessions; dancing workshops are given every Thursday. The **Bacchus Brasserie** (Guardwell, tel. 021/772382) offers dining and dancing to the over-25s. Jazz buffs will enjoy **Creole** (Pearse St., Kinsale, tel. 021/774109) which features live New Orleans jazz sessions nightly in summer.

Tigh de Barra in Clonakilty (Pearse St., tel. 023/33381) is a focal point for West Cork's traditional musicians, many of whom live in the nearby Irish-speaking area. **Dunmore House** (Muckross, Clonakilty, tel. 023/33352) features local artists in cabaret on Tuesdays and a family night with dancing and talent competitions on Thursdays.

Killarney Singing bars are popular in Killarney, where a professional leads the singing and encourages audience participation and solos. Try **The Laurels** (Main St., tel. 064/31149). Killarney is strict on "Over 21s, Neat Dress Essential," and this is the rule at the **Kenmare Rooms** in the East Avenue Hotel (East Ave., tel. 064/32522), which offers a live cabaret with big names in the summer. The charge here includes admission to **Revelles Disco. Scott's Hotel Gardens** (College Rd., tel. 064/31060) and **Gleneagles** (Muckross Rd., tel. 064/31870) are the summer hot spots, offering big-name cabaret acts, singing bars, and discos.

Kerry Try the **Kingdom Bar** (Kenmare, tel. 064/41361) for traditional music; for folk music, head for the **Strand Hotel** (Waterville, tel. 0667/4248). Just about every bar on the Dingle Peninsula offers music every night in July and August—or so it seems, if you're looking for a quiet one! **O'Flaherty's** (Bridge St., Dingle, no tel.) is a fine place for traditional music. For sing-along and dancing, try **An Reált—The Star Bar** (The Pier, Dingle, no tel.). In Tralee, ballad sessions are more popular than traditional Irish music. If you're looking for the latter, call 066/25965—the *seisún* (having a good time) hotline—which will tell you where the action is. For ballad sessions, check out **Kirby's Brogue Inn** (Rock St., no tel.) and **Jim's Cottage Bar** (Edward St., no tel.). **Horan's Hotel** (Clash St., tel. 066/21933) has disco music and cabaret acts nightly during July and August; on weekends only during the off-season.

Limerick **Foley's Bar** (Lower Shannon St., tel. 061/48783) has a ballad or traditional session every night, except Wednesday. Traditional music is featured at **Nancy Blague's Pub** (19 Denmark St., tel. 061/46327) on Tuesday and Sunday. The **Glory Hole Bar** (George Hotel, O'Connell St., tel. 061/44566) has sessions every night, and there is late-night disco at **Tropics** (also in the George Hotel) Friday through Sunday. More nighttime entertainment can be found weekends at **Whispers Nightclub** (Cruise's Royal Hotel, O'Connell St., tel. 061/44977).

8 The West

Introduction

by Alannah Hopkin

As any Dubliner will tell you, the West is distinctively different from the rest of Ireland. Within Ireland, the West refers to the region that lies west of the River Shannon; most of this area falls within the old Irish province of Connaught. The coast of this region is situated at the western extremity of Europe, facing its nearest neighbors in North America across 3,200 km (2,000 mi) of Atlantic Ocean. While the East, the Southwest, and the North were influenced by either Norman, Scots, or English settlers, the West escaped systematic resettlement, and, with the exception of the walled town of Galway, remained purely Irish in language, social organization, and general outlook for far longer than the rest of the country. The land in the West, predominantly mountains and bogs, did not immediately tempt the conquering barons. Oliver Cromwell was among those who found the place thoroughly unattractive, and he gave the Irish chieftains who would not conform to English rule the choice of going "to Hell or Connaught."

It was not until the late-18th century, when better transport improved communications, that the West started to experience the so-called foreign influences that had already Europeanized the rest of the country. The West was, in effect, dragged out of the 16th century and into the 19th. You will notice that all buildings of interest in the region date either from before the 17th century or from the late-18th century onwards.

Today, many people maintain that the West is the most typically Irish part of the country. It features the highest concentration of Irish-speaking communities and the best traditional musicians in the Republic. Many residents still live on small farms rather than in towns and villages (towns were unknown in pre-Christian Irish society); especially in winter, the smell of turf fires still pervades the region.

Like the Southwest, the population of the West was decimated by famine in the mid-19th century and by mass emigration from then until the 1950s. A major factor in the region's recovery from economic depression has been the attraction to visitors of its sparsely populated mountain landscape and long indented coastline, with its many lakes and rivers. Tourism's development, however, has been mercifully low-key. Apart from a seaside promenade and fun palace at Salthill, just outside Galway, the area has seen no major investment in public amenities. Instead, additional land has been acquired for the Connemara National Park. Despite the sufficient number of top-class accommodations and the many charmingly converted country-house hotels in the region, nothing intrudes on the simple attractions of its rugged, unspoiled countryside. The existence of some of the best angling in Europe on the West's rivers, lakes, and seas accounts for many regular visitors. Most holiday cottages are built according to the model of the traditional thatched cabin. The residents of the West also encourage the revival of cottage industries such as knitting, weaving, and woodworking; the provision of bed-and-breakfast in existing homes; and informal sessions of traditional music in small bars. The lack of razzmatazz makes the West an ideal destination for travelers on a tight budget. The place comes alive between June and September. April, May, and October are good times for an off-peak visit. Outside these months many places will be closed; nightlife options and restaurant choices become very limited. During the winter, weather can be harsh, with gales and rain sweeping in from the Atlantic day after day.

Essential Information

Arriving and Departing by Plane

Airports and Airlines The West's most convenient international airport is **Shannon** (tel. 061/61444), 25 km (16 mi) east of Ennis in the Southwest (*see* Essential Information, Chapter 7). **Carnmore Airport** (tel. 091/52874), near Galway City, and Horan International Airport (tel. 094/67222), at Knock in County Mayo, are used mainly for internal fights, with steadily increasing U.K. traffic. A small airport for internal traffic only is also located at Knockrowen, Castlebar, in County Mayo (tel. 094/22853). Flying time from Dublin is 25–30 minutes to all airports.

Flights from the U.S. No scheduled flights run from the United States to Galway or Knock; use Shannon Airport (*see* Essential Information, Chapter 7).

Flights from the U.K. **Aer Lingus** offers daily flights from London's Heathrow Airport to Galway and Knock via Dublin; the trip takes about two hours. **Ryanair** has at least one flight a day to Galway from London's Luton Airport; flying time is 70 minutes. The company also flies to Knock once a week from Birmingham, Coventry, and Bradford and daily from London's Luton Airport; flying time is 80 minutes.

Between the Airport and the Cities Carnmore Airport is located 6½ km (4 mi) from Galway City. No regular bus service is available from the airport to Galway, but most flight arrivals are taken to Galway Rail Station in the city center by an airline courtesy coach. Inquire at the time of booking. A taxi from the airport to the city center costs about £7.

If you're flying from Dublin to Horan International Airport in Knock, you can pick up your rental car at the airport. Otherwise, inquire at the time of booking about transport to your final destination: no regular bus service is available from Horan International Airport.

Arriving and Departing by Car, Train, and Bus

By Car Leave Dublin by the N4, picking up the N6 in Kinnegad for Galway City. The 204-km (127-mi) journey between Dublin and Galway takes about three hours. From Cork City take the N20 to Mallow and the N21 to Limerick City, picking up the N18 Ennis–Galway road in Limerick. The drive from Cork to Galway lasts 209 km (130 mi) and takes about three hours.

From Killarney the shortest and most pleasant route is the N22 to Tralee, then the N69 through Listowel to Tarbert and the ferry across the Shannon Estuary to Killimer in County Clare, joining the N68 in Kilrush. The drive from Killarney to Galway lasts 193 km (120 mi) on this route and takes just under three hours. The ferry leaves Tarbert every hour on the half hour and takes 20 minutes, avoiding a 104-km (65-mi) detour through Limerick City. It costs £6 one-way, £10 round-trip. (Ferries leave Killimer every hour on the hour.)

By Train Galway City, Westport, and Ballina are the main rail stations in the region. For County Clare, travel from Cork City, Killarney Town, or Dublin's Heuston Station to Limerick City (tel. 061/315555) and continue the journey by bus.

Trains for Galway, Westport, and Ballina leave from Dublin's Heuston Station (tel. 01/366222). The journey time to Galway is three hours; to Ballina 3¾ hours; and to Westport 3½ hours. For train passenger inquiries, call 091/62141 in Galway, 096/21011 in Ballina, 098/25253 in Westport.

By Bus **Bus Éireann** operates a variety of Expressway services into the region from Dublin, Cork City, and Limerick City to Ennis, Galway City, Westport, and Ballina, the principal depots in the region. Expect bus rides to last about one hour longer than the time by car.

For bus passenger inquiries, call 01/366111 in Dublin, 021/504422 in Cork, and 061/313333 in Limerick.

Getting Around

A car is virtually essential to get around in the West, especially during September through June. Although the main cities of the area can be easily reached from the rest of Ireland by rail or bus, transport within the region itself is sparse and badly coordinated. If a rental car is out of the question, your best option is to make Galway your base and take day tours (available only mid-June–Sept.) west to Connemara and south to the Burren, and a day or overnight trip to the Aran Islands. It *is* possible to explore the region by local and intercity bus services, but you will need lots of time and patience.

By Car The West has good wide main roads (National Primary Routes) and better than average local roads (National Secondary Routes), both known as "N" routes.

However, if you stray off the beaten track on the smaller Regional ("R") or unnumbered routes, particularly in Connemara and County Mayo, these mountain roads can be hazardous. Besides being narrow, steep, and twisty, they are frequented by untended sheep, cows, and ponies who are grazing "the long acre" (as the strip of grass beside the road is called) or simply straying in search of greener fields. If you find a sheep in your path, just sound the horn and the creature will get out of the way. A good maxim for these roads is "you never know what's around the next corner." Bear this in mind, and adjust your speed accordingly. Hikers and cyclists constitute an additional hazard on narrow roads in the summer.

Within the Connemara Irish-speaking area, road signs will be in Irish only. The main signs to recognize are Gaillimh (Galway), Rós an Mhil (Rossaveal), An Teach Doite (Maam Cross), and Sraith Salach (Recess). A good touring map, available locally through news agents and Tourist Information Offices, will give both Irish and English names where needed.

If you haven't already picked up a rental car at Shannon Airport (*see* Getting Around by Car, Chapter 7), try the following:

Galway City and Vicinity: Avis (tel. 091/68901), **Budget** (tel. 091/66376), **Hertz** (tel. 091/61837), **Johnson and Perrott** (tel. 091/68873), and **Murray's** (tel. 01/62222).

Horan International Airport, Knock: Avis (tel. 094/67252), **Murray's** (tel. 01/681777), and **South County Self Drive (Thrift Rent-a-Car,** tel. 01/806005).

By Train Rail transportation is not good within the West. The major destinations of Galway City and Westport/Ballina are situated on different branch lines. Connections can only be made between Galway and the other two cities by traveling inland for about an hour to Athlone (for inquiries, *see* Arriving and Departing by Train, above).

By Bus In July and August, the provincial bus service is augmented by daily services to most resort towns. Outside these months, many coastal towns receive only one or two buses per week. Bus routes are often slow and circuitous, and service can be erratic. A copy of the Bus Éireann timetable (45p from any station) is essential. The main bus stations are located at **Ennis** (tel. 065/24177), **Galway City** (Ceannt Station, tel. 091/62131), **Westport** (Railway Station, tel. 098/25253), and **Ballina** (tel. 096/21657).

By Ferry to the Aran Islands From mid-May to early September, a ferry departs from Galway City Docks at 9:30, 1:30, and 6:30. This ride is the longest sea crossing available—about 48 km (30 mi)—and takes about three hours. It costs £15 round-trip and can be booked at the Aran Ferries desk in the Tourist Information Office (TIO, Victoria Pl., Eyre Sq., tel. 091/63081). The TIO will also arrange bed-and-breakfast accommodations on the islands.

Most people opt for the one-hour crossing (about 16 km/10 mi) from Rossaveal, which is located 32 km (20 mi) west of Galway by car. This ride costs £12 round-trip. The boat ride is arranged by **Island Ferries,** which has a booking office opposite the TIO on Victoria Place in Galway City (tel. 091/61767). The company provides a coach connection from Galway to Rossaveal. Car parking is free on the quay at Rossaveal. Five sailings a day from Rossaveal are scheduled during the summer months (weather permitting) at 10:30, 12:30, 1:30, 6, and 6:30. Bicycles are transported free, and price discounts are available for families, students, and groups.

If you are heading for Inishere, the smallest island, the shortest crossing is from Doolin in County Clare (*see* Tour 1, below).

Frequent interisland ferries are available during the summer months, but tickets are not transferable, so ask the captain of your ferry about his interisland schedule if you plan to visit more than one island; otherwise, your trip can become expensive.

By Plane to the Aran Islands **Aer Arann** (tel. 091/55437) offers four flights daily on weekdays, and two flights on Saturday and Sunday during July and August. The flights call at all three of the Aran Islands and leave from Carnmore Airport near Galway. The flight takes about 15 minutes.

The Apex fare, paid for seven days in advance, is £35 round-trip (the same rate for groups of four or more passengers). The regular fare of £45 round-trip includes an option of one night's bed-and-breakfast on the islands. For £30, you can fly one-way and travel one-way by boat from the Galway City docks. Ask about other special offers at the time of booking.

Important Addresses and Numbers

Tourist Information The Irish Tourist Board provides free information service, tourist literature, and an accommodations booking service at its **Tourist Information Offices** (TIOs).

Main Offices **Ennis** (tel. 065/28366), **Galway City** (Victoria Pl., Eyre Sq., tel. 091/630081), **Horan International Airport, Knock** (tel. 094/67247), and **Westport** (tel. 098/25711). These offices are open all year weekdays 9–6 and Saturday 9–1.

Other Offices **Achill** (tel. 098/45384), **Aran Islands (Inishmore)** (tel. 099/61263), **Ballina** (tel. 096/22422), **Castlebar** (tel. 094/21207), **Clifden** (tel. 095/21163), **Cliffs of Moher** (tel. 065/81171), **Kilkee** (tel. 065/56112), **Kilrush** (tel. 065/51047), **Lahinch** (tel. 065/81474), **Lisdoonvarna** (tel. 065/74062), **Salthill** (Galway City; tel. 091/63081), and **Thoor Ballylee** (near Gort, tel. 091/31436). These offices are open July and August only, weekdays 9–6 and Saturday 9–1.

Emergencies **Police, fire,** and **ambulance** in all areas: dial 999 toll-free.

Doctors and Dentists **County Clare: Mid-Western Health Board** (tel. 061/316655); **Counties Galway and Mayo: Western Health Board** (tel. 091/51131).

Pharmacies **Galway: Matt O'Flaherty** (39 Eyre Sq., tel. 091/62927). **Westport: O'Donnell's** (Bridge St., tel. 098/25163).

Guided Tours

Orientation Tours The only full- and half-day guided tours in the region start from Galway. **CIE** offers a choice of full-day tours covering Connemara, the Burren and the Atlantic coast, Westport and Achill Island, Carraroe, and South Connemara (cost of all tours: £9 adults, £4.50 children), and half-day tours to Cong or South Connemara (cost: £6 adults, £3 children). Tours run from mid-June to early September only, with the widest choice available between mid-July and mid-August. Book in advance at Galway City's Ceannt Railway Station (tel. 091/62141) or the Salthill Tourist Information Office (tel. 091/63081), which also serve as departure points.

Galway Tours runs a day tour through Connemara and County Mayo, and another to the Burren in July and August and on certain bank holiday weekends. Tickets can be booked at the Tourist Information Offices in Galway City (Victoria Pl., Eyre Sq., tel. 091/630081) or Salthill (tel. 091/63081).

Walking Tours Galway City's **Tourist Information Office** (Victoria Pl., Eyre Sq., tel. 091/630081) has details of walking tours of Galway, which are organized on an occasional basis.

Exploring the West

Allow at least four days for exploring the region, and six days if you aim to visit the Aran Islands and/or Achill Island. Although distances between sites are not great, most of the tours in this chapter use the scenic but slower national secondary routes, on which 80 km (50 mi) to 112 km (70 mi) a day is a comfortable target.

Highlights for First-time Visitors

The Burren (*see* Tour 1)
Clifden (*see* Tour 3)
The Cliffs of Moher (*see* Tour 1)
Connemara National Park (*see* Tour 3)
Dun Aengus, Inishmore (*see* Tour 2)
Kylemore Abbey (*see* Tour 3)
Salmon Weir Bridge (*see* Tour 2)
Westport, Clew Bay (*see* Tour 3)

Tour 1: The Burren and Beyond—West Clare to South Galway

Numbers in the margin correspond to points of interest on the West map.

1 The tour starts in **Ennis,** the county town of County Clare, 25 km (16 mi) west of Shannon Airport on the main road (the N18) to Galway. **Ennis,** a pleasant if physically unremarkable town, is a major crossroads and a convenient stopping place between the West and the Southwest. It has always fostered traditional music, especially fiddle playing and step dancing (a kind of square dance). The Fleadh Nua festival in Ennis at the end of May attracts both performers and students of Irish music who sing and dance in a series of concerts, workshops, and lectures.

Two statues in town bear witness to the part that the people of Ennis have played in Irish democracy. On a tall limestone column above a massive pediment in the town center stands a statue of Daniel O'Connell (1775–1847), "The Liberator" (*see* Tour 3, Chapter 7), who was a member of Parliament for County Clare between 1828 and 1831, the time at which he was instrumental in bringing about Catholic Emancipation. Outside the Courthouse (in the town park, beside the River Fergus, on the west side of Ennis) stands a larger than life-size bronze statue of Eamon De Valera (1882–1975), who successfully contested an election here in 1917 that launched his political career. Although De Valera was born in the United States, his maternal forebears were from County Clare. He was the dominant figure in Irish politics during this century, serving as prime minister for most of the years from 1937 until 1959, when he resigned as leader of Fianna Fáil, the party he had founded; he went on to serve as president until 1973.

From Ennis, the main tour heads for the coast, which has been a playground for many generations of Irish people. If the season or the weather does not favor relaxing on sandy beaches and playing 18-hole golf courses, we suggest you take a shortcut, leaving Ennis on the N85 and joining the tour again at Lahinch, which is 32 km (27 mi) from Ennis.

The main route follows the N68 from Ennis to Kilrush (43 km/27 mi). (Those crossing from County Kerry by the Tarbert–Killimer ferry can join the tour at Kilrush, 5 km/3 mi west of Killimer.) The N68 is a good stretch of relatively straight two-lane highway passing through a thinly populated region of small farms. Many visitors remark on the smallness of the farms in the West, the great majority being between 30 and 100 acres, and some no more than small holdings. In order to make a living, most of these farmers or their spouses (in some cases both) have a second job, such as fishing, running a B&B, or

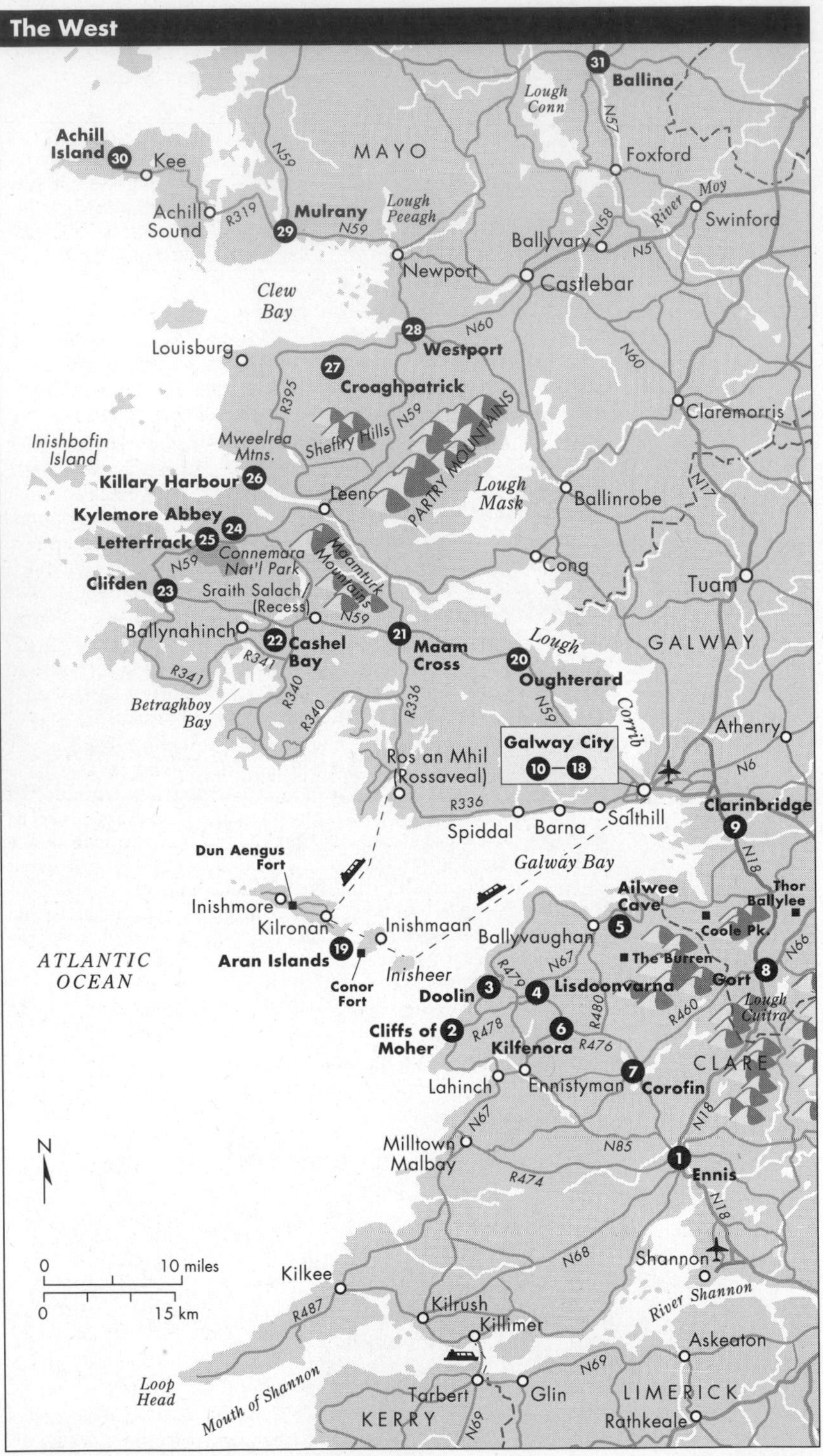
The West
Ballina
Lough Conn
N57
Achill Island
Kee
MAYO
Foxford
N59
Achill Sound
R319
Mulrany
Lough Peeagh
N59
River Moy
Swinford
Ballyvary
N58
N5
Newport
Castlebar
Clew Bay
N60
Westport
Louisburg
Croaghpatrick
N60
R395
Claremorris
N59
Inishbofin Island
Mweelrea Mtns.
Sheffry Hills
PARTRY MOUNTAINS
Killary Harbour
Leenane
Lough Mask
Ballinrobe
N17
Kylemore Abbey
Letterfrack
Connemara Nat'l Park
Maamturk Mountains
N59
Cong
Clifden
Sraith Salach/ (Recess)
N59
Tuam
Ballynahinch
Cashel Bay
R341
Maam Cross
Lough
GALWAY
R341
Oughterard
R340
R340
R336
N59
Corrib
Betraghboy Bay
Athenry
Galway City
Ros an Mhil (Rossaveal)
N6
R336
Clarinbridge
Spiddal
Barna
Salthill
Dun Aengus Fort
Galway Bay
N18
Ailwee Cave
Thor Ballylee
Inishmore
Kilronan
Inishmaan
Ballyvaughan
Coole Pk.
ATLANTIC OCEAN
Aran Islands
The Burren
N66
Inisheer
N67
R479
Gort
Conor Fort
Doolin
Lisdoonvarna
Lough Cutra
R480
R460
Cliffs of Moher
R478
Kilfenora
R476
CLARE
Lahinch
Ennistyman
Corofin
N67
N18
N
Milltown Malbay
N85
Ennis
R474
N18
0
10 miles
N68
Shannon
0
15 km
Kilkee
River Shannon
R487
Kilrush
Killimer
Askeaton
N69
Loop Head
Mouth of Shannon
Tarbert
Glin
LIMERICK
KERRY
N69
Rathkeale

other seasonal work. The rest rely on government subsidies or unemployment benefits, but few of them would change their way of life for a more lucrative one away from the land.

Kilrush is a small market town based on a formal layout dating, like most towns in West Clare, from the mid-19th century. Streets radiate from a large central square, the widest one leading to the harbor and the docks. This plan creates the impression that the town (pop. 3,000) is bigger than it actually is. You'll find pleasant walks and picnic tables in the **Kilrush Woods,** a mature 420-acre forest on the east side of town that is freely accessible.

Kilkee, which is 12 km (8 mi) west of Kilrush on the N68, is a popular holiday resort with safe bathing both in the waters along its long sandy beach and in deep rock pools known as Pollock holes, which do not dry out at low tide. The latter attract scuba divers as well as swimmers. From Kilkee, you can take an excursion to Loop Head Lighthouse on the R487 (about 38 km/ 24 mi round-trip). Loop Head is at the northern tip of the mouth of the Shannon, the very end of its long estuary.

The main route heads north up the coast on the N67. Sandy beaches and more Pollock holes can be found by taking a left off the main road at any sign that indicates "Strand" and traveling for about 2½ km (1½ mi). The shortcut joins the main tour on the N67 at **Lahinch,** another resort village, which has two 18-hole golf courses. From here, take the R478 for the Cliffs of Moher. For the first time on this coast, the road narrows and starts to climb. It twists past small whitewashed farms and green fields with glimpses of the sea on the horizon.

2 The best way to appreciate the magnificent **Cliffs of Moher** is to walk the short distance from the car park to O'Brien's Tower, which is located at the cliffs' highest point. The car park is a favorite spot with performers, and if you're lucky you will find some free entertainment, including step dancers, fiddle players, or even a one-man band. Next to the car park, take a look at the Visitor Center, which has leaflets explaining various aspects of the cliffs' natural history, as well as a crafts shop and tea room. *Visitor Center, tel. 065/81565. Admission free. Open Mar.–Oct. 26, daily 10–6.*

The cliffs rise vertically out of the sea as an 8-km (5-mi) wall that reaches at some points to a height of about 185 m (600 ft). The stratified deposits of five different rock layers can be seen in the striations of the cliff face. The shelves of rock on the cliffs are home to numerous sea birds, including a large colony of puffins. On a clear day the Aran Islands and the mountains of Connemara are visible to the north, while the lighthouse on Loop Head and the mountains of Kerry may be seen to the south.

Follow the R478 from the cliffs inland toward Lisdoonvarna. A detour, signposted on the left as "Roadford/Doolin" on the
3 R479, is a must for music lovers. **Doolin,** a tiny village consisting almost entirely of B&Bs, hostels, and pubs, claims three of the best pubs in Ireland for traditional music. This village is a magnet for young musicians, some of whom camp out here for the whole summer learning from the resident virtuosos.

On Doolin Pier, about 1½ km (1 mi) outside the village, local fishermen sell their catch fresh off the boat—lobster, crayfish, salmon, and mackerel. From mid-March until October (weather permitting), a regular ferry service takes visitors for a 30-minute ride to Inisheer, the smallest of the Aran Islands (*see* Tour 2, below). *Ferry, tel. 065/77086. Cost (round-trip): £10 adults, £5 children. Over 10 sailings daily mid-Mar.–Oct.*

4 Retrace your route to the R478 and turn left for **Lisdoonvarna,** a spa town featuring several sulfurous and iron-bearing springs with radioactive properties, all containing iodine. The town grew up in the late-19th century to accommodate visitors who wished to "take the waters." Its buildings reflect a mishmash of architectural styles: mock Scottish baronial, mock Swiss chalet, mock Spanish hacienda, and mock American motel. Lovers of kitsch will find the town delightful, while others may condemn it as tacky.

Lisdoonvarna is the traditional vacationing spot for the West's bachelor farmers, who used to congregate here in late September once the harvest was in with the vague intention of finding themselves a wife. (Irish farmers are notoriously shy with women and reluctant to marry, often postponing the event until their mid- or late-fifties.) This tradition has been resurrected as the Matchmaking Festival, which takes place in Lisdoonvarna during late September and early October. Middle-aged singles dance to the strains of country and western bands, and a talent contest is held to find the most eligible bachelor. An increasing number of women from the United States are trying their luck at the festival and are usually guaranteed a good time, if not a husband. By contrast, in July and August, the town is a favorite holiday spot with the Irish under-thirties, who dance the night away in a more contemporary style.

Lisdoonvarna Spa and Bath House has been renovated and is worth a visit if you're curious about health cures. The water offered here for drinking contains iron and magnesia and tastes quite as vile as most spa water. The bathing water can be enervating but is comparatively pleasant. Electric sulfur baths, massage, and wax baths are available, as well as a sauna and a solarium. The spa complex is on the edge of town in an attractive parkland setting. *Tel. 065/74023. Admission free to complex. Sulfur baths: £5 (book in advance). Open early June–early Oct., daily 10–6.*

Lisdoonvarna is situated in the heart of **The Burren,** and as you travel 16 km (10 mi) north on the N67 toward Ballyvaughan, the landscape becomes rockier and stranger. Instead of Irish green, gray is the prevailing color. The word Burren means "great rock." The Burren consists of fissured limestone known as *karst,* which is exposed in great irregular slabs with deep cracks between them known as pavements. This plateau appears, from a distance, so dry that nothing could grow on it, and its landscape reminds many visitors of the surface of the moon. In fact, underneath the rough, scarred surface of the Burren are spectacular caves, streams, and potholes. "Turloughs"—seasonal lakes that disappear in dry weather—appear on the plateau's surface. In the cracks of the rocks, an amazing variety of wildflowers and plants can be found, which are at their best from mid-May to mid-June. Botanists are particularly intrigued by the cohabitation of Arctic and Mediterranean plants. Many of these plants are so tiny as to be invisible from the car window, so make a point of exploring some of this rocky terrain on foot.

Just outside Ballyvaughan, you'll see a signpost to the right for
5 the **Ailwee Cave,** the only such chamber in the region accessible to those without spelunking expertise. This vast 2-million-year-old cave is illuminated for about 1,000 m (3,300 ft) and contains an underground river and waterfall. *Tel. 065/77036. Admission: £2.70 adults, £1.40 children. Open mid-June–Sept. 1, daily 10–7; Sept. 2–Nov. 1, daily 10–6.*

From the cave, return to the R480 and continue south, taking a
6 right after about 16 km (10 mi) on to the R476 for **Kilfenora.** Here, the tiny **Burren Display Center,** a modest audiovisual display with additional exhibits, explains all you'll want to know about The Burren's geology, flora, and archaeology. *Tel. 065/88030. Admission: £1.70 adults, £1 children. Open June–Aug., daily 9:30–7:30; Mar. 9–May 31 and Sept.–Oct., daily 10–5:30.*

Have a look at the tiny church beside the Display Center before leaving. The ruins of a small 12th-century church, once the **Cathedral of St. Fachnan,** have been partially restored as a parish church. There are some interesting carvings in the roofless choir, including an unusual life-size skeleton. In a field about 50 m (165 ft) to the west of the ruins is an elaborately sculpted high cross that is worth examining even though parts of it are badly weathered.

Retrace your route on the R476, carrying on for about 16 km (10
7 mi) to **Corofin.** Here, those in search of their Irish roots will want to visit the **Clare Heritage Center,** which offers a genealogical service and do-it-yourself advice. It also features a display on the history of the West of Ireland in the 19th century, covering culture, traditions, emigration, and famine, as it exposes some grim statistics. In 1841, for example, the population of County Clare was 286,394. Fifty years later, famine and emigration had more than halved this number to 112,334, and the population continued to decline, reaching an all-time low of 73,597 in 1956. (It is now heading for the 90,000 mark.) *Tel. 065/27955. Admission: £1.50 adults, 50p children. Open Apr.–Oct., daily 10–6; Nov.–Mar., weekdays 9–5.*

Another site in Corofin that should appeal particularly to archaeology buffs is the **Dysert O'Dea Castle Archaeology Center,** a 15th-century castle on the edge of town, with an exhibition on the antiquities of The Burren. Twenty-five monuments stand within a 1½-km (1-mi) radius of the castle; these date from the Bronze Age to the 19th century, and all of them are described at the center. *Tel. 065/27722. Admission: £1.50 adults, children 50p. Open May–Sept., daily 10–7.*

From Corofin, leave The Burren by taking the R460 north for 24 km (15 mi) to Gort; turn left (north) on to the N18. In the
8 center of **Gort** (a dull little town), look out for a sign on the right for **Thoor Ballylee.** Admirers of the poet W.B. Yeats (1865–1939) will want to take the detour 5 km (3 mi) up the N66 to visit the Norman tower that Yeats bought as a ruin in 1916 for the sum of £35. He repaired it and lived there intermittently until 1929. This handsome stone building beside a tranquil mill stream is now fully restored with Yeats's original decor and furniture. An audiovisual display is available on the Nobel

Prize-winning poet and his works. *Tel. 091/31436. Admission: £1.50 adults, 50p children. Open May–Sept., daily 10–6.*

Return to the N18 and continue north for Galway City. Just outside Gort on the left-hand side is **Coole Park,** former location of the home of Yeats's patron, Lady Augusta Gregory (1859–1932). Once a center for the Irish literary revival, the house fell derelict after her death and was demolished in 1941. The park is now a national forest and wildlife park, with picnic tables. The only reminder of its literary past is the Autograph Tree, a copper beech on which many of Lady Gregory's famous guests carved their initials, including George Bernard Shaw, Sean O'Casey, and Douglas Hyde, the first president of Ireland. *No phone. Car park: £2. Open daily 10–dusk.*

As the road runs farther north you will see fields hedged by dry stone walls made of gray boulders piled on top of each other; mortar is not used in the walls' construction. They are a typical feature of the West of Ireland, as are the long evenings caused by the sun slowly sinking over the Atlantic on the western horizon. As you approach Galway City you will catch an occasional glimpse of the sea on your left. This is Oyster Country, where the famous Galway oyster grows.

9 **Clarinbridge,** 19 km (12 mi) south of Galway City, is the place to stop and sample these shellfish, if there is an "R" in the name of the month of your travels. The new oyster season is launched with an Oyster Festival, a must for mollusk eaters, held annually in and around the town on the last weekend in September. From Clarinbridge, follow the signs for Galway City, which will take you to Eyre Square. Expect a few delays along the way in July and August when traffic is at its peak.

Tour 2: Galway City and the Aran Islands

10 Many Irish people consider **Galway** to be the best city in the Republic. This compact, lively, and informal place possesses a distinctive cosmopolitan charm. Good road and rail links with the capital make Galway and the surrounding region a favorite weekend destination for jaded Dubliners. The city, which has always attracted writers and artists, features two small but internationally acclaimed theater companies (*see* The Arts and Nightlife, below). Its university is a center for Gaelic culture, where many students take their degrees in the Irish language. Galway's predominantly young and well-educated population has attracted several multinational companies to its industrial estates, and the town positively buzzes with energy.

Galway is the largest city in the West of Ireland with about 37,000 residents; it is situated at the head of Galway Bay, where the River Corrib flows from the Lough down to the sea. Across the wide entrance to Galway Bay lie the three Aran Islands with their distinctive Irish-speaking communities. Galway has always been the chief trading post for the islands, and it is the most practical place from which to organize an excursion to them. If you can possibly make time for even a day trip by air to one of these islands, it will be a unique experience and a topic of conversation long after your visit to Ireland is over. Such a trip will also greatly enhance your understanding of Irish folkways and Gaelic culture.

Galway celebrated the 500th anniversary of its charter as a city in 1984 with a great display of civic pride, which has scarcely abated in the intervening years. The people here have plenty to be proud of. In the early 1980s, Galway was the first city in Ireland to discourage bland, international-style neon and plastic commercial signs and facades by reviving the old Irish tradition of hand-painted wooden shop signs with Gaelic lettering. The city has been further enhanced by the installation of well-designed modern sculptures, floral hanging baskets, and window boxes.

The founders of Galway were Anglo-Normans who arrived in the mid-13th century and fortified their settlement against "the native Irish," as local chieftains were called. Galway became known as the City of the Tribes because of the dominant role in public and commercial life of the 14 families who founded it. Their names are still common in Galway and elsewhere in Ireland and recur regularly in any account of Irish history and culture: Blake, Bodkin, Browne, D'Arcy, French, Kirwan, Joyce, Lynch, Morris, Martin, Skerret, Athy, Dean, and Font.

Numbers in the margin correspond to points of interest on the Galway City map.

Old Galway is best explored on foot—indeed, in July and August when the tourist season is at its peak and traffic on its narrow streets becomes heavy, walking is virtually the only way to get around. The major point of orientation for the visitor is
11 **Eyre Square,** the center of the city. The square is dominated on its southeast side by the solid four-story limestone facade of the **Great Southern Hotel** (Eyre Sq., tel. 091/64041), built to coincide with the arrival of the railway in the mid-19th century. The bus station and Ceannt Rail Station are just behind the hotel on Station Road, on the left-hand side as you face the hotel. **The Tourist Information Office** is located on Victoria Place on the right-hand side of the hotel. *Tel. 091/630081. Open weekdays 9–6, Sat. 9–1.*

The grassy central area of Eyre Square is known as **Kennedy Park,** in honor of John F. Kennedy, who visited the city in 1963, five months before his assassination. The park is dominated by a beautiful 6-m (20-ft) steel sculpture, which stands in the midst of a fountain pool. The work, installed in 1986, takes the form of brown sails that are seen on the traditional sailing boats, known as Galway hookers; these boats were used until the early part of this century to carry turf, provisions, and cattle across Galway Bay and out to the Aran Islands. The genial stone figure with a pipe, seated beside the steel sculpture, is Padraic O'Conaire, a pioneer of the Irish-language revival at the turn of the century. So ascetic was this great storyteller that when he died in a Dublin hospital in 1928 his only possessions were his pipe, his tobacco, and an apple. The monument beside the park fountain, known as the Browne Doorway, was taken in 1905 from a town house belonging to the family of that name. This doorway features the 17th-century coats of arms of both the Browne and Lynch families. Keep an eye out for similar if less elaborate versions of the entranceway as you walk around the old part of town. The bronze cannons in Kennedy Park were presented at the end of the Crimean War to the Connaught Rangers, recruits to a famous regiment of the British army from the West of Ireland.

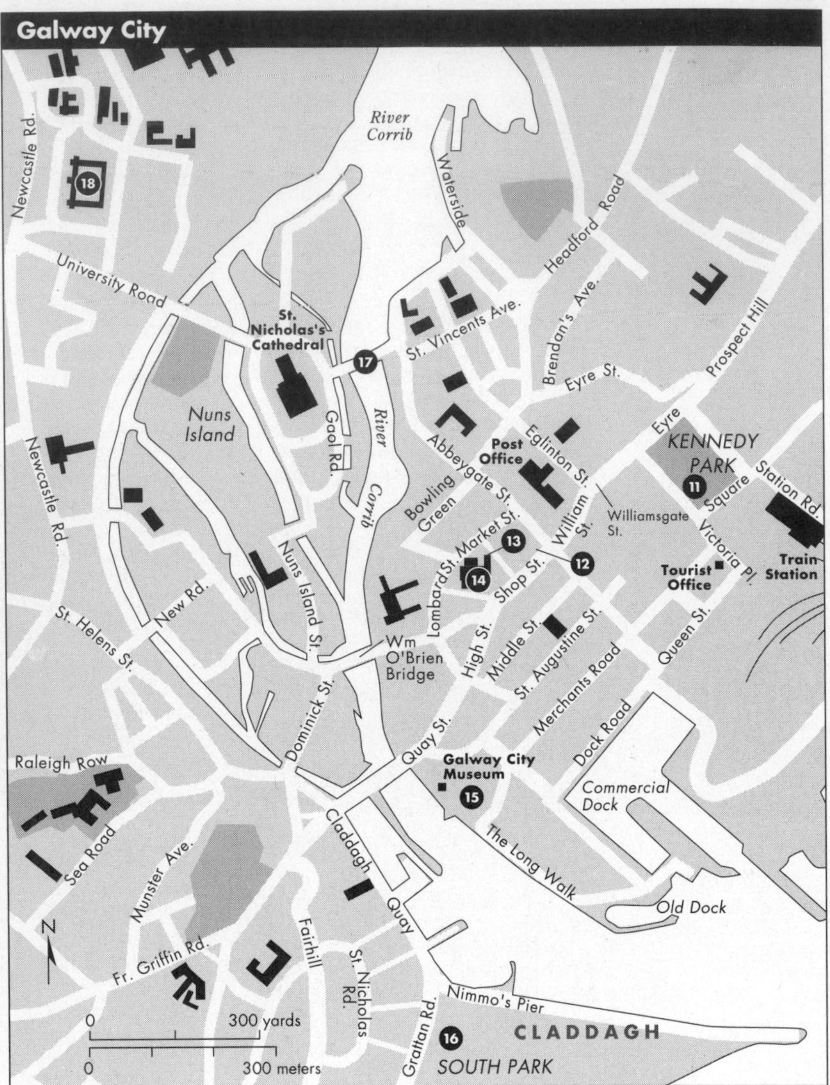

Claddagh, **16**
Collegiate Church of St. Nicholas, **14**
Eyre Square, **11**
Lynch's Castle, **12**
Lynch Memorial Window, **13**
Salmon Weir Bridge, **17**
Spanish Arch, **15**
University College, **18**

Leave Eyre Square by Williamsgate, which is a small street on your left as you stand at the top of the square with your back to the Great Southern Hotel. The **General Post Office** is located on Eglinton Street, the first street off Williamsgate to your right.
12 Next, continue straight ahead down William Street to **Lynch's Castle,** now a branch of the Allied Irish Bank, on the corner of Shop Street. This edifice is the best remaining example of a merchant's town-castle; a number of these fortified houses were inhabited by the leading families of Galway in the 16th and 17th centuries. Lynch's Castle features decorative details on its stone lintels that are usually found only in southern Spain; the building serves as a reminder of the close trading links that once existed in the 16th and 17th centuries between Galway and Spain.

To visit two of Galway's more famous sights, turn right at Lynch's Castle into Abbeygate Street, then take the first left,
13 at Market Street. Here you will find the **Lynch Memorial Window** embedded in a stone wall above a built-up Gothic doorway. At this spot, according to legend, James Lynch FitzStephen, mayor of Galway in the early 16th century, condemned his son to death after he had confessed to murdering a Spanish visitor. When no one could be found to carry out the execution, Judge Lynch hanged his son himself before retiring into seclusion.

Market Street leads to Lombard Street and the entrance to the
14 **Collegiate Church of St. Nicholas,** which was built by the Anglo-Normans in 1320 and enlarged in the 16th century. The church contains many fine carvings and gargoyles dating from the late Middle Ages. According to legend, Columbus once prayed here, because Galway was his last port of call before setting off on his voyage to discover the New World. The story, of course, is impossible to prove; but it's not totally implausible. On Saturday mornings, a traditional street market, held in the shadow of the church, enlivens the already busy city center. *Admission free. Open daily 8–dusk.*

If a browse around the shops is more enticing than the two previously mentioned attractions, continue from Lynch's Castle straight down (south) **Shop Street, High Street,** and **Quay Street,** investigating also the alleys and lanes on your left. (The same area can be reached from the Collegiate Church of St. Nicholas by following Lombard Street as it continues into Cross Street, where it finally meets the junction of Quay Street and High Street.) This section of town is considered the heart of fashionable Galway, where visitors will find all the city's best restaurants, bars, boutiques, art galleries, and crafts, antique, and book shops. This vibrant part of town with narrow winding streets, brightly painted shops, and unconventionally dressed locals charms both tourists and residents.

Time Out **Noctan's** (or **Tig Neactain,** to Irish speakers; 17 Cross St., tel. 091/66172) is a bar with old-fashioned partitioned snugs on the corner of Quay Street and Cross Street. It serves an excellent and inexpensive selection of imaginative bar food at lunchtime. This place attracts actors, writers, artists, musicians, and students; although it can be noisy, it is the city's in place to meet and to find out what's happening locally in the arts.

Leave the maze of streets on Galway's Left Bank by walking downhill toward the River Corrib. Ignore the bridge straight ahead (which leads to the nearby modern seaside resort, 15 Salthill, and turn left toward the **Spanish Arch,** which is visible at the far side of the car park. This structure, another reminder of Galway's past links with Spain, was built in 1594 to protect the quays where Spanish ships unloaded cargoes of wines and brandies. Beside the arch is the **Galway City Museum,** which contains an interesting selection of material relating to local history. *No tel. Admission: 50p adults, 30p children. Open June–Aug., daily 10–1 and 2–5.*

In this part of the city, the **River Corrib** is famous for its large population of mute swans. Pause and admire these stately 16 birds while looking across the estuary to the **Claddagh** on its west bank. This district was once an Irish-speaking fishing village outside the walls of the old town, which retained its own strong, separate identity until early this century. Unfortunately, the Claddagh's traditional thatched cottages were replaced by a conventional housing plan in the 1930s, and not much remains today of its unique traditions besides a piece of jewelry called the Claddagh ring, featuring two hands clasped in friendship around a heart. It is still used by many Irish people as a wedding ring. Reproductions in gold or silver are a favorite souvenir of Galway.

17 A riverside walk from O'Brien's Bridge to the **Salmon Weir Bridge** is signposted upriver from the Spanish Arch. In season —from mid-April to early July—shoals of salmon are visible from the bridge, lying in the clear river water before making their way upstream to the spawning grounds of Lough Corrib. This view is one of the most popular and memorable sights in Galway.

Galway's **Catholic Cathedral,** on an island forming the west bank of the River Corrib beside the Salmon Weir Bridge, was dedicated by Cardinal Cushing of Boston in 1965. The building features cut limestone with Connemara flooring, a copper dome, and all manner of expensive ornamentation. The 1960s were not a good period for Irish architecture, and its indelicate design lacks divine inspiration.

18 If an excursion to the campus of **University College** interests you, follow University Road to the west of the cathedral back on to the mainland, turning right into the quadrangle at the second corner after about ½ km (¼ mi). The pleasant Tudor-Gothic style quadrangle was completed in 1848, three years after the founding of the university. Its library boasts an important archive of Celtic-language materials, and it also hosts courses in July and August in Irish studies for overseas students.

The Aran Islands

Numbers in the margin correspond to points of interest on The West map.

For details on getting to the Aran Islands, *see* Getting Around, Essential Information, above.

Something very special about small inhabited islands creates a magnetic attraction for certain travelers. In the case of the 19 **Aran Islands,** the attraction is enhanced by their geography—the same weird limestone rock that is found on The Burren (*see* Tour 1, above), lifted in great ramparts against the pounding Atlantic Ocean—and their Irish-speaking inhabitants, who have inherited the lands and traditions of a hardy, plain-living fishing and farming folk. All islands have their idiosyncrasies, but the Aran Islands are more unusual than most.

Over the years they have attracted a number of writers and artists, including J.M. Synge (1871–1909), who learned Irish on Inishmaan and wrote his play *Riders to the Sea* about its people. The film *Man of Aran,* made on Inishmore in 1932 by the American director Robert O'Flaherty, is a classic documentary recording the islanders' dramatic battles with sea and storm. Since those days the islanders have benefited enormously from 20th-century progress; they now have multichannel television, a daily air service to Galway (subsidized by the government), outboard motors on their currachs, and all the modern conveniences in their homes. Yet these island folk retain a certain singularity from the mainland people, preferring a simpler kind of home decor, very plain food, and a strong sense of community. Crime is virtually unknown on the islands; you will find no locks on the doors of your B&B, and its front door latch is left permanently open. Many of the islanders have sampled life in Dublin or the cities of the United Kingdom and the United States, but they often return home by choice, some of them in time to raise their families on the islands, whose population remains stable.

Inishmore, the largest of the islands, with a population of 900, and the closest to the Connemara coast, is also the most commercialized, its appeal slightly diminished by the existence of some road traffic. In the summer, ferries arriving at **Kilronan,** its main village and port, are met by minibuses and pony and cart drivers, all anxious to show visitors "the sights." For the energetic, the best way to see the island is by bicycle. (Bring your own or hire one from the shed on the quay—no telephone.) The island is more than 8 km (5 mi) long and about 3 km (2 mi) wide at most points, with an area of 7,640 acres, making it just a little too large to explore comfortably on foot in a day.

Leaving Kilronan, you will notice the tall, dry (unmortared) stone walls enclosing diminutive fields that are a feature of the islands. The stone walls enabled the farmers to clear the land of rocks, while at the same time they created a buffer against the Atlantic gales. The farmers then had to "manufacture" soil by combining sand and rotted seaweed—the only available materials. As the road climbs the hill beyond Kilronan, you have access to panoramic views of the Connemara coast. Footpaths lead across the fields to both stony and sandy beaches, most of them contained in small deserted coves.

The main attraction on Inishmore is **Dun Aengus,** one of the finest prehistoric monuments in Europe, dating from about 2000 BC. The fort is spectacularly situated on the edge of a 90-m (300-ft) high cliff overlooking a sheer drop. The defenses consist of three rows of concentric circles, but who was defending themselves against whom is a matter of conjecture. Visitors have a great view of the island and the Connemara coast from the innermost rampart. *Admission free. Freely accessible.*

Inishmaan, the middle island in both size and location, has a population of about 300 and can be comfortably explored on foot—in fact, you have no alternative! This island features several antiquities—Conor Fort, a smaller version of Dun Aengus; the ruins of two early Christian churches; and a chamber tomb known as the Bed of Diarmuid and Grainne dating from about

2000 BC. Visitors can also take wonderful cliff walks above secluded coves.

On Inishmaan, the traditional Aran lifestyle is most evident. Until the mid-1930s or so, the women of Aran dressed in thick, red woolen skirts to keep out the Atlantic gales, while the men wore collarless jackets, baggy trousers made of homespun tweed with *pampooties* (hide shoes without heels, suitable for walking on rocks), and a wide hand-plaited belt called a *críos* (pronounced and most islanders don the famous hand-knitted Aran sweaters with their intricate designs and symbols, though nowadays they accompany them with jeans and sneakers. The origins of these designs gives an idea of the hardships endured by the islanders down the years: a body lost at sea could be identified by the pattern on its sweater as each district had its own pattern. Often this design was the only means of identification.

It is possible to explore **Inisheer,** the smallest and flattest of the islands, on foot in an afternoon, though if the weather is fine you may be tempted to linger on the long sandy beach that lies between the quay and the airfield. In the summer, Inisheer's population of 300 is augmented by high school students from all over Ireland attending its language school. Only one stretch of road about 450 m (500 yd) long links the airfield and the village.

The **Church of Kevin,** signposted to the southeast of the quay, is a small early Christian church that gets buried in sand by the storms every winter. Every year the islanders dig it out of the sand for the celebrations of St. Kevin's Day on June 14. A pleasant walk through the village takes you up to **O'Brien's Castle,** a ruined 15th-century tower open free to the public, which sits on top of a rocky hill—the only hill on the island.

Nature lovers will enjoy a ramble to "the back of the island," as its uninhabited side facing the Atlantic is called. No beaches can be found on the back of the island, but people do swim off the rocks. It is worth making a circuit of the island to get a sense of its unique tranquillity. A maze of footpaths runs between the high stone walls that divide the fields. On Inisheer, the fields are so small that they can only support one cow each, or two to three sheep. Those that are not cultivated or grazed turn into natural wildflower meadows between June and August, overrun with harebells, scabious, red clover, ox-eye daisies, saxifrage, and tall grasses. It seems almost a crime to walk here—but who can resist taking a rest in the corner of a sweet-smelling meadow on a sunny afternoon, sheltered by high stone walls with no sound but the larks above and the wind as it sifts through the stones? These singular moments make a visit to the Aran Islands worthwhile.

Tour 3: Through Connemara and County Mayo

Numbers in the margin correspond to points of interest on The West map.

Connemara is the name given to the western part of County Galway that lies between Lough Corrib and the Atlantic. Its moorland is dominated by the Maamturk Mountains and the Twelve Bens range to the north and is fringed by a deeply indented Atlantic coastline with innumerable creeks, bays, and small harbors. Population in this area is sparse, even on the lowland plains, which are mainly bog. Connemara National Park, in the north of the region, covers some 4,900 acres.

Two main touring routes—inland and coastal—lead through Connemara. Those who have traveled out from Galway City to Rossaveal on the R336 coastal route through Salthill, Barna, and Spiddal will have noticed how this, once one of the most impressive and unspoiled coastal roads in Ireland (and in an Irish-speaking area), has been scarred by ill-sited and badly de-thatched cabins that you see in the West are holiday homes; local residents prefer to live in garish, concrete one-story homes; a strident Spanish hacienda style, totally out of keeping with the local climate, is particularly favored. These new buildings are deplored by most visitors, including leading architects and environmentalists, but are stoutly defended by the bungalow-dwellers themselves. To avoid a second look at these eyesores, those starting from Rossaveal should follow the continuation of the R336 northwards to Maam Cross, joining this tour there on the N59.

If you start from Galway City, get on the well-signposted outer-ring road and follow signs for the N59—Moycullen, Oughterard, and Clifden—the inland Connemara route.

After about 32 km (20 mi), just past the village of Rosscahill, look out for a signpost on the right-hand side to **Aughnanure Castle.** This six-story stone tower house was built in the 16th century by the O'Flahertys, a ferocious Irish clan who made frequent raids on Galway City at the time. The large square building stands beside the River Drimneen in the midst of a field that is often grazed by sturdy Connemara ponies—a local breed whose shaggy good looks and strong character have made them world famous. *No tel. Admission: 60p adults, 25p children and senior citizens. Open mid-June–mid-Sept., daily 10–6. Key with caretaker rest of year.*

20 Return to the main road and continue on the N59 to **Oughterard** (pronounced "Ook-ter-ard"), a small and pretty village close to the shore of **Lough Corrib.** The lough is signposted to the right in the village center, less than 1½ km (1 mi) up the road, which explains why Oughterard is one of Ireland's leading angling resorts. In the summer from mid-June to early September, local boatmen offer trips on the lough, which has several islands. It is also possible to take a boat trip to **Cong** on the other side of the lough. This unusual village of small Gothic-style cottages was the location of the John Ford movie *The Quiet Man,* starring John Wayne, which was filmed in 1951. The boat docks beside Ashford Castle, now a luxury hotel where President Reagan stayed during his visit in 1984. **Inchagoill Island** (the Island of the Stranger), midway between Oughterard and Cong, is a popular destination for a half-day trip; it features several early Christian church remains. *Cost of boat rides subject to negotiation—expect to pay about £6 per person.*

Pick up the N59 again in Oughterard, where it continues west beside a string of small lakes. The sudden appearance of their shining blue water reflecting the blue sky is a typical
21 Connemara sight on a sunny day. **Maam Cross** (where the Rossaveal road joins this tour) is literally just a crossroads, apparently in the middle of nowhere. It was once an important meeting place for the people of north and south Connemara, and the location of a big monthly cattle fair, which still sur-

vives. Walkers will find wonderful views of Connemara by heading for any of the local peaks visible from the road.

Between Maam Cross and Recess (a distance of 16 km/10 mi), you will find some of the best scenery in Connemara. A short walk to either side of the main road will lead you to the shores of one of the many small loughs in the area: Stop and linger if the sun is out—even intermittently. It is the quality of the light filtering through the clouds that gives such splendor to the distant, dark-gray mountains and creates fascinating patterns on the brown-green moorland below. In June and July, the light lasts in the sky until almost 11, and it is worth taking a late evening stroll to observe the sun's reluctance to set.

If the weather is allowing the light to play its tricks, try to take a 26-km (16-mi) detour to the left about 3 km (2 mi) beyond Recess, following signposts for Cashel Bay (first right on the R340, second right on the R342) and then Ballynahinch (third right on the R341). If it is raining, however, stay on the main road for 19 km (12 mi) from Recess to Clifden.

22 **Cashel Bay** is a quiet, extremely sheltered angling center at the head of Bertraghboy Bay. General de Gaulle is among the many people who have sought seclusion here. Take it easy on the narrow mountain roads—stray sheep and bolting Connemara ponies are regular hazards, along with cyclists and reckless local drivers. The final turn on to the R341 takes you along the shores of **Ballynahinch Lake** and into more wooded country. Woodland in this part of the world indicates the proximity of a "big house," whose owner can afford to plant trees for pleasure and prevent them from being cut down for fuel. You will see a sign on the left-hand side for **Ballynahinch Castle,** now a small hotel but once the home of the Martin family, one of whom, Richard Martin (1754–1834), known as Humanity Dick, was the founder of the Royal Society for the Prevention of Cruelty to Animals.

Time Out Drive through the gates of **Ballynahinch Castle** (Ballinafad, Co. Galway, tel. 095/31006) and slowly up its well-kept driveway. Nonresidents are welcome here, and the **Fisherman's Bar** in the castle basement serves inexpensive bar lunches year-round. You can also take scenic walks through the woodlands by the lake on the castle's 350-acre estate.

A left turn back on the N59 will take you for 16 km (10 mi) to
23 **Clifden,** by far and away the prettiest "town" in Connemara. In most places, Clifden, with 1,381 residents, would be called a village, but out here it is looked on as something of a metropolis. Clifden offers a good selection of small restaurants, lively bars with music most nights in the summer, some very pleasant accommodations, and excellent walks. These features, as well as its location between the mountains and the sea, have made it a popular base for touring Connemara by car.

The town, perched high above Clifden Bay with its back to the mountains, has a profile enhanced by the tapering spires of its two churches. At first glance, however, it does not appear to lie beside the sea at all. The seashore is, in fact, best discovered on foot, by taking a short (2 km/1¼ mi) walk along the quay road through the grounds of the ruined **Clifden Castle.** The castle was the home of John D'Arcy, who founded the town in 1815, giving it its distinctive layout of a wide main street on a long ridge with a parallel street below it. The town is a sleepy place out of season, but it teems with visitors in July and in August, when the mid-month **Clifden Connemara Pony Show** (equestrian events and sales accompanied by exhibits of Irish arts and crafts) is a main attraction.

To appreciate Clifden's almost Alpine location, we suggest you take the aptly named **Sky Road,** signposted at the west end of town, a high narrow circuit of about 5 km (3 mi) via Kingstown; you'll enjoy the breathtaking scenery above the precipitous shores of Clifden Bay.

Time Out Try the **D'Arcy Inn** (Main St., tel. 095/21146), a Tudor-style bar in the center of town, for a quick pub lunch or a light evening meal. Inexpensive, plain Irish fare—Irish stew or poached salmon, accompanied by plenty of spuds—is served either in the upstairs restaurant or in a small room at the back of the bar.

Next, continue on the N59 from Clifden toward Letterfrack (14 km/9 mi) through the **Inagh Valley,** which is flanked by two impressive mountain ranges with distinctive conical-shape peaks that rise almost directly to over 600 m (1,968 ft) without any foothills.

Kylemore Valley, between the Twelve Bens and the Dorruagh Mountains, the latter naturally forested, is one of the more conventionally beautiful stretches of road in Connemara. The road passes over three lakes; if you have not already stopped at the
24 sign for **Kylemore Abbey,** you will certainly do so ¾ km (½ mi) later to look back at this fantastic turreted gray-stone building, which is visible across a reedy lake with a backdrop of wooded hillside. The abbey was built as a private home in 1864 by Mitchell Henry, a member of Parliament, and is now a convent of Benedictine nuns, who run a girls' boarding school here. The location is sheer heaven, almost enough to tempt one to take up the religious life.

The nuns welcome visitors to their well-stocked crafts center and simple cafeteria, and the grounds are freely accessible most of the year. Ask at the crafts shop for directions to the Gothic Chapel, a tiny replica of Norwich Cathedral built by Mitchell Henry on the abbey grounds. *Tel. 095/41113. Admission free. Crafts shop open Mar. 17–Nov. 1, daily 10–6; cafeteria open Easter and May–Oct. 15, daily 10–6; grounds open Feb.–Dec. 24, daily 10–6.*

About 8 km (5 mi) beyond Kylemore, signposted in the village
25 of **Letterfrack,** is the **Connemara National Park Visitor Center.** Drop in for details of the many excellent walks and beaches in the area. Some of the shorter (under 2 km/1¼ mi) walks can be followed from the main road on carefully laid out gravel paths, though most visitors will want to venture farther afield. *Tel. 095/41054. Admission free. Car park: £1. Open Apr.–Oct., daily 10–6.*

Beyond Letterfrack the road travels for some miles alongside
26 **Killary Harbour,** a narrow fjordlike inlet that runs for 16 km (10 mi) between the mountains, with its northern shore located in County Mayo. The harbor offers an extremely safe anchorage, 13 fathoms (78 ft) deep for almost its entire length and sheltered from storms by mountain walls. The rafts floating in

Killary Harbour belong to fish-farming consortia who are artificially raising salmon and trout in cages beneath the water. This is a matter of some controversy all over the West, with some people fearing the long-term effect of pollution from certain fish-farming practices on wild salmon and trout; others welcome the employment opportunities.

At **Leenane,** another tiny village, we leave Killary Harbour and County Galway to head up into County Mayo. If the weather is good and you're seeking more mountain scenery, take a detour to the left about 1½ km (1 mi) beyond Leenane on the R335, through the Doolough Valley between Mweelrea Mountain and the Sheeffry Hills and on to Westport via Louisburgh. Many lovers of the West claim that this section is the region's most impressive and unspoiled stretch of scenery. It will add about 24 km (15 mi) to your journey. Otherwise take the N59 from Leenane direct to Westport, a distance of 32 km (20 mi).

27 Look out on either road for the great bulk of **Croaghpatrick,** a 762-m (2,500-ft) mountain with a conical tip. On clear days a small white building is visible at its summit; a wide path ascends to it. The latter is the Pilgrim's Path, which about 25,000 people, many of them barefoot, follow each year in order to pray to St. Patrick in the oratory on its peak. The traditional date for the pilgrimage is the last Sunday in July, but the climb can be made in about three hours (round-trip) on any fine day and is well worth it for the magnificent views of the islands of Clew Bay. The climb starts at **Murrisk,** a village about 8 km (5 mi) outside Westport on the R335 Louisburgh road.

28 **Westport** is by far the most attractive town in County Mayo, situated on an inlet of Clew Bay, a wide expanse of sea dotted with islands and framed by mountain ranges. It is unusual in that it was planned by an architect, James Wyatt, in the late-18th century when he was employed to finish nearby Westport House (*see* below). Streets radiate from the central Octagon, and a charming riverside mall is lined with tall lime trees. The town remains a popular fishing center and has several good sandy beaches close by. An old-fashioned farmers' market is held on Thursday mornings on the Octagon; work clothes, harnesses, tools, and children's toys are for sale. You will discover some equally old-fashioned shops—ironmongers, drapers, and the like—by wandering around the streets that lead to the Octagon.

Time Out For something a little different along picnic lines, try the takeouts offered at the inexpensive German-owned **Continental Cafe** (High St., Westport, no tel.) or sit at an outside table on the sidewalk and sample the home-baked goods, soups, and salads. Health-food lovers will regard this place as an oasis in the wilderness.

The Quay is clearly signposted from the Octagon, about 2 km (1¼ mi) outside town. Visitors will find some good bars down here, as well as a choice of decent restaurants (*see* Dining, below). The main attraction on the Quay is **Westport House,** a stately home built on the site of an earlier castle and completed in 1788 by architect James Wyatt for the marquess of Sligo. The rectangular three-story house is furnished with late-Georgian and Victorian pieces. Family portraits by Opie and Reynolds, old Irish silver, and a collection of old Waterford glass are all on display. The home is superbly situated beside a lake with a small formal garden. However, its charm is sadly diminished for some visitors by rampant commercialization that extends even to video games in the old dungeons, which belonged to the earlier castle. The once tranquil grounds have given way to a small amusement park for children and a children's zoo. Sensitive souls should try to arrive early, when it is less likely to be busy. *Tel. 098/25430. Admission: £4.50 adults, £1.75 children. Open mid-May–May 31 and Aug. 26–mid-Sept., Mon.–Sat. 2–5; June 1–29, Mon.–Sat. 2–6; June 30–Aug. 25, Mon.–Sat. 10:30–6; mid-May–mid-Sept., Sun. 2–6.*

If the weather does not favor a visit to **Achill Island,** which offers cliff walks, sandy beaches, and deep-sea fishing, take the N60 from Westport House to Castlebar, the inland county town, then the N5 to Ballavary, the N58 to Foxford, and the N57 to Ballina. The total drive from Westport House to Ballina is 50 km (31 mi).

For Achill Island, take the N59 to **Newport,** a pleasant village on the Beltra River, which is popular from March to September with salmon fishermen. The N59 follows the shores of Newport
29 Bay (the northern shore of Clew Bay) to **Mulrany,** where the R319 branches off to the left for Achill.

30 **Achill Island** is one of those places that can be heaven on earth in good weather because of its splendid scenery. Accommodations and facilities, however, are very basic, so if the weather is too cold or wet to enjoy the outdoors, you'll probably be bored. A short causeway leads from the mainland to Achill Sound, the first village on the 147-sq-km (57-sq-mi) island. Achill, the largest island off the Irish coast, is mainly bogland and wild heather. The main road runs through rhododendron plantations to Keel, which has a 3-km (2-mi) beach, with amazing cathedrallike rock formations in the cliffs at its east end. Alternatively, take the longer scenic route signposted "Atlantic Drive." Until a few years ago, the people of Achill made a very poor living. Even as recently as the 1960s, some families were reliant on "remittances" from family members who had emigrated to the United States or England. Tourism has improved things, as has the establishment of cottage industries (mainly knitting) and shark fishing, which is popular from April to July.

To reach Ballina, retrace your steps to Mulranny and turn left on to the N59. The road runs for about 24 km (15 mi) across desolate, almost uninhabited bog, some of which has had its turf cut away down to rock level by successive generations' searching for fuel. The road then takes a right at Bangor across another long (32-km/20-mi) stretch of bog to Ballina.

31 **Ballina,** with a population of about 7,500, is the largest town in County Mayo and has quite a bit of light industry. Fishing for salmon and trout on the River Moy and nearby Lough Conn is its chief attraction. The town center is untidy and generally uninteresting; unless you plan to stay here for the fishing, you will probably want to drive straight through Ballina and continue for 59½ km (37 mi) on the N59 to Sligo Town.

Off the Beaten Track

While in Galway City, admirers of the writer James Joyce (1882–1941) will want to visit **Nora Barnacle House,** home of his Galway-born wife. The building is located in Bowling Green, adjacent to the Collegiate Church of St. Nicholas (*see* Tour 2: Galway City and the Aran Islands, above). Joyce stayed in the house many times. It contains memorabilia of the Barnacle family and papers relating to Joyce. *No tel. Admission: suggested voluntary donation of at least £1. Open weekdays 10–5.*

A **Corrib Cruise** from Wood Quay at the Galway City Docks is a from the car if you're touring. It lasts 1½ hours and travels 8 km (5 mi) up the River Corrib and about 6 km (3½ mi) around Lough Corrib. *Tel. 091/63081; ask for Aran Ferries. Cost: £4 adults, £2 children. Cruises May–Sept., daily at 3, July–Aug., daily at 1 and 4:30.*

If you like small, peaceful islands, take a trip to **Inishbofin,** which is 12 km (7½ mi) off the coast of Connemara. The island is about 6 km (3½ mi) by 8 km (5 mi), and has a population of 180. Cliffs, sandy beaches, small lakes, and a sheltered harbor are its main attractions. Inishbofin is popular with walkers, botanists, and naturalists. The Galway City Tourist Information Office (tel. 091/63081) will book your lodging on the island. Ferries (tel. 095/45806 for times and prices) leave daily from Cleggan, a small fishing village near Clifden, 1½ hours from Galway City.

Shopping

Shoppers can hunt for crafts, Irish-made clothing, jewelry, antiques, and memorabilia in the West. The major shopping areas can be found in Galway City and Ennis, and their most interesting shops carry the above-mentioned items. Connemara offers a large concentration of crafts shops; it is the best place in Ireland to buy an Aran sweater—either a traditional off-white design, or plain linen and cotton Aran-style knits in jewellike red, green, or blue.

Galway City is the place to buy a Claddagh ring (*see* Tour 2: Galway City and the Aran Islands, above). On the Aran Islands, sally rods are woven into attractive baskets (once used for potatoes or turf); colorful woven belts, known as **críoses** (pronounced "krishes"), are hand-plaited from strands of wool. Hand-woven woolen or mohair shawls or rugs provide an affordable touch of luxury. Musical instruments, traditionally made furniture, Connemara marble jewelry, modern lead crystal, batik, handmade beeswax candles, tweed place mats, and dried flower arrangements are among the many other attractive and interesting items—apart from tweeds and sweaters—to be found in the West. The majority of crafts shops mentioned below will mail items for overseas visitors.

County Clare (West)

Doolin **Crafts Gallery and Workshop** (beside the cemetery and church, tel. 065/74309) carries only Irish-made goods, including sweaters, modern lead crystal, linen, lace, and tweed. A jeweler's workshop and a resident batik maker are also available.

Ennis **The Belleek Shop** (36 Abbey St., tel. 065/29607) carries Belleek china, Waterford crystal, Donegal Parian china, as well as Lladro, Hummel, and other collectible china. **Flax In Bloom** (Abbey St., tel. 065/20833) offers women's and teenagers' fashions with an emphasis on Irish design and classic fabrics. **The Sweater Shop** (41 O'Connell St., tel. 065/20950) sells designer knitwear. At **Clare Business Center** (Francis St., tel. 065/20166) you'll find Peadar O'Loughlin, violin maker; Rosemary Cullen, jewelry maker; Bridin Twist, dress designer; and Patchouli, which sells patchwork rugs and hangings. **Fancy That** (11 Abbey St., tel. 065/28887) stocks Irish Dresden, Royal Winton, Stephen Pearce pottery, porcelain dolls, prints, and original paintings. Stop off at **Honan Antiques** (Abbey St., tel. 065/28137) for Victorianan items and mementos.

Lahinch **Design Ireland** (tel. 065/81480) is a small shop that carries Irish-made goods, including sweaters, linen, tweed, and other fine gift items.

County Galway

Clifden **Millar's Connemara Tweeds** (Main St., tel. 095/21038) is a general crafts and art gallery with a good selection of traditional tweeds and handknits. **The Celtic Shop** (tel. 095/21064) features good-quality general crafts. **Fire and Fleece** (tel. 095/35955) carries designer knitwear.

Galway City **Browne Doorway** (17 Eyre Sq., beside the Great Southern Hotel, tel. 091/65757) stocks general crafts and gift items. Try **House of James** (Castle St., tel. 091/67776) for the best in modern household items, as well as high fashion (Irish-made) clothing. Browse in **Treasure Chest** (William St., tel. 091/67237) for china, crystal, gifts, and classic clothing. **Padráic O'Máille** (Dominick St., tel. 091/62696) carries Aran sweaters, handwoven tweeds, and classically tailored clothing. Stop at **T. Dillon & Sons** (William St., tel. 091/61317) for jewelry; the store claims to be the original makers of the Claddagh ring. **Kenny's Bookshop** (High St., tel. 091/62739) offers five floors of books of Irish interest, mainly secondhand and antiquarian, as well as prints, maps, and a small art gallery.

Kylemore **Kylemore Abbey** (tel. 095/41113) sells sweaters, gifts, and general crafts items.

Letterfrack **Connemara Handcrafts** (tel. 095/41058) is a large roadside shop with an extensive selection of crafts and women's fashions made by Avoca Handweavers.

Recess **Joyce's** (tel. 095/34604) is a roadside shop carrying an imaginative selection of modern ceramics, handwoven shawls, and other good-quality crafts, in addition to books of Irish interest and a gallery of original paintings and small sculptures.

Spiddal **Mairtín Standún** (tel. 091/83108), a family-run drapery store, has expanded into a well-stocked crafts shop specializing in local handknits and tweeds.

County Mayo

Ballina **De Danaan Antiques** (Teeling St., tel. 096/21063) stocks old and antique country pine furniture. Try **Maguire Martin Showrooms** (Tone St., tel. 096/22598) for Victorian and Edwardian furniture, porcelain, paintings, and memorabilia. **Victorian Village Antiques** (Pearse St., tel. 096/22127) carries Victorian furniture and bric-a-brac.

Foxford **Woolen Mills and Craft Shop** (tel. 094/56104) is a factory outlet for top-quality blankets, rugs, and tweeds.

Westport **O'Reilly and Turpin** (Mill St., no tel.) features knitwear, handwoven items, and pottery. Stop at **John O'Brien** (Shop St., tel. 098/25169) for tweeds, Aran sweaters, and Irish linen. **Westport Antiques and Art Center** (Lodge Rd., tel. 098/26132) offers pine and country furniture and mementos.

Sports

Participant Sports

Bicycling Bicycles can be rented by the day or by the week. Traffic is generally light on roads other than the national primary routes, but bear in mind that this is a very hilly region. All Tourist Information Offices in the West provide lists of suggested cycle tours. The Irish Tourist Board publishes a leaflet, "Cycling Ireland" (£2), which describes four circuits that can be made in the West.

Bicycle Rentals **County Clare—Doolin: Mrs. Josephine Moloney, The Horse Shoe** (tel. 065/74006); **Ennis: Michael Tierney** (17 Abbey St., tel. 065/29433); **Kilfenora: Lynch & Howard** (tel. 065/84079); **Kilkee: Williams Ltd.** (Circular Rd., tel. 065/56041).

County Galway—Clifden: John Mannion (Railway View, tel. 095/21160); **Galway City: Europa Bicycles** (Hunter's Building, Earl's Island, tel. 091/63355); **Round the Corner** (Queen St., Victoria Pl., Eyre Sq., tel. 091/66606); **Renvyle: Gerard Coyne** (Tullycross, tel. 095/43450).

County Mayo—Achill Island: Achill Sound Hotel (tel. 098/45245); **O'Malley's Island Sports** (Keel P.O., tel. 098/43125); **Ballina: W.J. Kearney** (Abbey St., tel. 096/21249); **Cong: O'Connor's Garage** (tel. 092/46008); **Westport: J.P. Breheny & Sons** (Castlebar St., tel. 098/25020).

Board Sailing and Dinghy Sailing **Galway Sailing Center** (Rinville, Oranmore, tel. 091/94527) offers dinghy sailing and board sailing on Lough Corrib or on coastal waters. Instruction is also available. **Little Killary Adventure Center** (Salruck, Connemara, Co. Galway, tel. 095/43411) provides sailing and windsurfing instruction on sheltered coastal waters. One- and two-week courses in sailing and board sailing are available at the **Glénans Center,** based on an otherwise uninhabited island in Clew Bay near Westport. Contact the Center's head office (28 Merrion Sq., Dublin, tel. 01/611481).

Fishing Game fishing for wild Atlantic salmon, wild brown trout, and sea trout is one of the main attractions of the West. The salmon and brown trout season runs from March through September, closing earlier in some waters. Generally, fishing is at its best between mid-May and mid-June. The sea trout season starts in late May and also ends at the end of September. Details of the numerous fisheries in the area are available from the local Tourist Information Offices, or consult the Irish Tourist Board leaflet "Angling Ireland" (£1.80). Similar leaflets are available on coarse angling and sea angling.

Shore fishing is available all along the coast. Boats can be hired from April to October for deep-sea fishing (about £15 per person per day) from the following ports: **County Clare:** Doonbeg, Liscannor, Ballyvaughan; **County Galway:** Roundstone, Clifden, Cleggan, Inishbofin Island. **County Mayo:** Westport, Ballina, Belmullet, Killala.

Fishing tackle, bait, and licenses can be obtained at **Freeny's** (High St., Galway City, tel. 091/62609), **Murt's** (7 Daly's Pl., Wood Quay, Galway City, tel. 091/61018), **John Walkin** (Tone St., Ballina, Co. Mayo, tel. 096/22442), and **Patrick Kelly** (Bridge St., Lower Westport, Co. Mayo), tel. 098/25982.

Fitness Clubs Only two hotels in the region allow nonresidents to use their fitness facilities.

The **Connemara Gateway** has an unusual indoor pool beneath a glass-topped dome. *Oughterard, Co. Galway, tel. 091/82328. Admission: £3 adults, £2 children; sauna £2, tennis court £1. Open daily 10–8.*

The **Downhill Hotel** features a sports complex with a 12-m (39-ft) indoor oval pool, a sauna, a Jacuzzi, a gym, two squash courts, and three tennis courts. *Ballina, Co. Mayo, tel. 096/21033. Admission: £4 per day for use of all facilities. Open weekdays 3–11; Sat. 10–9; Sun. 10–7.*

Golf The West features some of the most challenging and ruggedly scenic courses in the country. Greens fees vary from £4 for a nine-hole course to £30 for a championship course, averaging about £10 per round for 18 holes. Courses are geared to visitors and are generally uncrowded, but it is always advisable to call beforehand.

County Clare The championship course at **Lahinch Golf Club** (Lahinch, tel. 065/81003) offers challenging links following the natural contours of the dunes. The 6,186-m (6,702-yd) course has hosted many great golfing occasions since it opened in 1892. The new Lahinch course, known as the **Castle Course** (same tel.), offers a more carefree round of seaside golf, with shorter holes than the championship course. **Dromoland Golf Course** (Newmarket-on-Fergus, tel. 061/71144) is one of the most scenic in the country, set in a 700-acre estate of rich woodland in the grounds of the Dromoland Castle Hotel. It has a natural lake that leaves little room for error on a number of holes. **Ennis** features an 18-hole parkland course (Drumbiggle Rd., tel. 065/24074) overlooking the town. Exhilarating 9-hole courses overlook the sea at **Spanish Point** (Miltown Malbay, tel. 065/84198), **Kilrush** (Ennis Rd., tel. 065/51138), and **Kilkee** (East End, tel. 065/56048).

County Galway The **Connemara Golf Club** (Ballyconneely, near Clifden, tel. 095/21153), which opened in 1973, is situated on a dramatic stretch of Atlantic coastline; the course measures 6,560 m (7,107 yd), and its par 72 is rarely matched. The **Galway City Golf Club** (Blackrock, Salthill, tel. 091/22169) is situated inland, although some of the fairways run close to the ocean. **Oughterard Golf Club** (tel. 091/82131) features a parkland course suitable for novices and those who wish to improve their games. **Tuam** (Barnacurra, tel. 093/24354) and **Ballinasloe** (Rosgloss, tel. 0905/42126) also offer 18-hole courses.

County Mayo **Westport Golf Club** (Carrowholly, tel. 098/25113), beneath Croughpatrick Mountain, overlooks Clew Bay; designed by Fred Hawtree in the early 1970s, it has twice been the venue for the Irish Amateur Championship. **Castlebar Golf Club** (Rocklands, tel. 094/21649) is a moderately challenging parkland course. Nine-hole courses are located at **Achill** (tel. 098/43202), **Ballina** (tel. 096/21050), and **Mulrany** (tel. 098/36262).

Hiking The West features excellent hiking country, although as yet there are only two signposted trails. **The Burren Way** runs from Ballinalacken, just north of Doolin, to Ballyvaughan on the shores of Galway Bay, a distance of about 20 km (12½ mi). The trail runs through the heart of the limestone landscape of The Burren, with ever-changing views of the Aran Islands and Galway Bay. The 73-km (45-mi) **Western Way** extends from Oughterard on Lough Corrib through the mountains of Connemara and South County Mayo past Killary Harbour to Westport on Clew Bay; this trail includes some of the finest mountain and coastal scenery in Ireland. For other routes, consult "Irish Walk Guides—The West," a pamphlet available at local Tourist Information Offices.

Horseback Riding Horses and ponies can be hired by the hour. Expect to pay about £6 for a hack, and about £9 if instruction or the use of indoor facilities is included.

County Clare **Clonmore Riding Center** (Clonmore Lodge, Quilty, tel. 065/87020) offers trekking and residential riding vacations.

County Galway **Aille Cross Equestrian Center** (Aille Cross, Loughrea, tel. 091/41216) features trekking, trail riding, and hunting. **Cashel House Hotel Riding Center** (Cashel, Connemara, tel. 095/31001) offers scenic treks. **Errislannan Manor Connemara Pony Stud and Riding Center** (Clifden, Connemara, tel. 095/21134) provides mountains treks, instruction, and courses for children. **Hazelwood House and Stables** (Creganna, Oranmore, tel. 091/94275) also offers trekking.

County Mayo **Claremorris School of Equitation** (Lisduff, Claremorris, tel. 094/71684) features show jumping and forest riding. **Drummindoo Stud and Equitation Center** (Castlebar Rd., Westport, tel. 098/25616) welcomes beginners and children.

Tennis The West isn't a popular place for playing tennis because of its wet and windy climate. Some hotels have one or two courts (*see* Lodging, below). Nine courts at the **Galway Lawn Tennis Club** (Threadneedle Rd., Salthill, tel. 091/22353) are available to nonmembers at £4 per hour. Nonmembers can also use the facilities at the **Tennis and Badminton Club** (Ennis, Co. Clare, tel. 065/21430). A public court is situated on Newport Road in Westport in County Mayo, and four public courts may be found in Ballina beside the River Moy on the N59 Sligo road.

Yacht Charters **Connemara Yacht Charters** (Drinagh Harbour, Errislannan, Clifden, Co. Galway, tel. 095/21332) has one five-berth cruiser available. Michael Clarke of **Western Ocean Yacht Charters** (5 New Docks, Galway City, tel. 091/65589) operates skippered charters along the Connemara coast.

Spectator Sports

Hooker Racing No longer used as working boats to carry turf and provisions, a small fleet of hookers is maintained and raced by enthusiasts. These solid, heavy broad-beamed sailing boats with distinctive gaff-rigged brownish-red sails participate in frequent races on Galway Bay in July and August. The main events take place in Carraroe in County Galway on the last weekend in July, and in Kinvara in County Galway (on the opposite southern shore of Galway Bay) on the third weekend in August.

Horse Racing Many small events are held throughout the year in the West, including trotting races, pony races, beach derbies, and the like. Local Tourist Information Offices can provide details. The main event is the **Galway Races,** which start on the last Monday in July and continue until the following Saturday. This boisterous, full-scale festival attracts a massive crowd; all manner of sideshows are set up, featuring entertainers, card sharps, Gypsy fortune-tellers, rifle ranges, and open-air concerts.

Dining and Lodging

Dining Because the West has a relatively short high season—from mid-June to early September—and a very quiet off-season, it does not offer as big a choice of small owner-operated restaurants as other parts of Ireland. Often the best place to eat will be a local hotel—Sheedy's Spa View in Lisdoonvarna, for example, which has one of the few excellent chefs in County Clare, or Rosleague Manor in Letterfrack; hotel dining will be described within the Lodging entries, below.

The dominant style of cooking in the West is best described as "country house cooking"; it relies on dishes that could be prepared by an enthusiastic host for a private dinner party at home—for instance, homemade pâté or seafood cocktail, followed by tournedos or salmon hollandaise, and chocolate mousse for dessert. Even at Drimcong House (near Galway City), home of one of Ireland's most acclaimed chefs, the emphasis is on fresh local produce prepared in relatively simple ways, albeit with the perfection that only a master can achieve.

Although restaurants in this region are less expensive than elsewhere in the country, portions are extremely generous. You'll find it hard to stick to a diet here; salads and fresh fruit are scarce on menus in this part of the world. But the quality of the meat (especially spring lamb, steak, chicken, and duck) and the seafood (especially oysters, salmon, and sea trout) is truly outstanding. Lobster, crayfish, crab, scallops, and mussels are available throughout the summer. Galway Bay's famous oysters are at their best when there is an "R" in the month; the oyster season officially opens in September and closes at the end of April.

The great majority of restaurants in the West are happy with a "casual but neat" appearance, so we have not indicated any dress code. The main exceptions are the grander (i.e., Moderate and Expensive) country-house hotels, where anyone in the cocktail bar or dining room after 7 PM will be expected to wear jacket and tie.

Category	Cost*
Expensive	over £20
Moderate	£15–£20
Inexpensive	under £15

**per person for appetizer, main course, and dessert, excluding drinks and 10% tip.*

Lodging The West features some of Ireland's best country-house and castle hotels, some distinguished regular old and new hotels, and a good choice of inexpensive B&Bs. Ashford and Dromoland Castles are undoubtedly the star hotels of the region, but lesser-known (and less expensive) places such as Ballynahinch Castle and Cashel House Hotel, both in Connemara, offer a similar degree of comfort on a smaller, more intimate scale.

The region has a shortage of moderately priced hotels (particularly in Galway City), but by way of compensation, there are some wonderful bargains in the lower price range. One of the great attractions of staying in the West, whatever the price range, is the restful atmosphere of so many of the hotels and guest houses, situated, very often, in the middle of a large private estate beside a lake or river, overlooking the Atlantic and/or distant mountain ranges.

Accommodations are extremely busy in July and August, and the best places also get booked up in May, June, and September, particularly at weekends. Be sure to book well in advance. Many visitors to the West enjoy outdoor activities, such as fishing, golfing, walking, and horseback riding; facilities for other sports, such as tennis courts or indoor pools, are scarce. So are television sets in bedrooms, even in hotels listed in the Expensive category. Rooms also do not always have direct-dial phones.

Category	Cost*
Very Expensive	over £100
Expensive	£75–£100
Moderate	£50–£75
Inexpensive	under £50

**All prices are for a standard double room, excluding taxes and service.*

Highly recommended restaurants and hotels are indicated by a star ★.

Achill Island

Lodging **Ostan Gob A'Choire (Achill Sound Hotel).** This small waterside hotel is in the village you first approach on the island from the mainland. The solid two-story town house has a brick-and-plate-glass bedroom extension. All bedrooms offer a sea view, but the nicer ones with tweed curtains and reproductions of Georgian furniture are located in the old building. The smaller new rooms are already a little frayed at the edges, but they are spotlessly clean and have pleasant views of the sound. *Ceilís*

(Irish dancing and song) are available in the bar most weekends. *Achill Sound, Co. Mayo, tel. 098/45245. 36 rooms with bath. Facilities: bar, restaurant. V. Closed Oct.–Mar. 22. Inexpensive.*

The Aran Islands

Inishmaan has no hotels, and the other islands have only one each. However, you'll find no shortage of B&Bs on the islands—most of them in simple family homes—even at peak times. The best way to book is through the Galway City Tourist Information Office (Victoria Pl., Eyre Sq., Galway, tel. 091/630081). Each island has at least one restaurant with a wine license that serves plain home cooking. Most B&Bs will provide a packed lunch and an evening meal (high tea) on request.

Inishere
Lodging

Hotel Inishere. This pleasant modern low-rise in the middle of the island's only village is located a few minutes' walk from the quay and the airstrip. The simple whitewashed building with a slated roof and half-slated walls offers bright, plainly furnished rooms with rust brown carpets and beige spreads. A new section of five rooms was added in 1990; they are slightly larger than the other 10 rooms. The restaurant (open to nonresidents) is the best bet on the island, although all the food (including fish) is imported frozen from the mainland. *Lurgan Village, Inishere, Aran Islands, Co. Galway, tel. 099/75020. 15 rooms, 5 with bath. Facilities: bar, restaurant. No TV or direct dial in rooms. No credit cards. Inexpensive.*

Inishmore
Lodging

Johnston Hernon's Kilmurvey House. Situated in the island's second village about 6½ km (4 mi) from the quay and the airport (accessible by minibus), this rambling stone farmhouse, more than 200 years old, is the first choice of many visitors (about 60% of them American) to the island. Four large rooms in the old house are furnished with hand-me-downs, and four modern rooms in a new extension have built-in furniture. *Kilmurvey, Inishmore, Aran Islands, Co. Galway, tel. 099/61218. 8 rooms. Facilities: restaurant with wine license, residents only. No TV or direct dial in rooms. No credit cards. Inexpensive.*

Ballina

Dining

Tullio's. This restaurant is part of a smart Victorian pub in the town center. The fin de siècle art-nouveau decor features an elaborate etched stained-glass window, a molded plaster ceiling, striped moiré wallpaper, a dark-green Turkish carpet, brass oil lamps, and well-upholstered velvet chairs. Cheerfully elegant rather than formal, the brightly lighted dining room with lively background music is frequented by Ballina's lawyers, businessmen, and vacationing fishermen. The dishes combine traditional French and Italian cuisines and come in very generous portions. Half duckling à l'orange, turbot Veronique (served with grapes in a sauce), and *escalope milanese* are among the extensive à la carte choices, but if you're really hungry, go for the five-course set menu. *Pearse St., Ballina, Co. Mayo, tel. 096/21890. Reservations advised weekends. MC, V. Moderate.*

Lodging

Beleek Castle. Approached through a turreted gate house on the edge of town, the castle stands on a hill at the end of about 1½ km (1 mi) of private road. Although it was built in the mid-

18th century of cut stone in the Gothic style with stepped turrets and leaded casements, it feels more like a small medieval castle than anything from the Georgian period. The vast lobby behind a heavy studded front door features flagstone floors and a carved overmantel towering some 3 m (10 ft) above the turf fire. The best of the generally spacious rooms are Nos. 1 to 6, at the front of the house; these all have either four-poster or ornate beds and are decorated in the Regency style, with delicate white-painted furniture—in contrast to the rough-hewn decor and massive furniture downstairs. Everything possible in the restaurant is flambéed at your table, including the Irish coffee. This place doesn't seem all that genuine, yet the secluded location is indeed idyllic. *Ballina, Co. Mayo, tel. 096/22061. 16 rooms with bath. Facilities: fishing, shooting. 2 bars, restaurant. AE, DC, MC, V. Expensive.*

Downhill Hotel. Delightfully situated on 40 wooded acres beside a gushing tributary of the River Moy (just off the N59 Sligo road at the entrance to town), this hotel is a popular spot with fishermen and outdoor types. The late-Victorian main house feels a little gloomy downstairs, but it is comfortable. Rooms in the new wing tend to be smaller than those in the main house, but the former have good views of the river across the garden. Rooms in the main house feature Georgian-style furniture with tastefully coordinated quilts and drapes. The sporting facilities offered here are the best for miles around. *Ballina, Co. Mayo, tel. 096/21033. 50 rooms with bath. Facilities: indoor heated pool, gym, sauna, Jacuzzi, solarium, 2 squash courts, snooker, 3 tennis courts, fishing. 2 bars, restaurant. AE, DC, MC, V. Expensive.*

Ballyvaughan

Dining ★

Claire's. Look for a crafts shop with the name Manus Walsh over the door. He's Claire's husband, and her pretty little restaurant, overlooking a leafy garden, is behind his shop. This dining spot has pine walls covered with greenery and batiks, rush-seated pine chairs, and a bright yellow candle in a bottle on each table. You can taste the freshness in the simple but imaginatively prepared food, including such entrées as panfried plaice with orange butter, and sirloin steak with Irish whiskey mustard sauce. *Ballyvaughan, Co. Clare, tel. 065/77029. Reservations advised. MC, V. Wine license only. Open May–Sept., dinner only. Moderate.*

Lodging ★

Gregan's Castle Hotel. This quiet, well-run large Victorian country house, surrounded by award-winning gardens, is located at the base of the aptly named Corkscrew Hill (on the N67, midway between Ballyvaughan and Lisdoonvarna) and overlooks the gray mountains of The Burren and Galway Bay. All bedrooms are individually furnished with Georgian and Victorian antiques and William Morris wallpaper; older ones feature molded plaster ceilings. The spacious new rooms on the ground floor have private patio gardens but lack the splendid views of the first-floor rooms. *Ballyvaughan, Co. Clare (via Galway), tel. 065/77005. 16 rooms with bath. Facilities: croquet, bar, French restaurant (jacket and tie required). No TV in rooms. MC, V. Closed Nov.–mid-Mar. Expensive.*

Cashel Bay

Lodging

Annilaun House. This mid-Victorian shooting lodge was built for the earl of Zetland and was known until this year as Zetland House. On a hill overlooking the secluded Cashel Bay, the hotel is popular with fishermen, hunters, and townsfolk in search of a rural retreat. Bedrooms are decorated in floral chintz and overlook the garden. The "minisuites" with a sea view in the old house are twice as large as the other rooms and are furnished with late-Victorian antiques. Your best bet is one of the middle-grade "superior" rooms in the converted coach house: all offer sea views, highly polished mahogany antiques, velvet armchairs, and fully tiled bathrooms with decorated washbasins. *Cashel Bay, Co. Galway, tel. 095/31111. 19 rooms with bath. Facilities: fishing, shooting, horseback riding. Bar, restaurant. AE, DC, MC, V. Closed Nov.–Easter. Expensive.*

★ **Cashel House.** This place has more antiques per square foot than any other hotel in Ireland. Dermot McEvilly claims that he acquired his extensive collection of antiques and curios when they were cheaper than new pieces; you'll admire the intricately carved oak tables, Beidermeyer bureaus, gilt mirrors, Georgian bookcases, ormolu clocks, and other knickknacks liberally scattered around the lobby, the lounge, the library, and the downstairs corridors. A favorite hideaway for sophisticated French and American guests, as well as Ireland's elite, this luxurious country house also features an award-winning 50-acre garden of exotic flowering shrubs, woodland walks, and Connemara ponies grazing out back. Bedrooms are furnished with a generous mix of antiques and curios and have king-size beds, which are canopied in the 13 minisuites. Each room overlooks some aspect of the richly planted garden and has plain wool carpets, nicely coordinated pink-and-green drapes and spreads, and brass bedside lamps. For a sea view, ask for a front room. *Cashel Bay, Co. Galway, tel. 095/31001. 28 rooms with bath. Facilities: horseback riding, tennis court, private beach, bicycle rental, fishing. AE, DC, MC, V. Expensive.*

Clarinbridge

Dining

Paddy Burke's. Once a simple village bar on the main Ennis–Galway road, this long, low-ceilinged, 200-year-old thatched cottage, divided into three separate eating areas, is now a world-famous seafood restaurant. The bar itself verges on the dingy side; ask for a table in the restaurant's adjoining room, furnished with oak-topped tables and solid chairs. Copper pans and sporting prints adorn the walls. Oysters are the thing to eat here; if they're not in season, try king scallops Mornay or monkfish in a garlic, cream, and white-wine sauce. *Clarinbridge, Co. Galway, tel. 091/96107. Reservations advised; essential in July and Aug. MC, V. Moderate.*

Moran's Oyster Cottage. Signposted off the main road on the south side of Clarinbridge, this waterside thatched cottage, the home of the Moran Family since 1760, offers a simply furnished restaurant at the back that only serves seafood. If oysters are not in season, try the seafood special (smoked salmon, crab, prawns, and crab claws with homemade brown bread) or a bowl of garlic mussels. *The Weir, Kilcolgan, Co. Galway, tel. 091/96113. Reservations advised. AE, MC, V. Inexpensive.*

Clifden

Dining **Doris's.** Owned and run by a young German couple, this establishment occupies two small floors of one of the oldest houses in town. At this restful place with plain white walls, lots of natural wood, tweed drapes, dark-red carpets and napery, you'll find upstairs both a harpist (most evenings) and an open turf fire. The cook, Doris, describes her cuisine as Mediterranean, but the menu also reveals some Asian influence: vegetable pilaf and grilled pork are both served, along with Andalusian chicken salad, *tournedos à la chasseur* (filet mignon with a tomato, onion, and pepper sauce), and a good selection of seafood. *Clifden, Co. Galway, tel. 095/21427. Reservations advised weekends and July–Aug. AE, DC, MC, V. Moderate. Closed Dec. 16–Jan. 3. Moderate.*

Lodging **Abbeyglen Castle.** Perched on a hilltop about 1 km (½ mi) outside Clifden overlooking the town and bay, this white-turreted fake castle (the crenellations were added only a few years ago) on 12 acres of steep grounds provides a stunning view over the church spires of Clifden to mountains, lakes, and the sea. A large dining room looks out to the wonderful view. Try to get a front room; the back rooms face an overgrown garden. Bedrooms are comfortable with side tables and matching chintz spreads and drapes, but in some rooms, the modern veneered furniture shows signs of wear. The bar is a lively and romantic spot on summer evenings. *Sky Rd., Clifden, Co. Galway, tel. 095/21201. 42 rooms with bath. Facilities: outdoor heated pool, tennis court, pitch-and-putt, sauna, solarium, snooker, helipad, bar, restaurant. AE, DC, MC, V. Closed Jan. Expensive.*

★ **Rock Glen Manor House.** Cross the bridge at the west end of town and go 2½ km (1½ mi) down the Roundstone road (the R341) to find this beautifully converted shooting lodge, built in 1815. On windy days, a tiny Connemara pony, Gregory, stands sentinel at the entrance gates and enjoys the breeze. Riding boots and tennis rackets in the hall make this feel more like a private home than a top-class hotel, as does the warm welcome from owner-manager Evangeline Roche. The ground floor is generously furnished with Victorian antiques; the large sunny drawing room, with plump white armchairs, magazines, books, and board games, offers a turf fire. Rooms vary in size and appeal; the best are situated on the first-floor front with sea views, but all the rooms are nicely furnished in the Georgian style, with fluffy mohair or chintz bedspreads, brass curtain rails and bedside lamps, and fully tiled bathrooms. Small-paned teak windows provide restful scenic views. Most guests are fly/drive tourists and others who appreciate the sedate and leisurely atmosphere of traditional country life that has been carefully re-created here. The Victorian-style restaurant, which serves fresh local produce, is worth a visit. *Clifden, Co. Galway, tel. 095/21035. 29 rooms with bath. Facilities: snooker, tennis court, bar, restaurant (dinner only). AE, DC, MC, V. Closed Nov.–Feb. Moderate.*

Dun Aengus. A B&B only a few minutes up the road from the Abbeyglen, this is the highest house in Clifden, with a positively vertiginous view over the bay and town that has to be seen to be believed. The large modern building has a weather-slated roof and a top story above the whitewashed ground floor. Simply fitted rooms are decorated with modern pine and candlewick spreads, and they have fully tiled bathrooms. Rooms numbered 1 to 4 share the singular view, as does the breakfast room. *Mrs. M. Ryan, Dun Aengus, Sky Rd., Clifden, Co. Galway, tel. 095/21069. 6 rooms with bath. Facilities: snooker, TV lounge (no TV or direct dial in rooms). Evening meal June–Aug. (BYOB). No credit cards. Inexpensive.*

Cong

Lodging **Ashford Castle.** This American-owned and -managed large, gray-stone turreted castle on the edge of Lough Corrib, surrounded by neatly manicured lawns and gardens, will fulfill every first-time visitor's dream of a genuine Irish castle. The high-ceilinged interior is lavishly furnished with priceless antiques and top-quality reproductions. Large 19th- and 20th-century oil paintings in gilt frames hang from the castle's carved stone walls above polished wood paneling, illuminated by crystal chandeliers. However, as old hands will tell you, the place is a far cry from the unpredictable charms of the "Real Ireland." The only Irish people you'll meet here, apart from the staff, are the gold Rolex set. The bedrooms in the discreetly added new wing are disappointingly like any other luxury hotel rooms; although they're beautifully furnished in the Georgian style, they have low ceilings and are boxy. Among the 20 "deluxe" rooms and six suites are the sunny ground-floor rooms occupied by then President Reagan on his 1984 state visit; they still feature the extra-long bed especially made for him and gold bath taps. "Deluxe" rooms have wonderful views of the river, lake, or gardens, generous sitting areas, heavily carved antique furniture, and extra-large bathrooms. The suites are vast and faultless, furnished with Georgian antiques and blissfully comfortable. *Cong, Co. Mayo, tel. 092/46003. 82 rooms with bath. Facilities: fishing, 9-hole golf, horseback riding, jaunting car, 2 tennis courts, clay-target shooting, 2 bars, 2 restaurants. AE, DC, MC, V. Very Expensive.*

Ennis

Lodging **The Old Ground.** This rambling creeper-clad building in the town center, dating from the early 18th century and much added to over the years, is a comfortable, well-established hotel that has retained its past elegance. The lodging serves as a popular base for Americans, especially golfers. The old house's attractive bedrooms offer pine bedheads, brass bedside lights, and candy-striped wallpaper. Some rooms overlook the busy main street, so try to get one facing the gardens. Smaller rooms in the new wing have the same tasteful combination of pine and brass. Be sure to look at the lovely old silver and the large Georgian sideboards in the dining room. *Ennis, Co. Clare, tel. 065/21247. 60 rooms with bath. Facilities: bar, restaurant. AE, DC, MC, V. Expensive.*

West County. A striking glass conservatory runs the length of the facade of this modern low-rise hotel on the edge of town (on the N18 Limerick road). It's a lively place, geared to the tour-bus trade, yet its roomy, pleasantly decorated public area can handle the crowds. Bedrooms feature wood-veneer furniture, speckled carpet, and floral drapes and spreads. The best rooms are located at the front overlooking the gardens; the rest have a view of the car park. *Ennis, Co. Clare, tel. 065/28294. 109 rooms with bath. Facilities: snooker, minigym, sauna, fish-*

ing, 2 bars, 2 restaurants, nightclub with live entertainment. AE, DC, MC, V. Moderate.

Fanore

Dining **Admiral's Rest.** You can guess from the nautical bric-a-brac on view that this place belongs to a retired naval man—one John Macnamara, who is an expert on The Burren's wildlife. (Ten inexpensive B&B rooms are available in the next-door bungalow.) The restaurant is housed in a modernized cottage on the coast road between Lisdoonvarna and Ballyvaughan, just across the road from the sea, which is visible through the large oval windows. Decor is rugged but stylish, including varnished stone floors, stone-topped tables, *sugán* (rope-seated) chairs, an open wood and turf fire, and posies of wildflowers on the tables. Seafood, such as lobster, mussels, or crab claws in garlic butter, is the mainstay of the simple menu, but you can also order a grilled T-bone steak, Irish stew, or a spicy vegetarian salad. *Fanore, Co. Clare, tel. 065/76105. Reservations advised. Wine license only. AE, MC, V. Closed Nov.–Easter. Inexpensive.*

Galway City

Dining ★ **Drimcong House.** To reach this exceptional country-house restaurant 19 km (12 mi) out of town on the N59 Oughterard/Clifden road, drive through the village of Moycullen; you'll see the driveway on your right. Gerry Galvin, the owner-chef, is one of the best cooks in Ireland. His wife Marie supplies the kitchen with herbs and unusual vegetables, all organically grown on the Galvins' land and virtually unavailable elsewhere in the West. The restaurant is housed in a modest, symmetrical two-story farmhouse, probably dating from the late-17th century. Leather place mats are set on solid oak tables, and the dining room is decorated with prints, cartoons, and original paintings by contemporary Irish artists. Gerry's cooking is distinguished by its simplicity; the exceptional menu might include hot oyster broth; monkfish marinated in olive oil and spring herbs, and then panfried and served on a leek sauce; or rack of Connemara lamb with an herby port-wine sauce. *Moycullen, Co. Galway, tel. 091/85115. Reservations advised. AE, DC, MC, V. Open Tues.–Sat. dinner only. Closed Christmas–mid-Mar. Expensive.*

Malt House. A small, busy bar in an alley off High Street in old Galway's center adjoins this restaurant's small ground-floor dining room, with a large bay window, a beamed roof, and rough cast walls. Tables are fairly close together, but nicely set with pink and green napery. Popular with locals on special occasions as well as with visitors, the lively spot specializes in seafood prepared in the classic French style; good choices are lobster, scallops, and the house special, prawns supreme in garlic cream. Other recommended dishes include boned duckling Gascony, served with potato stuffing and cherry sauce, or veal St. Augustine, made with cranberry sauce topped with pear and blue cheese. (A simpler, inexpensive menu featuring steaks and seafood is available at the bar.) *Olde Malte Arcade, High St., Galway, tel. 091/67866. Reservations advised. AE, DC, MC, V. Closed Sun. Expensive.*

Oyster Room. The main restaurant of the Great Southern Hotel, this establishment is by far the most formal place to dine in

Galway, a city noted for its easygoing informality. The high-ceilinged connecting rooms just off the lobby are suitably hushed, decorated in pale pink and green tones and featuring thick carpets, elegantly draped windows, tall gilt mirrors, and brass lamps. Tables with comfortable velvet-upholstered chairs are well spaced. The conservative French-Irish cuisine showcases the famous local seafood. Specialties include breast of chicken, stuffed with white crabmeat in Noilly Prat sauce and garnished with crab claws, and fresh Corrib salmon, served with fish and spinach mousse and baked in phyllo pastry. *Great Southern Hotel, Eyre Sq., Galway, tel. 091/64041. Reservations advised. Jacket and tie required. AE, DC, MC, V. Expensive.*

★ **Noctan's.** A small menu (with a choice of three fish and three meat dishes and one vegetarian main course, as well as appetizers and desserts) is served in the first-floor room above one of the most famous bars in the old town's Left Bank. The Swiss chef describes his cooking as *cuisine de marché*—the dishes offered are determined by that morning's marketing. Fillet of salmon Florentine, served with spinach in a cream sauce, and steak fillet Marianne, which is grilled and finished with brandy, are local favorites. The mildly Bohemian ambience features an open fire, filled with dried grasses in the summer, and a tiny red-walled corner room, which is decorated with old theatrical prints. An odd assortment of Victorian chairs surround the different-size tables, which are likely to be occupied by leading lights in Galway's thriving performing arts and visual arts scenes. *17 Cross St., Galway, tel. 091/66172. Reservations advised. MC, V. Dinner only. Closed Sun.–Mon. Moderate.*

The Brasserie. French in ambience and decor, American in cuisine, this cheerful place—with bright red bentwood chairs, apple green walls, and floral oilcloth on the tables beneath a brass ceiling fan—is situated right next door to the Taibhdhearc Theater and a stone's throw from the Druid Theater. The restaurant is known for its barbequed ribs. Tacos, pizzas, chicken Kiev, and steak are the alternatives, and the menu has a good selection of waffles and homemade ice cream. Service is friendly and informal, and the piped music is muted. *Middle St., Galway, tel. 091/61610. Reservations advised weekends. AE, MC, V. Closed Sun. and public holidays. Inexpensive.*

Conlon's. Known for its low prices and very fresh fish, this old Galway institution is located just off Eyre Square opposite the General Post Office. The upstairs area is mainly for takeouts; the simple, café-style restaurant in the basement features a tiled black-and-white floor, wood-paneled walls, and plastic-topped tables. Start with the famous chowder, followed by breaded strips of assorted fish, smoked haddock, or cod Mornay, all of them served with either chips or salad. This is also one of the cheapest and most reliable places in the area to eat oysters in season. *Eglinton St., Galway, tel. 091/62268. Wine license only. No reservations. No credit cards. Inexpensive.*

Lodging

★ **Ardilaun House.** This lovely 19th-century house lies at the end of a tree-lined avenue in a quiet suburb, midway between the city center and the Salthill promenade—about five minutes' drive from both. The peaceful public rooms overlooking the gardens have open fires in the large marble chimneypieces, fresh flower arrangements, and Regency-style furniture. The original house has been discreetly extended to allow for additional lodging space. The individually designed bedrooms feature a pink, gray, or green color scheme and Irish-made mahogany furniture with brass trim. All the fully tiled bathrooms have heated towel racks and marble sinks. For views of the bay, book a top-floor even-numbered room. Other rooms, which are just as pleasant, overlook the flower garden, shrubberies, and a fountain. *Taylor's Hill, Galway, tel. 091/21433. 91 rooms with bath. Facilities: restaurant, 3 bars, sauna, gym, and Jacuzzi. AE, DC, MC, V. Expensive.*

Galway Ryan. A number of modern low-rise hotels dating from the late '60s are situated on the outskirts of Galway, and the Ryan is the most attractive of these. Located 5 km (3 mi) from the city center, on the ring road, the hotel enables you a quick getaway from Galway during the morning rush hours. The public rooms are spacious and well-lighted but have anonymous modern decor. Each large bedroom, decorated in gray and beige tones, features a sitting area and a window the length of one wall that overlooks the hotel gardens. *Dublin Rd., Galway, tel. 091/53181. 96 rooms with bath. Facilities: bar, restaurant. AE, DC, MC, V. Expensive.*

★ **Great Southern.** Built in 1845 to coincide with the arrival of the railway in the area, this imposing limestone-faced hotel overlooking the main square of the town is still the best address in town after a century and a half. As soon as you walk into the large, thickly carpeted lobby through heavy glass-paneled wooden doors with large brass handles, you know that you've arrived at one of Europe's grandest old-fashioned hotels; this solid and luxurious establishment retains a great sense of tradition. Rooms are fairly big and combine the best of old and new, with tall ceilings and windows, tastefully muted coordinated color schemes, and Georgian-style tables and chairs. Ask for a back room on the fifth floor if you want a view of Galway Bay. It's worth visiting the rooftop swimming pool to enjoy an extraordinary panorama of the city and Galway Bay. In the evening, guests can sample French-Irish cuisine at the formal Oyster Room (*see* Dining, above) or have a drink in the lobby at the charming Railway Bar and Lounge. *Eyre Sq., Galway, tel. 091/64041. 120 rooms with bath. Facilities: indoor heated pool, sauna, plunge pool, restaurant, 2 bars. AE, DC, MC, V. Expensive.*

Skeffington Arms. The Skeff, on the west side of Eyre Square, attracts a loyal clientele who like its central location and the sense of history that still pervades this shabby Victorian landmark after innumerable refurbishments (most recently in 1989). The large, fully modernized bar on the ground floor is popular with both young and old. Guests approach rooms up a wide, top-lighted stairway, a relic of the Skeff's Victorian heyday. All bedrooms feature plain woolen carpets and floral drapes as well as odd bits of old furniture. The best and most spacious rooms are Nos. 3, 4, 6, and 10, overlooking the square. *28 Eyre Sq., Galway, tel. 091/63173. 22 rooms with bath. Facilities: 2 bars, 2 restaurants. AE, DC, MC, V. Closed Dec. 24–26. Moderate.*

Anno Santo. Situated 300 m (320 yd) from the sea on a residential road in Salthill (about an eight-minute drive from the city center), this small hotel has been run by the Vaughan family since 1950. A two-story bedroom wing has been added to the original, rather overdecorated bungalow. The upstairs rooms are smaller but brighter than the downstairs ones. Carpets with dizzying designs, plywood headboards and closets, and white candlewick spreads will not win any design awards, but the bedrooms are spotlessly clean. Guests of all nationalities stay here, mostly on fly/drive vacations, and the Vaughans are friendly and full of helpful touring advice. *Threadneedle Rd., Salthill, Galway, tel. 091/23650. 13 rooms with bath. Facilities: bar, restaurant. AE, DC, MC, V. Closed Dec. 24–Jan. 7. Inexpensive.*

Kilkee

Dining **Manuel's Seafood.** About 1½ km (1 mi) north of Kilkee, this modern restaurant, perched on a hill, looks out across fields to Kilkee Bay. It's a family business, with Manuel (Irish-born of Italian descent) waiting tables and his German wife, Doris, in the kitchen. Rustic pine tables and tweed-seated chairs stand on a gaily tiled floor, while the walls are adorned with scallop shells and dried shellfish. The menu includes black sole grilled on the bone, lobster Thermidor, garlic chicken breasts, and a vegetarian daily special. *Corbally, Kilkee, Co. Clare, tel. 065/56211. Reservations advised weekends and June–Aug. Wine license only. Dinner only. DC, MC, V. Closed mid-Sept.–Easter. Moderate.*

Knockferry

Lodging **Knockferry Lodge.** A half-hour drive from Galway City (21 km/13 mi—turn right off the N59 in Moycullen), this is an excellent base for visiting the city as well as Lough Corrib and Connemara. Owners Des and Mary Moran encourage visitors using this secluded modern fishing lodge on the lake shore to stay longer than just one night—the longer you stay, the lower the rate. The Morans like to share their local knowledge with guests and encourage them to get to know each other around the turf fire after dinner. Bedrooms are pretty and simple with modest antiques, Laura Ashley curtains and drapes, and hanging ferns in the half-tiled bathrooms. *Roscahill, Co. Galway, tel. 091/80122. 10 rooms with bath. Facilities: fishing (boats for hire), billiards, bar, restaurant (wine license only). No TV or direct dial in rooms. MC, V. Closed Nov.–Apr. Inexpensive.*

Lahinch

Lodging ★ **Aberdeen Arms.** This beautifully refurbished Victorian seaside hotel is a model of its kind, offering elegance and comfort in a friendly, easygoing ambience. It is popular with golfers, and humorous golfing prints hang on the dark-paneled walls of the bar and grill room. Ask for one of the new rooms that face the sea and feature spectacular skylights and windows. All rooms are large and tastefully decorated with built-in, cream-colored melamine closets, plain carpets, and matching cream floral drapes and spreads; some offer Georgian-style tables and chairs. The main dining room offers an excellent and varied menu of French-Irish cuisine; the hotel also serves one of the best breakfasts in the county. *Lahinch, Co. Clare, tel. 065/81100. 55 rooms with bath. Facilities: snooker, minigym, sauna, Jacuzzi, 10 tennis courts, 2 restaurants, 2 bars. AE, DC, MC, V. Moderate.*

Letterfrack

Lodging

Rosleague Manor. This pink, creeper-clad two-story Georgian house stands amid wooded grounds overlooking Ballinakill Bay and the mountains of County Mayo and Connemara. The clutter of walking and shooting sticks beneath the grandfather clock in the hall sets the tone of this fairly informal small country-house hotel. The best rooms are located on the first-floor front, overlooking the bay. All the solidly comfortable bedrooms are furnished with well-used Victorian and Georgian antiques, four-posters or large brass bedsteads, and drapes that match the William Morris wallpaper. The expensive, award-winning restaurant features seafood and homegrown vegetables. *Letterfrack, Co. Galway, tel. 095/41001. 13 rooms with bath. Facilities: tennis court, sauna, bar, restaurant. No TV in rooms. AE, MC, V. Expensive.*

Lisdoonvarna

Lodging

Ballinalacken Castle. This is not a castle but a sprawling Victorian lodge with bow windows that stands beside the 16th-century O'Brien castle ruins. Located 4 km (2½ mi) outside Lisdoonvarna on a hill, it commands a panoramic view of the Atlantic, the Aran Islands, and, across Galway Bay, the Connemara Hills; the hotel is surrounded by 100 acres of wildflower meadows. The interior is much less impressive, yet the room rates are very reasonable. Bedrooms come in all different shapes and sizes; some have marble fireplaces and very high ceilings, and all have splendid views. The furniture throughout the lodge is a haphazard mix of hand-me-downs, modern stuff, lovely old Irish oak, and sumptuous inlaid bureaus. *Lisdoonvarna, Co. Clare, tel. 065/74025. 6 rooms, 4 with bath. Facilities: bar, restaurant (dinner only), TV lounge (no TV or direct dial in rooms). No credit cards. Closed early Oct.–mid-May. Inexpensive.*

Sheedy's Spa View. Originally a 17th-century farmhouse, this is now a small, friendly hotel that has belonged to the Sheedy family since 1855. It is only a short walk from both the town center and the spa wells. Rooms are well cared for, simple, and spotlessly clean; most of them offer a Georgian-style coffee table and chairs. The award-winning, moderately priced Orchid Room restaurant serves an outstanding five-course set menu featuring French-Irish cuisine prepared by Patsy Sheedy and her internationally trained son, Frankie. *Lisdoonvarna, Co. Clare, tel. 065/74026. 11 rooms with bath. Facilities: bar, restaurant (dinner only, bar food at lunch), tennis court, TV lounge. No TV in rooms. AE, DC, MC, V. Closed Oct.–Mar. Inexpensive.*

Mulrany

Lodging

Mulrany Bay Hotel. Midway between Westport and Achill Island, overlooking the north shore of Clew Bay, this rambling old hotel was built in the 1890s and, frankly, has seen better days. However, the sea view and 100 acres of wooded gardens are ample compensation for the garish carpets and tatty modern furniture downstairs. It's a characterful place that appeals to individualists, including, presumably, the late John Lennon, who stayed in the Lennon Suite—a suitably weird set of rooms up in the eaves—in 1968. Ask for a front room with a bay window—No. 104, for example—or, failing that, any room in the old house, most of which have plain oatmeal-colored carpets, floral duvets, and modern veneered furniture with a small sitting area. Smaller, darker rooms in the new wing are used only in July and August. *Mulrany, Co. Mayo, tel. 098/36222. 52 rooms, 45 with bath. Facilities: tennis court, sauna, yoga room, snooker, bar, restaurant. No TV in rooms. AE, DC, MC, V. Closed mid-Nov.–Easter. Moderate.*

Newmarket-on-Fergus

Lodging ★ **Dromoland Castle.** Situated 13 km (8 mi) from Shannon and 9½ km (6 mi) from Ennis, this luxury hotel is a popular first stop with affluent American and French visitors. The original 16th-century O'Brien castle was pulled down early in the 19th century and replaced with an impressive turreted Gothic-style stone building that is now the hotel. The castle stands beside a lake, surrounded by well-landscaped formal gardens in their own neatly kept park. The hotel interior was recently given a face-lift by New York interior decorator Carlton Varney. Wide, thickly carpeted corridors are flanked by stone walls graced with large ancestral portraits. Bedrooms overlook the old Queen Anne stable yard and feature Regency-style furniture and a pleasant pink or green color scheme. A cut-glass decanter of complimentary sherry is found in every room. The vast suites have ruched drapes on the tall windows, great views over the park, and museum-quality antiques, many of them Irish-Georgian. *Newmarket-on-Fergus, Co. Clare, tel. 061/71144. 73 rooms with bath. Facilities: 18-hole golf course, lake fishing, bicycles, shooting (Nov.–Jan.), 2 tennis courts, billiards. AE, DC, MC, V. Very Expensive.*

Newport

Lodging **Newport House.** This Georgian mansion is strictly for those who will feel at ease in a rather grand and elegant private home. The handsome creeper-covered building beside the Newport River dominates the little town. Beyond a small, tidy lobby are spacious reception rooms furnished with gilt-framed family portraits, Regency mirrors, delicate Regency chairs, hand-woven Donegal carpeting, and crystal chandeliers hanging from ornate stucco ceilings. The sweeping staircase, top lighted by a lantern and a glass dome, leads to a light, airy gallery and the bedrooms. These are bright and less elaborate than the public rooms, which have pretty chintz drapes and a mix of Victorian antiques and merely old furniture. Most bedrooms have sitting areas and good views of the river and gardens; those that do not have such compensations as the enormous Jacobean four-poster in room No. 10. *Newport, Co. Mayo, tel. 098/41222. 19 rooms with bath. Facilities: fishing, horseback riding, snooker, bar, restaurant. No TV in rooms and no TV lounge. AE, DC, MC, V. Expensive.*

Oughterard

Lodging **Connemara Gateway.** An adventurously designed modern low-rise building with traditional gray slated roofs above white-washed walls, this hotel, about 1 km (½ mi) outside the village on the Galway side of the N59, combines the best of old and new. The traditional Irish cottage is the theme of the lobby and the bar, both of which are decorated with wooden and cast-iron artifacts, old country pine furniture, and large chintz sofas. The modern room furnishings are enhanced by floral wall panels, matching floral drapes, and fluffy mohair coverlets; all bedrooms have a small sitting area beside the large teak framed windows affording views of the gardens and the distant hills. Although the hotel takes in a lot of tour bus trade, this does not spoil its carefully fostered charm. *Oughterard, Co. Galway, tel. 091/82328. 62 rooms with bath. Facilities: fishing, indoor heated pool, sauna, tennis court, bar, restaurant. AE, DC, MC, V. Closed Jan. Expensive.*

★ **Currarevagh House.** Turn right in the village square and follow the twisting road signposted "Lakeshore" for about 6 km (4 mi) to find this very special, secluded place, pronounced "Curra-reeva." It's a genuine, unspoiled, old-fashioned country house in which breakfast is still laid out Edwardian buffet style on the dining room sideboard and the afternoon tea ritual is observed in the drawing room. A terrifying tiger skin hangs on the staircase, and other stuffed hunting trophies jump out at you from the dark wood paneling. Magnificent displays of fresh flowers, gathered from the 150 wooded acres, adorn the lobby and sitting rooms, where plump white armchairs tempt you to a seat in front of marble fireplaces with open turf fires. Rooms are furnished with modest antiques and family hand-me-downs (successive generations of the Hodgson family have lived here since it built the house in 1846). All bedrooms in the main house have different, slightly haphazard color schemes; the front ones overlook Lough Corrib, while others offer an equally pleasant view of the gardens (including rhododendrons, azaleas, camelias, and hydrangeas) and the mountains. The bedrooms in the new wing blend in successfully with the old house. They are more conventionally furnished with built-in furniture in dark polished wood, and overlook both the lake and garden. *Oughterard, Co. Galway, tel. 091/82312. 15 rooms with bath. Facilities: fishing (boats for hire), tennis court, private beach (lakeside), croquet, TV room, bar, restaurant. No TV or direct dial in rooms. No credit cards. Closed Oct.–Easter except for parties of more than 8. Moderate.*

Recess

Lodging

★ **Ballynahinch Castle.** Turn left off the N59 at the sign for the castle between Recess and Clifden, and after about 3 km (2 mi) look out for a fairy-tale green-and-white-painted gate lodge on the right. The castle is really a large house built in the late 18th century, on the site of an O'Flaherty castle beside the Ballynahinch River; it's a favorite retreat of statesmen and movie stars—including ex–U.S. President Gerald Ford and actor Alec Guinness. Visitors can walk in the property's 40 wooded acres, and they have access to excellent fishing and shooting facilities. Ballynahinch achieves great comfort without undue ostentation; the tiled lobby with Persian rugs, for example, has two inviting leather chesterfields in front of an open fire. The wide corridors, carpeted in Turkish red, feature prints and old photos of Connemara hanging on the walls. The biggest bedrooms, in the discreetly added new ground-floor wing, have four-poster beds, Georgian-style mahogany furniture, and floor-to-ceiling windows overlooking the river. Rooms in the old house are equally comfortable and quiet (they do not have televisions). *Balinafad, Recess, Co. Galway, tel.*

095/31006. 28 rooms with bath. Facilities: fishing, shooting, tennis court, croquet, bar, restaurant. AE, DC, MC, V. Expensive.

Westport

Dining

The Asgard. This restaurant is situated in a small room above a pub, but it has its own separate entrance and a small anteroom with an open fire for pre-dinner cocktails. White damask cloths cover the tables in the red-carpeted and red-draped dining room, which is decorated with large nautical prints and cooled by a brass ceiling fan. Service is friendly and professional. Cream of nettle soup, roast stuffed duckling with orange sauce, and fillet of sole vermouth are typical items on the menu of this popular and reliable eating place. *The Quay, Westport, tel. 098/25319. Reservations advised. Dinner only (award-winning, inexpensive bar food at lunch). AE, DC, MC, V. Moderate.*

Quay Cottage. A tiny waterside cottage has been gutted and cleverly converted into an atmospheric, informal wine bar and shellfish restaurant. Fishing nets, glass floats, lobster pots, and greenery hang from the high-pitched roof with exposed beams. All manner of nautical bric-a-brac also decorate the place. The dining room features sturdy rush-seated chairs at the polished oak tables and an open fire on evenings and rainy days. The lively place attracts a youngish crowd, in search of a good time as much as of good food. Try the chowder special (a thick vegetable and mussel soup), garlic butter crab claws, or a half-pound steak fillet, and be sure to sample the homemade brown bread. *The Quay (beside Westport House), Westport, tel. 098/26412. Reservations advised evenings and Sunday lunch. Wine license only. AE, DC, V. Closed mid-Dec.–Jan. Moderate.*

Lodging

Hotel Westport. This glass and aluminum hotel, a five-minute walk from the town center, is quiet and convenient, surrounded by lawns and overlooking the grounds of Westport House. The lobby, bar, and restaurant, decorated in an art-nouveau style, have heavy mahogany and stained-glass partitions. All bedrooms in the two-story bedroom wing are identical but pleasant, with Georgian-style mahogany bureaus and tables, off-white floral comforters, and good-quality, fully tiled bathrooms. *Westport, Co. Mayo, tel. 098/25122. 49 rooms with bath. Facilities: bar, restaurant (dinner only). AE, DC, MC, V. Moderate.*

Olde Railway Hotel. By far the best bet in the town center, this Victorian railway hotel offers both character and comfort. Fishing trophies, Victorian plates, framed prints, and watercolors brighten up the solidly furnished lobby and lounge. A mix of Victorian and old pieces furnishes the individually decorated bedrooms. Room No. 209 features a heavy Victorian bed and a river view. No. 114 has a Victorian chaise longue and a large Georgian wardrobe. Some rooms, such as No. 109, have simpler, white-painted furniture. All the bedrooms are sunny with ruched Austrian blinds. The front bar can be a lively spot, with good, inexpensive lunches and live music in the evening during high tourist season and weekends. *The Mall, Westport, Co. Mayo, tel. 098/25166. 20 rooms with bath. Facilities: fishing, restaurant (dinner only), 2 bars. AE, DC, MC, V. Moderate.*

The Arts and Nightlife

The Arts

Visual Arts/ Galleries Although many painters, sculptors, ceramic artists, weavers, and textile makers are based in the West, no major center exists for exhibiting in the region. Small exhibitions, however, can be found in crafts shops, restaurants, bars, and hotel lobbies during the peak tourist season.

The following small galleries are worth checking out for exhibits of reasonably priced painting, sculpture, stonework, ceramics, prints, wall hangings, and batiks by local artists: **Clifden, Co. Galway: Stanley's** (tel. 095/21039); **Millar's** (tel. 095/21038); **Ennis, Co. Clare: De Valera Library** (tel. 065/21616); **Galway City: Penny's** (High St., tel. 091/62739); **University College** (tel. 091/24411); **Oughterard, Co. Galway: Bridge Cottage Gallery** (tel. 091/82407); **Recess, Co. Galway: Joyce's** (tel. 095/34604); **Spiddal, Co. Galway: Stone Art Gallery** (tel. 091/83355); **Westport, Co. Mayo: Westport Antiques and Art Center** (Lodge Rd., tel. 098/26132).

Theater Galway City has two small but famous theaters. **An Taibhdhearc** (Middle St., tel. 091/62024), pronounced "Awn Tie-vark," was founded in 1928 by Hilton Edwards and Micheal Macliammoir as the national Irish-language theater. It continues to produce first-class shows, mainly of Irish works in both the English and the Irish language.

The **Druid Theater** (Chapel Lane, tel. 091/68617) is a comparatively young group of actors who have built up an excellent reputation over the past 10 years for adventurous and accomplished productions, mainly of 20th-century Irish and European plays, that regularly travel to the Royal Shakespeare Company's small stage in London.

Nightlife

Pubs form the basis of nightlife in the West. In fact, they are more or less the only form of nightlife around. Most large towns have a disco (usually an annex of a hotel or bar) patronized mainly by the under-thirties on Saturday or Sunday night, starting at about 10:30 and finishing at 1 or 2. In Galway City, the discos are located in the Salthill area. Expect to pay £2.50 to £5 cover charge.

In Ennis, an Irish cabaret evening is presented at the **West County Hotel** (tel. 065/28421) every Tuesday and Friday from early June to late September, with the option of dinner and show (cost: £17.50) or show only (cost: £4.50). Also in Ennis, **Cois Na hAbhna** (tel. 061/71166), a stage show featuring traditional music, song, and dance, takes place at 8:30 PM on Saturdays in June and September, and on Mondays, Thursdays, and Saturdays in July and August.

Pubs Traditional music performances can take place spontaneously at any time, but the pubs listed below have built up a reputation for music, and they foster it by engaging professional musicians to play for at least part of the evening. Such music sessions usually start at about 9:30. Saturday and Sunday are the busiest nights, but in July and August many of these places have music every evening. In general (unless there's a special big-name act), there's no admission charge for these sessions. If you're really enjoying yourself, it is good form to ask the barman to take drinks to the musicians, or do it yourself during the breaks.

Traditionally, everyone present at a spontaneous session pays their dues by contributing to the entertainment in turn. In the larger pubs, it is impossible to observe this custom; instead each musician, as in a jazz session, will take a solo turn. But if you're privileged enough to be included in a small session, try to have someone in your group ready to sing, play music, or tell a good joke. Your participation is an excellent way to make friends. The following places all feature traditional and folk music unless otherwise indicated:

County Clare **Ballyvaughan: Monk's Pub** (no phone); **Burren: Linnane's Pub** (New Quay, tel. 065/78120); **Doolin: Gus O'Connor's** (tel. 065/74168); **McDermott's** (no phone); **McGann's** (tel. 065/74133); **Ennis: Brandon's** (70 O'Connell St., tel. 065/28133); **Brogan's** (24 O'Connell St., tel. 065/29859); **Patrick's Pub** (Market St., tel. 065/28747); **Ennistymon: Nagle's** (Main St., tel. 065/71606); **Kilfenora: Vaughan's Pub** (no phone); **Lahinch: O'Dwyer's 19th** (no phone); **Lisdoonvarna: The Roadside Tavern** (no phone).

County Galway **Aran Islands: American Bar** (Kilronan, Inishmore, tel. 099/61130); **Clifden: Abbeyglen Castle Hotel** (tel. 095/21070); **Letterfrack: The Bard's Den** (tel. 095/41042); **Galway City: Sally Long's Music Bar** (rock and disco; tel. 091/65756); **The Quays** (Quay St., tel. 091/61777); **Noctan's** (Cross St., tel. 091/66172); **Garravanes** (Shop St., no phone); **Murray's Piano Bar** (cocktail music, Hotel Salthill, Salthill, tel. 091/22448); **Oughterard: Faherty's** (tel. 091/82194).

County Mayo **Achill Island: Alice's Harbor Inn** (Achill Sound, tel. 098/45138); **Achill Sound Hotel** (tel. 098/45245); **Ballina: Downhill Hotel** (tel. 096/21033); **Claremorris: Dalton Inn** (live rock, folk, and disco; tel. 094/71408); **Mulrany: Campbell's Tavern** (tel. 098/36234); **Westport: Ardmore Pub** (The Quay, no tel.); **Hogan's** (The Octagon, no tel.).

9 The Northwest

Introduction

by Andrew Sanger

British travel writer Andrew Sanger is the author of several popular guidebooks; he contributes frequently to several publications, including The Guardian, The Daily Telegraph, *and* The Sunday Times.

In the wild wet grass-and-heather hills of Donegal, Leitrim, and Sligo, the three counties in the remote Northwest, you'll find some of Ireland's most majestic scenery. Cool, clean waters from the roaring Atlantic Ocean slice the landscape into long peninsulas of breeze-swept rocky crests, each one remote from the next. The lower country, at least where it is covered by layers of moist bog, cuts open to reveal dark brown peat underneath; although this area may be thought less pretty than the rest of the region, it has a haunting, lonely appeal.

Tucked into the folds of the Northwest's hills, modest little market towns and unpretentious villages with muddy streets go about their business quietly. In the squelchy peat bogs, cutters working with long shovels pause to watch and wave as you drive past. Remember to drive slowly along the country lanes, for around any corner you may find a whitewashed thatched cottage with children playing outside, a shepherd leading his flock, or a bicycle-riding farmer wobbling along in the middle of the road.

Keep in mind, though, that the whole region—and County Donegal, in particular—attracts a good share of visitors during July and August; this is a favorite vacation area for people who live in nearby Northern Ireland. To be frank, a few places are quite spoiled by popularity with tourists and careless development. The Rosses Peninsula on Donegal's west coast, still sometimes described as beautiful, is marred by too much building. Also, Bundoran, on the coast between Sligo Town and Donegal Town, a cheap-and-cheerful family beach resort full of so-called "Irish gift shops" and "amusement arcades," is another place to pass by rather than visit. On the whole, though, the Northwest is big enough, untamed enough, and grand enough to be able to absorb all of its summer (and weekend) tourists without too much harm.

Something in the turbulent Atlantic air blows over these hills—a sense that the past is not so far away, a lilting half-heard Celtic tune that soothes the soul yet fires the imagination. County Donegal has the country's largest Gaeltacht (Irish-speaking area). Driving in this part of the country, you'll be amused, frustrated, and delighted by turns whenever you come to a crossroads: signposts show only the Irish place names, often so unlike the English versions as to be completely unreadable. All is not lost, however—any good map generally gives both the Irish and the English names, and locals are usually more than happy to help out with directions (in English), sometimes with a yarn thrown in. County Donegal was part of the indomitable ancient kingdom of Ulster, which was not conquered by the English until the 17th century. By the time they were driven out in the 1920s, the English had still not eradicated rural Donegal's Celtic inheritance.

If the whole of Ireland is a land of seemingly infinite diversity, in the Northwest even the air, the light, and the colors of the countryside change like a kaleidoscope. Look once, and scattered snow-white clouds are flying above tawny-brown slopes. Look again, and suddenly the sun has brilliantly illuminated some magnificent reds and purples in the undergrowth. The inconstant skies brighten and darken at will, bringing out a whole spectrum of subtle shades within the unkempt gorse and heather, the rocky slopes merging into somber peat and grassy meadows of scintillating green.

Not only close to the bracing ocean shore but also farther inland, water in all its forms dominates the Northwest; countless lakes, running streams, and rivers wind through lovely pastoral valleys. Be prepared for plenty of rainfall, as well; don't forget to carry a raincoat or umbrella. Although, as a kind local may inform you, the "brolly" acts purely as a talisman: "For it's only when you *don't* have it with you that the rain will really come down" is a piece of local wisdom.

Essential Information

Arriving and Departing by Plane

Airports The principal international air arrival point to the Northwest is the small airport at Charlestown, near Knock. Usually known simply as **Knock Airport,** the official name is **Horan International Airport** (tel. 094/67222). **Eglinton Airport** (tel. 0504/810784), at Derry City, a few miles over the border, receives flights from the U.K. airports of Manchester and Glasgow and from Dublin. Eglinton is a particularly convenient airport for reaching northern County Donegal. Small local airfields are also located at **Carrickfinn** (tel. 075/48232) near Dungloe and **Sligo Airport** (tel. 071/68280 or 071/68318) at Strandhill, 8 km (5 mi) from Sligo Town.

Airlines from the U.K. **Ryanair** offers direct flights daily to Knock Airport from London and other British airports. **Aer Lingus** has direct flights daily to Knock Airport, Eglinton Airport, and Sligo Airport from Dublin. **Loganair** provides direct flights daily to Eglinton Airport from Manchester and Glasgow, and to Carrickfinn Airport near Dungloe (four flights weekly) from Glasgow.

Between the Airports and Your Destination

By Car For car renters, Knock Airport is convenient—just 54½ km (34 mi) south of Sligo Town; a car rental desk is located at the airport. You can also pick up rental cars at Sligo and Eglinton (Derry) airports.

By Bus If you aren't driving, Knock Airport becomes less attractive, as you'll have no easy public transportation link to your destination, except the local bus to Charlestown (11 km/7 mi away). You also cannot rely on catching a bus at the smaller airports, except at Sligo Airport, where buses run from Sligo Town to meet all flights.

By Taxi Cabs usually stand waiting outside Knock Airport to meet incoming flights, but passengers arriving at the other airports may have to phone a local taxi company. Phone numbers of taxi companies are available from airport information desks and are also displayed beside pay phones inside the airport terminal.

Arriving and Departing by Car, Train, and Bus

By Car Sligo, the largest town in the Northwest, is relatively accessible on the main routes. The N4 travels the 224 km (140 mi) direct from Dublin to Sligo but you need to allow at least four hours for this journey. The N15 continues from Sligo Town to

Donegal Town and proceeds from Donegal Town to Derry City just over the border in the province of Northern Ireland. The best approach for anyone driving up from the West and the Southwest is on the N17, connecting Sligo to Galway.

By Train Sligo Town is linked by a direct train line to Dublin. From Dublin three trains a day are available, and the journey takes 3 hours and 20 minutes. The trip costs £16 one-way, £21 round-trip. The train stops at Ballymote (20 minutes from Sligo), at Boyle (40 minutes), and Carrick-on-Shannon (50 minutes). However, if you want to get to Sligo Town by rail from other provincial towns, you'll be forced to make some inconvenient connections and take roundabout routes. The rest of the region has no railway services. Contact **Irish Rail** (tel. 01/366222).

By Bus **Bus Éireann** (tel. 01/366111) can get you from Dublin to Sligo Town in four hours for a round-trip fare of £8. Two buses a day from Dublin are available. Another bus route, three times a day from Dublin, gets to Letterkenny in the heart of County Donegal in 4¼ hours, via a short trip across the Northern Ireland border, for £9 one-way, £12 round-trip. Other Bus Éireann services connect Sligo Town to other towns all over Ireland; for these connections, call 071/2152.

Getting Around

By Car
Driving Roads are uncongested, but in some places they are in a poor state of repair. In the Irish-speaking areas, signposts are written only in the Irish (Gaelic) language, which can be confusing. You need to prepare beforehand for this by checking the Irish names of places on your route.

Car Rentals You can rent a car in Sligo Town from **Murray's Europcar** (tel. 071/684000), or at Sligo Airport from **Johnson & Perrott** (tel. 071/68280). At Knock Airport, cars may be rented from Avis (tel. 094/67252). A medium-sized four-door costs around £40 per day with unlimited mileage (inclusive of insurance and taxes), or around £240 per week. Avis rentals tend to be a little more expensive than other companies. If you're planning to mostly tour northern County Donegal, you may find it more convenient to rent a car in Derry City from **Hertz** (tel. 0504/360420). If you're planning to take a rental car across the border to Northern Ireland, inform the company in advance and check the insurance position.

By Bus **Bus Éireann** services operate out of Sligo Town (tel. 071/60066) and Letterkenny (tel. 074/21309) to destinations all over the region, as well as to other parts of Ireland. Fares are economical. From Sligo Town, you can reach almost any point in the region for under £2. The fare all the way to Dublin from Sligo is only £5 one-way, £8 round-trip. Several other local bus companies link towns and villages in the Northwest, including **Funtrek** (tel. 01/730852) and **McGeehans** (tel. 075/46101).

Important Addresses and Numbers

Tourist Information The main visitor information center for the whole Northwest region is the Tourist Information Office (TIO) in **Sligo Town** (Áras Reddan, Temple St., tel. 071/61201). Sligo is in the extreme south of the region; if you are traveling in County Donegal in the North, try the TIO at **Letterkenny** (Derry Rd., tel. 074/21160) in a small chalet-type modern building about 1.6 km (1 mi) out of town. Both TIOs are open year-round: Sept.–May, weekdays 9–1 and 2–5; June, Mon.–Sat. 9–1 and 2–6; July–Aug., Mon.–Sat. 9–8, Sun. 10–2.

The following TIOs are open only during the summer months (usually first week in June to second week in September):

Bundoran, County Donegal (Main St., tel. 072/41350).

Carrick-on-Shannon, County Leitrim (On the river quay, tel. 078/20170). Information for County Leitrim and its county town.

Donegal Town, County Donegal (Quay St., tel. 073/21148).

Dungloe, County Donegal (In the village center, tel. 075/21297).

Emergencies Call 999 for **police, fire,** or **ambulance** services.

Main Police Stations **Carrick-on-Shannon** (tel. 078/20021), **Donegal Town** (tel. 073/21021), **Letterkenny** (tel. 074/22222), and **Sligo Town** (tel. 071/42031).

Hospitals **Letterkenny General Hospital** (High Rd., Letterkenny, Co. Donegal, tel. 074/22022) and **Sligo General Hospital** (Dromahair Rd., Sligo Town, Co. Sligo, tel. 071/42161).

Guided Tours

County Sligo's Tourist Information Office (tel. 071/61201) in Sligo Town organizes courtesy tours of the area, twice daily, lasting 1¼ hours. The guides are generally students, so a tip of 50p would be welcomed. **Lough Gill Cruises** (tel. 071/62540) runs agreeable 1¾-hour guided tours of the Lough, with commentary on connections to Yeats's writing. The cruises depart from the landing stages at Doorly Park Gates, at the eastern end of Sligo Town, and cost around £5. For a friendly, relaxed minibus tour of the area with a knowledgeable guide, call **John Houze** (tel. 071/42747) for his morning tour around Lough Gill (cost: £4.50 adults, £2 children, under 6 free) and his afternoon tour north of Sligo Town to Drumcliff, Lissadell House, and Creevykeel (cost: £5.50 adults, £2 children, under 6 free). **Bus Éireann** (tel. 071/60066 in Sligo, 074/21309 in Letterkenny) offers useful budget-priced one-day guided coach tours of the Donegal Highlands and to Glenveagh National Park. These tours start from Bundoran, Sligo Town, Ballyshannon, and Donegal Town.

Exploring the Northwest

Highlights for First-time Visitors

Ardara (*see* Tour 2)

Donegal Town (*see* Tour 2)

Glenveagh National Park (*see* Tour 3)

Grianan Ailigh, for the view of Lough Swilly (*see* Tour 3)

Lough Gill (*see* Tour 1)

Sheephaven Bay, from Rosguill Peninsula to Horn Head (*see* Tour 3)

Tour 1: Yeats Country—Sligo Town and Environs

Numbers in the margin correspond with points of interest on the Yeats Country and Around Donegal Bay and Sligo Town maps.

This tour, which covers the most accessible part of the Northwest, visits a pleasant, peaceful countryside of lakes, farms, and woodland on the border of Counties Sligo and Leitrim. If you are familiar with the romantic poems of W. B. Yeats, it will undoubtedly bring to mind some of his best writing. Yeats knew intimately all these villages and landscapes and eloquently celebrated many of them in verse. Often on this route, you'll have glimpses of "bare Ben Bulben's head," as he called flat-topped Ben Bulben Mountain, which looms over the western end of the Dartry range.

1 Begin this tour at **Sligo Town,** although you may not be staying in the town itself; the most interesting accommodations are located a few miles out. This busy marketplace is very much the region's principal community. With a population of about 17,000 inhabitants, it is the only town of any size in the whole of Northwest Ireland. Sligo is centered around two bridges across the River Garavogue, and its name in Irish, Sligeach, means "place of shells." This lovely riverside location, squeezed onto a narrow strip of land between the Atlantic and Lough Gill, often became a battleground in its earlier days. The community was attacked by Viking invaders in the 9th century and, later, by a succession of rival Irish and Anglo-Norman conquerors. In 1245, Sligo was fortified by the most successful of these victors, Maurice FitzGerald, earl of Kildare, although nothing is left now of his medieval castle.

Modern-day Sligo offers visitors only modest sights, but it does deserve a stroll, especially because of its close associations
2 with W. B. Yeats and all the talented Yeats family. At the **Yeats Building** beside Hyde Bridge, an annual Yeats Summer School is established every August, when guest speakers are invited to lecture on the world-renowned poet and his contemporaries. During the rest of the year, occasional exhibitions and other lectures on the writer are held in the area.

Yeats's brother, Jack, was a famous painter in his day; he once said, "I never did a painting without putting a thought of Sligo in it." Yeats's father, John, had a considerable reputation as a portraitist. Many of the works of these two artists, including portraits of W.B., are displayed with paintings by other Irish
3 artists at the **Sligo County Library and Museum,** on Stephen Street. Several pictures with connections to the Yeats family were donated by a New York stockbroker, James A. Healey, whose mother emigrated to the United States in 1884. Other items at the museum that can be seen on request are a collection of Yeats's first editions and other intriguing memorabilia, such as the author's personal letters and the Irish tricolor flag that draped his coffin when he was buried at nearby Drumcliff. *Stephen St., tel. 071/2212. Admission free. Library open Tues.–Sat. 10–1 and 2–5, and also 7–9 on Tues. and Thurs. Museum open June–Sept., Tues.–Sat. 10:30–12:30 and 2:30–4:30.*

Yeats Country and Around Donegal Bay

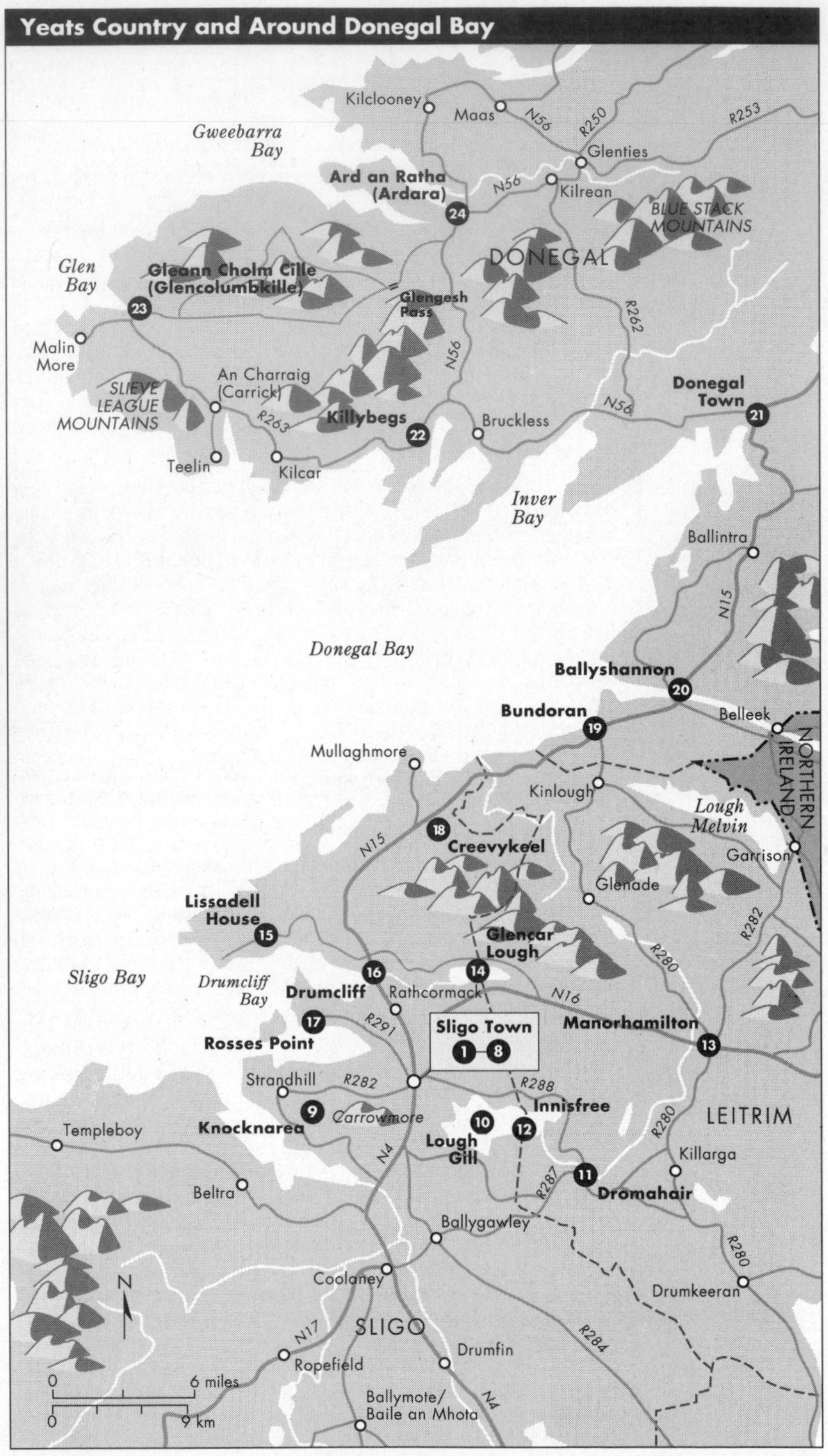

Courthouse, **5**
Dominican Abbey, **6**
St. John's Cathedral, **7**
Sligo County Library and Museum, **3**
13th-century Abbey, **4**
Tourist Information Office, **8**
Yeats Building, **2**

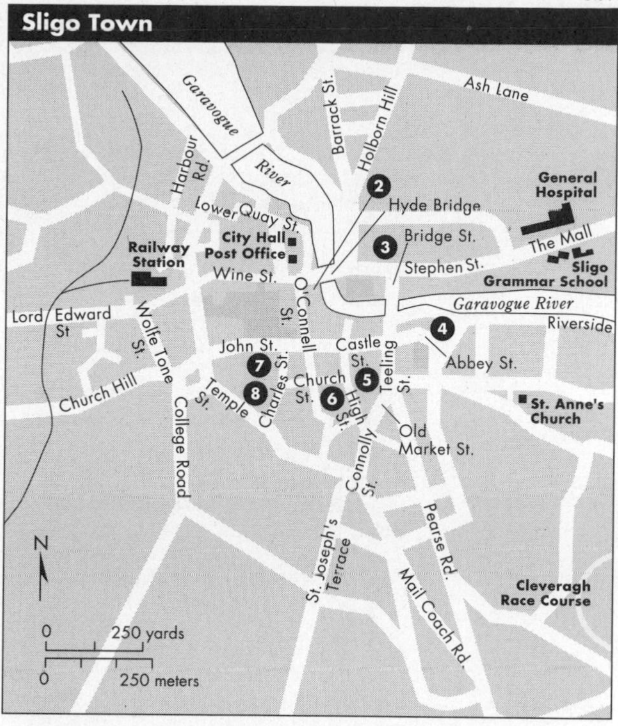

To find Sligo's only existing relic of the Middle Ages, walk down Bridge Street, nearly opposite the library and museum. Cross the river and turn left into Abbey Street, and here you'll find
4 the rather forlorn ruins of the **13th-century Abbey,** built for the Dominicans by Maurice FitzGerald. After a fire in 1414, it was extensively rebuilt, only to be destroyed again by Cromwell's Puritans in 1641. Some fine stonework remains, especially in the 15th-century cloisters. *Admission free. Usually open—if not, key with caretaker (currently Mr. A. McGuinn, 6 Charlotte St.).*

Retrace your steps, turning left into Teeling Street to see the
5 **Courthouse.** Compared with the generally simple style of most Irish country architecture, this Victorian Gothic edifice is distinctly elaborate with its flamboyant, turreted Gothic exterior; it is not open to casual visitors. After it was built, the structure became a symbol for English power. The Courthouse takes its inspiration from the larger Law Courts in London.

Continue beyond the Courthouse into Old Market Street right
6 onto High Street, passing the new **Dominican Abbey,** and left onto Church Street. At the end of Church Street, turn right onto Charles Street. You will notice along these streets that Sligo has numerous churches of all denominations. Presbyterians, Methodists, and even Plymouth Brethren are represented here, as well as Anglicans (Church of Ireland) and, of course, Roman Catholics. According to the Irish writer Sean O'Faolain, "The best Protestant stock in all Ireland is in Sligo." The Yeats family were part of that stock. At the end of Charles

Street, turn left onto John Street. If the door is unlocked, step
7 inside the **St. John's Cathedral** (Church of Ireland) on John Street; you'll find in the north transept a memorial to Susan Mary Yeats, mother of W.B. and Jack. *Admission free. No set hours.*

8 County Sligo's **Tourist Information Office,** useful for the whole of the Northwest, is located nearby on Temple Street near the corner of Charles Street.

Time Out One of Sligo's best pubs is **Hargadon's** (O'Connell St.), an atmospheric old place with cozy private snugs (rooms). On the same street nearby, **Beezie's** (tel. 071/45239) is a lively, popular bar and restaurant serving reasonably priced "Tourist Menu" meals (typical Irish meat dishes with two vegetables).

Numbers in the margin correspond with points of interest on the Yeats Country and Around Donegal Bay map.

Rising to the west of Sligo, and clearly visible from town, is
9 **Knocknarea** (328 m/1,083 ft), the "cairn-heaped grassy hill" that once caught Yeats's imagination. To drive out for a closer look at this evocative peak, take the Strandhill road out of town (the R292; it goes due west, following Sligo Bay). After 8 km (5 mi), a left turn brings you closer to the hilltop, though you will have to get out and walk to reach the summit, where you will have a good view of the mountains of Counties Donegal and Sligo. The huge cairn at its summit, a heaped-stone monument made with 40,000 tons of rock, is traditionally believed to commemorate "passionate Maeve," as Yeats called her, a 1st-century AD Celtic queen of Connaught who is the heroine of many Irish legends. Archaeologists argue, though, that the cairn is more likely a 3,000-year-old tomb.

Strandhill, at the foot of Knocknarea, is an unremarkable seaside resort, though it does have a good sandy beach and one unusual attraction called Dolly's Cottage, a typical 19th-century rural dwelling that serves now as a folk museum in which members of the Irish Countrywomen's Association sell their homemade wares. Some evenings, folk music sessions are held here. *Admission free. Open July–Aug., daily 3–5.*

A short drive southeast of Knocknarea is another small hill, **Carrowmore,** at the top of which several megalithic remains cover a broad area. Unfortunately, many have been badly damaged, but this is Ireland's largest single group of Stone Age monuments. Most are communal tombs dating back to 4000 BC. You can reach Carrowmore on the minor road back to Sligo Town. The whole trip around Knocknarea and back into town is about 16 km (10 mi).

Next, head from Sligo Town toward the shores of beautiful, gen-
10 tle **Lough Gill.** You can, if you prefer, make this trip by boat excursion from Sligo, traveling along the Garavogue into Lough Gill on the cruiser *Queen Maeve* (*see* Guided Tours, above). But if you're driving, get onto Stephen Street and take the N16 out of town (signposted to Manorhamilton and Enniskillen). Turn right almost at once onto the R286. Within minutes you will find some of the most scenic country imaginable, with rich woodland affording gorgeous views onto the lake so adored by the young Yeats. In fact, Lough Gill in Irish means simply "Lake Beauty." The legend is (there would have to be a legend

about such a place) that the bell from Sligo's Abbey lies at the bottom of the lake and that those who are without sin can hear it pealing. No one has ever reported hearing it.

The wooded estate and Georgian house on the right of R286, sitting on the north bank of the lough, is **Hazelwood.** Built in 1731, this structure was one of the earliest of several fine Palladian mansions designed by the German architect Richard Castle, who was responsible for many of Ireland's grandest houses. Hazelwood is currently in use as business premises. On the other side of the road is another pretty lake, **Lough Colgagh,** and you'll also see signposts leading to the **Deerpark Monument.** From the name, you might expect to see a statue in some deer enclosure; in reality, the monument is a complicated set of ritual burial chambers dating back to about 3500 BC. To see them, walk about 10 minutes from the road into a forest plantation. When you arrive, you will find a collection of stone structures arranged in a rough rectangle about 15 by 45 yards, with a central court tomb, as well as two sets of tombs on the east side and one on the west. Close by you can see the ruins of an ancient *cashel* (fortified settlement) with simple concentric stone ramparts.

Continuing from the Deerpark Monument, stay with the R286 for 12.8 km (8 mi), until it drops down toward the waterside. They say an Englishman's home is his castle, and it was certainly true of **Parke's Castle,** on the right as the road dips down. This sturdy fortified house was constructed in the 17th century by an English gentleman settler who needed the strong fortifications to defend himself against a hostile populace. What made relations worse is that he obtained his building materials mainly by dismantling a historic fortress on the site, which had belonged to the clan leaders of the O'Rourkes of Breffni (this district used to be called Breffni). The entrance fee includes a short video show on the castle and local history. A snack bar is available. *Tel. 071/64149. Admission: £1. Open June–Sept., daily 10–6.*

About 1.6 km (1 mi) farther, the road twists away from the lake, following the River Bonet toward Dromahair. Just at the edge of the village, you can pause first to ponder the story behind **The Old Hall,** a fine riverside mansion on the river's right bank (signposted; not open to visitors). It was built in 1626 for another unwelcome English landowner, Sir William Villiers, who constructed his house from stones taken from the ruins of an important O'Rourke castle that stood right next door. In that old fort, in the year 1152, Tiernán O'Rourke lived with his pretty wife, Dervorguilla, until one day their castle was attacked by Dermot MacMurrough, king of Leinster, who managed to persuade Dervorguilla to run away with him. O'Rourke was furious and formed an alliance with all the other Irish chieftains to bring MacMurrough to justice.

O'Rourke did get his wife back, but MacMurrough then sought help from the Plantagenet king of England, Henry II, who sent one of his best men, Strongbow, to fight beside MacMurrough against the Irish kings. And so began the Anglo-Norman invasion of Ireland, the start of the long effort by England to conquer the Irish.

On the other side of the River Bonet stand the handsome remains of **Creevelea Abbey,** reached by a few minutes' walk along a footpath. In fact not an abbey but a friary, Creevelea was founded for the Franciscans in 1508 by a later generation of O'Rourkes. It was the last Franciscan community to be founded before the suppression of the monasteries by England's King Henry VIII. Like many such ruined abbeys, the place still has religious meaning for the local people, who treat it with reverence. One curiosity of this abbey is the especially large south transept; notice, too, its endearing little cloisters, with well-executed carvings on the pillars of St. Francis of Assisi. *Signposted at Dromahair. Admission free. Accessible all day.*

Real Yeats fans will want to cast eyes on nearby Innisfree, the "Lake Isle" around which the poet weaved his enticing imagery:

"I will arise and go now, and go to Innisfree . . .
And live alone in the bee-loud glade.
I hear lake water lapping with low sounds by the shore;
While I stand on the roadway, or on the pavements grey,
I hear it in the deep heart's core."

To reach Innisfree, drive through the neat and tidy little village
11 of **Dromahair** to take the R287, the minor road that heads back
along the south side of Lough Gill toward Sligo Town. Turn
right at a small crossroads, after a mile or so, where signposts
12 point to **Innisfree** (pronounced *Inish Free*). A little road leads
down to the lakeside, from where you can see the island just offshore. The small tree-covered island is not the haven of peace that it must have been when Yeats wrote those words—excursions arrive by boat from Sligo Town, and visitors traveling by car turn up throughout the day.

A little beyond the Innisfree turnoff lies **Dooney Rock,** across the water on the southeastern end of the Lough Gill; this is where the poet daydreamed, contemplated the lake's islands, and imagined a fiddler on the rock who made "folk dance like a wave of the sea."

Come back along the R287 toward Dromahair, but instead of
turning into the village, continue driving (the road number
13 changes to R280) toward **Manorhamilton.** This small rural town
was built in the 17th century for the Scottish Planter (colonist settling on Irish lands confiscated from Catholic owners) Sir Frederick Hamilton. Sir Frederick had been given the local manor house by Charles I of England (hence, the town's name). The manor itself is now an ivy-covered ruin, and there's not much to see here. The surrounding scenery, however, is superb. Take the N16, signposted to Sligo Town, for about 9½ km
(6 mi) until you reach the little turning that heads right to
14 **Glencar Lough.** The turn is signposted "waterfall," and you'll
discover several waterfalls here, with a parking lot and footpath leading to one of the highest. The lake is fed by the River Drumcliff and other streams at the foot of the Dartry Mountains: "Where the wandering water gushes/ From the hills above Glen-Car," as Yeats saw it.

Stay on Lough Glencar's right bank, and you'll reach a fork in the road: a left heads back to the N16 and Sligo Town, a right weaves across the country toward the N15 and the villages of Drumcliff and Carney. You want to take the right, but even if you miss it, almost any other right turn off the N16 will lead you in the same direction.

15 Next, stop at **Lissadell House** (signposted from the N15), near Carney, beside the Atlantic waters of Drumcliff Bay. This impressive aristocratic residence has belonged to the distinguished Gore-Booth family since it was built in 1834. The family became good friends of W. B. Yeats, who recalled seeing the house often as a child from his grandmother's carriage. Later, in 1894, he was invited to visit the house and became acquainted with the two Gore-Booth daughters, Eva and Constance. He recalled their meeting in verse: "The light of evening, Lissadell,/ Great windows open to the south./ Two girls in silk kimonos." Eva became a poet, while sister Constance went on to lead a dramatic political life as a fiery Irish nationalist, taking a leading role in the 1916 Easter Rising against the British.

Lissadell House is now open to the public, with tours of the house, a craft shop, and refreshments. A copy of Yeats's poem "In Memory of Eva Gore-Booth and Con Markiewicz" is displayed on a sign beside the main gate at the entrance, and aficionados of all things Yeatsian will certainly find the house interesting if only for the associations with the poet. Others may prefer to wander the grounds. The interior is typical of 19th-century aristocratic country homes. The woods of the Lissadell estate have become a forestry and wildlife reserve—a fine place for bird-watchers, it serves as a home to Ireland's largest colony of the Barnacle Goose, along with several other species of wildfowl. *Tel. 071/63150. Admission: £1.50 adults, 50p children. Open May–Sept., Mon.–Sat. 2–5:15.*

Double back from Lissadell, through Carney, in the direction of Drumcliff. Just north of Carney, by the way, the legendary Battle of the Book took place in AD 561, one of the earliest and most acrimonious cases in the whole history of copyright law.

St. Columba, a recluse and missionary who established Christian
churches and religious communities in Northwest Ireland, is
thought to have been the founder of a monastic settlement around
16 575 at **Drumcliff,** east of Lissadell and Carney on the N15. The
monastery flourished for many centuries, but all that is left of it
now is the base of a Round Tower and a richly carved High
Cross dating from around 1000. These remains stand close together by the road. More notable now is the fact that W. B. Yeats lies buried with his wife, George, in an unpretentious grave in the grounds of Drumcliff's plain and simple Protestant church, opposite the High Cross. Yeats actually died on the French Riviera in 1939; it took almost a full decade for his body to be brought back to Drumcliff in accordance with his wishes. In the poem "Under Ben Bulben," he spelled out not only where he was to be buried but also what should be written on the tombstone: "Cast a cold Eye/ On Life, on Death./ Horseman, pass by!" Today you can stand in the churchyard and read those words cut into the gray headstone. It is easy to see why the curious, flat-topped Ben Bulben (536 m/1,730 ft) made such an impression on the poet; the mountain gazes calmly down upon the small rural church, and at the same time it faces the mighty Atlantic.

Before returning to Sligo Town, for another sight of the Atlantic breakers you can turn right off the N15 at Rathcormack and
17 take a trip out to **Rosses Point,** where Yeats and his brother,
Jack, often stayed during their summer vacations. This popular seaside and leisure area with good safe sandy beaches and

fine views is around 6 km (4 mi) from the N15 and is clearly signposted. Two popular sportmen's havens, the County Sligo Golf Club and the Sligo Yacht Club, are also located here. From Rosses Point, the drive is just 8 km (5 mi) straight back to Sligo Town on the R291.

Tour 2: Around Donegal Bay

The soaring Donegal hills beckon from the horizon as you travel north to Donegal Town from Sligo Town. The rolling coastal fields break open here and there to give startling views across the waters of Donegal Bay. The whole stretch from Sligo Town to Donegal Town has become the Northwest's most popular vacation area, but this is certainly no Miami or Côte d'Azur. You'll pass a few small and unremarkable seashore resorts, and, in some places, you may find that haphazard and fairly tasteless construction detracts from the scenery. In between these minor resort developments, the traveler encounters wide-open spaces free of traffic and full of fresh air. The most interesting part of this tour lies on the north side of the bay—all that rocky indented coastline due west of Donegal Town. That's where you'll breathe a sigh of relief and enter the true away-from-it-all world of County Donegal.

Take the N15 from Sligo Town in the direction of Donegal Town. The whole County Sligo coastal region is dotted with numerous prehistoric sites; 16 km (10 mi) after you pass Drumcliff
18 (*see* Tour 1, above), you'll reach, at **Creevykeel,** one of Ireland's best megalithic court-cairns. The site (signposted) lies off the road, just beyond the edge of the village of Cliffony. You'll see a burial area and an enclosed open-air "court" where rituals were performed around 2500 BC.

Here you're crossing the county line into Donegal, but the first
19 town reached could hardly be less typical of the area. **Bundoran** is one of Ireland's most popular seaside resorts, yet it remains remarkably unsophisticated, with little to offer except a long seafront development favored by Irish and Northern Irish family vacationers. While its souvenir shops and amusement arcades are not very appealing, it does have certain attractions. You'll find first-class golf facilities available on the edge of town at Aughrus Head, as well as horseback riding, and good fishing is 6½ km (4 mi) away at Lough Melvin. North of the town center you'll find another handsome beach at Tullan Strand, washed by the kind of waves that thrill surfers. Between the main beach and Tullan, some weird cliffside rock formations have been sculpted by the Atlantic's power. Something of a local spectacle, these natural creations have been given whimsical names such as the Fairy Bridges, the Wishing Chair, and the Puffing Hole (this last one blows wind and water from the waves pounding below).

Continue on the N15 for another 6½ km (4 mi) to reach
20 **Ballyshannon,** which rises gently from the banks of the River Erne. On the left-hand side of the road as it reaches the town, you'll see the factory of **Donegal Parian China** (tel. 072/51826), which produces exquisite fine chinaware and porcelain. Stop at the factory for one of the free 15-minute tours that are given all day from May to September. (You may be more familiar with chinaware from the older **Belleek Pottery,** which straddles the Republic–Northern Ireland border 6½ km/4 mi away. Both

companies produce a delicate cream-colored pottery of great value and elegance.)

Lough Erne marks an ancient frontier, and the Ballyshannon River crossing was for centuries the gateway into the Ulster region. Through the medieval period Ballyshannon was the southern stronghold of the O'Donnell clan, whose lands eventually became County Donegal. Today, Ballyshannon is a peaceful little town with mountain views; the surrounding area offers great opportunities for anglers because the local river and estuary are both teeming with fish. The town was also the birthplace of the prolific Irish poet William Allingham. Each year in early August, the normally quiet village springs to life with a grand festival of folk and traditional music (*see* The Arts and Nightlife, below).

Time Out In its triangular central area, Ballyshannon has several bars and places to grab a snack. The biggest and most popular pub is the green-shuttered **Seán Óg's,** which serves light Irish meals all day and features traditional music in the evenings.

Stay on the N15 toward Donegal Town, 21 km (13 mi) away. About a mile before you arrive in town, a sign on the right points to **Donegal Craft Village,** rather a grand name for a small roadside complex of new crafts shops. You can shop for imaginative pottery, handwoven goods, and ceramics and stop off at
21 a coffee shop that sells snacks. Then continue on into **Donegal,** turning past the town's small harbor amid trees on the edge of Donegal Bay. Here you'll find a view across the water, with its tiny islands and wooded banks, that is tranquil and delightful. The road brings you into a triangular main area called the Diamond (a common name for the central square of a former Plantation town). Donegal is a small, carefully-designed place, with a population of less than 2,000. Rebuilt in the 17th century, it still preserves a touch of the dignity of that era. Its history actually goes back a lot further than that Plantation period when Protestant colonists were planted on Irish property confiscated from their Catholic owners. Donegal was previously known in Irish as *Dun na nGall,* or "Foreigners' Fort." The foreigners in question were Vikings, who in the 9th century set up camp here to facilitate their pillaging and looting. After they had been driven out, the town was taken over by the powerful O'Donnell clan (originally Cinel Conail), who made it the capital of Tyrconail, their extensive Ulster territories.

Near the north corner of the Diamond, clan leader Hugh O'Donnell built **Donegal Castle** (in fact, a fortified tower house rather than a castle) in the 1470s. More than a century later, this structure was the home of his descendant Hugh Roe O'Donnell, who faced the might of the invading English. He was to be the last clan chief of Tyrconail. As the English made steady gains, in 1602 he went to Spain to rally reinforcements from his allies there and died overseas. The Irish faction at Donegal Castle was defeated by English forces and it came into the possession of Sir Basil Brooke. In 1610, he reconstructed the little castle, making it much more lordly and luxurious, and adding the fine Jacobean fortified mansion with towers and turrets that can still be seen today. Inside, note the large ornate fireplaces carved with Brooke's crest. *Tirchonaill St. Admission free. In summer months, unrestricted access; in winter, key from the caretaker (ask locally).*

In 1474, Hugh O'Donnell founded a monastery by the waterside of Donegal Town for the Franciscans, but it was partially destroyed by gunpowder in 1601 during a war with English invaders. Despite the damage, it was probably in this monastery that the *Annals of the Four Masters* were written from 1632 to 1636. This important tome chronicles the whole Celtic history and mythology of Ireland from earliest times up to the year 1618. The Four Masters were four monks who believed (correctly, as it turned out) that Celtic culture was doomed after the English conquest, and they wanted to preserve as much of it as they could. At the National Library in Dublin, you may see facsimile pages of the monks' work (the original is kept under lock and key). The monastery's gaunt ruins, impressive more for the location than for what survives of the buildings, can still be seen on the bank of Donegal Bay, just a few paces from the town center and sheltered behind a sea wall. What remains is the choir, south transept, and two sides of the cloisters. *Freely accessible.*

A monument to the Four Masters is situated in the Diamond. Around the three sides of the Diamond, you'll find popular bars, a couple of good old-fashioned hotels, and several shops stocked with high-quality Donegal tweeds and knitwear. Donegal Town has long been one of two principal marketplaces where the county's handcrafts are brought down from the hills to be sold to the rest of the world (the other is the village of Ardara; *see* below). Homespinning has almost disappeared now, but handweaving and knitting still contribute to the livelihood of thousands of country people. In small workshops attached to their rural cottages, they produce top-grade hand knits as well as what is regarded as the finest tweed in the world. Donegal Tweed is the name of a universally recognized style of cloth—a sturdy woolen fabric both soft and hard wearing, with distinctive mixed muted colors—that is still at its best when made in these Donegal mountains.

What makes the Donegal area so perfect for tweed-making? The natural humidity of the air is important, as is the extremely soft water of the River Eske that drains off the peat bogs and is used to wash the wool. If you've the time and inclination, and wish to judge the difference in quality, you might find it worthwhile to shop around the region for your hand knits and tweed clothes—several village outlets have lower prices than in Donegal Town (*see* Shopping, below).

One well-known shop on the Diamond is **Magee's,** a general clothing store founded in 1866. The original Mr. Magee handed down his business in 1887 to his young cousin Mr. Temple, and the company, now providing suitings to top department stores and clothing manufacturers all over the world, is still owned and run by the Temple family. Much of the stock that carries Magee's label is made in the store's own factory beside the River Eske, only a short walk from the shop. Magee's tweed jackets are said to be among the best in the world, yet they are not expensive if you buy them here. A tour of the weaving factory is fascinating, if a little rushed. You'll see how old-fashioned handwork can be combined with the most modern electronic looms, the two complementing each other. Signs around the factory explain to visitors what is going on. *The Diamond, tel. 073/21100. Free factory tour (lasts around 10 min). No definite times: the first tour starts at about 11, the last at about 3.*

Time Out If you feel hungry before or after looking at **Magee's,** you won't need to leave the shop to find a bite to eat. The store has its own restaurant on the premises, serving snacks and simple dishes such as baked potatoes, quiches, and salads, or scones and cakes ideal for an inexpensive afternoon tea.

The main road west is the N56, which runs slightly inland from a magnificent shoreline of rocky inlets with great sea views; it's worthwhile turning off the road from time to time to catch a better sight of the coast. About 6½ km (4 mi) out of Donegal Town, the N56 skirts **Mountcharles,** a bleak hillside village that looks back across the bay. Stay on the N56, which takes you through **Bruckless,** where you'll locate a good bed-and-breakfast accommodation, the 18th-century Georgian **Bruckless House** (tel. 073/37071; *see* Dining and Lodging, below). Don't be too impressed by the Round Tower in the churchyard here, which is not an authentic medieval structure but a 19th-century belfry. Soon after Bruckless, the N56 turns inland across the bogs toward Ardara, but this tour stays by the shore.

The road number now becomes R263, which runs through at-
22 tractive heathland and wooded hills down to **Killybegs.** This thriving little fishing port takes one by surprise, with its big trawlers from Spain and France moored in its welcoming harbor. Although it is by far the most industrialized place along this coast, the village retains a certain charm because of its waterfront setting. Killybegs also serves as a center for the manufacture of Donegal hand-tufted carpets. Examples of this much-sought-after product have found their way into such varied places as the White House and the Vatican.

After Killybegs, the R263 narrows, climbs, and twists, giving even better views of Donegal Bay before descending again into pretty **Kilcar,** a traditional center of tweed-making. The next village, signposted by its Irish name **An Charraig (Carrick),** clings to the foot of the Slieve League Mountains, whose color-streaked ocean cliffs are the highest in Ireland and among the most spectacular. To see them, you'll have to do some serious walking on a difficult coastal path, starting out from the Irish-speaking village of **Teelin,** a mile south from Carrick.

After another 8 km (5 mi), crossing barren moorland, the road
23 reaches **Gleann Cholm Cille (Glencolumbkille).** This tiny, spread-out hamlet clings to the rockbound harbor of Glen Bay, looking straight out to the pounding Atlantic. The name of this dramatic spot means St. Columba's Glen (or, alternatively, Columba's Glen Church), and the legend is that St. Columba, a Christian missionary (*see* Drumcliff, above), lived here for a while during the 6th century with a group of followers. Some 40 prehistoric cairns are scattered around the village, and these have become connected locally with the St. Columba myths. The **House of St. Columba,** on the clifftop rising north of the village, is a small oratory said to have been used by the saint himself. Inside, stone constructions are supposed to have been his bed and chair. Every year on June 9, starting at midnight, local people make a two-mile barefoot procession called *An Turas* (the journey) around 15 medieval crosses and ancient cairns, collectively called the Stations of the Cross.

The **Folk Village** near the beach in Glencolumbkille is an imaginative museum of rural life. The exhibit is arranged as a group of traditional-style cottages—representative of three centuries—which are described on a guided tour. The dwellings are true to the old life, with bare earth floors and very basic living conditions. The complex also offers a crafts shop, where high-quality local handmade products can be bought. There's also a tea shop with snacks. *No phone. Admission: £1.50. Open Easter–Sept., Mon.–Sat. 10–8, Sun. noon–3.*

From Glencolumbkille, if you drive 25½ km (16 mi) up and over the scenic curves of **Glengesh Pass** with a succession of switch-
24 backs, you'll go down to the sea again at **Ard an Ratha** (**Ardara**—say it with the accent on the *last a*). This unpretentious, old-fashioned hamlet of low, pale cottages among the green and brown hills is fortuitously situated at the head of a lovely ocean inlet. For centuries, Ardara has been an important wool-trading center, where great cloth fairs were held on the first of every month. Nowadays, a Weavers' Fair and Vintage Weekend is held only once a year, as near to July 1 as possible, and it has more to do with music, dance, and having fun than with selling homespuns. Ardara actually enjoys traditional music all year round; it has a large number of charming and popular pubs, though several seem to be doubling as shops.

Though the cloth fairs have died out, cottage workers in the surrounding countryside still provide Ardara (and County Donegal) with very high-quality handwoven cloths and, especially, hand knits. If you fancy a chunky Aran sweater, you'll find few better or less expensive places to look for one than this area. You'll have several stores to choose from (*see* Shopping, below). During the summer, Ardara attracts quite a large number of visitors and verges on being overcrowded. Yet the tourists make little real impact: Ardara holds loyally to its own traditions and history.

Time Out The long-established **Nesbitt Arms** (tel. 075/41103) in the village center is a reasonable place for a drink and a snack.

The N56, the Donegal coast's narrow and unfrequented "main road," runs through Ardara. Heading south to return to Donegal Bay and Donegal Town (40 km/25 mi), the road runs first across peat bogs—waterlogged grasslands of tawny, tweedy colors ruled across with black lines where the turf has been cut. North from Ardara, the road takes an erratic course up to **Dungloe** (40 km/25 mi), where you can begin the next tour.

Tour 3: Northern Donegal

Numbers in the margin correspond with the numbered points of interest on The Northern Peninsula map.

Traveling on northern County Donegal's country roads, you'll feel that you have escaped at last from all the world's hurry and hassle. True, the county's largest town, Letterkenny, is up here. And Letterkenny, with a population of 6,500, even has a set of traffic lights—the only traffic lights in the whole of the county. For the rest, you'll discover almost nothing but scenery: broad island-studded loughs of deep dark tranquillity; unkempt, windswept, sheep-grazed grasses on mountain slopes; ribbons of luminous greenery following sparkling streams; and the mellow colors of wide bog lands, all under shifting and changing cloudscapes. This tour, apart from Inishowen Peninsula, which is included as a separate excursion at the end, could take anywhere from one day to a week, depending on precisely how low a gear you slip into after a few breaths of Donegal air. You can cut the tour short if necessary, but try your best to catch the rewarding Fanad and Rosguill peninsulas and the drive around Sheephaven Bay.

25 We'll start from **Letterkenny;** although it may be the least attractive or interesting place on this whole tour, it is pleasingly down-to-earth. The bustling town center is just a single long street, lined with an array of small shops and pubs and dominated by an imposing 19th-century church. The main Donegal Tourist Information Office, loaded with maps, literature, and advice, can be found 1.6 km (1 mi) south on the Derry road, N13. *Tel. 074/21160. Open Sept.–May, weekdays 9–5; June, Mon.–Sat. 9–6; July–Aug., Mon.–Sat. 9–8, Sun. 10–2.*

The best thing about Letterkenny is its close proximity to great scenery in every direction. Take the R245 northward out
26 of town for 13 km (8 mi) to **Ramelton** (or Rathmelton, though the pronunciation is the same). A handsome little former Plantation town, it climbs uphill from a river harbor close to Lough Swilly. The village was the birthplace of Francis Makemie (1658–1708), who preached here before emigrating and founding the American Presbyterian church. Take the waterside road (the R247), which runs beside one of the loveliest of
27 Donegal's big fjordlike ocean inlets, **Lough Swilly.**

28 After 11 km (7 mi), you'll reach **Rathmullen,** an ancient harbor village among green fields, with little houses looking across curving Lough Swilly to the Inishowen hills on the other side. The view is especially good from the ruins of a 16th-century Carmelite fortified priory at the top of the village. Rathmullen's modest harbor, below, was once important; here, English naval officers, posing as ordinary merchant seamen, captured Red Hugh O'Donnell in 1587. They invited him aboard to taste some of their "cargo of foreign wines," and the sociable clan leader fell for it. Once on board, he was shipped to imprisonment in Dublin Castle. After six years he escaped and returned to Donegal with added determination to defend his homeland—but to no avail. In 1607, Rathmullen's harbor was the scene of the Flight of the Earls—the great exodus of Ulster nobility that brought to an end the 13-year war with the English. The million-acre Ulster territories became part of the English domain, and two years later the Plantation era began, the root cause of the "Troubles" that are still continuing across the border in Northern Ireland. The old fort near Rathmullen dock is what remains of a Martello Tower. Six of the towers—fortified defenses built in case Napoleon's army should invade to support the Irish cause—were erected around Lough Swilly. Just north of the village, **Rathmullan House** (tel. 074/58188) is a top-class country-house hotel. It is one of the best accommodations in the Northwest and has an excellent restaurant (*see* Dining and Lodging, below).

Extending north from here is the barren and rock-strewn
29 **Fanad Peninsula.** The signposted **Fanad Scenic Drive** takes you 27 km (17 mi) up beside Lough Swilly to low-lying Fanad Head at its northern tip, then down again through the tiny resort village of **Kerrykeel,** with views of long and narrow Mulroy Bay

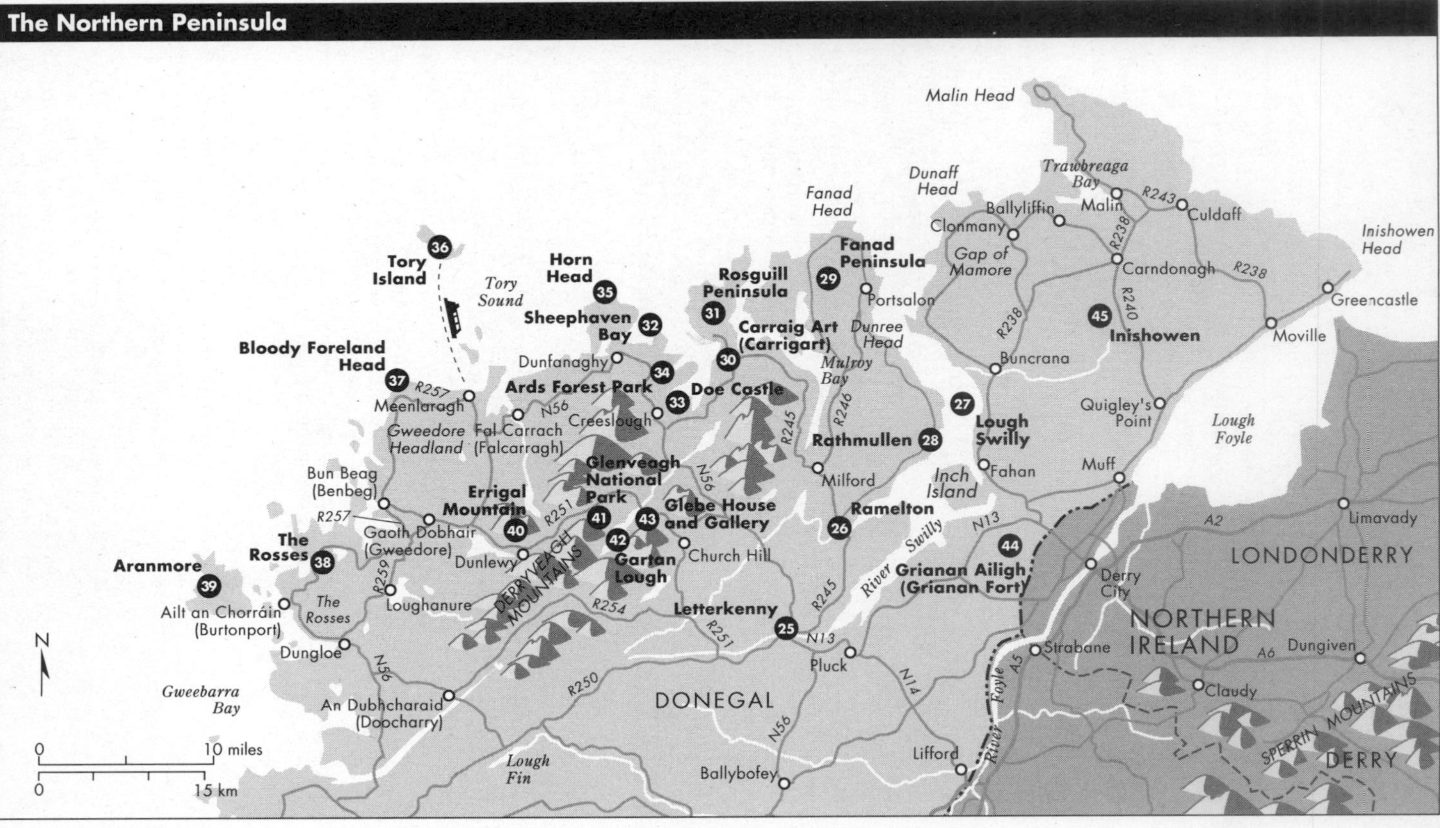
The Northern Peninsula
Malin Head
Trawbreaga Bay
Dunaff Head
Fanad Head
Malin
Culdaff
Ballyliffin
Clonmany
Gap of Mamore
Carndonagh
Inishowen Head
Greencastle
Moville
Fanad Peninsula
29
Portsalon
Rosguill Peninsula
31
45
Inishowen
Tory Island
36
Tory Sound
Horn Head
35
Sheephaven Bay
32
Carraig Art (Carrigart)
30
Dunree Head
Mulroy Bay
Buncrana
Bloody Foreland Head
37
Dunfanaghy
Ards Forest Park
34
33
Doe Castle
27
Lough Swilly
Quigley's Point
Lough Foyle
Meenlaragh
Creeslough
Gweedore Headland
Fal Carrach (Falcarragh)
Rathmullen
28
Glenveagh National Park
41
Milford
Inch Island
Fahan
Muff
Bun Beag (Benbeg)
Errigal Mountain
40
Glebe House and Gallery
43
Ramelton
26
Limavady
Gaoth Dobhair (Gweedore)
The Rosses
38
Aranmore
39
Dunlewy
42
Gartan Lough
Church Hill
River Swilly
Grianan Ailigh (Grianan Fort)
44
Derry City
LONDONDERRY
Ailt an Chorráin (Burtonport)
The Rosses
Loughanure
DERRYVEAGH MOUNTAINS
Letterkenny
25
NORTHERN IRELAND
Dungloe
Pluck
Strabane
Dungiven
Claudy
Gweebarra Bay
An Dubhcharaid (Doocharry)
DONEGAL
River Foyle
SPERRIN MOUNTAINS
DERRY
Lough Fin
Ballybofey
Lifford
R257
R259
R251
R254
R250
R245
R246
R238
R240
R243
N56
N13
N14
A2
A5
A6
N
0 10 miles
0 15 km

twisting and turning on the other side. If you want to cut the journey short, you can take the back road direct from Rathmullen to Kerrykeel for 9½ km (6 mi).

Time Out Passing through Kerrykeel, you might want to take advantage of its dining spots and bars. **The Village Restaurant** (tel. 074/50062), a family-run establishment, is the best place around for good home-cooked meals all day. The menu has plenty of choices, including three-course lunches at under £6. *Open June–Sept., daily. Closed the rest of the year Sun., Mon., Tues.*

After another 6½ km (4 mi) you'll reach sprawling **Milford;** turn
30 right onto the R245 to follow Mulroy Bay round to **Carraig Airt**
(Carrigart). The small village, with a lot of charm and many old-
fashioned taverns, gives access via a slender isthmus to
31 **Rosguill Peninsula,** which is extremely beautiful with its rocky
heart and its fringe of sand dunes and beaches. The signposted
Atlantic Drive circles the peninsula. This area is not as far off
the beaten track as you might think; you'll see several caravan
sites and self-catering cottages, popular with visitors from
Northern Ireland. At the little resort of **Downings,** visitors enjoy a long sandy beach, good fishing, and a chance to buy directly from **McNutts Homespun Tweeds Factory.** Westward are
32 views of the shallow, meandering inlets of **Sheephaven Bay.**

The R245 follows round the sandy shores of the Bay, first run-
33 ning down from Carraig Airt to the imposing waterside **Doe**
Castle, a tall weatherbeaten tower at the center of a complex
structure enclosed within sturdy defenses. The castle occupies
the southern end of Sheephaven Bay, at the foot of **Muckish**
Mountain just inland. The building is further protected by the
sea on three sides and by a rock-hewn moat on the fourth. Described by attacking English forces in 1587 as "the strongest
fortress in all the province," the impressive edifice dates back
at least to 1440, when it became the home of MacSweeney Doe,
one of the "gallowglasses" (from the Irish *gall o glach*)—
foreign mercenaries employed by the O'Donnell clan. Despite
the castle's present poor condition, it was still occupied by his
descendants until 1890. MacSweeney Doe's curiously carved
tombstone is fixed to the southwest tower of the outer wall.
Near Creeslough. Admission free. Usually open. If locked, in-
quire at caretaker's cottage on approach path.

You'll pass through adjacent **Creeslough** (pronounced *creesh-*
34 *la*), where the road becomes the N56, to reach **Ards Forest Park**
after a couple of miles. Clinging to Sheephaven Bay's southwest shore, the 1,188-acre national park is the former wooded
estate of a Capuchin friary; the friary itself is still occupied by
the Capuchins. Within the grounds are four prehistoric fortified sites and one dolmen. If the weather is fine, the park's forest trails and picnic sites provide a welcome opportunity to
enjoy some air and exercise. *Tel. 074/38021. Admission £1*
adults or £3 per family. Open daily 8 AM–9 PM.

Another 8 km (5 mi) on the N56 brings you into **Dun Fionnachaid (Dunfanaghy),** a tidy former Plantation village on the very edge of Sheephaven Bay. When the tide goes out, the vast sand flats of Killyhoey Beach are uncovered and the sea recedes into the far distance, but as it rises again the sands are submerged in double-quick time. On the west side of the village, the signpost to **McSwyne's Gun** (McSwyne is the old spelling of MacSweeney) leads to a huge natural blowhole that gives out a deafening bang when the tide rushes in during rough weather.

Time Out In Dunfanaghy, the **Carrig Rua** (tel. 074/36133)—the name's Irish for "red rock"—and **Arnold's** (tel. 074/36208) are both traditional village hotels on Main Street, offering decent unpretentious local fare at about £6 for lunch.

35 A little back road runs from Dunfanaghy up to **Horn Head,** the most spectacular of County Donegal's Atlantic headlands. From its sheer 186-m (600-ft) cliffs, you have access to great views along the coast to the other headlands ranged one behind the other. And bird-watchers will love it here—the cliffs are home to hundreds of seabirds, including puffin and guillemot.

From this point westward, the terrain is rougher, wilder, and rockier; you're also likely to hear the Irish language being spoken. The N56 reaches round 11 km (7 mi) to **Fal Carrach (Falcarragh),** the site of an Irish-language college.

Another 13 km (8 mi) around the rugged seashore, in good weather, you can catch a ferry from **Meenlaragh** (near
36 Gortahork) to **Tory Island.** Though just 14½ km (9 mi) offshore, Tory is strangely inaccessible; the weather is rarely right, and the currents are often difficult. Although the island is desolate, rocky, and barren—without a single tree—it has been inhabited since prehistoric times. The local people talk their own Irish dialect and refer to the mainland as "Ireland," considering themselves almost as a separate miniature nation. You'll find medieval and prehistoric relics scattered all over the ocean-battered landscape, notably the **Round Tower** of pink granite, partly ruined but still with its conical cap poised on the cliffs. At the island's eastern end, **Balor's Fort** is a prehistoric fortress, supposed to have been the residence of Balor, the terrifying one-eyed Celtic god of night and darkness. Tory Islanders are not above believing in such things. At the center of the island, the **wishing stones** have the power, it is said, to destroy enemies. Still talked about today is the time, in 1884, when the stones were turned against the British gunboat *Wasp* that came filled with police to collect taxes—which Tory Islanders are unaccustomed to paying. The ship sank, and all but six of the crew were lost. Most of the islanders don't earn enough to pay tax in any case and live simple lives as fishermen. Quite a few, however, have unexpected sidelines as artists, ever since 1968, when the well-known Irish painter Derek Hill chanced to meet islander James Dixon; Dixon felt that he could do a better job of painting than Hill. Many other Tory Island residents thought they could, too, and today the Tory Island artists, depicting their own life and landscape in a naive style, are widely acclaimed and have exhibited abroad.

Because no accommodation is available on Tory Island, be sure to ask before making the crossing to ensure that a return will be possible the same day. Returning to Meenlaragh on the mainland, you're on the edge of the **Gweedore** headland, which you can follow round on the R257, the coast road. Gweedore is rocky, sparsely covered with heather and gorse, and low-lying
37 until you reach its farthest point, **Bloody Foreland Head.** This dramatic name for once does not recall the slaughter of some

historic battle but describes instead the vivid red hues of the gaunt rock face when lighted up at sunset.

Follow the shore road south another 13 km (8 mi) to **Bun Beag (Benbeg)** and **Croithli (Crolly),** at the meeting between Gwee-
38 dore and the next distinctive headland, called **The Rosses.** On both Gweedore and The Rosses, the bleak but dramatic terrain has not benefited from a liberal sprinkling of modern bungalows.

The Rosses, though similar to Gweedore, is more beautiful. The coast road, the R259, struggles over the unbelievably stony and inhospitable landscape, crisscrossed with water channels and strewn with myriad ponds. Yet quite a number of people manage to survive here, many of them Irish speakers. The decline of population and living standards was reversed by Patrick Gallagher (1873–1964), who became known as Paddy the Cope. Son of a poor local family, he left school at 10, went to Scotland as a farmhand, and saved enough money to return home in the 1950s and buy a smallholding of his own. Gallagher, very affectionately remembered throughout the area, persuaded the citizens around The Rosses to set up cooperatives to bring in new farming methods and machinery, as well as cooperatively owned stores to keep prices down.

Staying on the R259, after 16 km (10 mi) you will reach **Ailt an Chorráin (Burtonport),** which claims to land more salmon and lobster than any other fishing port in Ireland. This village is
39 the departure point for a trip over to **Aranmore,** 6½ km (4 mi) offshore. Aranmore means "big island," and it is indeed the largest and most populous of County Donegal's rocky offshore fragments. The ride out takes 25 minutes and costs £2 (seven crossings daily), but although fairly accessible, the island still feels remote and ungoverned. It has been inhabited for thousands of years—witness the prehistoric fort on its south side—and offers good fishing, as well as striking cliff scenery and views back onto The Rosses.

If you drive 6½ km (4 mi) farther round the coast, the R259 rejoins N56 at **An Clochan Liath (Dungloe),** a pleasant little fishing town regarded as the capital of The Rosses, though you'll find little to do or see here.

Next, start the journey back to Letterkenny. The N56 takes you direct to Croithli (Crolly) in 13 km (8 mi), a quicker journey than going back along the coast road. Stay on the N56 north until you're a couple of miles beyond **Gaoth Dobhair (Gweedore)** village, on the little River Clady, and take the R251 to skirt the
40 south side of **Errigal Mountain** to the village of **Dunlewy,** altogether only about 13 km (8 mi) from Crolly. This whole drive features great scenery, some of the best in County Donegal. Serene Errigal looks especially grand from Dunlewy. Follow the R251 round as the road is edged northward by the **Derryveagh Mountains.**

After 16 km (10 mi), the road brings you to the main gate of
41 **Glenveagh National Park.** You must leave your vehicle at the entrance; a shuttle bus will take you farther into the park, or you may walk. Also at the gate, you'll see a Visitor Center with a permanent exhibition on the local way of life and on the influence of climate on the park's flora and fauna. The 24,000-acre protected wilderness has a thick carpet of russet-colored heath and dense woodland that rolls down the Derryveagh slopes into

the broad open valley of the River Veagh (or Owenbeagh). At the center of the park is the dark and clear **Lough Beagh,** and on a ledge overlooking the long narrow lake stands the elaborately battlemented **Glenveagh Castle,** a most improbable edifice that looks exactly like what it is: a 19th-century folly. For all that, it's actually a grand, luxurious house inside, and its exotic, extensive gardens are also a sheer delight. Beyond the castle, footpaths lead into more remote sections of the park, where you may suddenly chance upon a herd of shy red deer or catch sight of a soaring falcon.

These Glenveagh lands were always known as a remote and beautiful region. They were brought together under single ownership by a ruthless gentleman farmer, John George Adair, who gradually acquired the estate, including its hundreds of poor tenants, between 1857 and 1859. In 1861, he evicted all the tenants without compensation and destroyed their cottages. Adair had the lakeside castle built in 1870, but immediately he went to live in Texas. Adair died in 1885 without returning to Ireland, but his wife, Cornelia, perhaps intrigued by the thought of her husband's castle, crossed the Atlantic to make Glenveagh her home. She lived extravagantly and spent a fortune to make the four different gardens and the walks as lovely as they are today; it was she who planted the luxuriant rhododendrons here. In 1984, the last owner of Glenveagh, U.S. millionaire Henry P. McIlhenny, generously presented the estate to the nation, after years of carefully maintaining and restoring the area. *Glenveagh National Park, Church Hill, Letterkenny, tel. 074/37088 or 074/37090. Admission: £1 adults, 40p children, 70p senior citizens. Several footpaths are available, including Derrylahan Nature Trail, a 1.6-km (1-mi) signposted trail. Guided walks can be arranged. Open Easter, and June–Sept. daily 10:30–6:30. Guided tours of the castle: £1 adults, 40p children, 70p senior citizens. May–Oct., Tues.–Sun. 10:30–6:30.*

Time Out A cafeteria conveniently located in the park's Visitor Center serves such café food as fish and chips, or tea and scones. A full meal will cost you about £5.

---

42 It is 13 km (8 mi) from Glenveagh on the R251 to reach **Gartan Lough** (close to Church Hill village), although the lake is technically within the national park and is administered partly by the park authorities.

The lake and its surrounding mountain country are marvelously beautiful. St. Columba was supposedly born here in AD 521, and the legendary event is marked by a huge cross (at the beginning of a footpath into the national park). Nearby, you'll find other dubious "relics" of the saint that are popularly believed to possess magical powers, such as the Natal Stone, where he is thought to have first opened his eyes, and the Stone of Loneliness, where he is said to have slept.

43 More satisfying is a visit to **Glebe House,** which consists of a fine Regency manor and 25 acres of gardens that are situated on the northwest shore of the lake, just off the R251. The former home of the distinguished artist Derek Hill, it now serves as a remarkable gallery displaying Hill's extensive art collection, which includes works by Picasso, Renoir, and other great Impressionists; paintings by Yeats's brother, Jack; and intriguing

examples of the work of the Tory Islanders (*see* above). The decoration and furnishings of the house, including original William Morris wallpaper, are worth a look as well. In 1981, Derek Hill handed over this treasure trove of art to the nation. *Church Hill, tel. 074/37071. Admission: £1. Open Easter and May–Oct., Tues.–Sat. 11–6:30, Sun. 1–6:30.*

If you want to learn more about St. Columba and his times, return to the R251 and turn right almost at once onto the R254 in Church Hill. Straight away you'll arrive at the **Colmcille Heritage Centre.** This exhibition and interpretation center features medieval manuscripts, stained glass, and displays tracing the decline of the Celtic religion and the rise of Ireland's Christianity. *Gartan, Church Hill, tel. 074/21160. Admission: £1. Open May, Sept., Oct., Mon.–Sat. 11–6:30, Sun. 1–6:30; June–Aug., Mon–Sat. 10–6:30, Sun. noon–6:30.*

If you stay on the R251, you'll be back in Letterkenny after 16 km (10 mi). One more major peninsula in the region is worth exploring—the huge Inishowen, the most northerly part of Ireland. This grandly wild piece of land remains unspoiled despite a string of small and untempting coast resorts. For the 160-km (100-mi) Inishowen circuit, plus the 64-km (40-mi) round-trip to reach it from Letterkenny, you would need to allow at least a whole day. If time is short, however, you can easily see the best of Inishowen in a much shorter time.

44 If nothing else, visit the Celtic fort **Grianan Ailigh (Grianan Fort).** Take the main Derry road, the N13, from Letterkenny. After 29 km (18 mi), keep a look out for signs to Buncrana, because the easy-to-miss sign for the fort is opposite. Instead of turning to Buncrana, take the narrow lane that climbs and turns for more than a mile to reach the fortress, on top of a 251-m (810-ft) hill. The most striking thing here is the site itself, with an immense panorama of the rolling Donegal and Derry landscape below. To the north, you're given an exquisite aerial view of the Swilly estuary, flowing around Inch Island into Lough Swilly. On either side rise the hills, often partly veiled by mists, of the Fanad and Inishowen peninsulas.

As for the fort, what you'll see is a circular stone enclosure—the diameter is about 23½ m (76 ft)—that you can enter through a gate (open most of the year). Inside, you'll find further concentric defenses, with passages within the walls and earth ramparts that surround a sturdy central structure. No one knows when Grianan Fort was built, but it was probably an Iron Age fortress: its position was accurately recorded in the 2nd century AD by the geographer Ptolemy of Alexandria. Later it became the seat of Ulster's O'Neill chieftains and remained so for many centuries despite serious attempts made by their enemies to destroy it, especially in the year 674 and again in 1101. The present-day fortress, however, owes a good deal to overzealous "restoration" in the 1870s; before that, it was in ruins. *Freely accessible.*

Go back to the N13 and cross straight over to take the Buncrana turning. When you meet the R238, another main road coming from Derry City—the town is only 8 km (5 mi) away—turn left.
45 You're now on **Inishowen,** a green pastoral peninsula with a solid mountainous interior, enclosed by Lough Swilly on one side, Lough Foyle on another, and the battering Atlantic to the north. Following the R238, you pass **Fahan,** with its monastic

ruins, and **Buncrana,** a popular down-market beach resort much favored by people from Derry City. It has a 14th-century O'Docherty tower that gradually became part of an 18th-century mansion. Shortly after you pass Buncrana, turn left at the fork in the road away from the R238 to stay by the coast, driving past the 19th-century fort on **Dunree Head,** up and over the spectacular viewpoint of the **Gap of Mamore,** down toward **Dunaff Head** where Lough Swilly opens into the ocean. Rejoin the R238 at **Clonmany** and take it through **Ballyliffin,** another small resort town with an O'Docherty tower on the beach.

Time Out Ballyliffin is a convenient place for a snack or meal. Try **The Strand Hotel** (tel. 077/76107), a likable family-run establishment offering well-prepared home-cooked lunches, with a three-course menu for under £8.

By the junction of the R238 and the R240, you'll see a church with a curious remnant of early Christianity against one wall, the decorated 7th-century **Donagh Cross,** accompanied by a couple of pillar stones. The strange carvings on the stones clearly date from a pre-Christian period. Turn the corner into **Carndonagh,** a village featuring several more medieval monastic remains. The road then runs up beside **Trawbreaga Bay,** through picturesque **Malin** village on the waterside up to **Malin Head,** Ireland's most northerly point. Although it does have good views, Malin Head is not as dramatic a spot as some of the other headlands.

Take the signposted route across the peninsula from Malin Head to **Moville,** a sleepy waterside resort on the Lough Foyle side. The drive takes 8 km (5 mi) from here to the peninsula's rocky eastern tip, **Inishowen Head.** On the way, at **Greencastle,** you'll see the fortifications of foreigners who tried to control the nine counties of Ulster: a 14th-century Anglo-Norman fortress and an English fort built five centuries later to defend against French support for the Irish. The drive along the lough shore toward Derry City is attractive but punctuated by small, uninteresting villages that cater at modernized pubs to day (or evening) visitors from Derry. If you want to turn away from Derry toward Letterkenny before reaching the border, take the R239 from **Muff** to **Bridge End,** where, incidentally, you can find one of the most attractive of Ireland's many new Catholic churches.

Off the Beaten Track

Ballymote and Carrowkeel Start out by traveling about 11 km (7 mi) from Sligo Town south on the N4. Turn right onto the N17 and right again onto an unfrequented minor road, the R293, between meadows and woods for a further 13 km (8 mi) toward **Ballymote,** a tiny, appealing village. Once a place of importance with an imposing castle, it is now in ruins. A powerful Anglo-Norman Ulster earl, Richard de Burgo, built the fortress in the 14th century, and for centuries afterward it stood firm against any English conquest of the Northwest. The castle's six towers still stand. Close by is another ruin, that of the Franciscan friary where the *Book of Ballymote* was written in 1391. This tome, now located at the Royal Irish Academy in Dublin, holds tremendous significance to historians, because it enabled them to unravel the secrets of the old Ogham alphabet. This system of writing with just 20 letters was inscribed on Celtic standing stones, especially those dating from about the 4th and 5th centuries.

If you would like to see a major Bronze Age site, head down the unnumbered road that goes the 8 km (5 mi) from Ballymote to Castlebaldwin. From here, you'll be able to walk to the large **Carrowkeel** burial ground. It takes awhile to get up to the site, but you'll see 14 cairns (you can actually go inside three of them) and a panoramic view when you arrive.

The Leitrim Lakes The hilly landscape of unspoiled County Leitrim is dappled with clean cool lakes. Anglers love this area because its peaceful waters are filled with fish. Despite a liberal sprinkling of villages, in reality the county is almost uninhabited. Even its largest town, bright and bustling **Carrick-on-Shannon,** has a population of less than 2,000 people. The town has plenty of lively bars, and you can hire a boat here to tour the Shannon. Carrick is a good base for a quick look around the vicinity. Take the R280 north from the town to **Drumshanbo** at the tip of huge **Lough Allen.** From here, the R208 turns back to **Drumcong** village and the small lakes **Scur** and **St. John.** Where the R208 meets the R202, turn right for Fenagh, and then right again onto the R209 to return along the south side of the lakes into Carrick. If you were to continue beyond Fenagh, you would reach **Mohill,** birthplace of Turlough O'Carolan, the 18th-century blind harpist regarded as the last of the Celtic bards. His most famous composition was adapted for "The Star-Spangled Banner." South of Carrick, labyrinthine back lanes meander across the broad **Shannon** and the lakes—**Boderg, Bofin,** and **Kilglass**—that straddle the river.

Lough Derg This site is really out of the way, yet tens of thousands determinedly beat a path to this lonely lake, ringed by heather-clad slopes, throughout the period from Whitsunday to the Feast of the Assumption (that is, from June to mid-August). In the center of the lough, Station Island, which is known as St. Patrick's Purgatory, is one of Ireland's most popular pilgrimage sites, even though it is also the most rigorous and austere of such sites in the country. Pilgrims stay on the island for three days, taking no sleep and no food except black tea and dry toast. They walk barefoot around the island, on its flinty stones, to pray at a succession of shrines. The pilgrimage has been followed since time immemorial; during the Middle Ages, it attracted large numbers of devotees from foreign lands.

You can reach the shores of Lough Derg by turning off the main Sligo–Donegal road (N15) onto the minor Pettigo road (R232), which hauls itself over the Black Gap and descends sharply into the border village of Pettigo, about 21 km (13 mi) from the N15. From here, take the Lough Derg (8 km/5 mi) access road. *If you would like to know more about St. Patrick's Purgatory in order to become a pilgrim, write: Reverend Prior, Lough Derg, Pettigo, Co. Donegal. Nonpilgrims may not visit the island June–mid-Aug.*

Shopping

The outstanding specialties of the Northwest are high-quality handwoven tweeds and hand knits. Smart traditional tweed sports jackets, comfortable yet long-lasting, are one of the best buys. The region is also a good place to purchase Aran sweaters; they are knitted with distinctive crisscross patterns and are made of plain undyed wool. The sweaters are also soft but durable. Not so long ago, these warm weatherproof pullovers were worn by every County Donegal fisherman, usually made to a design belonging exclusively to his own family. Patterns are not so secret now, allowing greater variety in the knitwear, but all the sweaters have that unmistakable Aran look. High-quality machine-made tweeds are also available. All these wool-based items have been made here for centuries, and you'll find that prices are astonishingly low. You'll also want to look out for locally made parian china, a thin, fine, and pale product of very high quality and workmanship. Elaborate flower motifs and a "basket weave" design are two distinctive features of this china, which has been a specialty of Belleek, on the Donegal–Fermanagh border, for more than 100 years. In recent years, it has also developed in and around Ballyshannon.

Ardara

This attractive village features several stores that sell handweaving and locally made knitwear. Nowadays the stores usually commission goods directly from cottage outworkers and provide them with the wool and patterns. Prices are about as low as you'll find anywhere. You can get an especially good deal on handsome, chunky Aran hand-knitted sweaters (£30–£70). You'll find cardigans (similar prices) and scarves (£12) in the same style. You can pick up a pure wool handwoven tweed tie for about £4. A wide choice of ready-to-wear tweeds are carried in all the stores; good-quality tweed sports jackets for women (up to about £150) as well as men (up to £80) are a bargain. The shops here also stock a selection of traditional Irish products from other parts of the country (glassware and linen, for example). The main stores, all recommended, are **Kennedy's** (tel. 075/41106), at the top end of the main street; **John Molloy** (tel. 075/41133), on the Killybegs road; and **C. Bonner & Son** (tel. 075/41196), on Front Street.

Ballyshannon and Belleek

Donegal Irish Parian China (tel. 072/51826), situated just south of Ballyshannon on the N15, is the Republic's largest manufacturer of parian china. Visitors are welcome to take free 15-minute tours of the workshops (May–Sept., daily 9:30–4:30) and can take advantage of lower factory prices. Traditional methods of manufacture are used, and most of the work is done by hand. The least expensive items, miniature vases, cost around £8. A full tea set starts from £170.

From Ballyshannon, the R230 runs along the south bank of the River Erne toward Belleek. Right beside the Garda (Irish police) checkpoint, 1.6 km (1 mi) before the border to Northern Ireland, you'll find **Celtic Weave China** (tel. 072/51844), a small family business that produces high-quality parian china. The company specializes in the basket-weave design and in elaborate floral decoration, creating many one-of-a-kind pieces on commission for prestigious organizations around the world. A single piece of china will be made to your own specifications if you wish. Extremely delicate-looking handpainted china "flower baskets" are also available (though in fact this type of chinaware is not as fragile as it appears). Most pieces cost under £100.

Continue on the same road, into Belleek in Northern Ireland, where **Belleek Pottery** stands beside the Erne River. This is the best-known producer of Belleek chinaware. The visitor center here acts as a showroom for the company's wide range of elegant products. Although this is not within the limits of our Northwest region, you'll find Belleek china in the shops of Donegal and Sligo (*see* also Chapter 10).

Donegal Town

Donegal Town has long been the principal marketplace for the region's wool products. There are several smaller shops retailing local handweaving and knits, but the town's principal store is **Magee's** (tel. 073/21100), which occupies a prime position on the Diamond, the town's central area. Look especially for items with Magee's own label; the store has its own factory in town making garments and fabrics for major clothing companies and big-name department stores. Tweed jackets cost around £115 for men and £100 for women; men's suits are priced at £175, and ladies' suits at £185; skirts cost about £50. Aran sweaters are also available from around £65–£75. You can even buy Magee's best-quality tweed by the roll at £16 per yard. For a smart handcrafted hat of tweed and Irish linen, stroll five minutes up Tirconaill Street, past the castle and the post office, to **Hanna's Hats** (tel. 073/21084). About 1.6 km (1 mi) south of town, right beside the main N15, the **Donegal Craft Village** is a complex of new workshops where you can buy pottery, handweaving, and ceramics from local young craftspeople and watch the items being made.

Kilcar

For a fine selection of handwoven goods and other local crafts, stop off at **Studio** (tel. 073/38194). The store also features a tea shop on the premises.

Killybegs

County Donegal's exclusive hand-tufted carpets are made at Killybegs by **Donegal Carpets** (tel. 073/31021).

Sligo Town

For a large selection of hand-knit and hand-loomed sweaters and all other woolen goods, try **P. F. Dooney & Son** (36 O'Connell St., tel. 071/2274). **Cosgrove's of Sligo** (32 Market St., tel. 071/42809), which retains its original 19th-century shop front, stocks fine foods to satisfy hungry tourists; it also has a crafts section with a selection of pottery, watercolors, and other works by local artists.

Sports

Participant Sports

Bicycling Bicycle rentals are available in **Ardara** from **Donal Byrne** (West End, tel. 075/41156), in **Carrick-on-Shannon** from **Geraghty's** (Main St. tel. 094/31019), in **Donegal Town** from **C. J. Doherty** (Main St., tel. 073/21119), in **Ramelton** from **Hugh Whoriskey** (tel. 074/51022), and in **Sligo Town** from **Gary's Cycles** (Quay St., tel. 071/45418). Many of these rental shops have mountain bikes for cycling in rough hill country. The Northwest is mostly hard but rewarding cycling country, with some steep climbs and strong winds at times, but with plenty of low-cost accommodations, marvelous scenery, and empty roads. These conditions are perfect for keen cyclists, but others may also prefer to use a bike simply for some gentle meandering around a small area.

Bird-watching Bird-watchers have access to a large variety and population of bird life on County Donegal's northern headlands. Most of the bird species are not resident; huge numbers of winter and summer migrants land here. Bird sanctuaries are located on **Inch Island** in Lough Swilly (with a considerable number of whooper swan in the fall), on the **Lough Foyle** shore of Inishowen (with wigeon, waterfowl, and waders in the fall), at **Horn Head** (with Ireland's largest colony of razorbill, as well as puffin and guillemot), and at **Sheskinmore Lough** (with geese, ducks, and waders) near Ardara. The sand and mud flats of **Sligo Bay** attract geese, and in the grounds of **Lissadell House** at Rosses Point, you'll find flocks of barnacle geese. For more information contact the **Irish Wildbird Conservancy** (Southview, Church Rd., Greystones, Co. Wicklow, tel. 01/875759).

Fishing No license is needed for sea fishing. For game fishing (salmon and sea trout), the license costs £10 for 21 days, or £25 for a full season. For all coarse and pike angling, a license costs £5 for 21 days or £10 for a year; senior citizens are exempt from these latter costs. A composite license covering all freshwater fish is available for £40. The licenses can be obtained for County Donegal from the **Northern Regional Fishery Board** (Ballyshannon, tel. 071/51435) and for Counties Sligo and Leitrim from the **North-Western Regional Fisheries Board** (Ballina, Co. Mayo, tel. 096/22623). Some tackle shops are also permitted to sell licenses.

Tackle Shops **County Donegal: John McGill** (Main St., Ardara); **O'Doherty's** (Main St., Donegal Town); and **Pat Barrett** (Bundoran).

County Leitrim: The Creel or **Geraghty's** (both on Main St., Carrick-on-Shannon) and **Aodh Flynn** (Manorhamilton).

County Sligo: Barton Smith (Hyde Bridge, Sligo Town).

Fishermen will find that the best area for brown trout is located around Bundoran, including Lough Melvin. In western County Donegal, you'll have good opportunities for catching sea trout. Plenty of salmon and brown trout live in the rivers of southern County Donegal and northern County Sligo. More brown trout can be found in the loughs near Dunfanaghy in northern County Donegal, near Bundoran on the border of Donegal and Sligo counties, and in the border area of Sligo and Leitrim counties.

Pike anglers and coarse anglers can cast their lines in the abundant County Leitrim lakes.

Golf The Northwest has a large number of nine- and 18-hole courses, most in seaside locations, and several of them are world-class. For a full list, you'll need to contact the Irish Tourist Board or local Tourist Information Offices. The Northwest's best 18-hole courses, which all welcome visitors, include **Bundoran Golf Club** (tel. 072/41360), on the cliffs above Bundoran beach; **Donegal Golf Club** (tel. 073/21262), at Murvagh; **County Sligo Golf Club** (tel. 071/77134) at Rosses Point, which has hosted just about every Irish championship; **The North West Golf Club** (tel. 074/61027), near Buncrana on Inishowen Peninsula; **Rosapenna Golf Club** (tel. 074/55301), 24 km (15 mi) northwest of Letterkenny; and **Enniscrone Golf Club** (tel. 096/36297), in the midst of lovely scenery close to the Enniscrone resort on the County Sligo coast about 14½ km (9 mi) north of Ballina. Expect to pay greens fees of around £10 a day.

Hiking Trails in the Northwest provide the experienced walker with challenging opportunities. It helps to be able to read a map, and on high ground you're wise not to take any chances with the weather, which can suddenly become wet and misty. The mountain districts (such as the Blue Stacks, near Donegal Town) offer rough walks with dramatic views. There are long-distance footpaths across County Donegal, in County Leitrim, and around Lough Gill in County Sligo. For information about these walking routes, contact **Field Officer, Long Distance Walking Routes Committee** (Cospoir, 11th floor, Hawkins House, Dublin 9). Good shorter trails are also accessible, clearly marked, within Glenveagh National Park in northwest County Donegal.

Horseback Riding/Pony Trekking For hacking, trekking, and other horseback sport by the hour, the day, or for longer periods, contact **Carrigart Riding Stables** (tel. 074/55114) at the foot of the Rosguill Peninsula; **Lenamore Stables** (tel. 077/84022), at Muff on Inishowen Peninsula; **Rockhill Trekking Centre** (tel. 074/50012), at Kerrykeel on the Fanad Peninsula; **Stracomer Riding School** (tel. 072/41787), at Bundoran on the south County Donegal coast; and the **Evans Stables** (tel. 073/37071), at Bruckless on the north coast of Donegal Bay. To canter along sandy beaches interspersed with cliff walks, try **The Old Rectory Stables** (tel. 071/63221), in Drumcliff at the foot of Ben Bulben. Several other establishments offer full riding vacations including lodging; the details are shown in a leaflet from the Irish Tourist Board, or for more information, contact **The Association of Irish Riding Establishments** (Mespil Hall, Kill, Co. Kildare, tel. 045/77208 or 045/77299).

Surfing For **surfing,** head to Strandhill, Rossnowlagh, and Bundoran on the south County Donegal coast (if you need to rent equipment), or to Marble Strand and Rosapenna in north County Donegal (if you have all your own gear). These areas offer excellent conditions for world-class surfing. Ask the **Irish Surfing Association** (Tigh-na-Mara, Rossnowlagh, Co. Donegal, tel. 073/21053) for more specific information.

Dining and Lodging

Dining

by Andrew Sanger and Georgina Campbell

The Northwest is not usually considered a great gastronomic center. You can expect meals to be generally plain and simple, but the servings are generous, with a filling portion of potatoes. Still, the food ingredients used in dishes are of good quality and are locally produced. Fish, fresh from the sparkling clean rivers and loughs, could hardly be better. The region has only a few fine restaurants of distinction. In the rural districts, your best bet is to choose a hotel or guest house that can provide a decent evening meal as well as breakfast.

Category	Cost*
Very Expensive	over £20
Expensive	£15–£20
Moderate	£10–£15
Inexpensive	under £10

**per person for a typical three-course meal, including tax and service but excluding drinks.*

Lodging

Although the Northwest is a far-flung corner of Ireland, the choice of good bed-and-breakfasts and small hotels in the region is excellent because of the constant influx of visitors, particularly in July and August. The traditional provincial hotels in Sligo Town, Donegal Town, and the small coastal resorts in between, have been modernized and equipped with all the necessary comforts, yet they retain the charm that comes with older buildings and their sense of personalized service. However, away from these areas, your options are more restricted, and your best overnight option, with some exceptions, is usually a modest guest house offering bed, breakfast, and an evening meal.

Many of the modern Irish guest houses recommended below are similar to one another in what they have to offer: they are often one-story buildings with undistinguished contemporary furniture and not much character. Many provide peat fires and merely adequate meals. For the most part, however, visitors will find hosts friendly, helpful, and concerned about keeping their properties clean and well-maintained.

A particular pleasure may be gained by staying in an Irish-speaking home. With a little bit of luck, the local Irish Tourist Information Offices can be helpful in making a booking with a family who speaks Irish. In Counties Donegal, Leitrim, and Sligo, you can also stay at some first-class country-house hotels where you are welcomed with gracious professionalism.

Category	Cost*
Very Expensive	over £80
Expensive	£60–£80
Moderate	£40–£60
Inexpensive	under £40

**All prices are for a standard double room, including breakfast and tax.*

Highly recommended restaurants and hotels are indicated by a star ★.

Ardara

Dining and Lodging

Bay View House. On the outskirts of the village, this modern, well-kept bungalow offers bed and breakfast, as well as a peaceful location with superb sea views. You can relax in front of a peat fire in the guest lounge with picture windows, and enjoy tasty traditional Irish home cooking in the dining room. *Mrs. Bennett, Bay View House, Portnoo Rd., Ardara, Co. Donegal, tel. 075/41145. 7 rooms with shower. Facilities: tea-making equipment in rooms, games room, dining room. Book evening meal before noon. V. Closed Nov. 16–Feb. Inexpensive.*

Greenhaven House. Another good B&B, this establishment is an excellent value for the money. Located only a few minutes from the village, the comfortable modern one-story home has its own gardens and marvelous views of the nearby mountains and bay. You'll be warmed by a peat fire in the lounge and wake up to a hearty breakfast. The family who runs the place can advise you on shopping for handknits and other items. *Mrs. Eileen Molloy, Greenhaven House, Portnoo Rd., Ardara, Co. Donegal, tel. 075/41129. 6 rooms with shower. No evening meal. No credit cards. Closed Oct.–Feb. Inexpensive.*

★ **Woodhill Guest House.** This spacious home of the Yeats family (no relation to the famous poet) stands on 4 acres of wooded grounds only ½ km (¼ mi) from the village. The residence once belonged to the Nesbitts, former landlords of Ardara. The house has a cream-colored Victorian exterior, but parts of the interior date back to the 17th century. The fine front public areas feature high ceilings and marble fireplaces; the hall has a lovely round table and stained glass window. Bedrooms are less grand but large, offering superb mountain views. You'll find this an amiable, relaxed place, with frequent Irish folk music sessions presented in the bar. The best feature here is the high-quality home-cooked food. The moderately priced restaurant seats 40 and attracts visitors and locals alike. Cordon bleu à la carte meals, in a French-Irish style, rely upon fresh local ingredients. Typical dishes include salmon with garlic and spinach sauce, accompanied by seasonal vegetables; or rack of lamb with herbs that are picked from the family garden. The elaborate desserts are also all homemade. The breakfast eggs, by the way, couldn't be fresher because the Yeatses have their own hens. *Mr. and Mrs. Yeats, Woodhill Guest House, Donegal Rd., Ardara, Co. Donegal, tel. 075/41112. 5 rooms without* *bath. Facilities: restaurant, bar, fishing, clay-pigeon shoots. AE, MC, V. Inexpensive.*

Ballymote

Dining and Lodging ★

Temple House. Well off the beaten track, and undoubtedly one of the most unusual B&Bs anywhere, this vast country mansion with a pillared entrance is outwardly gray and austere; the approximately 100 rooms are decorated and furnished in the Georgian and Victorian styles, with highly polished mahogany tables and sideboards, and the original rugs. This is not a country-house hotel, but a working, organic farm, surrounded by more than 1,000 acres of land. It belongs to Sandy and Deb Perceval and has belonged to their family since 1665. Within the grounds, you'll find the ruins of the original fortified manor house, built to incorporate a historic Knights Templar castle; guests can also visit formal terraced gardens and a private lake with waterside footpaths. The huge bedrooms feature authentic Victorian curtains, marble-top washstands, polished floorboards, dressing tables, and huge shuttered windows. Deb Perceval prepares a good evening meal, using farm-fresh produce; top-class wines are served. The traditional Irish breakfasts are generous. The Percevals make no pretense of offering modern facilities. Among the six bedrooms, all have hot and cold water but only one has a full private bath. No television is available. *Mrs. D. Perceval, Temple House, Ballymote, Co. Sligo, tel. 071/83329. 6 rooms, 1 with bath. Facilities: boating, shooting, fishing; golfing and horseback riding about 24 km (15 mi) away. AE, V. Moderate.*

Ballyshannon

Dining and Lodging

Danby House. Just 1.6 km (1 mi.) out of town on the coast road, you'll discover this pleasant guest house and restaurant with its own walled gardens, set on 20 acres of grounds overlooking the Erne estuary of Donegal Bay. The white-and-black building with shuttered windows dates from 1820 and features large, well-proportioned rooms with impressive fireplaces. Bedrooms are furnished with antiques, including mahogany wardrobes, dressing tables, and four-poster beds. The house features one of the best French-Irish restaurants (with moderate to expensive meals) in the area. The high-ceilinged dining room, decorated in peach and brown tones, was once a private ballroom; unfortunately, guests may find it gloomy because of the dim lighting. The children of owner-chef Derry Britton serve generous portions of country food, including homegrown vegetables; local free-range duck, prepared in orange and fig sauce; and a variety of seafood, supplied daily from nearby Killybegs. Langoustines are used in an unusual appetizer, and the specialty of the house, pil-pil, consists of lightly grilled prawns served hot in earthenware dishes with lots of garlic, courgettes, shallots, and fresh coriander. *Rosnowlagh Rd., Ballyshannon, Co. Donegal, tel. 072/51138. 5 rooms with bath. Facilities: dining room, bar, fishing, riding (20 stables). AE, MC, V. Inexpensive.*

Bruckless

Dining and Lodging ★

Bruckless House. A two-story 18th-century farmhouse on the north side of Donegal Bay, this unusual B&B stands on 19 acres of woods, gardens, and a meadow where Irish draft horses and Connemara ponies roam. Public rooms have a fine view of Bruckless Bay; their Asian decor reflects years spent in Hong Kong by the owners, the Evans family. The more conventional but comfortable bedrooms share a large bathroom upstairs. Guests enjoy wholesome dinners that use fresh produce from the Evanses' garden, milk and cream from the resident cow, and seafood straight from the bay. Nearby visitors can drive to the Glencolumbkille Folk Museum and Ardara, and along the Donegal coastline. *Mrs. C. J. Evans, Bruckless House, Bruckless, Co. Donegal, tel. 073/37071. 5 rooms, 2 with bath. AE, DC, MC, V. Dinner must be booked by noon. Closed Oct.–Mar. Moderate.*

Castlebaldwin

Dining ★

Cromleach Lodge. Christie and Moira Tighe run this highly regarded restaurant (with excellent accommodations also available), situated on a hillside overlooking Lough Arrow, 5 km (3 mi) off the N4 at Castlebaldwin. All the windows have panoramic views, making each table in the three small dining rooms equally desirable. An extensive six-course table d'hôte menu is priced according to the choice of the main course, and makes use of fresh ingredients in attractively presented dishes with light sauces. A typical meal could begin with grilled goats' cheese, served with salad, followed by a soup such as fresh lobster bisque. Fresh fillet of turbot with chablis and chive sauce or salmon with saffron and lemon sauce are some of the seafood choices. Loin of lamb with rosemary juice or fresh breast of duck with juniper sauce are other favorites. A good choice of desserts includes a selection of fresh fruits individually marinated in different flavored syrups (such as apricots in Grand Marnier or kiwis in lemon and Pernod), a terrine of two chocolates layered with pistachio nuts, a selection of homemade ices, Irish farmhouse cheeses, and homemade petits fours. *Lough Arrow, Castlebaldwin, Co. Sligo, tel. 071/65155. Reservations advised. Dinner Mon.–Sat.; Sun. dinner fortnightly. Closed Dec. 23–31. AE, DC, MC, V. Moderate–Expensive.*

Collooney

Dining and Lodging ★

Markree Castle. Fans of Knockmuldowney House (formerly at Strandhill, west of Sligo Town) will be pleased to learn that this huge, five-story gray stone castle is the family home of Charles Cooper, Knockmuldowney's one-time proprietor; the building looks Victorian, but it actually dates to the 17th century. Mr. Cooper and his wife, Mary, are again welcoming bed-and-breakfast guests, and they're also keeping the name Knockmuldowney Restaurant for evening meals. The house, situated on a 1,000-acre estate, features fine Edwardian and Victorian mahogany furniture throughout, an oak-paneled hall, and ornate Louis XIV plasterwork in the first-floor dining room. The comfortable bedrooms are furnished in the same rich, heavy period style, but the bathrooms have been modernized; rooms provide garden or river views. The dining room has been restored with 19th-century green and beige decor and plenty of gilding. Mrs. Cooper prepares the delectable French meals with Anglo-Irish touches. Two table d'hôte menus are offered; one is a reasonably priced set five-course menu, and the other has about five choices for each course. Recommended dishes include stuffed mushrooms mornay and Egyptian lemon chicken, which is marinated in garlic, lemon juice, and oil and then baked in butter. Bailey's Blackberry Mist—a mousse made with blackberry puree and Bailey's Irish Cream liqueur —is a favorite dessert, served with homemade biscuits. On Sunday, a traditional lunch is available with a choice of two roasts or fish. Guests will also enjoy afternoon tea with biscuits, banana bread, and fruit cake. *Markree Castle, Colloney, Co. Sligo, tel. 071/67800 (11 km/7 mi south of Sligo Town). 15 rooms with bath. Facilities: restaurant. AE, DC, MC, V. Expensive.*

Donegal Town

Dining

Harvey's Point. Open in 1989, this Swiss-owned restaurant at the foot of the Blue Stack Mountains is situated in a 20-room hotel complete with helipad. One end of the split-level wood-paneled dining room directly overlooks Lough Eske. The establishment features warm peach decor, Tiffany lamps, and unusual locally made granite-top tables. The French cuisine leans toward a nouvelle presentation, with several lobster entrées on the menu; it might be served whole with a choice of two sauces, alongside rice and mussels, or garnished with tomatoes and red cabbage. Fisherman's Platter, a selection of five kinds of fish, is also served with two sauces, and sirloin steak is served with demiglaze sauce, topped with garlic butter. A special dessert is homemade ice cream with profiteroles and chocolate sauce. *Lough Eske, Donegal, Co. Donegal, tel. 073/22208. Reservations required. Jacket and tie advised. MC, V. Moderate–Expensive.*

Dining and Lodging

★ **St. Ernan's House.** For a restful stay, it's hard to imagine anything better than this cream-colored, two-story, 19th-century hotel, built by a nephew of the duke of Wellington, on a wooded Donegal Bay island; the house is reached by a causeway only a short distance south of town. Its attractive bedrooms are furnished with antiques and have superb views of the bay. The grand dining room features silk drapes and wallpaper in a green-and-gold Regency stripe pattern. Tables are laid traditionally with white linen, and the entrées make use of fresh local produce, especially fish, prepared in the Irish country-house style. The five-course dinner changes nightly, but a typical menu might include white crabmeat in lime mayonnaise as an appetizer, followed by grilled salmon hollandaise, steamed cod with asparagus tips and chablis sauce, or baked lamb with rosemary and apricot sauce. Desserts tend to be well-established favorites such as pears bordeaux (poached in red wine) or crème caramel. *Brian and Carmel O'Dowd, St. Ernan's House, St. Ernan's Island, Donegal, Co. Donegal, tel. 073/21065. 11 rooms with bath. Facilities: dining room (dinner open to nonguests). MC, V. No children under 6. Closed Nov.–Easter. Moderate.*

Hyland Central. Opening onto Donegal's central square, this family-run hotel offers a warm and friendly traditional atmosphere and a good location. Public areas retain a touch of Old World style, but the comfortable bedrooms (some of them quite spacious) lack character with their rather ordinary modern furniture. Many rooms have a view of lovely Donegal Bay. The large dining room with efficient, smart waitresses serves good, filling food. The hotel is a favorite with business travelers, vacationers, and locals who come for a drink or a meal. *The Diamond, Donegal, Co. Donegal, tel. 073/21027. 60 rooms with bath or shower. Facilities: dining room, gardens, indoor pool, solarium, games room. AE, MC, V. Moderate.*

Dromahair

Dining and Lodging

Drumlease Glebe House. This quiet Georgian country-house hotel, a perfect base for exploring Yeats Country, is situated on its own grounds beside the village. Although the exterior may seem a bit austere, the interior is a haven of civilization and comfort minutes from Lough Gill. Rooms are graced with striking antique furniture, lovely oil paintings, and pine floors. The attractive bedrooms with multipaned windows are all different, each with matching wallpaper, spreads, and drapes. The river at the bottom of the garden is full of trout and salmon. Dinners are prepared in the hearty Anglo-Irish style, with such classics as roast beef and Yorkshire pudding; they are graciously served by candlelight on polished tables set with Irish crystal and silver. *Dromahair, Co. Leitrim, tel. 071/64141. 8 rooms, 6 with bath. Facilities: dining room, fishing, gardens, outdoor pool. AE, MC, V. No children under 15. Expensive.*

Dunfanaghy

Dining and Lodging

Arnold's Hotel. A favorite with Irish vacationers, this friendly hotel run by the Arnold family provides unassuming, relaxed accommodations and generous traditional Irish meals. The best rooms overlook the landscaped garden. The Arnolds initiate special-interest courses for guests, such as painting and bird-watching. *Main St., Dunfanaghy, Co. Donegal, tel. 074/36208. 36 rooms, 26 with bath. Facilities: bar, baby-sitting, games room, tennis. AE, DC, MC, V. Closed Nov.–Mar. Inexpensive.*

Carrig Rua Hotel. On the shore of Sheephaven Bay, this unpretentious, popular two-story white hotel is an ideal base for exploring northern Donegal and Glenveagh National Park. Friendly and modestly priced, the bed-and-breakfast establishment caters to the tastes of Irish family vacationers, especially from across the border. Children are also made very welcome. The inviting modern rooms have new furniture and carpeting, and some offer bay views. Meals served here are plain, simple, and abundant in the traditional Irish style. *Main St., Dunfanaghy, Co. Donegal, tel. 074/36133. 22 rooms with bath or shower. Facilities: bar, baby-sitting. AE, V. Inexpensive.*

Fahan

Dining

Restaurant St. John's. This restored Georgian house enjoys a lakeside setting. You'll find a cozy, old-fashioned atmosphere, with open fires, pictures of old Derry, and red decor in the dining room, although white Donegal linen is used for tablecloths and napkins. Owner-chef Reg Ryan specializes in uncomplicated home cooking, but he is fastidious about his ingredients, and uses only local produce in the peak of its season and homegrown organic vegetables. Homemade bread is baked daily to serve with fresh garden soups and pâtés. The two six-course table d'hôte menus (one moderate, the other expensive) both give good value for the money. Look for irresistible seafood appetizers, such as hot crab in garlic butter and cream or monkfish, deep-fried in a very light batter and served with homemade mayonnaise. Fillets of brill with herbs and fennel sauce or Donegal rack of lamb, served with apple and mint jelly, are typical main courses. Desserts include homemade ice creams and carrageen moss soufflé. *Fahan, Co. Donegal, tel. 077/60289. Reservations advised. Dress: casual. Dinner only. Closed Mon., Christmas Day, and Good Friday, and 2 wks in Feb. DC, MC, V. Moderate–Expensive.*

Letterkenny

Dining and Lodging

Mount Errigal Hotel. One of County Donegal's smartest and most modern hotels, although not at all posh, this property appeals to both business and family vacation visitors. Service here is friendly and professional. Private events and conferences are often staged here, and the bar remains a favorite for locals seeking a relaxed night out. The clean and comfortable bedrooms are efficiently arranged, with characterless, pale-colored furnishings. The Glengesh, the hotel's softly lit restaurant, serves popular Irish cooking; it features Edwardian-style brass and glass decor. *Ballyraine, Letterkenny, Co. Donegal, tel. 074/22700. 56 rooms with bath or shower. Facilities: restaurant, 2 lounge bars, disco, games room, facilities for disabled guests, video, sauna, baby-sitting. AE, DC, MC, V. Moderate.*

Rathmullen

Dining

Water's Edge Restaurant. Dawn and Kevin Cairns run this restaurant with panoramic views in a converted row of old cottages on the western shore of Lough Swilly. The cozy, romantic dining spot is two-tiered, with wooden beams, oak tables, deep burgundy red decor, and colored linen tablecloths and napkins. The mixed international menu is influenced by the owners' travels but based squarely on fresh local ingredients and seasonal availability; fish is the main strength in summer, while steaks, chicken, duckling, and scallops appear more often in winter. If you like seafood, don't miss the Water's Edge Special, a mixture of fresh fish and shellfish—such as clams, lobster, salmon, and mussels—cooked in white wine and garlic and topped with Roquefort cheese. A popular dessert is Queen Sofia's Delight, a rich meringue-based sweet made with seasonal fruit and fresh cream. *The Ballyboe, Rathmullen, Co. Donegal, tel. 074/58182 or 58138. Reservations advised. Dress: casual but neat. Dinner year-round; light lunches in summer (June–Sept.) only. Closed Christmas Eve. DC, MC, V. Moderate–Expensive.*

Dining and Lodging
★

Rathmullan House. One of Ireland's most enticing and popular country-house hotels, this rambling, cream-colored, two-story mansion, dating from the 18th century, features large bay windows, fine antiques and oil paintings, and prize-winning gardens; its lawns stretch down to a deserted sandy beach. The public areas, including a drawing room, an impressive library, and a coffee room, are the height of elegance, but they're also informal and friendly. Bedrooms vary from old-fashioned basic to grand, but all of them feature antiques and light-colored wallpaper and curtains. Ask for a room facing Lough Swilly. The light-filled pavilion dining room with a tented ceiling has pink and green decor, silk drapes, and views of the gardens and the lake from the windows. Two table d'hôte menus—roasts and seafood with fresh produce—are available in the Irish country-house style. A typical menu might include poached salmon with black butter or roast lamb with herb stuffing and red currant jelly, followed by a sweet dessert or Irish farmhouse cheese. Breakfast, consisting of fresh fruit compotes, carrageen moss pudding, and other hot or cold dishes, is a specialty here. The hotel is well situated for visiting the Donegal coast, Glenveagh National Park, and the Glebe House and Gallery. *Rathmullen, Co. Donegal, tel. 074/58188. 19 rooms, 16 with bath and shower. Facilities: dining room, bar, gardens, heated indoor pool, sauna, steam room, tennis, croquet. No TV in rooms. AE, DC, MC, V. Closed Nov.–Easter. Expensive.*

Fort Royal Hotel. On 18 acres of grounds beside Lough Swilly, this spacious, comfortable hotel, once an aristocratic private home, is a decent, less-expensive alternative to the Rathmullan House (*see* above). It attracts a regular clientele who enjoy its relaxed professionalism and marvelous location. Rooms are clean and meals are satisfactory. *Rathmullen, Co. Donegal, tel. 074/58100. 19 rooms, 16 with bath or shower. Facilities: bar, gardens, golf, tennis, squash. AE, DC, MC, V. Closed mid-Oct.–Mar. Moderate.*

Riverstown

Dining and Lodging ★

Coopershill. A three-story Georgian farmhouse in 500 acres of private woods and farmland, this fine stone abode has been home to seven generations of the O'Hara family since it was constructed in 1774. It provides an ideal place for a quiet vacation. Large public rooms are furnished with appealing period antiques and overstuffed furniture, and deer heads hang in the vast hallways. The spacious bedrooms reflect the same antique style (with no televisions) and most have four-poster or canopy beds. In the tranquil dining room overlooking the woods, Irish-style meals and a wide choice of wines are served by candlelight from a grand sideboard with family silver. The menu, which changes nightly, includes roast beef or lamb, fresh vegetables, and special soups. Guests can walk on the grounds amid undisturbed wildlife. *Coopershill, Riverstown, Co. Sligo, tel. 071/65108. 6 rooms with bath. Facilities: dining room, garden, private fishing, boating. AE, MC, V. Closed Nov.–Mar. 23. Expensive.*

Rossnowlagh

Dining and Lodging

Sand House Hotel. This large modern hotel, located right on Donegal Bay, makes a peaceful, well-located base for sightseeing the bay coastline. It has a mock "manor house" exterior, and access to a 3-km (2-mi) stretch of sand. The renovated, well-kept bedrooms are beautifully decorated with antiques. Choose between a sea view at the front, or back rooms overlooking a golf course. You'll find the staff solicitous and cheerful. The efficient restaurant caters to the plain hearty appetites of Irish vacationers looking for something special. Fresh seafood, including Donegal Bay oysters and mussels, is the daily specialty, but meat dishes are also given special attention. *Rossnowlagh, Co. Donegal, tel. 072/51777. 40 rooms with bath or shower. Facilities: restaurant, bar, baby-sitting, children's playroom, games room, golf, surfing club, tennis. AE, DC, MC, V. Closed Nov.–Easter. Expensive.*

Sligo Town and Environs

Dining
★

Reveries. One unique attraction of this smart restaurant 8 km (5 mi) from town is the romantic Rosses Point view of Knocknarea, Sligo Bay, and Oyster Island. The other draw is Paula Gilvarry's first-class cooking, which makes this one of the Northwest's best dining spots. Dark wood tables with matching chairs are elegantly set with blue linen cloths, matching china, and fine crystal. The chef makes expert use of fresh local ingredients, especially fish and homegrown vegetables, in her adventurous dishes prepared in an individualized nouvelle style. Start perhaps with apple, cheese, and leek tart in carrot and mustard sauce. Main courses include a venison stir-fry with peppers and bamboo shoots, or pork with herb topping and basil cream sauce. Guests can choose from a good wine list and an exceptional cheese board with some 30 varieties. Desserts are equally inviting. *Rosses Point, Co. Sligo, tel. 071/77371. Reservations advised. Dress: casual. AE, MC, V. Open Tues.–Sat. for dinner only; Sun. dinner fortnightly. Closed for 2 wks in Nov. and 4 days at Christmastime. Moderate.*

Bonne Chère Restaurant. Popular for years with Sligo residents seeking a decent meal at modest prices, this big restaurant in the town center features a relaxed ambience with a pleasant colonial decor. The well-prepared food comes in generous portions, ranging from simple traditional meals such as bacon and cabbage or stews to chicken curries reflecting the African origins of proprietors Anne and Michael Welch. In the evening, meat and fish grills predominate. The name, by the way, doesn't mean "pricey," but is a rather old French literary way of saying "good food." *45 High St., Sligo, Co. Sligo, tel. 071/42014. Reservations advised. Dress: casual. AE, MC, V. Open 8 AM–10:30 PM. Inexpensive–Moderate.*

Dining and Lodging

Ballincar House Hotel. In its peaceful 6-acre wooded grounds between Sligo Town and Rosses Point, this out-of-town, leisure-oriented vacation hotel, formerly a private home, is convenient for exploring Yeats Country or the Donegal Bay coast. Its modern bedrooms with private baths and televisions may lack the charm of some other houses in the area, but the restaurant is highly recommended, specializing in seafood, such as lobster mornay and salmon. Because of the hotel's popularity, you're advised to reserve rooms way in advance. *Rosses Point Rd., Sligo, Co. Sligo, tel. 071/45361. 20 rooms with bath or shower. Facilities: restaurant, bar, gardens, tennis, sauna, solarium, squash. AE, DC, MC, V. Closed Dec. 23–Jan. 23. Moderate.*

Sligo Park Hotel. A mile out of town on the N4 (main Dublin road), this modern, well-run property, surrounded by trees and pastures, doesn't have much character. Its predictable, reliable comforts (private baths, phones, and televisions in each room) appeal to business travelers, but it also makes a reasonable base for visitors to Yeats Country. The hotel offers dancing, a disco, or piano entertainment on some evenings. *Pearse Rd., Sligo, Co. Sligo, tel. 071/60291. 62 rooms with bath or* *shower. Facilities: restaurant, bar, gardens, secretarial services, laundry services. AE, DC, MC, V. Moderate.*

The Arts and Nightlife

The Arts

The rustic and underpopulated Northwest features few serious arts activities and events. If you're in the right place at the right time, however, you can attend or participate in several entertaining festivals. Ask at the Irish Tourist Board Information Offices for up-to-date advance booking information, or check announcements in the local press, including *The Donegal Democrat, The Leitrim Observer,* and *Sligo Champion.*

Theater In early June, during the **Ballyshannon Drama Festival,** the town hosts different drama companies for a program of mainly Irish plays. Sligo Town's **Hawk's Well Theatre** often features interesting theater programs. It brings in amateur and professional companies from all over Ireland (and occasionally from Britain) to stage a wide variety of shows. Most of the summer season is devoted to the works of popular Irish playwrights. *Temple St., Sligo, tel. 071/61526. Amateur shows: £3.50; professional shows: £4.50. Tues.–Sat. evenings.*

Music At the beginning of August, on the bank holiday weekend, the normally quiet town of Ballyshannon hosts one of Ireland's largest and best folk music events, the **Ballyshannon Music Festival.** Visitors can hear both well-known and unknown folk and traditional musicians as they entertain in a riverside location. Impromptu performances occur at pubs. A party atmosphere prevails, attracting up to 12,000 visitors annually.

Fleadh Cheoil, the annual Irish festival of traditional music, has been held in Sligo Town for the past two years and is scheduled to be held there again in 1991 during the last weekend in August.

Hawk's Well Theatre in Sligo Town (*see* above) puts on concerts from time to time, including classical performances.

Nightlife

An evening out in the rural Northwest is generally an evening at a lively, popular pub with live music. Always ask locally at your hotel if there is a nearby pub with "sessions," which are small-scale, informal performances of traditional folk music. For other entertainment though, especially if you want something a little more sophisticated, you may have to look long and hard. Some hotels or large pubs, particularly at resort towns in season, put on a disco or dance on certain days of the week, or have performances by local groups with an emphasis on country-and-western music. These events generally don't deserve a special journey but can be entertaining if they are nearby.

For a small, old-fashioned village, Andara in County Donegal offers a surprising number of pubs, with many of them offering evenings of traditional music. **Peter Oliver's** bar provides music almost every night. **Nancy's,** which is perhaps one of the smallest pubs in the whole of the Republic, finds space for a folk group several nights a week.

In Donegal Town, **The Abbey Hotel** (tel. 073/21014), on the Diamond, features weekend dancing and Irish folk music during the week. Letterkenny, also in County Donegal, offers folk music, jazz, or dancing on weekends at the **Mount Errigal Hotel** (tel. 074/22700). Sligo Town's **Southern Hotel** (tel. 071/62101) and **Sligo Park** (tel. 071/60291) have bands, country-and-western shows, and discos during the whole week.

10 Northern Ireland

Introduction

by Andrew Sanger

If Celtic legends are true, the giant Finn MacCool threw down the Giant's Causeway off the coast of Northern Ireland and marched across it in a few strides to reach the shores of Scotland, later returning to his homeland with equal ease. The story isn't entirely implausible. The channel between Scotland and Ireland, though turbulent, has never been much of a barrier to people moving in both directions, and the ancient Irish province of Ulster always had close ties with its neighbor on the other side of the water.

Thanks largely to that strong Scottish influence, Ulster and Ulstermen have always been somehow separate from the rest of Ireland. Nearly 2,000 years ago the people of Ulster built the Black Pig Dyke—a great ditch and earth barrier—to mark the border between themselves and the other Irish regions to the south. To the southerners and to would-be conquerors, Ulster was always known as a tough, indomitable land, home of a warlike people. The "Red Hand" at the center of its flag tells a typically ferocious tale: Two great Celtic warriors raced from Scotland to Ireland's northern coast to settle a dispute between them for possession of Ulster. The first to touch the foreign land could call it his own. In the last moments, one of the rivals cut off his own hand and threw it onto the shore and so, by blood and sacrifice, won Ulster.

Present-day Northern Ireland, a division under the rule of the United Kingdom, includes six of Ulster's nine counties (the others—Donegal, Cavan, and Monaghan—lie in the Irish Republic) and retains a sense of isolation today. The hard-headed and industrious Scottish Presbyterians imported to make Ulster a bulwark against Ireland's Catholicism have had a profound and ineradicable effect on the place. Not least of the Scottish legacies are the North's distinctive accents. Northern Ireland has more factories, neater-looking farms, better roads, and more two-story redbrick houses (which are typical in Britain) than does the Republic. Of course, you'll also see, in Protestant districts, some of the odder manifestations of the pro-British Loyalists' zeal: curbstones and lampposts painted in the British colors of red, white, and blue; entwined British and Ulster flags fluttering from tall poles raised in pocket-handkerchief front yards; and countless signs and crests declaring proud devotion to Ulster and the Queen.

For all that, the national frontier, which separates British Northern Ireland from the Irish Republic, is of little consequence to visitors, or even to residents, who may cross it freely at any time. The only inconvenience is that of waiting in line to be eyed warily by British soldiers, who are on the lookout for militant Republicans. No one should be deterred from traveling here on that account. The "Troubles"—almost always confined to a few city streets whose names come up again and again on news broadcasts—are not as bad in reality as they look on the screen. The truth is that Northern Ireland has a considerable number of attractions worth visiting and some of the very best of Irish scenery on its County Antrim coast and in the tranquil green lake country of County Fermanagh. It also maintains close links with the United States and Canada, to which many Ulstermen have emigrated in the last century.

From the Norman period onward, the English made greater and greater inroads into Ireland, endeavoring to subdue what they believed (probably quite correctly) was a potential enemy and a collaborator with that great adversary of England's naval might, Catholic Spain. Ulster proved the hardest part to conquer, but in 1607, Ulster's Irish nobility were beaten, and left their homeland in a great exodus known as the Flight of the Earls. Most went to Spain, abandoning their lands forever to confiscation by the English crown. The English distributed the territories among individuals called Planters—the name given to staunch Protestants from England and, even more often, from Scotland who came to Ireland to farm, work, and colonize. New Protestant towns were built, and Catholics became subjected to harshly repressive laws. Inevitably, tension between the two religious groups increased, often flaring into violence toward the end of the 19th century.

In the parliamentary elections of 1918, almost the whole of Ireland voted for Sinn Féin, the party that believed in independence for all of Ireland; in the six counties, however, the majority of votes went to the Nationalists (who were demanding Home Rule—local autonomy within the United Kingdom), and, especially in Counties Down and Antrim, to the Unionists (who wanted nothing less than to remain an integral part of the United Kingdom). In 1921, by a majority, leading Irish politicians in Dublin agreed to allow the North to remain in British hands, in exchange for complete independence for Ireland's remaining 26 counties. The North established its own parliament housed in the imposing Stormont building just east of Belfast.

Although the "sectarian" conflict has clearly more to do with politics than religion, visitors may be surprised by the high degree of religious observance in the North. Protestants divide about equally into Anglicans and a variety of more or less austere nonconformists, especially Presbyterians. From the 1880s to the 1920s, the Nationalist movement included many Protestants. However, the passage of time caused positions to become more entrenched, rather than less. The Unionists today are closely identified with the "planted" Protestant population, while the Nationalists or Republicans are inextricably associated with the native Irish community, which is almost entirely Catholic.

In the 1960s, after 40 years of living beneath the permanent Protestant majority, the Catholics launched a civil rights movement to demand equal rights in jobs, housing, and opportunities. The severity with which this was put down led to the return of direct rule from London and, at the same time, to a rebirth of the Irish Republican Army (IRA), which had lain dormant for decades. The war between the IRA and the British establishment has continued ever since. At the same time, Protestant paramilitary organizations wage their own war against the IRA. In an effort to undermine the extremism of both sides, in 1985 the London and Dublin governments signed the Anglo-Irish Agreement, which gives the Irish government a consultative voice in Northern Ireland's affairs.

The good news is that this tactic seems to be working, and in the last five years the political climate in Northern Ireland has become more relaxed. In 1990, a Fair Employment Commission was set up to integrate workplaces, and in the same year new legislation brought integration to schools, which had both been traditionally segregated into Protestant and Catholic institutions. More and more people on both sides of the sectarian divide show a sincere willingness to make compromises and want only to live in peace with their neighbors. At the extremes, however, the violence between diehard Nationalists and fanatically pro-British Loyalists still continues.

For this reason, visitors to Northern Ireland still have to exercise a little care. Certain areas have seen frequent frightening incidents, particularly the poor working-class districts—both Protestant and Catholic—in west Belfast, and similar neighborhoods in Derry. Yet apart from these easily identified danger spots, Northern Ireland (including these two cities) is as tranquil, inviting, and friendly as the rest of the country.

Essential Information

Arriving and Departing by Plane

Airports and Airlines

Aldergrove Airport, or **Belfast International** (tel. 08494/22888), is Northern Ireland's principal air arrival point, situated 30½ km (19 mi) from Belfast. **Belfast City (Harbour) Airport** (tel. 0232/457745) is the second airport, 6½ km (4 mi) from Belfast. It receives flights from U.K. provincial airports and from Luton (near London). **Eglinton Airport** (tel. 0504/810784) is 8 km (5 mi) from Derry City.

Flights from Britain

British Airways (tel. 0232/240522) and **British Midland Airways** (tel. 0232/225151) operate most flights into Belfast. By far the cheapest flights are offered by **Capital Airlines** (tel. 0532/505550) and **Brittania** (tel. 0582/405737). Other main airlines include **Loganair** (tel. 041/8893181) and **Air UK** (tel. 0345/666777).

Frequent services throughout the day to Belfast are scheduled from London Heathrow, London Gatwick, and 17 other U.K. airports. Flights take about 1¼ hours from London. British Airways' and British Midland Airways' shuttle services between London and Belfast are walk-on, no-reservation flights, and the airlines claim that no passenger will be turned away—another plane will be added if a scheduled flight is overbooked. Direct flights from Paris on Air France and from Amsterdam on Schiphol also arrive in Belfast. Scheduled flights to Belfast from the United States and Canada are routed via London, but sometimes charter services fly direct to Belfast from New York and Toronto. Eglinton, Derry City's airport, receives flights from Manchester, England, and Glasgow, Scotland, via Loganair.

Between the Airports and the Cities

Belfast: Ulsterbus (tel. 0232/320011) operates a shuttle bus every ½ hour (cost: U.K.£3 one-way, U.K.£5 round-trip) between the Aldergrove Airport and the Belfast city center. From the Belfast City Airport, you can travel into Belfast by train from Sydenham Halt to Central Station (East Bridge St.) or catch a taxi from the airport to your hotel.

Derry City: If you arrive at Eglinton Airport (8 km/5 mi from Derry City), you will need to call a taxi (tel. 0504/261911 or 0504/44100 or 0504/43813) to get to your destination.

Arriving and Departing by Car, Ferry, Train, and Bus

By Car While many roads from the Irish Republic into Northern Ireland have been closed, drivers can choose from a score of legitimate crossing points, as well as from another score of "unapproved" routes across the border. Visitors should expect an army checkpoint at all approved frontier posts, but few formalities are practiced. The fast N1/A1 road connects Belfast to Dublin (160 km/100 mi); sometimes you'll encounter delays at the border on this road (*see* Staying in Northern Ireland in Chapter 1).

By Ferry **Belfast Ferries** (tel. 051/922–6234; nine-hour crossing) offers car ferries to Belfast from the English port of Liverpool. **Sealink Ferries** (tel. 077/622620; 2½ hours) provides car ferries to Larne from Stranraer, Scotland, and **P&O European Ferries** (tel. 058/12276; 2½ hours) has car ferries to Larne from Cairnryan, Scotland.

By Train The Belfast–Dublin Express train travels nonstop between the two cities in two hours. Six trains run daily in both directions (three on Sundays).

By Bus Northern Ireland's bus company **Ulsterbus** (tel. 0232/32011) crosses the border to connect with the Republic's **Bus Éireann** (tel. 01/746301 in Dublin) services. The ride from Dublin to Belfast takes four hours, with a change at Monaghan. Buses to Belfast also run from London and from Birmingham, making the Stranraer ferry (tel. 077/622620) crossing.

Getting Around

By Car
Driving In general, drivers will find that in Northern Ireland the roads are in much better shape, signposting is clearer, and gasoline is cheaper than in the Irish Republic. Northern Ireland visitors, however, must deal with army checkpoints; a soldier may ask you a few questions, or even wish to search your luggage; you'll pass through more quickly if you cooperate politely. Bad rush-hour delays can occur getting in and out of Belfast on highways A6 and A2. But on the whole, driving is quicker and easier in Northern Ireland than in areas south of the border.

Parking Always make sure you are not in a "control zone," where it is prohibited to leave a vehicle unattended. Most town centers are control zones, with free car parks situated within walking distance.

Car Rentals Visitors can choose among several local rental companies, but car rental isn't cheap. A compact car costs U.K.£80–U.K.£100 per week (including taxes, insurance, and unlimited mileage). If you're planning to take a hired car across the border into the Republic, inform the company and check its insurance procedures. The following are some of the main rental offices. **Belfast: Avis** (Great Victoria St., tel. 0232/241414) and **Godfrey Davis** (58 Antrim Rd., 0232/757401). **Aldergrove Airport: Avis** (tel. 08494/22333), **Godfrey Davis** (tel. 08494/23444), and **Hertz** (tel. 08494/22533). **Belfast City Airport: Avis** (tel. 0232/240404). **Derry City: Hertz** (tel. 0504/360420).

By Train Northern Ireland Railways runs only three rail routes: Belfast–Derry via Coleraine, Belfast–Bangor along the shore of Belfast

Lough, and Belfast–Dublin. Rail Runabout tickets allow seven days' unlimited travel (cost: U.K.£27). For information contact: **Northern Ireland Railways** (17 Wellington Pl., Belfast, tel. 0232/230671), **Belfast Central Station** (East Bridge St., tel. 0232/230310), and local rail stations.

By Bus Visitors can take advantage of frequent and inexpensive Ulsterbus links between all Northern Ireland towns. The main bus stations in Belfast are located behind the **Europa Hotel** on Great Victoria Street and on Oxford Street near the Central Railway Station. A good bet for touring by bus is a Freedom of Northern Ireland Ticket, which allows unlimited travel (cost: U.K.£6 a day or U.K.£17 for a week; prices subject to change). For all specific fare and schedule details, call **Ulsterbus** (tel. 0232/320011). Within Belfast, visitors have access to good city bus service. All routes start from Donegall Square; you'll find a kiosk there where you can pick up a timetable. For **Citybus** inquiries, call 0232/246485.

Important Addresses and Numbers

Tourist Information The main information center for the whole of Northern Ireland is the **Tourist Information Office** (TIO) located in Belfast, which provides maps, advice, and information on every attraction in Belfast and the province, including upcoming events and festivals. *River House, 48 High St., tel. 0232/246609. The TIO is scheduled to move in 1991 to St. Anne's Ct., opposite St. Anne's Cathedral (same phone number). Open weekdays 9–5:15; Easter–Sept., also open Sat. 9–2.*

Year-round local offices are located at **Armagh** (40 English St., tel. 0861/527808), **Carnlough** (Post Office, Harbour Rd., tel. 0574/85210), **Carrickfergus** (Town Hall, tel. 09603/51604), **Derry City** (Foyle St., tel. 0504/267284), **Downpatrick** (Down Leisure Centre, Market St., tel. 0396/613426), **Enniskillen** (Lakeland Visitor Centre, Shore Rd., tel. 0365/23110), **Giant's Causeway** (Visitor Centre, tel. 02657/31855), **Larne** (Larne Harbour, tel. 0574/70517), **Newcastle** (Central Promenade, tel. 03967/22222), **Newry** (Arts Centre, Bank Parade, tel. 0693/66232), and in more than a dozen other Northern Ireland towns. During June through August, many more towns and villages open tourist information offices.

Emergencies For **police, ambulance, fire,** or **coast guard,** dial 999 in all of Northern Ireland. The **main police station** (tel. 0232/650222) in downtown Belfast is located at 6–10 North Queen Street.

Hospitals In Belfast, the main hospitals with emergency rooms are **Belfast City Hospital** (Lisburn Rd., tel. 0232/329241) and **Royal Victoria Hospital** (Grosvenor Rd., tel. 0232/240503). In Derry City, **Altnagelvin Hospital** (Belfast Rd., tel. 0504/45171) has an emergency room.

Weather In Belfast, call Weathercall at 438544 (area code: 0232, if you're calling outside Belfast).

Banks and Money Exchange

Northern Ireland uses British currency, and Irish *punts,* or pounds, are not accepted. Rates change rapidly, but the British pound is worth a little more than the Irish (*see* Irish Currency in Chapter 1). You'll sometimes be given bank notes, drawn on Ulster banks, that are valid only in Northern Ireland; be sure not to get stuck with a lot of these when you leave because they will be difficult to change at banks back home. As in the Irish Republic, credit cards are not widely accepted outside the main towns. Main banks are open weekdays 10–3:30. Changing money outside banking hours is possible at **Thomas Cook** branches at Belfast Airport (open weekdays 7 AM–8 PM, weekends 7 AM–10 PM) and 11 Donegall Place (open Mon.–Sat. 9–5:30).

Guided Tours

Orientation Tours

Citybus offers a Belfast city orientation tour that takes in the city's shipyards and heads out from the city center as far as Stormont (9½ km/6 mi east) and Belfast Castle on Cave Hill to the north. *Milewater Rd., tel. 0232/246485. Cost: U.K.£3.25 adults, U.K.£1.75 children, including afternoon tea. City tour leaves Castle Place June–Sept., Tues., Wed., and Thurs. at 2 PM.*

Ulsterbus (Milewater Rd., tel. 0232/331577) operates half-day or full-day trips during June to September from Belfast to the Glens of Antrim, the Giant's Causeway, the Fermanagh lakes, Lough Neagh, the Mourne Mountains, and the Ards Peninsula.

Special-Interest Tours

Giant's Causeway/ Bushmills

If you're seeing the province without a car, you could have difficulty reaching the Giant's Causeway. Apart from a tour to that destination from Belfast, Ulsterbus has also teamed up with the Old Bushmills Distillery to run the **Bushmills Bus,** an open-top tour bus running from Coleraine to the Giant's Causeway via the coast resorts; you also visit Bushmills to observe whiskey-making. *Tel. 0232/331577. Cost: U.K.£2 adults, U.K.£1 children and senior citizens. Bus leaves Coleraine Mon.–Sat. 9:20, 11:30, 2:10, and 4; Sun. 2:10 and 4 only.*

Lower Lough Erne

Kestrel is a 63-seat water bus operated by **Erne Tours** (tel. 0365/22882); it sets off from Round O pier at Enniskillen during the summer for a two-hour trip on beautiful Lough Erne. On weekdays, the boat makes a half-hour stop at Devenish Island to allow visitors to see Ireland's best round tower. From May to June there are Sunday trips at 3 PM, and occasionally at other times of year.

Exploring Northern Ireland

Along the shores of Northern Ireland's coasts and lakes, green gentle slopes descend majestically into hazy, dark-blue water, against a background of more slopes, more water, and huge cloud-scattered skies. If time is short, you might decide to skip Belfast. (If you arrive by plane, you can easily bypass Northern Ireland's capital because the Belfast Airport is several miles from the city.)

You certainly won't need to stick rigidly to the route in this guide. Belfast and Derry, however, do deserve a visit, if possible. Belfast is a naturally lively, friendly city; with the decline in the number of dangerous incidents, you'll discover a new joie de vivre in the air. Derry, it must be said, still presents a few problems, although much of the bad housing has been swept away; new developments are being built both in the suburbs and in the small city center. British fortifications remain much in evidence, though, and soldiers patrol in force. Derry's center is still enclosed by its medieval walls, making it one of Europe's best-preserved examples of a fortified town.

If you want to see only one small area with plenty of variety, the best choice would be a stay in or near Enniskillen, in County Fermanagh. The town itself is bright and bustling; Lough Erne close by has magnificent lake views, as well as one of Ireland's most impressive round towers on Devenish Island. On the other side of Enniskillen stands Castle Coole, one of the most graceful mansions of 18th-century Anglo-Irish nobility.

Highlights for First-time Visitors

The Giant's Causeway (*see* Tour 2)
The Glens of Antrim (*see* Tour 2)
Lower Lough Erne (*see* Tour 3)
Ulster Museum (*see* Tour 1)
Victorian (and older) pubs in Belfast (*see* Tour 1)

Tour 1: Belfast

Numbers in the margin correspond with points of interest on the Northern Ireland and the Belfast maps.

1 **Belfast** is quite unlike any other city, Irish or British. Its unique charisma derives from a curious mixture of identities, its sense of separateness, and, of course, the notoriety it has received as a center of conflict. Belfast also combines the hard-headed proletarian quality of a large industrial town with the dignified self-confidence of a respectable and well-to-do provincial capital. It was a great Victorian success story, a boomtown whose prosperity was built on trade: Linen and shipbuilding brought in most of the wealth. Now Belfast struggles against decline; linen is no longer a major industry here, and shipbuilding has suffered severe setbacks. The quaysides along the River Lagan, however, are still impressively active, and the dry dock is one of the world's largest.

The city's central district, lying west of the docks, extends from the City Hall to St. Anne's Cathedral. The area is alive with commerce, shops, cafés, pubs, and historic (but now modernized) streets. Large redbrick or white Portland stone Victorian banks, as well as offices and department stores, occupy this old heart, symbols of Belfast's high standing before the creation of the Irish Free State. Now the whole of this district is pedestrianized for security reasons; the roads are closed to traffic by sturdy green railings with police checkpoints. There's no sign, though, of any trouble. The bitterness of the '70s appears to have been left behind.

Perhaps the most astonishing thing about Belfast is its setting —high wild heath-green slopes rise abruptly at the end of the city-center streets. Until the Plantation period at the beginning of the 17th century, Belfast was an insignificant village called *Beal Feirste* (meaning "Sandbank Ford"). In the 1600s the district, formerly belonging to Ulster's ancient O'Neill clan, was granted to Sir Arthur Chichester, who was from Devon in southwest England. Chichester's son was made earl of Donegall, and he initiated the building of the town; he is remembered in many of the street names. A century later, French Huguenots (i.e., Protestants) fleeing persecution settled here, bringing their valuable skills in linen work. In the 18th century, Belfast saw a phenomenal expansion, with the population doubling in size every 10 years. The religious sectarian divide appeared during the 19th century when Presbyterian ministers began to preach bitterly against the town's Catholic residents. But the town's growth continued, factories were built, and industry expanded. In 1849, Queen Victoria paid a visit, and she is recalled in the names of buildings, streets, bars, monuments, and other places around the city. In the same year, the university opened and took the name Queen's College. Victoria granted Belfast full city status in 1888. Today its population is 400,000—one-third of all Northern Ireland's citizens.

When the working day is over, Belfast's central area closes down and the life of the town shifts south. Great Victoria Street down to Shaftesbury Square is known as the **Golden Mile,** though it is not quite as glittering as the name implies and is only about a third of a mile in length. Beyond it, down University Road to Stranmillis Road, is the **University Area.** Chances are that as well as drinking and eating in these two parts of the city, you'll also be staying nearby. The University Area is the safest part of town and features many good bed-and-breakfasts and guest houses. Belfast's best centrally located hotel, the
2 **Europa** (tel. 0232/327000), at the northern end of Great Victoria Street, makes a good starting point for a walking tour of the city center.

Many Belfast residents trace an improvement in the atmosphere of their city, and especially an upsurge in evening enter-
3 tainments, to the reopening in 1980 of the **Grand Opera House,** next door to the Europa. This typical Victorian theater, built in 1895, retains its original richly decorated auditorium, where heavy gilt moldings, ornamental plasterwork, and frescoes depict Asian themes. Although the city already had a lively theater with its own company, the Lyric in south Belfast, the Opera House attracted bigger, diverse audiences upon its reopening. Today it mounts touring performances of all kinds: musicals, operas, and children's plays, as well as conventional theater. The best way to see and enjoy this immaculate example of Victoriana is to attend a performance. *Great Victoria St., tel. 0232/241919. Seats range from U.K.£1.50 to U.K.£25.*

Turn right from the Opera House on to Howard Street to reach Belfast's central Donegall Square, dominated by its columned
4 and domed **City Hall** (built 1906). To appreciate the classical style and the setting of the building, first take a walk right round Donegall Square. In the gardens you'll see statues of Queen Victoria; a monument commemorating the unlucky ocean liner *Titanic,* which was built in Belfast; and a short column in honor of the U.S. Expeditionary Force, which landed in the city on January 26, 1942—the first contingent of the U.S. Army to land in Europe. Then step inside the City Hall; the public entrance is located at the rear of the building. If it happens to be a Wednesday morning, you can join the weekly guided tour and be shown the Council Chamber, the Great Hall, and the Reception Room. If not, you may at least walk into the Entrance Hall, to the foot of the Grand Staircase. Here you'll discover a riot of ornamental marble inlays and decora-

Northern Ireland

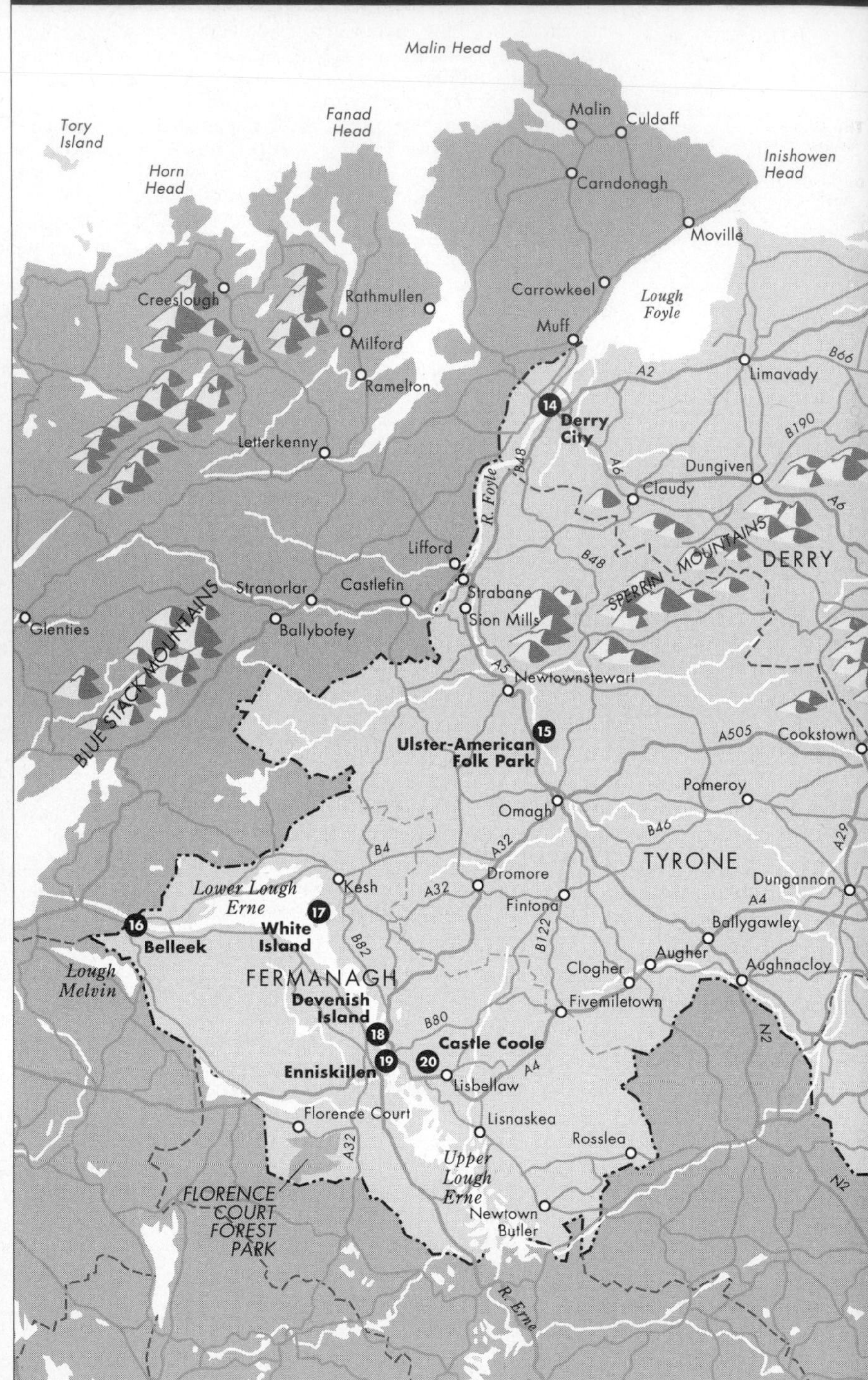

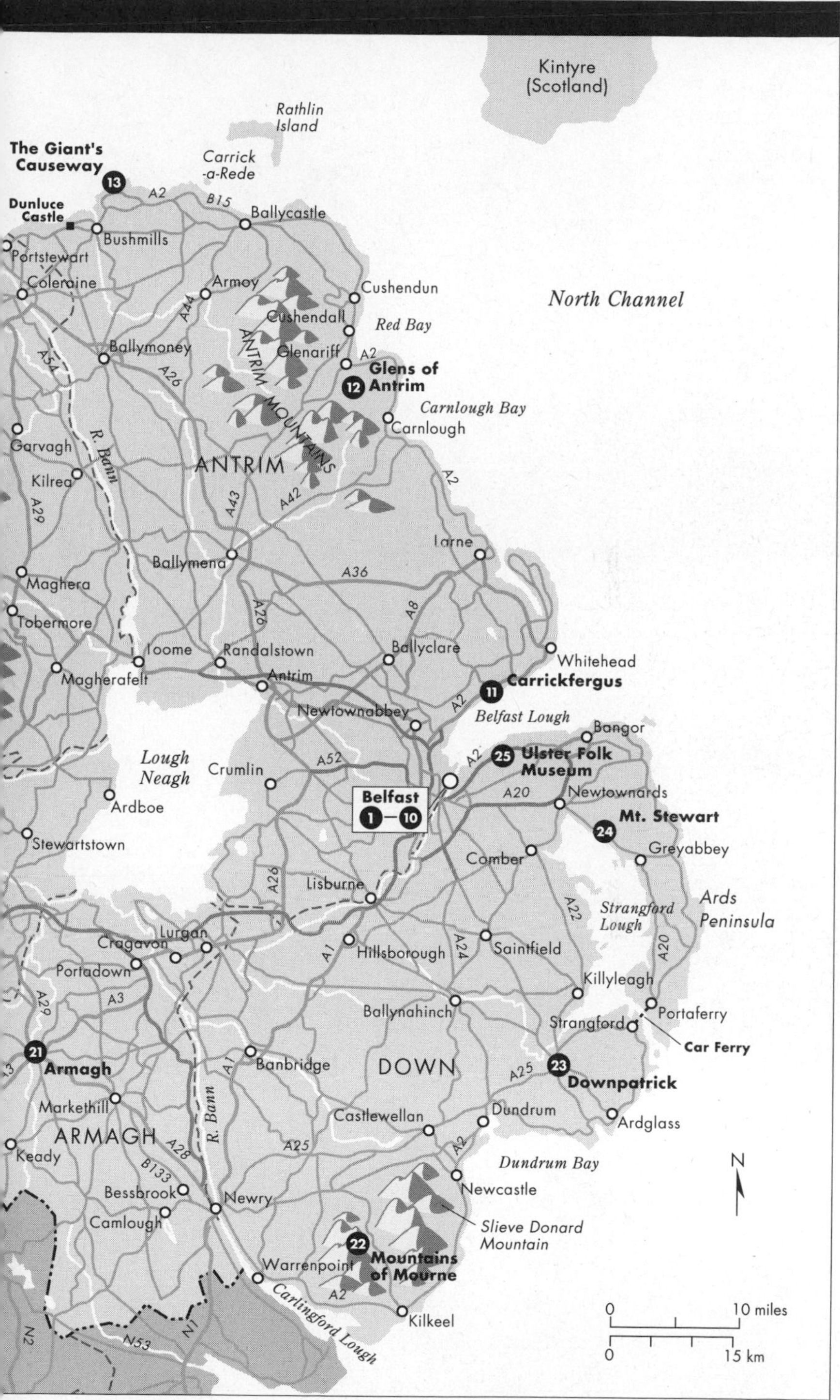

Kintyre (Scotland)
Rathlin Island
The Giant's Causeway
Carrick -a-Rede
Dunluce Castle
Ballycastle
Bushmills
Portstewart
Coleraine
Armoy
Cushendun
Cushendall
Red Bay
North Channel
Ballymoney
Glenariff
Glens of Antrim
ANTRIM MOUNTAINS
Carnlough Bay
Carnlough
Garvagh
Kilrea
R. Bann
ANTRIM
Larne
Ballymena
Maghera
Tobermore
Toome
Randalstown
Ballyclare
Whitehead
Magherafelt
Antrim
Carrickfergus
Newtownabbey
Belfast Lough
Bangor
Ulster Folk Museum
Lough Neagh
Crumlin
Belfast
Newtownards
Ardboe
Mt. Stewart
Stewartstown
Comber
Greyabbey
Lisburne
Strangford Lough
Ards Peninsula
Lurgan
Cragavon
Hillsborough
Saintfield
Portadown
Killyleagh
Ballynahinch
Portaferry
Strangford
Car Ferry
Armagh
Banbridge
DOWN
Downpatrick
Markethill
Castlewellan
Dundrum
Ardglass
ARMAGH
Keady
Dundrum Bay
Bessbrook
Newry
Newcastle
Camlough
Slieve Donard Mountain
Mountains of Mourne
Warrenpoint
Carlingford Lough
Kilkeel
N
0 10 miles
0 15 km

Albert Memorial Clock Tower, **7**
Botanic Gardens, **9**
City Hall, **4**
Europa Hotel, **2**
Grand Opera House, **3**
Northern Ireland Tourist Office, **6**
Queen's College, **8**
St. Anne's Cathedral, **5**
Ulster Museum, **10**

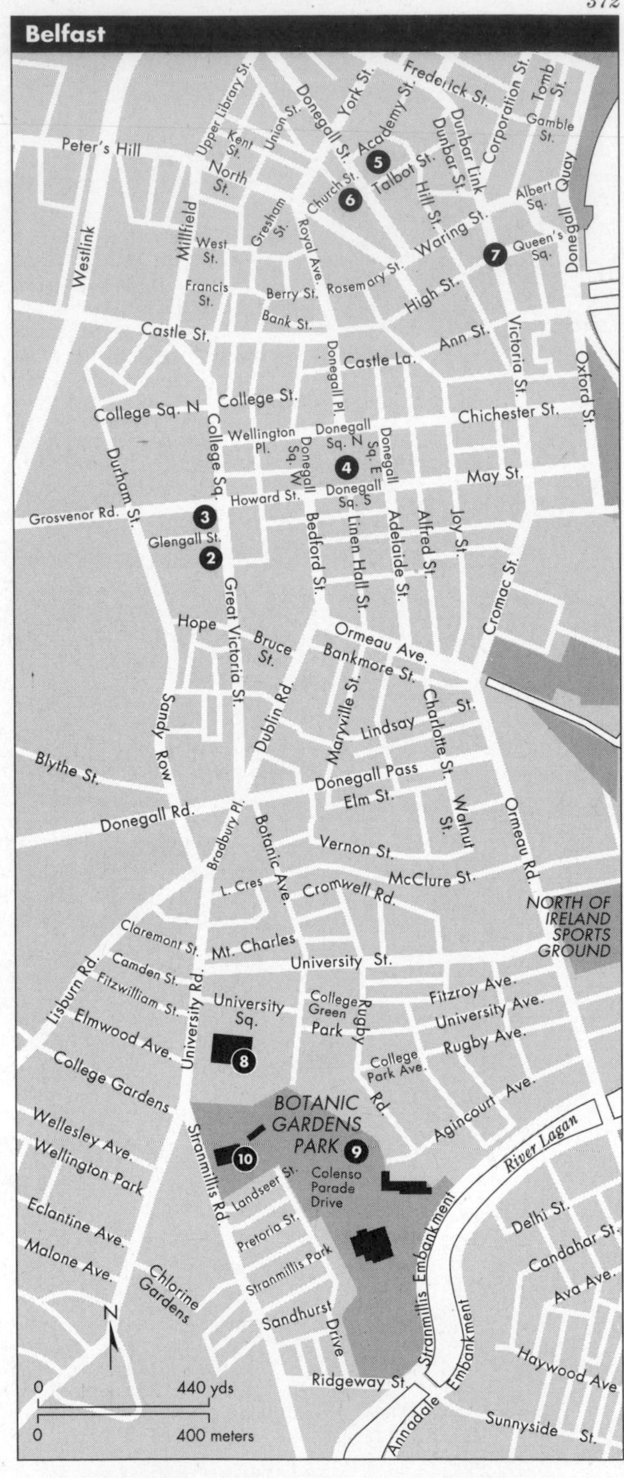

tive plasterwork reaching up toward the dome. *Donegall Sq., tel. 0232/320202. Admission free. Guided tours: Wed. 10:30.*

You'll notice many buses waiting on the western and eastern sides of Donegall Square. This is the terminus for all city buses. The gray building on Donegall Square's northwest corner (at the junction with Wellington Place) is the **Linen Hall Library.** This comfortable private library, founded in 1788, is not really a tourist attraction, but you may want to stop here. Besides being a perfect hideaway for relaxing with a newspaper, the library has an unparalleled collection of local historical documents. Paintings and prints that show Belfast views and landmarks adorn the walls. The artworks are for sale and make excellent and original souvenirs or gifts. *17 Donegall Sq. N, tel. 0232/321707. Visitors may join the library for 1 mo at a cost of U.K.£2. Open Mon.–Wed. and Fri. 9:30–6, Thurs. 9:30–8:30, Sat. 9:30–4.*

Step round the corner of the library on to **Donegall Place,** Belfast's main shopping street. You'll pass through the security gates into the pedestrians-only zone. Stroll up to Royal Avenue, a continuation of Donegall Place.

Time Out Belfast offers dozens of intriguing pubs packed with relics of the Victorian and Edwardian periods. At the start of Royal Avenue, turn left into Bank Street to find **Kelly's Cellars,** a typical traditional bar with character. Specialties include Ulster fry (fried bacon, sausages, egg, etc., with potato bread) and champ 'n' sausages (champ is creamy mashed potato with chopped spring onions), each for less than U.K.£2. Two centuries ago, Kelly's Cellars was the regular meeting place of a militant Nationalist group, the Society of United Irishmen, whose leader, Wolfe Tone, is remembered as the founder of Irish republicanism.

---

5 To see **St. Anne's Cathedral,** continue to the end of Royal Avenue (crossing North Street), and then turn right on to Donegall Street. St. Anne's, a large edifice built at the beginning of this century, could almost be considered the spiritual headquarters of the province's Anglican establishment. Frankly, though, this is not an especially beautiful building. Its somber heaviness and deep rounded arches are hallmarks of the Irish neo-Romanesque style. Lord Carson, who was largely responsible for keeping the six counties inside the United Kingdom, is buried here beneath a suitably austere plain gray slab. Almost opposite the cathedral in St. Anne's Court, off North Street, you
6 will find the new premises of the main **Northern Ireland Tourist Office** (scheduled to open in early 1991). Behind St. Anne's Cathedral, you'll find a run-down area of narrow cobbled back streets and abandoned warehouses; this district is due for a major overhaul, with new construction and businesses already promising to revive the neighborhood.

Walk south down to Waring Street (it runs at the bottom of both Hill Street and Donegall Street), turn left toward the Lagan River, then right into busy Victoria Street. From here, as you
7 walk toward the leaning **Albert Memorial Clock Tower,** you'll be able to see parts of Belfast's famous shipyards and two of the world's largest cranes, dubbed Samson (108 m/350 ft high) and Goliath (143 m/462 ft). At the clock tower, named for Queen

Victoria's husband, Prince Albert (though he never came to Northern Ireland), turn right on to High Street.

Off High Street, and especially down to the parallel Ann Street, run narrow lanes and alleyways called entries. Though mostly cleaned up and turned into chic shopping lanes, they manage to hang on to something of their former raffish character. Wandering along these lanes you'll discover some unique pubs with authentic Victorian interiors. For example, take a look inside **The Morning Star** (Pottinger's Entry, nearly opposite the tourist office) with its large windows and fine curving bar. **White's Tavern** (Winecellar Entry, off the High St.) is Belfast's oldest pub, founded in 1630. Although it has been considerably updated, it still has a warm and comfortable ambience, with plush seats and a big open fire.

Follow Ann Street back to Donegall Place, then retrace your steps through Donegall Square to Great Victoria Street.

Time Out You might want a drink (and maybe a plate of oysters) in Belfast's best-preserved pub, the **Crown Liquor Saloon** (tel. 0232/325368), which is directly opposite the Europa Hotel on Great Victoria Street. The Crown, owned by the United Kingdom's official conservationist charity, The National Trust, dates back to the end of the 19th century and has been kept in immaculate condition with opulent ornamentation, richly carved woodwork around cozy snugs (private rooms), leather seats, colored tiles, and abundant mirrors.

The Europa and the Crown bar mark the start of **The Golden Mile,** so-called because most of Belfast's evening life takes place in bars and restaurants here. The Crown is far from being the only impressive old pub on this stretch. Indeed, if you would like to try another Victorian bar with more locals and fewer visitors, you only have to walk into **Robinson's,** next door to the Crown. **The Beaten Docket,** on the other side of the Crown, is snazzier and appeals to a younger crowd.

8 The **University Area** is centered on **Queen's College** (set well back from University Rd.), which was constructed in the 1840s. Queen's is modeled on the colleges at Oxford University in England, with their spires, turrets, and fine stonework. **University Square,** adjacent to Queen's, is another architectural treasure with its Georgian terraces.

9 Spreading out beside Queen's, the 19th-century **Botanic Gardens** provide a welcome haven of quiet and greenery. A pretty highlight of the gardens is the 150-year-old curved iron-and-glass Palm House, the oldest such structure in the world. *Stranmillis Rd., tel. 0232/324902. Admission free. Gardens open daily dawn–dusk. Palm House open weekdays 10–5, weekends 2–5.*

10 Within the gardens, to the left of the main entrance, the **Ulster Museum** offers three floors devoted to the history and prehistory of Ireland in general and Northern Ireland in particular, together with a considerable collection of 19th- and 20th-century fine art. In the natural history section, you'll see, among other things, a skeleton of the now-extinct Irish giant deer. The museum's centerpiece is the fabulous jewelry and gold ornaments (as well as cannon and other armaments) recovered from the Spanish vessel *Girona*, sunk off the Antrim coast

in 1588. Perhaps the most imaginative, user-friendly sections are on the first floor—one colorfully traces the rise of Belfast's crafts, trade, and industry; the other tells the story of the Nationalist movement and explains the separation of Northern Ireland from the rest of the country. Visitors have access to a little café on level three. *Stranmillis Rd., tel. 0232/381251. Admission free. Open weekdays 10–5, Sat. 1–5, Sun. 2–5.*

The road south divides at the Botanic Gardens. Stranmillis Road leads into **Stranmillis,** a perfectly safe neighborhood with a cultured air and a choice of eateries. The community reaches over to the riverside towpath along the Lagan. **Malone Road** joins the river farther south, close to the out-of-town **Giant's Ring** (off Ballyleeson Road), a large, neolithic earthworks focused on an impressive *dolmen* (Celtic monument made of large stone slabs). To get this far, unless you're a keen walker (it's possible to come all the way on the Lagan towpath) you'll be happier driving in a car or taking a bus: bus No. 22 passes close to the site, and on the return journey it will take you back to Donegall Square.

Tour 2: Around Counties Antrim and Derry

Numbers in the margin correspond with points of interest on the Northern Ireland map.

This circular route starts and finishes in Belfast, passing through some fair-sized towns, but most of the way you're driving in open country. Scenery is the best thing about Northern Ireland, but the region has much more to offer. For example, you'll discover the roots of several Ulstermen who became distinguished Americans. To follow the whole tour as described here could take an unhurried three or four days.

Begin this tour by heading north out of Belfast along the industrialized west shore of Belfast Lough. Cave Hill (*see* Off the Beaten Track below), rising to the left, makes a popular day excursion for city dwellers.

11 Take the busy A2 toward **Carrickfergus.** This town on the shore of the lough grew up around **Carrickfergus Castle,** one of the first and one of the largest of Irish castles, which is still in good shape. Impressively located on a rock ledge, it was built in 1180 by John de Courcy, provincial Ulster's first Anglo-Norman invader. The castle stood as a bastion of British rule right up until 1928, at which time it was still an English garrison. In fact, when Carrickfergus was enclosed by ramparts at the start of the 17th century, it was the only English-speaking town in Northern Ireland. Not surprisingly, this was the loyal port where William of Orange chose to land on his way to fight the Catholic forces at the Battle of the Boyne in 1690. However, the English did have one or two small setbacks, including the improbable victory in 1778 of John Paul Jones, an American privateer, over the British warship HMS *Drake*. That, by the way, was America's first naval victory during the Revolutionary War. After the sea battle, the inhabitants of Carrickfergus stood on the waterfront and cheered Jones because they supported the American Revolution.

Walk through the castle's 13th-century gatehouse into the Outer Ward; continue into the Inner Ward, the heart of the fortress. Here stands the five-story Keep, a massively sturdy building with walls almost 2½ m (8 ft) thick. Inside the Keep, you'll find a Cavalry Regimental Museum with historic weapons and an impressive vaulted Great Hall. These days, Carrickfergus Castle hosts entertaining medieval banquets (inquire at a local tourist office); if you're here at the beginning of August, you can enjoy the annual Lughnasa festival, a lively medieval costume entertainment. *Tel. 09603/51273. Admission: U.K.75p adults, U.K.35p children under 16. Open Apr.–Sept., daily 10–6; 10–4 Oct.–Mar., daily (closed all year Sun. AM).*

Other structures that remain from Carrickfergus's past are St. Nicholas's Church, dating from the 13th and 14th centuries, and the handsomely restored North Gate in the town's medieval walls. **Dobbins Inn** (tel. 0574/51905) on the High Street has been a popular hotel for more than three centuries. While in Carrickfergus, you might like to take a look at the **Andrew Jackson Centre,** in a thatched cottage a mile northeast of the town. This exhibit tells the tale of U.S. president Jackson, whose parents emigrated from Carrickfergus in 1765. This cottage was not their home, but it probably resembles it.

As you head away from the town on the A2, you'll pass through the village of **Eden,** where **Castle Dobbs** was the home of Arthur Dobbs, the 18th-century British governor of North Carolina. A mile and a half (2½ km) off the road, signposted on the left, **Dalway's Bawn,** built in 1609, is the best surviving example of an early *bawn,* or fortified farmhouse occupied by a Protestant Planter. Stay on the A2 to **Larne,** and pass through this workaday port town.

Soon after Larne, the coast of County Antrim becomes spectacular. Wave upon wave of high green hills curve down into the hazy sea, and the views are thrilling. The lower slopes are lush and intensively farmed, but rugged, too, while green moorland covers the rounded summits. Broad, rich glens, or valleys, cut through the hills toward the sea. In the 86 km (54 mi) between
12 Larne and Ballycastle there are nine magnificent **Glens of Antrim.** The journey by these glens is mostly along a small, winding two-lane road close to the sea. **Carnlough** (24 km/15 mi out of Larne) is a little resort made of white limestone. It features an endearing harbor within stone walls and a small tourist office inside the post office.

Time Out Carnlough's **Londonderry Arms** (20 Harbour Rd., tel. 0574/85255) is a fine old traditional inn by the harbor. It dates back to the 17th century and once belonged to Winston Churchill. Fresh seafood is, of course, the specialty—try the seafood gratiné or the lobster—and substantial homemade wheat bread is served as well.

Beyond Carnlough the scenery becomes even more attractive. **Glenariff,** opening on to Red Bay at the village of Glenariff (also known as Waterfoot), is considered the loveliest of the glens. At neighboring **Cushendall,** you'll see a curious fortified square tower of red stone—a 19th-century jailhouse—standing at a crossroads in the middle of the village. If you would like a break from the Antrim coast, stay on the A2 direct to Ballycastle. But if you would prefer to stay by the sea, turn left at the tower in the direction of **Cushendun,** a tiny jewel of a village. From this part of the coast you can see the Mull of Kintyre on the Scottish mainland. The coast road rejoins the A2 after a few miles and descends—passing the ruins of the former Franciscans' 16th-century **Bonamargy Friary**—into **Ballycastle,** the glens' main resort, at the northern end of the Glens of Antrim drive.

Every year since 1606, on the last Tuesday in August the town has hosted its **Oul' Lammas Fair,** a modern version of the ancient Celtic harvest festival Lughnasa. Ireland's oldest fair, this is a highly popular two-day event at which sheep and wool are still sold alongside more modern shopping stalls. If you're here at this time, treat yourself to the fair's traditional snacks, "dulse and yellow man" (edible seaweed and rock-hard yellow toffee). If you happen to be at Ballycastle in June, you might find yourself in the middle of the **Fleadh Amhran agus Rince,** a lively three-day music and dance folk festival.

From Ballycastle you have a view of *L*-shape **Rathlin Island,** where in 1306 the Scottish king Robert the Bruce took shelter in a cave and was inspired to continue his armed struggle against the English by watching the patience of a spider spinning its web. It was on Rathlin in 1898 that Guglielmo Marconi set up the world's first radio link, from the island's lighthouse to Ballycastle. If the sea is not too rough (which it often is), a daily boat excursion journeys to the rocky windswept island; only 9½ km (6 mi) away from shore, Rathlin can take an hour to reach. Make sure that you'll be able to return the same day.

Follow the shore road (B15) to **Carrick-a-Rede,** famous for one simple thing: a rope bridge. The bridge, swinging 25 m (80 ft) above the crashing sea, is the insecure-feeling link between the mainland and a salmon fishery on a tiny island 18½ m (60 ft) offshore. The walk across the bridge is pretty scary, but perhaps that's why almost every man, woman, and child passing this way likes to try it. *Admission free. Bridge open daily May–Sept.*

Another 8 km (5 mi) along the coast brings you to Ireland's
13 strangest and most impressive geological curiosity, **The Giant's Causeway.** This bizarre sight consists of huge masses of mostly hexagonal pillars of volcanic basalt, clustered like honeycomb; about 37,000 of these columns extend down the cliffs, far into the sea. They were supposedly created from boiling lava crystallizing as it burst into the sea; the lava came from an underground fissure that stretched from Northern Ireland to the Scottish coast. According to legend, however, the columns were created when the giant Finn MacCool threw stepping-stones into the sea to make a causeway over to the Scottish island of Staffa.

Arriving by car, at first you'll reach a cliff-top parking lot beside the **Visitor Centre,** which provides displays about the area and an audiovisual exhibition explaining the formation of the causeway coast. To reach the causeway itself means a round-trip journey on foot of about 3 km (2 mi). If you can't face such a trek, a minibus from the Visitor Centre will take you to the site. You can walk or scramble over the rocks (beware: they can be slippery and dangerous), some of which have been given whimsical names such as the Organ, the Harp, and so on. Farther out, Port-na-Spania is the spot where the 16th-century Spanish Armada galleass *Girona* went down on the rocks. The ship was carrying an astonishing cargo of gold and jewelry, some of which was recovered in 1967 and is now on display in the

Ulster Museum in Belfast (*see* Tour 1: Belfast, above). Beyond that, Chimney Point is the name given to one of the causeway structures on which the Spanish fired, thinking that it was Dunluce Castle, which is 8 km (5 mi) west. *Giant's Causeway Visitor Centre, Causeway Head, near Bushmills, tel. 02657/ 31855. Car park: U.K.£1. Audiovisual exhibition: U.K.£1 adults, U.K.50p children. Static exhibition: U.K.50p adults, U.K.30p children and senior citizens. Open July–Aug., daily 10–7. Closes earlier according to demand, rest of year.*

Time Out The pleasant little tearoom in the Visitor Centre provides wholesome snacks at moderate prices. Enjoy panoramic sea views while you enjoy the cakes and scones.

Just inland from The Giant's Causeway about 3 km (2 mi) on the A2 is **Bushmills,** the village whose distillery produces the original, the best, and the most famous of Irish whiskeys. Enthusiasts of this elegant firewater who would like to see how it is made should call ahead at the Bushmills Distillery to join one of the guided tours. *Tel. 02657/31521. Admission free. Tours Mon.–Thurs. mornings and afternoons, Fri. mornings only.*

About 5 km (3 mi) west of Bushmills, still on the A2, the **Dunluce Castle** ruin lies dramatically on a cliff top. Originally a 13th-century Norman fortress, it was captured in the 16th century by the indomitable local MacDonnell clan chiefs, who enlarged it, making it an important base for controlling the area. Maybe they expanded the castle a little too much, for in 1639 the kitchens and the cooks plummeted into the sea. *Admission: U.K.60p adults, U.K.30p children and senior citizens. Open Apr.–Sept., Mon.–Sat. 10–7, Sun. 2–7; Oct.–Mar., Mon.–Sat. 10–4, Sun. 2–4. Closed 1–1:30.*

To reach **Coleraine,** either take the A2 to the small resort of Portrush and turn inland on the A28 or turn back to Bushmills and take the B17 from there—either way, you'll drive about 13 km (8 mi) to Coleraine from Dunluce Castle. At Coleraine, cross the River Bann into County Londonderry (or Derry). The Bann, which cuts through Northern Ireland, marks the boundary between the fiercely Protestant counties Antrim and Down, and the other four counties.

Take the A37 west from Coleraine through **Limavady,** with its Georgian main street. At No. 51, in the year 1851, Jane Ross noted down the tune played by a traveling fiddler and called it "Londonderry Air," later to become better known as "Danny Boy." While staying at an inn on Ballyclose Street, William Thackeray (1811–1863) wrote his rather lustful poem "Peg of Limavaddy," about a barmaid. Among the many Americans descended from Ulster emigrants was President James Monroe, whose relatives came from the Limavady area.

14 As the road turns down toward **Derry City,** the neat terraces rising gently from the Foyle Valley come into view. The town appears attractive and inviting, which is astonishing because of its reputation as one of Europe's most troubled cities. In reality, here as in Belfast, the publicity is out of proportion to the actual situation, though as always, it is extremely prudent to avoid wandering about in certain sections of town, notably Bogside and Creggan. The name of the city, by the way, is now officially Derry, although staunch Loyalists (including many government departments) still like to call it by its old Planta-

tion period name, Londonderry. The county, though, is still called Londonderry. The "London" part of the name was tacked on in 1613 after the Irish nobility were thoroughly trounced and the city and county were handed over to the Corporation of London, which represented London's merchants. They brought in a large population of Protestants, built new towns for them, and reconstructed Derry within the **City Walls,** which survive almost unchanged to this day.

These substantial ramparts of gray stone, pierced by eight gates (originally four), are about 8 m (25 ft) high and as much as 9 m (30 ft) thick. The walls are only 1.6 km (1 mi) all round, which indicates how small the walled area is. These days, Derry extends far beyond this fortified center; most of the life of the town actually takes place outside the walls. The best way to get the feel of Derry's history is to stroll along the parapet walkway atop the ramparts. The walkway has been closed for some time, but it is scheduled to be reopened for guided walks by mid-1991. If the ramparts walkway is still closed during your visit, a near-complete circuit can be made at ground level. The best starting point is Shipquay Gate on the north side, beside the ornate Victorian **Guildhall,** with convenient parking close by. The town's Tourist Information Office is located on Foyle Street, two minutes on foot from the Guildhall car park.

Over the centuries, the sturdy ramparts withstood many fierce attacks and were never breached, which explains Derry's coy soubriquet, "The Maiden City." The most celebrated siege occurred from 1688 to 1689, when James II (the Catholic king trying to regain the throne of England) reached the town with his army, expecting to be welcomed by Derry's governor, Colonel Lundy. But 13 Protestant apprentice boys had stolen the keys of the city gates; after throwing Lundy outside, these lads locked the gates to prevent James's entry. James, undeterred, blockaded the town with the intention of starving it into submission. Of the 30,000 people within the walls, a quarter of them died of hunger before reinforcements arrived from William of Orange (the Dutch Protestant claimant to the English throne). The blockade was broken, and James was forced to withdraw. The whole event is proudly recalled by Derry's Protestant community—now a minority of the population—who still hold colorful ceremonial marches in honor of the apprentice boys, reenacting the Protestants' triumph and annually burning an effigy of the hated Governor Lundy.

From Shipquay Gate, walk along Union Hall Street. You'll pass **O'Doherty's Tower** (where an Interpretation Center is planned to open in 1991 to tell the Derry City story) and turn up toward **Butcher Gate,** on the west side, which opens onto the Catholic Bogside district. The graffito "Doire Cholmcille" near this gateway is the old Irish name for Derry City—Columba's Oak. A five-minute walk downhill outside Butcher Gate into the Bogside will take you to **Free Derry Corner,** one of the city's compelling modern curiosities, a surviving gable wall, from a demolished terrace of houses, that is painted with the bold words YOU ARE NOW ENTERING FREE DERRY. From here you can see **Roaring Meg,** one of the original cannons from the 1688–89 siege, which still looks out from Double Bastion, a fortified corner on the ramparts. Go back inside Butcher Gate, and continue on Magazine Street to **Bishop Gate.** Here you'll discover one of the most extraordinary features of the walls: The British army is still using them to defend the city. Bishop Gate, opening on to the Fountain Area, a Protestant quarter on the south side, is under exceptionally heavy guard.

Within the walls, Shipquay Street climbs steeply to the central square, the Diamond. On the way it passes an attractive new development lying to the right (look for sign, THE VILLAGE). Beyond the Diamond, if you walk on Bishop Street Within, you'll pass **St. Columb's Cathedral.** Built in 1633 in simple Planter's Gothic style, the church is a treasure house of Derry Protestant emblems, memorials, and relics from the 1688–89 siege.

Time Out Among the several modest cafés suitable for a snack or lunch break in Derry City, one of the most agreeable is **The Boston Tea Party.** This small tea shop is situated in the new development called The Village, which is reached down an alley nearly opposite the Richmond Shopping Centre on Shipquay Street. Boston, by the way, has surprising links with Derry dating back to the 17th and 18th centuries, when many Derrymen escaped their hardships at home by emigrating to that U.S. city and other parts of the New World.

Tour 3: Around Counties Tyrone, Fermanagh, Armagh, and Down

From Derry City, head across County Tyrone toward Enniskillen. Take the A5 south via Strabane to Omagh. For a delightfully rustic alternative route, drive along the minor road B48, which skirts the foot of the **Sperrin Mountains. Strabane** does not offer much to hold your interest, apart from the well-preserved 18th-century **Gray's Print Shop** (49 Main St., tel. 0504/884094). John Dunlap (1746–1812), who apprenticed here as a printer before emigrating to Philadelphia, founded America's first daily newspaper, *The Philadelphia Packet*, in 1771, and was also the man who printed and distributed the American Declaration of Independence. James Wilson, grandfather of President Woodrow Wilson, also emigrated. The original **Wilson family home,** a simple thatched cottage, still with much of the original 18th-century furniture, survives at Dergalt, 3 km (2 mi) along the Plumbridge Road. It can be visited by knocking at the farmhouse next door, still owned and worked by the Wilson family.

About 27 km (17 mi) south from Strabane on the A5, just 5 km (3
15 mi) from Omagh, you'll reach the **Ulster-American Folk Park,** which has been designed to re-create a Tyrone village of two centuries ago, a log-built American settlement of the same period, and the docks and ships that the emigrants to America would have used. The centerpiece of the park is an old whitewashed cottage, now a museum, which is the ancestral home of Andrew Mellon, the U.S. millionaire banker. Another thatched cottage is a reconstruction of the boyhood home of Archbishop John Hughes, founder of New York's St. Patrick's Cathedral. Exhibitions trace the contribution of the Northern Irish people to American history. The park also features a crafts shop and café. *Camphill, Co. Tyrone, tel. 0662/3292. Admission: U.K.£2 adults, U.K.£1 children. Open Easter–Sept., Mon.–Sat. 11–6:30, Sun. and holidays 11:30–7; Oct.–day before Easter, weekdays 10:30–5. Last admission 1½ hrs before closing.*

Drive south through **Omagh,** County Tyrone's capital, taking the A32 in the direction of Enniskillen. After 9½ km (6 mi), turn right onto the B4 to the village of **Kesh,** beside **Lower Lough Erne.** The best of this highly scenic lake can be seen by driving from Kesh to Enniskillen on the shore road (B82). Lovers of Belleek pottery should first skirt the northern edge of
16 the lake to reach **Belleek,** where this distinctive fine porcelain is made. You can tour the **Belleek Pottery Ltd.** factory, where original methods of manufacture are still used; you can purchase some of the pottery, and enjoy a snack in the tea shop. *Tel. 0365/65501. Admission free. Tours Mon.–Thurs. 9:30–4:15; Fri. 9:30–3:15.*

Just a mile across the border, on the road to Ballyshannon in County Donegal, you can visit **Celtic Weave China** (tel. 072/51844), a small operation making handmade fine pottery similar to the items made in Belleek (*see* Shopping, below).

On the journey beside Lough Erne, apart from pausing to catch your breath at the lovely views of green hills extending down to the still lake water, you should also stop at **Castle Archdale Country Park,** signposted down a narrow road about 6½ km (4 mi) from Kesh, where there's a lakeside marina, an open-air country museum, and a World War II exhibition featuring the Battle of the Atlantic. *Tel. 03656/21333. Admission free. No set hours.*

From Castle Archdale a June–September ferry (tel. 0365/22711; cost: U.K.£1; no boat Mon.) takes passengers to see the
17 weird Celtic carved figures on **White Island.** After you drive 13 km (8 mi) farther from Castle Archdale Park, where the B82 joins the A32, a small sign shows the way to catch the little boat from April–September (tel. 0365/22711; cost: U.K.£1; no boat
18 Mon.) over to **Devenish Island.** The extensive but ruined 12th-century monastery on Devenish features Ireland's best example of a round tower and a richly carved high cross.

19 Another 5 km (3 mi) south along the A32 brings you to **Enniskillen,** the pleasant capital of County Fermanagh, with its town center strikingly situated on an island in the River Erne between Upper and Lower Lough Erne. At the riverside, the 16th-century **Water Gate** is handsomely turreted, and part of the 15th-century **Castle Keep** contains the local history collection of the **Fermanagh County Museum** (tel. 0365/25050) and the polished paraphernalia of the **Royal Inniskilling Fusiliers Regimental Museum** (tel. 0365/23142). Beyond the West Bridge lies Portora Royal School, established in 1608 by King James I. Its grounds contain the ruins of Portora Castle. Writers Oscar Wilde and Samuel Beckett were both educated at Portora Royal School. The town's other sights are admittedly modest. Yet the spires of its 19th-century churches and town hall lend a certain charm to this friendly town. One satisfying journey to make from Enniskillen is a complete tour of Lower Lough Erne, allowing a full day to really enjoy it.

Time Out Among the several relaxed and welcoming old pubs in Enniskillen's town center, the one with the most appeal is **Blakes of the Hollow** on the main street, a place hardly altered since it opened in 1887. Its name derives from the facts that the heart of the town lies in a slight dip or hollow and the pub's landlord is named William Blake. Don't ask if he's related to the great poet of the same name—everybody does, and he isn't!

About 11 km (7 mi) south from Enniskillen on the A4 and the A32, **Florence Court** deserves a visit if you have the time. One of the most impressive of Northern Ireland's grand Anglo-Irish mansions, it was built in the 18th century for John Cole, father of the first earl of Enniskillen. The house features abundant rococo plasterwork, 18th-century furnishings, and a fine porcelain collection. You can stroll around the estate grounds, and have a snack and coffee at the tea shop. *Tel. 036582/249. Admission: U.K.£1.50 adults, U.K.75p children. Open June–Aug. Wed.–Mon., closed Tues.; Apr., May, Sept., weekends only. Grounds open 10–1 hr before sunset. House open 2–6.*

Next, drive east from Enniskillen on the A4, the main Belfast road (from Florence Court, backtrack on the A32 to Enniskillen), and 3 km (2 mi) from town, you'll see signs pointing to
20 **Castle Coole** on the left. Another of the graceful mansions of the Anglo-Irish ruling class of the 18th and 19th centuries, this home is considered the finest of them all. The house stands in its own landscaped oak woods and parkland at the end of a long tree-lined driveway. In perfect Palladian symmetry, white colonnaded wings extend from either side of the white neoclassical mansion. In a recent restoration, anything not in keeping with the original design was removed. Inside, too, everything —from the lavish plasterwork to sumptuous period furniture —reflects the taste and wealth of its first owners, the earls of Belmore. Castle Coole is still the home of the present earl of Belmore. *Enniskillen, Co. Fermanagh, tel. 0365/22690. Admission: U.K.£2 adults, U.K.£1 children. Open Easter and June–Aug., Fri.–Wed. 2–6, closed Thurs.; May and Sept., weekends and holidays only; rest of year, grounds open, house closed.*

Continue in an easterly direction along the A4, through drumlin-dotted farmland (drumlins are tiny hillocks). At Augher village, pick up the A28 on the right.

After a 40-km (25-mi) drive, the road reaches the small but an-
21 cient ecclesiastical city of **Armagh.** Despite some pleasing Georgian streets (especially The Mall, east of the town center), the heart of Armagh can seem drab, and it suffers from having been a trouble spot in the religious conflict. Here St. Patrick founded a church, and the town has remained a religious center until the present day. In fact, *two* Armagh cathedrals are dedicated to Ireland's patron saint. Despite the 1921 partition of Ireland into two parts, the seat of the Catholic Archbishop of All Ireland remains in Armagh, as does the seat of the Archbishop of the Anglican Church of Ireland.

The pale limestone Victorian Gothic **Catholic Cathedral** with two pale spires, on a hill at the north end of town, is best seen from a distance; it is dedicated to St. Patrick. Nearer the town center, a squat battlemented tower identifies the **Protestant Cathedral,** in simpler early 19th-century Perpendicular Gothic style. It stands on the site of much older churches and contains several relics of Armagh's long history, including sculpted pre-Christian idols. This cathedral claims to be the burial place of Brian Boru, the great High King—that is, King of all Ireland —who drove the Vikings out of Ireland in the 11th century.

Walk down College Street, turning off English Street in the town center, to the broad Georgian esplanade called The Mall. At the north end of the green stands the 19th-century Courthouse, and at the other end, a dominating jailhouse. On the corner of The Mall East, the **Royal Irish Fusiliers Museum** (in Sovereign's House, tel. 0861/522911) features exhibits that illustrate part of the story of Britain's efforts to control this part of Ireland from the 1798 Rebellion onward.

On a completely different note, about 200 yards from the museum up College Hill—a continuation of College Street at the north end of the Mall—is Armagh's main attraction, the **Astronomy Centre and Planetarium.** It contains fascinating exhibits including models of spacecraft, video shows of the sky, and hands-on computer displays. The Observatory here has been in continuous use since 1791. *Tel. 0861/523689. Admission: U.K.£2 adults, U.K.£1.50 children under 18 and senior citizens. Open daily 1:30–4:45.*

Next, leave Armagh on the A28, driving toward Newry. Instead of going the whole way on the main road, after about 9½ km (6 mi), you'll have a more enjoyable drive if you take the B133, on the right. This will lead you through a rustic drumlin landscape of vivid green pastures. The appearance of villages changes as you return toward the River Bann; houses and farms begin to resemble homes and farms in Britain rather than those in the Republic. **Bessbrook** is a "model village" built in 1846 by Quaker linen manufacturer John Grubb Richardson. It has a naive, dreamlike, toy-town quality, with its neat terraces and picture-book village stores. Richardson decreed that there would be no pubs at Bessbrook. Maybe that explains why there are no fewer than six in the neighboring village, Camlough. **Derrymore House,** a thatched cottage with a well-tended garden outside of Bessbrook, is the place where in 1800 the fateful Act of Union was drafted.

From Bessbrook, the drive is only 3 km (2 mi) to the middle of **Newry,** a town with a history of vigorous Irish nationalism, despite having the first Protestant church in Ireland, St. Patrick's. Though still standing, the church has been altered a great deal since it was put up in 1578, having been frequently damaged and repaired. Some 18th-century buildings in Newry survive, especially on Upper Water Street and Trevor Hill, notably the White Linen Hall. On weekends and market days, Irish citizens fill the town, coming from across the Northern Ireland border, only 6½ km (4 mi) away, to take advantage of lower prices in the North.

Follow the east bank of industrialized Carlingford Lough and then the wild Irish Sea to **Newcastle.** On the way you'll be cir-
22 cling the atmospheric and unspoiled **Mountains of Mourne,** which "sweep down to the sea" (in the words of a popular song) from 620-m (2,000-ft) summits. This area was long considered ungovernable, its hardy inhabitants living from smuggling contraband into the numerous rocky coves on the seashore. Much of the Mourne range is still inaccessible, except on foot. The countryside of high windswept pasture and moorland, threaded with bright streams, is perfect for away-from-it-all walkers. Newcastle is the main center for visitors to the hills. Looming above the town is **Slieve Donard,** its panoramic 870-m (2,805-ft) summit grandly claiming views into England, Wales,

and Scotland—"when it's clear enough," or, in other words, rarely!

23 **Downpatrick,** 19 km (12 mi) away from Slieve Donard on the A2, used to be called plain and simple Down, but the town is proud of a suspected association with St. Patrick and changed its name in his honor. St. Patrick was a 5th-century Briton who, captured by the Irish, became a slave in the Down area; he escaped to France, where he learned about Christianity, and bravely returned to try to convert the local chiefs. Although it is not true that Patrick personally brought a new faith to Ireland (there was already a bishop of Ireland before Patrick got here), he must have been a better missionary than most because he did indeed win influential converts. The clan chief of the Down area gave him land at the village of Saul, near Downpatrick, to build a monastery.

Downpatrick's hilltop cathedral, built in 1790, preserves parts of some of the earlier churches and monasteries that have stood on the site since the 6th century. Even before that time, the cathedral site had long been an important fortified settlement (Down takes its name from the Celtic word "Dun," a fort). In the churchyard, a somber slab has been inscribed "Patric"—it's supposedly the saint's tomb, which is a bit of a fraud since no one knows where Patrick is buried. It might be here, at Saul, or, some scholars argue, more likely at Armagh. A lot of such mystery and legend surrounds Patrick. For some hard fact, visit the **St. Patrick Heritage Centre** next to the cathedral; it's housed, together with the **Down Museum,** inside a former 18th-century jail. *The Mall, tel. 0396/5218. Admission free. Open weekdays 11–5, weekends 2–5. Closed Sept.–June, Mon.*

From Downpatrick, head northeast on the A25 to Strangford (13 km/8 mi) and the **Ards Peninsula.** You'll have to cross Strangford Lough on the car ferry from Strangford to Portaferry, both quiet fishing villages with old fortifications to guard this once-strategic channel, which joins the lough to the sea. At **Strangford, Castle Ward** is an 18th-century mansion in a bizarre mixture of styles—classical on one side, Gothic on the other. The 700-acre estate has a "Victorian pastimes center" for children, a wildfowl collection, a restaurant, an information office, and the old tower house, which once guarded the shore. Holiday cottages are available for rentals as well. *Located .8 km (½ mi) west of Strangford on south shore of Strangford Lough, tel. 0396/86204. Admission: U.K.£1.50 adults, U.K.75p children. House open May–Aug., Fri.–Wed. 1–6; closed Thurs. Estate open year-round, dawn–dusk.*

The ferry crossing from Strangford to **Portaferry** takes 10 minutes or less, and boats leave every half hour throughout the day all year long.

Time Out On the Portaferry waterside, **The Portaferry Arms** (tel. 02477/28230), an old, unpretentious bed-and-breakfast, has a full menu of inexpensive snacks and lunches. Take a window seat and watch the unhurried activity on the quay and the relaxed routine of the tiny ferry as it chugs to and fro across the lough.

Before moving on, you may like to take a look at Portaferry's unusual **Northern Ireland Aquarium,** which has models of the underwater environment in Strangford Lough and examples of

70 species that call the lough their home. Some of these creatures may not be what you expect—seal and some large, long-lived species of fish still live in the lake. *Northern Rope Walk, Portaferry, tel. 02477/28062. Admission: U.K.£1.20 adults, U.K. 60p children and senior citizens, children under 5 free. Family ticket U.K.£3. Open Apr.–Aug., Mon.–Sat. 10–6; Sun., afternoons only. Sept.–Mar., Tues.–Sat. 10:30–5; Sun., afternoons only.*

The A20 makes its way north from Portaferry up the lake shore. Strangford Lough is not really a lake; it is joined to the sea by the channel you crossed at Portaferry, and might be better described as a fjord. Although Strangford Lough is deep in the middle, it rises to shallow banks dotted with rounded islands (actually submerged drumlins). In fact, its original Norse name was *Strang Fjord* (Strong Fjord), referring to the powerful current that flows into and out of the water with every tide. Huge populations of wildfowl gather in and beside the water.

24 **Mount Stewart,** signposted on the right around 21 km (13 mi) from Portaferry, is the grand 18th-century family home of the marquesses of Londonderry. The marvelous landscaped gardens give the impression that the owners had more money than they knew what to do with; they created luxuriant flower beds, elaborate hedges, and planned views, and they populated the grounds with surprising stone carvings of rare and extinct creatures. The octagonal Temple of the Winds is a copy of a similar little structure in Athens. *Newtownards, tel. 024774/387. Admission: U.K.£3 adults, U.K.£1.50 children. Open June–Aug., Wed.–Mon. 1–6, closed Tues.; May, Sept., Oct., weekends and public holidays only.*

On the A20, from Newtownards west to Belfast direct is only 16 km (10 mi), but it's worth detouring via **Bangor** (6½ km/4 mi
25 from Newtownards on the A21) to visit the **Ulster Folk Museum,** which is also 11 km (7 mi) from Belfast on the A2. Devoted to the province's social history, the open-air museum is set in some 70 acres around Cultra Manor and encircled by a larger park and recreation area. It brings Northern Ireland's past vividly to life with a score of reconstructed buildings brought here from around the region; these structures represent different facets of Northern Ireland life—a traditional weaver's dwelling, terraces of Victorian town houses, an 18th-century country church, a village flax mill, a farmhouse, and a rural school. You start your visit with the Folk Gallery, which explains the background of each building. Across the main road (by footbridge) is the Transport Museum, with exhibits showing every kind of transport, including a miniature railway on Saturdays during the summer. *Cultra, near Holywood, tel. 0232/428428. Admission: U.K.£1.50 adults, U.K.80p children and senior citizens. Open May–Sept., Mon.–Sat. 11–6, Sun., afternoons only; Oct.–Apr., Mon.–Sat. 11–5, Sun., afternoons only. May–June, till 9 PM Wed.*

Off the Beaten Track

Belfast's Churches An amazing variety of religious denominations is represented in Belfast. The oldest is **Knockbreda Parish Church** (Church of Ireland), on Church Road, off the A24 on the south side of the city. This dark, sturdy, and atmospheric structure was built in 1737, the work of architect Richard Cassels, who designed many of Ireland's greatest mansions. It quickly became *the place to be buried—witness the vast 18th-century tombs in the churchyard. The* **First Presbyterian Church** (Rosemary St.) dates from 1783 and has an interesting elliptical interior. It hosts lunchtime concerts. **St. Malachy's** (Roman Catholic; Alfred St.), built in 1844, features some fine stonework, including an astonishing fan-vaulted ceiling. By the riverfront is one of the most appealing churches, **Sinclair Seamen's Church** (Presbyterian; Corporation Sq. off Donegall Quay). It was designed by Charles Lanyon, the architect of Queen's University, and has served the seafaring community since 1857. A maritime theme pervades the building; even the pulpit is shaped like a ship's prow.

Cave Hill On fine weekends, it seems that half of Belfast makes its way up to this airy hill north of the city center, where you'll find walks and fine views of the city spread out below. Up here visitors can also visit the zoo, the grand 19th-century baronial mansion **Belfast Castle** (now a restaurant), and, at the summit, the ancient earthworks of **MacArt's Fort.**

East Tyrone Tour 2 makes a quick dash across this large and most rural of Northern Ireland counties, but you may want to explore the area further. North of Omagh, the country is pretty and rustic, with small farm villages within sight of the bare Sperrin Mountains. Heading east from the town on the A505, you'll discover a pensive landscape of moist heath and bog. Left of the road, **Beaghmore** is a strange Bronze Age ceremonial site preserved for millennia beneath the blanket of peat: it has seven stone circles and 12 cairns. Farther along, the A505 reaches **Wellbrook Beetling Mill** (Corkhill, tel. 06487/51735; admission: U.K.£1), where locally made linen was first "beetled," that is, pounded with noisy water-driven hammers to give it a smooth finish. The mill is kept in working order by the National Trust. About 6½ km (4 mi) beyond Wellbrook is **Cookstown,** an odd Plantation village with a single broad main street more than 1½ km (1 mi) in length. From here, head down on the back lanes to **Lough Neagh,** the largest lake in the British Isles (396 sq km/153 sq mi) and noted for an abundance of eels. On its shore at **Ardboe** stands a remarkable 10th-century high cross. It is huge—more than 5½ m (18 ft) tall—and richly carved with biblical scenes.

Shopping

The best of Northern Ireland's traditional products, many made according to time-honored methods, includes exquisite linen and superior handmade woolen garments that are usually associated with the Republic of Ireland. Handmade lacework also remains a skill among the countrywomen of some Northern Ireland districts. Visitors should look out for hand-cut crystal glassware from County Tyrone. Highly regarded as well is the mellow cream-colored parian china of Belleek. Not only is it beautiful, but this china may also prove to be a good investment, because old Belleek always goes up in value.

At the other end of the price scale, handcrafted miniatures of the legendary leprechaun make an inexpensive and amusing (if predictable) souvenir. Blackthorn walking sticks are another popular memento from the province. Polished granite stones from the Mountains of Mourne provide a pretty reminder of a haunting corner of the province.

Belfast

Belfast's main shopping streets include Donegall Place, High Street, Royal Avenue, and several of the smaller streets connecting with them. The whole area is traffic-free (except for buses), so visitors will find it pleasant to wander and window-shop. **Anderson McAuley** (Donegall Pl., tel. 0232/326681) stocks a good selection of linen, Tyrone crystal, Belleek china, and miniatures. **Smyth's Irish Linens** (14 Callender St., behind Marks & Spencer, no phone) carries a great selection of handkerchiefs, tablecloths, napkins, and other linen goods that make excellent souvenirs or presents. If you've an interest in bric-a-brac, visit the **Variety Market,** a flea market you'll find on May Street every Tuesday and Friday morning.

Gifts

China Anyone who's driving around Lower Lough Erne will find themselves passing through the village of Belleek, which sits right on the border with the Republic, beside the sparkling River Erne. On the riverbank stands the Visitor's Center of **Belleek Pottery Ltd.** (tel. 0365/65501), producers of world-famous Belleek chinaware and porcelain. The center is a factory, a showroom, a permanent exhibition, a Belleek pottery museum, and a café all under one roof. On weekdays, a tour of the factory starts every half hour. You'll find hardly any noise in the workshops, however—everything at Belleek is handmade, using the exact process that was invented in 1857. Look around the showroom to choose items to own or give. Prices are high. A cup and saucer costs about U.K.£25. A bowl in a basket-weave style (very typical of Belleek) could cost you around U.K.£300. *Tel. 0365/65501. Admission free. Tours Mon.–Thurs. 9:30–4:15; Fri. 9:30–3:15.*

Celtic Weave China Ltd (Cloghore, Ballyshannon, Co. Donegal, tel. 072/51844) is a one-family outfit just across the border from Belleek on the Ballyshannon road. You'll find them on the left side of the road as you approach the Garda (police) checkpoint on the Irish Republic side. Celtic Weave specializes in the intricate basket-style design, decorated with sprays of colorful china flowers. The company's work has an excellent reputation, and many pieces are made on commission.

Glassware Visitors can watch classic pieces of full lead crystal being mouth-blown and hand-cut at **Tyrone Crystal** (Killybrackey, Dungannon, Co. Tyrone, tel. 08687/25335). Tours are conducted on weekdays—phone ahead for tour times.

Sports

Northern Ireland is a favorite destination for connoisseurs of the great outdoors. Yet no matter how many people come here, the province offers a great deal of space, few crowds, and perfectly tranquil waterways and countryside. A free brochure, "Holiday Breakaways," from the Northern Ireland Tourist Board, details hotels and guest houses that especially suit sports and outdoor enthusiasts.

Participant Sports

Bicycling Roads are good and fairly traffic-free, so cycling is popular. There's no need to have a bike of your own—many towns have rental firms. Bicycle rentals cost around U.K.£3.50–U.K.£4 a day, U.K.£20 for a week. In Belfast, rent from **Ernie Coates** (108 Grand Parade, tel. 0232/471912) or **Bike It** (4 Belmont Rd., tel. 0232/471141). Local Tourist Information Offices can offer suggestions for good cycling routes.

Bird-watching The province has as wide a range of habitats for birds as could possibly be packed into such a tiny area, and there is a wealth of species to satisfy all bird lovers. The best time to come is winter, but even in the summer months visitors can participate in first-class bird-watching, especially on the Antrim uplands, all down the Antrim coast, and on the offshore islands. For wildfowl and wading birds, the shores of Lough Neagh and Strangford Lough are exceptional. For information, ideas, and details of field-study groups, contact Northern Ireland Tourist Information Offices and the **Royal Society for the Protection of Birds** (Belvoir Park Forest, tel. 0232/692547).

Fishing With a 606-km (466-mi) coastline, part on the Atlantic and part on the Irish Sea, as well as major loughs and an abundance of unpolluted rivers, Northern Ireland is a great place for anglers. Set your rod for shark and conger off the Antrim coast, for big skate and tope in Strangford Lough, and for salmon and rainbow trout in the Glens of Antrim.

To catch game fish—salmon and trout—you'll need a license from either the **Fisheries Conservancy Board** (1 Mahon Rd., Portadown, tel. 0762/334666) or the **Foyle Fisheries Commission** (8 Victoria Rd., Derry, tel. 0504/42100), depending on where you're fishing. The license cost is U.K.£9 for 15 days. In addition, you must get permission from the owner of the land where you plan to fish and you may have to pay a charge. If the landowner is the **Department of Agriculture** (Stormont, Belfast, tel. 0232/63939), you'll have to pay for an additional permit (cost: U.K.£13 for 15 days, or U.K.£5 a day). You don't have to approach these bodies individually: All licenses and Department of Agriculture permits are available from the Northern Ireland Tourist Board in Belfast (tel. 0232/231221) or the **Lakeland Visitor Centre** (Enniskillen, tel. 0365/23110), as well as from a number of tackle shops around the province. In some areas, you'll need a license for coarse fish—pike, roach, and bream—costing around U.K.£5 and available mainly from local tackle shops.

Scores of tackle shops are situated around the province, and 10 of them are located in Belfast. Here are a few useful addresses in main angling areas: **J. A. Knaggs** (Main St., Ballinamallard, tel. 036581/321), **R. Bell** (38 Ann St., Ballycastle, tel. 02657/62520), **Carlton Park Fishing Centre** (Belleek, tel. 036565/8181), **Smyth's** (1 Park St., Coleraine, tel. 0265/43970), **Lakeland Tackle and Guns** (Sligo Rd., Enniskillen, tel. 0365/23774), **Four Seasons** (80 Main St., Newcastle, tel. 03967/25078), **Hook, Line & Sinker** (43 South St., Newtownards, tel. 0247/811671).

Golf Northern Ireland features more than 70 golf courses—many in spectacular coastal settings—that welcome visitors. Greens fees vary from about U.K.£7 to U.K.£15. A course is nearly always within reach of your hotel, with a dozen golf clubs within

8 km (5 mi) of Belfast. The **Royal County Down** (Newcastle, tel. 03967/23314) is considered by many golfers to be one of the finest courses in the world. Another championship course is at the **Royal Portrush Golf Club** (Portrush, Co. Antrim, tel. 0265/822311). All golf courses and clubs are listed in the Northern Ireland Tourist Board Information Bulletin No. 17, "Golf—Where to Play," available from main tourist offices.

Hiking Northern Ireland has plenty of magnificent walking country. The **Ulster Way,** in particular, is for the serious hiker, a 896-km (560-mi) trek right around the six counties. Apart from the ability to read a map, no special skills are needed, and the terrain never demands more than a pair of stout walking shoes. Of course, visitors do not have to walk the whole trail; some sections are easier than others, and some of the best stretches are clearly marked. The **Sports Council for Northern Ireland** (House of Sport, Upper Malone Rd., Belfast BT9 5LA, tel. 0232/381222) can give advice about the Ulster Way and sells books covering each section of the route. Anyone who would like to try their hand at tougher walks in the hills should obtain the excellent and informative little handbook in the Irish Walks series, No. 4, *The North East,* by Richard Rogers. It gives precise details of 45 hill walks, complete with descriptions of the wildflowers you'll see along the way. For hikes in the Mountains of Mourne, you can obtain maps and details of suggested routes from **The Mourne Countryside Centre** (91 Central Promenade, Newcastle, Co. Down, tel. 03967/24059).

Horseback Riding/Pony Trekking Sitting on the back of a horse or pony is a great way to travel into places that are out of bounds for motorists. Woodland, beaches, and rough country become accessible on guided rides, some suitable for complete beginners. Some 35 riding and trekking centers are located around the province, and several of them offer accommodations. Trekking rates are mostly U.K.£4–U.K.£5 an hour, with small reductions for children. The most convenient center in the Belfast area is **Lagan Valley Equestrian Centre** (172 Upper Malone Rd., Belfast, tel. 0232/614853). The center is open Monday through Saturday throughout the year, and it charges an hourly rate of U.K.£5 adults, U.K.£4 children (minimum age 7). The center runs pony treks through the Lagan Valley Regional Park, as well as residential summer camps. If you're over in the Enniskillen/Lough Erne area, **Drumhoney Stables** (Lisnarick, 5 km/3 mi west of Irvinestown, tel. 03656/21892) can teach you to ride, take you on a pony trek through Castle Archdale Country Park, or even rent you a pony and trap (suitable for two adults and up to four children). Hourly rates are U.K.£6 adults, U.K.£4.50–U.K.£5 children. The stables also have residential accommodations.

Lake and River Cruising Inland cruising on the Erne waterway—777 sq km (300 sq mi) of lakes and rivers—is one of Northern Ireland's major treats. Upper and Lower Lough Erne are enclosed by some of Ireland's finest scenery and are studded with more than 100 little islands. Out on the lakes and the River Erne, which links them, you'll have all the solitude you want, but you'll also find company at loughside hostelries. To hire a good standard-size boat, contact **Erne Charter Boat Association** (Lakeland Visitor Centre, Enniskillen, Co. Fermanagh, tel. 0365/23110). Expect to pay at least U.K.£300 for a four-berth cruiser.

Spectator Sports

Ask any tourist office for the leaflet of the year's *Events*, which shows the dates and times of major sports occasions. Look out especially for the **hurling** and **Gaelic football** events. Dates of local matches are listed in local newspapers. During the summer, you'll come across **cricket** matches being played throughout the province. One oddity is the ancient precursor of bowls, called **bullets,** which is still played in County Armagh. It involves throwing bowls (originally they were cannonballs, hence the name) along a narrow winding country lane; the first to cover 3 km (2 mi) is the winner. The All-Ireland Championship for this sport is held in early August.

Dining and Lodging

Dining

Northern Ireland cuisine is similar to cooking in the Republic; it features good-quality fresh local fish and meat, prepared in a simple style. Acceptable French and other Continental dishes, except in Belfast, will be difficult to find. Vegetables receive an unimaginative treatment, and you'll find a heavy emphasis on potatoes, which are often served in two different ways on the same plate. Yet the hearty, unpretentious home cooking available is tasty, nourishing, and above all *filling*, because portions tend to be huge.

Visitors will not find much on the menu that is unfamiliar. Ulster Fry, an inexpensive café and pub dish, is something like an Irish breakfast: a sizzling portion of bacon, sausages, tomatoes, and eggs, served with potato bread or soda bread. Champ is another potato dish, this time a creamy, buttery mash with spring onions. Some other traditional favorites that remain popular include Guinness soup, oysters from Strangford Lough, Ardglass herring, and smoked salmon from Ballamena. Be sure to check out the variety of freshly baked breads, which you can sample at teatime. Tea, especially when described as high tea, is usually served around 6 PM; it's a full meal of breads and buns, accompanied with sandwiches or savory hot dishes, and followed by fruit cake. Among the delicious baked fare are scones (white or wholemeal), farls (triangular griddle cakes leavened with soda and buttermilk), potato bread (solid stuff, sometimes eaten fried), and wheaten bread (dark brown, very heavy). Most pubs will serve a pot of tea and a plate of scones.

Quite apart from cafés, pubs, and restaurants, Northern Ireland has discovered the convenience of fast food. Wine bars are another upcoming kind of eatery; in reality these are just restaurants with a good wine list. Most diners, though, still prefer to take a pot of tea with their food.

Without being formal, the Northern Irish tend to dress soberly. Men often wear a jacket and tie when dining out; but if you prefer to dress more casually, that is quite acceptable at most establishments. By the standards of the Republic or the United States, or even by the rest of the United Kingdom, restaurant prices are surprisingly moderate. Tax is usually included in the price of a meal. A service charge of 10% may be indicated on the bill; it is customary to pay this, unless the service was bad.

Category	Cost*
Very Expensive	over U.K.£20
Expensive	U.K.£15–U.K.£20
Moderate	U.K.£10–U.K.£15
Inexpensive	under U.K.£10

* *per person for a typical three-course meal, including tax and service but excluding drinks.*

Lodging

Northern Ireland has some good modern hotels but hardly any lodging in the more expensive categories. Travelers often find that the most enjoyable accommodations are low-cost guest houses (often family-run), offering bed and breakfast. Most B&Bs provide an evening meal as well, if needed. Visitors can choose from the humblest terraced town houses or farm cottages to the grandest country houses. Dining rooms of country-house lodgings frequently reach the standard of top-quality restaurants.

Northern Ireland's six youth hostels have not been listed here. For their details contact **Y.H.A.N.I.** (56 Bradbury Pl., Belfast BT7 1RU, tel. 0232/324733). All accommodations in the province are inspected and categorized by the Northern Ireland Tourist Board, who publish all names, addresses, and ratings in the handbook *Where to Stay* (U.K.£2.50).

Category	Cost*
Very Expensive	over U.K.£80
Expensive	U.K.£60–U.K.£80
Moderate	U.K.£40–U.K.£60
Inexpensive	under U.K.£40

**All prices are for a standard double room, including breakfast and tax.*

Highly recommended restaurants and hotels are indicated by a star ★.

Belfast

Dining
★

Roscoff. Several locals consider this bright, uncluttered restaurant with a 1930s period influence, situated in the Golden Mile area, to be one of the best dining spots in Northern Ireland. You're likely to overhear the chat of barristers and British Government ministers at other tables. The specialty is Breton fish and seafood dishes (Roscoff is a port on the Brittany coast); portions are generous and accompanied with large quantities of vegetables. One of the delicious appetizers is hearts of Cos lettuce with Parmesan cheese; as a main course you might try the roast monkfish: three pieces of fish served with thin, crisply fried noodles in a tangy sauce, flavored with Chinese spices. For dessert, sample an individual Tarte Tatin, a French apple pie baked to perfection and served with freshly made ice cream. *Shaftesbury Sq. (at the end of Great Victoria*

St.), tel. 0232/331532. Reservations advised. Jacket and tie advised. AE, DC, MC, V. Closed Fri. PM *and Sun. Very Expensive.*

★ **Restaurant 44.** This establishment in the Golden Mile area has a warm Edwardian look with a terra-cotta and brown color scheme, mirrors, wood-paneled walls, and subdued lighting. The dishes with an Italian influence include an appetizer of warm smoked duck salad with a tarragon and lime dressing, and the main course Treasures of the Sea (slices of turbot, salmon, sole, and other fish in a creamy tomato sauce with a tang of Pernod, Cointreau, and dry vermouth). A rich chocolate "ganache" (truffle cake) is recommended for dessert. *44 Bedford St., tel. 0232/244844. Reservations required. Jacket and tie advised. AE, DC, MC, V. Closed Fri.* PM *and Sun. Expensive.*

Bananas. Adjoining Restaurant 44, with the same owners and kitchen, Bananas is as good as its neighbor. It features a colonial-type decor, with cane furniture, a plain wood floor, and ceiling fans. Palms grow in flowerpots that are made from old chimneys. The mixed international menu includes Continental and Asian cuisines. You might start with baked oatmeal herring in mustard sauce, followed by a main course of spiced marinated chicken with banana *raita* (a cool yogurt dip). Vegetable *thali* consists of a selection of several Indian dishes. One of the best desserts is Irish coffee ice cream, made on the premises. *44 Bedford St., tel. 0232/244844. Reservations required. Dress: informal. AE, DC, MC, V. Closed Fri.* PM *and Sun. Moderate.*

★ **La Belle Epoque.** Relaxed and intimate, this well-established restaurant offers a French charm, with Art Nouveau decor reminiscent of Paris. The French moderne classique menu features pigeon breast in raspberry sauce as an appetizer, and an excellent main course of pheasant in a cream and wine sauce. For dessert, you can't go wrong with the freshly made fruit sorbets. *103 Great Victoria St., tel. 0232/323244. Reservations advised (required on weekends). Dress: casual. DC, MC, V. Closed Sun. Moderate.*

The Strand. Situated in the popular University Area, this bistro attracts students and professors alike with its adventurous and unusual menu. Recommended dishes include chicken pancakes, peanut plaice, or cod in coconut and apple sauce. For dessert try the cream-laden gateaux. Several vegetarian entrées are available. *12 Stranmillis Rd., tel. 0232/682266. Reservations advised. Dress: casual. AE, DC, MC, V. Moderate.*

★ **Saints and Scholars.** This University Area restaurant offers two distinct sections. The downstairs "Library" has bookshelves on the walls, but the lively, noisy, and cheerful ambience could hardly be less studious. Upstairs, you'll find a calmer and more comfortable cream-colored dining room. One of the special appetizers is mousse of Arbroath smokies (smoked haddock with butter). Main dishes include a hearty cassoulet (rich meaty stew with duck, sausages, and beans) and Seafood Harmony (a selection of baked or poached fish, with sauce thermidor). Many vegetarian dishes are available, such as mushrooms stuffed with cream cheese and avocado. The rich dessert crepes, made according to a recipe from the Danish royal court, are truly fit for a king. *3 University St., tel. 0232/325137. Reservations required. Dress: casual. AE, DC, MC, V. Inexpensive.*

Lodging

★ **Culloden Hotel.** Located 8 km (5 mi) from the city center on the A2, this former 19th-century Scottish baronial mansion stands grandly amid 12 acres of woods and parkland. The public areas feature ornate woodwork, Louis XV chandeliers, decorative plasterwork, and stained glass. Bedrooms, both in the original section and in a newer wing, feature silk and velvet decor and fine views. The excellent dining areas include the large French Mitre Restaurant with mahogany tables and a garden view and a Grill Bar, which serves both snacks and meals. The hotel is situated in a peaceful part of town, close to the Ulster Folk Museum. *142 Bangor Rd., Holywood, Co. Down BT18 0EX, tel. 02317/5223. 93 rooms with bath. Facilities: restaurant, grill bar, tennis, squash, croquet, games room, snooker, laundry, 24-hr room service. AE, DC, MC, V. Very Expensive.*

Europa Hotel. This popular modern high-rise city-center hotel has long attracted visiting journalists and businessmen. What it lacks in period charm is compensated for by the polite and efficient staff and the comfortable ambience. Bedrooms are blandly decorated but they are clean and functional and offer all the modern conveniences, including central heating, and TV. The hotel, conveniently located near the Opera House, is only 1.6 km (1 mi) from the train station and 6½ km (4 mi) from the airport. *Great Victoria St., Belfast BT2 7AP, tel. 0232/327000. 200 rooms with bath. Facilities: café, bar, restaurant, secretarial services, laundry, 24-hr security. AE, DC, MC, V. Very Expensive.*

★ **Wellington Park Hotel.** Formerly a private residence, this attractive Georgian-style establishment is considered the best lodging available in the Queen's University area of town. Many evening visitors enjoy the relaxed bars, live music, and good food at this friendly family-run hotel. The quiet bedrooms are well-designed with built-in wooden furniture; some of them feature loft sleeping areas. *21 Malone Rd., Belfast BT9 6RU, tel. 0232/381111. 50 rooms with bath or shower. Facilities: bar, restaurant, laundry. AE, DC, MC, V. Expensive.*

★ **Ash-Rowan Guest House.** Former award-winning restaurateurs Sam and Evelyn Hazlett own and run this outstanding B&B in a spacious Victorian home. Every bedroom has been decorated in a tasteful individual style, and each has a private bath and TV. Guests have access to a library. Breakfasts and dinners, prepared by the owners, are first rate. This no-smoking house is located on a tranquil, residential street near Queen's University and the Ulster Museum. *Mrs. E. Hazlett, 12 Windsor Ave., Belfast BT9 6EE, tel. 0232/661758. 4 rooms with bath. MC, V. Closed Dec. Moderate.*

Camera House. Mrs. Drumm runs this delightful B&B in a brick Victorian house with bay windows. Bedrooms are clean, cheerful, and simply furnished. You'll appreciate the friendly welcome and the generous breakfasts. *Mrs. A. Drumm, Camera House, 44 Wellington Park, Belfast BT9 6DP, tel. 0232/660026. 11 rooms, 7 with bath or shower. MC, V. Inexpensive.*

The Cottage. Aptly named, this lovely little B&B in Mrs. Muldoon's immaculate white home, located 8 km (5 mi) east of Belfast, has a charming flower-filled garden in the back. It's as rural a setting as you're likely to find so close to the city center. The traditional country-house decor combines beautiful antiques and modern comforts in the bedrooms. *Mrs. E. Muldoon, The Cottage, 377 Comber Rd., Dundonald, Belfast*

BT16 0XB, tel. 0247/878189. 3 rooms, 1 with bath. No credit cards. Inexpensive.

Carrickfergus

Dining and Lodging

Dobbins Inn. Still thriving after more than three centuries, this modest family-run hotel on High Street attracts locals to its convivial bar, especially during live music performances on Sunday, Monday, and Tuesday evenings. The adequate bedrooms offer private baths, TVs, and tea-making equipment. High tea is available, and the DeCourcy restaurant serves an acceptable dinner. *6–8 High St., Carrickfergus, Co. Antrim, BT38 9HE, tel. 09603/51905. 13 rooms with bath. Facilities: restaurant, baby-sitting service. MC, V. Moderate.*

Coleraine Area

Dining and Lodging

★

Blackheath House. Situated 13 km (8 mi) south of Coleraine, this fine country house surrounded by magnificent countryside was built as the home of the 18th-century bishop of Derry. The brown structure is within close driving distance of golf courses and the Causeway Coast beaches and cliff walks; the home retains a genteel character and stands amid 2 acres of landscaped gardens; among its more modern comforts is an indoor swimming pool. The large bedrooms—including a four-poster room, a French Colonial room, and a pine room—have been individually decorated with a mixture of modern and antique furniture. The drawing room, with a fine marble fireplace, is filled with old pieces of furniture. Down in the cellars lies MacDuff's, a first-class expensive restaurant, open to nonresidents, where proprietors Joseph and Margaret Erwin provide excellent meals prepared with farm-fresh meats and local vegetables, game, and seafood. The menu offers steak in blue cheese sauce, sole in a sauce of tomato and herbs, and a good wine list. Breakfasts are filling, with a generous Ulster Fry. *112 Killeague Rd., Blackhill, Coleraine, Co. Londonderry BT51 4HH, tel. 0265/868433. 6 rooms, 5 with bath. Facilities: pool, restaurant (closed Sun. and Mon.). No credit cards. Moderate.*

Greenhill House. This charming Georgian country house about 13 km (8 mi) south of Coleraine is run by Elizabeth and James Hegarty and provides a peaceful retreat. Guests enjoy the pleasantly decorated bedrooms, the substantial breakfasts, and the excellent dinners of locally caught fish, Ulster beef, and homemade bread and cakes. *24 Greenhill Rd., Aghadowey, Co. Londonderry BT51 4EU, tel. 0265/868241. 7 rooms, 6 with bath. No credit cards. Closed Nov.–Feb. Inexpensive.*

Lodging

Camus House. Follow the road along the Bann valley south from Coleraine; 6½ km (4 mi) out of town, you'll arrive at this appealing Georgian farmhouse that dates back to 1685. Today it's a relaxed and gracious guest house, elegantly furnished, with a snug sitting room with a stone fireplace. Proprietor Mrs. Josephine King provides a friendly atmosphere and a hearty breakfast. The pleasant bedrooms, decorated in pastel colors, have tasteful modern furnishings, reading lamps, and large closets. *27 Curragh Rd., Coleraine, Co. Londonderry BT51 3RY, tel. 0265/42982. 3 rooms without bath. No credit cards. Inexpensive.*

Derry City

Dining and Lodging

White Horse Hotel. In the countryside overlooking Lough Foyle, yet only 8 km (5 mi) northeast of Derry City on the road to Limavady, this former inn has been enlarged into a comfortable modern hotel that caters to business and vacation visitors. Bedrooms are clean and unpretentiously furnished, with TVs and tea-making equipment. Locals and guests alike enjoy the good Irish meals served at the relaxed grill bar or smarter restaurant. *68 Clooney Rd., Campsie, Co. Londonderry BT47 3PA, tel. 0504/860606. 50 rooms with bath. Facilities: bar, restaurant, 24-hr valet service. MC, V. Moderate.*

Downpatrick/Ards Area

Dining and Lodging

Portaferry Inn. Standing on the quayside (or "strand") overlooking the narrow channel that connects Lough Strangford to the sea, this centuries-old whitewashed inn offers well-kept, simply furnished double rooms. The main action takes place in the popular bar and restaurant, where unadventurous but competent breakfasts, lunches, and dinners are briskly served. *10 The Strand, Portaferry, Co. Down, BT22 1PE, tel. 02472/28231. 5 double rooms with bath or shower. Facilities: restaurant, bar/lounge, boat mooring, laundry. AE, DC, MC, V. Moderate.*

Enniskillen and Environs

Dining and Lodging
★

Jamestown House. Tucked away in lush tranquil countryside near Lower Lough Erne and 11 km (7 mi) from Enniskillen, this dignified country house dates from 1760 and is run by Arthur and Helen Stuart. The large, attractive bedrooms feature modern furnishings, and elegant drawing and dining rooms contain older fine polished mahogany pieces. Staying here is just like visiting friends in the country. A river runs through the grounds—Mr. Stuart is keen on angling and advises visitors on the best spots to fish in the area. Breakfasts and the expensive set dinners are both generous and satisfying. *Magheracross, Ballinamallard, Co. Fermanagh, tel. 036581/209. 3 rooms, 2 with bath or shower. No credit cards. Moderate.*

Glens of Antrim

Dining and Lodging

Ballygally Castle. At the Larne end of the North Antrim coast drive, 40 km (25 mi) from Belfast, you'll find an impressive little castle, complete with pointed turrets, facing the Ballygally Bay, that was built by a Scottish lord in 1625. After centuries of defending itself from invaders, the castle now cheerfully invites visitors to sample a good night's sleep and hearty breakfast within its substantial stone walls; modern plumbing and central heating have been skillfully integrated into the old Scottish-style design, but a recent extension, unfortunately, does not complement the castle architecture. Bedrooms, some of them located in the castle turrets, have been individually decorated with comfortable furnishings. In the dining room a decent table d'hôte evening meal is served (to music, on Saturdays), and a Sunday high tea is also available. *Ballygally Castle, 274 Coast Rd., Ballygally, Co. Antrim BT40 2RA, tel.*

0574/83212. 30 rooms with bath. Facilities: bar, dining room, baby-sitting, fishing on grounds. MC, V. Moderate.

Londonderry Arms. This ivy-covered traditional hotel by Carnlough Harbour, built as a coaching inn in 1848, features a lovely seaside garden, unique antique carved furnishings, regional paintings and maps, and Georgian period decor. The lodging once belonged to Sir Winston Churchill, and since 1947, it has been owned and run by the O'Neill family. A dozen of the bedrooms feature Georgian antiques, and the rest offer functional contemporary decor. Rooms 2, 8, and 9 are recommended for their spaciousness and good views. The hotel serves a substantial traditional Irish meal that relies on local seafood; bread and scones are homemade. Traditional Irish music is provided during the summer months. *Harbour Rd., Carnlough, Co. Antrim BT44 0EU, tel. 0574/885255. 21 rooms with bath. AE, DC, MC, V. Moderate.*

Mountains of Mourne Area

Dining and Lodging

Slieve Donard Hotel. A lavish redbrick monument to Victoriana, this turreted hotel stands like a palace on spacious green lawns at one end of Newcastle's 6½-km (4-mi) sandy beach. Guests will feel as if they are stepping back to the town's turn-of-the-century heyday as an elegant seaside resort, even though rooms now have every modern comfort. Ask for a room overlooking the water. The relaxed gatehouse pub/dining room serves adequate seafood dishes; folk music is presented every Saturday night. For daytime relaxation, walk the airy promenade or visit the Royal County Down Golf Club, right next door. *Downs Rd., Newcastle, Co. Down BT33 0AH, tel. 03967/23681. 120 rooms with bath. Facilities: pub/dining room, recreation center with 2 tennis courts and indoor pool. AE, DC, MC, V. Expensive.*

The Arts and Nightlife

The Arts

Just about all Northern Ireland's arts and cultural activity is concentrated in Belfast. The *Belfast Telegraph* newspaper lists arts events. The high point of the province's cultural year is the **Belfast International Festival of Arts,** lasting a couple of weeks each November. It offers a full schedule of dramatic and musical events centered at Whitla Hall, at Queen's University. The **Belfast Folk Festival** in September is a weekend of traditional foot-tapping Irish music and dance at downtown locations.

Film

Cannon Cinema (Great Victoria St., tel. 0232/322484), with four screens, and **Curzon Cinema** (Ormeau Rd., tel. 0232/641373), with three screens, are two of several city-center movie theaters showing new British and American releases and big box-office favorites.

Queen's Film Theatre is Belfast's "art" cinema, with two screens showing domestic or imported movies. *University Sq. Mews, off Botanic Ave., tel. 0232/667687. Open during university semesters only.*

Music

The Ulster Hall (Linenhall St., tel. 0232/241917) is the large city-center concert hall where classical orchestral pieces are performed; the center is the home base of the Ulster Orchestra. The hall has a splendid Victorian organ, so organ recitals are often held. Sometimes rock concerts are also scheduled here.

Whitla Hall (Queen's University, tel. 0232/245133) hosts classical concerts and recitals throughout the year.

Harberton Theatre (Harberton Park, Balmoral, tel. 0232/661302), in the southwest suburbs, is the home of the Ulster Operatic Society, which presents concerts and musicals.

Grosvenor Hall (Glengall St., tel. 0232/241917) is the place for some down-home music; this is the place to find country-and-western, gospel, and folk concerts.

Theater and Opera

The Arts Theatre (Botanic Ave., tel. 0232/324936), near the University Area, specializes in laugh-a-minute comedies and lightweight productions.

The Grand Opera House, a beautifully restored Victorian playhouse, has no company of its own but books shows from all over the British Isles and sometimes further afield. It puts on a constant stream of plays of widely differing kinds, plus occasional operas and ballets. *Great Victoria St., tel. 0232/241919. Tickets: U.K.£1.50–U.K.£25.*

The Group Theatre is a showcase for Belfast's local dramatic societies. *Bedford St., tel. 0232/329685. Tickets: U.K.£2–U.K.£2.50.*

The Lyric Theatre, in the south of Belfast, stages thoughtful drama played by its resident company and draws most of its inspiration from traditional Irish culture. *Ridgeway St., tel. 0232/381081. Tickets: Mon.–Thurs. all seats U.K.£5, Fri. and Sat. U.K.£6.*

Nightlife

A night out in Northern Ireland usually means an evening at a pub—that's where most entertainment takes place. The most popular pubs are those lively, convivial places where traditional Irish folk music is played frequently, and often quite spontaneously. They can be found in towns and villages all over the province, and the best way to locate them is to ask where to find a "singing pub." Pubs, by the way, close around 11:30 PM.

Belfast
Golden Mile Area

Robinsons (next to the Crown Liquor Saloon, Great Victoria St., tel. 0232/329812) is a popular pub appealing to a young crowd. **The Beaten Docket** (also next to the Crown, tel. 0232/242926) is a noisier modern pub that attracts an even younger crowd than Robinsons; it features up-to-the-minute music. **Limelight** (Ormeau Ave., no phone) is a disco nightclub with cabaret on Tuesday, Friday, and Saturday, and music on other nights. **The Linenhall** (Clarence St., tel. 0232/248458) is a pub with a music lounge, where jazz is performed on Monday, Wednesday, and Saturday, and rock music on Thursday.

University Area

The Eglantine (tel. 0232/667994) and **The Botanic** (tel. 0232/660460), known as the Egg and the Bot, respectively, to their student clientele, are two big, popular disco pubs facing each other across Malone Road.

City Center/Docks

Pat's Bar (Prince's Dock Rd., tel. 0232/744524) and **Maddens** (Smithfield, no phone) are popular pubs with first-rate sessions of traditional music. **The Rotterdam** (Pilot St., tel. 0232/746021) features folk, jazz, and blues performers. **Kelly's Cellars** (Bank St., tel. 0232/324835) offers blues on Saturday nights.

Index

Personal Itinerary

Departure *Date*

Time

Transportation

Arrival *Date* *Time*

Departure *Date* *Time*

Transportation

Accommodations

Arrival *Date* *Time*

Departure *Date* *Time*

Transportation

Accommodations

Arrival *Date* *Time*

Departure *Date* *Time*

Transportation

Accommodations

Personal Itinerary

Arrival *Date* *Time*

Departure *Date* *Time*

Transportation

Accommodations

Arrival *Date* *Time*

Departure *Date* *Time*

Transportation

Accommodations

Arrival *Date* *Time*

Departure *Date* *Time*

Transportation

Accommodations

Arrival *Date* *Time*

Departure *Date* *Time*

Transportation

Accommodations

Personal Itinerary

Arrival *Date* *Time*

Departure *Date* *Time*

Transportation

Accommodations

Arrival *Date* *Time*

Departure *Date* *Time*

Transportation

Accommodations

Arrival *Date* *Time*

Departure *Date* *Time*

Transportation

Accommodations

Arrival *Date* *Time*

Departure *Date* *Time*

Transportation

Accommodations

Personal Itinerary

Arrival *Date* *Time*

Departure *Date* *Time*

Transportation

Accommodations

Arrival *Date* *Time*

Departure *Date* *Time*

Transportation

Accommodations

Arrival *Date* *Time*

Departure *Date* *Time*

Transportation

Accommodations

Arrival *Date* *Time*

Departure *Date* *Time*

Transportation

Accommodations

Addresses

Name

Address

Telephone

Name

Address

Telephone

Name

Address

Telephone

Name

Address

Telephone

Name

Address

Telephone

Name

Address

Telephone

Name

Address

Telephone

Name

Address

Telephone

Name

Address

Telephone

Name

Address

Telephone

Name

Address

Telephone

Name

Address

Telephone

Name

Address

Telephone

Name

Address

Telephone

Name

Address

Telephone

Name

Address

Telephone

Fodor's Travel Guides

U.S. Guides

Alaska
Arizona
Boston
California
Cape Cod
The Carolinas & the Georgia Coast
The Chesapeake Region
Chicago
Colorado
Disney World & the Orlando Area
Florida
Hawaii
Las Vegas
Los Angeles
Maui
Miami & the Keys
New England
New Mexico
New Orleans
New York City
New York City (Pocket Guide)
New York State
Pacific North Coast
Philadelphia
Puerto Rico (Pocket Guide)
The Rockies
San Diego
San Francisco
San Francisco (Pocket Guide)
The South
Texas
USA
The Upper Great Lakes Region
Vacations on the Jersey Shore
Virgin Islands
Virginia & Maryland
Waikiki
Washington, D.C.

Foreign Guides

Acapulco
Amsterdam
Australia
Austria
The Bahamas
The Bahamas (Pocket Guide)
Baja & the Pacific Coast Resorts
Barbados
Belgium & Luxembourg
Bermuda
Brazil
Budget Europe
Canada
Canada's Atlantic Provinces
Cancun, Cozumel, Yucatan Peninsula
Caribbean
Central America
China
Eastern Europe
Egypt
Europe
Europe's Great Cities
France
Germany
Great Britain
Greece
The Himalayan Countries
Holland
Hong Kong
India
Ireland
Israel
Italy
Italy 's Great Cities
Jamaica
Japan
Kenya, Tanzania, Seychelles
Korea
London
London Companion
London (Pocket Guide)
Madrid & Barcelona
Mexico
Montreal & Quebec City
Morocco
Munich
New Zealand
Paris
Paris (Pocket Guide)
Portugal
Rio de Janeiro
Rome
Saint Martin/ Sint Maarten
Scandinavia
Scandinavian Cities
Scotland
Singapore
South America
South Pacific
Southeast Asia
Soviet Union
Spain
Sweden
Switzerland
Thailand
Tokyo
Toronto
Turkey
Vienna
Yugoslavia

Special-Interest Guides

Cruises and Ports of Call
Smart Shopper's Guide to London
Healthy Escapes
Shopping in Europe
Skiing in North America